MACARTHUR AND THE AMERICAN CENTURY

MacArthur and the American Century

A Reader

EDITED BY
WILLIAM M. LEARY

UNIVERSITY OF NEBRASKA PRESS
LINCOLN AND LONDON

Acknowledgments for the use of previously published material appear on pages 505–7, which constitute an extension of the copyright page.
All photographs are courtesy of the MacArthur Memorial Archives, Norfolk VA.
Photo 1 (#00000014) belongs to the MacArthur Memorial and is reprinted by permission; all others are U.S. Signal Corps or U.S. Navy photographs.

Manufactured in the United States of America
∞
Library of Congress Cataloging-in-Publication Data
MacArthur and the American century: a reader / edited by William M. Leary.
p. cm.
Includes bibliopgraphical references (p.) and index.
ISBN 0-8032-2930-5 (cl.: alk. paper)
1. MacArthur, Douglas, 1880–1964.
2. MacArthur, Douglas, 1880–1964—Influence.
3. Generals—United States—Biography.
4. United States. Army—Biography.
5. United States—History, Military—20th century.
I. Leary, William M. (William Matthew), 1934–
E745.M23 2001
355'.0092—dc21
[B]
00-044736

For Stanley L. Falk
Distinguished scholar, wise mentor, good friend

CONTENTS

Illustrations

Maps

Introduction

William M. Leary

It is intriguing to imagine what historians might have written about Douglas MacArthur had he faded into obscurity after stepping down as army chief of staff in 1935. It certainly seems unlikely that he would have attracted much attention beyond a handful of scholars. At best, his life might have been the topic for a dissertation that might or might not have been published, depending upon the literary and analytical skills of the author.

MacArthur, it would be noted, had a distinguished military career, at least in the institutional sense. The son of a Civil War hero who rose to three-star rank and command of U.S. forces in the Philippines during the turbulent years that followed the Spanish-American War, MacArthur compiled an impressive record at West Point. Graduating in 1903 at the top of his class and as first captain of the Corps of Cadets, he received his commission as a second lieutenant in the Corps of Engineers.

Over the next ten years MacArthur saw duty in a variety of military postings in the Philippines, Panama, and the United States. In 1914 he conducted a hazardous reconnaissance mission during the U.S. occupation of Veracruz, Mexico, and was recommended for the Medal of Honor. To MacArthur's immense disgust he failed to receive the high honor.

MacArthur was serving on the general staff of the War Department when the United States entered World War I in April 1917. He suggested and then implemented a plan to form a National Guard division that would be composed of units from several states. MacArthur became chief of staff of the resultant Forty-second Infantry, or "Rainbow" Division.

The Forty-second Division went into combat in France early in 1918. Colonel MacArthur, in his turtleneck sweater and long purple muffler, quickly made his mark on the field of battle. Whether personally leading a patrol through enemy lines or standing coolly aloof in the midst of incoming artillery fire, he seemed to lead a charmed life. Usually individuals who believe that they are invulnerable to enemy fire are among the first to fall in battle. But there are those rare soldiers whose survival can only be attributed to divine intervention—or incredible good luck. MacArthur, himself, credited the Almighty.

Promoted to brigadier general in June 1918 (after the personal intervention of Chief of Staff Peyton C. March), MacArthur went on to command a brigade in the Forty-second and, briefly, the entire division. Recommended for but again denied the Medal of Honor, his impressive list of battlefield awards included two Distinguished Service Crosses, seven Silver Stars, and two Purple Hearts.

Thanks to the efforts of General March, an old friend of his father's, MacArthur received a plum postwar assignment: superintendent of the U.S. Military Academy. Although the posting allowed him to retain his brigadier's star, MacArthur faced a daunting challenge. West Point, he found, was firmly rooted in the nineteenth century. Furthermore, the academy's academic board, dominated by senior faculty members, was determined to keep it that way.

MacArthur was equally determined to bring about change in his beloved institution. Thanks to his dynamic leadership the curriculum was modernized and the quality of instruction improved. He abolished the traditional summer camp for cadets, largely a social affair, in favor of basic infantry training. He curbed the worst abuses of hazing and formalized the honor code, placing its administration in the hands of the cadets. A firm believer in the benefits of athletic participation in the shaping of officers, he promoted intercollegiate athletics and instituted a new program of intramural sports.

In his three years as superintendent MacArthur brought West Point into the modern world. His role in shaping the twentieth-century West Point was comparable to that of Sylvanus Thayer in the nineteenth century. Although his immediate successors tried to turn back the clock, MacArthur's reforms could not be reversed, at least not for long.

Despite his exemplary performance MacArthur failed to receive his second star—which he felt he deserved. Instead, he was sent to the Philippines in 1922 as commander of the Military District of Manila. The assignment abroad, which the recently married MacArthur initially resisted, would prove a turning point for his later career. Having served in the islands as a junior officer, MacArthur had a deep affection for the Philippines and the Filipino people. Although not known as an especially

gregarious person, he managed to cultivate a number of prominent individuals who were destined for places of high power in the government
of the islands.

After a year in his administrative assignment in Manila MacArthur
returned to the field as commander of a brigade in the recently formed
Philippine Division. This led, in turn, to command of the division and, in
January 1925, to his second star. At the time MacArthur was the youngest
major general in the army.

MacArthur spent the next three years in the United States, mainly
in charge of corps areas, before returning to Asia in October 1928
as commander of the Philippine Department. During his twenty-two-
month tour of duty he solidified his relationships with the elite of Filipino
society while contemplating schemes to defend the islands in the event
of attack. Believing that the existing war plan was unrealistic, MacArthur
embraced the idea of creating a large Filipino self-defense force. At the
time, however, nothing could be done to implement the scheme.

In August 1930 MacArthur was summoned home to claim the prize
that had eluded his father: chief of staff of the United States Army. At
fifty years of age he had reached the pinnacle of the military hierarchy,
thanks largely to the support of President Herbert Hoover's secretary of
war, Patrick J. Hurley.

MacArthur could not have taken the army's top job at a worse time.
The nation's economy was in a tailspin, and Hoover was determined
to slash federal spending. The military was a prime target for budget
cuts, at least in part because of deepening isolationist sentiment in the
country. Many Americans believed that the United States had been
lured into World War I by a conspiracy of munitions makers, or by
British propaganda, or by bankers—take your pick. In any event, U.S.
participation in the European conflict had been a mistake, a mistake that
should never be repeated. The American people—or most of them—saw
no need for a strong military establishment.

MacArthur soon found himself fighting administrative battles on two
fronts. He did everything in his power to preserve the army's dwindling
resources and strenuously lobbied Congress for funding, even to the
point of making political enemies. At best his efforts only slowed the
process of the army's decline. By the end of 1932 he believed that the
nation's military strength had fallen below the point of safety.

MacArthur also spoke out against the growing antiwar movement in
the country. Military conflict, he argued, was part of the human condi-

tion. The best way to preserve peace—even ensure national survival—was to be prepared to fight. His message that weakness only invited aggression was ignored.

The year 1932 saw the nation mired in the depths of the Great Depression. It also marked the most controversial episode in MacArthur's career—at least to that point—when he was called upon to deal with the Bonus Expeditionary Force (BEF). MacArthur's conduct during this sad episode was questioned at the time—and later as well. Whether or not he exceeded his orders and displayed unseemly zeal in routing the BEF veterans remains debatable. Certainly he embraced the notion that the BEF was led by communists, and he made some rather extreme public statements. Nonetheless it should be remembered that the new president, Franklin D. Roosevelt, reappointed MacArthur for a second term as army chief of staff.

The situation for the army under the new Democratic administration was no better than it had been under Hoover. MacArthur continued to fight against budgetary cuts while implementing a modest reform program. When the army was called upon to manage Roosevelt's Civilian Conservation Corps, MacArthur responded with an alacrity that pleased the president.

MacArthur stepped down as chief of staff in 1935. Had his career ended at that point, what might a biographer have concluded about him? A stellar combat soldier in World War I, MacArthur stood out as an academic innovator when he brought about fundamental reforms at the U.S. Military Academy. He went on to become chief of staff at a difficult time in the nation's history and made a valiant effort to preserve the fighting ability of the army. Swept up in the controversy surrounding the BEF, he (a) did his duty or (b) acted inappropriately and damaged his reputation. His career provides valuable insight into the institutional character of the army during the first third of the twentieth century.

MacArthur's biography, if published at this point in his career, likely would have been done by an academic press and would have attracted a small audience of specialists in military history. It seems doubtful that additional studies of his career would ever have been necessary.

We know, of course, that the "end" of MacArthur's career in 1935 proved only a prelude to the next sixteen years that would see the general thrust into worldwide prominence and into the center of numerous controversies. The beginning of this phase of MacArthur's life came with a call from the Philippines.

The summons that ultimately would place MacArthur on the center of the world stage came from Manuel Quezon, first president of the new Philippine Commonwealth. With the islands scheduled to receive their independence in 1946, Quezon was concerned about the country's security. He wanted MacArthur, whom he had come to know and admire during the 1920s, to serve as his military adviser and supervise the development of a force that would be capable of defending the Philippines when the Americans left. The task appealed to MacArthur and he accepted Quezon's lucrative offer.

Between 1936 and 1941 MacArthur worked on what was envisioned as a ten-year plan to develop a viable military force for the Philippines. At the center of his scheme was the creation of a Swiss-style citizen army that would be led by a small group of professional soldiers in the event of war. In addition, a force of bombers and torpedo boats would be needed to ensure the security of the islands.

Inadequate funding from both the U.S. and the Philippine governments soon caused the program to fall far behind schedule. It probably did not matter much in the end; MacArthur's defense scheme likely would not have succeeded in any event.

In July 1941 worsening relations with Japan caused President Roosevelt to recall MacArthur to active duty as commander of U.S. Army forces in the Far East, and to federalize Filipino defense units. Ten new Filipino divisions were to be raised and trained, with additional troops to be sent from the United States. MacArthur would even receive the bombers—B-17s—that he had wanted as an important component of his defense strategy.

It all came too little and too late. By the time the Japanese attacked Pearl Harbor on December 7, 1941, Filipino mobilization had hardly begun and most of the promised American reinforcements had not yet sailed from the United States. Several squadrons of B-17s, however, had arrived in the islands—just in time to be destroyed by Japanese air attacks.

Naturally MacArthur's conduct during the early days of the war was later the subject of considerable scrutiny. The general's critics faulted him for failing to take prompt action to protect his air force and for neglecting to stock adequate supplies for his troops in Bataan. Yet, either despite or because of his leadership, the Philippines held out for five long months in the face of determined Japanese forces.

Evacuated to Australia at President Roosevelt's orders, MacArthur was hailed as a national hero by both Americans and Australians at a time when the Allies were desperate for heroes. Instead of bearing the responsibility for the worst defeat in American history and suffering an ignominious sacking like Pearl Harbor's commanders had, he was praised by Washington for his heroic defense against what seemed unstoppable Japanese assaults. Gen. George C. Marshall, the army's chief of staff, even arranged for MacArthur to receive his long-desired Congressional Medal of Honor.

MacArthur's campaign along his jungle road to Tokyo—from Australia, across New Guinea, and into the Philippines—became controversial and was destined to generate a torrent of books and articles. Some writers heaped praise on MacArthur, emphasizing his determination, boldness, skilled use of air power and amphibious forces, and inspirational leadership. They believed he overcame immense logistical problems and a constant shortage of men and material to conquer a stubborn and well-led enemy.

Other authors raised questions about the viability of the entire strategy in the Southwest Pacific, seeing MacArthur's political machinations as responsible for a waste of resources. Arrogant and vain, MacArthur was far better at generating favorable publicity for himself than at waging war. Victories often came about despite rather than because of his leadership. Much of the credit for the defeat of Japanese forces should go to his talented subordinates in the field.

The controversies surrounding MacArthur's generalship during World War II are unlikely ever to be resolved. Both his admirers and critics, however, might agree on one point: MacArthur was extraordinarily lucky. And, as Napoleon once commented, this quality should be prized above all others when it comes to waging war.

The end of World War II marked the spread around the world of American power and influence. In Japan MacArthur possessed a unique authority. Designated as the Supreme Commander for the Allied Powers (SCAP), he oversaw a fundamental reconstruction of the conquered nation with little outside interference. MacArthur used his great power to dismantle Japan's military structure, formulate a new constitution that emphasized democratic principles, and bring about far-reaching economic and social reforms.

Critics of MacArthur have pointed out that the policies governing the rebuilding of Japan were in fact formulated in Washington, not Tokyo. This was true, but MacArthur embraced these policies and implemented them with gusto. Without question he was responsible for setting Japan's course for the next fifty years. If he had done nothing else of note during his career this alone would have entitled MacArthur to a position of prominence in the American century.

North Korea's invasion of South Korea in June 1950 turned Mac-Arthur's attention once more to the battlefield. Following initial setbacks for his United Nations forces, he dismissed pleas for caution and launched a bold invasion at Inchon. Many things could have gone wrong but the gods of war again smiled on MacArthur. His troops promptly defeated the enemy in the south then pushed north across the thirty-eighth parallel. All thoughts of a quick victory, however, vanished when China intervened before the end of the year. MacArthur wanted to expand the war but his superiors in Washington had different global priorities. His all-too-public disagreement with these priorities caused President Truman to relieve him of command in April 1951.

MacArthur's career ended in controversy. Hailed by most Americans as a hero when he returned to the United States, public enthusiasm soon faded. He spent the final years of his life in virtual seclusion in New York City's Waldorf-Astoria Hotel.

The selections that follow should be taken as an introduction to Mac-Arthur's lengthy and noteworthy career. If one of the most distinctive features of the American century has been the expansion of the United States across the Pacific Ocean, Douglas MacArthur—the Far Eastern general—surely must be credited with playing a major role, for good or ill, in shaping the character of the American impact on Asia. The controversies surrounding the spread of American influence are mirrored in his actions. Though MacArthur can be criticized, he cannot be ignored.

CHRONOLOGY

1880	Born on January 26 at U.S. Army Arsenal, Little Rock Barracks, Arkansas
1893–97	Attended West Texas Military Academy
1899–1903	Student at U.S. Military Academy; graduated first in a class of ninety-four cadets
1904–13	Served in Philippine Islands, Panama, and United States as an engineering officer
1913–17	Appointed to general staff of War Department
1917–19	Chief of staff (later, brigade commander), Forty-second Infantry Division, American Expeditionary Force
1919–22	Superintendent, U.S. Military Academy
1922–25	Served in Philippine Islands
1925–28	Commanded corps areas in the United States
1928–30	Commander, Philippine Department
1930–35	Chief of staff, U.S. Army
1935–41	Military adviser to the Philippines; field marshal in Philippine army
1941	Recalled to active duty with U.S. Army in July as commander, U.S. Army Forces, Far East
1942	Designated commander, Southwest Pacific Area, following defeat in the Philippines
1943	Conducted New Guinea campaign
1944	Returned to Philippines, wading ashore on Leyte on October 20
1945	Accepted Japanese surrender on September 2; appointed Supreme Commander, Allied Powers, Far East (SCAP)
1945–50	Instituted reforms in occupied Japan
1950	Appointed commander in chief, United Nations Forces, Far East, following North Korean invasion of South Korea in June
1951	Relieved of command by President Truman on April 11
1964	Died in Washington DC on April 5; buried at MacArthur Memorial, Norfolk, Virginia

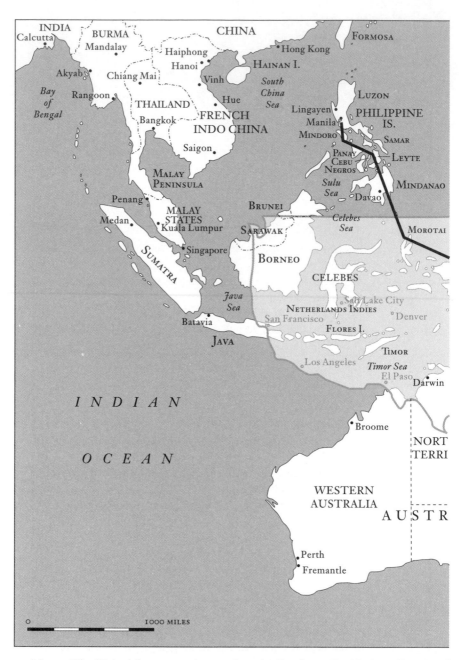

Map 1. The United States superimposed on the Southwest Pacific Area. Reprinted from *Reports of General MacArthur*, vol. 1, *Campaigns of MacArthur in the Pacific* (Washington: GPO, 1966).

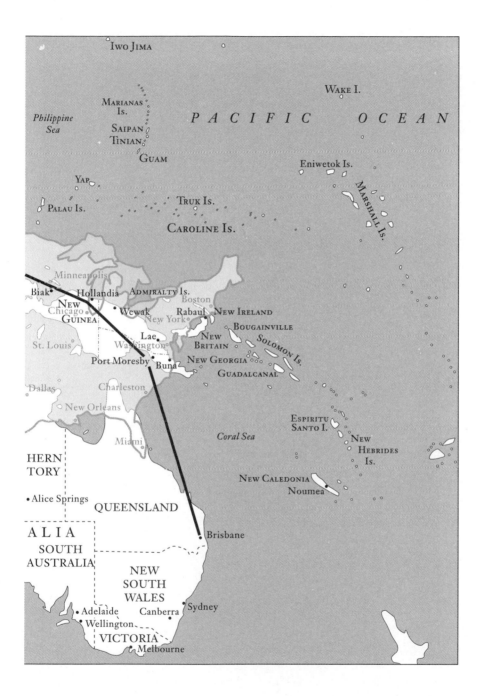

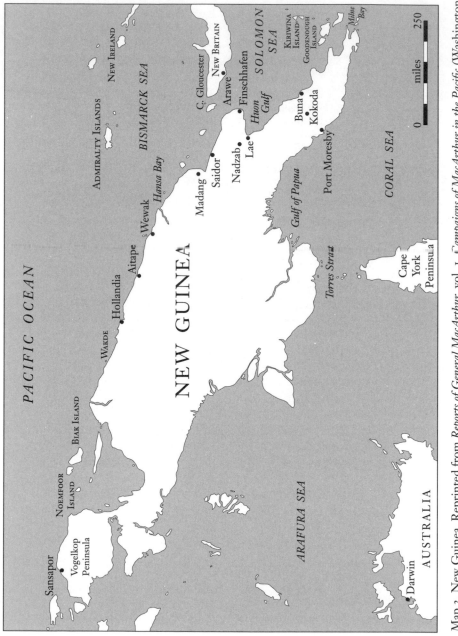

Map 2. New Guinea. Reprinted from *Reports of General MacArthur*, vol. I, *Campaigns of MacArthur in the Pacific* (Washington: GPO, 1966).

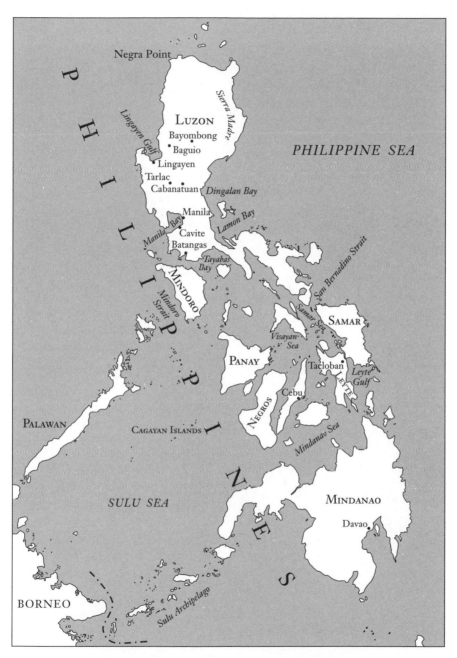

Negra Point

PHILIPPINES

Lingayen Gulf

Sierra Madre

LUZON
• Bayombong
• Baguio
• Lingayen
Tarlac •
• Cabanatuan   Dingalan Bay

PHILIPPINE SEA

• Manila
Manila Bay
Cavite
Batangas   Lamon Bay

Tayabas
Bay

MINDORO

Mindoro
Strait

San Bernadino Strait

Samar Sea

SAMAR

Visayan
Sea

PANAY

Tacloban

Leyte
Gulf

LEYTE

Cebu

NEGROS

Cagayan Islands

PALAWAN

Mindanao Sea

SULU SEA

MINDANAO

Davao •

BORNEO

Sulu Archipelago

Map 3. The Philippines. Reprinted from *Reports of General MacArthur*, vol. 1, *Campaigns of MacArthur in the Pacific* (Washington: GPO, 1966).

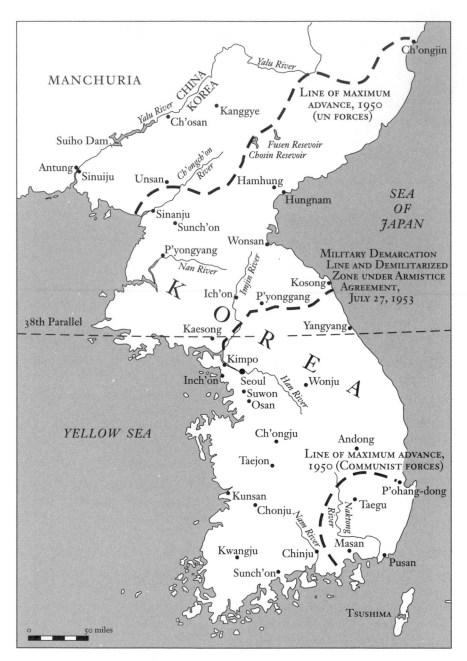

Map 4. Korea. Reprinted from Robert F. Futrell, *The United States Air Force in Korea*, *1950–1953*, rev. ed. (Washington DC: U.S. Air Force, 1983).

1. Growth to Maturity

Let Us Remember

Douglas MacArthur

Addressing the annual reunion of the Veterans of the Forty-second Infantry Division in Washington DC *on July 14, 1935, MacArthur treated his wartime comrades to an idealized view of the place of the American soldier—and the United States—in history. In a rhetorical style that was rooted in the nineteenth century he spoke against the prevalent antiwar sentiment in the country and called for preparedness.*

Mr. President and gentlemen of the Rainbow Division, I thank you for the warmth of your greeting. It moves me deeply. It was with you I lived my greatest moments. It is of you I have my greatest memories.

It was seventeen years ago—those days of old have vanished, tone and tint; they have gone glimmering through the dreams of things that were. Their memory is a land where flowers of wondrous beauty and varied colors spring, watered by tears and coaxed and caressed into fuller bloom by the smiles of yesterday. Refrains no longer rise and fall from that land of used-to-be. We listen vainly, but with thirsty ear, for the witching melodies of days that are gone. Ghosts in olive drab and sky blue and German gray pass before our eyes; voices that have stolen away in the echoes from the battlefields no more ring out. The faint, far whisper of forgotten songs no longer floats through the air. Youth, strength, aspirations, struggles, triumphs, despairs, wide winds sweeping, beacons flashing across uncharted depths, movements, vividness, radiance, shadows, faint bugles sounding reveille, far drums beating the long roll, the crash of guns, the rattle of musketry—the still white crosses!

And tonight we are met to remember.

The shadows are lengthening. The division's birthdays are multiplying; we are growing old together. But the story which we commemorate helps us to grow old gracefully. That story is known to all of you. It needs no profuse panegyrics. It is the story of the American soldier of the World War. My estimate of him was formed on the battlefield many years ago and has never changed. I regarded him then, as I regard him now, as one of the world's greatest figures—not only in the era which witnessed his achievements but for all eyes and for all time. I regarded him as not only one of the greatest military figures but also as one of the most stainless; his name and fame are the birthright of every American citizen.

The world's estimate of him will be founded not upon any one battle or even series of battles; indeed, it is not upon the greatest fields of combat or the bloodiest that the recollections of future ages are riveted. The vast theaters of Asiatic conflict are already forgotten today. The slaughtered myriads of Genghis Khan lie in undistinguished graves. Hardly a pilgrim visits the scenes where on the fields of Chalons and Tours the destinies of civilization and Christendom were fixed by the skill of Aetius and the valor of Charles Martel.

The time indeed may come when the memory of the fields of Champagne and Picardy, of Verdun and the Argonne shall be dimmed by the obscurity of revolving years and recollected only as a shadow of ancient days.

But even then the enduring fortitude, the patriotic self-abnegation, and the unsurpassed military genius of the American soldier of the World War will stand forth in undimmed luster; in his youth and strength, his love and loyalty, he gave all that mortality can give. He needs no eulogy from me or from any other man; he has written his own history, and written it in red on his enemy's breast. But when I think of his patience under adversity, of his courage under fire, and of his modesty in victory I am filled with an emotion I cannot express. He belongs to history as furnishing one of the greatest examples of successful and disinterested patriotism. He belongs to posterity as the instructor of future generations in the principles of liberty and right. He belongs to the present—to us— by his glory, by his virtues, and by his achievements.

The memorials of character wrought by him can never be dimmed. He needs no statues or monuments; he has stamped himself in blazing flames upon the souls of his countrymen; he has carved his own statue in the hearts of his people; he has built his own monument in the memory of his compatriots.

The military code which he perpetuates has come down to us from even before the age of knighthood and chivalry. It embraces the highest moral laws and will stand the test of any ethics or philosophies ever promulgated for the uplift of mankind. Its requirements are for the things that are right, and its restraints are from the things that are wrong. Its observance will uplift everyone who comes under its influence. The soldier, above all other men, is required to perform the highest act of religious teaching—sacrifice. In battle and in the face of danger and death he discloses those divine attributes which his Maker gave when He created man in his own image. No physical courage and no brute instincts can take the place of the divine annunciation and spiritual uplift which will alone sustain him. However horrible the incidents of war may be, the soldier who is called upon to offer and to give his life for his country is the noblest development of mankind.

On such an occasion as this my thoughts go back to those men who went with us to their last charge. In memory's eye I can see them now—forming grimly for the attack, blue-lipped, covered with sludge and mud, chilled by the wind and rain of the foxhole, driving home to their objective and to the judgment seat of God. I do not know the dignity of their birth, but I do know the glory of their death. They died unquestioning, uncomplaining, with faith in their hearts and on their lips the hope that we would go on to victory.

Never again for them staggering columns, bending under soggy packs, on many a weary march from dripping dusk to drizzling dawn. Never again will they trudge ankle-deep through the mud on shell-shocked roads. Never again will they stop cursing their luck long enough to whistle through chapped lips a few bars as some clear voice raised the lilt of "Madelon." Never again ghostly trenches, with their maze of tunnels, drifts, pits, dugouts—never again, gentlemen unafraid.

They have gone beyond the mists that blind us here and become part of that beautiful thing we call the Spirit of the Unknown Soldier. In chambered temples of silence the dust of their dauntless valor sleeps, waiting. Waiting in the chancery of Heaven the final reckoning of Judgment Day: "Only those are fit to live who are not afraid to die."

Our country is rich and resourceful, populous and progressive, courageous to the full extent of propriety. It insists upon respect for its rights, and likewise gives full recognition to the rights of all others. It stands for peace, honesty, fairness, and friendship in its intercourse with foreign nations.

It has become a strong, influential, and leading factor in world affairs. It is destined to be even greater if our people are sufficiently wise to improve their manifold opportunities. If we are industrious, economical, absolutely fair in our treatment of each other, strictly loyal to our government, we, the people, may expect to be prosperous and to remain secure in the enjoyment of all those benefits which this privileged land affords.

But so long as humanity is more or less governed by motives not in accord with the spirit of Christianity, our country may be involved by those who believe they are more powerful. Whatever the ostensible reason advanced may be—envy, cupidity, fancied wrong, or other unworthy impulse may direct them.

Every nation that has what is valuable is obligated to be prepared to defend against brutal attack or unjust effort to seize and appropriate. Even though a man be not inclined to guard his own interests, common decency requires him to furnish reasonable oversight and care to others who are weak and helpless. As a rule, they who preach by word or deed "peace at any price" are not possessed of anything worth having, and are oblivious to the interest of others including their own dependents.

The Lord Almighty, merciful and all-wise, does not absolutely protect those who unreasonably fail to contribute to their own safety, but He does help those who, to the limit of their understanding and ability, help themselves. This, my friends, is fundamental theology.

On looking back through the history of English-speaking people, it will be found in every instance that the most sacred principles of free government have been acquired, protected, and perpetuated through the embodied, armed strength of the peoples concerned. From Magna Charta to the present day there is little in our institutions worth having or worth perpetuating that has not been achieved for us by armed men. Trade, wealth, literature, and refinement cannot defend a state— pacific habits do not insure peace nor immunity from national insult and national aggression.

Every nation that would preserve its tranquility, its riches, its independence, and its self-respect must keep alive its martial ardor and be at all times prepared to defend itself.

The United States is a pre-eminently Christian and conservative nation. It is far less militaristic than most nations. It is not especially open to the charge of imperialism. Yet one would fancy that Americans were the most brutally blood-thirsty people in the world to judge by the frantic efforts that are being made to disarm them both physically and morally. The public opinion of the United States is being submerged by a deluge of organizations whose activities to prevent war would be understandable were they distributed in some degree among the armed nations of Europe and Asia. The effect of all this unabashed and unsound propaganda is not so much to convert America to a holy horror of war as it is to confuse the public mind and lead to muddled thinking in international affairs.

A few intelligent groups who are vainly trying to present the true facts to the world are overwhelmed by the sentimentalist, the emotionalist, the alarmist, who merely befog the real issue, which is not the biological necessity of war but the biological character of war.

The springs of human conflict cannot be eradicated through institutions but only through the reform of the individual human being. And that is a task which has baffled the highest theologians for 2,000 years and more.

I often wonder how the future historian in the calmness of his study will analyze the civilization of the century recently closed. It was ushered in by the end of the Napoleonic Wars which devastated half of Europe. Then followed the Mexican War, and the American Civil War, the Crimean War, the Austro-Prussian War, the Franco-Prussian War, the Boer War, the Opium Wars of England and China, the Spanish-American War, the Russo-Japanese War, and finally, the World War—which, for ferocity and magnitude of losses, is unequaled in the history of humanity.

If he compares this record of human slaughter with the thirteenth century, when civilization was just emerging from the Dark Ages, when literature had its Dante; art, its Michelangelo and Gothic architecture; education, the establishment of the famous colleges and technical schools of Europe; medicine, the organization of hospital systems; politics and the foundation of Anglo-Saxon liberty, the Magna Charta—the verdict cannot be that wars have been on the wane.

In the last 3,400 years only 268—less than 1 in 13—have been free from wars. No wonder that Plato, the wisest of all men, once exclaimed, "Only the dead have seen the end of war!" Every reasonable man knows that war is cruel and destructive. Yet, our civilization is such that a very little of the fever of war is sufficient to melt its veneer of kindliness. We all dream of the day when human conduct will be governed by the Decalogue and the Sermon on the Mount. But as yet it is only a dream. No one desires peace as much as the soldier, for he must pay the greatest penalty in war. Our Army is maintained solely for the preservation of peace—or for the restoration of peace after it has been lost by statesmen or by others.

Dionysius, the ancient thinker, twenty centuries ago uttered these words: "It is a law of nature, common to all mankind, which time shall neither annul nor destroy, that those that have greater strength and power shall bear rule over those who have less." Unpleasant as they may be to hear, disagreeable as they may be to contemplate, the history of the world bears ample testimony to their truth and wisdom. When looking over the past, or when looking over the world in its present form, there is but one trend of events to be discerned—a constant change of tribes, clans, nations; the stronger ones replacing the others, the more vigorous ones pushing aside, absorbing, covering with oblivion the weak and the worn-out.

From the dawn of history to the present day it has always been the militant aggressor taking the place of the unprepared. Where are the empires of old? Where is Egypt, once a state on a high plane of civilization, where a form of socialism prevailed and where the distribution of wealth was regulated? Her high organization did not protect her. Where are the empires of the East and the empires of the West which once were the shrines of wealth, wisdom and culture? Where are Babylon, Persia, Carthage, Rome, Byzantium? They all fell, never to rise again, annihilated at the hands of a more warlike and aggressive people; their cultures memories, their cities ruins.

Where are Peru and old Mexico? A handful of bold and crafty invaders destroyed them, and with them their institutions, their independence, their nationality, and their civilization.

And saddest of all, the downfall of Christian Byzantium. When Constantinople fell, that center of learning, pleasure, and wealth—and all the weakness and corruption that goes with it—a pall fell over Asia and southeastern Europe which has never been lifted. Wars have been fought these nearly five centuries that have had for at least one of their goals the bringing back under the Cross of that part of the world lost to a wild horde of a few thousand adventurers on horseback whom hunger and the unkind climate of their steppes forced to seek more fertile regions.

The thousand years of existence of the Byzantine Empire, its size, its religion, the wealth of its capital city were but added incentives and inducements to an impecunious conqueror. For wealth is no protection against aggression. It is no more an augury of military and defensive strength in a nation than it is an indication of health in an individual.

Success in war depends upon men, not money. No nation has ever been subdued for lack of it. Indeed, nothing is more insolent or provocative or more apt to lead to a breach of the peace than undefended riches among armed men.

And each nation swept away was submerged by force of arms. Once each was strong and militant. Each rose by military prowess. Each fell through degeneracy of military capacity because of unpreparedness. The battlefield was the bed upon which they were born into this world, and the battlefield became the couch on which their worn-out bodies finally expired. Let us be prepared, lest we, too, perish.

> They will tell of the peace eternal,
>   And we would wish them well.
> They will scorn the path of war's red wrath
>   And brand it the road to hell.
> They will set aside their warrior pride
>   And their love for the soldier sons.
> But at the last they will turn again
>   To horse and foot and guns.
>
> They will tell of the peace eternal,
>   The Assyrian dreamers did.
> But the Tigris and Euphrates
>   Ran through ruined lands,
> And amid the hopeless chaos
>   Loud they wept and called their chosen ones
> To save their lives at the bitter last,
>   With horse and foot and guns.
>
> They will tell of the peace eternal,
>   And may that peace succeed.
> But what of a foe that lurks to spring?
>   And what of a nation's need?
> The letters blaze on history's page,
>   And ever the writing runs,
> God, and honor, and native land,
>   And horse and foot and guns.

MacArthur as West Point Superintendent

Stephen A. Ambrose

In his history of West Point Stephen Ambrose gives high marks to MacArthur for leading the military academy into the twentieth century. MacArthur modernized the curriculum, codified the honor code, created a system of intramural athletics, and sponsored other fundamental reforms in an institution that was highly resistant to change. His three years as superintendent proved a formative time in the evolution of his beloved West Point.

"If Sylvanus Thayer was the Father of the Military Academy, then Douglas MacArthur was its savior." So William A. Ganoe decided, and there was much truth in what he said.[1] MacArthur rescued the Academy in a time of crisis; like Thayer, he changed its orientation, turning it from a self-centered institution that was oblivious of the society that created it into an institution alive to its responsibilities. MacArthur's challenge was essentially the same as Thayer's—to turn out graduates demonstrably useful to the United States. The country's needs had changed—it no longer required a public institution for civil engineers; it did need a cadre of professional soldiers able to lead civilian soldiers in war involving the large masses of society—but the principle remained the same. Still, MacArthur could not blindly follow Thayer. Most of his practical problems were entirely different from those Thayer faced. The Father of the Military Academy had the active support of the army and the West Point faculty, while his opposition came from outside the establishment. MacArthur had to overcome the intense and sometimes fanatical resistance of the old graduates and the Academic Board, while he found his strongest supporters among the ranks of civilian educators and commentators.

In the broadest sense MacArthur's task was more difficult than Thayer's, for Thayer did not have to struggle against the tyranny of the past. MacArthur's chief problem was not to formulate specific new approaches or ideas but to effect a general breakthrough. If he could do that, if he could get the Academy to recognize and accept the need for change, the need to throw out some of the antiquated methods, the rest would come sooner or later. He did do so, and that was his greatest contribution.

MacArthur found on his arrival a surly Corps of Cadets whose morale was faltering and an academic program that was badly disorganized. The cadets the War Department had admitted in 1918 had been promised graduation in June, 1919, but when the war ended, the date was delayed to 1921; in disgust, over one hundred members of the class resigned. The 1918 graduates who had been ordered back to the Academy for additional training as "commissioned officers unassigned" were furious and made no attempt to hide their feelings. The Academic Board favored an immediate return to the four-year course, but Congress fixed the term at three years.[2]

MacArthur's most pressing problem was the length of the course, and his first task, which was also among his easiest, did resemble Thayer's. MacArthur protested that the congressional attempt to save money by reducing the course to three years was misguided. "The government's expenditures for military needs are a form of national insurance from which come dividends year by year," he said. "A comparatively small outlay by the United States will serve in future wars to lessen the tremendous expense and the loss of blood for which no money can repay when the unforeseen tragedy is upon us."[3] For one of the few times in his career as Superintendent, MacArthur had the support of the old graduates and the Academic Board. They all urged Congress to reconsider, none more strongly than General Pershing, who firmly declared in a public letter to Representative John J. Morin, "Four years is none too great a time for the character forming . . . [that is] the greatest advantage of West Point."[4] Congress gave in and allowed the Academy to return to the four-year course.

During the debate over the length of the course the *New York Times* raised what is conceived to be a related issue. In supporting the reduction of the course to three years, the newspaper declared, "We need less 'pipeclay' and less seclusion at the Military Academy—in one word, more democracy. During their four years' term the cadets see about as little of the world as the inmates of a convent. When they graduate they know little of human nature, and the only men they have handled are themselves."[5]

MacArthur agreed with everything the *Times* said, except that he could not see how it related to three versus four years, and the main trend of his administration would be to move the Academy in the direction the newspaper urged. MacArthur also found support for his ideas from the President Emeritus of Harvard University, Dr. Charles W. Eliot. In a far-reaching, yet detailed criticism, Eliot declared in 1920 that in the first place no American college should accept "such ill-prepared material as West Point accepts. Secondly, no school or college should have a completely prescribed curriculum. Thirdly, no school or college should have its teaching done almost exclusively by recent graduates of the same school or college who are not teachers and who serve short terms." Turning to results, which the Academy always cited as proof of the perfection of the system, Eliot charged that "during the Great War, West Pointers were unable to adapt to new methods in the fields of supply and procurement, because of their stifling training."[6]

Colonel James G. Steese, of the War Department General Staff, prepared a more or less official answer to Eliot. After taking up Eliot's points one by one ("The entrance requirements at West Point are about equivalent to those of the average college of the United States"), Steese concluded: "We admit that West Point is hard, and we admit that it is narrow. We consider that it is well that at least one institution should continue in the United States which holds that the duties of its students are more important than their rights."[7]

Someone in the War Department should have checked with the Superintendent at West Point before firing off an answer to Eliot. MacArthur, it turned out, not only agreed with the Harvard president but went further. In his first annual report, MacArthur explained his thinking. He assumed West Point's mission was to provide officers capable of leading men in future wars. At the Academy, it had always been thought that this unchanging mission could best be accomplished with unchanging methods. MacArthur disagreed. "Until the World's War," he pointed out, "armed conflicts between nations had been fought by . . . a small fraction of the populations involved. These professional armies were composed very largely of elements which frequently required the most rigid methods of training, the severest forms of discipline, to weld them into a flexible weapon for use on the battlefield." But all that had changed. "Early in the World's War it was realized to the astonishment of both sides that the professional armies . . . were unable to bring the combat to a definite decision. It became evident that war was a condition which involved the efforts of every man, woman and child in the countries affected."

The rousing of the nation to arms brought about an entirely different kind of army. Now officers had to lead men who represented the sturdiest parts, and not the scurviest, of society, men eager to fight who only had to be told where and how. Discipline was no longer a problem, so the old rules and methods no longer sufficed. A new type of officer was needed, one "possessing an intimate understanding of the mechanics of human feelings, a comprehensive grasp of world and national affairs, and a liberalization of conception which amounts to a change in his psychology of command."[8] Or, as MacArthur put it more succinctly to Ganoe, "How long are we going on preparing for the War of 1812?"[9]

As long ago as the early part of the nineteenth century, the Prussian Minister of War, Leopold von Boyen, had compared the two approaches to war. "The old school places all its trust in the standing army," he said, while "the modern school believes . . . that the country cannot be defended by a standing army alone. . . . The old school believes that arbitrary authority and discipline alone makes soldiers, the new school that it is necessary for the army to follow changing civilian custom. . . . The old school wishes to consider military questions without the participation of the public; the new school holds that the defense of the state is impossible without the material and moral co-operation of the entire nation."

MacArthur announced that he intended to do away with cadet provincialism, increase cadet responsibility, especially so as to prevent as much as possible the automatic performance of stereotyped functions and develop initiative, bring the Academy into a newer and closer relationship with the army at large, substitute subjective for objective discipline, broaden the curriculum to keep it abreast of the best civilian thought on education, and in sum "deliver a product trained with a view to teaching, leading, and inspiring the modern citizen" in the next war.[10]

The Academic Board was astonished. No Superintendent since Lee had made any internal changes at the Academy without consulting the Board and obtaining its approval, and none since Thayer had even dreamed of such far-reaching changes. The Board liked neither MacArthur's methods nor his objectives. The members, senior men all (five had been professors when MacArthur was a plebe), felt themselves responsible for the integrity of the Academy; Superintendents came and went, but they stayed on. MacArthur soon faced the active hostility of a majority on the Board; his only supporters with any power in the administration were his adjutant, Ganoe, and his commandant, Robert M. Danford; and only Danford had a vote on the Board.

It was in the nature of the institution that the Board's opposition would be effective. Many years later Ganoe, who in the meantime had served for nearly a decade in civilian universities, said he had never discovered another "group so powerful and deeply entrenched."[11] The members had tenure, status, and an intimate knowledge of the workings of the Academy, while the Superintendent was a transient who was fortunate if the knew the right questions to ask. The Superintendent had one vote on the Board, which was therefore controlled by the professors. The Board had authority to determine the time allocated to each department, to conduct and grade examinations, to grant diplomas, to recommend cadets for commissions, to choose textbooks, and to suggest changes in the course of study or methods of instruction.[12]

Thus great power rested in the hands of the members of the Board, most of whom felt in 1919 that the only change needed was an immediate return to the pre-war system that had bred the great leaders of World War I. MacArthur himself quickly saw one reason for this attitude. "The professors are so secure, they have become set and smug," he told Ganoe. "They deliver the same schedule year after year with the blessed unction that they have reached the zenith in education." They did not have to compete for grants, promotions, or chairs; they had no need to fear deans, presidents, trustees, or regents. They retained their "highly respectable and regarded position by merely going along."[13]

Under the circumstances, MacArthur was at a distinct disadvantage. His personality did not help. A supreme egotist, he found it difficult to pay proper respect to the professors or to work a tone of deference into his voice when he talked to them. He badly hurt their feelings by announcing his intentions without consulting with them or asking their advice. He felt a strong sense of mission and considered his program so obviously necessary that he never explained it fully to the Board; the members, consequently, saw him as a brash young man meddling in areas he did not understand. MacArthur understood what he was about, in fact, and had carefully studied the problems before coming to his conclusions, but the Board never knew this, and he never took its members into his confidence.

There was a certain aura about MacArthur that prevented people from getting close or really understanding him or his aims. One cadet of the time remembered, "Neither I nor the vast majority of my class ever saw the general, except when he was walking across diagonal walk, apparently lost in thought, his nose in the air, gazing at distant horizons as his publicity photos always portrayed him throughout his career." He shocked everyone with his unconventional uniform, which included a sloppy cap from which he had removed the wire stiffener and a short overcoat. Pershing had strictly forbidden such dress, so the impression MacArthur gave was that "he was not only unconventional but perhaps a law unto himself." MacArthur's habit of returning salutes with a casual lift of his ever-present riding crop added to the impression, especially since the Academy prided itself on being punctilious in matters of military courtesy.[14]

MacArthur's majestic bearing and his astonishing record of accomplishment intimidated people. He did nothing to dispel this attitude and allowed very few men to get close to him. Indeed, he took such pleasure in his own superiority that not many tried. One result was that the distance between the Superintendent and the Academic Board grew even greater. Another problem was that MacArthur knew he would be at the Academy for five years at best, and he felt a sense of urgency which was totally absent in the Board, whose members had been there for decades and would stay on long after MacArthur was gone. They saw no need to hurry. Neither understood the other.

The professors were not unaware that there were things wrong with West Point, that some traditions and practices could be defended only on the ground that they had always been. What the Board feared was that any tampering with the framework would bring the entire edifice tumbling down. MacArthur saw things differently; to him it seemed obvious that unless the building was shored up and repaired by making long-needed changes, the whole structure would rot away. Both the Superintendent and the Academic Board wanted to preserve the century-old system—MacArthur, when he assumed his duties, said, "We have to hold fast to those policies typified in the motto of the Academy, DUTY-HONOR-COUNTRY"—but their approach was so different that there was no possibility of their working together.

MacArthur did try; he made more of an effort to meet the Board halfway than it did to meet him, although both the Superintendent and the members strove to keep surface relations friendly. Only once did the deep but underlying hostility come into the open. One of MacArthur's proposals was to bring to the Academy as instructors Regular Army officers who had graduated from civilian institutions and gave promise of being excellent teachers. Like Eliot, he thought the inbreeding at West Point had gone much too far, and he suspected that the professors were bringing back as instructors those former cadets whom they had liked without making an attempt to secure the best teachers. He asked the War Department to prepare a list of those potential instructors who would meet his criteria. Then he explained his plan to the Academic Board. A stuffy silence followed. Finally, one of the oldest members of the Board delivered his opinion. The plan, he said, was a step backward. The instructor from outside simply could not fit into the section room, could not handle the cadets, could not appreciate the West Point system. It was bound to fail. As the professor sat down, MacArthur quietly pointed out that non-graduates were already instructing in the department of modern languages and in the gymnasium with great success. He contin- ued to defend his idea, but the professor began to interrupt more and more frequently. Soon he was cutting in on the middle of MacArthur's sentences. Finally the Superintendent exploded. He banged his fist on the table and shouted, "Sit down, sir. I am the Superintendent!" He looked around the room, then added, "Even if I weren't, I should be treated in a gentlemanly manner."[15]

Failing to persuade the professors by his arguments, the Superinten- dent decided to send them to civilian institutions to see for themselves the great strides that were being made in education. He himself did not inspect any civil schools, but he read widely—he was especially well versed in John Dewey's writings on education—and was aware of what they were doing and accomplishing. The professors resented the implication that they had anything to learn from civilians and resisted, but he required them to spend one month of each year at another school of their own choosing to observe and absorb new methods and ideas. The program was not a great success, but a few of the professors did admit that they had learned something.[16]

This was the age of the social sciences, and MacArthur hoped that the professors' observations at the civilian schools would persuade them to add a whole new series of courses. In time he asked the members of the Board for courses in psychology, sociology, economics, and political science, all designed to broaden the cadet's education and prepare him for his new responsibilities. The Board gave MacArthur a combined course in economics and political science—even that did not get under way for some years—and nothing else.[17] And, as if in reply to MacArthur's pro- gram, in 1920 the Academic Board stated in its report on the curriculum, "The Military Academy is intended to impart a specialized training for a specialized purpose, and this purpose is not the same as that of any civilian institution."[18]

MacArthur next tried visiting the professors individually in their offices and attending sections himself. Neither procedure had ever been employed before. Through these methods he was able to induce some professors to make some changes. In modern languages, he persuaded the professor to eliminate the past system of daily marking for those cadets who had no preparation for the particular language, thus encouraging the deficient cadets to make known their difficulties and permitting the instructors to help them. The English department put more emphasis on public speaking, organizing a course in the subject and a debate team. It also required each cadet to read two newspapers daily and discuss the day's news in the first ten minutes of class. In natural philosophy the professor agreed to allow the cadets to use a slide rule; in drawing, more time was spent on maps; chemistry added lessons on the internal-combustion engine; the department of military art and history abandoned the detailed study of the campaigns of the Civil War and substituted for them the campaigns of World War I; in history, more emphasis was placed on the Far East.[19]

The changes were coming too fast for the Academic Board, but MacArthur was winning some of the members over. In 1921 he got a majority of the Board to agree to recommend three changes: instructors should spend the first year of their appointment to the Academy at civilian universities, taking courses in the particular study they would teach; each professor would visit three separate institutions of higher education as an observer each year; to relieve the isolation, more general lectures by men of authority and reputation would be given to the entire Corps.[20] That was something, but in relation to what MacArthur had hoped to accomplish it was not very much. Owing to the hostility of the Board, the curriculum was the area in which he was least successful in his efforts to reform.

On other matters MacArthur did not need to consider the Board. Its authority was limited to the curriculum, and it was outside that area he had his great successes. One of his first acts was to abolish Fort Clinton, the area east of Trophy Point where summer camp was held. It was a drastic break with one of West Point's oldest and most hallowed traditions. For over a century the cadets had gone to camp to do a little drilling in the morning, rest or gossip in the afternoon, and attend formal hops in the evening. It was a carefree life, a welcome respite after the academic year, marked by excellent food served by civilian waiters in a magnificent mess hall, by band concerts, and by guard duty pranks. Social life at the Academy revolved around summer camp, and the officers—and their wives—were shocked when MacArthur terminated it. But he was determined to produce soldiers, men who knew something of the army and of their profession beyond fancy uniforms and formal hops. During his Superintendency the cadets spent their summers at Camp Dix, New Jersey, training with Regular Army troops under the guidance of career sergeants who were delighted with the opportunity to put the cadets through a program of basic training. When it was finished, MacArthur made the cadets march back to West Point, with full gear and no help from enlisted men.[21]

MacArthur had another objective in sending the cadets to Camp Dix; he wanted to introduce them to at least a portion of the outside world. This was a major part of his program, and he did everything he could to accomplish it. When he went to the Academy, West Point was still following the system set up by Thayer, and the only time in four years that a cadet got away from the post was the summer furlough at the end of his Third Class year. There was no Christmas leave, no leave of absence. Cadets were allowed off the post only on horseback, and then they were on their honor not to dismount or halt. They had absolutely no contact with civilians. MacArthur himself later recalled the situation. "They had no opportunity to familiarize themselves with the mores and standards of people in the world without," he said, "so that when they graduated and mingled freely with their fellows, they had no common background of knowledge and awareness. They were thrust out into the world a man in age, but as experienced as a high school boy. They were cloistered almost to a monastic extent."[22]

Working from his premise that West Point was created and supported by the nation in order to provide leaders in war—officers, that is, who could lead citizen-soldiers—MacArthur did all he could to see to it that cadets came into contact with civilians. In large part, expanding the horizons of the cadets meant allowing them more privileges, something which brought down on the Superintendent the wrath of the old graduates. Unlike the Board, the alumni had no power and could only grumble or sometimes rant. MacArthur gave the cadets $5.00 a month in cash, to spend where and how they chose. He granted upperclassmen six-hour leaves on week ends, except during the summer months, when they received two-day leaves, a relative freedom that allowed them to go into New York City. "They acquire by their small business transactions and by their contact with the outside world," MacArthur explained, "the beginnings of an experience which will be of value to them when they graduate." During the spring term, First Classmen could walk out of the gates at will. All cadets were allowed to receive packages from home as ordinary mail and no longer had to submit them to a tactical officer for inspection. MacArthur gave First Classmen the status of junior officers in their social relations with the officers of the post, which meant they could make calls, attend parties, and even play cards with the officers and their wives. The three upper classes were allowed to organize themselves, electing a president, vice-president, and other officers.[23]

Nothing upset the alumni and the professors more than MacArthur's liberalization of the regulations. Allowing the cadets to enjoy more freedom struck, it was believed, at the very structure of the Academy. For over a century West Point had been a place of rhythm and harmony, a place where behavior was governed by strict regulations, a place that substituted order and the collective will for presumption and individualism. But it was not just the loss of serenity implicit in MacArthur's program that bothered the old grads, not just the painful knowledge that there would be times when no one in authority would know where the cadets were or what they were doing; rather they had a substantial objection. Order, discipline, and a sense of community were necessary to the efficient working of an army, and MacArthur seemed to be destroying them all.[24]

The principle was that in the army, and thus at West Point, the individual's needs must be subordinate to those of society. MacArthur was in full agreement with this basic dictum of the military ethic; what he feared was that West Point had gone too far and in its enforced conformity had lost sight of its, and the army's, duty to society. The dictum was true only in its broadest sense; in specific terms, West Point and the army had to recognize that the nature of war itself had changed, was constantly changing. Here was the crux of the matter, the proposition the Old Guard could never accept; to them only tactics changed. A new type of officer was needed, one who could subordinate his own needs but at the same time could lead civilians who had an advanced concept of their rights and who were reluctant to accept the military ethic. In fact, the citizen-soldiers often found their motivation in fighting the exact opposite of the military ethic.

MacArthur himself could say, "In many businesses and professions the welfare of the individual is the chief object, but in the military profession the safety and honor of the states become paramount,"[25] but in modern war it was not enough merely to state the theory. Officers had to *convince* civilians acting as soldiers of its necessity for the duration of the conflict, and they could never do so unless they understood the civilians. In turn, they would never understand the civilians unless they shared some experiences with them.

All of this is not to say that West Pointers had, before MacArthur, subscribed to some kind of *ancien régime* system of values, as was sometimes asserted. Graduates were, after all, Americans before they became cadets, and they represented their society. Even had it tried to do so—and it never did—the Academy could not have changed the cadets from Americans into professional European soldiers who scorned those who engaged in pursuits for profit. Grant, Sherman, McClellan, Halleck, and many others were extensively engaged in real estate, manufacturing, railroading, and other business activities before the Civil War. The concept of "honor" held by French officers shocked Eisenhower and the other American generals who dealt with them in 1942. And General Mark Clark used a commercial metaphor to describe one of those dealings: "Darlan was a political investment forced upon us by circumstances, but we made a sensational profit in lives and time through using him."[26] For the European professional, honor and glory may have sufficed; for the American soldier, true representative of his society, efficiency and results counted. General Matthew Ridgway, who graduated two years before MacArthur became superintendent, opposed officers who wasted lives for "glory." He could also make the statement, "All lives are equal on the battlefield. . . . The dignity which attaches to the individual is the basis of Western civilization."[27] Nevertheless, before MacArthur, the emphasis had been placed on unquestioning obedience and the subordination of the individual to the group. And certainly there had been no attempt to introduce cadets to the civilian world which they served and from which the soldiers in the next war would come. This opportunity MacArthur tried to provide.

Part of his program was to turn out officers whom the ordinary citizen-soldier would respect. He had been greatly impressed during the war with how much better athletes among the officer corps performed than did non-athletes and with how much enlisted men admired athletes. The West Point physical fitness program was already better than that offered by any college, but MacArthur decided to extend it, to the point that it eventually became an *idée fixe* at the Academy. Quoting John Dewey— "There is an impossibility of insuring general intelligence through a system which does not use the body to teach the mind and the mind to teach the body"—he introduced what he correctly believed to be "one of the most complete physical regimes in any institution in the world." He centered his program around competitive athletics, not the individual or group calisthenics which American boys have always hated. The key was a program of intramural athletics, with each company fielding a team in each sport—football, baseball, soccer, lacrosse, tennis, basketball, track and field, and golf and polo. All cadets were required to participate. The play was so rough, especially in intramural football, that the cadets came to call it "intra-murder." MacArthur was delighted with the results. "Nothing more quickly than competitive athletics brings out the qualities of leadership, quickness of decision, promptness of action, mental and muscular coordination, aggressiveness, and courage," he said. "And nothing so readily and so firmly establishes that indefinable spirit of group interest and pride which we know as morale."[28] Or, as he put it in the lines he had carved on the stone portals of the gymnasium:

Upon the fields of friendly strife
Are sown the seeds
That, upon other fields, on other days
Will bear the fruits of victory.[29]

MacArthur's success with the athletic program was offset by his failure in his dealings with Congress. He asked for two things—an extensive building program and a doubling of the size of the Corps of Cadets— and got neither. In both cases he was really too late; during the war, when Congress appropriated nearly any amount the army asked for, he might have received the money he needed for construction. He once told Danford that during the war everyone connected with West Point must have been sound asleep. "Here, while we spent billions on the Army, not a penny of it came to West Point!" He repeatedly asked Congress for money to build and in one report included extensive drawings of needed construction, but to no avail.[30]

He had the same experience in his attempts to double the size of the Corps. It had been increased in 1916 to a total of 1,334, but the army had also grown, so West Point was only furnishing one-third of its officers. MacArthur argued that, since the overwhelming trend of public opinion was opposed to a large standing army and preparations for war, it was all the more necessary to "increase the small leaven of professionally trained experts to train the great masses of the citizen soldiery which must be improvised in time of strife."[31] But Congress did not increase the Corps until 1935, when it allowed a total of 1,960 cadets.

MacArthur, supported and prodded by the Chief of Staff and remembering his own experiences as a plebe, made the elimination of hazing one of his major goals.[32] Others had tried to achieve this end before him, with no success. Superintendents Ernst and Mills had attempted to use the cadet officers of the First Class to control hazing by ordering them to make sure the Second and Third Classmen did not exert unnecessary authority upon the plebes, but the system never worked, for the First Classmen would not turn in their fellow cadets. Superintendent Scott tried to curb the practice through extremely rigorous regulations, which among other things gave him greater and more arbitrary power, but without the co-operation of the cadets he was helpless. Superintendent Tillman, who suffered through some unfavorable publicity when the Academy underwent a hazing investigation during World War I, also studied the problem closely. He knew that West Point had more trouble than civilian colleges with hazing because the authorities had countenanced the practice, and he charged that for the most part no "serious efforts" had been made to eliminate it. It was difficult to eradicate because tradition held that hazing had always been practiced, because each class knew that its predecessor had indulged in the practice, and because the alumni openly supported it. Tillman's idea, which MacArthur would appropriate as his own, was to put selected upperclassmen in charge of the plebes, giving them recognized and specified authority.[33]

Tillman did not have time to inaugurate his system, and when MacArthur took over, hazing was at its height. The barking, hissing, and snarling of upperclassmen to plebes was more than one cadet, Stephen Bird, could stand, and he committed suicide on New Year's Day, 1919. In trying to stop the practice, however, MacArthur met his stiffest resistance from the graduates, who had come to regard hazing as West Point's most hallowed tradition, and of the cadets themselves. One of his first acts was to meet with a selected group of First Classmen and ask them to study the Fourth Class orientation system and report on it. He charmed the First Classmen by treating them in a friendly, informal manner and even offering them cigarettes, which was against regulations, but he was not able to get what he wanted from them. Eventually they did draw up a pamphlet on plebe customs, listing "acceptable" and "unacceptable" hazing practices, but the upperclassmen simply would not abandon the "tradition." Hazing continued pretty much as it had since the Civil War.[34]

Perforce, MacArthur used sterner methods. One day in 1920 Commandant Danford came to see him and the two began talking about hazing. Danford recalled that early in his army career he had been at Fort Riley, Kansas, where he was given charge of some sixty recruits. Danford trained them just as he would have a plebe in Beast Barracks. After three days his commanding officer called him in and admonished him, "Mr. Danford, we do not handle the American soldier the way a Yearling handles a Plebe at West Point." Danford went on to tell MacArthur that Beast Barracks ought to be abolished; the system terrified incoming cadets, gave them and the upperclassmen who had charge of them a totally wrong impression of army discipline, and was a chief factor in the continuance of hazing. MacArthur agreed, and he and Danford worked out a new system. Beast Barracks would henceforth be run not by upperclassmen but by commissioned officers of the army, and only they would have charge of and contact with the plebes. It was a momentous change, and the alumni set up a howl, but to no avail as long as MacArthur was Superintendent.[35]

Another change in discipline came when MacArthur, with Danford's help, abolished the "skin list." Under the old system, whenever a tactical officer saw an infraction of the regulations or something else amiss during his inspections, he would make a note of the offense, something like, "Smith, T. H.—Grease spots on floor at ten A.M." Taken together, these "skins" made up the skin list, which was read before the Corps in the evening. If Smith had no excuse, he would accept his demerits; if he had one, he would carefully write it out in the prescribed form. A day or two later the tactical officer would just as carefully either accept the excuse and remove the skin or not, as he saw fit. In the latter case Smith could again file an excuse, on which the tactical officer would make another endorsement. Sometimes the notes went back and forth for weeks. Danford wanted to do away with the system, substituting for it a company orderly room on the ground floor of each barracks. There, at a stated hour each day, the tactical officer could handle delinquencies verbally, looking the cadet in the eye and treating him, as a means of teaching him the responsibilities of command, just as a company commander in the army treated his enlisted men.[36]

One of MacArthur's contributions to the Academy has since become

West Point's proudest possession. It is the Honor Committee and the codified honor code. The honor system at West Point dates back to Sylvanus Thayer, who established the principle that a cadet's word is always accepted and consequently that a cadet is expected always to tell the truth. But neither Thayer nor his successors ever spelled out the code or established any investigating and enforcing agency. Sometimes cadets took matters into their own hands, as in 1871 when members of the First Class learned that two plebes had lied to Commandant Emory Upton. Fearful that the cadets would be dismissed by the Academy only to be reinstated by Congress, they took the guilty plebes outside the post, forced them to put on civilian clothes, gave them $50.00, and instructed them never to return. News of the incident soon reached Congress, which investigated, censored Upton and Superintendent Pitcher—both believed the First Class had acted badly but from commendable motives—and reinstated the plebes. Undeterred, the cadets organized a Vigilance Committee, consisting of representatives from each company, to continue the practice, and it continued for years.[37]

The esteem in which West Pointers hold the honor system was best expressed by a 1915 graduate, Dwight D. Eisenhower, shortly after World War II. "I think that everyone familiar with West Point would instantly agree that the one thing that has set it definitely apart from every other school in the world is the fact that for a great number of years it has not only had an 'honor' system, but that the system has actually worked," Eisenhower said.[38] But MacArthur realized that if the honor system were to continue it would have to be on some regular foundation—Vigilance Committees had a habit of changing rules in midstream. He therefore created an Honor Committee, selected by the cadets themselves, which interpreted the honor system to the Corps and brought violations into the open so that the guilty could be discharged by constituted authority. Its procedures and rules were codified, but it had no punitive power. It acted, in effect, as a grand jury, reporting possible violations to the Commandant.[39]

The six general principles of the code are: (1) lying, quibbling, evasion, or a resort to technicalities in order to shield guilt or defeat the spirit of justice are not tolerated; (2) a cadet who intentionally violates the honor system should resign at once and offenders are never granted immunity; (3) anything to which a cadet signs his name means irrevocably what is said, both as to letter and spirit; (4) no intentional dishonesty is condoned; (5) every man is honor bound to report any breach which comes to his attention; and (6) the Corps, individually and collectively, is the guardian of its honor system.

In practice, the effect of the system is that when a cadet tells a tactical officer that his absence after hours is legitimate, his word is accepted; when sections take examinations, the members have their books before them, the instructor leaves the room, and no man cheats; when one section has an examination before the noon meal, which the members of that section take with members of another section that will take the same examination that afternoon, no one discusses the test.

Another MacArthur innovation, which again flew in the face of current American trends, was the military efficiency and conduct rating. In civilian institutions in the twentieth century the dedication was to scholarship, as opposed to the "whole man" concept of the pre–Civil War era, and a sharp distinction was made between academic grades and delinquency demerits, between scholarship and conduct. Harvard led the way in 1869 when it began to rank students on the basis of academic grades alone. Character no longer counted in grading. All that mattered was classroom performance.[40] MacArthur was aware of this trend, which was accepted nearly everywhere by the time he became Superintendent, but he did not approve of it. To him character, the "whole man," was just as important as classroom brilliance. Thus he continued to count demerits in the general standings, but he went further. Military bearing, leadership and personality, military efficiency, athletic performance, and cadet participation in such activities as choir or the YMCA all counted. Cadets were rated periodically by the other cadets in the company on their leadership ability and on other elements of military character, and by the tactical officer attached to the company. The results counted heavily in the final class standings.[41]

Before the Civil War, when West Point was a leading scientific institution, not much was said about character development there, especially since Yale, Princeton, and other such institutions were specializing in that field. After 1865, however, when the civilian institutions began to feel that the whole man could not be educated in traditional ways and simultaneously began to surpass the Academy as practical schools, West Point increasingly maintained that it was different from (and, though no one ever said it publicly, better than) the colleges because of its emphasis on character development. MacArthur approved of this emphasis—no one felt this aspect of the West Point mission more deeply than he did. But he also knew that character development could become a catch phrase, devoid of meaning, that it was difficult to define at best and had to have its roots in reality if it were to retain any meaning. He felt that cadets could be high-minded, clean-living men in an age that ridiculed such phrases, but only if they saw some meaning to those virtues and only if they saw some connection between what they were doing at the Academy and what they would be doing as army officers. The graduates feared that cadets would be contaminated by any contact with the outside world; MacArthur feared they were doomed without it. He was trying to preserve the best in the West Point system, but few understood this and even fewer were willing to rally to his side.

In January, 1922, less than three years after he assumed his duties, MacArthur learned that the Chief of Staff, John J. Pershing, was ordering him to duty in the Philippines. Insofar as he normally could have expected to stay at the Academy for at least four years, the order came as a shock. Immediately West Point, the army, and to a certain extent the nation were alive with rumors. The most obvious explanation was that pressure from the Academic Board and the alumni had forced Pershing and the War Department to relieve the young Superintendent. MacArthur himself hinted as much when he told Ganoe that General Fred W. Sladen, of the class of 1890, was to be his replacement. "I fancy it means a reversal of many of the progressive policies which we inaugurated," MacArthur commented.[42] One young officer stated publicly that the traditionalists in the army were removing MacArthur because he was not Prussian enough.[43] There is, however, no evidence to support the charge.

The official War Department explanation was simple. It kept a roster of general officers available for foreign service, and when MacArthur's name came to the top of the list he was more or less automatically transferred to the Philippines. The explanation, though probably true, satisfied practically no one. In February a fresh rumor cropped up. MacArthur had just announced his engagement to Mrs. Cromwell Brooks, a Philadelphia widow (he married her on February 14 in Palm Beach, Florida). The story was that Pershing had also been a suitor for the hand of Mrs. Brooks and when he lost her decided to punish MacArthur by sending him to the Philippines.

"It's all damn poppycock," Pershing told reporters when asked about the rumor. "If I were married to all the ladies to whom the gossips have engaged me I would be a regular Brigham Young." MacArthur also vehemently denied the allegation.[44] Another story that reached the newspapers was that MacArthur was going to hand in his resignation from the army.[45] Nothing came of it, and in June MacArthur quietly turned the Academy over to Sladen.

The Old Guard may have had nothing to do with MacArthur's transfer, but they certainly welcomed it. In his first year as Superintendent, Sladen did all he could to return to the old ways. He abolished the practice of sending the cadets to Camp Dix for the summer and instead rebuilt the old summer camp, rather smugly noting, "The experience of the summer has proved conclusively that the practice, prevailing for more than a century before 1920, of maintaining a summer camp at West Point for military instruction was based upon sound principles." In the English department, the required daily reading of newspapers was dropped. Sladen did away with MacArthur's practice of granting frequent leaves to upperclassmen and would not allow the cadets to possess cash. He returned Beast Barracks to the upperclass cadets.[46] MacArthur and his innovations, seemingly, had been safely laid to rest.

But that was not really so. MacArthur had brought a new spirit to the Academy, a willingness to experiment, to break with tradition, to question everything, that could never be shut out. Slowly his innovations would be restored, his ideas accepted. If Sylvanus Thayer dominated West Point in the nineteenth century, Douglas MacArthur dominated it in the twentieth. The chief difference was that Thayer had sixteen years in which to impose his personality and ideas, while MacArthur had but three.

Notes

1. Ganoe, *MacArthur Close-Up*, 167.
2. *Annual Report of the Superintendent* (West Point, 1919), 3–5.
3. MacArthur, *Reminiscences*, 78.
4. Baumer, *West Point*, 18–19.
5. *New York Times*, May 21, 1919.
6. *Ibid.*, May 9, 1920.
7. *Ibid.*, May 30, 1920.
8. *Annual Report of the Superintendent* (West Point, 1920), 3–5.
9. Ganoe, *MacArthur Close-Up*, 30.
10. *Annual Report of the Superintendent* (West Point, 1920), 3–5; Boyen is quoted in Ropp, *War in the Modern World*, 153.
11. Ganoe, *MacArthur Close-Up*, 35.
12. John W. Masland and Laurence I. Radway, *Soldiers and Scholars; Military Education and National Policy* (Princeton, 1957), 174–76, has an excellent

discussion of this problem. The authors point out that the Superintendent has a status comparable in some respects to that of a political minister who assumes control of a department of professional civil servants. If the Superintendent wants to make far-reaching changes, he must recognize that he may not be around long enough to see them through, and he has no assurance that they will be continued by his successors. The point is especially well taken if one thinks in terms of the minister in a European multi-party system, such as the Fourth Republic in France.

13. Ganoe, *MacArthur Close-Up*, 88–89.

14. W. S. Nye to author. December 3, 1964, in author's possession. Colonel Nye goes on to point out, "Likely my impression is a superficial one, for by all accounts MacArthur was a man of superior intellect and great leadership ability. All that granted, I think it must be conceded that he was also a man of boundless ambition, and a great actor. All great men, generals included, need such attributes."

15. Ganoe, *MacArthur Close-Up*, 97–99; Danford, writing in *Assembly*, XXIII (Spring, 1964), 13, remembered MacArthur's expression as "Sit down, Sir, I'm talking."

16. Ganoe to author, February 27, 1965, in author's possession; *Assembly*, XXIII (Spring, 1964), 18–19.

17. *Annual Report of the Superintendent* (West Point, 1920), 20–22.

18. Quoted in *ibid.*, 6.

19. *Annual Report of the Superintendent* (West Point, 1921), 23–25; *ibid.* (West Point, 1922), 13.

20. *Ibid.* (1921), 15–17.

21. *Assembly*, XXIII (Spring, 1964), 11; Ganoe, *MacArthur Close-Up*, 33; *New York Times*, August 19, 1920.

22. MacArthur, *Reminiscences*, 81.

23. *Annual Report of the Superintendent* (West Point, 1922), 7–8; *ibid.* (1921), 11–12; Baumer, *West Point*, 173–74.

24. Allen Guttmann, "Political Ideals and the Military Ethic," *The American Scholar*, XXXIV (Spring, 1965), 221–37, has an excellent discussion of the military ethic.

25. Quoted in *ibid.*, 231.

26. Quoted in *ibid.*, 228.

27. Quoted in *ibid.*, 232.

28. *Annual Report of the Superintendent* (West Point, 1922), 11; Baumer, *West Point*, 188–89; *Assembly*, XXIII (Spring, 1964), 11.

29. MacArthur, *Reminiscences*, 82.

30. *Assembly*, XXIII (Spring, 1964), 14.

31. *Annual Report of the Superintendent* (West Point, 1921), 10–13.

32. MacArthur, *Reminiscences*, 81.

33. Superintendent's Annual Report, 1918, in *Annual Report of the War Department* (Washington, 1918), I, 1423–24.

34. *Assembly*, XXIII, (Spring, 1964), 9; Nye to author, December 3, 1964, in author's possession. Nye reports that one of his classmates who attended the meeting said later that "he thought MacArthur to be somewhat of a poseur and not very frank or sincere with the cadets." I am deeply indebted to Colonel Nye for his help on this chapter; he was kind enough to grant me a long interview, to put his comments in writing, and to give me permission to quote him.

35. Ganoc, *MacArthur Close-Up*, 103–7.

36. *Ibid.*, 120–21.

37. Ambrose, *Upton*, 72–75.

38. *Report to the Superintendent by the* USMA *Committee on Service Academies* (West Point, 1949), 77–78.

39. *Ibid.*, 78; *Assembly*, XXIII (Spring, 1964), 9.

40. Rudolph, *American College*, 348.

41. *Annual Report of the Superintendent* (West Point, 1920), 10.

42. Ganoe, *MacArthur Close-Up*, 157.

43. *New York Times*, February 5, 1922.

44. *Ibid.*, February 10, 1922.

45. *Ibid.*, February 8, 1922.

46. *Annual Report of the Superintendent* (West Point, 1923), 7.

Douglas MacArthur

Dwight D. Eisenhower

While serving in Washington as assistant executive to the secretary of war (1929–33) and special assistant to the chief of staff (1933–35), Dwight D. Eisenhower decided to "jot down from time to time impressions of people with whom I came in contact." He believed that at some point in the future "it will be fun to review these to determine whether my impression was a permanent one." His initial views of MacArthur are insightful and at times erroneous, especially concerning MacArthur's lack of political ambition. After years of close association with MacArthur, Eisenhower would have cause to revise his opinions of his superior, and not in a favorable direction.

Douglas MacArthur, General, Chief of Staff

Fifty-two years old. Essentially a romantic figure. I have done consider-able personal work for him, but have seen far less of him than of other seniors now in the dept. Very appreciative of good work, positive in his convictions—a genius at giving concise and clear instructions. Consid-eration of the principal incidents in his career leads to the conclusion that his interests are almost exclusively military. He apparently avoids social duties as far as possible—and does not seek the limelight except in things connected with the Army and the wd. Magnetic and extremely likable. Placed a letter of commendation on my record—and has assured me that as long as he stays in the Army I am one of the people earmarked for his "gang."

In my opinion he has the capacity to undertake successfully any position in govt. He has a reserved dignity—but is most animated in conversation on subjects interesting him. I doubt that he has any real political ambition—and in these days of high powered publicity and propaganda—I do not expect to see him ever prominently mentioned for office outside the wd.

Most people that have known Gen. MacA. like and admire him to a degree. These same people, however, almost without exception profess themselves to be incapable of understanding his policies with respect to the Army's commissioned personnel. The mention of any kind of promotion system involving selection seems to be anathema to him—and he will tolerate no suggestion of "forced elimination." Generally speaking in naming officers for promotion to Brig. Gen. he seems to select the older and senior ones—regardless of qualifications. In this one thing even those who have known him longest seem to consider him reactionary and almost bigoted. In my own part, while some of his "makes" have astounded me, I know that there is nothing personal in his attitude toward this matter, and that the policy he is following has been adopted only after careful study and consideration on his part. The chief of these reasons I believe to be a hatred of favoritism and special privilege.

He is impulsive—able, even brilliant—quick—tenacious of his views and extremely self-confident. It might be remarked too that he has not appointed some of his new Brigadiers under any delusions as to their abilities. He is too shrewd for that!! The answer is that, in his opinion at least, he is pursing a course representing the lesser of two evils.

The Army and the Bonus Incident

John W. Killigrew

As John Killigrew of the American University points out, the use of regular troops against the unarmed civilians of the Bonus Expeditionary Force was a public relations disaster for both the army and Chief of Staff MacArthur. He goes on to argue, however, that the criticism was largely undeserved; MacArthur, for his part, was only following the orders of his superiors. Other scholars who have examined this episode have been more critical of MacArthur's performance.

One of the most controversial incidents that involved the Army during the depression years, and one which brought it into the political arena and the focus of public debate, was the use of the Regular Army to disperse the bonus marchers in Washington during the summer of 1932. The Regular Army had been used infrequently in the past to put down civil disturbance, the most recent incident which had an impact on public opinion being the use of federal troops during the Pullman Strike in Chicago during 1895.[1]

In early June 1932, with the arrival of the bonus people in Washington, Congress sought to make available to them Army cots, blankets, tents, surplus clothing, and medical and mess facilities. The War Department opposed such a scheme on the grounds that utilization of Army stocks would cause such depletion as to "require replacement with additional appropriations." By mentioning the increased cost of any proposal the Army was confident it could parry congressional importunities. Congress was told that its plans to house and clothe the bonus people with military supplies violated the "basic principles" of the War Department and the Army hoped that there would be no further discussion of the matter.[2]

In the opinion of the Army the motley assemblage of veterans congregating in Washington was hardly worthy of aid and comfort; indeed, the War Department was concerned with the possibility of serious disturbances and some anxiety that the development of close relationships between the bonus marchers and the troops would have a deleterious effect on the reliability of the latter in case they were called out for riot duty. According to one officer who participated in the eviction of the bonus people this factor made some impression on the War Department: "Initially, the relations between the troops and the Marchers were so good as to cause some concern among War Department staff officers who, unlike the officers on duty with the troops, were somewhat doubtful about the reliability of the troops if their services were needed."[3]

General Douglas MacArthur, the Chief of Staff, was alert to the possibility that the concentration of disaffected and unemployed people in Washington, petitioning *en masse* before Congress, was a potential source of unrest and perhaps violence. Soon after the arrival of these people in the capital he took precautionary action to prepare the Army for any eventuality. Early in June the Chief of Staff wired all corps area commanders that in case any bonus marchers passed through their respective corps areas it should be determined if any communist elements were present. The corps area commanders were directed to "report in secret code" to Washington indicating the presence of communist elements and the names of the leaders of the bonus marchers with "known communistic leanings."[4] The Army felt that if it had the ultimate responsibility for the maintenance of law and order in the national capital such information was of critical value in forming a sound estimate of the situation in reference to potential trouble in Washington. But of greater significance this radiogram reflected the fact that the Army was seriously concerned over the potentiality of disturbances and violence throughout the country as a result of unemployment and the social and economic upheaval brought on by the depression. It seemed therefore to the General Staff that prudence required planning for this very real probability.

In general the replies of the corps area commanders to the General Staff reflected the ignorance of the subordinate commanders in respect to the composition of the bonus marchers, and because of the lack of reliable information they were unable to appraise intelligently the social and political makeup of the various groups heading for Washington. The corps area commanders had only rumors or little known facts as a basis for their replies, and obviously did not think that the presence of communists, as a source of potential violence, was a serious matter. From Baltimore, the Commander, III Corps Area, reported that there were no known information of communists within the bonus group that had left this city, but that there was a "general feeling of unrest . . . to the general effect that some serious trouble is likely to arise at an early date."⁵ This was the only report from the nine subordinate territorial commanders that indicated the possibility of trouble for the War Department in Washington. In fact the general tenor of the replies was likely to soothe the concern of the beleaguered War Department in the capital. General Edward L. King reported from Atlanta that communists and troublemakers were "making little effect on southern bonus marchers."⁶

General Malin Craig wired from the Presidio that the bonus units leaving the West Coast for Washington had announced that they would not tolerate any communist elements and that to his knowledge there was no evidence of communist influence. Indeed, Craig added, among the bonus marchers from the West Coast "discipline" and "conduct were excellent."⁷ In respect to the bonus people that had already concentrated in Washington G-2 reported to the Chief of Staff that of twenty-six "so-called" leaders of the Bonus Army, three were reported to be communist or affiliated with communist organizations.⁸

MacArthur's concern and anxiety over the possibilities of trouble was further reflected in the fact that in early June two experimental vehicles from Aberdeen Proving Ground, a T-4 armored car and a 75mm self-propelled gun, were ordered to Fort Myer to be available in case trouble ensued in the nation's capital.⁹

At the same time the Chief of Staff directed that the War Department's "White Plan," which contemplated the employment of the Regular Army in Washington in case of emergency, be revised. The Commanding General of the 16th Brigade, comprising the Regular Army units in and around Washington, prepared the new plan and forwarded it to MacArthur. According to this plan,

> the greater part of the bonus marchers have thus far resisted all attempts of the Communists to gain control of them but there are a number of well-known Communist leaders here and they are claiming credit for the instigation of the march.
>
> Any demonstration therefore will almost certainly contain ex-soldiers without a desire for Communist affiliations and Communists themselves who will try by overt acts, possibly of violence, to commit the veterans.
>
> Our operations, therefore, should contemplate giving an opportunity to the non-Communist veterans to disperse, but of course the tactics employed

must depend on the commander on the spot and the character of the emergency.

For this reason, tear gas grenades are provided which would be used in sufficient numbers to be effective if the character of the disorder did not require more drastic action at once.

The operation plan went on to direct that in case of an emergency the assembly area for the troops would be the Ellipse in the rear of the White House facing Constitution Avenue. The plan also directed that the "White House, Treasury Buildings, Bureau of Engraving and Printing and the Capitol are critical points and their protection primarily must be foreseen."[10]

Early in July Congress appropriated money for the return of the veterans to their homes and over 5,000 of the estimated 12,000 veterans then in Washington left the city. By the end of July there was estimated to be around 5,000 members of the "BEF" (Bonus Expeditionary Force) in Washington.[11] Congress adjourned on July 16 without passing a bonus bill and there seemed no apparent reason why the BEF should remain in the capital.

On July 21 the bonus people were informed by the Washington police that eviction of the BEF from government-owned buildings along Pennsylvania Avenue, between the Capitol and the main business district of Washington, would begin within twenty-four hours. These buildings were in the process of being demolished in order to make way for a proposed park, and the absence of plumbing made the sanitation problem acute. The order was postponed and the threat of a showdown between the police and the BEF forestalled. On July 27 the order was reissued and eviction began on the morning of the 28th. After one building had been cleared a fight between the police and some of the bonus marchers ensued and one of the latter was killed by police gunfire. News of the fight brought additional bonus marchers to the scene, and early in the afternoon the District Commissioners reported to Hoover that the situation was out of control.[12]

This development was followed by Hoover ordering the Regular Army to disperse the bonus marchers and presumably evict them from Washington. At 2:55 P.M. on the afternoon of July 28, the Secretary of War issued the following order to MacArthur: "The President has just informed me that the civil government of the District of Columbia has reported to him that it is unable to maintain law and order in the District.

You will have United States troops proceed immediately to the scene of disorder. Cooperate fully with the District of Columbia police force which is now in charge. Surround the affected area and clear it without delay.

Turn over all prisoners to the civil authorities.

In your orders insist that any women and children who may be in the affected area be accorded every consideration and kindness. Use all humanity consistent with due execution of this order."[13]

The 16th Brigade, numbering about 600 troops from the 3rd Cavalry, 1st Tank Regiment, and the 12th Infantry Regiment were alerted at 1:40 P.M. to assemble at the Ellipse on the afternoon of the 28th. The discrepancy in the time factor between the alert at 1:40 P.M. and the order from Hurley, more than an hour later, is explained by the fact that Hoover requested the District Commissioners to inform him in writing that the situation was out of hand before orders were actually given to use Regular troops. At 3:50 P.M. General Perry Miles reported to MacArthur for orders at the Old State-War-Navy Building at the corner of 17th Street and Pennsylvania Avenue. MacArthur showed Miles the order from Hurley, and informed him also that as Chief of Staff he would accompany the Army, "not with a view of commanding the troops but to be on hand as things progressed, so that he could issue necessary instructions on the ground." At 4:10 P.M. General Miles issued his field order at the Ellipse giving his subordinate commanders instructions for the move against the bonus marchers. At 4:30 P.M. the advance to the "affected area" began. This area consisted of portions of Pennsylvania Avenue between the Capitol and the main part of the Washington business district. The main BEF camp was located east of the Capitol across the Anacostia River.[14]

According to one officer who participated in the dramatic advance up Pennsylvania Avenue on that warm summer afternoon in 1932, the "affected area" below the Capitol was

> a fantastic mixture of rioters, spectators, shoppers, streetcars, baby carriages, police, infantry, and officers from the War and Navy Department in civilian clothes.
>
> The rioters, well-supplied with bricks and hunks of concrete, also had considerable shelter in the partly dismantled buildings. An infantry squad with fixed bayonets quickly pushed its way into the building where the police had been resisted most successfully, ignored the rioters and went at the double

up the stairs to the roof. . . . The cavalry, operating with drawn sabers, largely to keep the rioters from grabbing at bridles, cleared the avenue, and the long job of pushing the rioters out of the center of Washington and across the Anacostia River began.

Initially, there was considerable resistance and the troops had several casualties from rock showers. The task was made more difficult by the necessity of halting before advancing to give time to innocent spectators to get out of the way. This, unfortunately, also gave the rioters time to reorganize and to get more bricks, and also time to try to get around the flanks of the troops and infiltrate with the general public back toward Pennsylvania Avenue.[15]

By 8:00 P.M. the "affected area" along Pennsylvania Avenue had been cleared and the bonus marchers had been pushed out of the center of Washington to their encampment across the Anacostia River, and the first phase of the incident had ended. At 9:00 P.M. the 16th Brigade was ordered to proceed to the Anacostia Flats, the area of the BEF bivouac, and evacuate all bonus marchers from the area. Hurley's original order to MacArthur did not indicate exactly what the Army was to do after the "affected area" near the Capitol was cleared, and it appears that MacArthur gave the order to clear the Anacostia camp area at the direction of the President. According to one student of the incident it is "inconceivable that any troop movements were carried out contrary to his (Hoover's) express command."[16] The movement of the Army into Anacostia to disperse the BEF camp was one event that was most severely criticized. Hoover's critics considered that to drive the bonus people out of their only place of shelter during the night was a rather harsh measure. However, the President's decision was probably based on the realization that had the BEF been given time to organize their forces, a much more serious situation might have developed. Any appraisal of Hoover's action must take into consideration the fact that for eight weeks the city's inhabitants had been annoyed by the presence of thousands of bonus marchers.[17]

Anacostia Flats lies some two miles or so southeast of the Capitol. Here on low ground along the east bank of the river the BEF had erected its makeshift camp. Crossing the Anacostia River bridge at 11th Street the infantry formed a line for "direct pressure" southward through the general camp area with cavalry units covering the left flank, the right flank being covered by the river. General Miles reported the following vivid, if not too clear, account of the ensuing operation.

The occupants of the Bonus Marchers' camp were allowed until 11:15 P.M. to remove their property and evacuate. At 11:15 P.M. the Infantry began its movement. . . . The movement forward was assisted by searchlights furnished by a fire truck provided by the Metropolitan Police Department. Little resistance was met in the camp except on the part of individuals, most of whom were intoxicated. When the (Infantry) Battalion reached the heights south of the camp, the right flank company was greeted with a shower of rocks. Companies K and I moved up the escarpment to the railroad track and drove the mob to the Northeast, using gas. . . .

While this was going on the mob which had been driven off the property just south of the flats had foregathered with a crowd estimated at about 2,000 which had formed along the south edge of the flats. About this time a large part of the mob started a movement toward the Southeast part of the burning camp apparently with a view of flanking the troops. . . . Colonel Kunzig had also noticed the movement of the mob and had "Assembly" blown on the bugle. The Battalion reformed and the mob fell back into Anacostia. At 2:00 A.M. the troops bivouacked.

The next morning cavalry reconnaissance determined that the BEF had evacuated the Anacostia Flats area, and at noon the Army was ordered to return to Washington and evict remaining bonus marchers from areas of Southwest Washington. During July 29, success in disbursing the BEF and the "steady exodus" of the bonus people from all camps in Washington proper indicated that the Army could be returned to their regular posts during the evening. MacArthur announced that he intended to "relieve all troops by night."[18]

The final report of the incident by the infantry regiment commander noted that the use of tear gas and the resulting surprise, along with a lack of leadership in the BEF, insured success for the Army. This officer noted after the initial action by the troops there was a "barrage of profanity, the throwing of missiles and the return of tear gas grenades." He commented that many spectators joined with the bonus marchers in using "insulting language toward the troops," and that some of the BEF tried to fraternize with the regulars and get them to disregard their orders. Analyzing the participation of the troops in this sensitive duty, the officer reported: "The troops met this duty with forbearance and restraint and throughout the operations remained calm and collected notwithstanding the resistance and insulting remarks of both Bonus

Marchers and spectators. They used tactful force and were intent on accomplishing their mission effectively and satisfactorily."[19]

The report of the officer who commanded the cavalry units that participated in the incident went into greater detail. According to his report: "Prior to the disturbance the officers, men and animals were put through a thorough course of training in anticipation of their being called upon for Riot Duty against the BEF. The attitude of all therefore was well defined and general. As far as this command was concerned it was purely impersonal. All took the attitude that the duty was just another job although a difficult one requiring unusual control. At no time was any sympathy shown to the Bonus Marchers." It was reported that up to the time the bonus marchers showed active resistance the cavalry troopers displayed no resentment. Upon receiving the rock showers of the BEF the troops became antagonistic: "During this fight they (the Cavalry troops) became thoroughly angry but were easily restrained after each trotting charge. The punishment and casualties received were taken as a matter of course. On the second day the general attitude was more antagonistic and the men would undoubtedly have used their permitted weapons more severely if resistance had been encountered." Success in putting down the riotous bonus people, according to this officer, was "due to the serious intention of the regulars to handle the situation" and this led to the conviction among the BEF that it was "hopeless to oppose the regular troops. . . ." At the same time various spectators and others obtained a "lasting lesson in the effectiveness of regular troops during disorders."

In addition, the opportunity to point out the value of mounted troops in this sort of civil disturbance was not missed. According to the report, the horse, non-toxic gas, and the saber are more effective than the rifle and the bayonet in civil disturbances, because the time interval during contact, before the latter are used as a deadly weapon, is considerably shorter compared to cavalry weapons. The report emphasized: "Undisciplined people on foot will not withstand the advance of the mounted man and they are universally afraid of being trampled by the horse. The saber was a great aid as a punishing power. The flat of the saber was used plentifully and the point some—mainly in threatening those showing an inclination to turn during retreat." The report concluded by urging that the Army give more publicity to its operations against the BEF on July 28–29 so that a "conviction in the general mind that it will act relentlessly and will use at once any amount of force necessary to destroy resistance will result in its mere presence being sufficient to end many disorders."[20]

The result of this unique affair had an unfortunate effect on the Army: The use of regular troops against unarmed civilians from a public relations point of view was a disaster. The liberal reform element in American political tradition, intrinsically distrustful of the professional military class, considered this display of force by the Regular Army vivid evidence of the danger of "militarism." Certainly the incident played directly into the hands of the anti-militarist and pacifist groups throughout the country.

MacArthur associated himself with an extremely unpopular and unpleasant duty and consequently received the continuing opprobrium of liberal critics. Although he was executing an order of the Commander-in-Chief, the Chief of Staff insured for himself the relentless antagonism of his critics for directing the use of federal troops against civilians. Coming at the eve of the presidential election of 1932, the eviction of the BEF from Washington served to associate in the popular mind the Army with the Hoover Administration. To those persons throughout the country who were buffeted by economic distress and unemployment the incident seemed cogent evidence that the Army was on the side of the "established order" that was held responsible for the economic situation of the nation. Since the Army is an agent of the Government it is by the very nature of things on the side of the established order.

If, as it has been alleged, the entire affair was the work of communist conspirators, who sought to defame and besmirch the Army in the mind of the public, their work was only too successful.[21] Regardless of the fact that the troops did not use unnecessary force and did not fire a shot, nor inflict a serious casualty, in general public opinion the Army has always been reproached and ridiculed for the eviction of the BEF from Washington in the summer of 1932.

One particular criticism of its role in the bonus episode touched the Army in a most sensitive spot. This criticism was that the Army had prepared special plans and instructions in respect to handling the bonus marchers, and thus had forced the President's hand. In a sense, knowledge that the Army was prepared for any eventuality and capable of evicting the bonus people, thus relieving the Hoover Administration of a most distasteful liability, may have made it easier for the District Commissioners and President Hoover to solve their dilemma. But the Army believed that in preparing for a civil disturbance it was not forming policy, and that the formation of plans and preparations for handling riots was dictated by prudence and sound military procedure. One protest from the American Civil Liberties Union to President Hoover contained the above criticism. MacArthur was indignant over the implication that he conspired to use force against the BEF, and denied that he had issued any special instructions for handling domestic riots. Smarting against criticism of the Army's general planning policy the Chief of Staff requested Hoover to ignore the charges of the ACLU: "Absolutely no instructions have been issued from the War Department at any time during my incumbency of the office of Chief of Staff dealing with any riot troubles or disturbances, and any effort to show any activities along those liens due to the depression are simply fabrications."[22]

Notes

1. "Federal Aid in Domestic Disturbances," *Senate Document 263*, 67th Cong., 2nd Sess. (Washington, 1922). Regular Army troops had been used three times between 1900 and 1932: Nevada—1907, Colorado—1914, and West Virginia—1921.
2. Ltr, Acting Secretary of War Frederick H. Payne to Hon. J. J. McSwain, Chairman House Comm. on Military Affairs, June 25, 1932. AG Bonus (5–28-32), Section 1, Record Group 94, Records of The Adjutant General's Office, The National Archives (hereafter RG 94, NA).
3. Maj. Gen. H. W. Blakeley, "When the Army was Smeared," *Combat Forces Journal*, II (February 1952), 28.
4. Memo, AC/S G-2 for the AG, June 10, 1932, for radiogram to all corps area commanders, AG 240 Bonus (5–29-32), Section 1, RG 94, NA.
5. Ltr, CG 3rd Corps Area to AG, July 5, 1932. AG 240 Bonus (5–28-32), Section 1, RG 94, NA.
6. Tel, King, Fort McPherson, to AG, June 11, 45. WVR, AG 240 Bonus (5–28-32), Section 1, RG 94, NA.
7. Tel, Craig to AG, June 14, 1932. WAF 61, AG 240 Bonus (5–28-32), Section 1, RG 94, NA.
8. Memo, AG for the Chief of Staff, June 12, 1932. AG 24 Bonus (5–28-32), Section 1, RG 94, NA.
9. Ltr, Chief of Ordnance to CO Aberdeen Proving Ground, June 4, 1932. The crews of these vehicles were told that if any person asked the purpose of the trip to Washington they were to reply that the vehicles were to be available in the capital in case anyone wanted to view the latest developments in mechanized equipment. Folder entitled: Rpt of Operations Against Bonus Marchers, 1932, Mil. Dist. of Washington, A46–458, Record Group

98, Records of United States Army Commands, The National Archives (hereafter, RG 98, NA).

10. Memo, Brig. Gen. Perry Miles, CG 16th Brigade, for the Chief of Staff, June 4, 1932. Folder entitled: Rpt of Operations Against Bonus Marchers, 1932, Mil. Dist. of Washington, A46–458, RG 98, NA.

11. Blakeley, "When the Army Was Smeared," p. 28.

12. William C. White and W. W. Waters, BEF *The Whole Story of the Bonus March* (New York: John Day Company, 1933), pp. 175–220. Waters claims that he was "commander" of the BEF. His account of the incident is critical toward the Hoover Administration for its efforts to force the situation after Congress adjourned and evict the bonus marchers from Washington so that it would be relieved of a political liability during the presidential campaign. Waters exonerates MacArthur and the Army but claims that the situation was never out of hand and that the Army need not have been called out to evict the BEF. For a judicious and excellent account of the incident see: Bennett M. Rich, *Presidents and Civil Disorders* (Washington: Brookings Institution, 1941), pp. 150–177.

13. Ltr, Hurley to MacArthur, July 28, 1932. AG 240 Bonus (5–28-32), Section 1, RG 94, NA.

14. Ltr, General Miles, CG 16th Brigade, to Chief of Staff, sub: Rpt of Operations against the Bonus Marchers, August 4, 1932. This letter consisted of Miles's post-action report of the operation. Folder entitled: Rpt of Operations against Bonus Marchers, 1932. Mil. Dist. of Washington, A46–458, RG 98. (Hereinafter cited as Rpt of Operations, 16th Brig.)

15. Blakeley, "When the Army Was Smeared," p. 29.

16. Rich, *The Presidents and Civil Disorders*, p. 175.

17. *Ibid.*, pp. 175–76.

18. Rpt of Operations, 16th Brigade.

19. Ltr, CO 12th Inf Regt to CG 16th Brigade, Washington DC, Aug. 6, 1932. Folder entitled: Rpt of Operations against Bonus Marchers, 1932, Mil. Dist. of Washington, A46–458, RG 98, NA.

20. Ltr, CO 2nd Sqd, 3rd Cav Rgt, to the CG 16th Brigade, August 5, 1932. Folder entitled: Rpt of Operations against Bonus Marchers, 1932, A46–458, Mil. Dist. of Washington, RG 98, NA.

21. Blakeley, "When the Army Was Smeared," p. 26.

22. Ltr, Chief of Staff to Lawrence Richey, Secretary to the President, August 12, 1932. AG 240 Bonus (5–28-32), Section 3, RG 94, NA.

The Defense of the Philippines

Douglas MacArthur

In an address to the faculty and students of the Command and General Staff School at Baguio on August 3, 1936, military adviser MacArthur defended his recently formulated defense plan for the Philippine Islands. MacArthur envisioned the creation of a Swiss-style large reserve force that would be led in time of war by a small group of professional soldiers. The geography of the Philippines, he emphasized, would give the advantage to the defenders. As later events would demonstrate, his analogy between the Philippines and Gallipoli was erroneous.

The basic military problem facing the Philippine Government is whether with its present resources of population and wealth it can develop a defensive force capable of withstanding a more powerfully armed opponent. Does the old boxing adage, so often quoted in athletic circles, "A good big man will always defeat a good little man," unfailingly apply in war? The answer is that the axiom would apply only if the two opponents should meet the issue of combat under practically identical conditions. If each could concentrate its entire army in the vital battle area, and if each were compelled to solve substantially similar problems of supply, transportation, reinforcement, and tactical operation, the larger army would always win. But this equality of conditions never exists in warfare, and war has therefore shown many startling reversals in which the apparently weaker opponent achieved victory. From the classic Biblical example of David and Goliath through the successful Revolutionary War which established American independence, the history of the world is replete with illustrative examples.

In the case of the Philippines, it would be an impossibility for any potential enemy to bring to the Philippine area anything like a preponderant portion of his army. He would indeed have difficulty in concentrating into the vital area as large a force as the Philippine Army which would oppose him. Any conceivable expeditionary force might actually find itself outnumbered.

This country has the enormous defensive advantage of being an island group. Hundreds of miles of water separate it from any other land. The protective value of isolation has time and time again been demonstrated in military history. No other operation in warfare is so difficult as that of transporting, supplying, and protecting an army committed to an overseas expedition. The English Channel has been the predominant factor in the freedom from invasion enjoyed by the British Islands throughout their modern history of many wars. Although Europe has, time and again, seethed with supposedly invincible armies, of which at least two have made elaborate and definite preparations for the invasion of the Island Kingdom, never since modern armies have come into being with their enormous size and huge amounts of impedimenta has Great Britain been compelled to drive off a land attack from its shores. The British Navy has, of course, been a powerful factor in sustaining this security. But in this dual combination of defenses, the ocean obstacle has been the first and more important, and the Navy has been the one to increase the effectiveness of the first.

The United States undoubtedly owes its existence as an independent nation to the friendly Atlantic. The War of the Revolution would have most certainly resulted in ignominious defeat for the Colonies had geography separated them from the mother country by a mere land frontier rather than by 3,000 miles of ocean. In the War of 1812 this factor again permitted the Colonies to withstand the forces of the mightiest empire then existing and preserved the American nation from resubmission to British control.

In the case of the Philippine Islands, we have then as its first favorable factor in solving its defensive problem a geographical separation from every possible land enemy. It is true that there is no thought of attempting to develop here a powerful battle fleet. But it is pertinent to point out that the major duty of a great fleet is to preserve overseas communication. Inshore defense is only a subsidiary function. This function for the Philippines will be performed by flotillas of fast torpedo boats, supported by an air force. Due to the exclusively defensive posture of the Philippine nation, great battle fleets are not necessary to insure its preservation. The islands themselves are to be developed as a citadel of defensive strength and the essential function of air and naval forces will be that of denying transports the opportunity of anchoring close to Philippine shores for the debarkation of troops and supplies.

The threat to large surface ships residing in small fast torpedo boats supported by air detachments was recently indicated in the Mediterranean. It is significant that following the lesson there demonstrated, Great Britain, Germany, and other powers are following the Italian example in adding this particular weapon as an important category in defensive equipment.

But geography did not cease its defensive favors to the Philippines when it made them an isolated group. Nature has studded these islands with mountainous formations, making practicable landing places for large forces extremely few in number and difficult in character. The vital area of Luzon, in which dwell approximately 7 million Filipinos, presents in all its long shore line only two coastal regions in which a hostile army of any size could land. Each of these is broken by strong defensive positions, which if properly manned and prepared would present to any attacking force a practically impossible problem of penetration.

But nature has still further endowed the Philippines with defensive possibilities: 60 per cent of the national terrain consists of great forest areas, impenetrable by powerful military units. The mountainous terrain, the primeval forests, and the lack of communications, combine to create a theater of operations in which a defensive force of only moderate efficiency and strength could test the capabilities of the most powerful and splendidly equipped army that could be assembled here.

Other islands of the Archipelago possess similar defensive possibilities. In some instances no practicable landing places for large forces exist. In every case determined troops at the shore line could deny landing to an attacker of many times their own number.

It is a human trait to magnify the potentialities of an enemy and to underestimate one's own strength. Too often we are apt to take counsel of our own fears. In contemplating the defense of the Philippines we should visualize the enormous effort necessary to launch and prosecute a huge overseas campaign. The difficulties to be overcome by the aggressor in such a situation are not even dimly understood by the layman. Only those who have participated in or witnessed the extraordinary expenditure of energy and money required in such operations can appreciate the obstacles that invariably stand in the way of success. In the World War the United States had practically to change the entire course of its industrial activity in order to send to France the forces required there. Billions upon billions of dollars were poured into the venture and over 100,000,000 people devoted their full energy to its success. Yet, in spite of the fact that its expeditionary forces were dispatched to permanent ports and bases that were in the firm possession of American allies, and no tactical operations of any kind were required in order to establish it ashore, more than a year elapsed before the American Army could place a single complete division on the battlefront.

The amount of shipping that must be withdrawn from commercial activity and transformed into vessels suitable for troop transportation is so great as to present, in itself, a major problem, even to a power rich in maritime resources. To transport 300,000 men with essential equipment and supplies for only 30 days requires approximately 1,500,000 tons of shipping. The greatest total maritime tonnage of any nation operating in the Pacific Ocean is but 4,700,000 tons. These figures give only a faint indication of the serious logistical problems that must be solved whenever an overseas expedition is proposed.

Of all military operations, the one which the soldier dreads the most is a forced landing on a hostile shore. It is at that time he is at his weakest, the enemy at his strongest. His transport frequently arrives at the end of an unpleasant voyage. Crowded accommodations and generally unpleasant conditions have not tended to improve his morale. At the critical moment his ships are forced to come to a standstill in order to undertake the debarkation of the attackers in small boats. At this time motionless targets, they are subjected to an intensive attack from fast-moving torpedo boats and even faster-whirring bombers of the air. Each small boat, with only a fraction of men, has to make its way in through a pitiless fire of artillery, machine guns and musketry—a fire of deadly accuracy because delivered from prepared and protected positions. Yet through this veritable holocaust his small unprotected boat with no means of effective response to the enemy fire must reach the shore, perhaps through a dangerous surf, to discharge its occupants in an attempt to build up a firing line to overcome an emplaced enemy. Subject to desperate counterattack on the beach, perhaps engulfed in poisonous waves of gas, deprived of the inspirational presence of great masses of his comrades, he has always the feeling that goes with a forlorn hope. Lucky indeed the command that can achieve success on such a day and in such a way.

The outstanding World War example of an overseas operation accompanied by landing against a defended shore was the Allied operation at Gallipoli. In the initial stages of that abortive campaign the Gallipoli Peninsula was very inadequately defended and the early naval bombardments encountered only antiquated forts. While it is true that the land attacks were poorly coordinated and failed to achieve the element of surprise because of the warning given the defenders through naval bombardments, still errors of omission and commission of this type are invariably characteristic of attempted landings against defended beaches. The complete failure of the Allied attack is a matter of history. The only point in mentioning it here is to remark that it emphasized again for all students of warfare the tremendous difficulties attendant upon overseas operations and to indicate the degree of reluctance with which any General Staff would commit a major portion of its army to a venture of this character.

In contemplating such an attack any government would have an additional cause for hesitation. This is the tendency of wars to spread and draw into the maelstrom of battle nations that originally had no apparent cause for participating in the quarrel. The World War illustrated this tendency with particular emphasis. Any government that should prepare and send overseas a force of sufficient strength to attack the Philippines would have to consider carefully the possibility of any other potential enemy taking advantage of the situation and entering the contest at a time when the aggressor was seriously committed and possibly even embarrassed in the Philippines.

The layman might attempt to deprecate the force of the considerations I have just enumerated by quoting the experience of Italy in its conquest of Ethiopia. In doing so, he would be guilty of a fundamental error in reasoning, because the implied analogy is almost completely false. The conditions under which Italy invaded and conquered Ethiopia were fundamentally different from those that will exist here after the Defense Plan has reached its full development. Let me amplify:

Ethiopia had no army worthy of the name. Ethiopian troops were sketchily equipped with weapons largely medieval in their characteristics. Ethiopian forces were torn by internal strife; they had no effective leadership; they were loosely organized, and were in fact totally lacking in every phase of modern organization, equipment, and training. Italy was not required to make a landing against a defended shore line. She had two principal land bases from which to begin the campaign, namely, Italian Somaliland and Eritrea. Even so, press reports indicated that the initial mobilization for the campaign began months and months before the first troops were actually shipped, and were so extensive as to test the capacity of Italian resources.

I have no hesitancy in stating, and I believe that my professional opinion in this matter would be substantiated by every General Staff in the world today, that had Ethiopia adopted an adequate system of military development ten years ago and thereafter continued faithfully to organize, train, and equip its military forces in that concept, the Italian armies would not be in Addis Ababa today. More than this, I do not believe that under such conditions the military conquest of Ethiopia would have been attempted.

In the face of this wealth of facts and lessons favoring the defensive potentialities of an island empire, the query naturally arises as to why there should be any serious question as to the ability of the Filipinos to defend themselves with reasonable effectiveness. The answer again is a very simple one. It is because the United States has never stationed in this American possession a sufficient force to defend the Islands against land attack. Since the end of insurrection days the American Army, including its Filipino contingent, has averaged about 10,000 men. With defending forces represented by this pitifully small garrison and with the broad Pacific lying between them and their nearest supporting troops, it was appreciated by all that the Philippines could not be held against strong surprise land attack. This fact was thoroughly understood by the professional soldier and sailor who repeatedly protested and complained, "The Philippines cannot be successfully defended with its present garrisons." By the layman, however, the modifying phrase was ignored and it was translated into the slogan "The Philippines cannot be successfully defended," and this shibboleth finally attained the dignity of an expression of popular opinion. No conclusion could be more false. An adequate garrison can defend the Philippines for as long as available supplies and provisions will sustain the Army and its supporting population. Considering the productivity of these Islands in the matter of food, this period of feasible defense will undoubtedly extend, once the necessary training has been accomplished and the necessary equipment accumulated, far beyond the capacity of any attacker to maintain a large expeditionary force in these territorial waters.

The defensive possibility in the Islands is not entirely an academic question. The Philippine insurrection of almost forty years ago gave us a valuable lesson along this line. In that campaign a poorly equipped and loosely organized force of irregulars, which probably never exceeded 20,000 in its total strength, compelled the American Government, with its bases thoroughly established here and with complete command of the ocean, to support large forces here engaged in bitter field campaign for a period of several years—forces which at one time numbered almost 100,000 men. Had the Filipino Army been properly organized and adequately equipped, the resources in men and money expended by the American Government would have been multiplied many-fold.

Another great advantage accrues to an army when it serves a government whose military policy is purely and passively defensive such as it is here. Under such conditions the Army as a whole and in each of its parts is not diverted by extraneous objectives and missions, but rather is permitted to concentrate its full attention on one specific problem in one specific area. Each unit of the defending army may then, in any future war, operate on a battlefield thoroughly known to its officers and men— on a battlefield in which every part has been thoroughly prepared with the single purpose of preventing penetration by the enemy. The relative advantage enjoyed by a force occupying ground deliberately selected and organized for defense was proven by World War experience to be represented in a numerical advantage of some four or five to one.

The respect accorded to any army organized for a definite and specific defensive task, as in the present instance, is well illustrated in the case of Switzerland. The military system applying in that country more closely parallels the Philippine plan than does any other now in existence. The Swiss Army has no objective except to defend the homeland, within its own national boundaries. It has taken advantage of every geographical feature to increase its tactical power and to make more difficult the problem of any potential invader. So clearly have the general staffs of Europe appreciated the strength of a nation organized and prepared to defend itself with the full power of its citizenship, that for decade after decade, Switzerland, although its population numbers little more than one-fourth that of the Philippines, has maintained its territory inviolate and has successfully avoided entry into any of the conflicts that have engulfed other nations of Europe.

If there are those who scoff at the thought that Filipinos can successfully defend themselves, when once their citizenry has been trained in the profession of arms and equipment in reasonable amounts has been accumulated, let us not forget that the idea of Philippine self-sufficiency in this respect is essentially a new idea. Scoffers will never be lacking when any new concept is advanced. Usually, however, they are found among those who know little or nothing of the facts, but who arrogate to themselves the dogmatic wisdom of popular slogan and glib generality. Those who lightly regard the difficulties of conquering the Philippines know nothing of war themselves and next to nothing about the actual potentialities of the Filipino people, Philippine assets, and Philippine terrain. They forget that this country is numerically stronger than such nations as Turkey, Switzerland, Yugoslavia, Sweden, Siam, Portugal, Persia, Norway, Hungary, Greece, Finland, Czechoslovakia, Denmark, Chile, Argentina, Austria, Bulgaria, and many others now armed to the teeth. Canada has about two-thirds of the population strength of the Philippines. Mexico about the same population as the Philippines. Brazil is the only nation besides the United States in the American continents, including North, South, and Central America, that has a greater population. Indeed, only fourteen nations in the world, I have been informed, have a greater population than the Philippines. In the general staffs of the world, I assure you, you would find no dissenting voice to the assertion that, when the Philippine Defense Plan has reached fruition, it will represent a defensive strength that will give hesitation to the strongest and most ruthless nation in the world. Let me remind you that there were a multitude of skeptics who maintained that Fulton's steamboat would not float, that the Arnacal flight would not reach Madrid, that the Wright brothers would not get their airplane off the ground, that Ericsson's *Monitor* would be a dismal failure, and that Marconi was a visionary at best, and possibly a lunatic at the worst. Defeatists have always been present to greet every new thought, every new idea, and every new attempt at constructive progress. Defeatists laughed at America's attempt to free herself from British control, but today the United States is possibly the most powerful nation in the world.

Defeatists ask how, within the ten years' military budget of $80 million, can a sufficient force be equipped including an air component and an offshore patrol of torpedo boats. Planes cost $30,000 each, boats $35,000. The ten-year budget provides $10 million for the air components, $5 million for the Off-Shore Patrol. To complete the fiscal analysis in broad outline, $30 million go to the Regular force and $35 million to the Reserves. With this latter personnel serving as a civic duty, practically without professional remuneration, a large and adequate part of this latter sum is available for military supply and equipment. Parenthetically, the yearly defense budget amounts to about 22 per cent of the estimated annual governmental income, much less than in most countries.

Only recently I saw two moving pictures that reminded me of this type of defeatist opposition. One portrayed the story of Louis Pasteur and the world's continued and incessant skepticism which so jeopardized his efforts. The other was the film showing the knock-out of Joe Louis by the German Schmeling. Ninety-nine per cent of the sporting world vociferously proclaimed the impossibility of such an outcome. Why? They did not know the facts; they refused to listen to such an unbiased and clear thinking expert as Damon Runyon when he intimated the possibility that the German would reach his goal. He based his conclusion solely upon fact not upon blind hysteria and imitative ballyhoo and thereby arrived at a correct estimate.

I wish to reiterate my fixed opinion that when the Philippine Defense Plan reaches fruition the people of these Islands will be in a favorable posture of defensive security. The question, of course, is one that no sane man would care to see resolved in the only way that it can ever be answered finally and conclusively—namely, by the test of conflict. But so far as the study of history and some considerable experience with armies and with warfare can lend a color of value to my opinion, I am certain that no chancellery in the world, if it accepts the opinions of its military and naval staffs, will ever willingly make an attempt to willfully attack the Philippines after the present development has been completed.

Finally, this one impelling question naturally presents itself as lying at the heart of the issue here involved. "If the Philippines does not prepare for its own defense, to maintain its own security and to preserve its own independence, how are these functions to be performed?" Surely, no other race or nation will expend its youth and its treasure for the defense of this Archipelago. Yet, we know that defenselessness invites aggression and that when unprotected, economic and political independence cannot continue to exist. Pacific habits do not insure peace. Trade, wealth, literature, and refinement cannot defend a state. If others are not to perform these functions for the Filipinos, certainly they must gird themselves for the task. Without security there can eventually be only slavery. With slavery will come national death.

Douglas MacArthur and Manuel Quezon: A Note on an Imperial Bond

Carol M. Petillo

Carol Petillo, a doctoral student at Rutgers University in the late 1970s, raised serious questions about MacArthur's acceptance of a $500,000 payment from the government of the Philippines in the dark days following the Japanese attack on the islands. Although she acknowledges that it is impossible "to determine conclusively all the reasons behind this exchange," she speculates that the payment goes far in explaining aspects of MacArthur's conduct in 1942—and later.

The links by which imperial powers controlled their colonies varied over time. Ranging from the raw power of Spain with its advantages of horses and muskets to the more subtle American progressive school teachers and knowledgeable money-lenders, the connections between governors and governed existed at both the institutional and personal levels. The national wealth of a colonial power grew through the advantages of privileged trade, cheap labor, and the plantation economy; the personal wealth of the representatives of the colonial power was sometimes increased through the perquisites of office, some acknowledged, others carefully camouflaged. The document examined in the following pages is an example of one of the ways this personal wealth was quietly increased.

Executive Order #1, issued on January 3, 1942, by Manuel Quezon, president of the Commonwealth of the Philippines, conveyed $640,000 from the Philippine Treasury to the personal bank accounts of General Douglas MacArthur, commanding general of the United States Army Forces in the Far East (USAFFE), his chief of staff, General Richard K. Sutherland, his deputy chief of staff, General Richard J. Marshall, and his personal aide, Colonel Sidney L. Huff. Although the principals involved in this exchange left no other evidence to explain this document's meaning,[1] a careful search of the records of related government offices indicates that this exchange was more than just another way of extricating funds from the beleaguered Philippines.[2] Indeed, there is every reason to believe that Executive Order #1 was a transaction between two men of great personal power: one who desperately needed aid for his countrymen and security for himself and his family, the other holding the means by which both believed these ends could be achieved.

This document, found in the recently opened papers of Richard K. Sutherland in the National Archives, Washington DC,[3] reads as follows:

FORT MILLS, CORREGIDOR

PHILIPPINES

BY THE PRESIDENT OF THE PHILIPPINES

EXECUTIVE ORDER NO. 1

General Douglas MacArthur, United States Army, was appointed Military Adviser to the Commonwealth of the Philippines, with the approval of the President of the United States, upon its inauguration in November, 1935. General MacArthur, assisted by the American Military Mission which he formed, devised original plans and methods to develop the national defense of the Philippines. The Military Mission was the instrument which enabled the Government of the Commonwealth to train and equip an army. During bitter assaults by shortsighted or misguided critics of my national defense policy the Military Mission, on many occasions, bore the brunt of the attack and contributed immeasurably to the successful fulfillment of my plans. These officers forged the weapon that is now striking the blows on the field of battle that earn for the Philippines the priceless right to be recognized on its own merit as an equal in the brotherhood of arms by the nations of the world. A magnificent defense has earned the plaudits and admiration of the world. That no troops have ever done so much with so little is due primarily to the outstanding generalship that made possible the skillful maneuvers that saved the lives of thousands of our soldiers despite the overwhelming force that confronted them. But it is in the importance of the accomplishment of General MacArthur and the Military Mission rather than in their deeds themselves that makes them transcendent. They stand as the outpost of victory of individual freedom and liberty over slavery and tyranny in the mighty struggle that engulfs the world. Win or lose, live or die, no men have ever carried a heavier burden or weightier responsibility with greater resolution and determination. The record of their services is interwoven forever into the national fate of our people.

In recognition of outstanding service to the Commonwealth of the Philippines and pursuant to the authority granted me by Commonwealth Act Number One and especially by the Emergency Powers Law, the officers named below are hereby granted recompense and reward, however inadequate, for distinguished service rendered between November 15, 1935 and December 30, 1941 as indicated below:

General Douglas MacArthur $500,000 U.S. Currency
Major General Richard K. Sutherland $ 75,000 U.S. Currency
Brigadier General Richard J. Marshall, Jr. $ 45,000 U.S. Currency
Lieutenant Colonel Sidney L. Huff $ 20,000 U.S. Currency

Done at Fort Mills, Corregidor, Philippines this third day of January, in the year of our Lord, nineteen hundred and forty-two and of the Commonwealth of the Philippines, the seventh.

[Sgd. Manuel L. Quezon]
By the President:
[Sgd. Basilio J. Valdes]
Secretary to the President.</SIG>
Fort Mills, Corregidor,
Philippines,
February 19, 1942.

Received from His Excellency, the President of the Commonwealth, the sum of ONE MILLION TWO HUNDRED EIGHTY THOUSAND PESOS, (P1,280,000.00). In the event that orders issued to the Chase National Bank by radio on February 15, 1942, directing the transfer of certain funds, are not carried out, these funds will be applied to that purpose; otherwise, they will be held for the account of the Government of the Commonwealth of the Philippines.

Fort Mills, P. I.,
February 25, 1942.

Received from General Douglas MacArthur the sum of ONE MILLION TWO HUNDRED EIGHTY THOUSAND PESOS (P1,280,000) which have been held by him for the account of the Commonwealth Government for special purposes specified by the President of the Commonwealth.

(Sgd.) MANUEL ROXAS Lt. Col.,
In Charge of Philippine Treasury.
Certified to be a true copy:
S. L. HUFF,
Lt. Col., A. D. C.,

The conditions under which this document was executed help to explain its meaning. Douglas MacArthur was recalled to the regular United States Army to command USAFFE in July 1941 after serving more than five years as military advisor to the Philippine Commonwealth.[4] As military advisor, MacArthur received a salary of 36,000 pesos ($18,000) per year and personal yearly allowances of 30,000 pesos ($15,000). In addition, he insisted upon, and was given a seven-room, fully air-conditioned suite atop the Manila Hotel, equal in comfort to that of the American governor general's residence which had been Malacanang Palace until the inauguration of the Commonwealth.[5] From 1935 to 1937, the General remained on active duty in the United States Army and thus continued to receive his salary as a major general in addition to the Philippine emoluments. (After 1937, when he chose retirement rather than reassignment, his United States Army pension replaced the major general's salary.) The General, as well as the staff of the Military Advisor's Office, was permitted the additional salary and allowances under an act of Congress passed in 1926 which authorized the President to assign military advisors to certain foreign countries and which allowed such advisors "to accept from the government to which detailed offices and such compensation and emoluments thereunto appertaining as may be first approved by the Secretary of War or by the Secretary of the Navy, as the case may be." This act was revised in May 1935 to include the Philippine Islands.[6]

During the six-year period from 1935 to 1941, the General attempted to develop in the Philippines a citizen army patterned after that of Switzerland and partially supplied by the U.S. Department of War.[7] Despite criticism from Washington planners and some Philippine leaders,[8] he optimistically dismissed the assumptions of WAR PLAN ORANGE, which argued that in case the Philippines were attacked by Japan the best that could be expected would be a holding action in northern Luzon until aid could arrive from the United States.[9]

On December 8, 1941, Japanese bombers began their onslaught against the Philippines. Within two weeks, it had become painfully clear that MacArthur's original plan to repel the invaders at the beaches would not succeed, and he was forced to reorganize his armies for a stand on Bataan and Corregidor as WAR PLAN ORANGE had originally outlined. On December 24, the USAFFE staff, accompanied by some members of the High Commissioner's Office and token representation of the Commonwealth government, prepared to move its headquarters to Fort Mills on Corregidor and declare Manila an open city. Although the seriously ill Quezon argued that he could best serve his people by staying with them in Manila, MacArthur, supported by his superiors in Washington, persuaded Quezon that his place was with a government in exile, safe from Japanese pressure.[10]

The days following the move to Corregidor were desperate indeed. Crowded into the narrow laterals of Malinta Tunnel with little hope of safe passage out of the situation, those present were naturally fearful. When the Japanese began their full-fledged air attack on the fortress on December 29, these concerns reached a new high. The solemn inaugural ceremony, which took place the next afternoon, marking the beginning of Manuel Quezon's second term as Commonwealth president did little to raise the spirits of those present.[11]

Neither the published accounts nor unpublished papers of any of those involved reveal all that went on at the January 1, 1942, meeting held at MacArthur's headquarters on Corregidor. A diary of those days says only that "late this afternoon an important dispatch was received from the War Department. The General held a conference at his quarters, Generals Sutherland and Marshall and Colonels Willoughby and Huff attended.[12] Later, President Quezon was called in. Still later, Mr. Sayre attended. A reply was drafted in conference."[13]

The dispatch referred to in this entry argued for the evacuation of Manuel Quezon from Corregidor to the United States.[14] While MacArthur's response insisted that this was "too hazardous to attempt," Quezon was quoted as having "no preference" regarding the move. What becomes clear from reading the remainder of USAFFE's long response is that the evacuation suggested by Washington indicated to those on Corregidor who read it that the War Department was not optimistic about the relief of the Philippines. In an attempt to reverse this attitude, MacArthur issued his most impassioned plea up to that point, arguing for "the immediate combined effort of all resources of the United States and her allies by land, sea, and air."[15] In the aftermath of this exchange, Executive Order #1 was issued on January 3, 1942, and then apparently held in abeyance until February 15.

From January 3 until February 15, 1942, communiques between Washington and Corregidor reflected the growing realization that the USAFFE troops would not be relieved. The consequent disillusionment of the troops and their leaders culminated in the February 8 dispatch from Fort Mills in which Quezon suggested surrender and neutralization of the islands; MacArthur seemed to acquiesce, arguing that "the temper of the Filipinos is one of almost violent resentment against the United

States."[16] Reaction in Washington on February 9 brought conferences between Secretary of War Henry L. Stimson, General George C. Marshall, and President Franklin D. Roosevelt, and resulted in Roosevelt's now famous response "emphatically deny[ing] the possibility of this government's agreement to the political aspects of President Quezon's proposal." Granting MacArthur authorization to capitulate "the Filipino elements of the defending forces," the President acknowledged MacArthur's "desperate situation" and again suggested the evacuation of the High Commissioner, President Quezon and his Cabinet, and the General's wife and son. The dispatch clearly conveyed the message, however, that MacArthur's responsibility was to keep United States troops fighting because "it [was] mandatory that there be established once and for all in the minds of all peoples complete evidence that the American determination and indomitable will to win carrie[d] on down to the last unit."[17]

Although some accounts of the reaction at Fort Mills to Roosevelt's message have suggested that a furious Quezon attempted to resign and return to Manila, the principals involved at the time made no such claim.[18] Other dispatches indicated that the period from February 9 to February 12 was one of indecision on the part of the Philippine president and heightened concern in Washington. However, on February 12 the debate appeared to have drawn to a close with Quezon's acquiescence in the United States advice.[19]

On February 15 the British surrendered Singapore, underlining with abundant clarity the desperate position of the Filipinos and the forces attempting their defense. On the same day MacArthur wired the War Department of Quezon's desire to transfer $640,000 via Executive Order #1 to MacArthur, Sutherland, Marshall, and Huff.[20] Although there is no direct evidence connecting this radiogram and one from Fort Mills to Washington on the 16th,[21] it is significant that after several statements arguing that Quezon could not safely be evacuated, MacArthur, one day after the transfer of funds was ordered, reversed his position and decided that indeed the president's evacuation could be achieved. On February 20, just after he received verification of the transfer, this decision was carried out and Quezon headed south toward the unoccupied islands on the submarine Swordfish.[22]

Meanwhile in Washington, officials in the War Department and the Department of the Interior (the Division of Territories and Island Possessions) spent some of the time between February 16 and February 20 in correspondence with the Chase National Bank where Commonwealth funds were held, assuring the bank officials that the transfers should be made and that "the original radiogram was shown to the President of the United States and to the Secretary of War and they were informed of the action taken."[23] On February 18 John Prentice, assistant cashier of the Chase National Bank, wired the director, Division of Territories and Island Possessions, that the transfers had been completed. On February 19 a letter from Prentice to the director confirmed that the transaction had been made as directed by the radiogram of February 15 and Executive Order #1. Shortly thereafter, the War Department relayed this information to Quezon.[24]

Since efforts to reach persons who participated in this exchange have met with failure,[25] and since the principals involved are all dead and did not refer to this episode in any of their published accounts or private papers, it is impossible to determine conclusively all of the reasons behind the exchange of funds and the connection of the exchange to subsequent developments. The incident does, however, suggest several possible conclusions which help to explain questions long asked by students of the period:

1. MacArthur's chief biographer has suggested that "some of MacArthur's reactions and behavior in early 1942 are hard to comprehend apart from the context of his personal ties and devotion to the Philippine nation and its president, Quezon." Although the retreating USAFFE troops clearly were under-supplied, MacArthur refused to contradict Quezon's order that critical rice and sugar supplies not be moved from the provinces within which they were bought and where they were available to the resident Filipinos. At other times, bombing schedules were delayed on the demand of the Philippine president.[26] In the light of Executive Order #1, we must ask if MacArthur's "personal ties and devotion to the Philippine nation" were influenced by half a million dollars provided by its president, Quezon.

2. Since the War Department's wire to the Chase National Bank clearly stated that both President Roosevelt and Secretary Stimson had seen the Quezon radiogram and since a copy of that wire was found in the Roosevelt Papers, we must assume that MacArthur's superiors in Washington understood the possibility that their commanding general felt angry and abandoned and might therefore refuse to follow orders or somehow undermine American policy. Perhaps they believed that their acceptance of this exchange was a necessary expedient to insure MacArthur's and, in turn, Quezon's cooper-

ation in creating the vision of "American determination and indomitable will" which Roosevelt demanded in his message of February 9. The fact that Secretary of Interior Harold L. Ickes looked askance at but did not interfere with the exchange lends credence to this point.[27]

3. Since MacArthur and Quezon clearly had not decided on the feasibility of Quezon's departure until mid-February, it is possible that notice of the completed transfer of funds influenced MacArthur's decision to evacuate the Philippine president on February 20. As Stimson and Roosevelt hoped, the Commonwealth president would be much less likely to negotiate with the Japanese from exile in the southern islands, Australia, or the United States.

4. MacArthur's vehement insistence, throughout the war, on the necessity of approaching Japan through the Philippines may have been partly influenced by the knowledge that Quezon, in exile in the United States, certainly expected such a strategy and might even have believed that he and the General had a prior understanding to that effect.

5. Finally, one of the most controversial debates of this period takes shape around the question of why MacArthur felt called upon to free Manuel Roxas while he imprisoned the other members of the collaborationist government who were captured with Roxas after the invasion of the Philippines in 1944. According to one eyewitness account, the telephone call in late April 1945 from Roxas at Sixth Army Headquarters at San Fernando, Pampanga, to General Sutherland at MacArthur's headquarters in Manila effected his release.[28] Perhaps Roxas's signature on the sheet attached to Executive Order #1 was a reminder to the recipients of the $640,000 of the confidential exchange which Roxas had witnessed on Corregidor and an additional reason for MacArthur's often reconfirmed trust in the man who would shortly become the first president of the Philippine Republic.

The complete explanation of this exchange lies buried beneath the rationalizations, ambivalences, and secrecy of the participants. While it is possible that both those approving and those accepting the $640,000 in question may have believed that their action was protected by the congressional act which allowed for the establishment of the office of military advisor, it would seem that the July 26, 1941, order which transferred the staff of that office to USAFFE would preclude this interpretation. Since they had been reassigned to a U.S. force, it can be argued that MacArthur and the other three officers involved were once again subject to regular

U.S. Army rules, which state in part that "every member of the Military Establishment, when subject to military law, is bound to refrain from . . . Acceptance by an officer of a substantial loan or gift or any emolument from a person or firm with whom it is the officer's duty as an agent of the government to carry on negotiations."[29] Certainly it is doubtful that the act of 1926 was meant to allow exchanges of this size to occur under conditions such as those on Corregidor in early 1942. The moral implications are even more complex and ambiguous. In the period in which it occurred, this "recompense and reward" was not without precedent, although the amount involved certainly would make it one of the largest gifts of its kind. President Quezon could have believed that he was acting in the best interests of his countrymen, as perhaps he was. However, the acceptance of these gifts totaling $640,000 by officers on active duty with the U.S. Army from the treasury of an impoverished country is more difficult to justify. It is the historian's responsibility to lay bare such transactions in order to encourage further research, debate, and understanding of their meaning and implications for both the past and the present.

Notes

This introduction is based on research made possible by grants from the U.S. Army Center of Military History, the Eleanor Roosevelt Institute, and the Philippine National Library.

1. In an effort to confirm the main points of this research, I have examined the private papers of Manuel Quezon, Philippine National Library (PNL), Manila; Douglas MacArthur, MacArthur Memorial Bureau of Archives (MMBA), Norfolk VA; Richard K. Sutherland, Modern Military Branch (NNMM), National Archives (NA), Washington DC; Richard J. Marshall, United States Army Military History Institute (MHI), Carlisle Barracks PA; and Francis Sayre, Library of Congress (LC), Washington DC. No record of the papers of Naval Lt. Sidney L. Huff (later commissioned in the U.S. Army) could be found, but neither his book, *My Fifteen Years with General MacArthur* (with Joe A. Morris, New York, 1964), Douglas MacArthur's *Reminiscences* (New York, 1964), Francis Sayre's *Glad Adventure* (New York, 1957), nor Manuel Quezon's *The Good Fight* (New York, 1946) mentions the transaction which is described below.

2. The corroborating documents found in Files of Division of Territories and Island Possessions, "9-7-4 Banking," Legislative and Natural Resources Branch (NNFN), NA, were found by this author earlier than Executive Order

#1 and were originally believed to perhaps reflect methods of legitimately conveying funds out of the Philippines. A search of File "9–7-43 Money," NNFN, NA, however, provided ample evidence that there existed very complex, carefully-outlined, and carefully-controlled methods for such transfers, none of which were followed in the transfer of funds initiated by Executive Order #1.

3. A letter of thanks mentioning but not describing this executive order may be found in Quezon to MacArthur, Feb. 20, 1942, RG 10, VIP files, MMBA. In an effort to determine why this document had not been published with other Philippine executive orders from this period, I visited the Malacanang Library in Manila, repository of Philippine government documents, and was told by the archivist in charge that no executive orders had been issued between December 1941, when Quezon left Manila, and May 1942, when he arrived in Washington. It is true that many of the earlier executive orders issued by the Commonwealth government during the period 1936 to 1941 were not published and much of the official record had been destroyed during the Japanese occupation. Consequently, it is small wonder that the records pertaining to this order were lost or destroyed and never missed by the postwar Philippine government.

4. The most complete account of the years under discussion in this summary are in D. Clayton James, *The Years of MacArthur* (2 vols., New York, 1970 and 1975), I, 479–619, II, 3–99; and Frazier Hunt, *The Untold Story of Douglas MacArthur* (New York, 1954), 167–259; more generalized accounts from participants include Quezon, *The Good Fight*, and Sayre, *Glad Adventure*. Specific documents relating to MacArthur's appointment may be found in RG 1, 10, 17, and 18, MMBA; OF 25t, OF 400 and PSF 102, Franklin D. Roosevelt Library (FDRL); AG 093.5 Phil. Islands, Old Military Branch (NNMO) and file 6166–111, Bureau of Insular Affairs, NNFN, NA.

5. Quezon to MacArthur, Dec. 31, 1935, RG 10, VIP files, MMBA; "Memorandum of the Terms of Agreement...," 1935, RG 1, MMBA; "The Vargas-Saulo Interviews" (second interview), 29, and (fourth interview), 67; and Domingo C. Abadilla, "The Manila Hotel Story," Sept. 29, 1975, Vargas Foundation (VF), Manila; Quezon to MacArthur, Oct. 25, 1935, Quezon Papers, PNL. The calculation is based on the rate of exchange during the 1930s which was regulated by the U.S. government and did not fluctuate.

6. *U.S. Statutes at Large*, XLIV, 565 (1927), XLIX, 218 (1936). For correspondence relating to MacArthur's retirement in 1937, see Craig to MacArthur, Aug. 24, 1937, file PSF 102, FRDL.

7. "Report on National Defense in the Philippines" (Manila, 1936), RG 1, MMBA; Craig to MacArthur, Aug. 5, 1936, file AG 093.5, NNMO, NA; MacArthur to Quezon, June 1, 1935, RG 17, MMBA.

8. For a discussion of the on-again-off-again support of the War Department, see Louis Morton, *Strategy and Command: The First Two Years* (Washington DC, 1962), 46–68. See also Camilio Osias, ed., *The Philippine Forum* (Manila, 1935–1937) in which Osias, a member of the Philippine National Assembly, reported his own disagreements as well as those of others with MacArthur's strategy.

9. WAR PLAN ORANGE, devised in 1904, was regularly updated prior to this period and was revised early in 1934 when it became clear that the U.S. Congress would approve legislation establishing the Philippine Commonwealth. The last revision occurred in 1938 and held until replaced by RAINBOW 5 in early 1941. See Morton, *Strategy*, 22, 36, 41–42, 86–91, 131–139.

10. For the best account of the Philippine defense during the months between December 8, 1941, and its capitulation in May 1942, see Louis Morton, *The Fall of the Philippines* (Washington DC, 1953). For accounts of the move to Corregidor, see MacArthur, *Reminiscences*, 136; and James, *Years*, II, 30.

11. Although the tension of the last week in December on Corregidor is discussed in all of the recollections of the period, a particularly detailed account is in Sayre, *Glad Adventure*, 230–251.

12. It is important to note that the four USAFFE officers who participated in the early part of this meeting were the men who had the closest and most personal relationships with MacArthur and were almost continuously at his side during these days. See James, *Years*, II, 77–80. Three of these men were rewarded by Executive Order #1. Colonel Willoughby's exclusion is unexplained by any of the evidence discovered thus far.

13. "Diary, General Douglas MacArthur, Commanding General, United States Army Forces in the Far East," 44, RG 2, USAFFE, MMBA.

14. John Jacob Beck, *MacArthur and Wainwright, Sacrifice of the Philippines* (Albuquerque, 1974), 58–59; Morton, *Fall*, 239.

15. MacArthur to George C. Marshall, Jan. 1, 1942, file AG 381, Dec. 41, Far East Situation, NNMM, NA.

16. MacArthur to Marshall, Feb. 8, 1942, No. 2275, NNMM, NA.

17. Roosevelt to MacArthur, Feb. 9, 1942, No. 1029, Item #8, Exec. #10, Quezon File, NNMM, NA.

18. For an account of Quezon's violent reaction to the Roosevelt message, see James K. Eyre, Jr., *The Roosevelt-MacArthur Conflict* (Chambersburg PA, 1950), 40–41. MacArthur, *Reminiscences*; James, *Years*; and Quezon, *The Good Fight*, do not mention Quezon's reactions.

19. For the clearest account of this exchange, see Beck, *MacArthur*, 96–110.

20. MacArthur to Chase National Bank, Feb. 15, 1942, Radio No. 285, file PSF 64, FDRL; and MacArthur to the Adj. Gen., Feb. 15, 1942, Files of Division of Territories and Island Possessions, "9-7-4 Banking," NNFN, NA.

21. MacArthur to Marshall, Feb. 16, 1942, No. 296, file AG 381, NNMM, NA.

22. Beck, *MacArthur*, 116; MacArthur, *Reminiscences*, 152; James, *Years*, 11, 96–98; Sayre, *Glad Adventure*, 240.

23. Deane to Brown, Feb. 17, 1942, "9-7-4 Banking," NNFN, NA; "Memo for Record," Feb. 20, 1942, file OPD 004.2, NNMO, NA. In 1939 the Bureau of Insular Affairs of the War Department, which handled Philippine matters, was disbanded and the administration was transferred to the Division of Territories and Island Possessions under the direction of the Department of the Interior. See Rowe to Watson, May 31, 1939, file OF 25b, FDRL.

24. Radio No. 1063, 2120142 to CG, USAFFE, mentioned in "Memo for Record," Feb. 20, 1942, file OPD 004.2, NNMO, NA. Records which seem to corroborate this transfer may also be found on miscellaneous bank statements from 1946 in "Old Tax Papers," RG 10, MMBA.

25. A letter from this author to General J. R. Deane, USA Ret., has met with no response. Officials in the Department of the Interior of the Interior state that they have no addresses nor information concerning the persons whose names appear on the memorandums involved.

26. James, *Years*, II, 90–91.

27. It is clear in the accounts of official Washington during this period that almost no one outside of those directly involved was aware of the Philippine gift. However, in the diary of Harold Ickes (microfilm edition, reel 5), entry dated April 5, 1942 (LC), the Secretary of the Interior, whose department had been actively involved in the correspondence relating to the transfer and kept the only complete file thereof, recounted a discussion with Philippine Commissioner Joaquin Elizalde concerning the matter. Ickes stated that Elizalde "confirmed the $500,000 credit to MacArthur . . . [and] said that it was not extra compensation paid by the Philippine Government but I thought that he acted just a little embarrassed." Ickes, who mistakenly believed that General Jonathan Wainwright was also a recipient of Philippine funds, went on to ask "Why was it necessary to place such large sums of money to the credit of General Wainwright and General MacArthur." The Henry Lewis Stimson diaries (microfilm edition), Manuscripts and Archives, Yale University Library (New Haven CT), on the other hand, are silent concerning this matter. (Stimson seldom revealed his personal feelings about matters discussed in the diary.) It is perhaps significant, however, that Stimson's assessment of MacArthur, whom he had known since World War I, was generally sympathetic prior to this period, but became noticeably critical after February 1942. See, for example, the Stimson diaries, XXXVII, 5 (microfilm edition, reel 7), entry dated Jan. 2, 1942, and XXXVIII, 54 (microfilm edition, reel 7), entry dated March 23, 1942.

28. Although extensive discussion of these issues may be found in the popular and scholarly literature since 1946, perhaps the most complete study is David Joel Steinberg, *Philippine Collaboration in World War II* (Ann Arbor, 1967).

For the eyewitness account of the details of Roxas's capture and subsequent release, see Dale Pontius, "MacArthur and the Filipinos," *Asia*, XLVI (1946), 436–440, 509–512.

29. The regulation violated may be found in Army Regulations 600–10, Par. 2e (9) (War Department, Washington DC, Dec. 6, 1938), NNMO, NA. The best explanation of the implications of this regulation is to be found in *The Officer's Guide* (8th ed., Harrisburg, Pa., 1942), 381–382. See also Articles 95 and 96, "The Articles of War," in *A Manual for Courts-Martial, U.S. Army* (Washington DC, 1928), 224; and *The Code of the Laws of the United States of America, 1934* (Washington DC, 1935), 18 U.S.C. 91, and 10 U.S.C. 1565, 1567, 1568.

An Exchange of Opinion

Paul P. Rogers and Carol M. Petillo

Paul Rogers of Virginia Polytechnic Institute and State University, who served as a stenographer on Corregidor in 1942, takes a more benign view of the half-million-dollar payment to MacArthur. Carol Petillo, in her response, makes clear that she is not persuaded by his arguments.

The article of Carol Petillo which appeared in the February, 1979, issue of this journal and the subsequent flurry of publicity produced a predictable protest from the wide circle of Douglas MacArthur devotees and an equally predictable twitter of delight from those who believed a flaw had been found in the MacArthur image.[1]

I was assigned as stenographer to MacArthur and his chief of staff, Richard Kerens Sutherland, on October 20, 1941. I was taken to Corregidor and was evacuated to Australia. I served as secretary and office manager until September 1945. I witnessed the events discussed by Petillo. I typed many of the documents involved. I had close intimate contact with MacArthur and Sutherland. I have studied the documents and I have pondered their significance. I have challenged my memory and my judgments.

Sutherland's diary records that at three in the afternoon of February 13, 1942, MacArthur walked into Lateral Three of Malinta Tunnel and spent half an hour discussing with his chief of staff "highly secret matters of policy." One hour later Sutherland began to work on the "composition, at the direction of General MacArthur, of important Executive Order for President Quezon." Sutherland worked at the task until eight that evening. He prepared the draft of Executive Order Number One and gave it to me to be typed. I returned the typed copy to him. He read it and handed it to MacArthur. MacArthur read the paper and returned it to Sutherland commenting that the amounts hardly compensated for income they had lost during their service with the Military Mission. MacArthur walked out of Lateral Three leaving the paper with Sutherland, who continued to work until eleven.[2]

After Sutherland left his desk for the night, I made the daily entry in my Corregidor diary. With some hesitation I decided to record the event, but to camouflage the facts I changed the word "order" to "act." I changed MacArthur's $500,000 to $50,000, then changed Sutherland's $75,000 to $45,000 to keep it in line with amount recorded for MacArthur. The amounts given to Richard J. Marshall and Sidney L. Huff were recorded without change. It was not very cleverly done but it satisfied my sense of propriety. The affair was buried in the diary entry. As a matter of honor I did not discuss it during the war or after. I had been accepted into a position of trust and I would not violate the obligation my position imposed upon me.[3]

The Executive Order[4] would not have been taken to Quezon before February 14. At two that afternoon MacArthur, President Manuel L. Quezon, High Commissioner Francis B. Sayre, and Sutherland met to discuss the "disposal of money and securities, and on matters of high policy."

A dispatch of February 15 directed the transfer of funds by Chase National Bank.[5] In Washington DC, action was delayed while the request was discussed by General George C. Marshall, Secretary of War Henry L. Stimson, and President Franklin D. Roosevelt. The matter was referred to Secretary of the Interior Harold L. Ickes for final action. Five days were required to reach a decision. The official memorandum for record states that there is no record of approval by Ickes. Nevertheless, Chase National Bank made the transfer and so notified the Adjutant General on February 18.[6]

On Corregidor there was some sense of urgency in view of Quezon's imminent evacuation. To guarantee payment, an equivalent amount of Philippine currency was segregated, boxed, and delivered to Sidney Huff who acted for MacArthur with the understanding that it would be returned to Manuel Roxas, who acted for Quezon, if the transfer were confirmed. The receipt was signed on February 19.[7] Quezon had radioed Chase National on February 18 asking confirmation. Confirmation was received on February 25 after Quezon had left Corregidor. The box of currency was returned to Roxas for Quezon who by then was in Panay. Quezon was notified on February 27 of the fact of the confirmation.[8]

The transfer of the currency made no more sense than my diary entry. If Roosevelt had not approved the transfer of funds through the banks, the entire affair would have been annulled. Physical possession of a box of currency would have raised significant legal problems. Eventually, the large amount of currency would have to be presented for redemption and difficulties would have been encountered. MacArthur and Sutherland would have known this. As in the case of my diary entry, the useless stratagem relieved everyone's sense of propriety.

Richard Sutherland was the most capable officer in MacArthur's command. In a very real way he "ran" MacArthur's war. Later in the war he and MacArthur would have difficulties but at this time they were close friends. During World War II, where the conduct of the war was concerned, MacArthur and Sutherland acted as one even after their friendship had dissolved. It hardly detracts from MacArthur's stature to assert that he made effective use of a fine chief of staff and recognized that he had one, a fact which biographers should note.

There is no evidence in the diary or elsewhere which would justify accepting January 3, 1942, as the date of action. I am convinced that the order was written on February 13 and backdated. The choice of February 13 seems to create a dilemma because backdating appears to be unnecessary. However, it may indicate only that the matter had been discussed as early as January 3 with action delayed until such time as Quezon's evacuation had been agreed upon.

There is no clear record as to who actually originated the action. One might assume that Quezon raised the matter with MacArthur and asked that MacArthur put the document in final form. Or, on the contrary, one might argue just as reasonably that MacArthur raised the issue with Quezon and was told to prepare a document. Or it may be that MacArthur and Sutherland prepared a document and presented it to Quezon for signature accompanied by pleas for justice and charity or by threats of retribution. There is no evidence. I am inclined to believe that the matter was first discussed by MacArthur and Quezon, and that Quezon more likely raised the possibility of some recognition of MacArthur's services. It is likely that the affair might have been discussed privately as early as January. Quezon and MacArthur talked daily about many things.

The problem of motivation will be difficult to resolve unless one works from the position that the parties were reasonable and prudent men who expected that the transaction would be judged by the standards of their peers. The record discloses no attempt to hide the matter. The various documents which effected the transfer of funds were dispatched through War Department channels. MacArthur and Quezon would have expected them to be delivered to Marshall and by him to Stimson and Roosevelt. Ickes controlled Philippine finances and he inevitably would be called into the discussion. MacArthur, as Chief of Staff, had been a member of the Roosevelt administration, knew Stimson and Ickes, and was acquainted with the probable course of events which must follow receipt of such a dispatch from Corregidor at a time when both these men were still quivering from the shock of Quezon's proposal to neutralize the Philippines. Roosevelt had an opportunity to block the transfer of funds and did not do so and thereby gave the matter whatever legality was required presumably because he believed it to be in the national interest. Whether in the eyes of Divine Justice it was moral or immoral, one must suppose that Divine Justice will find a solution when human frailty is unable to do so.

There is strong historical precedent for such a grant, and given a legitimate desire to reward a faithful general, the method is not particularly questionable. As for the amount involved, it is impossible to know how to place a fair value on such services. MacArthur was not one to underestimate the value of his own performance. It is understood in academe as well as in the military that only a fool undervalues his worth and that it is better to ask for too much than to ask for too little. MacArthur records that during his tour as Chief of Staff an attempt was made to reduce General John J. Pershing's pension. MacArthur appeared before the Senate Appropriation Committee to speak in Pershing's behalf. He "spoke of the tribute accorded General Douglas Haig in England. Haig was Pershing's counterpart during World War I. After the war, Haig was promoted to field marshal and received, in addition to a life trust of nearly $9,000 a year, a trust fund of nearly half a million dollars, yielding an income of about $30,000 a year."[9]

One portion of a sentence in Quezon's memoirs also may be relevant: " . . . the Filipino returns lavishly, with a loyalty that knows no bounds, the affection and confidence of those whom he has elevated to high office."[10] On the day of Quezon's departure from Corregidor he wrote a long letter to MacArthur to express in personal terms the feeling which had been expressed officially by Executive Order Number One. The letter is reproduced here in full.[11]

MALACAÑAN PALACE

MANILA

Fort Mills, P.I.

February 20, 1942

My dear General MacArthur:

Although I have given official recognition to the services you have rendered to the government of the Commonwealth and to the Filipino people in my Executive Order No. 1, series of 1942, I feel that I must write you this letter, which partakes of an official as well as private character, in order to tell you how grateful I am, my own family, and the members of my whole staff for the kindness and generosity with which we have been treated here; and to ask you to convey to all the officers within your command, particularly to General Moore, our deep gratitude.

As I have already told you, I would have remained here to the very bitter end, if you deemed it necessary for me to stay. I am going only because you and I have agreed that the cause for which we are fighting can be best promoted by my being in the unoccupied territory where I could render you help and assistance by keeping up the morale and determination of my people to stand by America. But I am leaving you with a weeping heart, for you and I have not only been friends and comrades; we have been more than brothers. My thoughts will always be with you and your dear wife and my godson. If better days should come to all of us, as I hope they will, I expect that the memory of these hectic days will strengthen our friendship and cooperation even more. I am leaving my own boys, the Filipino soldiers, under your care. I know that you will look after their welfare and safety and that, above all, you will see to it that their names may go down in history as loyal and brave soldiers.

With my love to you, Jean and the boy, in which all my family joins, I say good-bye till we meet again. May God ever keep you under His protection.

Sincerely yours,

/s/ Manuel Quezon

Gen. Doug MacArthur

Commanding General, USAFFE

Fort Mills, P.I.

Too much has been made of the apparent vacillations with respect to the evacuation of Quezon. There was never any doubt that Quezon *must* leave Corregidor. The problems arose with respect to timing, method, and ultimate destination. The timing was dictated by uncertainty as to the impact of Quezon's departure on the Filipino troops in Bataan. January was too soon. April would have been too late.

The method of evacuation was complicated by Quezon's health. His doctors did not feel he could survive a trip by submarine. MacArthur's radiogram concerning this fact was intended to apprise Roosevelt of a possible disaster and to transfer to Roosevelt the onus of responsibility for it. A surface vessel involved substantial risk of capture and death. The evacuation plan provided for both contingencies. Quezon finally agreed to the submarine for the initial stage of the evacuation. A submarine had to be called in from patrol and there was no certainty that one would arrive. The date actually chosen for Quezon's evacuation was determined by the arrival of *Swordfish* at Corregidor.

Quezon's inner conflicts concerning evacuation are reflected in the documents, his own record, and others as well. They are not difficult to understand. MacArthur went through the same agonies when his turn came. On March 11 when I typed the order for Master Sergeant Rogers to leave Corregidor, I felt the same conflict: a great shame intensified by the fact that I also felt great relief. None had a choice. Quezon, MacArthur, and I were all under orders to leave. Quezon might agonize and protest but the thought of his daughters in the hands of Japanese soldiers was reason enough to do what common sense and orders from Washington already dictated.

Conclusions drawn in the Petillo article as problems for further investigation are interesting excursions into mystery story writing and are discussed seriatim.[12]

1. The criticisms of MacArthur's behavior to which Petillio refers are taken from a secondary source. The secondary source picked them out of primary sources without any apparent evaluation. The question is not whether MacArthur was criticized but whether any other course of action would have been possible or productive of better results. All military decisions represent a compromise between civilian and military needs. MacArthur's loyalty to the Filipinos and Quezon has never been doubted. Even if there had been no loyalty, ninety-five percent or more of the troops engaged were Filipinos and Quezon's requests would have carried great weight. In addition to all of this, the decisions referred to were made in early December. Executive Order Number One was issued in February. Were the decisions made in anticipation of the grant?

2. Does one really believe that Roosevelt was afraid that MacArthur, in anger, would cast aside reputation and honor after long years of faithful service?

3. Petillo is incorrect in stating that Quezon's evacuation had "clearly" not been decided until mid-February. The fact of evacuation was accepted in January; the precise details as to when and how were not decided until February. As of February 10 MacArthur was already under orders to arrange the evacuation of Quezon. As it turned out, Quezon had left Corregidor before the transfer of funds was completed.[13]

4. MacArthur's attitude with respect to liberation of the Philippines was shared unequivocally by Roosevelt. The promise to liberate the Philippines made by Roosevelt on January 30 and on February 10 committed the United States to this action as a matter of national honor.[14] The desire to attack Japan by way of the Philippines reflected not only MacArthur's sense of obligation to the Filipinos but his own sense of future command possibilities. If the Philippines were by-passed, the supreme command would go to Admiral Chester Nimitz and MacArthur would be left in limbo. All of this may seem to be important, but the decision to move to Japan through the Philippines was made on strategic and tactical grounds, supported by all Pacific commanders, by Roosevelt and Marshall in Washington, with only Admiral Ernest King demurring.

5. No documentation supports the view that Manuel Roxas should have been treated as a criminal of war. He was the third ranking power in the Philippines. Had Roxas taken an oath of allegiance to Japan, everything else to the contrary, he would have been hanged. It was accepted as a fact that Sergio Osmeña's term as president would be a limited one and that at the first election he would be replaced. In the traditional hierarchy, Roxas was the next man in line and at the time he seemed to be as essential to political stability as the Emperor of Japan was held to be a year later.

As to the violation of established procedures in making the disbursement, it must be remembered that after December 24, 1941, the Government of the Commonwealth of the Philippines did not exist except in the persons of Quezon and the half dozen men with him on Corregidor who acted under emergency powers. They were men without a country to govern. There were no procedures, personnel, or records by which Quezon could legitimize expenditures. A document in the MacArthur/Sutherland Secret File, Philippine Government Section, Quezon 135, which carries Sutherland's notation, "Mr. Rogers—File," describes this dilemma. The document contains an inventory of currency of the Commonwealth which records the disbursement of the funds without any details of the transaction. The document records that Quezon did not have in his possession, even in Washington after the evacuation, a copy of the Emergency Powers legislation which had been enacted before the Japanese occupation of manila. Her certainly would not be aware personally of the intricate details of administrative regulations spelled out either in the regular procedures or in the emergency powers.

The discovery of Executive Order Number One reflects commendable determination. It was not easily located. I acknowledge without hesitation the scholarly perseverance and desire for truth which is reflected by the discovery. Scholarly integrity demanded that the discovery be made public. The public is entitled to know of the affair and to judge it.

A man's character and achievement are reflected in an amalgam of incidents. Given the complexity of human existence it would be foolish to expect a career to be devoid of some incident which could be turned to criticism. An untutored or a frivolous mind may read into such an incident what he chooses, smirking because he has neither the wisdom nor the understanding which is required to take the full measure of the man's accomplishment. The scholar does not have such freedom. He carries in his hands the reputation of the men he studies. Their achievements entitle these men to a fair hearing.

I am willing to reaffirm a judgment which is based upon my own experience, still firmly held after forty years of serious thought about the matter. I watched MacArthur four years in defeat and in victory. His habitual behavior revealed generosity, sensitivity, sympathy, understanding, and a genuine concern for subordinates. When praise and encouragement failed to spur them to action, he did not hesitate to use any other stratagems necessary to enforce his will. MacArthur was truly a fine man driven by a deep sense of duty and destiny, tempered always by humanity and justice. His historical greatness has been confirmed. He has passed into legend. During the years I served MacArthur I did not see anything or hear anything which would impugn his character. There is nothing in any of the documents seen by me during the war or in those I have seen since which cause me to question this judgment.

Rejoinder by Carol Petillo

As I read the opening paragraphs of Paul Roger's statement, my expectations mounted. Finally, it appeared, an actual observer of the 1942 exchange would address the many questions which my research had raised, and which I had only partially answered in my original article (*Scapsphr*, February 1979, my response to Justin Williams (*Scapsphr*, August 1980), and in my recently published book, *Douglas MacArthur: The Philippine Years* (Indiana University Press, 1981). I was soon disappointed. Despite his references to documents which other scholars have not yet been permitted to see, and his certainty concerning an episode which he must recall from a distance of more than forty years, the major portion of Rogers's argument relies on opinion and evaluations which have long been questioned by students of modern American and Philippine history. Since space is limited here, I will refer interested readers to coverage of this debate in the earlier mentioned publications, and response to only a few of Rogers's allegations.

Much of his argument is easily refuted. Perhaps the most obvious fault of logic is his comparison of MacArthur's acceptance of Philippine money to General John J. Pershing's pension fight or the reward given to General Douglas Haig by Great Britain after World War One. In both of these cases, the men in question were being rewarded by the same governments that they had served exclusively throughout their long careers. In the MacArthur episode, possible conflicts between the Philippine and United States interests in this period raise very different issues and make the comparison invalid.

Even more difficult to accept is Roger's contention that the exchange was, on the one hand, honorable and based on historical precedent and yet, on the other hand, it required by his own judgment efforts "to camouflage the facts." Admittedly, there are those in the military (and in academe) who perpetually "ask for too much, [rather than] too little." There are others who do not. As evidence of this reality, I would refer Rogers and those who support his position to the words of another military officer who, when offered the same opportunity by Manuel Quezon only a few months after the issuing of Executive Order Number One, refused it with these words:

> I carefully explained to the President [Quezon], that I deeply appreciated his thought and was grateful for his expressions of gratitude, but that *it was inadvisable and even impossible for me to accept a material reward for the services performed.*
>
> I explained that while I understood this to be unquestionably legal, and that the President's motives were of the highest, the danger of misapprehension

or misunderstanding on the part of some individual might operate to destroy whatever usefulness I may have to the allied cause in the present War. . . . [Emphasis in the original; Dwight D. Eisenhower is referring to services performed for the Philippine Commonwealth during his tenure as MacArthur's Chief of Staff between 1935 and 1939. This statement may be found in Manuel L. Quezon to Major General Dwight David Eisenhower, June 20, 1942, and Memorandum for Record, June 20, 1942, "Manuel Quezon" folder, Dwight David Eisenhower, Pre-Presidential Papers, 1916–1952, Dwight D. Eisenhower Library.]

As I have stated elsewhere, the legal assumption which Eisenhower made is beyond the field of my expertise, although I'm convinced that a good argument could be made for the contrary position. The point which I want to reinforce, however, is that there were those of talent and ambition in circumstances similar to MacArthur's in 1942 who chose a different path and who clearly understood why such action was required.

As those who have followed this debate from its beginning will realize, there are many other aspects of Roger's argument and innuendo to which I might respond. In the interest of space, however, I will limit the remainder of my rejoinder to only two more points:

1. A close reading of my discussion of the criticisms of MacArthur's military decisions during the period of late 1941 and early 1942 will reveal that my major "secondary source" was D. Clayton James's exhaustive study, *The Years of MacArthur* (2 vols., New York, 1970 and 1975). To suggest that James's work is not evaluative of its sources is to reveal a painful unfamiliarity with the quality of his scholarship and its fundamental place of importance in the vast MacArthur literature.

2. Many have followed the course and focus of my work since I began the project at Rutgers University in 1976. They will confirm, I believe, that I was in no way ever determined to find Executive Order Number One or any other evidence of its nature. I approached my dissertation research seriously, but with no preconceived notions regarding my ultimate interpretation of the General. When the document appeared, however (and, by the way, any scholar who asked for permission to see the Sutherland Papers at the time of my research could have come upon the same information), I was urged by several advisors to make it public. I would be either naive or dissimulative if I did not admit that my motives for doing so probably included both "scholarly integrity" and personal ambition. None of this changes the nature of the evidence nor the serious questions which it

raises. I agree with Rogers that no career is likely "to be devoid of some incident which could be turned to criticism," but I would argue that in this instance, the incident was serious and made even more noteworthy precisely because, for some people, MacArthur "has passed into legend." Is history better served by truth, even if not fully understood, or by myth that romanticizes historical figures beyond human recognition?

As Rogers suggests at the outset, public response to my findings is divided—but into three camps rather than two. One group is made up of those who for either personal or ideological reasons identify with MacArthur and the values which he has come to represent, and feel threatened by anything they perceive as an attack on his place in history. Another group is composed of those who delight in the exposure of fault in any public figure. Yet a third group consists of those who have the sophistication to understand that unconscious motivations, ambivalence in regard to authority, and a reaction to the enormous stress engendered by the situation might help to explain the General's action in 1942. For this admittedly small third group, it is not difficult to sort out MacArthur's honorable actions from those that are less so, nor to admit the General's importance to modern American history without feeding the legend which he has become.

When the first salvo of this battle was fired in February 1979, I urged "further research, debate and understanding" concerning the questions which I had raised. The response has been far greater than I expected, and one which I suspect will continue for some time to come. Nonetheless, I have taken my position, published several statements expanding and explaining my original research, and revealed my own philosophical perspectives in the process. My research interests have moved to other topics, and my energies must be devoted to new work. Therefore, with my very best wishes to those who continue to be engaged by the debate, this response must serve as notice of my retirement from the fray.

Notes

1. Carol M. Petillo, "Douglas MacArthur and Manuel Quezon: A Note on an Imperial Bond," *Pacific Historical Review*, XLVII (1979), 107–117.
2. "Brief Summary of Action in the Office of Chief of Staff," box 2, RG 2, MacArthur Memorial Archives. A description of MacArthur's World War II office files will be found in my unpublished manuscript, "MacArthur and

Sutherland," which is filed with my "Corregidor Diary" in the MacArthur Memorial Archives, although neither are yet available to the public.

3. Paul P. Rogers, "Corregidor Diary." Only Sutherland, Marshall, and Huff had been members of the Military Mission. Charles A. Willoughly and other officers joined MacArthur after the Mission had been dissolved and reconstituted as United States Army Forces in the Far East.

4. Box 4, Item 27, Sutherland Papers, RG 200, National Archives. All of the materials in Item 21 were kept with other records in filing cabinets in my office.

5. MacArthur to Agwar [Adjutant General, War Dept.], Number 285, Feb. 15, 1942. I typed this radiogram but I have not found a copy in MacArthur's files. Franklin D. Roosevelt Library, PSF 64, contains Roosevelt's copy. MacArthur's signature is the ritual signature which was required on all official correspondence. The effective signatures are those of Jose Abad Santos, Secretary of Finance, and Manuel Quezon. When this message was received in Washington, two copies were sent to the Secretary of the General Staff. He in turn sent a paraphrase copy to Chase National Bank.

6. Memo for Record, WPD 004.2 (2–20-42), will be found in (Section 1) (Case 1), RG 165, National Archives; J. R. Deane to C. F. Brown, Feb. 17, 1942, File 9–7-4 Banking, RG 126, National Archives.

7. Attached to Executive Order Number One.

8. USAFFE 40, USAFFE Section, MacArthur/Sutherland Secret File, box 15, folder 1, RG 4, MacArthur Memorial Archives. The same materials will be found in Item 3, Sutherland Papers, RG 200, National Archives. The receipt signed by Roxas is attached to Executive Order Number One. USAFFE 58 is located with USAFFE 40.

9. Douglas MacArthur, *Reminiscences* (Greenwich CT, 1965), 101.

10. Manuel L. Quezon, *The Good Fight* (New York, 1946), 221.

11. Personal File, box 2, RG 2, MacArthur Memorial Archives.

12. No attempt will be made to document the numerous sources which provided the basis for my comments. A fully documented statement would run far beyond the bounds of this limited paper. Specific documents are cited.

13. USAFFE 25, USAFFE Section, MacArthur/ Sutherland Secret File, box 15, folder 1. This material is also in Item 3, Sutherland Papers.

14. USAFFE 11 and 25, USAFFE Section, MacArthur/Sutherland Secret File, box 15, folder 1.

2. World War II

The Lessons of History

Douglas MacArthur

MacArthur's actions during World War II would absorb the attention of a battalion of historians in the years to follow. At a luncheon on April 19, 1963, that marked the announcement by Columbia College of Columbia University of a chair in international history in his honor, MacArthur gave his views on the challenging nature of the historian's task.

Words can but inadequately describe the depth of my gratitude for the honor you do me. The over-generous introduction by the distinguished Governor of this great state—the presence here of so eminent an assemblage of leaders whose resourceful wisdom and penetrating vision contribute so much to the strength of the nation—and the action of Columbia college in authorizing a chair in international history to bear my name—all leave me with a sense of the most profound appreciation. I thank you from the bottom of an old soldier's heart.

If there is one thing I have learned during my long years of experience it is that if we would correctly solve the problems of the present and chart a safe course into the future we must study and weigh and understand the manifold lessons of which history is the great—indeed the only— competent teacher. For as Cicero put it eighty years before the birth of Christ, "Not to know what happened before one was born is always to be a child."

What then is history? That is the subject of as many different and conflicting views as there are philosophers-statesmen-soldiers and authors. Thus Plutarch complained, "So difficult a matter is it to determine the truth of anything by history." Yet Cicero said, "History indeed is the witness of the times—the light of truth." General George Meade of Civil War fame—after victory by the Union—observed cynically, "I don't believe the truth will ever be known and I therefore have great contempt for history." But General Robert E. Lee—after defeat—took a more philosophical view. "The march of providence is so slow," he said, "and our desires so impatient—the work of progress is so immense and our means of aiding it so feeble—the life of humanity is so long—that of the individual so brief—that we often see only the ebb of the advancing ways—and are thus discouraged. It is history that teaches us to hope." Napoleon took a particularly cynical view that history "is but a fable agreed upon. Historians are like sheep—they copy that which their predecessors have written . . . without troubling themselves to inquire into reasons or even probabilities." Similarly cynical was Thomas Jefferson. "A morsel of genuine history," he lamented, "is a thing so rare as to be always valuable."

Ralph Waldo Emerson expostulated, "I am ashamed to see what a shallow village tale our so-called history is. There is less intention in history than we ascribe to it. We impute deep-laid far-sighted plans to Caesar and Napoleon—but the best of their power was in nature—not in them." While to the contrary, Thomas Carlyle held that "Universal history—the history of what man has accomplished in this world—is at bottom the history of the great men who have walked here." The Duke of Wellington—long after Waterloo—complained, "I should like much to tell the truth—but if I did I should be torn to pieces—here and abroad!" And years later—after the surrender at Appomattox—General Lee observed in similar vein, "The time is not come for impartial history. If the truth were told just now it would not be credited."

This cynicism toward history finds reflection in the views of countless others. Thomas Carlyle: "Happy the people whose annals are blank in history books." Robert Walpole: "Anything but history—for history must be false." Voltaire: "The history of the great events of this world is hardly more than the history of crimes. How much charlatanry has been put into history—either by astonishing the reader with prodigies—by titillating human malignity with satire—or by flattering the families of tyrants with infamous praise." Edward Gibbon said, "History is little more than the register of crimes—follies and misfortunes of mankind." And John Quincy Adams once cryptically observed, "The public history of all countries—and all ages—is but a sort of mask—richly colored. The interior working of the machinery must be foul." "Historians," Benjamin Franklin complained, "relate—not so much what is done—as what they would have believed."

Few philosophers or writers or leaders in the arts and sciences speak kindly of history. For the historians who seek to chronicle contemporary events—with few exceptions—are animated by those most human of emotions, bias and prejudice. Few—if any—can meet the test laid down by Cicero: "The first law is that the historian shall never dare to set down what is false—the second—that he shall never dare to conceal the truth—the third—that there shall be no suspicion of either favoritism or prejudice." Edmund Burke drew a distinction between the historian who writes of the present and he who writes of the past. "We are very incorrupt and tolerably enlightened judges of the transactions of past ages," he said, "where no passions deceive and where the whole train of circumstances—from the trifling cause to the tragical event—is set in an orderly series before us. Few are the partisans of departed tyranny."

Samuel Johnson—in his *Life of Boswell*—gave this profile of an historian: "Great abilities are not requisite for an historian—for in historical composition all of the greatest powers of the human mind are quiescent. He has facts ready to hand—so there is no exercise of invention. Imagination is not required to any high degree—only about as much as is used in the lower kinds of poetry." But Macaulay summed up the rarity of competent historians by pointing out that "To be a really good historian is perhaps the rarest of intellectual distinctions." And Francis Bacon said, "It is the true office of history to represent the events—themselves—and to leave the observation and conclusions thereupon to the liberty and faculty of every man's judgment."

Despite his cynical estimate of historians, Napoleon did not underestimate the value of a knowledge and understanding of history in the development of the human mind. "History wants no illusions," he said. "It should illuminate and instruct—not merely give descriptions and narratives which impress us. Tacitus did not sufficiently study the mystery of facts and thoughts—did not sufficiently investigate and scrutinize their connection—to give posterity a just and impartial opinion. History should know how to catch men and peoples as they would appear in the midst of their epoch. It should take account of external circumstances which would necessarily exercise an important influence on their actions—clearly see within what limits that influence wrought. . . . The patrimony of history should be nothing but the truth. It is by that quality that it is rendered respectable and worthy to serve as a perpetual instruction to man."

Contemporary historians—biographers and other chroniclers of historic events—are probably no better nor worse than have been their predecessors through the ages. Not many possess that high degree of self-discipline which will permit them to rise above emotion. For bias and prejudice color many historical writings to confuse and mislead the student. His task must be to winnow out fact from fiction. It is my earnest hope that he who occupies this chair will diligently guide those under his tutelage through the man-made labyrinth of confusion and uncertainty with which the facts of history are so often enshrouded—that he will inculcate into their hearts and minds the knowledge that history is a sacred trust—that no written record is worth more than the integrity of the writer—that he include in his curriculum ample and accurate accounts of the life and works of the men and women of action who have developed our industries—who have forged our great nation from a wilderness—and who have advanced our liberty and freedom. His will partly be the responsibility that the fires of patriotism and sacrifice burn brightly in the soul of this and future generations. For in such history lies the fountainhead of those human forces which alone can preserve us as a free nation.

Douglas MacArthur and the Fall of the Philippines, 1941–1942

Duncan Anderson

Praised at the time for his heroic stand in the Philippines during the early days of the war in the Pacific, MacArthur came under a barrage of criticism from historians in the postwar years. In his examination of the topic Duncan Anderson, senior lecturer in the Department of War Studies at Sandhurst, contends that responsibility for the debacle should be widely shared.

Promotion to a Far East or Pacific command in 1941 was the worst fate to befall any rising "star" of the American or British officer corps. The débâcle at Pearl Harbor destroyed Admiral Husband E. Kimmel, Commander-in-Chief of the Pacific fleet, and General Short, commander of United States Army forces in Hawaii: both were immediately relieved of command and never again employed on active service. Two months later in Burma, the British generals Lieutenant General Hutton and Major General John Smyth met the same fate. Languishing in Japanese POW camps, Major General Christopher Maltby, British commander in Hong Kong and Lieutenant General Arthur Perceval, British commander in Malaya, had ample time to ruminate on their ruined careers. Although Major General Gordon Bennett, officer commanding the 8th Australian Division, managed to avoid capture in Singapore, the hostile reception he met on his return home was worse. Like Kimmel, Short, Hutton and Smyth, he was never again given an active posting.

By early 1942 only one Allied "star" still shone in the Far East— General Douglas MacArthur, Commander of U.S. Army Forces Far East (USAFFE). MacArthur's success seems all the more dazzling set against the darkness which had descended on Kimmel, Short, Hutton and Smyth— men with whom, ironically, he had much in common. Like Kimmel and Short, MacArthur had been surprised by the Japanese and lost much of his air strength from the outset. His troops, like Perceval's and Hutton's, proved unequal to the Japanese and were soon in retreat. The sarcastic nickname given MacArthur by his men—"Dugout Doug"—scarcely suggested confidence in his leadership. These doubts were shared by a number of Washington officials. Brigadier-General Dwight D. Eisenhower, MacArthur's former aide, now head of the Pacific War Plans Division, General George Marshall, Army Chief of Staff, and President Franklin D. Roosevelt, all thought MacArthur even more culpable than Kimmel or Short given the nine hours warning between Japan's surprise attack on Pearl Harbor and their attack on the Philippines. Yet when, in March 1942, MacArthur escaped from Bataan, only weeks before its final fall, Australia gave him a hero's welcome—quite unlike the frosty reception met by their own general, Bennett, the previous month. Rewarded with his country's highest decoration, MacArthur was appointed commander of the newly created South West Pacific Area.

The fall of the Philippines was the worst defeat yet suffered by the United States, a source of national humiliation. But instead of extinguishing MacArthur's star it added new lustre to it. American public opinion was almost uniformly on his side. It was widely believed that MacArthur's generalship had been brilliant; this alone had kept United States and Filipino troops fighting on long after the fall of Singapore, Rangoon and Java. Bataan and Corregidor became American household names. Blame was pointed at Roosevelt, Marshall and the United States Navy, the latter for timidity in failing to deliver to MacArthur the supplies promised by Washington. Some of MacArthur's more fanatical admirers considered Admiral King and General Marshall lucky to have escaped a Court Martial, and Roosevelt, impeachment and trial before the Senate. A Congressional Medal of Honor and command of a theatre were the very least MacArthur deserved.

Immediately after the war, MacArthur's role as a triumphant general ruling a conquered Japan rendered his reputation unassailable. Some high Washington officials and many former Philippine prisoners-of-war were unable to share in the adulation. But the hagiographic portrait of MacArthur produced in 1946 by his admiring successor in command, General Wainwright, immediately diminished the dangers of dissent. The first challenge to the "received" version of the First Philippine Campaign came not from a former prisoner-of-war but from MacArthur's former airforce commander, General Lewis Brereton. *The Brereton Diaries*, published some months after *General Wainwright's Story*, raised some disturbing questions about MacArthur's handling of the campaign. Brereton implied that MacArthur's negligence was largely responsible

for the success of the surprise Japanese bomber attack which had devastated American air bases at Luzon on the first day of the war. By
now Louis Morton was compiling information for his official history
of the First Philippine Campaign. His doubts about MacArthur's prewar
defence plans were strong enough to furbish an article in *Military Affairs*
(1948). A year later, the first book by a former prisoner-of-war, Colonel
Ernest B. Mullin's *Bataan Uncensored*, recounted a tale of ineptitude in
high places. When Morton's *The Fall of the Philippines* appeared in 1953,
it demanded a major critical re-evaluation of MacArthur's generalship.

This was slow to happen. By 1953, all eyes were focused on MacArthur's recent conduct of the Korean War. On 11 April 1951 Truman had
relieved MacArthur of command of the United States forces in Korea.
Depending on one's political viewpoint, MacArthur's plans to expand
the limited Korean War into China would have either purged the world
of the evils of communism or plunged it into an atomic holocaust. Not
surprisingly, during the 1950s and 1960s historians and political scientists
were more interested in the postwar phase of MacArthur's controversial
career than in dredging up the issue of the Philippines. But Volume 1 of
Clayton James's definitive biography (1970) marked the start of a gradual
shift in interest back to MacArthur's Second World War career.[1] Since
then, younger historians such as Carol Petillo and Michael Schaller have
followed up Clayton James' leads to develop a comprehensive critique of
MacArthur's generalship during the Philippines campaign.[2] Numerous
charges are levelled at MacArthur—failure to raise and train an effective
army, failure to perceive the true nature of the threat, failure to respond
with sufficient flexibility to changed circumstances. The catalogue of
errors which emerges reads like a "how-not-to" guide for would-be-
generals.

Fifty years ago, MacArthur's defence of Bataan and Corregidor secured him a niche in America's pantheon of heroes. Recent scholarly
scepticism has dislodged him from that niche, demoted him from su-
perstar to failed actor, no better than Kimmel or Short. Or (to vary
the metaphor) MacArthur looks less like a star than a supernova, a
blaze of light without substance. But the new critique of MacArthur
seems oddly uneven. It blames him for things over which he had no
control, such as the effectiveness of the Philippine Army or shifts in
u.s.-Japanese relations, and exonerates him from failures for which he
was personally responsible, such as the collapse of his administrative
system in Bataan or the plummetting morale of his troops. Pendulums in

historical scholarship always swing from one extreme to another before a balanced appraisal can be reached: it is the aim of this chapter to give the pendulum a backward nudge.

Douglas MacArthur took up the post of military adviser to the Commonwealth of the Philippines in December 1935. No-one could have been more delighted than the islands' president, Manuel Quezon. Ten years earlier, during MacArthur's second tour of duty as commander of the Philippines' American garrison, Quezon had been impressed by MacArthur's marked preference for the social company of prominent Filipinos rather than American expatriots. By 1935, MacArthur was America's most distinguished serving officer, having just completed five years as Army Chief of Staff in Washington. His controversial political reputation by no means deterred Quezon, since MacArthur's politics were sympathetic to the Philippines' interests. Roosevelt's newly elected Democrat administration had ample reason to dislike MacArthur, who only three yeas before had enraged liberal America by clearing protesting ex-servicemen (the bonus marchers) from their encampments by the Anacostia River outside Washington. MacArthur was closely associated with the Republican party. He was a personal friend of Herbert Hoover and John Rand, founder of the Sears Roebuck empire and major funder of Republican campaigns, and was even tipped within the party for presidential nomination. Quezon, worried that Roosevelt might thrust independence on the Philippines even before the projected date of 1946, had double reason to welcome MacArthur to Manila. Despite occasional disagreements, Quezon and MacArthur's friendship lasted for the six years the general spent on the Philippines. MacArthur's integration into the Filipino élite involved extensive business investments, high rank in the Masonic Lodge, and close family ties with Quezon, whom he requested to act as his baby son's godfather in 1938.

MacArthur's task between 1935 and 1941 was to create a defence for the Philippines. His own ideas about its scope and role differed radically from those held by the United States War Department and Navy, who, since the start of the century, had viewed America's possession of the Philippines as a strategic liability rather than an asset. In 1919 Japan's acquisition of German islands in the North Pacific which dominated communications between Hawaii and the Philippines heightened this sense of liability. The series of Orange (Japan) War Plans (WPO) developed by Washington steadily reduced the role of the United States garrison, the "Philippine Department," from an active to a defensive one. In the event of war, the garrison would merely "hold" the Bataan Peninsula and the forts dominating the entrance to Manila Bay while the United States Navy battled across the Pacific to the rescue. MacArthur's plans were far more ambitious. His national Philippine Army—some 200,000 men, annually trained and backed by a small airforce and a substantial force of torpedo boats—would be able to defend the entire archipelago.

The Army's War Plans Department voiced its reservations as early as the spring of 1936. They thought MacArthur's project at best unrealistic, at worst dangerous. The Philippine legislature was prepared to raise only an inadequate eight million dollars per year. Bureaucratic inefficiency and corruption (according to Eisenhower's diaries during his spell as MacArthur's aide between 1935–9) further reduced that sum.[3] Washington officials who feared insurrection from disaffected Filipino natives insisted that all modern weapons for Bataan's defence be stored on the fortress island of Corregidor: they saw the main danger to Philippine security as an internal one posed by Sakdalista guerrillas. They thought MacArthur's needs would be best served by a small, division-sized, highly trained gendarmerie, one which could slot into existing American defence plans were war to break out before independence. This force could help defend the Bataan Peninsula alongside the Philippine Scouts and the small American garrison.

MacArthur's recent critics have asserted that Eisenhower and the War Department were right at the time to censure his defence plans.[4] But criticisms made with the benefit of hindsight distort historical teleology: they presuppose that MacArthur was preparing for only one contingency, the full-scale Japanese invasion that actually occurred in 1941. In 1935, the threat of war with Japan seemed remote, even to the Japanese Navy, who thought conflict impossible before the early 1950s. Although Japan's subsequent involvement in China after July 1937 exacerbated U.S.-Japanese relations, it made an attack on the Philippines seem less rather than more likely. In 1935, MacArthur was planning ahead for a post-independence army for the Philippines, one which would fulfil his classical ideals of military training as a prerequisite for citizenship. His National Army would train and meld the disparate ethnic, linguistic and racial groups on the islands into a distinct Philippine identity.

Clayton James, Schaller and others argue that the threat of war, even if remote in the late 1930s, was looming closer by the early summer of 1940. The defeat of France and Holland, coupled with Britain's apparent military impotence, now offered the Japanese the tempting target of vulnerable European Asian empires. An attack on the Philippines seemed an active possibility: this should, they assert, have prompted MacArthur to revert to a defence scheme which would fit in with the latest version of the Orange War Plan, wpo3.[5] But by this stage MacArthur's sense of personal identity was intimately bound up with the future of the Philippines. He had resigned from the United States Army in 1937, the year after he had accepted the role of Field Marshal of the new Philippine Army. The limited and defeatist implications of wpo3 were anathema to him; also to his supporters in the Philippine legislature, who would be reluctant to supply the same level of funding for a smaller, less nationalistic army. MacArthur's training in Washington military politics had alerted him to the potential conflict between narrowly-conceived defence plans and larger political issues.

Modern critics universally condemn the optimism with which MacArthur presented his defence plans to the Philippine legislature between 1936 and 1941. This could be excused as a necessary exercise to ensure the continued funding of his army but unfortunately MacArthur used the same glowing terms in the reports he sent back to Washington. Historians of the Pacific War believe that the cumulative impetus of these unrealistic assessments led Roosevelt, in the wake of Japanese moves on Indo-China in early July 1941, to reverse American policy on the Philippines a few weeks later. MacArthur had repeatedly assured Washington that with just a little more help from the United States, his army could hold the Philippines. Between August and November, heavy bombers, modern fighters, thousands of tons of supplies and some 8,000 personnel were rushed across the Pacific. All that these last-minute efforts achieved, assert MacArthur's critics, was to increase the toll of the Bataan Death March.[6]

The theory that MacArthur was responsible for transforming American defence policy in the Western Pacific presupposes that within only a matter of weeks he had managed to convert Roosevelt, Marshall and the other Chiefs of Staff to his own views. But Washington as always fully briefed about the numerous shortcomings of MacArthur's Philippine Army. Eisenhower had spelt them out clearly to the War Department after returning from the islands in December 1939. On 4 June 1941, the Secretary of War and the Secretary of the Navy approved a new war plan (Rainbow 5) based on the assumption that the Philippines neither could nor should be defended.[7] The report Marshall received twelve days later from Major General Grunert, commander of the Philippine Department, analysed the state of the Philippine Army in terms which confirmed rather than dispelled Eisenhower's previous doubts.[8]

If Washington remained unconvinced by MacArthur's plans, what made the government change its policy? The concentration of scholarly interest on the stream of optimistic communiques flowing from Manila to Washington has diverted critical attention from some fundamental changes which were then taking place in the Administration's policy-making machinery. On 20 June, the disparate elements which had comprised the Army Air Corps had been formed into the United States Army Air Force. This was far more than a mere change of name—an important byproduct was the establishment of an independent Air War Plans Division.[9] On 23 June, Roosevelt signed an executive order authorising the acceleration and expansion of the production of heavy bombers—the B-17 and the B-24.[10] Any schemes the new Air War Plans Department now drew up could be very ambitious indeed.

On 2 July, attention was focussed on the Pacific when Japanese forces landed in southern Indo-China, a move which threatened not only the British and Dutch Asian empires but also the United States' supplies of rubber, tin and bauxite. For the next three weeks, various federal departments struggled to find an acceptable response. Defence plans for the Philippines were drawn up by the new Air War Plans Department, whose chief, Colonel Harold L. George, had served as an observer on Dowding's staff during the Battle of Britain. George's division produced a blueprint for a defence of the Philippines by aircraft operating without the assistance of land or naval forces. What he called a "strategical defensive" could be established, he argued, by the deployment of 340 heavy bombers and 130 fighters to Luzon. The commander of the Air Force, General "Hap" Arnold, and the Secretary for War, Henry Stimson, took up the plan enthusiastically.[11] On 25 July, Stimson urged Roosevelt to authorise the despatch of large numbers of heavy bombers and fighters to the Philippines.[12] Two days later, Roosevelt announced a dramatic hardening in American policy towards Japan—the freezing of Japanese assets in the United States which, along with similar British and Dutch moves, cut off Japan's supplies of oil. On the same day, Marshall recalled MacArthur to the United States Army and appointed him Lieutenant General commanding a combined Philippine Army–Philippine Department command, the United States Army Forces Far East. On 1 August Marshall told MacArthur of the official change in

United States Pacific policy—the Philippines were now to be defended—and promised him substantial help. From that time until well after the Japanese attack on 8 December, Marshall always reassured MacArthur that help was on the way.

The sequence of events in June and July 1941 makes plain that the reversal of American policy on Philippine defence had nothing whatever to do with MacArthur's assurances about the efficiency of his troops. Contrary to the accepted version of events, the decision was made in Washington and *imposed* on MacArthur. The high class claims MacArthur had made for his Philippine Army later supplied Stimson, Roosevelt and Marshall with a convenient scapegoat when their own policy failed. MacArthur never realised he was not responsible for Washington's apparent change of heart. Obsessed with a land battle, he had in fact wanted military equipment and American advisers rather than aircraft. But when Brereton, commander of the new Far Eastern Air Force, arrived on 3 November, MacArthur greeted him warmly with the words, "Lewis, you are just as welcome as the flowers in May."[13] Between August and early December, an eight million dollar airfield improvement and construction programme gave the Philippines some forty completed and semi-completed airfields and the largest concentration of war planes outside the United States. Of the 8,000 American servicemen who arrived on the islands during this period, 5,600 were Army Air Force.[14] Impressive though the effort was it was all too little, too late. The Japanese struck on 8 December, nearly four months earlier than MacArthur had predicted.

Shortly after midday on 8 December, Japanese air attacks on Clark and Iba Fields in central Luzon wiped out many of the United States Air Force's heavy bombers and fighters. Manila, forewarned, but not forearmed, had received news of Pearl Harbor more than nine hours earlier. Finding the guilty party responsible for Luzon is a historical detective game only marginally less popular than solving the Pearl Harbor mystery. Was it MacArthur, or Brereton, his airforce commander, or Major General Sutherland, his new Chief of Staff? Or all three? Historians trying to reconstruct the events of those crucial nine hours have failed to reach a majority verdict. Brereton's diaries supply us with a seemingly unimpeachable defence. At 5:30 on the morning of the 8th, he sought an audience with MacArthur for permission to carry out an airstrike on Japanese airfields on Formosa. Sutherland refused him entry on the grounds that MacArthur was too busy. Brereton's urgent phone calls elicited MacArthur's belated approval for a photo reconnaissance mission over Formosa upon which any bombing mission would be based. Had that mission been authorised at 5:30 it might have pre-empted a Japanese strike and would have cleared Clark Field of the B-17s.

Although MacArthur, as Commander United States Army Forces Far East, was technically responsible, Brereton's defence for the days leading up to 8 December looks shaky. He delayed carrying out MacArthur's command to send the United States Air Force's heavy bombers to Del Monte Field in northern Mindanao (well out of Japanese range). Del Monte Field was still under construction and ground space was limited. But Brereton's motives for delay may have been more dubious. Notorious for his socialising, drinking and womanising, he had planned a party to end all parties for American air crews at the Manila Hotel on the night of 7 December, one which MacArthur's orders would have forced him to cancel. The party went ahead. Brereton did not get back until after 2 A.M. Woken by the news of Pearl Harbor at 3:30, he was almost certainly still drunk and probably not alone. Sutherland (on record as advising Brereton to down some coffee) may have refused him admittance to MacArthur for being the worse for wear. In any other context, Mac-Arthur's decision to base an airstrike on evidence gathered from photo reconnaissance would have seemed prudent rather than over-cautious. The success of aerial bombing raids usually depended on an accurate knowledge of the target.

The argument about the delay in airstrike authorisation is a red herring: the real blame lay at Washington's door for allowing the latest American aircraft to gather in the Philippines without proper protection. On the day itself a number of chance factors coalesced to produce the disaster. Brereton, conscious of the vulnerability of his B-17s sitting stationary on the airfields, had ordered them up early that morning, covered by fighter protection. When authorisation for an airstrike came through at 12 P.M., he ordered the B-17s and P-40s down for essential preparation and refuelling. In that brief period, when the skies over Luzon were clear, the Japanese bombers, whose take-off had been delayed for several hours by heavy fog over Formosa, flew over Clark and Iba Fields and could scarcely believe their luck; rows of American aircraft grouped on the fields while ground crews moved fuel lines and trailers of ammunition and bombs across the runways. It took them less than half an hour to break the back of the United States Far Eastern Air Force. Brereton should have kept a fighter screen aloft. But responsibility for the Luzon disaster ultimately points back to the Washington bureaucracy—

Stimson, Marshall, Roosevelt, "Hap" Arnold and the Air War Plans staff. In their rush to get the latest aircraft to Luzon as quickly as possible they had neglected the vital matter of protection. The heavy bombers, which could travel to Luzon independently, arrived well in advance of essential hardware such as radar sets, communication equipment, and anti-aircraft guns. Under normal circumstances, the sequence would have been reversed: first air fields with bomb-proof hangars and anti-aircraft guns, then a radar and communications net tied to widely deployed fighter squadrons, last of all the heavy bombers. Washington and the Air War Plans Department took a gamble and lost.[15]

Although MacArthur can be exonerated for the Clark and Iba Field disasters, historians have argued that the islands' sudden dramatic loss of air power should have forced him to activate wpo3 at once.[16] But was the case so clear-cut on 8 December? If the decision depended solely on the state of his embryonic Philippine Army, then MacArthur was clearly in the wrong. Mobilisation, begun on 1 September, was due to be completed by 15 December. As the nine divisions finished their training, they were deployed in the three defensive commands into which MacArthur had divided the islands: three divisions to central and southern islands (the Visayas and Mindanao), two to southern Luzon, and four to north Luzon under Major General Wainwright's command. The Philippine troops were ragged at the seams. They had rifles and webbing but no proper uniforms. Their makeshift fatigues of denims, canvas shoes and straw hats barely distinguished them from ordinary Filipino peasants. Disciplined by ncos only slightly less ignorant than themselves, their military training had not extended much beyond grasping basic commands and loading and firing weapons. Transport was minimal; any trucks beyond the paltry twenty assigned to each division had been requisitioned or stolen. The large shipments of equipment which arrived in Manila by early December proved mostly useless. Ammunition left over from 1918 was often defective, and the field guns lacked sights. The Philippine "artillery regiments" were little more than gangs of curious peasants playing with obsolete guns.[17]

By December 1941, the regular strength of the usaffe had grown to 30,000. Over half that number were tied up in service detachments and the Air Force: of the remaining 15,000 who served on the front line, 10,000 belonged to the Philippine Division. MacArthur concentrated them in a reserve position near Manila alongside two newly arrived tank battalions and a field regiment of self-propelled guns, adding as

leaven the best of his newly raised divisions—5,000 men drawn from
the Philippine constabulary. MacArthur's reserve amounted to 20,000
well trained troops, supported by over a hundred tanks and about two
hundred self-propelled guns and field-guns.

Was he wrong to risk pitting this force against the Japanese in ma-
noeuvre warfare? Critics have suggested that by this stage MacArthur
had retreated into a fantasy world, cushioned from reality by sycophantic
staff and an imperious Sutherland who controlled access to his offices.[18]
But MacArthur may have had perfectly good reasons (ones overlooked
by historians) for his delay in activating WPO3. Although MacArthur's
Philippine Army was far from ready, Marshall's radio message on 8
December had guaranteed him "every possible assistance within our
power."[19] MacArthur believed that reinforcements would arrive any day.
On 13 December, a convoy carrying 70 fighters and dive-bombers was
re-routed from the Central Pacific to the Philippines via Australia under
the protection of the United States Asiatic Fleet. Two days later, Marshall
radioed MacArthur that another 160 fighters and dive-bombers were
being loaded aboard two fast transports, and that an additional fifteen
heavy bombers had been directed to the Philippines. On 22 December,
he promised another 80 B-17s and B-24s via Africa and the Indian Ocean.
He even allayed MacArthur's fears that the Japanese advance might
cut the resupply link: "The heavy bombers beginning to flow from
this country via Africa to your theatre should be able to support you
materially even if compelled initially to operate from distant bases. They
will be valuable also in co-operating with naval forces and smaller aircraft
in protecting your line of communications. The great range, speed and
power of these bombers, should permit, under your direction, effective
surprise concentrations against particularly favorable targets anywhere
in the theater."[20]

Thus MacArthur had every reason to expect the imminent arrival of
large numbers of war planes. Withdrawal to Bataan, with its one small
airfield, would have seemed extremely premature. Had he abandoned
the central Luzon airfields in mid-December, he would simultaneously
have abandoned any chance of retrieving the situation. Resumption of
an American command had not converted MacArthur to the advantages
of WPO3. He was still a Philippine field marshal who knew that his mostly
Filipino troops would interpret an American withdrawal as a sign that
their commander was ready to sacrifice their families to the Japanese.

Although MacArthur rejected the cautionary policy of WPO3 he did not use his troops to try to ward off every single Japanese landing. He knew that the small Japanese landings at Vigan and Aparri on the north coast of Luzon (10 December) and at Legaspi in the extreme south-east (14 December) were diversions. The only place on the Luzon coast where a large-scale landing was possible was Lingayen Gulf, about 100 miles north-west of Manila. It was here that he concentrated the divisions of Wainwright's North Luzon Force.

Morton and James, the two leading authorities on the campaign, have suggested that MacArthur harboured more reservations about the outcome of a battle between his own men and the Japanese invaders than is commonly supposed. On 13 December, MacArthur apparently told Quezon that he might need to activate WP03 very quickly. Some of his officers inspecting defences at Lingayen seemed unduly concerned about the location of withdrawal routes.[21] This scarcely constitutes evidence. Substantial counter-evidence (overlooked by Morton and James) lies in the decisive nature of MacArthur's logistic arrangements, which can scarcely be open to misinterpretation. Since 8 December, trainload after trainload of supplies had been shifted from Manila to depots around Lingayen. On 18 December, when MacArthur's code-breakers gave him definite information that a large Japanese convoy was heading to Lingayen, he actually *increased* the supply flow to Lingayen rather than diverting it to Bataan. By 21 December, North Luzon Force's depots were crammed with some 18,000 tons of supplies. No general planning a token defence would have created advance depots on such a scale.[22] In addition MacArthur sent north from his reserve the crack 26th Cavalry of the Philippine Scouts and one of his newly-arrived tank battalions.

Would MacArthur have made a stand on Lingayen had he realised the disparity between his Philippine Army and the Japanese troops? He knew full well that his Filipinos weren't up to American standards, but neither, he thought, were the Japanese. All that he had heard about Japanese soldiers pointed to weakness and inefficiency: they had been unable to defeat the peasant militias of China after more than three years of war, and had been humiliated by the Red Army in the border clashes of 1938 and 1939, the same Red Army which was in turn humiliated by the militia of Finland in November 1939. The odds that a Japanese landing on Lingayen would succeed were not as high as they later appeared. By the third week in December, the Japanese had launched nine amphibious operations. Six of these had been successful because unopposed: of the three that had been opposed, two ended in defeat and one in near disaster.[23] A Japanese invasion force heading for Lingayen Gulf would have to run the gauntlet of American submarines and aerial assault as well as coping with the high surf and uncertain weather conditions of December.

MacArthur could have amply justified his decision to stand at Lingayen. But in his *Reminiscences* he chose to skirt round the issue, devoting only two paragraphs to a suspiciously simplified account. According to MacArthur, on 22 December a large Japanese convoy entered the gulf and disgorged six divisions totalling 80,000 men—about twice the number of his 40,000 defenders. The Japanese already knew the locations of the defenders' strong points and easily avoided them. MacArthur claimed that what really prompted his decision to reactivate WPO3 was the news of a fresh Japanese landing at Lamon Bay, only forty miles south-east of Manila. He apparently suddenly realised that the Japanese commander General Homma intended "to swing shut jaws of a great military pincer, one prong being the main force that had landed at Lingayen, the other the units that had landed at Atimonan." Under these circumstances all he could do was pull back into Bataan to avoid a trap.[24]

What makes MacArthur's account so extraordinary is that it contradicts Louis Morton's meticulous historical analysis of the Lingayen landings published some twelve years earlier. Morton had pointed out that the Japanese landings had been far from easy. Although the United States Asiatic Fleet's submarines had proved only a minor deterrent, high winds and pounding surf had capsized landing craft and caused many of the Japanese invaders to swim ashore without arms or equipment. Moreover, Homma commanded not 80,000 men but only 43,000, about the same number that Wainwright had concentrated around Lingayen Gulf. Defending troops can rarely have been in such a favourable situation: mass slaughter of the Japanese should have been a likelihood. But after scrutinising dozens of unit diaries, Morton discovered only one instance of Filipino resistance.[25] The mere suspicion that the Japanese were coming was enough to panic the Filipinos, who by dawn were streaming south-east around the head of the gulf. Wainwright attempted a counter-attack, throwing the 26th Cavalry, elements of the provisional tank battalion, and Brigadier General Clyde Selleck's 71st Division of the Philippine Army against the Japanese. Never having trained together, the tanks and cavalry were unable to coordinate their activities. The Japanese drove both units back and by early afternoon of 23 December their patrol probes had produced widespread panic and chaos in Selleck's division.

It was this factor above all others that finally prompted MacArthur to activate WPO3. Although Lamon Bay was only forty miles from Manila, the route between crossed country so rugged that it would have taken the advancing Japanese more than a week to get from one location to the other. The south-eastern jaw of MacArthur's "great military pincer" would have closed so slowly that any potential prey would have had ample warning to escape.[26] It seems not insignificant that MacArthur punished the inept Selleck far more severely than any of his other failed divisional commanders. He was the only brigadier-general dismissed from command and reduced to the rank of colonel.

On 24 December the full implications of WPO3 came home to Mac-Arthur. He was now no longer the commander of what had been, in effect, a theatre—he had been reduced to caretaker of a soon-to-be beleagured fortress. Implementation of WPO3 entailed ordering Hart and Brereton to reduce their respective headquarters and withdraw to the south, Hart to Java and Brereton to Australia. MacArthur saw Hart go with little regret. Hart's small surface fleet had withdrawn at the outbreak of hostilities and his submarines had proved singularly ineffective. His dealings with MacArthur, which only just bordered on the civil, reflected the long-standing animosity between MacArthur and the United States Navy which had always precluded co-ordination of Philippine defence policy.[27]

MacArthur felt Brereton's loss more keenly. When his squadrons had first touched down on the islands, MacArthur had seen them as confirmation that after five years, Washington had at last decided to take his own plans for Philippine defence seriously. Even the disasters at Clark and Iba fields had not shaken MacArthur's confidence. Believing that Marshall's promised reinforcements would enable him to regain control of the air by early January, MacArthur dreamt of winning a land campaign against the Japanese in the Western Pacific while the United States Navy cowered in the Eastern. That dream now lay in ruins. Brereton's role was reduced to sustaining and developing aerial supply lines against the Japanese.

The relocation of HQ Asiatic Fleet and HQ USAAFFE were only two of the decisions MacArthur made on 24 December. Few generals have ever made as many sweeping command changes all on one day.[28] Apart from shutting down his naval and air headquarters, MacArthur shifted his own headquarters and the United States High Commission together with President Quezon and the entire Philippine Government to the Malinta tunnel complex on the fortress island of Corregidor. Simultaneously, he created two entirely new corps-level headquarters, one a rear-echelon HQ in Manila to oversee the withdrawal of forces to Bataan, the other on Bataan itself to organise the defenders. He also announced widespread changes in appointments: he sacked one divisional commander (Selleck), promoted another divisional commander (Jones) to the command of South Luzon Force, and transferred the South Luzon Force commander, General Parker, to the command of the Bataan Peninsula. Historians have acknowledged the confusion that inevitably ensued, but few have recognised its full implications.[29] It nearly led to the loss of one of MacArthur's corps, it certainly contributed to the ineffectiveness of supply movements to Bataan, and it seriously interfered with efforts to construct a sound defence scheme for the peninsula.

MacArthur's sweeping command changes have escaped censure because historians have focussed on the most successful single aspect of the operation: the carefully planned and well-rehearsed withdrawal of Wainwright's North Luzon Force. This movement had been practised since the early 1920s: there could have been few officers with Philippine service who were not familiar with the phasing of the withdrawal from stop-line to stop-line. The retreat began on Christmas Day and by 31 December North Luzon Force reached the fifth and final stop-line anchored on the Angat River at Baliuag, a position about ten miles north of Manila Bay which covered the main road from Manila to Bataan as it wound round the head of the bay and bridged the wide, steeply banked Pampanga River at Calumpit.

Apart from some minor skirmishes, the North Luzon withdrawal went like clockwork. But the parallel withdrawal of South Luzon Force gives a very different impression of MacArthur's generalship. MacArthur failed to give clear directives to Jones, who lacked the benefit of pre-planning for his extremely difficult task of co-ordinating a simultaneous retreat of three separate columns along three routes divided by lakes and jungle-clad mountains. The sudden withdrawal of any one force would leave the flanks of the other two exposed. This is precisely what happened at 3 A.M. on 25 December when Japanese patrols penetrated the front of the middle column, the 1st Regiment of the 1st Philippine Division, who rapidly withdrew towards Manila. A furious Jones caught up with them a few hours later: but news of MacArthur's command changes had not yet filtered through and the regiment's Filipino commander refused to take orders from him.

By 28 December, South Luzon Force was holding the Japanese at bay at Tiaong, still some forty miles south west of Manila. That same day MacArthur's Corregidor headquarters issued an order for the immediate withdrawal of South Luzon Force via Manila to Bataan. But the next day, 29 December, that order was countermanded by HQ Manila, which sent South Luzon Force back south-east again instructing them to hold the Japanese at bay for as long as possible. That Japanese had, of course, used the intervening hours to advance and occupy the Tiaong position. South Luzon Force grudgingly dug a new defence line. They were forced to abandon it the next day when HQ Corregidor ordered them to retreat north as quickly as possible and be across the Calumpit Bridges by 6 A.M. on 1 January 1942.

As South Luzon Force rolled through Calumpit on New Year's Eve, MacArthur radioed Jones again to inform him that he was now to take charge of the Agnat River defence line and hold it until the last troops had pulled through Calumpit. He was then to withdraw over the bridges and blow them up behind him. Unfortunately, MacArthur forgot to relay this information to General Wainwright, the North Luzon Force commander. On the afternoon of 31 December, Wainwright arrived at Jones's new headquarters in Plaridel, a town just south of Baliuag, to conduct the final defence. Wainwright ordered Jones to pull back his troops: Jones replied that he was now in command and intended to fight the battle very differently. Brigadier General Stevens, commander of 91st Division, joined in the argument. The three generals were interrupted by news that the Japanese were now in Baliuag and that the defenders were retiring south. This unexpectedly solved the question. Just after 6 A.M. the last of South Luzon Force passed over the Pampanga River blowing up behind them the bridges at Calumpit.

This complex operation was concluded successfully almost despite MacArthur, whose confusing last-minute changes in headquarters, commands and leadership nearly caused disaster. Within a five-day period, contradictory orders had had South Luzon force dancing up and down like a yo-yo: retreat, advance, retreat, advance, retreat. Even the most loyal Filipino private must have harboured a few doubts about his commander. Furthermore, MacArthur had inadvertently created a situation where two generals, Wainwright and Jones, each believed himself in command. Had events not overtaken them, they would have issued dangerously contradictory orders to troops about to fight the enemy.

Historians have been less forgiving of MacArthur's mishandling of wpo3's logistic aspects. wpo3 entailed withdrawal of supplies as well as troops—supplies intended to sustain some 43,000 men for the possible six months it would take before the United States Pacific Fleet came to the rescue. The town of Cabanatuan contained a vast rice depot on which civilian Manila depended. MacArthur's critics point out that its supplies would have fed Bataan for five years: MacArthur's threat to court-martial any logistic officer who laid a finger on them looks like another example of his readiness to sacrifice his troops' welfare to Filipino politics. All this is another red herring. The Manila warehouses were always well-stocked, and there was no real shortage of supplies, only a difficulty in moving them. General Drake, MacArthur's Quartermaster, calculated on 8 December that it would take at least two weeks to move supplies to Bataan sufficient for wpo3. MacArthur refused to authorise the operation, instructing Drake instead to stock the depots in the Tarlac area in preparation for the anticipated battle for Lingayen Gulf. By 22 December, 35 trainloads, carrying 18,000 tons of supplies, had been shifted north.

Two days later, Drake learnt that wpo3 was now in effect. He faced the near impossible task of saving the contents of the depots as well as shifting to Bataan supplies for perhaps twice as many men in half the original time. The railway system was defunct; Japanese bombers had already destroyed rolling stock and scared away native train crews. Motor transport was by now out of the question. On 8 December, Drake had the foresight to requisition 1,000 civilian trucks for supply purposes, but by 24 December most had been commandeered by American and Filipino units during the move to Lingayen. Drake's only hope now was that troops retreating through big depots such as Tarlac or Fort Stotsenberg would have the sense to carry off with them some of the supplies to last for the projected six-month siege. Few did. But even fully loaded, they could not have carried away more than 30 per cent of the depot contents. They took only about 5 per cent: most of the residue fell into the hands of the advancing Japanese.[30]

Water transport was still a possibility. Even on 8 December, Drake had started to requisition supplies from merchant ships still docked in Manila Bay. Between Christmas Eve and the New Year, Drake scraped together a fleet of some 300 barges to carry supplies between Manila and Bataan. But docking facilities on Bataan limited unloading to six barges at a time. Manila dockyard's skilled Filipino stevedores had disappeared in terror of Japanese bomb attacks: their replacements, American and

European civilian volunteers responding to radio broadcasts for help, were far slower. Few of the barges themselves could make more than 3 knots an hour. It took them more than ten hours to get to Bataan. Not surprisingly, most only managed one trip before the fall of Manila on 2 January 1942.[31]

In these circumstances, Drake's achievement in shifting more than 30,000 tons of supplies to Bataan and Corregidor was impressive. But the singular lack of communication between MacArthur and his quartermaster led to severe problems. Drake gave top priority to military supplies and ammunition. Corregidor never ran short of these, but men could scarcely eat bullets. When the first returns of unit strength came in, MacArthur had been amazed to read that he had some 80,000 troops on Bataan, with a further 26,000 civilians. He immediately suspected this was an exaggeration: the usual inflation of figures made by troops trying to secure ample rations. When the figures proved correct, the ration situation looked grim. Drake calculated rations would last for fifty days at most. Even the most stringent exploitation of Bataan's natural resources—fish, rice and Caribou—would not secure adequate supplies for 180 days. The low priority given to medical supplies was equally worrying. The malaria that infested Bataan during the summer season did not seem a major threat in January: but by March the one month's supply of quinine and handful of mosquito nets would scarcely stave off an epidemic. MacArthur, who had suffered badly from malaria during his earlier service on Bataan in 1906, should have been more percipient.[32]

Historians seem to have assumed that defence lines on Bataan were adequate. But because MacArthur had forbidden any advance work on them (perhaps fearing the negative impact on Filipino morale), the task that faced General Parker on 24 December was formidable.[33] Speed was essential, but haste led to mistakes. The most serious was the abandonment of Fort Wint, an island outpost only marginally less important than Corregidor itself. Fort Wint dominated the entrance to Subic Bay, Bataan's north-western shore. Its guns, trained on the western side of the Bataan Peninsula, would jeopardise any attempted landings. But on Christmas Eve Fort Wint's commander, Colonel Napoleon Boudreau, learnt that he had 24 hours in which to dismantle his guns and evacuate to Bataan. The task was impossible: on 25 December, the garrison withdrew, leaving the Japanese a Christmas present of all their fixed guns, some mobile guns, and several thousands rounds of 155 mm ammunition.[34]

United States Engineers began arriving on Bataan on 25 December. The peninsula had been thoroughly surveyed over the decades (MacArthur had assisted in the task as a junior officer) but too little time remained to make use of these detailed plans to construct man-made defence lines and obstacles. Bataan's excellent natural defences partly compensated: a tangle of steep jungle-clad mountains sandwiched between narrow coastal plains running down the eastern and western sides. The U.S. Engineers, basing their calculations on the average capacity of their own troops, pronounced as impassible the rugged Mount Natib Massif in the centre of the peninsula's twenty-mile neck. They thought that a forward defence line across the eastern and western coastal plains would prove sufficient, the inland flanks of both lines anchored on the eastern and western slopes of Mount Natib. Mt. Natib's forbidding terrain would deter any Japanese from attempting the ten-mile gap between the eastern and westernmost American units. Some six miles south, the engineers began work on a rear battle line which, skirting the northern slopes of Mt. Samat, ran all the way across the peninsula. If and when the Japanese breached this, the battle for Bataan would be over.[35]

After establishing his new Corregidor headquarters, MacArthur began to reorganise the forces retreating into the peninsula. He placed Wainwright in charge of I Corps, three Philippine Divisions assigned to the rugged western side of the defence line. He assigned Parker to command II Corps (four Philippine Divisions and the Philippine Scouts) which he sent to the eastern side of the defence line. The ten-mile front was defended by some 40,000 men, supported by about 100 guns. The Japanese commander on the spot, General Nara, attempted an assault on the Abucay line on 9 January, based on the false supposition made by Homma's intelligence that MacArthur's troops numbered only a demoralised 25,000. His own troops, reduced to 6,000 effectives by the demands of the southern campaign for the Indies, faced odds of 1 to 6: inevitably they failed to break through II Corps' position and were soon beaten back.

Carlos Romulo, MacArthur's press officer, described the battle for the Abucay line in these terms. "MacArthur had set his wickedest trap and launched his first great attack against the Japanese at Abucay. He had set it with banked tiers of hidden artillery. He let the advancing Homma legions come on in a tremendous offensive, luring them into ambush. He did not fire until the Japanese army was in close range. Then thousands were fed to the hungry mouths of our guns at the slaughter of Abucay."[36]

Swashbuckling stuff: but Romulo's account, like most of MacArthur's press releases, oversimplifies and over-glamorises history. In reality the Japanese recovered rapidly from their initial reverse. Infiltrating through the jungle they located the Mount Natib gap, worked their way round the flanks of both Parker's and Wainwright's Corps, broke the cohesion of the Philippine Army Divisions, fought off American and Filipino counter-attacks and by 26 January had forced the defenders back to the Mount Samat line. General Nara then overplayed his hand. Now down to only 4,000 effectives, he attempted battalion-sized infiltration of the new defence line and battalion-sized landings near the southern tip of Bataan. The defenders now outnumbered the Japanese by 20 to 1. There was an unglamorous inevitability about Nara's decision to break off battle in the second week of February to await reinforcements.

The difference between Romulo's purple prose account of the Abucay line battle and the grey historical reality underscores the blurring of truth and fiction so characteristic of MacArthur's Philippine years. Historians have condemned as vulgar propaganda the stream of communiqués, despatches and press accounts flowing from Corregidor, all of which exaggerated and valorised MacArthur's central role as general leading his troops to victory.[37] Philippine jungle warfare was scarcely so heroic. But MacArthur, steeped in military history (he owned more than 4,000 volumes on the subject) may have been modelling himself, consciously or unconsciously, on great generals of the past, Napoleon, Washington and Lee. An avid film-goer, historical movies such as *The Buccaneer* may also have supplied MacArthur with the model for the bird's eye view sweep of the panoramic battle-field described in his *Reminiscences*. "Our headquarters, called 'Topside,' occupied the flattened summit of the highest hill on the island. It gave a perfect view of the whole panorama of the siege area. As always, I had to see the enemy, or I could not fight him effectively. Reports, no matter how penetrating, have never been able to replace the picture shown to my eyes."[38] Bataan proved a test of generalship, but not in the way MacArthur believed. Conditions in the Pacific and Asia rarely allowed generals to demonstrate their prowess with corps-sized thrusts and rapier-like ripostes. Battles were won by junior officers and NCOs in bitter attritional slogging-matches. Good generalship meant being able to inspire your men to fight that little bit harder for that little bit longer. Often the only way a general could help his men was by his morale-boosting presence. Vandergrift on Guadalcanal, Moreshead in New Guinea and Slim in Burma all discovered this truth. So in time did MacArthur, but not during the First Philippines Campaign.

Historians have paid too little attention to MacArthur's responsibility for the administrative collapse on Bataan. The shortage of food and medical supplies was made far worse by inefficient distribution: in such circumstances the usual formula applied—the closer to the front, the more distant the supply source and the more inadequate the rations. Front-line troops went short while rear echelons ate well. There was little MacArthur could do to improve the supply lines themselves: rough tracks hacked out over jungle-clad hills on which trucks often broke down. But he might have cracked down far earlier on the problem of discipline in the rear areas which enabled armed gangs of deserters to loot supplies. The Philippine Army military police he sent to guard the depots proved infinitely corruptible. By the time MacArthur considered publicly executing looters and deserters, the problem was so widespread that such a solution would have been impossible to implement. Front-line morale plummeted: empty bellies were bad enough, but rumours that rear area troops never went hungry and the food in Corregidor was ample, even luxurious, caused massive resentment. The rumors were not entirely unfounded. The bacon, ham, fresh vegetables, coffee, milk and jam which Wainwright found available in Corregidor when he took over from MacArthur in March 1942 had long since disappeared from Bataan.

Short rations led to low morale and severe malnutrition. After rations were cut from January's barely adequate level of 2,800 calories a day to March's starvation diet of 1,000, troops were forced to forage or die. Minor ailments became major ailments and vitamin-deficiency diseases proved debilitating. By 8 March, malaria affected over one third of all front-line units. Lack of training in even elementary hygiene precautions meant that common diarrhoea and dysentery ran rife through native Filipino troops when they fell back to fixed positions. They drank stagnant water and failed to sterilise their mess gear. Their latrines were neither properly constructed nor properly used. Once again, administrative inefficiency made the initial shortage of resources and supplies critical. As commander of the Philippines, MacArthur was ultimately responsible.

The swelling tide of complaints which reached Corregidor might have prompted MacArthur to go and see for himself but he ventured out of the underground labyrinth of his island fortress only once. Here he was most surely to blame. When his troops chanted the refrain "Dugout Doug MacArthur lies ashaking on the Rock" (ironically to the tune of the "Battle Hymn of the Republic") they were only acknowledging with bitter humor the absence of leadership which left them feeling as if they were fighting in a void. MacArthur might have made a world of difference to troop morale by a few unexpected tours of inspection, some unannounced appearances among his men. Simply the rumor that MacArthur was doing *something* to solve the problems of ration shortages, deserters and looters would have helped forge that vital link between high command and troops and sustained their fighting spirit. Instead he became a virtual recluse.

In a famous photograph taken in March 1942 of USAFFE HQ in the Malinta tunnel, MacArthur, wearing his cap of Field Marshal of the Philippine Army, leans back on his chair. The mask of stoic fortitude which fixes his features betrays more than a hint of boredom. How was MacArthur spending the long days, if not in active service? As he himself remarked wittily to Romulo, "The sword may rest, but the pen never does."[39] Historians have been fascinated by the stream of communiqués which flowed to Washington from Corregidor during the 78 days MacArthur was in residence. Like Lieutenant General Arthur Perceval signalling from Fort Canning to his superior General Sir Archibald Wavell in Java, MacArthur pleaded for reinforcements. Unlike Perceval, when he realised they were not in the offing, he refused to keep a respectful silence and began instead to play the role of arm-chair strategist, arbitrarily advising Washington on lofty matters of American defence policy. He urged the abandonment of the "Europe first" strategy, suggested that America should press the Soviet Union to open up a front against Japan in Manchuria, and demanded that the Pacific Fleet abandon its timid defensive posture and launch a carrier strike against the Japanese home islands. Although immured on a remote Philippine island fortress, MacArthur found it difficult to stop behaving like the Chief of Staff he had been just six years earlier.

Washington officials found MacArthur's "advice" embarrassing but it made no difference to their policy. They could not ignore his more public manipulation of American opinion. It was no coincidence that of all the prominent journalists who gathered in Manila by 1941, Melville and Annalee Jacoby, correspondents for *Time* and *Life* magazines, should have been among those who ended up on Corregidor. MacArthur thoughtfully provided them with radio telephone links to the United States. He even wrote the copy which he broadcast on the radio station "Voice of Freedom," set up soon after his arrival on Corregidor with the help of his friend Carlos Romulo. Romulo remembered MacArthur as a "continual source of stimulation": he would pace up and down the headquarters lateral and then burst in upon his press officers: " 'I have an idea!' That is one of his pet phrases. And he would go to his desk to scribble rapidly the suggestion for a broadcast or communiqué that had come to him. 'Think it over and see if you can improve upon it,' he would always say, tossing it across the desk."[40] MacArthur either wrote or co-authored 140 communiqués—exciting, vivid and often wholly imaginary accounts of the campaign in which he always emerged as a military genius thwarting Japan's evil designs again and again. His troops on Bataan who knew the reality found the stream of propaganda nauseating. "Voice of Freedom" broadcasts, ostensibly designed to boost Filipino morale, probably had the opposite effect. But enraptured American radio audiences hung on his every word. By the end of 1941, MacArthur was on the front cover of *Time*, and by early 1942 MacArthur-mania was sweeping the United States.

All this caused serious problems for Washington when it came to deciding what to do with MacArthur. Eisenhower was all for leaving him on Corregidor, where his histrionic talents equipped him perfectly for the role of heroic commander of a doomed fortress. This was a minority view (though one shared by the Navy).[41] Two other suggestions were raised—one that he should escape to Mindanao to lead resistance and perhaps become a guerilla chieftan, the other that he escape to Australia and take command of the United States forces assembling there.

Marshall really had only one option open to him. He simply could not allow MacArthur, a former Chief of Staff and a national hero, to fall into Japanese hands. On 4 February he first broached the subject of evacuating MacArthur from the Philippines.[42] The dispatch confirmed MacArthur's long-standing suspicions that Washington was preparing to abandon the Philippines. He embarked on a series of byzantine manoeuvres in a last attempt to manipulate American policy. On 8 February, Washington received three communications from Corregidor: one from Quezon, one from High Commissioner Sayre, one from MacArthur. Quezon proposed that the United States should grant immediate independence to the Philippines, which would then be neutralised. Japanese and United States forces would be withdrawn by mutual consent and the Philippine Army disbanded. Sayre and MacArthur endorsed Quezon's request, MacArthur adding that "the temper of the Filipinos is one of almost violent resentment against the United States. Every one of them expected help, and when it has not been forthcoming, they believe they have been betrayed in favour of others."[43]

The immediate reaction in Washington as one of shocked surprise. Recovering, Roosevelt and Marshall authorised Eisenhower, the one man in Washington with deep insights into MacArthur's psychology, to draft a reply under Roosevelt's signature which reached MacArthur on 9 February. Eisenhower hit MacArthur where he knew it would hurt most. He was instructed to capitulate his Filipino forces if necessary: but "American forces will continue to keep the flag flying in the Philippines as long as there remains any possibility of resistance." MacArthur should remember, continued Eisenhower, that "the duty and the necessity of resisting Japanese aggression to the last transcends in importance any other obligation now facing us in the Philippines." MacArthur probably never realised that this despatch was composed by his former aide: it would have heaped insult upon injury.[44] On 11 February, an angry MacArthur assured Roosevelt, "I have not the slightest intention in the world of surrendering or capitulating the Filipino element of my command . . . there has never been the slightest wavering of my troops." He firmly intended to fight "to destruction" on Bataan and then Corregidor. He would arrange for the evacuation of Quezon and Sayre (they left by submarine a few weeks later) but he and his family would "share the fate of the garrison."

MacArthur had slammed the ball firmly back into Washington's court. The likely reaction of the American public to the death of their hero, his wife and baby son, gave Washington officials many sleepless nights. Marshall sent MacArthur a radiogram which urged him to reconsider. MacArthur ignored it. On 15 February, the day Perceval surrendered Singapore, MacArthur sent Marshall a despatch urging an immediate American naval offensive in the Pacific. This extraordinary game was brought to an end on 22 February when Roosevelt gave MacArthur a direct order to leave Corregidor for Australia where he would assume command of a new South-West Pacific theatre. This was one of the few orders MacArthur ever obeyed, but even then it was used as a basis for negotiations. MacArthur decreed that he would only leave when the situation was right, by which he meant not just the situation on Bataan but elsewhere. Significantly, his departure from Corregidor on 12 March came three days after the surrender of Java and the Japanese occupation of Rangoon. MacArthur knew the Japanese were pouring reinforcements into the Philippines and that the next assault would finish the Bataan garrison. It did, and Bataan surrendered on 9 April. A month later Corregidor also surrendered. By this time MacArthur, firmly ensconced in Melbourne as Commander in Chief of the new Southwest Pacific Area, was beginning his campaign to return to the Philippines.

Notes

1. D. Clayton James, *The Years of MacArthur*, Vol. I, (London, 1970).
2. See Carol M. Petillo, *Douglas MacArthur: The Philippine Years* (Bloomington IN, 1981), and Michael Schaller, *Douglas MacArthur the Far Eastern General* (New York, 1989).
3. Robert Ferrell (ed.), *The Eisenhower Diaries* (New York, 1981), pp. 19–20.
4. See, e.g., James, I, 502–9; Schaller, p. 34.
5. Schaller, p. 45; James, I, 537; Ronald H. Spector, *Eagle Against the Sun* (New York, 1985), pp. 72–4.
6. James, I, 609; Schaller, p. 49; Spector, p. 73.
7. W. F. Craven and J. L. Cate, *The Army Air Forces in World War II*, I (Chicago, 1948), p. 139.
8. James, I, 581.
9. Craven and Cate, p. 145.
10. General H. H. Arnold, *Global Mission* (London, 1951), p. 159.
11. Craven and Cate, p. 178; Mark S. Watson, *Chief of Staff Pre-War Plans and Preparations* (Washington, 1950), pp. 438–440.
12. Watson, pp. 445–6.
13. Louis Morton, *The Fall of the Philippines* (Washington, 1953), p. 67.
14. Morton, p. 49.
15. Lewis H. Brereton, *The Brereton Diaries: The War in the Air in the Pacific, Middle East and Europe, 3 October 1941–8 May 1945* (New York, 1946), pp. 34–44; Craven and Cate, pp. 203–210; Arnold, pp. 271–3; Morton, pp. 80–90.
16. James, *The Years of MacArthur*, Vol. II (London, 1975), 27; Gavin Long, *MacArthur as Military Commander* (London, 1969), p. 67.
17. Morton, pp. 25–30.
18. Long, p. 67; James, II, 28.
19. Morton, p. 146.
20. Alfred D. Chandler (ed.), *The Papers of Dwight David Eisenhower*, I (Baltimore, 1970), 21.
21. Morton, pp. 160–163; James, II, 27.
22. Alvin P. Stauffer, *Quartermaster Corps: Operation in the War Against Japan* (Washington, 1956), p. 6.
23. Unopposed: Patani, Singora (8 December); Guam, Vigan, Appari (10 De-

cember); Legaspi (12 December). Opposed: Kotabharu (8 December); Wake (12 December); Hong Kong (17 December).

24. General Douglas MacArthur, *Reminiscences* (London, 1964), p. 124.

25. Morton, p. 131.

26. Morton, pp. 195–202; Karl C. Dod, *The Corps of Engineers: The War Against Japan* (Washington, 1966), pp. 80–82.

27. See e.g. Morton, pp. 164–6; James, II, 30; Long, p. 72; William Manchester, *American Caesar* (London, 1979), p. 218.

28. Morton, pp. 195–202.

29. Ernest B. Miller, *Bataan Uncensored* (Long Prairie MN, 1949), p. 75; Stauffer, p. 9; James, II, 33; Manchester, p. 215.

30. Stauffer, pp. 11–13.

31. Stauffer, p. 12.

32. Morton, pp. 367–370.

33. The official history of the Corps of Engineers makes clear the extraordinary fact that the surveying of defence positions was not underway until 2 January (Dod, p. 87).

34. Morton, pp. 279–280.

35. Dod, pp. 85–9.

36. Carlos P. Romulo, *I Saw the Fall of the Philippines* (London, 1943), p. 93.

37. See, e.g., James, II, 89; Schaller, p. 61.

38. MacArthur, p. 130.

39. Romulo, p. 106.

40. Romulo, p. 107.

41. Ferrell, p. 49.

42. Chandler, pp. 97–8.

43. James, II, 94–6.

44. Chandler, pp. 104–6.

MacArthur

An Australian Perspective

David Horner

David Horner is a member of the Strategic & Defence Studies Centre at the Australian National University and the author of numerous studies of Australia's role in World War II, including a superb biography of Gen. Sir Thomas Blamey. In an essay specially commissioned for this volume he assesses MacArthur's impact on Australia.

Gen. Douglas MacArthur spent only two and one-half years in Australia but it was perhaps the most crucial period of his military career. When his plane touched down at the remote northern town of Darwin on March 17, 1942, he had left his Philippines command facing certain defeat. Yet within a week of departing Australia for the last time on October 14, 1944, he was back in the Philippines as the triumphant commander of a liberating army. To many American commentators, however, and perhaps even to MacArthur himself, Australia was but a way station along a glittering road of success that led him from West Point to the Philippines (several times), to Mexico, the Western Front, Washington, Japan and, finally, to Korea. While American historians generally acknowledge that MacArthur's period in Australia was important, they give little attention either to his impact on Australia or to his relations with key Australians.

The perspective from Australian historians is somewhat different. MacArthur is one of the few non-Australians with an entry in the *Australian Dictionary Biography*. (Most of the others are British-born governors general and state governors.) MacArthur's impact on Australia was substantial. He dominated strategic affairs in Australia for all but four months of the Pacific War, and he also embodied the American-Australian alliance. This alliance, which began with the arrival of U.S. troops late in 1941, flourished under MacArthur and was finally cemented with the signing of the ANZU.S. Pact in February 1951 when, as it happened, MacArthur was again commanding Australian forces in action in Korea.[1] Half a century later Australian Defence Headquarters in Canberra is still dominated by the spire (with its crowning eagle) of the Australian-American memorial.

When MacArthur arrived in Australia in 1942 few Australians would have known of his disputes with President Roosevelt when he was chief of staff in the early 1930s, and they did not understand the destructive rivalry between the U.S. Navy and Army which polarized feelings about MacArthur in the U.S. services. Australians have an innate reluctance to indulge in hero worship of public figures. (In Australia it is called "cutting down the tall poppies.") But, as the Japanese advanced relentlessly south in the three months following the attack on Pearl Harbor, the Australians knew that they could not withstand a Japanese attack on their own. When it was announced on March 18 that MacArthur was to be supreme commander of a command soon to be known as the Southwest Pacific Area (SWPA), the Australian public's fears were eased immediately. Many Australians saw the "hero of the Philippines" as their national savior.

From the first day of his arrival in Melbourne on March 21, Mac-Arthur had an important impact on the government. For example, the deputy prime minister, Frank Forde, who met MacArthur at the railway station in Melbourne, was tremendously impressed. He recalled that faced by "the greatest catastrophe that could have happened, the country looked to America. . . . MacArthur was the man who would influence his government along the right lines."[2] MacArthur told him that "although the war clouds" were "black" he was "absolutely confident that with the backing and cooperation of the Government and people of my country, and the wholehearted support and cooperation of the Government and people of Australia, in the very near future naval vessels and aeroplanes, fighting personnel and weapons of war will be in Australian waters."[3] MacArthur also had a positive effect on the public. The *Brisbane Courier Mail* said that his arrival was "stirring news, the best news Australians have had for many a day." The *Melbourne Herald* observed that the "United States would not send its greatest contemporary soldier to a secondary war zone, and the fact that it regards Australia as a sphere of supreme importance is by far the most heartening circumstance which the Commonwealth Ministers have encountered since Japan's entry into the war." The *Sydney Daily Mirror* thought Australia had been "electrified" by MacArthur's appointment. A few days later Forde said that he was satisfied that MacArthur was "a master of strategy, and that under his direction the aggressive offensive, attacking policy will be developed to the highest possible degree."[4]

Civil-Military Relations

MacArthur had a unique relationship with the Australian government. Like Wellington in Portugal during the Peninsular War, he was a foreign general in command of another country's armed forces. Strategic direction came from the U.S. Joint Chiefs of Staff (JCS), but MacArthur had to be sensitive to the needs of the Australians. Furthermore, the civil agencies, which supported his forces, could be directed only by the Australian government. It was a mark of MacArthur's diplomacy that he retained the loyal support of the Australian prime minister, John Curtin, until the latter's death in July 1945.

MacArthur first met Curtin on March 26, 1942, when MacArthur traveled to Canberra to meet the Advisory War Council. Australian war policy was determined by the War Cabinet—a committee of the eight key ministers. But the Advisory War Council, which consisted of five War Cabinet ministers and five senior nongovernment members, had been set up to involve the opposition in major decisions concerning strategy and war policy. As five of the eight War Cabinet ministers also sat on the Advisory War Council, its decisions could be accepted as War Cabinet decisions and hence in early 1942 it was Australia's principal body for strategic direction.

MacArthur told the Advisory War Council that their first step was to secure Australia as the base from which a counteroffensive could be mounted toward the Philippines. This counteroffensive would depend on the speed with which men and equipment could be moved to Australia. He doubted whether the Japanese would try to invade Australia, but believed they would try to conduct raids and attempt to secure air bases in Australia. MacArthur suggested that coordination with the Australian government should be undertaken through the prime minister who was also minister for defense. Curtin, the leader of the Australian Labor Party that had come to power in October 1941, was a former journalist and trade unionist with no experience in military affairs. Despite their different backgrounds and experience, MacArthur and Curtin established a warm relationship.[5] "Mr. Prime Minister," said MacArthur, putting his hand on Curtin's shoulder, "we two, you and I, will see this thing through together. . . . You take care of the rear and I will handle the front."[6] At a dinner for all the parliamentarians MacArthur made a stirring address:

There is a link between our countries which does not depend upon the written protocol, upon treaties of alliance, or upon diplomatic doctrines. It goes deeper than that. It is that indescribable consanguinity of race which causes us to have the same aspirations, the same hopes and desires, the same ideals, and the same dreams of future destiny.

My presence here is tangible evidence of our unity. I have come as a soldier in a great crusade of personal liberty as opposed to perpetual slavery. My faith in ultimate victory is invincible, and I bring you tonight the unbreakable spirit of the free man's military code in support of our just cause.

We shall win or we shall die, and to this end I pledge you all the resources of all the mighty power of my country and all the blood of my countrymen.[7]

Over the next two weeks MacArthur and the Australian government refined the arrangements for strategic direction. The key figure in Australian strategic policymaking and in formalizing these arrangements was the secretary (that is, civil service permanent head) of the Defense Department, Frederick Shedden, who was also secretary of both the War Cabinet and the Advisory War Council.[8] On April 8 at a meeting in Melbourne with MacArthur, Shedden, and the commanders of the Allied Naval, Land, and Air Forces (Admiral Leary and Generals Blamey and Brett), Curtin explained that as defense minister he would be the link between the government and MacArthur, while MacArthur would have operational control of the Australian forces.[9] There would be no link between the government and the commanders of the Allied Naval, Land and Air Forces, as they were under MacArthur, but Blamey would have contact with Curtin on the basis of his position as commander in chief of the Australian military forces.

Australia's senior strategic decision-making body would be the Prime Minister's War Conference, consisting of MacArthur, Curtin, and any ministers or officers who might be summoned by the prime minister. Shedden would also be present, and he became the link between Curtin and MacArthur; as Curtin wrote to MacArthur on April 10, "if I should not be readily available, Mr. Shedden has my full confidence in regard to all questions of War Policy."[10]

Shedden's detailed minutes of the Prime Minister's War Conference provide a unique and vital record of Curtin's discussions with MacArthur. After the war these minutes were not made available to the official historians; when they asked Shedden (who remained defense secretary until 1956) to produce records of specific conversations he did so but did not volunteer other records. The official histories refer to some of the discussions between Curtin and MacArthur but, remarkably, make no mention of the formation of the Prime Minister's War Conference.

Thus with MacArthur's arrival the whole strategic decision-making structure was revised. Whereas previously the chiefs of staff had been the government's principal advisers on strategy and had been responsible for the operations in the defense of Australia, both responsibilities now rested with MacArthur. It is true that Curtin could still have received advice from the Australian chiefs, particularly Blamey, but, supported by Shedden he looked to MacArthur as his main source of advice.

Despite these positive developments, as days passed MacArthur became increasingly agitated about the delay in endorsing his directives. His leading biographer, D. Clayton James, observed that "two contradictory images of MacArthur emerged." The more public image was one of a supremely confident general who would lead his forces to victory while in private he appeared tired, bitterly disappointed, and at times seized by moods of despair.[11] Later Shedden recalled that there were two major crises in the relationship between Curtin and MacArthur. He claimed that in each case he acted as a go-between, putting proposals to each so as to minimize disagreement. The first crisis came in April 1942 when MacArthur discovered how few forces he had in Australia and "lost heart and wanted to give his job up."[12]

Shedden was referring to a meeting on April 14 when, in Curtin's absence, MacArthur urgently asked Shedden to call on him at his Melbourne headquarters. Shedden found MacArthur "somewhat depressed" at the delay in receiving his formal directive. He thought that if this "were in any way due to inhibitions which might be held by the Australian Government regarding an American officer commanding its Forces," he was willing to abandon the idea of a joint Allied command and merely command the U.S. forces while still cooperating with the Australians. Shedden reassured him that the government warmly supported the idea of an Allied command and, according to Shedden, "he appeared to be much happier at the conclusion of the interview."[13]

Shedden traveled immediately to Canberra and gave Curtin a letter for him to sign. Curtin had just been advised that the U.S. president had agreed to arrangements whereby the Australian government could "refuse the use of its forces for any project which it considered inadvisable."[14] Curtin signed the letter, advising MacArthur that his directive had been approved by the president and that the Australian government would assign its forces to his command. The letter continued:

> You have come to Australia to lead a crusade, the result of which means everything to the future of the world and mankind. At the request of a sovereign State you are being placed in Supreme Command of its Navy, Army and Air Force, so that with those of your great nation, they may be welded into a homogeneous force and given that unified direction which is so vital for the achievement of victory.
>
> Your directive, amongst other things, instructs you to prepare to take the offensive. I would assure you of every possible support that can be given you by the Government and people of Australia in making Australia secure as a base for operations, in assisting you to marshal the strength required to wrest the initiative from the enemy and, in joining with you in the ultimate offensive, to bring about the total destruction of the common foe.[15]

Shedden told Curtin that, following a talk with MacArthur, the letter "had removed his doubts."[16] At midnight on April 18, 1942, all combat units of the Australian armed forces except those serving in the European and Middle East theaters were assigned to MacArthur's command.[17] By this stage 38,000 American forces were in Australia, while the all-volunteer Australian Imperial Force (AIF) troops under his command totaled 104,000 and the militia, 265,000.

MacArthur's appointment was a substantial abrogation of Australian sovereignty, but in the emergency of early 1942 perhaps there was no other option. Though Australia had a large army, most of it was poorly trained and equipped. Two AIF divisions had served in the Middle East: one was still there and another was training in Australia. But the eleven militia divisions, which included large numbers of conscripts, had only recently gone onto full-time service. More important, the Royal Australian Navy (RAN) was relatively small and many of its ships were deployed away from Australia with British forces. The Royal Australian Air Force (RAAF) was in an even worse situation. It had many men under training, but large numbers were in Britain; those who remained were manning outmoded aircraft and these were few in number. Faced with the possibility of a Japanese invasion the Australians looked to the Americans for support.

Initially MacArthur had only small numbers of U.S. ships and planes but his mere presence gave Australia access to U.S. men and equipment that might not otherwise have been sent. As Field Marshal Dill, the

British military representative in Washington, put it in March 1942, "MacArthur will be a suction pump for reinforcements and military supplies to Australia. It is this quality rather than his generalship which makes him attractive in Australian eyes."[18] The first part of the statement was true but the Australian government also looked to MacArthur for military advice, seeking his views, for example, as to whether the Ninth Australian Division should be returned from the Middle East.

Fortunately, for the first year or more the Australian government's national strategy corresponded with MacArthur's ideas on how the war should be conducted, and they made common cause to the Joint Chiefs of Staff in Washington. Both MacArthur and the Australian government disagreed with the Allied policy of defeating Hitler first and both wanted reinforcements to be sent to the Southwest Pacific. MacArthur had vowed to return to the Philippines and needed additional forces for that mission. The Australian government had a genuine and realistic concern for the security of the country. Churchill's reputed statement that Australia could be recovered after the war had been won seemed less sensible when viewed from Canberra than from London.

Of course the Japanese never really planned to invade Australia. Although Curtin and his military advisers could be excused for expecting such an invasion between February and June 1942, after the Battle of Midway it was clear that the invasion would not materialize. Yet for a full year longer Curtin, urged on by MacArthur, used the threat of invasion to maintain the momentum of the Australian war effort and to request further American support for the SWPA.

Shedden's role as the link between MacArthur and the Australian government has not been fully appreciated. In his biography of MacArthur, James names thirty-seven people who met with MacArthur "individually or in a group fourteen or more times" between March 17, 1942, and August 28, 1945.[19] Only four Australians are mentioned: General Blamey (who met MacArthur seventy-six times), Curtin (thirty-eight meetings), Shedden (thirty-two meetings), and Blamey's chief of staff, Lieutenant-General Berryman (sixteen meetings), who was at MacArthur's headquarters for most of the last year of the war. This list, based on MacArthur's diary, overlooks the fact that though Shedden accompanied Curtin to almost all of his meetings with MacArthur he is generally not listed as being present at those meetings.

Shedden's private meetings with MacArthur were lengthy, and at times he traveled to MacArthur's headquarters in Brisbane for several days of meetings. For example, he met MacArthur several times over the periods of October 20–26, 1942, January 16–20, 1943, May 24–31, 1943, and November 29–December 1, 1943. Shedden's notes of the meetings in May 1943 alone filled fifty-seven typed foolscap pages. It seems that by early 1943 he had fallen under MacArthur's spell, for in January 1943 he wrote a record that is worth quoting at length.[20]

I always find General MacArthur's personality an interesting study and he really has to be closely studied to be properly understood. Some people, who should know better, dismiss him rather cheaply because of a certain demonstrative manner and his verbosity.

His demonstrative manner is due to his mercurial temperament. He has great enthusiasm for his work, but becomes depressed at the political frustrations which, in his view, shape world strategy, to the detriment of the Southwest Pacific Area. His verbosity is probably largely due to the fact that he keeps so exclusively to himself and his staff. This probably leads to a tendency to introspection and a desire to pour out his thoughts and feelings on anyone interested in his problems and views. Another result of this introspection is a tendency to suspect motives on occasions without sound grounds for them, with the consequence that, by dwelling on them, he may build up a view which is entirely contrary to the known facts.

Anyone who has had close relations with General MacArthur cannot come away without any other impression than that he has been in the presence of a great masterful personality. He has a broad and cultured mind and a fine command of English. He might be described as an American conservative who has faithfully maintained the standards of his British ancestors. He views with great disfavour the influence which foreign people have had in America on British standards. He is a great stickler for the status of his position.

I rank General MacArthur's expositions of strategy as equal to those of Admiral Sir Herbert Richmond, who is the greatest living writer on Naval history and strategy, and to Lord Hankey, who, as Secretary of the Committee of Imperial Defence, demonstrated the possession of a great strategical mind. General MacArthur has a profound knowledge of military art and history, is a shrewd judge of men, and, what is essential for a successful Commander, great personal courage and leadership, as was exemplified during the campaign in the Philippines. Though his Army was mainly Philippino [sic], it offered a stout resistance to the Japanese and this Army was entirely General MacArthur's creation.

At 63, he has shown that his mind has not lost its resiliency and that he has not been blindly wedded to orthodoxy in the art of war, by demonstrating in the New Guinea campaign how effectively land and air forces can be used in cooperation, and how air transport can be used when movement by land and sea is impossible.

General MacArthur is very proud of his post as Commander-in-Chief, Southwest Pacific Area, by reason of the unity of Naval, Military and Air control that is vested in him, and also because of the fact that he is a foreigner, commanding on the soil of a sovereign State, Allied Forces, of which the main part belong to the Government of the country in which he is located. He is extremely solicitous for the correctness of his relations with the Australian Government, to whom he feels greatly indebted for the set-up under which he works. . . .

Australia is very fortunate to have such an officer responsible for operations in the Southwest Pacific Area. General MacArthur says that should he commit a grave error in the conduct of operations, he will be the first to detect it and efface himself from the scene. The Government need have no fear of having to take distasteful action with his own Government, as he would not let the need arise. His influence, counsel and advice are having effects over the whole field of Service administration in Australia, and it is of great advantage to the Government that such a person should be available in addition to the Government's own advisers. He will certainly be missed when he moves his headquarters away from the mainland and our main contact with the higher direction of the war will again be confined to the Government's representatives in London and Washington.

Perhaps this description tells as much about Shedden as it does about MacArthur. He seems to have accepted uncritically MacArthur's claims about his own performance. The validity of the assertion that MacArthur's forces offered stout resistance in the Philippines is open to challenge, and Shedden was in no position to make this judgment. Shedden emphasized MacArthur's role in strategic decision-making in Australia and how much the government relied on his advice.

MacArthur similarly had a high opinion of Shedden and on February 5, 1943, wrote to Curtin to express his appreciation of Shedden's "splendid contribution to our success. While not in any sense serving under my command, his duties have been so identified therewith that I feel I owe him a deep obligation for the superior manner in which he has beneficially influenced many momentous problems and materially contributed to their successful conclusion." MacArthur recommended

that Shedden be given an "appropriate reward."[21] Despite the Labor government's reluctance to recommend knighthoods, in June 1943 Shedden
was made a Knight Commander of the Order of St. Michael and St.
George. The previous month, on Curtin's recommendation, MacArthur
had been appointed to the Grand Cross of the British Order of the Bath.

Curtin and Shedden maintained a close relationship with MacArthur
until late in the war. Both Australians deferred to MacArthur and the
Australian government held him in high regard. In May 1944 the Sydney Morning Herald observed that MacArthur had "displayed all the
qualities of an able diplomat as well as a great commander, and he has
won the eternal gratitude of the Australian people."[22] Curtin told the
Press: "His devotion to duty could not have been greater had he been an
Australian officer with a lifetime of service in the Australian Army. He is
a great genius."[23] After the successful landing at Luzon in January 1945,
the acting prime minister, Francis Forde, said that MacArthur "was one
of the greatest military leaders of the last 100 years."[24] For his part, in
his *Reminiscences* MacArthur wrote that Curtin was "the heart and soul
of Australia" and "one of the greatest of wartime statesmen."[25]

Reassessment

Over the past thirty years Australian scholars have increasingly scruti-
nized the relationship between MacArthur and Australia's political and
military leaders of the time. The most important historian in initiating
this reassessment was Gavin Long, the general editor of the twenty-two-
volume Australian official history series. Comments on MacArthur's role
are scattered throughout the official history volumes but generally they
are blandly factual. Dudley McCarthy's volume on the Papuan campaign, however, criticized MacArthur's conduct of that campaign, while
Long's volume on the final campaigns pointedly analyzed the command
relationships.[26] The otherwise excellent two volumes on the role of the
government do not tackle the question of the extent to which Curtin
and the government were in MacArthur's hands. The best early analysis
of MacArthur's performance as a commander, one covering his whole
career but with particular reference to his relations with the Australians,
is Gavin Long's *MacArthur as Military Commander*, published in 1969,
which has withstood the test of time remarkably well.[27]

Subsequent scholars have built upon the foundation provided by
Long's work and the official Australian records. John Hetherington's
biography of Field Marsh. Sir Thomas Blamey, based on Blamey's papers

(published in 1954 and in a more detailed edition in 1972), highlighted the problems faced by Blamey in his dealings with MacArthur.[28] As the works by Australian scholars have proliferated they have focused on at least ten key issues concerning MacArthur and his relations with the Australians.[29] The remainder of this chapter will briefly describe each of these issues.

Military Command Structure

In the Allied composition of its forces, the Southwest Pacific Area was unique among the theater commands set up in the Second World War. Some commands, such as the Pacific Ocean Area commanded by Adm. Chester Nimitz, were almost completely American. Other commands were Allied in nature but the main forces came from the two major Allies—Britain and the United States. For example, Southeast Asia Command, led by Britain's Adm. Lord Louis Mountbatten, included a majority of British or British-Indian forces with a smaller but still significant number of American forces. The Mediterranean Command under Gen. Dwight Eisenhower had large numbers of American and British forces, and later included Canadians, French, New Zealanders, and Poles. Similarly, Eisenhower's Allied Expeditionary Force in Europe included many nationalities but the principal forces came from the United States and Britain.

By contrast, the SWPA was a coalition of forces from the United States and Australia with only very small numbers from the Netherlands and New Zealand. In the three years and four months from the time when the command was set up in April 1942 until the Japanese cease-fire in August 1945, the Australian army provided the majority of MacArthur's forces and played the largest part in his land campaigns until the early months of 1944. Both the RAN and the RAAF also contributed substantial forces.

The management of this coalition of unequal allies posed particular problems. In 1942 Australia had a population of a little over 7 million people while the United States numbered some 135 million. The U.S. president, Franklin Roosevelt, and the British prime minister, Winston Churchill, together decided the shape of the Allied war effort; this was refined by the Combined Chiefs of Staff, which consisted of the chiefs of staffs of the two great powers. Australia had no role in this strategic decision-making.

As a major world power in the 1940s the United States was loath to place its forces under an Allied commander, but in certain circumstances was willing to do so. For example, in North Africa U.S. Army forces were placed under the Allied Land Commander, Gen. Harold Alexander. Later, at Normandy the U.S. land forces came under the command of Gen. Bernard Montgomery during the early stages of the campaign.

But in the SWPA it rankled to place American land forces under the commander of such a small country as Australia, and from the beginning MacArthur tried to find ways of ensuring that Americans did not serve under Australian command. Yet, until sufficient American land forces had arrived and been trained, MacArthur had to rely on the Australians for his offensives.

MacArthur's attitude was demonstrated in the composition of his headquarters, which was known as General Headquarters (GHQ) and was located in Melbourne and later in Brisbane. Although it was supposed to be an Allied headquarters it was staffed almost completely by Americans. When the U.S. Army chief of staff, Gen. George C. Marshall, urged MacArthur to include Australian officers, MacArthur replied that no qualified officers were available.[30] This was clearly untrue, since three Australian divisions had already fought several major campaigns in the Middle East and many officers had recent command and staff experience in operations. But MacArthur had his way; GHQ remained staffed almost completely by U.S. Army officers, so it was hardly a joint or Allied headquarters.

Below this level MacArthur's forces included the Allied naval, land, and air forces. MacArthur's naval forces were more powerful than those of the RAN and an American, Vice Adm. Herbert Leary, became commander Allied Naval Forces. This arrangement caused few command problems and the chief of the Australian naval staff became responsible for the close defense of Australia.

The RAAF had few modern aircraft but was expanding rapidly, as were the U.S. air forces in Australia as men and machines arrived from America. An American, Lt. Gen. George Brett, became commander Allied Air Forces. This organization had an unhappy history. MacArthur and other senior Americans were upset at Brett's policy of placing of U.S. air units under Australian commanders and in August Maj. Gen. George C. Kenney replaced Brett. He separated the Allied air forces and directly commanded the U.S. Fifth Air Force. The Australian operational air units were placed under an Australian commander, Air Vice-Marsh. William Bostock, who reported to Kenney. As will be discussed later, this arrangement caused command problems within the RAAF but, before long, the Americans provided the largest part of the available air forces and command of the air offensive was in American hands.

Command of the Allied Land Forces went to the commander in chief of the Australian army, Gen. Sir Thomas Blamey. That an Australian should command these forces seemed unchallengeable, for in mid-1942 the Australian army consisted of ten infantry divisions, two motor divisions, and one armored division. One of these divisions was still in the Middle East but the remainder were in Australia with some units in New Guinea.[31] By contrast there were only two undertrained U.S. divisions in Australia. Blamey had been a senior staff officer in the First World War and had already commanded the Australian forces in the Middle East during the Second World War.[32]

From the beginning MacArthur wanted to organize his forces as task forces so that Blamey would not command all the American land forces, but General Marshall insisted on a joint Allied headquarters. MacArthur, however, did not give up on the idea of forming task forces.

Just as there were few Australians at MacArthur's GHQ, few Americans reported to Blamey's Land headquarters. When Blamey asked MacArthur for U.S. officers he received little encouragement. MacArthur realized that the senior Australian staff officers had vastly more experience than their American counterparts and he warned Washington that the dispatch to Australia of poor officers would result in what he called a "black eye for U.S. when placed with experienced and capable Australian officers."[33]

The feeling at the time is shown when Maj. Gen. Robert C. Richardson visited Australia in June 1942 on behalf of the U.S. chief of staff. MacArthur offered Richardson command of the U.S. I Corps, which was then being formed in Australia. Richardson declined because he did not want to serve under Blamey's command. MacArthur wanted a U.S. corps headquarters arranged so that when it came to operations he could set up an American task force which would come directly under his rather than Blamey's command. The U.S. War Department was sympathetic to MacArthur's request, but had to acknowledge the needs of coalition warfare; as Maj. Gen. Thomas Handy, an assistant chief of staff at the War Department, put it, "the Australians have 350,000 troops and a little break for them seems to be necessary."[34]

Inevitably, when the Japanese began their offensive in Papua in July 1942 they were met by Australians of the New Guinea Force rather than by American troops. But, as the Japanese advanced over the rugged Owen Stanley Ranges toward Port Moresby, it was clear that New Guinea needed to be reinforced. MacArthur's first reaction was to send the Thirty-second U.S. Division to New Guinea to operate directly under GHQ in Brisbane. This would have produced an impossible command structure, with two separate superior headquarters in Australia commanding separate national forces in the one operational area.[35] Apparently Blamey talked MacArthur out of that folly, and instead the commander of the Australian I Corps, Lt. Gen. Sydney Rowell, was ordered to Port Moresby to command New Guinea Force. With him went the Seventh Australian Division.

In September 1942 MacArthur ordered Blamey to New Guinea to act as task force commander there, and in November MacArthur went to New Guinea to command the overall campaign himself. Before the end of the campaign MacArthur took action to remove Blamey from command of American troops. On January 11, 1943, he asked Marshall to send Lt. Gen. Walter Krueger from America "to give the U.S. Army the next ranking officer below General Blamey in the Allied Land Forces which is not now the case and is most necessary."[36] Soon after Krueger's arrival MacArthur formed Alamo Force to conduct the operations of the Sixth Army, which was to be commanded by Krueger. There were not yet enough troops to form a U.S. army in Australia but Krueger, who also commanded Alamo Force, "realized that this arrangement would obviate placing Sixth Army under the operational control of the Allied Land Forces."[37] Krueger's deputy chief of staff commented later that Alamo Force was created "to keep the control of Sixth Army units away from General Blamey."[38] This new command system was, in the words of Gavin Long, achieved "by stealth and by the employment of subterfuges that were undignified, and at times absurd."[39] Blamey knew what was happening but, realizing MacArthur's standing with his government, made no complaint.

Communiqués

The second issue concerned MacArthur's press communiqués. Soon after he assumed command he persuaded the Australian government to endorse an arrangement whereby all information concerning operations in the theater was to be released by his headquarters. Much has been written of the way MacArthur personally drafted many of his communiqués, which were often designed to enhance the work of his theater in comparison with other theaters. As Long wrote, the "exaggerations and sometimes mendacity of the communiqués were obviously aimed at the American public in general and Washington in particular."[40] For example, after the capture of Buna MacArthur announced the end of the Papuan campaign, while Admiral Halsey's South Pacific forces were still fighting on Guadalcanal. The Australian field commanders, as well as the American general, Robert Eichelberger, resented MacArthur's announcement, knowing that they faced more grim battles before the Japanese were eliminated. Fighting continued for almost three more weeks.

In a similar vein, MacArthur communiqués stated that in the battle of the Bismarck Sea in March 1943 Allied air forces sank some twenty-two Japanese vessels and destroyed over one hundred Japanese aircraft for the loss of four aircraft. When further assessments showed that Japanese losses were considerably fewer, MacArthur refused to amend the statement and even as late as 1945 he was sticking to the story of his original communiqués.

The Australians believed that the SWPA communiqués attributed successes by Australian troops to "Allied forces" while U.S. forces were always described as such. MacArthur's communiqués did not reveal that Blamey had arrived in New Guinea in September 1942. When MacArthur arrived in November, a communiqué announced his arrival and belatedly added that Blamey and Kenney were there as well. MacArthur also released news of U.S. combat troops in the battle area but, as the war correspondent George Johnston observed, the statement was phrased "in such a way as to give the impression that the Japs had been rolled back across the Owen Stanleys by the Americans."[41] The Sydney Morning Herald reported that "American forces have penetrated central and northern Papua to a point near Buna and the Japanese troops defending the strip of land from the Owen Stanley Range to Buna are menaced on several sides."[42] In fact no American troops had yet been in action. Australian war correspondents, like their American counterparts, had to have their reports cleared by U.S. authorities and could only describe Australian operations once they had been revealed in the communiqués.

The issue came to a head in January 1945 after troops of the First Australian Army had been in action in New Guinea, New Britain, and Bougainville from late October 1944 without being mentioned in the communiqués. As Gavin Long put it in the Australian official history: "Probably never in the history of modern war has so large a force, although in action, been hidden from public knowledge for so long."[43] After pressure from both the acting prime minister, Forde, and Blamey, on January 9 MacArthur released a meager bulletin, which at least enabled the Australian newspapers to publish the reports and photographs they had accumulated over the previous months. When Shedden told MacArthur about criticism of his communiqués, MacArthur replied that it was incongruous for the press to criticize him for failing "to aggrandize their current minor operations to make them appear to be of major importance. This represents an attitude of incorrigibility."[44] The communiqué problem continued until the end of the war.

Papuan Campaign

The Papuan campaign did not show MacArthur at his best and was shaped from the beginning by faulty strategic assessments. He disregarded intelligence reports that the Japanese were planning to strike at Port Moresby by advancing overland from the north coast of Papua, and instead planned an offensive to seize Rabaul. The Japanese beat him to the punch and landed near Buna on the night of July 21, 1942. Eventually, as mentioned earlier, MacArthur and Blamey ordered Lieutenant General Rowell, the headquarters of the First Australian Corps, and the Seventh Division to New Guinea.

When in late August the Japanese mounted major offensives at both Milne Bay and on the Kokoda Trail, MacArthur and GHQ reacted badly to the news of Australian reverses. The tense atmosphere in Brisbane is shown by a letter written by Blamey's chief of staff, Maj. Gen. George Vasey, to Rowell in Port Moresby: "You possibly do not realise that for GHQ this is their first battle and they are therefore, like many others, nervous and dwelling on the receipt of frequent messages. . . . It boils down to the question of who is commanding the army—MacArthur or TAB [Blamey], and it seems the sooner that is settled the better."[45]

In messages to Washington MacArthur began to blame the reverses not on faulty strategy or the superior numbers of the Japanese but on the poor quality of the Australian troops and commanders. As he said, "the Australians have proven themselves unable to match the enemy in jungle fighting."[46] Rowell, who the previous year had been chief of staff of the Australian I Corps in the Greek and Syrian campaigns, resented these criticisms, commenting at the time: "I do hope that there is a show-down [between Blamey and MacArthur]. Taking it by and large, we do know something about war after three small campaigns."[47]

As the Japanese advanced over the Kokoda Trail MacArthur became concerned that he was about to face another defeat. Indeed, after his earlier defeat in the Philippines he faced the prospect of losing his command. He therefore persuaded Curtin that Blamey should go to New Guinea to take personal command there. Long called it "a proposal that was not only unorthodox but unwise."[48] Blamey had full confidence in Rowell but had to obey. Unfortunately, Rowell took Blamey's arrival as showing a lack of confidence in his command. There was an intense clash of personalities and Blamey relieved Rowell of command of New Guinea Force. Lt. Gen. Edmund Herring succeeded Rowell, but Blamey also remained in Port Moresby. In effect he was now a task force commander— the very command arrangement that MacArthur had told Washington he wanted to institute several months earlier.

Blamey reaped the benefit of Rowell's careful planning, and at the beginning of October the counteroffensive began, back over the Owen Stanley Range toward the Japanese beachheads at Buna, Gona, and Sanananda. It was a grim battle against stubborn Japanese resistance, with Allied troops on short rations and suffering from malaria. Blamey was still under pressure from MacArthur, and with the latter urging greater speed Blamey felt compelled to relieve several more commanders.

The U.S. Thirty-second Division was brought forward from Australia, but it was a national guard division not fully trained for jungle warfare. Its initial attack on Buna was a disaster, and MacArthur immediately bypassed the chain of command and ordered it to "take Buna at all costs."[49] A week later there had still been no progress by the Americans.

Blamey used reports of American inactivity to counter MacArthur's earlier criticism of the Australians. According to Blamey's chief of staff, when the Australians were being driven back along the Kokoda Trail, "The jokes of the American officers in Australia, making fun of the Australian Army, were told all over Australia." He thought that MacArthur, MacArthur's chief of staff, Maj. Gen. Richard Sutherland, and Kenney were "not guiltless" among those who had made disparaging remarks.[50] On November 25, when MacArthur suggested bringing the Forty-first U.S. Division up from Australia to reinforce the Seventh Division, Blamey objected. Kenney, who was present, recorded: "Blamey frankly said he would rather put in more Australians, as he knew they would fight. . . . I think it was a bitter pill for General MacArthur to swallow."[51]

Upset and humiliated at reports that American soldiers had dropped

their weapons and run, MacArthur called his American corps commander, Major General Eichelberger, to Port Moresby and on November
30 told him "to take Buna, or not come back alive."[52] Eichelberger later
wrote: "At the time I did not realise General MacArthur was being
gloated over by the Australian high command who had been criticised
by him previously."[53]

By the time the Japanese were annihilated in late January 1943 the
Australians had deployed six infantry brigades to the area and the Americans four infantry regiments. The Japanese committed a little over
20,000 troops of whom 13,000 were killed. The Australians and Americans together suffered 8,546 battle casualties. Casualties from malaria
exceeded 27,000; those suffering from tropical disease numbered over
37,000. The Australians lost more than 2,000 killed; the Americans 600.
By comparison, in the Guadalcanal campaign, which took place at about
the same time, about 1,600 Americans were killed. Many Australians
resented the heavy casualties, which they attributed to MacArthur's
unreasonable demands for a speedy outcome.

The Militia Bill

Much controversy in Australia has revolved around the degree to which
Curtin relied upon MacArthur for advice on issues that should have been
decided by Australian leaders. One example concerned the employment
of militia troops, mainly conscripts, who were restricted by law to service
in Australian territory. In October 1942 the War Cabinet discussed with
the chiefs of staff the difficulty of sending additional forces to New
Guinea in view of the depletion in numbers of volunteer Australian
Imperial Force (AIF) troops. At that stage both AIF and militia troops
were fighting in New Guinea (which was Australian territory) but when
the fighting moved forward to Dutch New Guinea the militia would not
be able to be deployed. Yet conscripted American soldiers were already
serving in New Guinea.

At Curtin's request Shedden discussed the problem with MacArthur,
who said that it was nothing to do with him but, as an observer, he said
"that there was one serious flaw in the Government Policy—failure to
amalgamate the AIF and the AMF [Australian Military Forces, i.e., militia]
by some formula which, while not giving any credit to the Opposition,
would enable the Government to get out of what he felt would become
an increasingly difficult position." MacArthur "hoped that the Prime
Minister would find a way to act and would act quickly."[54]

Curtin felt his responsibilities deeply. Although he had been jailed briefly in the First World War because of his opposition to conscription, in November 1942 he announced that he would be introducing measures to allow Australians conscripted for service within Australia to continue fighting the Japanese as the battlefront moved northward. After persuading a special federal conference of the Australian Labor Party in January 1943, Curtin successfully moved the bill through Parliament the following month—a considerable political achievement. There were sound military and diplomatic reasons why Australia should have taken this action, and many people in Australia would have supported it but, nevertheless, it was a matter for the Australian government to decide, not a foreign general.

Command of the RAAF

Another example of MacArthur's influence over Curtin concerned the command of the RAAF. In April 1942 a relatively junior officer, Air Vice-Marsh. George Jones, was appointed chief of the air staff and soon found himself in bitter dispute with Air Vice-Marshal Bostock, the commander of the RAAF's operational forces, which came under the command of MacArthur's Allied Air Forces commander, Kenney.

In April 1943 in an attempt to overcome the problem the government decided to appoint an air officer commanding-in-chief (AOC-in-C) of the RAAF and asked the British government to provide a suitable officer. The Australian government contemplated appointing one of the British officers that had been suggested but was advised against it by MacArthur. A year later Curtin again tried to appoint a British officer as AOC-in-C, but MacArthur again counseled against it. This time Shedden could not support MacArthur, advising Curtin that the Americans preferred "the divided arrangement, because they can play one side off against the other."[55] With respect to the effect of these arrangements Shedden warned Curtin: "Some day there will be an outcry about the relatively poor RAAF effort in the South-West Pacific Area in relation to the resources allocated to the air effort." Curtin still followed MacArthur's advice.

The Manpower Crisis

The third example of MacArthur's influence came in mid-1943, when the Australian government was finding it increasingly difficult to meet all the demands on Australian manpower but also seemed incapable of deciding how to allocate the resources it had. Shedden therefore asked MacArthur to make a statement that Australia was now more secure and that there could be a small reduction in the numbers of men needed for the land forces.

As a result, in June 1943 MacArthur met with Curtin and assured him that "the threat of invasion to Australia had been removed."[56] He suggested that Australia should provide a maximum military effort until Rabaul was captured, and then reduce its military commitment to a land and air expeditionary force, enabling resources to be devoted to food production instead. In his memoirs Shedden described MacArthur's advice as "most helpful, even though as Commander-in-Chief, he could have been unduly demanding." He thought that MacArthur was sympathetic to Australia's position.[57] MacArthur had gone beyond advising Curtin on strategic policy for the SWPA, and was offering direct comment on balancing the Australian war effort, a matter that should have been the prerogative of the Australian chiefs of staff.

It was clear to Blamey, if not immediately clear to Curtin, that MacArthur's strategic policy was no longer appropriate for Australia. MacArthur wanted Australia to provide services for the American troops even though the Australian combat forces would have to be reduced. While MacArthur claimed that it was in Australia's interest to provide a substantial striking force, by October 1943 he was making plans to reduce Australia's offensive role.

The government's policy envisaged maintaining six divisions for active operations, the RAN at its existing strength, the RAAF at a strength of fifty-four squadrons, and the production of food for Great Britain. Military forces were necessary to guarantee an effective voice in the peace settlement, but not all the tasks could be achieved with the manpower available in Australia.

As the authors of the volumes of the official history covering the war economy, Sydney Butlin and Boris Schedvin, wrote, it was apparent that "the structure of command of the direct war effort was in disarray."[58] The War Cabinet was unable to balance the demands the military had for an increased role in offensive operations against the demands of those who saw Australia's most important duty as the supply of food and war equipment. Paul Hasluck, in his official history of the role of the government, wrote that there was an "absence of clear, firm, exact and prompt determinations on policy by those responsible for the higher direction of the war in Australia."[59] Butlin and Schedvin were even more critical. To them there was "a lack of leadership from the Prime Minister and the War Cabinet. . . . An important part of the problem which could not be readily resolved was MacArthur's domination of Curtin."[60]

Curtin did not always bend to MacArthur, although he acknowledged that the Australian war effort would be "governed by operational considerations determined by the strategical policy" of General MacArthur.[61] When MacArthur expressed reservations about Curtin's plans and said that he was still waiting on advice from Washington, Curtin would not be browbeaten. MacArthur quickly replied that he "accepted absolutely that it was for the Australian government to decide the nature and extent of its war effort."[62]

Nevertheless, Curtin was still under MacArthur's spell and in October 1943 said that if MacArthur "had been born in Australia and gone to [Australia's Royal Military College] Duntroon he could not have shown higher concern for Australia's interests."[63] In a broadcast in November 1943 Curtin said that he "was indebted to General MacArthur for the high statesmanship and breadth of world vision he has contributed to the discussion. The complete integration of our concepts, which has been a source of such strength, will continue to the end." Astonishingly, these last two sentences had been written by MacArthur himself; he had requested Curtin to add them to his statement.[64]

Papuan Campaign

During 1943 MacArthur found himself embroiled, perhaps inadvertently, in an Australian domestic political dispute. In the latter months of 1942 the minister for labor and national service, Edward Ward, had made several speeches in which he claimed that under the previous government there had been a plan to abandon the whole of northern Australia if the country were invaded. Despite mild rebukes from Curtin, Ward, the "firebrand from East Sydney," continued his allegations, causing the nongovernment members of the Advisory War Council to become restive at Curtin's failure to publicly repudiate Ward's statements.

Then, on March 17, 1943, at a conference to mark his first year in Australia, MacArthur told journalists that when he "came to Australia, the defence plan . . . involved North Australia being taken by the enemy. This was based on the conception of the 'Brisbane Line' of defence."[65] MacArthur was probably trying to counter Curtin's arguments that more attention needed to be given to the defense of continental Australia, but others have argued that he was "trying to display himself as a military god striding forward to meet the foe, erect and unafraid, while lesser men quailed and crumpled up in terror."[66] Whatever the reason, MacArthur maintained this view and, in his memoirs, recalled that "detailed plans were made to . . . lay desolate the land above the Brisbane Line. . . . I decided to abandon the plan completely."[67]

Ward seized on the term "Brisbane Line" and made further speeches claiming that this had been the defense plan until the change of government.[68] The opposition was incensed and raised the matter at the Advisory War Council. Shedden knew that the allegations about the Brisbane Line were inaccurate. Over a year earlier, at the Advisory War Council meeting on March 18, 1942 (the very day that MacArthur's appointment as commander in chief swpa was announced), the Australian chiefs had urged the formation of an Allied force of British and American naval units to attack the Japanese. They had recommended, and the council had affirmed, that Darwin and Port Moresby should be defended to the fullest extent possible and that every effort should be made to provide forces for these areas. Thus, by the time the AIF formations had begun to return from the Middle East and the swpa was being formed, the Australian government had decided to carry the fight to the Japanese just as soon as forces became available to do so.

In his memoirs Blamey recalled: "From the outset it had been decided between General MacArthur and myself that as soon as possible we would move to the offensive against Japan as far north as we could proceed. But it was essential first to ensure that the defence of vital areas should be secured."[69] Blamey's deployments, which had been begun by his predecessors and endorsed by MacArthur, kept most of the troops in southeast Australia. It was not until mid-May, after the success in the battle of the Coral Sea, that MacArthur directed army units (in limited numbers) to New Guinea. Knowing this background, Shedden wrote later that MacArthur's statement of March 17, 1943, about a Brisbane Line "was a flamboyant utterance for . . . no such plan existed."[70]

When Shedden visited MacArthur in Brisbane in late May 1943 he sought the general's reaction to the controversy. MacArthur thought the opposition would let the matter drop but maintained that Australia's home defense plan, "had, judging by the appreciation he saw after his arrival, been defeatist in outlook and preparations."[71] MacArthur was wrong about the opposition letting the matter drop, as it was soon being discussed in both the press and in Parliament.

In the midst of this debate Curtin announced a royal commission to investigate Ward's claims and, following normal procedure, relieved Ward of his ministerial duties pending the report being tabled in Parliament. Curtin also announced that he would be asking for the dissolution of Parliament in preparation for a federal election. The royal commission's terms of reference were confined to Ward's claims of a missing file and the question of whether he had been informed that it referred to the Brisbane Line. The royal commission found that there was no missing file. In the official history Paul Hasluck wrote that Ward's action in "creating a false impression" about the Brisbane Line "for political advantage was not novel. The novelty was in Curtin's conduct. His failure on this occasion to repudiate firmly suggestions which he must have known to be untrue fell below his customarily high standards of honesty and courage."[72] Years later Fred Daly, the only surviving member of the Curtin government, was asked whether Ward had been right in his allegations about the Brisbane Line. Daly's reply was short and to the point: "He must have been. We won the 1943 election, didn't we!"[73]

MacArthur's claims played on Curtin's mind, although for the present he took no action. On November 6, 1943, in a letter to Curtin MacArthur said in passing that it had never been his intention "to defend Australia on the mainland of Australia."[74] In view of MacArthur's further claim Curtin referred the matter to Blamey. After his staff had conducted a thorough study of the files, Blamey replied on January 28, 1944, that there was no justification for "MacArthur's statement."[75] As Blamey's biographer noted, "Even in a letter to his Prime Minister a serving soldier can hardly call his superior officer a liar. Blamey could not have gone closer to it than he did."[76]

Changing Command Relationships and the Philippines Campaign

After the Papuan campaign the command arrangements worked tolerably well during the major offensives in the second half of 1943. Blamey continued as commander Allied Land Forces but was also appointed commander New Guinea Force with the task of seizing Lae, Salamaua, Finschhafen, and Madang. Most of Blamey's land forces were Australian and he was supported by Australian and U.S. naval and air units. There were a number of command problems, such as planning for the Lae landing, the role of the Americans at Tambu Bay, and the reinforcement of Finschhafen, but in the main relations between Blamey and MacArthur were satisfactory. The campaign was highly successful.

In early 1944, however, the whole command relationship began to change. After months of hard campaigning the Australian divisions had been exhausted and most were withdrawn to Australia for rest and retraining. For the remainder of the year the Americans advanced along the north coast of New Guinea before landing in the Philippines in October. The landings were commanded by the Alamo Task Force and Krueger's Sixth Army, and Blamey had no role as commander Allied Land Forces.

MacArthur's rapid advance, the buildup of American divisions (which continued throughout the year), and Australia's manpower shortages presented the Australian high command with severe problems. The crucial question was whether MacArthur would use any of the Australian divisions in the Philippines. In March 1944 MacArthur told Curtin that the spearhead of his advance would be three Australian divisions and an American paratroop division. He said that the Australians would be commanded by an Australian corps commander and that Blamey would have a lesser role.[77] It is difficult to believe that MacArthur was completely frank with Curtin, for his outline plan for the capture of the Philippines made no mention of Australian units and the previous month he had told his staff that plans to use the Australians would probably not come off.

In April 1944 Curtin, Shedden, and Blamey left for a visit to the United States and Britain; while they were away they received news from Australia that MacArthur intended to use Australian troops on garrison duties in New Guinea and the Solomons. Determined to find a suitable mission for the Australian army, Blamey was attracted by a proposal then being developed by the British chiefs of staff for an advance from either northern Australia or West New Guinea into the Netherlands East Indies.

MacArthur was far from enthusiastic about these proposals. When he met Curtin and Shedden in Brisbane in June he expressed concern that the Australian divisions would not be ready in time for him to use them in the Philippines. MacArthur said that it was evident that Blamey, in his discussions in London, had been disloyal to him and to the command organization in the SWPA and, since Curtin supported the command organization, also disloyal to the prime minister. MacArthur said that "the position of Commander of the Allied Land Forces had now become a fiction—Blamey had refused to associate himself closely with MacArthur in the same manner as the Commanders Allied Naval and Air Forces, and because of his duties as Commander-in-Chief of the Australian Military Forces, he was rarely available when required."[78] While it is true that Blamey's duties caused him to spend much time in Melbourne, MacArthur had actively sought to exclude Blamey from his role as commander Allied Land Forces by establishing task forces. Blamey doubted that MacArthur would use the Australians in the Philippines, but Curtin told MacArthur that he had no intention of changing the existing command arrangement and that the employment of Australian troops should remain in MacArthur's hands.

Meanwhile, MacArthur began concentrating his forces for operations in the Philippines, and when he ordered Blamey to relieve the six American divisions engaged in garrison or holding operations in the Solomons and New Guinea, Blamey produced plans to use seven Australian brigades. MacArthur insisted that Blamey use twelve brigades—or four Australian divisions—thus making fewer Australian divisions available for use in the Philippines. The Australian divisions were not used for the invasion of the Philippines, but at various times during the latter months of 1944 and the early months of 1945 plans were floated to use two Australian divisions in the northern Philippines. None came to fruition as MacArthur had no intention of using the Australians in what he perceived as a purely American operation.

The British Commonwealth's plan to advance from northern Australia or West New Guinea into the Netherlands East Indies was never approved, but through his desire to preserve the AIF for these operations Blamey had given MacArthur the excuse that the troops were not ready. In so doing Blamey left himself open to MacArthur's charges that he was disloyal to the prime minister, thus making it even more certain that Curtin would support MacArthur.

In September 1944 MacArthur destroyed the myth that Blamey had any role as commander Allied Land Forces when he dissolved Alamo Force and gave orders directly to HQ Sixth Army. If the Australian I Corps were to be involved in the Philippines (which was still a possibility at this stage), MacArthur planned that it would come directly under the command of Sixth Army.

When MacArthur established GHQ at Hollandia in August 1944 Blamey moved his advanced headquarters there. But after the Americans landed on Leyte in October 1944 MacArthur moved his headquarters forward to that island and never returned to Australia. After his final and by some accounts emotional meeting with Curtin on September 30, 1944, Blamey never saw MacArthur again.[79] Blamey's headquarters was excluded from Leyte until eventually, in January 1945, a small liaison staff under Blamey's chief of staff, Berryman, joined GHQ. The liaison staff accompanied MacArthur's headquarters to Manila in early 1945, while Blamey's advance headquarters was established on the island of Morotai.

By early 1945 Blamey and the Australian government were becoming increasingly dissatisfied with the role of their forces within the Southwest Pacific. As Blamey observed in February 1945, a "feeling that we are being side-tracked is growing strong throughout the country."[80] There were two crucial issues: the future role of the Australian I Corps and Blamey's role as commander Allied Land Forces.

With respect to the first issue, Curtin, at Blamey's instigation, wrote to MacArthur about his plans for Australian I Corps.[81] If no definite plans existed then perhaps the Australian forces should be reduced considerably. MacArthur replied that he planned to use the corps in Borneo and the Netherlands East Indies.

A little later Curtin, again at Blamey's request, wrote to MacArthur about Blamey's role as commander Allied Land Forces. MacArthur replied bluntly that he had operated with task forces for the previous eighteen months and did not mention Blamey's position as commander Allied Land Forces at all. Curtin merely noted the reply. The Australian government had acquiesced in a situation which Blamey thought was intolerable. Curtin had been unable to disagree with Blamey about the rightness of the Australian position, but he equally had been unable to be firm with MacArthur.

The Final Campaigns

The Australian operations in Borneo in the last four months of the war throw additional light on the relationship between MacArthur and the Australian high command. The first operation was the capture of Tarakan in May 1945. Blamey approved the plans to capture the island because its oil fields and refinery would be useful and its airfield could support later operations in Borneo. However, after the landing the airfield could not be repaired in time for subsequent operations and the oil facilities were too damaged to be used during the war. One month later Australian troops landed at Brunei Bay. Later research has shown that MacArthur's and the joint chiefs' arguments that the British wanted a naval base at Brunei were hardly truthful.[82]

By this time Blamey and his senior commanders were more wary of MacArthur's proposed final landing, to be undertaken by the Seventh Australian Division at Balikpapan in southeastern Borneo. Neither Blamey, Lt. Gen. Sir Leslie Morshead, the corps commander controlling operations in Borneo, nor the commander of the Seventh Division could see any strategic purpose for the operation.[83] On Blamey's advice the acting Australian prime minister, Ben Chifley, suggested to MacArthur that the operation be canceled.[84] MacArthur promptly replied by telegram:

> The Borneo Campaign in all its phases has been ordered by the Joint Chiefs of Staff who are charged by the Combined Chiefs of Staff with the responsibility of strategy in the Pacific. I am responsible for the execution of their directives employing such troops as have been made available to me by the Governments participating in the Allied Agreement. Pursuant to the directive of the Joint Chiefs of Staff and under authority vested in me as Supreme Commander, Southwest Pacific Area, I have ordered the 7th Division to proceed to a forward concentration area and, on a specific date, to execute one phase of the Borneo Campaign.
>
> Australian authorities have been kept fully advised of my operational plans. The concentration is in progress and it is not now possible to substitute another Division and execute the operations as scheduled. The attack will be made as projected unless the Australian Government withdraws the 7th Division from assignment to the Southwest Pacific Area. I am loath to believe that your Government contemplates such an action at this time when the preliminary phases of the operation have been initiated and when withdrawal would disorganize completely not only the immediate campaign but also the strategic plan of the Joint Chiefs of Staff. If the Australian Government, however, does contemplate action along this line, I request that I be informed immediately in order that I may be able to make the necessary representations to Washington and London.[85]

MacArthur's blunt reply was hardly honest. The Australians did not know that the joint chiefs had reluctantly agreed to the Balikpapan operation only because MacArthur insisted that not to carry it out would "produce grave repercussions with the Australian government and people."[86] Now the Australians were being told that it had to be carried out because it had been ordered by the joint chiefs. Had the operation been canceled it is hard to see how it would have disorganized completely "the strategic plan of the joint chiefs." MacArthur's threat to make representations must be seen as pure bluff. His claim that there were "no specific plans as far as I know for employment of Australian troops after the Borneo campaign" while no doubt technically correct would appear to repudiate his earlier promises that AIF divisions would accompany him to Japan. The truth was that MacArthur wanted to capture Balikpapan so that he could show the Dutch government that he had made an attempt to recover part of their territory. It was not a reason that appealed to either the Australian government or the joint chiefs.

MacArthur's telegram arrived in Canberra on a Sunday while ministers were scattered in various parts of the Commonwealth. Shedden drafted a reply, took it to Curtin in hospital, and MacArthur was informed that the Australian government approved the operation. When the landing took place on July 1 a total of 229 Australians were killed and 634 were wounded. Japan did not surrender one minute earlier as a result of this action.

It is hard to know whether the Australian government's greater readiness to question MacArthur during this period was a result of increasing disillusion or whether it was partly a result of Curtin's illness and the fact that Chifley was acting prime minister. Chifley was a former engine driver who as treasurer had been a key minister for three and one-half years but had not been fully involved in the strategic direction of the war.

While the discussions about the Borneo operations were proceeding the First Australian Army was conducting operations in Bougainville, New Britain, and the Aitape-Wewak area of New Guinea. Initially the operations were given little publicity, which, as mentioned earlier, was a cause for some disquiet. Later, when the need for the operations was queried in Australia, Curtin wrote to MacArthur inquiring whether the campaigns were being conducted in accordance with his directive. MacArthur avoided the question but Blamey told the government that since MacArthur had provided the necessary landing craft for some of the operations he must have approved them. MacArthur retorted that although he had met a request for support, the operations were "unnecessary and wasteful of lives and resources."[87]

Chifley did not know quite what to do, but eventually, on July 21 after the death of Curtin and his rise to prime minister, he wrote to MacArthur and reminded him that as commander in chief he was responsible for the operation of the forces assigned to him. Australia's only right was to withhold forces, and the government had assumed that "even within the limits of discretion allowed subordinate commanders, their plans would be subject to your broad approval." He regretted that the government was "greatly embarrassed by your reply. It has publicly defended the wisdom of these operations."[88] This was the strongest letter written by an Australian prime minister to MacArthur, but the general never deigned to reply.

It would be a mistake to see MacArthur's relations with the Australian high command solely in terms of the personalities of men like Curtin, Shedden, and Blamey, although undoubtedly they were the key figures of the day. Nor should the picture be painted in terms of good or bad. MacArthur was a brilliant political general with long experience in dealing with politicians. Perhaps the Australian government was lulled into accepting his views wholeheartedly because of the happy coincidence between the general's views and their own in 1942. Inevitably a time would come when these views would diverge. For their part, in the emergency of 1942 Australia's political leaders probably had few options but to accept MacArthur's leadership.

Blamey was also an adept political general who was not afraid to meet MacArthur head-on. The problem came when Curtin accepted MacArthur's advice over that of the Australian general. This put Blamey in a weak position and made it more difficult for him to stand firm against MacArthur. Had Blamey been more tactful perhaps he might have been able to persuade Curtin to have more confidence in him, but Blamey was mistrusted by many members of the Australian Labor Party. In any case, invariably Shedden sided with MacArthur rather than with Blamey.

In retrospect perhaps the government should have sought to restructure the SWPA in late 1943 or early 1944. However, the government was hampered by the fact that the bulk of the naval and air forces were provided by the Americans. By force of circumstance Australia had achieved a larger than usual role in this alliance, mainly because it provided the logistics base and most of the ground troops until early 1944. Once the Americans moved away from the base and provided more ground troops of their own, Australia's influence waned.

If there is some doubt as to whether the command arrangements could have been renegotiated at the end of 1943, there was definitely a need for such a rearrangement at the end of 1944. By this time Curtin was sick and mistrustful of Blamey. MacArthur was still anxious to use the Australian I Corps somewhere, and perhaps Curtin could have used this lever. In the long run Curtin remained loyal to MacArthur. As he said in Parliament in 1943: "I make no pretence to being, in any way, a strategist in defence matters. I have a plain and simple rule to which I have adhered. It is that in all matters relating to the operational direction of the war, the sole responsibility shall rest upon the High Command. The duty of the Government consists in allocating to the High Command such forces as it seeks and such equipment as it calls for."[89]

In considering the relationship between MacArthur and the Australian high command there are many lessons for contemporary Australia in how to manage a coalition with a large and powerful friend. There is no easy solution, but such a relationship needs constant vigilance and astuteness if the smaller country is not to be trampled upon. Australia is still applying those lessons today.

MacArthur's relationship with the Australians highlighted his skill at the political and strategic level. It showed that a general at this level had to display qualities far beyond those expected from a successful general on the battlefield. In Blamey, MacArthur had a formidable opponent but, with the support of Curtin and Shedden, as well as the power of the United States, MacArthur held the trump cards. The experience of 1943 and 1944 dominated military and political thinking in Australia for the next fifty years.

Notes

1. For the signing of the ANZU.S. Pact see Robert O'Neill, *Australia in the Korean War 1950–53*, vol. 1, *Strategy and Diplomacy* (Canberra: Australian War Memorial and Australian Government Publishing Service, 1981), ch. 13.
2. Forde interview with E. D. and A. Potts, St Lucia, December 19, 1973, copy in MacArthur Memorial Military Archives (MMMA), Norfolk, Virginia.
3. Forde to Hetherington, September 29, 1970, Hetherington Papers, Australian War Memorial (AWM).
4. *The Courier Mail*, March 19, 1942; *The Herald*, March 18, 1942; *Daily Mirror*, March 18, 1942; *The Age*, March 24, 1942.
5. For MacArthur's meetings with Curtin see his daily appointments diary in MMMA: RG 5, SCAP, folder 6.
6. D. MacArthur, *Reminiscences* (New York: McGraw-Hill, 1964), p. 151.
7. *The Sydney Morning Herald*, March 27, 1942, p. 4.
8. In some U.S. books Shedden is described incorrectly as Australia's War or Defense Minister.
9. Minutes of Prime Minister's War Conference, Melbourne, April 8, 1942, National Archives of Australia (NAA): Shedden Papers, CRS A5954, item 813/2.
10. Curtin to MacArthur, April 10, 1942, NAA: CRS A5954, item 1598/2.

11. D. Clayton James, *The Years of MacArthur*, vol. 2, *1941–1945* (Boston: Houghton Mifflin Company, 1975), pp. 171–72.

12. Extracts from Gavin Long interview with Shedden, January 31, 1946, AWM 54, item 577/7/52. The second crisis came in late 1943 when Australia decided to reduce manpower allocated to the services.

13. Notes of discussion with General MacArthur, Commander-in-Chief, Southwest Pacific Area, April 14, 1942, NAA: CRS A5954, item 3/5.

14. Evatt to Curtin, April 12, 1942, NAA: CRS A5954, item 571/5.

15. Curtin to MacArthur, April 15, 1942, MMMA: RG 3.

16. Shedden Manuscript, book 4, p. 6, in NAA: Shedden Papers, CRS A5954.

17. Curtin to MacArthur, April 17, 1942, MMMA: RG 4.

18. Cable JSM 137, Dill to British chiefs of staff, March 24, 1942, Public Record Office (PRO), London: WO 106/3427.

19. James, *The Years of MacArthur*, vol. 2, appendix A.

20. Visit to Brisbane, January 16–20, 1943, Impressions of General MacArthur, notes by Shedden, NAA: CRS A5954, items 2/1 and 2037/6.

21. MacArthur to Curtin, February 5, 1943, MMMA: RG 4.

22. *Sydney Morning Herald*, May 5, 1944.

23. MacArthur, *Reminiscences*, p. 208.

24. *Daily Telegraph*, January 11, 1945.

25. MacArthur, *Reminiscences*, pp. 169, 208.

26. Dudley McCarthy, *South-West Pacific Area—First Year* (Canberra: Australian War Memorial, 1959); Gavin Long, *The Final Campaigns* (Canberra: Australian War Memorial, 1963), p. 599.

27. Gavin Long, *MacArthur as Military Commander* (Sydney: Angus and Robertson, 1969).

28. John Hetherington, *Blamey: Controversial Soldier* (Canberra: Australian War Memorial, 1972).

29. The key books are: D. M. Horner, *High Command: Australia and Allied Strategy, 1939–1945* (Sydney: George, Allen & Unwin, 1982); David Horner, *Blamey: The Commander-in-Chief* (Sydney: Allen & Unwin, 1998); David Day, *Reluctant Nation: Australia and the Allied Defeat of Japan 1942–1945* (Melbourne: Oxford University Press, 1992).

30. Signal, MacArthur to Marshall, June 15, 1942, National Archives and Records Administration (NARA): RG 165, OPD Exec 10, item 7D.

31. The militia divisions in Australia were the First, Second, Third, Fourth, Fifth, Tenth, First Motor, and Second Motor. Northern Territory Force was a division-sized formation with both AIF and militia units and was later to become the Twelfth Division. The AIF divisions in Australia were the Seventh and the First Armored. Of the three other AIF divisions, the Sixth was moving from Ceylon to Australia, the Eighth had been captured at Singapore, and the Ninth was still in the Middle East.

32. For a discussion of the relationship between Blamey and MacArthur see David Horner, "Blamey and MacArthur: The Problem of Coalition Warfare," in *We Shall Return! MacArthur's Commanders and the Defeat of Japan 1942–1945*, ed. William M. Leary (Lexington: University Press of Kentucky, 1988).

33. Signal AG 152, MacArthur to Adjutant General War, April 8, 1942, NARA: Sutherland Papers, Correspondence with War Department.

34. Minutes of conference, July 26, 1942, NARA: RG 165, OPD 333, item 17.

35. S. F. Rowell, *Full Circle* (Melbourne: Melbourne University Press, 1974), p. 110.

36. MacArthur to Marshall, January 11, 1943, MMMA: RG4.

37. Walter Krueger, *From Down Under to Nippon* (Washington: Combat Forces Press, 1953), p. 10.

38. Interview tapes, papers of Gen. George H. Decker, Carlyle PA, U.S. Army Military History Institute.

39. Long, *The Final Campaigns*, p. 599.

40. Long, *MacArthur*, p. 118.

41. George Johnston, *War Diary 1942* (Sydney: Collins, 1984), p. 128.

42. *Sydney Morning Herald*, November 9, 1942.

43. Long, *The Final Campaigns*, p. 37.

44. Shedden to MacArthur, January 31, 1945; MacArthur to Shedden, February 12, 1945, NAA: CRS A5954, box 75.

45. Vasey to Rowell, morning and afternoon August 28, 1942, AWM: Rowell Papers.

46. Signal, MacArthur to Marshall, August 30, 1942, NARA: RG 165, OPD Exec 10, item 23a.

47. Rowell to Vasey, August 30, 1942, AWM 54, item 225/2/5.

48. Long, *MacArthur*, p. 109.

49. Lida Mayo, *Bloody Buna* (Garden City NY: Doubleday, 1974, p. 120.

50. Berryman, quoted in Eichelberger dictations, book 2, pp. vii–122, vii–123, copy from Jay Luvaas.

51. George C. Kenney, *General Kenney Reports* (New York: Duell, Sloan and Pearce, 1949), p. 151.

52. Robert L. Eichelberger, *Our Jungle Road to Tokyo* (London: Odhams, 1951), p. 42.

53. Jay Luvaas, ed., *Dear Miss Em, General Eichelberger's War in the Pacific, 1942–1945* (Westport CT: Greenwood, 1972), p. 33.

54. Notes of discussions with Commander-in-Chief, Southwest Pacific Area, Brisbane, October 20–26, 1942, NAA: CRS A5954, item 2/7.

55. Shedden to Curtin, November 4, 1944, NAA: CRS A5954, box 238.

56. Minutes of prime minister's War Conference, June 7, 1943, NAA: CRS A5954, box 2.

57. Shedden manuscript, book 4, ch. 56, p. 4.

58. S. J. Butlin and C. B. Schedvin, *War Economy 1942–1945* (Canberra: Australian War Memorial, 1977), p. 110.

59. Paul Hasluck, *The Government and the People, 1942–1945* (Canberra: Australian War Memorial, 1970), p. 297.

60. Butlin and Schedvin, *War Economy 1942–1945*, p. 393.

61. War Cabinet Agendum 311/1943, July 13, 1943, NAA: CRS A2671, item 311/1943.

62. Notes of discussions with Commander-in-Chief, Southwest Pacific Area, November 29–December 1, 1943, NAA: CRS A5954, box 2.

63. Notes on talk between Sir Walter Layton and Curtin, October 22, 1943, PRO: PREM 3 159/2.

64. The statement is reproduced in MacArthur, *Reminiscences*, p. 183; evidence in the Shedden papers, NAA: CRS A5954, item 2037/6, shows that the statement dated November 28, 1943, was written by MacArthur and sent by teleprinter to Curtin.

65. George Johnston, "Eventful Year in South West Pacific, Island Moves by Japs Countered," *Argus* (Melbourne), March 18, 1943.

66. Hetherington, *Blamey*, p. 302.

67. MacArthur, *Reminiscences*, p. 162

68. For a full discussion see Paul Burns, *The Brisbane Line Controversy: Political Opportunism Versus National Security, 1942–45* (Sydney: Allen & Unwin, 1998).

69. Blamey's memoirs, ch. 3, p. 10, from T. R. Blamey.

70. Shedden manuscript, book 4, ch. 52, p. 5.

71. Notes of discussions with Commander-in-Chief Southwest Pacific Area, Brisbane, May 25–31, 1943, NAA: CRS A5954, item 2/3.

72. Hasluck, *Government and the People*, p. 717.

73. Daly to author, Canberra, 1980.

74. MacArthur to Curtin, November 6, 1943, NAA: CP290/16, bundle 1.

75. Blamey to Curtin, January 28, 1944, AWM: Blamey papers, 3DRL6643, item 4/22.

76. Hetherington, *Blamey*, p. 304.

77. Notes of discussion with Commander-in-Chief, Southwest Pacific Area, March 17, 1944, NAA: CRS A5954, box 3.

78. Notes of discussion with Commander-in-Chief, Southwest Pacific Area, June 27, 1944, NAA: CRS A5954, box 3.

79. Geoffrey Perret, *Old Soldiers Never Die: The Life of Douglas MacArthur* (New York: Random House, 1996), p. 414.

80. Blamey to Berryman, February 17, 1945, AWM: Blamey Papers, 3DRL6643, item 2/43.68.

81. Curtin to MacArthur, February 15, 1945, NAA: CRS A5954, box 570.

82. Horner, *High Command*, p. 396.
83. Brigadier Barham to Berryman, June 2, 1945, AWM: Berryman Papers.
84. Chifley to MacArthur, May 18, 1945, NAA: CRS A5954, box 570.
85. MacArthur to Chifley, May 20, 1945, NAA: CRS A5954, box 570.
86. Signal CA 51543, MacArthur to Marshall, April 12, 1945, NARA: RG 218, CCS 383 Pacific Ocean Area (6–10-43) sec 11. Joseph Forbes, "General Douglas MacArthur and the Implementation of American and Australian Civilian Policy Decisions in 1944 and 1945," in *Military Affairs* 49:1 (January 1985), argues that MacArthur followed the wishes of the Australian government and the joint chiefs. But he does not differentiate between the earlier operations at Tarakan and Brunei and the later operation at Balikpapan.
87. MacArthur to Chifley, May 20, 1945, NARA: Sutherland Papers, correspondence with Australian government.
88. Chifley to MacArthur, July 21, 1945, NARA: Sutherland Papers, correspondence with Australian government.
89. Commonwealth Parliamentary debates, February 11, 1943.

The Army in the Southwest Pacific

Stanley L. Falk

Stanley Falk, a widely published scholar who has served as chief historian for the U.S. Air Force and deputy chief historian for Southeast Asia at the U.S. Army Center of Military History, takes a critical look at the strategy employed by the United States for the defeat of Japan. He concludes that the emphasis on operations in the Southwest Pacific, in large part due to the "forceful presence" of MacArthur, was a waste of resources.

During the first two years of its World War II struggle against Japan, the U.S. Army sent nearly three-quarters of a million men to the Pacific. The great majority of these soldiers went to the South and Southwest Pacific—particularly the latter—and their numbers were to grow even more as the war continued.

The Army thus found itself locked very quickly in bitter combat with a stubborn and dangerous foe in an insular arena half-way around the world from home. Until that time, most of the Americans fighting in this strange and distant region had probably never heard of the Philippines, New Guinea, or the Solomon Islands, or of such exotic places as Bataan, Papua, Guadalcanal and other remote and alien locations. They had not imagined contending with thick, dark jungles; high, rugged mountains; sharp-edged grasses and strangling vegetation; fierce insects and blood-sucking leeches; and oppressive heat and choking dust that alternated with pelting tropical downpours, pervasive dampness and bottomless mud. Perhaps even more unexpected was the fierce and brutal nature of the enemy, who seemed frighteningly at home in this primitive and hostile environment.

If American GIS wondered what they were doing in these unlikely places—and were perhaps astonished that anyone would choose to fight in them—their surprise and concern were not without reason. Indeed, the heavy commitment of U.S. Army forces to the far Pacific constituted a major alteration of the prewar American plan for conflict with Japan. That plan had never projected sending American soldiers to the islands of the Southwest Pacific. It had, instead, directed that the U.S. Navy would do most of the fighting, that combat would take place in the Central Pacific, and that neither the Army nor the South Pacific would play more than a minor role.

The Army's huge involvement in that distant corner of the world was thus an unexpected strategic deviation. As the war progressed, it would become a costly and unnecessary diversion of resources from the primary strategy to defeat Japan and Germany.

The roots of this diversion lay in several interrelated factors. The first was America's long involvement with the Philippines and the dramatic presence in those islands of Gen. Douglas MacArthur. Another was the fact that the war was not simply the anticipated one between the United States and Japan alone but had instead grown into a global conflict of immense proportions. A third was the unexpected success of the initial Japanese offensive. The final factor was the mix of expedience, opportunism and interservice rivalry that dominated American Pacific strategy in World War II.

Ever since the U.S. acquisition of the Philippines at the turn of the century—what historian Samuel F. Bemis once termed our "great national aberration"—American strategists had wrestled with the problem of defending a remote archipelago so distant from our shores as to be virtually indefensible without a major commitment of resources far greater than this country was willing, or able, to make.

The primary threat to the Philippines came from Japan, so defense of the islands could only be considered within the overall American war plan for Japan. This plan was called Orange—under a system designating possible enemy nations by color—and was developed over several decades. It recognized that Japanese control of the islands of the Central Pacific interdicted the U.S. line of communications to the Philippines, making their easy defense all but impossible.

War Plan Orange, therefore, called for an American naval offensive to gain control of the central and western Pacific and defeat Japan by blockade and bombardment. The Philippines would be lost initially, but Manila Bay would be needed as a major western base for the U.S. fleet. The Army had the vital mission of holding Manila Bay until the fleet could fight its way through to it, however long this might take.

The growth of Japanese naval power in the late 1930s and the increas-

1. Captain and Mrs. Arthur
MacArthur with their sons
Douglas (*left*) and Arthur II,
c. 1887.

2. MacArthur as a cadet at West
Texas Military Academy, 1896.

3. Brig. Gen. Douglas MacArthur returns from France, 1919.

4. MacArthur as superintendent of West Point, c. 1921.

5. Chief of Staff MacArthur directs troops against the Bonus Expeditionary Force, July 1932.

6. Manuel Quezon makes MacArthur a field marshal in the Philippine army, August 24, 1937.

7. Gen. Thomas Blamey,
MacArthur, and Prime Minister
John Curtin, Melbourne, c. June
1942.

8. MacArthur at Port Moresby,
Papua New Guinea, December 25,
1942.

9. MacArthur, President
Roosevelt, Adm. Chester Nimitz,
Adm. William D. Leahy, Hono-
lulu, July 22, 1944.

10. MacArthur lands at Leyte, October 20, 1944.

11. MacArthur in front of his personal airplane, *Bataan*, 1944.

12. American flag raised on Corregidor, March 2, 1945.

13. MacArthur on the balcony of his office at City Hall, Manila, August 24, 1945.

14. MacArthur signs surrender document on uss *Missouri* in Tokyo Bay, September 2, 1945, as Gen. Jonathan Wainwright and Lt. Gen. Arthur Percival look on.

15. MacArthur's first meeting with Emperor Hirohito, September 27, 1945.

16. MacArthur greets Dr. Syngman Rhee, president of South Korea, upon arrival in Tokyo, February 16, 1950.

17. MacArthur and Chiang Kai-shek on Taiwan, July 31, 1950.

18. (*Left to right*) Gen. J. Lawton Collins, army chief of staff; MacArthur; Adm. Forest P. Sherman, chief of naval operations; and Adm. Arthur W. Radford, commander in chief, Pacific; Tokyo, August 21, 1950.

19. MacArthur views enemy dead following Inchon landing, September 17, 1950.

20. MacArthur and Lt. Gen. Walton H. Walker, commander of Eighth Army, Korea, 1950.

21. MacArthur and President Truman, Wake Island, October 15, 1950.

22. MacArthur addresses Joint Session of Congress, April 19, 1951.

23. MacArthur with his wife, Jean, and son, Arthur, Brewster, New York, summer 1951.

24. MacArthur and President Kennedy, New York, December 1961.

25. MacArthur reviews
Corps of Cadets, West Point,
May 12, 1962.

26. MacArthur at his final
birthday reunion dinner,
January 26, 1964.

ing chance that America might be involved in a war in Europe, however, made any prolonged defense of Manila Bay less and less probable. At best, the Army could hold the entrance to the bay for six months, by which time the Pacific Fleet might be able to breach the Japanese blockade and bring in a relief force.

By 1941, however, it seemed clear that early rescue of the Philippines would be impossible in the face of superior Japanese strength. War Plan Orange, moreover, had been subsumed into a far broader Rainbow Plan for an alliance war against multiple enemies, with top priority assigned to defeating Germany. The Philippines would thus fall to the Japanese and remain in their hands for whatever time it took to smash Germany and build up American forces for a Pacific counteroffensive.

This pessimistic view reckoned without the impressive stature and persuasive eloquence of Gen. MacArthur.

Gen. MacArthur's links to the Philippines went back many years and were forged especially in the late 1930s. In 1935, having completed his tour as U.S. Army chief of staff, he had become military adviser to the Philippine Commonwealth with the primary task of creating a Philippine army to defend the islands after their promised independence in 1944. Gen. MacArthur retired from the American Army in 1937, but in July 1941, with the war threatening, President Franklin D. Roosevelt recalled him to active duty. He now commanded all American and Philippine forces in the Far East, with the apparently hopeless mission of holding the Philippines against the expected Japanese invasion.

Gen. MacArthur believed firmly that with proper support the young Philippine army he was forming could defeat that invasion. Despite great difficulties in raising, equipping, organizing and training the Filipino forces, he reported only progress and increasing strength. In truth, however, the army he had created was one in name only, barely capable of the simplest operations and helpless before a determined Japanese assault. Nevertheless, his optimism and forceful arguments persuaded the War Department to give the Philippines its highest priority.

During the fall of 1941, Army ground and air reinforcements began reaching the islands in increasing numbers, but they were still far from sufficient for the task at hand. When war began, the crushing of the American Pacific Fleet at Pearl Harbor, the nearly simultaneous destruction of Gen. MacArthur's air force, and the rush of Japanese victories throughout the Pacific eliminated any further chance of helping the Philippines. By early January 1942, Filipino and American troops had been forced back into the shelter of Bataan Peninsula and Corregidor Island, guarding the entrance to Manila Bay in accordance with the Orange plan, but only awaiting their inevitable defeat.

In the weeks that followed, Gen. MacArthur bombarded Washington with calls for supplies and reinforcements. He also demanded an immediate Pacific offensive to prevent the fall of the Philippines, which, he warned, could lead to the loss of the entire Pacific and Asia. The "Germany-first" priority, he argued, should be dropped in favor of an all-out effort against Japan.

Although attempts to push supplies through the Japanese blockade had little success, leaders in Washington decided to establish and develop a base in Australia from which to support the Philippines. Stocked initially with supplies and reinforcements that were unable to break through to those islands, the Australian base soon took on significant proportions. Its creation was a key step in the alteration of prewar American Pacific strategy.

By mid-February, indeed, continued Japanese advances and the apparent threat they posed to Australia had precipitated an American decision to send an infantry division and supporting troops to that continent, thus committing the United States to Australia's defense. In the weeks that followed, additional Army units would move into New Caledonia and other islands along the Southwest Pacific strategic line of communications. By May 1942, more than a quarter of a million Army ground and air troops were in Australia, Hawaii and the island chain that linked them. These forces included six divisions and the equivalent of two others, as well as supporting combat and service troops and hundreds of combat aircraft.

While this commitment constituted no reversal of the Germany-first priority, the dispatch of major Army forces to the far Pacific was clear indication that that area would hardly starve for resources and that War Plan Orange had been significantly modified.

Meanwhile, late in February, in view of the deteriorating situation in the Philippines and throughout the Southwest Pacific, President Roosevelt had ordered Gen. MacArthur to leave Corregidor for Australia. There, he told him, he would head a new Allied command to be established to halt the onrushing Japanese.

The general's arrival in Darwin in mid-March 1942, coincided with an Allied agreement that the United States would bear primary responsibility for the war in the Pacific. Command was to be exercised by an American officer reporting to the U.S. Joint Chiefs of Staff. Gen. MacArthur quickly put in his bid for this assignment with his resounding "I shall return" to the Philippines declaration and his simultaneous announcement that he had been chosen to head "the American offensive against Japan."

Yet American command arrangements were still undecided. If the Orange concept of a Central Pacific naval offensive was to be followed, then it made obvious sense to give command to a naval officer, but the Army was dead set against relinquishing the entire Pacific area to the Navy, and, in any event, no naval officer outranked Gen. MacArthur or enjoyed anywhere near his prestige or popularity. The Navy, on the other hand, was hardly willing to cede the waters of the Pacific to a soldier, and it certainly was not going to turn the fleet over to Gen. MacArthur.

The only practical course was to establish two commands, dividing the Pacific and the war against Japan between them. Gen. MacArthur would head what was called the Southwest Pacific Area: essentially Australia and the zone north of it to the Philippines. The rest of the Pacific, designated the Pacific Ocean Areas, would be commanded by Adm. Chester W. Nimitz.

Gen. MacArthur's mission was basically defensive, to protect Australia and the line of communications, but his orders also stipulated that he was to hold Australia as a base "for future offensive action." In wording practically standard for this sort of a directive, they admonished him to "prepare to take the offensive." He proceeded to operate as if he had full authorization for a major counteroffensive to recapture the Philippines. He complained about the inadequacy of Australian forces under his command, called for a greater concentration of American resources in the Southwest Pacific and began planning offensive operations in New Guinea.

Gen. MacArthur's arguments for an early Pacific offensive were reflected in the views of another Pacific advocate in Washington, Adm. Ernest J. King, chief of naval operations. They differed, however, in the ultimate objective of this offensive. Gen. MacArthur's strategic eye was fixed on the Philippines. Adm. King urged an offensive through the Solomons and New Guinea to seize bases in the Carolines and Marshall Islands. This might lead to the Philippines, but, more important, it would open the Central Pacific naval assault envisioned in Orange.

Before any American counteroffensive could begin, however, the onrushing Japanese still had to be halted. In New Guinea, only a handful of Australians opposed them, and, by summer 1942, the Japanese were pressing across the mountainous spine of that huge island toward Port Moresby on the southeast coast. In a parallel advance, they were also preparing air bases in the southern Solomons to further consolidate their threat to the Hawaii-Australia line of communications.

In June, however, the American naval victory at Midway had opened the way for a limited counteroffensive against the Japanese. A month later, the Joint Chiefs of Staff directed Gen. MacArthur and Adm. Nimitz to begin a series of operations to capture the great Japanese base of Rabaul on New Britain. These operations constituted a major, three-stage campaign in the South and Southwest Pacific, with command arrangements reflecting the earlier decision to split the Pacific into two theaters.

The first stage of the campaign would be undertaken by Adm. Nimitz in what was called the South Pacific subtheater of his broad Pacific Ocean Areas Theater. South Pacific forces would open the drive on Rabaul by seizing bases in the southern Solomons. Then, in the second stage of the Allied counteroffensive, they would continue their advance up the Solomons while Southwest Pacific Area forces mounted a simultaneous parallel attack along the north coast of New Guinea. In the final stage of the campaign, both arms of the offensive would combine in a pincer movement to seize Rabaul. Adm. Nimitz would command the initial stage, but stages two and three would be under Gen. MacArthur.

The directive from the Joint Chiefs made no mention of a Central Pacific naval offensive nor, for that matter, of what might follow the seizure of Rabaul. But by continuing the earlier modification of Orange strategy, it made an irrevocable commitment of major Army forces to the South and Southwest Pacific.

The offensive began with the landing of the 1st Marine Division on Guadalcanal, in the southern Solomons, in August 1942. In the bloody fighting that followed, another Marine division and two Army divisions and a separate regiment had to join the battle before it ended in mid-winter. In February, finally, a third Army division seized islands just north of Guadalcanal in preparation for stage two of the drive on Rabaul.

The American invasion of Guadalcanal and the threat it posed to Japanese positions further north forced the Japanese to divert major resources from New Guinea to the Solomons. By mid-September, their drive on Port Moresby had ground to a halt. Under increasing pressure from Australian troops and American Army air units, the Japanese fell back on defensive positions around Buna and Gona on New Guinea's north coast. There, two Australian divisions were joined by a U.S. Army division and another American regiment in four months of bitter and costly combat that finally ended Japanese resistance in January 1943.

Thus, by early 1943, the great Japanese offensive into the southern Pacific had been stopped and thrown back upon itself. There was a pause in major operations by both sides as Allied and Japanese forces licked their wounds, tightened their helmet straps, and began to build up for future operations. The Japanese threat to Australia and the line of communications was ended; henceforth, the enemy could do no better than to defend his initial conquests, without any hope of extending them. The Allies, however, could now consider how to follow up their newly won initiative.

The first half of 1943 saw heavy air battles fought almost continuously over New Guinea and the Solomons, as both Japanese and Americans sought to gain aerial supremacy across this vast military arena. By late spring, the Americans had gained the upper hand, and thereafter would increasingly dominate the skies over the Southwest and South Pacific areas.

Their success was materially aided by the growing Allied ability to intercept, analyze and decipher Japanese signal communications, an impressive demonstration of which came in the crushing March 1943 Battle of the Bismarck Sea. Forewarned by signal intelligence that the Japanese were sending a major reinforcement convoy to eastern New Guinea, Gen. MacArthur's air arm struck heavily at the enemy transports and escorting destroyers. In three days of devastating attacks, the Army fliers wiped out most of the convoy, practically destroying an entire enemy division and forcing the Japanese to shift their defensive priority from the Solomons back to New Guinea. They sent no more major convoys to eastern New Guinea, and their position in the Solomons was weakening daily in the face of mounting aerial losses.

Meanwhile, thousands of miles to the northeast, Adm. Nimitz was preparing to eject Japanese forces from islands in the Aleutians captured nearly a year earlier during the abortive Midway operation. In May 1943, U.S. Army troops invaded the island of Attu and wiped out the defenders in three weeks of bitter combat. In attacking Attu, Adm. Nimitz had purposely bypassed the more heavily defended island of Kiska, forcing the Japanese to evacuate Kiska before it, too, could be assaulted and overwhelmed.

The practice of bypassing enemy strongholds in order to attack weaker defenses was soon adopted by Adm. Nimitz's forces in the South Pacific and by Gen. MacArthur in the Southwest Pacific. It became the standard technique in the subsequent Allied advance toward the Japanese home islands. It would, indeed, be quickly demonstrated in the campaign against Rabaul.

Stage two of that campaign got under way at the end of June 1943. Southwest Pacific forces advanced overland and by sea along the north coast of New Guinea, while Army and Marine units in the South Pacific began to climb the island ladder of the northern Solomons. By now, however, the need to capture Rabaul itself seemed less pressing, and the desirability of attacking that great bastion appeared even less so.

American air and naval supremacy in the Southwest and South Pacific had removed the necessity of using Rabaul as a base to cover further advances in New Guinea. In like manner, American plans to open a Central Pacific offensive through the Gilbert Islands in late 1943 eliminated the need for Rabaul as a staging area for the Carolines and Marshalls. Finally, while Japanese defenses of the strategic approaches to Rabaul had been battered, Rabaul itself and its 100,000 defenders still remained a difficult and extremely costly target. Indeed, any major effort to capture it would draw major Allied resources away from both New Guinea and the Central Pacific and delay for many months offensives in either area.

In late July 1943, therefore, the Joint Chiefs of Staff decided to drop plans to capture Rabaul in favor of bypassing and neutralizing it. The Rabaul area would be encircled, reduced by air and naval pressure, and left behind in the wake of continuing Allied advances.

This was soon accomplished. By the end of the year, South Pacific forces had secured the northern Solomons, while the advance in New Guinea had reached the Huon Peninsula and leaped the Dampier Strait to land in western New Britain. In these battles, the Japanese suffered heavy casualties and major losses in aircraft and warships. A devastating series of aerial strikes against Rabaul soon destroyed it as an offensive threat, even as Allied ground units were seizing key island positions surrounding that once powerful bastion. By early 1944, Rabaul was completely isolated, of no further use to the enemy as a strategic base.

The Japanese, indeed, had already acknowledged their impotence. Defeated in the Solomons and eastern New Guinea, driven from the

Aleutians, unable to replace their losses in men and material, and anticipating an early American offensive in the Central Pacific, they made the only prudent decision they could. On 30 September, 1943, Imperial General Headquarters wrote off eastern New Guinea, the Rabaul area, and, indeed, much of the Pacific to the advancing Allies.

Japanese forces would establish a new so-called absolute national defense zone inside a line running from western New Guinea north through the Carolines and Mariana Islands. Positions outside that line were to be defended by all means possible with the resources on hand, but there would be no further effort to reinforce or resupply those areas. For all practical purposes, Tokyo had abandoned them.

Less than two months later, the American Central Pacific drive got under way when soldiers and marines invaded the Gilbert Islands. With the U.S. Pacific Fleet increasing rapidly in size and strength, this great new offensive seemed to suggest a revival of the original Orange plan. In fact, however, it merely represented a continuation of the compromise on Pacific strategy and command that had characterized the first two years of the war. Henceforth, American forces would follow a two-pronged strategy of mutually supporting Pacific drives: a naval offensive under Adm. Nimitz through the Central Pacific and an Army push under Gen. MacArthur through New Guinea to the Philippines.

In retrospect, continuation of the Southwest Pacific advance was a mistake. The Central Pacific was the surest and straightest avenue to the heart of Japan, without any need for further seizure of real estate in the Southwest Pacific. Given the growing superiority of American air and naval power, the Central Pacific offensive assured swift destruction of the Japanese fleet and the early capture of bases from which air strikes and blockades could force the surrender of Japan itself. Indeed, by June 1944, barely seven months after Adm. Nimitz began his advance, he had reached the Marianas, practically on Japan's doorstep, while Southwest Pacific forces were still fighting in New Guinea.

The continued Southwest Pacific drive was clearly peripheral and subsidiary, attacking enemy troops that no longer threatened Allied interests and suffering heavy casualties that might otherwise have been avoided, nor did it have the early decisive impact on the war that the Central Pacific offensive achieved. Indeed, Japan's surrender would have come no later had Southwest Pacific ground forces simply remained in place in the final year and a half of the war and allowed the Japanese in that area to wither away under the mounting pressures of American air and seapower.

The only real accomplishment of the continued Southwest Pacific advance was the liberation of the Philippines from cruel Japanese occupation, but that would have come almost as quickly with Japan's surrender— and without the deaths of more than 100,000 Filipino civilians, the destruction of Manila and other cities, and the U.S. Army battle casualties of 10,000 in western New Guinea and more than 62,000 in the Philippines themselves. To these grim figures must be added nearly 10,000 Marine and Army casualties in the bloody Palau Islands campaign undertaken by Adm. Nimitz to support the Philippine invasion. This total of 82,000 American casualties—including nearly 16,000 dead—was well over twice the losses incurred in the Central Pacific drive to the Marianas.

The dual offensives through the Central and Southwest Pacific were clearly driven by the impetus of command and strategy compromises made early in the war. While the Joint Chiefs of Staff seemed to favor the Central Pacific advance, they continued to give the Southwest Pacific an almost equal priority. Thus the building of forces in Gen. MacArthur's theater continued unabated during 1944, more than doubling American troop strength there. By the time he invaded Luzon in January 1945, Gen. MacArthur commanded 15 American divisions, plus supporting combat and service units and sizeable Australian forces. Indeed, more U.S. Army ground forces would be committed to Luzon than had seen action in North Africa, Italy or southern France.

Thus, the initial small assignment of American troops to the defense of the Philippines, the establishment of an Australian base to support them, and the subsequent expansion of forces to hold the line of communications had mushroomed into an irreversible commitment to the Southwest Pacific Area. This commitment could well have been halted at the end of 1943, by which time the Japanese had been decisively neutralized as an offensive threat in that area. Army divisions later sent to the Southwest Pacific could have been used far better to meet the acute shortage of combat manpower in Europe and elsewhere, yet the momentum of the Southwest Pacific buildup, the forceful presence of Gen. MacArthur, and the pressures of interservice rivalries made inevitable the dual-pronged nature of American Pacific strategy.

In truth, however, the continued Southwest Pacific commitment was an unnecessary and profligate waste of resources, involving the needless loss of thousands of lives, and in no significant way affecting the outcome of the war.

Douglas MacArthur and the 1944 New Guinea Offensive

Stephen R. Taaffe

Stephen Taaffe of Trevecca Nazarene University, author of a recent study of MacArthur's 1944 New Guinea campaign, summarizes the findings of his research in this specially commissioned essay. Whether his generally positive view of MacArthur's military leadership represents the beginning of a trend among a new generation of historians of World War II remains to be seen.

Douglas MacArthur was no ordinary military commander. Unlike so many of his World War II contemporaries, many in the American public knew of MacArthur long before the conflict began as the son of another famous general, as a First World War hero, and as the 1930s army chief of staff who routed the Bonus Army. Rank and background aside, MacArthur stood out in other important ways. His courage under fire, keen intelligence, commanding presence, and total unwavering commitment to whatever cause he advocated inspired intense devotion from many who saw him as the embodiment of all that was good and noble in the American army. As one subordinate put it: "His mind was u beuutiful piece of almost perfect machinery. The surprising thing was that he kept it running so perfectly, stimulated almost exclusively by prodigious reading. . . . Rarely was he put to his mettle by other mortals. And when he was—if in his own military field—he was superb, dazzling."[1]

Unfortunately for the general's place in history, many others viewed MacArthur in a different light. To these people MacArthur was a vainglorious, manipulative, disobedient, deceitful, and pompous commander who frequently confused his own causes with those of his country, often needlessly risking the latter for the sake of the former. While almost everyone who came in contact with him acknowledged his considerable military talent, many also identified fundamental character flaws that prevented him from becoming a commander of the first rank. As one British officer wrote during World War II: "He is shrewd, proud, remote, highly strung and vastly vain. He has imagination, self-confidence, physical courage and charm, but no humor about himself, no regard for truth, and is unaware of these defects. He mistakes his emotions and ambitions for principles. With moral depth he would be a great man; as it is he is a near miss which may be worse than a mile."[2]

MacArthur's ability to provoke either intense devotion or fervent scorn continued long after he died. Some historians see him as a great and misunderstood military leader who fought bravely in World War I's trenches, guided the army through hard times in the 1930s, led the United States to victory in the Pacific War, and turned the tide in Korea until betrayed by the weak-willed and incompetent Truman administration. Other historians, however, portray MacArthur as a loose cannon who repeatedly disobeyed both his civilian and military superiors to seek his own aims, a man who often endangered his soldiers' lives pursuing counterproductive strategies. By this second interpretation MacArthur was no friend to either democracy or American interests. Such intense polarization often obscures efforts to stake out a realistic middle ground between these two extreme views.

The 1944 New Guinea offensive is one of World War II's lesser-known campaigns, but it serves as a valuable tool with which to evaluate MacArthur's abilities as a military commander. American Pacific War strategy was based on a two-pronged offensive toward Japan from Hawaii and Australia, with MacArthur leading the latter drive. In early 1944 MacArthur's Southwest Pacific Area (swpa) command confronted a series of Japanese bases scattered along New Guinea's north coast. MacArthur fulfilled his part of the "dual-drive" offensive by overwhelming or by-passing these Japanese positions as he moved toward the strategically vital China-Formosa-Luzon region. MacArthur not only managed to cross the New Guinea littoral in less than six months at the cost of only 11,300 casualties, but he also succeeded in using his victory to persuade the reluctant Joint Chiefs of Staff (jcs) to endorse a Philippines liberation campaign. Because he was able to invade the Philippines long before the navy was capable of mounting its proposed assault on Formosa through the central Pacific, MacArthur's strategic designs contributed greatly to the United States' cost-effective triumph in the Pacific War.

On one hand the New Guinea offensive showed MacArthur at his best. He was flexible in attaining his goals, gave his subordinates considerable autonomy to implement his directives as long as they did not interfere with his strategic timetable, eagerly grasped new technology and exploited available intelligence, and successfully melded the SWPA's disparate land, air, and sea units into a formidable force. On the other hand the campaign raised some troubling questions about MacArthur's command abilities. To wage the New Guinea offensive he developed an agenda independent of his superiors' agenda, twisted the truth when it served his purposes, and deployed his forces in ways that exposed them to unnecessary losses. Fortunately for him—and for the soldiers under his command—superior American resources and poor Japanese planning compensated for his shortcomings in New Guinea. Such advantages, however, would not always be available to him, and this goes a long way in explaining the defeats MacArthur suffered in Korea and elsewhere.

MacArthur and the Dual-Drive Decision

By early 1944 the Pacific War had clearly turned in the United States' favor. Allied victories in the Aleutians, Gilbert Islands, the Solomons, and Papua New Guinea had seriously dented the Japanese defense perimeter and all but isolated the big Japanese base at Rabaul on New Britain. Such successes, however, were not designed to bring Japan to its knees, but rather to maintain pressure on the enemy and secure Australia's communications line with the United States while the Allies focused on crushing Nazi Germany.

While American, Australian, and Japanese soldiers fought and died throughout 1943, the JCS pondered its next move. No one wanted to surrender the strategic initiative back to Japan, despite the American commitment to concentrate on beating Germany first, but consensus broke down on where to apply the pressure. Looking over their maps and charts and reports the JCS finally decided that a central Pacific offensive from Hawaii through the Japanese-held Mandate Islands—the Marshalls, Marianas, and Palaus—was the best way to reach the Japanese homeland. Such an offensive would provide the navy with plenty of room to deploy its growing number of aircraft carriers for a decisive battle with its Japanese counterpart, and the small islands were tailor-made for marine amphibious assaults. In addition, the Army Air Force (AAF) could station its new B-29 bombers on the Marianas and from there hurl them against vulnerable Japanese cities. The British and American Combined Chiefs of Staff (CCS) signed off on the proposal at the Sextant conference in Cairo in December 1943. As one CCS document said, "Due weight should be accorded to the fact that operations in the CP [central Pacific] promise at this time a more rapid advance toward Japan and her vital lines of communication; the early acquisition of strategic air bases closer to the Japanese homeland; and, of greatest importance, are more likely to precipitate a decisive engagement with the Japanese fleet."[3]

The JCS did not explicitly rule out a Philippines liberation campaign, but MacArthur was convinced that it was leaning in that direction.[4] As he saw it, the best way to win the war was by means of a SWPA-dominated offensive to that archipelago. He believed that prying the Japanese out of the small, heavily defended Mandates would be a slow and costly process that would not win the war anytime soon. A SWPA-led campaign to the Philippines, on the other hand, would save both time and American lives. MacArthur thought that Japanese defenses in the region were weak and nearby Australia could provide the SWPA with valuable logistical support. In addition, seizing the Philippines would cut Japan off from its vital Netherlands East Indies oil supplies, expose the Chinese coast to invasion, and tempt the Japanese navy into the decisive battle its American counterpart craved.[5]

Strategic constraints were certainly a crucial component to determining the Pacific War's course, but there was more to it than that. Pride, honor, and bureaucratic rivalries all played important roles. MacArthur believed that the United States had a moral obligation to liberate the Philippines that superseded most ordinary strategic considerations. His humiliating defeats at Bataan and Corregidor haunted him, and he was determined to redeem his pledge to return in triumph and liberate the archipelago.[6] Many naval officers, for their part, saw the Pacific War as *their* war, with Pearl Harbor, not Bataan, as the wrong to be righted. They were dead set against letting an army general, especially the despised MacArthur, lead them into Japan.[7] Like it or not, the consensus-bound JCS had to take into consideration such turf wars and personality clashes when it formulated Pacific War strategy. Summing things up, one army observer later noted, "I felt that the discussion really wasn't basically concerned about the best way to [win the war]. It was who was going to do it, and who was going to be in command, and who was going to be involved."[8]

MacArthur was by no means willing to meekly accept the JCS's Sextant conference decision that downgraded his command and his responsibilities, so throughout late 1943 and early 1944 he worked hard to reverse it in favor of a SWPA-led Philippines liberation campaign. Arguing against a central Pacific offensive on strategic grounds was merely one of several arrows in his quiver. Another was his formidable public relations machine. Although Pacific War strategy remained ambiguous, MacArthur and his headquarters acted in public as if a Philippines invasion was a foregone conclusion. Indeed, most newspapers accepted as given that such a campaign was the ultimate goal of MacArthur's operations, and MacArthur did nothing to discourage such speculation. Later on, after the dual-drive offensive began but before the JCS decided to assault the Philippines, MacArthur said at a Canberra, Australia, banquet in his honor: "Two years ago when I landed on your soil I said to the people of the Philippines whence I came 'I shall return.' Tonight I repeat these words, 'I shall return.' There is nothing more certain than our ultimate reconquest and liberation from the enemy of those and adjacent islands. One of the great offenses of the war will at the appropriate time be launched for that purpose."[9] This was not true; the JCS had authorized no such offensive, but such exhortation had its uses in rallying Americans back home to his banner. Public pressure might or might not compel the JCS to underwrite a Philippines liberation campaign, but MacArthur was undoubtedly aware that it would influence the politically sensitive President Roosevelt, who, if and when push came to shove, would be the ultimate arbiter of Pacific War strategy. As one subordinate noted, "He was a good enough tactician to know that the political threat back home of the name MacArthur was one of his most effective weapons in dealing with the political maestro in the White House."[10] If MacArthur could not directly convince the JCS to change its mind, then he could and did try to indirectly do so by creating a groundswell of support for a Philippines liberation campaign among the important officers in the Pacific. A late-January 1944 strategy conference at Pearl Harbor provided him with an opportunity to bring recalcitrant naval officers around to his way of thinking. MacArthur did not attend the meeting himself but instead relied on his subordinates to proselytize on his behalf. Their efforts were reinforced by doubts held by many attending naval officers of the viability of a central Pacific offensive due to recent heavy losses on Tarawa in the Gilbert Islands. Mulling things over, Pacific Ocean Areas (POA) commander Adm. Chester Nimitz agreed with MacArthur's officers that a SWPA-dominated offensive through the Philippines was probably the best way to go. Unfortunately for MacArthur, Nimitz's boss and JCS member Adm. Ernest King angrily rejected such suggestions.[11]

Finally, MacArthur was willing to resort to coercion to achieve his goals. SWPA Chief of Staff Maj. Gen. Richard Sutherland traveled to Washington in February and March 1944 to lobby the JCS to support

MacArthur's strategic ideas. MacArthur told Sutherland to relay to Army Chief of Staff Gen. George Marshall that he would interpret any decrease in his force or responsibilities—meaning a Pacific War offensive that did not include a Philippines liberation campaign—as a vote of no confidence in him. Under such circumstances, "my professional integrity, indeed my personal honor would be so involved that if otherwise I request that I be given early opportunity to personally present the case to the Secretary of War and the President before finally determining my own personal action in the matter."[12] It is hard to tell exactly what, if any, impact this had on Marshall, but no one in the JCS wanted to abdicate their responsibilities to the unpredictable Roosevelt, who had already shown a positive genius for disrupting American grand strategy.[13] The message does, however, indicate the lengths to which MacArthur was prepared to go to fight the Pacific War his way.

In the end MacArthur's various actions, as well as Marshall's own continuing doubts about the Sextant conference decisions, helped convince the JCS to take another look at Pacific War strategy. After a first glance, however, the JCS's resulting March 12, 1944, directive seemed to merely reiterate decisions made at Cairo the previous December. It said nothing about a Philippines liberation campaign, but instead reaffirmed, "[T]he most feasible approach to the Formosa-Luzon-China area is by way of the Marianas-Carolines-Palaus-Mindanao area, and that the control of the Marianas-Carolines-Palau area is essential to the projection of our forces into the former area."[14] The Joint Chiefs ordered MacArthur to conquer New Guinea and move on to the southern Philippines island of Mindanao, but this offensive was not a prelude to a full-scale invasion of the Philippines. Instead it was designed to support Nimitz's more important central Pacific campaign by diverting and tying down Japanese resources that might otherwise be moved out of New Guinea and stuffed into the Mandates.[15]

A second hard look at the JCS report, however, showed that MacArthur had not yet lost the strategic debate. The JCS wanted him to occupy Mindanao "preparatory to a further advance to Formosa either directly or *via Luzon* [emphasis added]."[16] Luzon was in the heart of the Philippines and any Philippines liberation campaign had to include its reconquest. If MacArthur could reach the China-Formosa-Luzon area before or at the same time as the navy-dominated POA offensive was taking place, he could reopen the strategic debate and push for a Luzon invasion as the opening round of a Philippines liberation campaign even though the JCS was not yet thinking along those lines. To do so, however, MacArthur had to move as rapidly as possible across New Guinea. The big island, in short, was more than just a road to the China-Formosa-Luzon region; it was a racetrack as well, with the navy running hard on a parallel lane to the north. The victor, as MacArthur interpreted things, would have a lot of say in determining ensuing strategy. MacArthur's desire for speed had a major impact on the way he conducted his New Guinea campaign.

MacArthur's actions in early 1944 were not those of a typical World War II general. His implicit and not-so-implicit threats to use his substantial political clout and connections, as well as his continuing strategic arguments, were major factors in pressuring the JCS to reexamine its plans. To be sure, on the surface the JCS did not cave in to MacArthur's demands, but its March 12 decision left Pacific War strategy vague enough to accommodate both the navy's and MacArthur's views until American forces reached the China-Formosa-Luzon region, at which point the joint chiefs would reopen the strategic debate and determine whether an invasion of Luzon or Formosa was necessary. In doing so the JCS bought MacArthur's continued cooperation and maintained interservice harmony in the Pacific for the time being. As events later demonstrated, there were certainly some advantages to the JCS's new dual-drive offensive, but this did not excuse MacArthur's egocentric efforts to disrupt Pacific War strategy if he did not get his way—or anyhow some indication that he might get his way later on if he played ball now. Unfortunately for MacArthur, during the Korean War he again tried to pressure his superiors to adopt his strategic views. That time, however, President Truman responded not by compromising but by relieving the general of his command.

Winning the New Guinea Campaign

To MacArthur New Guinea was valueless in and of itself. The big island derived its strategic significance from its geographical location between the SWPA's forces and the China-Formosa-Luzon region finish line. MacArthur was willing to do whatever was necessary to get there first and reopen the strategic debate in favor of a Philippines liberation campaign. He was not concerned *how* the SWPA got across New Guinea as long as it did so *quickly*. To that end he displayed considerable flexibility at the operational level throughout the New Guinea campaign. Any idea that promised to propel his offensive forward and save time and resources appealed to him, even if it entailed an increased risk of failure and American losses. As MacArthur saw things, although a slow and safe New Guinea campaign might reduce casualties in the short run it would almost certainly cost him his chance to liberate the Philippines in the long. If this happened the navy would be free to implement its unwise and counterproductive central Pacific–oriented strategies, which would ultimately cost the country far more in terms of time, blood, and treasure than anything he might do or fail to do in New Guinea.[17]

The Admiralties Islands invasion best demonstrated MacArthur's operational flexibility. Situated two hundred miles north of New Guinea, MacArthur wanted the Admiralties not only to completely cut off Rabaul from the rest of the Japanese empire but also to cover his northern flank and provide the SWPA with the air and naval bases it needed to spearhead his offensive across New Guinea. MacArthur planned to assault the islands on April 1, 1944, but in late February he received air reconnaissance reports that indicated that the Japanese might have abandoned the place. MacArthur saw this as an opportunity to accelerate his campaign and keep pace with the navy's central Pacific offensive by taking the islands immediately with a hastily assembled reconnaissance-in-force. In doing so he rejected both the arguments from some of his lieutenants that this would disrupt the SWPA's delicate logistical system and other intelligence reports that suggested that upwards of four thousand Japanese were there. To MacArthur the possible gains outweighed the potential losses. As he explained to a subordinate, "[It is] a gamble in which I have everything to win, little to lose. I bet ten to win a million, if I hit the jackpot."[18]

MacArthur's reconnaissance-in-force landed on the Admiralties on February 29, 1944, and quickly established a beachhead. In the following days repeated attacks from the all-too-real Japanese garrison almost wiped out the Americans, but they managed to hold out until help arrived. Once reinforced the Americans went on to secure the islands by the end of March. Even so it was a close call, and the price tag of fifteen hundred American casualties was relatively high considering the number of troops committed to the operation. MacArthur, however, believed that the hurried assault was well worth the risks and the cost. He estimated that seizing the Admiralties advanced his timetable by two months and the operation gave him the air and naval bases his offensive toward the China-Formosa-Luzon region required.[19] Moreover, the JCS was reconsidering its Sextant conference decisions when MacArthur launched his attack, and his success demonstrated to his superiors that the swpa was capable of moving rapidly across New Guinea. MacArthur had no regrets, and in fact he considered the operation one of his brightest maneuvers.[20]

MacArthur's flexibility extended beyond operational planning. During the New Guinea campaign he eagerly employed any available technological advantage that would accelerate his offensive. Because the campaign involved a series of amphibious landings up the big island's north coast, MacArthur's attitude toward this form of warfare played a big part in the offensive's success. The army developed all sorts of peculiar vehicles to get soldiers and their supplies and equipment from ship to shore, including fifty-feet-long all-steel lcms (landing-craft mechanized vehicles) that could carry sixty men or sixty thousand pounds of cargo onto a hostile beach, and cleated lvts (landing vehicles tracked) that could move onto shore and inland to furnish advancing troops with fire support. Even the humble bulldozer provided crucial service by opening beach exits, clearing fields of fire, and burying Japanese bunkers and pillboxes.

All these landing craft were manned by the army's seventy-three hundred–man strong Engineer Special Brigades (esbs), created specifically for this purpose when the navy proved unable to do the job. esbs not only moved men and equipment from ship to shore, they also provided effective covering fire. Each esb possessed some one thousand rocket tubes and eighteen hundred machine guns dispersed among all its landing craft. This gave them a tremendous wallop and went a long way toward explaining swpa's innumerable successful New Guinea amphibious landings. MacArthur had little to do with esb development but he was among the first to recognize its value. Throughout the war he did all he could to obtain and hold onto as many of them as possible, and at one point dismissed Marshall's suggestion that he give one of them up.[21]

MacArthur also recognized the value of the intelligence assets at his disposal. These included air photo reconnaissance, elite Alamo Scouts to reconnoiter beaches, and especially radio intercepts. By the time MacArthur launched his New Guinea offensive the Allies had broken many of Japan's most important codes. Collectively known as "ULTRA" intelligence, this top secret decryption of Japanese wireless military traffic enabled swpa headquarters to read many important Japanese radio messages. MacArthur used this information in planning and undertaking operations up the New Guinea coast. Most notably, ULTRA informed him that the Japanese expected swpa to attack their big base at Hansa Bay–

Wewak. Thus forewarned, MacArthur instead targeted lightly defended Hollandia, some 380 miles up the coast to the northwest, and seized it with minimal losses in April 1944. Without ULTRA MacArthur might have assaulted well-defended Hansa Bay–Wewak and suffered heavy losses, which would have slowed down his offensive and reduced the chances that he would ever get to liberate the Philippines. Instead, the successful Hollandia operation enabled the general to isolate some fifty-five thousand Japanese troops at Hansa Bay–Wewak, gave him important airdromes to support future operations, moved his forces well up the New Guinea coast, and saved him a couple months over his original timetable.[22]

To be sure, SWPA's intelligence assets were not foolproof and several times during the New Guinea campaign MacArthur's intelligence chief Maj. Gen. Charles Willoughby incorrectly analyzed the data collected, with unfortunate results. In June and July 1944, for instance, Willoughby proved unable to predict accurately when the Japanese would attack SWPA forces along the Driniumor River near Aitape, which caused confusion among the Americans and contributed to the nearly twenty-four hundred casualties suffered in the ensuing fighting there. Similarly, Willoughby's inability to determine Japanese intentions in the Wakde-Sarmi region played a role in the 158th Regimental Combat Team's unsuccessful assault on Lone Tree Hill in May 1944. MacArthur, however, was willing to risk such occasional intelligence mishaps because more often than not the information Willoughby collected and analyzed gave him opportunities to accelerate his campaign by taking advantage of Japanese weaknesses.

Finally, MacArthur received crucial support from his chief subordinates in the field. Although he intentionally kept his lieutenants out of the public spotlight by restricting their access to the press, MacArthur gave them considerable latitude to implement his strategic and operational plans as long as they achieved their objectives quickly.[23] As one put it, "[MacArthur] would organize an expedition, and give someone command, and then he did not interfere."[24] MacArthur's subordinates were not automatons who blindly followed orders, but rather strong-willed men who used their authority to influence the campaign in ways their boss sometimes did not anticipate. For example, SWPA ground forces commander Lt. Gen. Walter Krueger may very well have saved the Admiralties reconnaissance-in-force. MacArthur wanted the invasion force lean and mean, but a doubtful Krueger—without orders—increased the number of troops involved to over one thousand and sent in the Alamo Scouts to reconnoiter ahead of time. Krueger did not specifically disobey MacArthur's orders but he certainly twisted them so as to increase the chances for the operation's success. Without Krueger's initiative the Japanese might have wiped out the reconnaissance-in-force at its beachhead. Similarly, SWPA naval commander Vice Adm. Thomas Kinkaid decided on his own to leave behind two destroyers to watch the Admiralty Islands' beachhead, and the valuable fire support these vessels provided helped beat off the ferocious Japanese attacks. As one general later put it, "[The navy] didn't support us; they saved our necks."[25] By constantly taking the initiative and maintaining a can-do attitude, MacArthur's lieutenants contributed greatly to SWPA's victory in New Guinea.

In addition to fighting and winning battles, MacArthur's subordinates also played a part in SWPA's logistical success. MacArthur understood that winning battles was merely the first step in making geographical locations useful to his war effort. The Americans needed airfields, port facilities, roads, warehouses, fuel depots, and so on to successfully prosecute the Pacific War, but New Guinea's infrastructure bordered on the prehistoric. Moreover, MacArthur wanted the island transformed fast so he could continue his race to the China-Formosa-Luzon region. Here, too, SWPA commanders rose to the challenge by quickly turning primitive locales like the Admiralties, Hollandia, Biak, Sansapor-Mar, and Morotai into giant logistical complexes from which the Americans could stage, supply, and support operations further up the coast and toward the Philippines. Maj. Gen. Franklin Sibert, for instance, not only secured the Sansapor-Mar vicinity easily in July 1944, but he built new airfields from scratch that were ready for bombers a month later, in time to support the ensuing Morotai operation. Integrating New Guinea into the SWPA's logistical network was no easy task, but MacArthur's lieutenants managed to pull it off in a timely fashion in spite of the horrendous terrain and constant shortages of almost everything.

MacArthur was willing to give his subordinates considerable leeway on the operational and tactical level, but only as long as their actions did not slow down his all-important strategic timetable. When this happened he pressured Krueger to get his subordinates to hurry up, even if such haste risked increased American casualties. During the Biak operation, for example, Maj. Gen. Horace Fuller was unable to secure the island's three airdromes as rapidly as MacArthur wanted. MacArthur complained to Krueger and Krueger in turn leaned on Fuller until Fuller quit in disgust. Similarly, MacArthur's desire for celerity caused problems along the Driniumor River. Krueger ordered XI Corps commander Maj. Gen. Charles Hall to assume the offensive and eliminate Japanese forces attacking from Hansa Bay–Wewak. As Krueger interpreted the situation, waiting for the Japanese to show up and batter themselves against Hall's well-prepared Aitape defenses would take too much time and would deprive the SWPA of resources it needed to continue the drive toward the China-Formosa-Luzon region. On the other hand, attacking into the jungle would permit the Americans to retain the initiative and end the operation quickly, thus freeing up thousands of troops for bigger adventures to the west, even if such a strategy meant larger casualties than Hall's play-it-safe plan.[26] In the ensuing battle the Americans suffered heavy losses slugging it out with the Japanese in the dense jungle without as much firepower and logistical support as a defensive strategy promised, but Krueger concluded that such a strategy best fulfilled MacArthur's agenda. Whatever the short-term consequences, MacArthur's occasional heavy-handedness at the tactical level demonstrated that he knew exactly what role New Guinea played in his Pacific War strategy.

MacArthur's frequent refusal to interfere at the operational level paid off in other ways. He generally relied on his air, ground, and naval commanders to coordinate operational planning among themselves, and the give-and-take this entailed promoted flexibility and interservice harmony within the SWPA.[27] Only rarely did Krueger need to appeal to MacArthur to get air and naval commanders to fall into line. In addition, MacArthur's hands-off policy and his desire to reach the China-Formosa-Luzon region by whatever means possible encouraged his naval, air, and land commanders to improvise, often with stunning results. During the fighting in New Guinea the SWPA developed or improved new techniques such as colored smoke and lights to guide landing craft to the shore, elite Alamo Scouts to reconnoiter beaches before amphibious landings, naval demolition teams to clear beach obstacles, and AAF skip bombing to sink Japanese ships. Had MacArthur and his headquarters kept a tight rein on operations his subordinates might not have felt as free to experiment or to cooperate.

Prewar American military planners never envisioned waging war in a primitive, jungle-ridden place like New Guinea. Fortunately, MacArthur understood that the island posed a unique challenge to an American army that emphasized firepower, mobility, and material superiority.[28] To win the campaign MacArthur did not abandon traditional army tenets, but instead modified them to accommodate New Guinea's peculiar environment. The island had no road or rail network to promote mobility, so the SWPA turned to the sealanes to move rapidly up the coast. Although almost all SWPA operations were amphibious, MacArthur was also willing to use airborne troops when necessary, as during the Noemfoor operation. New Guinea's dense jungle made it difficult to deploy the large amounts of artillery that the army traditionally relied upon, so the SWPA instead fell back on air and naval support to rain down destruction on Japanese opposition. Finally, labor-saving devices such as bulldozers, angledozers, cranes, rollers, and power shovels enabled the Americans to scrape the airfields, docks, warehouses, and port facilities the SWPA needed to incorporate New Guinea into its logistical network. That the SWPA could afford to deploy and utilize such exotic equipment and weaponry was due in no small part to America's immense industrial production, and to MacArthur's willingness to take advantage of it.

Some Troubling Tendencies

By almost any measurement the New Guinea campaign was a resounding success not only for the Allies in general but also for MacArthur personally. The SWPA's offensive succeeded both in tying down a significant number of Japanese forces and in giving MacArthur the opportunity to persuade the JCS to commit itself to a Philippines liberation campaign. Moreover, SWPA casualties were relatively light, especially compared to those the POA command sustained in its concurrent campaign in the Marianas. MacArthur's generalship, however, was not flawless. In his desire for speed MacArthur made a number of errors that could have seriously damaged the American Pacific War effort and cost him his chance to invade the Philippines. Fortunately for the general, American advantages in intelligence collection, logistics, firepower, and numbers— as well as a number of Japanese miscues and problems—negated his mistakes and permitted him to successfully prosecute the campaign.

In order to liberate the Philippines MacArthur had to wage two wars: one against the Japanese in New Guinea and the other against detractors who opposed his strategic designs. MacArthur understood that the two conflicts were interrelated, and he believed that the best weapon against his domestic opponents in the navy and elsewhere was a rapid advance across New Guinea to the China-Formosa-Luzon region that would put him in a strong bargaining position to reopen the strategic debate deferred by the JCS's March 12 dual-drive offensive compromise.

To that end, throughout the New Guinea campaign MacArthur did his best to convince his superiors and the public that his offensive was proceeding smoothly and efficiently. Unfortunately for the general, things did not always work out that way; several times the SWPA's offensive ran into unexpected snags that upset MacArthur's fast timetable. In response, MacArthur on occasion deliberately misled his superiors and the public about his problems and progress. Such dissembling gave a false impression of the SWPA's war.

Shortly after American troops stormed ashore on the island of Biak on May 27, 1944, for example, MacArthur's headquarters issued a communiqué that stated, "For strategic purposes this marks the practical end of the New Guinea campaign."[29] Even Marshall accepted this rosy and somewhat premature scenario, at least for a while anyway. He radioed MacArthur two weeks later, "[I] send you my personal congratulations on the Aitape–Hollandia–Maffin Bay–Biak campaign which has completely disorganized the enemy plans . . . and has advanced the schedule of operations by many weeks."[30] MacArthur's communiqué, however, was not accurate or truthful. Throughout the New Guinea offensive the Japanese rarely opposed SWPA landings at the water's edge, but instead holed up inland away from powerful American naval support and made their stand there. Most of the fighting and the bulk of American casualties occurred miles from the beachhead days after the troops first came ashore. The Biak operation was no exception, and the Americans did not secure the island's three airfields until June 22, nearly a month after MacArthur's headquarters proclaimed victory. To be sure, MacArthur could argue that in New Guinea once his forces were safely ashore it was a matter of time until they gained their objectives against the isolated Japanese. However, for MacArthur *saving time* was the entire point of the campaign. From a strategic view the SWPA's victory in New Guinea was all but inevitable because the Japanese gradually wrote off most of the island as indefensible. The Japanese hoped that their comrades left behind along the big island's north coast could delay MacArthur's juggernaut long enough to permit them to make their stand to the west. The longer those isolated Japanese could hold out inland and prevent the SWPA from seizing or building the vital airfields necessary to continue its offensive, the harder it became for MacArthur to reach the China-Formosa-Luzon region ahead of or at the same time as Nimitz's POA and the less likely it was for him to successfully lobby for an invasion of the Philippines. By giving an inaccurate portrayal of his progress MacArthur conveyed the impression that his offensive was proceeding more smoothly than was actually the case. To be sure, there was nothing unusual about generals deceiving the public as to their problems, but failing to keep the JCS fully informed was an inexcusable military sin.

MacArthur's supporters frequently point to New Guinea as the origin of the general's brilliant leapfrog strategy. Here the SWPA first used in a big way its superior amphibious mobility to bypass inert Japanese strongpoints, thus avoiding heavy American casualties and rendering useless tens of thousands of isolated Japanese soldiers. Writing in his memoirs years after the war MacArthur explained his strategy toward these Japanese positions in New Guinea and elsewhere: "I did not intend to take them—I intended to envelop them, incapacitate them, apply the 'hit 'em where they ain't—let 'em die on the vine' philosophy. . . . There would be no need for storming the mass of islands held by the enemy. . . . I accordingly applied my major efforts to the seizure of areas which were suitable for airfields and base development, but which were only lightly defended by the enemy."[31] Indeed, during the New Guinea campaign things often worked out just as MacArthur remembered. For instance, the SWPA's Hollandia operation in April 1944 cut off some fifty-five thousand Japanese soldiers, and subsequent unopposed landings at Sansapor-Mar and Morotai also isolated large numbers of the enemy at Manokwari and Halmahera. Unfortunately there were also several occasions during the New Guinea campaign when the SWPA inadvertently attacked thousands of entrenched Japanese and suffered relatively heavy casualties. Sometimes such attacks were necessary to maintain MacArthur's demanding timetable. For example, the Americans invaded Biak because it possessed the only airfields around that were long enough to accommodate the bombers SWPA needed to support operations further west. MacArthur could have ordered the SWPA to build new airfields from scratch in an undefended area but that would have taken time that the general could not afford to spend. Despite the skill of American aviation engineers, airfield construction along the boggy New Guinea coastline was a difficult proposition, especially since the Japanese had already built on and fortified the good sites. MacArthur often, but not always, preferred to gamble that he could occupy enemy airstrips quickly. As events turned out, the Biak operation in particular cost more time and blood than he had anticipated.

On other occasions the SWPA attacked well-defended Japanese positions because MacArthur's headquarters misread available intelligence or because of poor command decisions in response to MacArthur's urgent desire for speed. This occurred not only along the Driniumor River but also at Wakde-Sarmi in May and June 1944. In the latter operation Krueger, on the basis of somewhat ambiguous intelligence reports, ordered American troops to pry the Japanese out of their positions in and around well-defended Lone Tree Hill so as to protect the American beachhead at Toem. Here, as at the Driniumor, Krueger responded to MacArthur's desire for speed by ordering a costly attack rather than following a safer but more time-consuming defensive strategy which, while leading to fewer American casualties, would have tied down significant SWPA resources needed to maintain the westward advance across New Guinea. In the end it took three weeks, two big assaults, and a good many wounds all around for the SWPA to seize Lone Tree Hill and its companions.

Throughout the New Guinea campaign MacArthur scattered his forces up and down the big island's long coastline, and it was not uncommon for the SWPA to wage several operations at once. In June 1944, for instance, American troops were simultaneously engaged at Biak, Wakde-Sarmi, and Driniumor River. Such dispersion was to some extent necessary due to New Guinea's horrendously difficult terrain and primitive facilities that made it impossible to move and supply troops long distances overland, but it was also the result of MacArthur's insistence on speed. He understood that mopping up took time and he was unwilling to wait to eradicate all Japanese opposition before pushing ahead to the next operation. Such a strategy, however, rendered the SWPA vulnerable to any Japanese counterthrust that might defeat the Americans in detail. To be sure, the Japanese on New Guinea had surrendered the strategic initiative but there was always the possibility of enemy attacks from outside of the theater.

This MacArthur discovered in June 1944 when the Japanese navy intervened in the SWPA in a major way to try to save the Japanese garrison on Biak in Operation Kon. Japanese naval officers feared that an American-held Biak could threaten their southern flank in their planned upcoming climactic battle with the American fleet in the Marianas, so they hoped to disrupt the SWPA's offensive there long enough to keep the island in Japanese hands until after the big battle they foresaw. Fortunately for the Americans the Japanese attack was haphazard and uncoordinated, and the SWPA was able to parry the thrust until Nimitz's mid-June assault on the Marianas convinced the Japanese navy to recall its forces in preparation for the disastrous Battle of the Philippine Sea. Even so it was a close call, especially after the Japanese damaged or destroyed a majority of the planes the SWPA had deployed on Wakde island, which at the time was the nexus of American air power in the area. The SWPA's near escape was due as much to Japanese confusion as to anything else, although dogged fighting by American and Australian airmen and sailors certainly played a part. To be sure, Kon could not have stopped MacArthur's campaign altogether but it might have crippled and delayed the New Guinea offensive long enough to cost the general his chance to reach the China-Formosa-Luzon region ahead of or at the same time as the navy. Here again, however, MacArthur was willing to run that risk in order to invade the Philippines.

In the larger sense, however, the SWPA's vulnerability to a sudden Japanese offensive such as Kon was the direct result of the JCS's dual-drive offensive which had deprived MacArthur of significant naval resources and had presented the Japanese with the opportunity to defeat the Americans in detail. Although American military doctrine emphasized concentration of force, the JCS was willing to sacrifice this tenet in order to preserve interservice harmony by permitting two big Pacific offenses. The joint chiefs were ultimately responsible for the grand strategy that gave the Japanese their opportunity in Kon, but MacArthur's stubbornness contributed to the formation of the dual-drive offensive that diluted the American counteroffensive across the Pacific in the first place. Moreover, MacArthur's insistence on speed made his SWPA forces even more vulnerable to Japanese counterattack than a more cautious offensive that reflected the JCS's conception of the campaign would have.

The New Guinea campaign was without a doubt one of MacArthur's most successful. In the space of six short months he streaked eighteen hundred miles across the big island, surrounded and bypassed tens of thousands of enemy soldiers, and did so with relatively few Allied casualties. In addition, he was able to use his victory to successfully lobby the JCS for a Philippines liberation campaign that began at Leyte in October 1944 and culminated in the Luzon invasion the following January. Throughout the offensive he kept his eyes on the ultimate prize and skillfully used the tools available to him to get there. He made some mistakes, but American technological, materiel, and logistic superiority more than compensated for them—that time.

MacArthur's view of his New Guinea campaign differed from that of the JCS. The joint chiefs saw the offensive as a diversion designed to pin down Japanese soldiers who might otherwise be deployed against the navy in the central Pacific. From this perspective some of MacArthur's actions were foolhardy and superfluous. A more cautious campaign would have just as easily fulfilled the JCS's agenda, and done so without endangering so many American lives in what was after all supposed to be a sideshow theater. To be sure, MacArthur was in the end able to accomplish the JCS's goals with few casualties and in record time, but he did so at great and perhaps unnecessary risk.

From MacArthur's perspective, on the other hand, waging the New Guinea campaign his way was justified and proper. He believed that the best way to win the Pacific War was via a Philippines liberation campaign not a POA-led offensive through the central Pacific to Formosa, and his strategy was geared toward that end. His strategic conceptions did not match his superiors' when the campaign began, but the joint chiefs' March 12 directive left him with enough wiggle room to carry out his agenda in New Guinea without explicitly disobeying orders, thanks in no small part to the pressure he exerted on them to modify their plans. Once he reached the China-Formosa-Luzon region MacArthur convinced the JCS that an invasion of the Philippines was a good idea, especially since the navy lacked the logistical support to mount an assault on Formosa anytime soon. MacArthur, on the other hand, was able to begin his attack on the archipelago in October 1944, thus preventing the Pacific War from stalling. Seen in this light MacArthur's conception of the New Guinea campaign was the correct one, despite the risks.

Notes

1. Edward Coffman and Paul H. Hass, eds., "With MacArthur in the Pacific: A Memoir by Philip F. La Follette," *Wisconsin Magazine of History* 64(2) (1980–81): 94.
2. Lt. Col. Gerald Wilkinson, as quoted in Michael Schaller, *Douglas MacArthur: The Far Eastern General* (New York: Oxford University Press, 1989), p. 74.
3. CCS 417/2, "Over-all Plan for the Defeat of Japan," December 23, 1943, *Records of the Joint Chiefs of Staff* (Frederick MD: University Publications of American, 1980–81) (hereafter cited as RJCS), pp. 1–2.
4. William Ritchie to George C. Marshall, September 22, 1943, Correspondence with War Department, MacArthur Memorial Archives, Norfolk VA (hereafter cited as MMA), RG 4, box 16, folder 4.

5. MacArthur to Marshall, October 31, 1943, Correspondence with War Department, MMA, RG 4, box 16, folder 4.

6. See, for instance, Daniel E. Barbey, *MacArthur's Amphibious Navy: Seventh Amphibious Force Operations, 1943–1945* (Annapolis: United States Naval Institute, 1969), p. 22; Robert L. Eichelberger, "MacArthur's Desire to Return to the Philippines, Dictations," Robert Eichelberger Research Collection at Duke University, Durham NC, box 73, pp. 352–54; and Ernest J. King and Walter Muir Whitehill, *Fleet Admiral King: A Naval Record* (New York: Norton, 1952), p. 538.

7. Barbey, *MacArthur's Amphibious Navy*, p. 183; Ritchie interview, June 24, 1971, from 1971 Interviews, James Collection, MMA, RG 49, box 4, p. 5; Interview with Robert G. Wood, *Army Senior Officer Oral Histories* (Frederick MD: University Publications of America, 1989), tape 30, p. 20.

8. Interview with Thomas H. Handy, September 8, 1971, from 1971 Interviews, James Collection, MMA, RG 49, box 3, pp. 25–26.

9. Douglas MacArthur, *A Soldier Speaks Out: Public Papers and Speeches of General of the Army Douglas MacArthur* (New York: Praeger, 1965), pp. 129–30.

10. Coffman and Hass, "With MacArthur in the Pacific," p. 93.

11. E. B. Potter, *Nimitz* (Annapolis: Naval Institute Press, 1966), pp. 282–83.

12. MacArthur to Richard Sutherland, February 26, 1944, radio communications (personal), Sutherland Papers, MMA, RG 30, box 7, folder 6, p. 4.

13. See Kent Roberts Greenfield, *American Strategy in World War II: A Reconsideration* (Baltimore: Johns Hopkins Press, 1963), pp. 49–79; Forrest C. Pogue, *George C. Marshall: Ordeal and Hope, 1939–1942* (New York: Viking Press, 1966), pp. 329–30; and H. H. Arnold, *Global Mission* (New York: Harper, 1949), pp. 323, 355–56.

14. JCS 713/4, "Future Operations in the Pacific," March 12, 1944, RJCS, p. 36.

15. "Future Operations in the Pacific," pp. 36–37.

16. "Future Operations in the Pacific," p. 37.

17. MacArthur to Marshall, October 31, 1943, Correspondence with the War Department, MMA, RG 4, box 16, folder 4.

18. Courtney Whitney, *MacArthur: His Rendezvous with History* (New York: Knopf, 1964), p. 107.

19. Roger O. Egeberg, *The General: MacArthur and the Man He Called Doc* (New York: Hippocrene Books, 1983), p. 35.

20. Egeberg, *The General*, p. 37.

21. See MacArthur to Marshall, September 18, 1943, Correspondence with the War Department, MMA, RG 4, box 16, folder 4.

22. Egeberg, *The General*, p. 44.

23. Coffman and Hass, "With MacArthur in the Pacific," pp. 93–94.

24. Thomas Kinkaid, *The Reminiscences of Thomas Cassin Kinkaid* (New York: Columbia University, Oral History Research Office, 1961), p. 334.

25. Barbey, *MacArthur's Amphibious Navy*, pp. 156–57.
26. Walter Krueger, *From Down Under to Nippon* (Washington DC: Combat Forces Press, 1953), pp. 71–72.
27. Kinkaid, *Reminiscences of Kinkaid*, pp. 358–59.
28. Douglas MacArthur, *Reminiscences* (New York: McGraw-Hill, 1964), pp. 155–56.
29. "GHQ Communiqué #780," May 28, 1944, SWPA press releases, MMA, RG 3, box 3.
30. Marshall to MacArthur, June 9, 1944, Official Correspondence, MMA, RG 3, box 1.
31. MacArthur, *Reminiscences*, p. 169.

MacArthur's Lapses from an Envelopment Strategy in 1945

D. Clayton James

D. Clayton James, author of the widely acclaimed three-volume biography of MacArthur, raises questions about the general's strategic moves in the Philippines in 1945 as well as his relationship with the Joint Chiefs of Staff. James views MacArthur's conduct as a forecast of the controversies that would rage during the Korean War.

The strategy which General of the Army Douglas MacArthur adopted in 1945 in the southwest Pacific campaign has received scant attention from historians. Symbolic of this neglect is the omission in the American Army's series on the Pacific conflict of a sequel to Louis Morton's *Strategy and Command: The First Two Years*, whose coverage ends in late 1943. The treatment of MacArthur's late-war strategy in most college-level textbooks on recent American or military history ranges from no mention whatsoever to propagation of a host of myths. This essay challenges three of those myths still widely believed: (1) That after the Joint Chiefs of Staff finally authorized an invasion of Luzon, the directive was subsequently implemented by MacArthur in the manner envisioned by his superiors; (2) that having gained credit, often justifiable, for brilliant moves bypassing strong Japanese forces, MacArthur continued to the war's end his policy of bypassing and thus neutralizing the enemy forces in his theater's rear areas, rather than attacking them; and (3)that during the final weeks preceding Japan's capitulation, the next major invasion that MacArthur had in mind was Operation Olympic, the landing on Japan's southernmost island, Kyushu, which was set for November 1945.[1]

Although MacArthur had proclaimed upon arriving in Australia in March 1942 that he would return to liberate the Philippines, the Joint Chiefs had not given much thought then to a long-range plan to defeat Japan, much less to a counteroffensive led by him. Indeed, the development of a plan that would most directly and rapidly bring about Japan's surrender did not become a seriously debated issue until well into 1943 when the Allied buildup in the Pacific warranted such consideration. The Joint Chiefs were flexible in their thinking at first and weighed a wide assortment of strategic alternatives for dealing with Japan. In no small measure because of pressures from MacArthur and Fleet Admiral Ernest J. King to give priority to the axis of advance each favored—respectively, the New Guinea-Philippines axis from the south and the central Pacific route from the east—the Joint Chiefs gradually narrowed down the alternatives to the seizure of either Luzon or Formosa as prerequisite to an invasion of Japan.

King had long objected to continuing a major offensive via the southwest Pacific axis, and by late spring 1944 Generals George C. Marshall and Henry H. Arnold were also increasingly critical of the liabilities of an attack on Luzon. Marshall felt that MacArthur's Luzon plan would be "the slow way" and "would take a very much longer time than to make the cut across" from the Marianas to Formosa.[2] MacArthur argued that the Formosa plan was militarily "unsound" whereas political, humanitarian, and strategic considerations "demand the reoccupation of the Philippines."[3] Through studies extending over a year and a half the Joint Chiefs and their committees had been steadfastly concerned with determining which plan would be the most logistically feasible, the most economical in manpower and materiel losses, and the most strategically decisive in producing the fall of Japan. They arrived at the decision in favor of MacArthur's proposal with reluctance and trepidation. By later September 1944, Admirals King, Chester W. Nimitz, and their planners admitted that the Formosa invasion was not practical in the near future due to insurmountable logistical difficulties. On 3 October the Joint Chiefs issued a directive authorizing the Luzon operation.

At the Yalta Conference in February 1945, while MacArthur's armies were fighting on Leyte and Luzon, the Joint Chiefs assured their British counterparts that they had no intention of committing United States forces to reconquer the rest of the Philippines (such as Mindanao, Panay, Negros, Palawan, Bohol, and Cebu) and the Netherlands East Indies. For several months, however, MacArthur had been working on his Victor Plan for the seizure of the remainder of the Philippines and his Oboe Plan for the invasion of the East Indies rather than leave the two large island groupings to wilt on the vine. In fact, he had decided as early as September 1944 to send Lieutenant General Robert L. Eichelberger's

Eighth Army to seize the rest of the Philippines as soon as General Walter Krueger's Sixth Army was securely entrenched on Luzon. A few weeks after the Lingayen beachhead on Luzon was established in January 1945, and while the Sixth Army was suffering severe losses in battles for Manila and other strong points on Luzon, MacArthur unleashed the Eighth Army in the reconquest of the Philippines to the south. By the time the Joint Chiefs changed their minds and issued a directive in April authorizing operations in the Philippines below Luzon, MacArthur's forces already had undertaken eight of the eleven major amphibious operations which proved necessary to secure that territory. Astoundingly, the Joint Chiefs resigned themselves to MacArthur's fait accompli and raised no objections to the eight operations conducted prior to their directive. Pondering the "mystery how and whence... MacArthur derived his authority to use United States forces to liberate one Philippine island after another" at a time when he "had no specific directive for anything subsequent to Luzon," Rear Admiral Samuel Eliot Morison, the distinguished naval historian, concludes that "the JCS simply permitted MacArthur to do as he pleased, up to a point."[4]

A variety of factors underlay MacArthur's motivation in attacking the previously bypassed Philippine islands. The Philippine political faction of Manuel Roxas, which had MacArthur's backing, was eager to have the areas south of Luzon liberated before the Philippine Congress convened in June, because political sentiments there were predominantly against President Sergio Osmeña. As it turned out, the freed southern congressmen helped the Roxas faction to attain majorities in the Philippine Senate and House. Also, MacArthur felt a strong duty to free the entire archipelago lest the bypassed enemy troops turn with vengeance upon hapless American prisoners and Filipinos, as had occurred in the Palawan massacre of December 1944.[5] Moreover, use of the Eighth Army, Seventh Fleet, and Thirteenth Air Force in these operations blocked their transfer by the Joint Chiefs to Nimitz's theater in the central Pacific, a possibility had they remained idle for long. In addition, MacArthur wanted the central and southern Philippines in order to establish air bases to cover his projected Borneo operations and to train and stage the expected huge influx of units from Europe for the invasion of Japan.

MacArthur's dispatch of the Eighth Army to the Japanese-held Philippine islands south of Luzon and his transfer there of three Sixth Army divisions had a crippling impact on Luzon operations. Especially in the hard-fought battles at Wawa Dam, Villa Verde Trail, and Balete

Pass, the lack of adequate troops and firepower was sorely felt by the Sixty Army. Operating against perhaps the ablest Japanese ground commander, General Yamashita, and the largest enemy army that American soldiers met during the Pacific war, the Sixth Army found itself locked in a costly, drawn-out, and frustrating campaign on Luzon, with Yamashita cornered but still fighting with over 50,000 troops when the war ended. MacArthur would have been wiser to have used the Eighth Army primarily to expedite the reconquest of Luzon, for few bases set up in the central and southern islands proved of value later and the beleaguered enemy garrisons south of Luzon were so isolated that they posed no threat to MacArthur's lines of communication or his future moves. The United States Army's official history states frankly that, for the most part, the southern campaigns "had no strategic importance" but "were designed for the purpose of liberating Filipinos, reestablishing lawful government, and destroying Japanese forces."[6] This was fortunately not general knowledge to the hard-pressed men of the Sixth Army during their bloody campaign on Luzon.

Continuing in the spring of 1945 to send his forces on tangents south of Luzon, MacArthur disregarded advice from Washington planners and the Australian high command in embarking on an invasion of Borneo. In early 1944 the Joint Chiefs had ordered staff studies on a possible seizure of petroleum-rich Borneo, but the idea was dropped because the undertaking would have drained MacArthur's resources, so powerful was the enemy's estimated strength in the Greater Sundas. Yet MacArthur offered a plan to the Joint Chiefs in February 1945 for an invasion of North Borneo by the Australian I Corps. He maintained that "90 days after the beginning of such an expedition it would be possible to begin operations for the production of crude oil,"[7] but the Army-Navy Petroleum Board in Washington countered that it would take a year or more. Nevertheless, at Yalta later that month the Combined Chiefs authorized him to invade "British Borneo," that is, Sarawak, Brunei, and North Borneo, if an invasion of Japan did not become possible before the end of 1945. Prime Minister John Curtin and General Thomas Blamey of Australia protested his proposed use of their nation's forces in Borneo, criticizing mainly the command arrangement and strategic wisdom of the plan. MacArthur, however, finally won them to a grudging acceptance of his scheme.

In March he came forth with his six-phase Oboe Plan, calling for the invasions, in order, of Dutch Borneo, Java, the rest of the Netherlands East Indies, and finally British Borneo. Interestingly, though his superiors had told him to go ahead with contingency plans for only an attack on British Borneo, his Oboe Plan relegated it to last among the East Indies operations he intended to stage. Without much enthusiasm for the idea, the Joints Chiefs in April approved a revised version of Oboe that included only landings at Tarakan (May), Brunei Bay (June), and Balikpapan (July). These operations along the eastern and western coasts of Borneo were successfully executed, with MacArthur providing strong American air, naval, and logistical support for the Australian I Corps.

While the American Eighth Army and the Australian I Corps were following MacArthur's southward tangents in 1945, the Australian First Army was committed to annihilating the bypassed enemy forces in Northeast New Guinea, Bougainville, and New Britain. MacArthur had informed Blamey in July 1944 that soon his First Army was to "assume the responsibility for the continued neutralization of the enemy in Australian and British territory and mandates in the [Southwest Pacific Area]."[8] Upon the arrival of the Australians that autumn, six American divisions were released to join the operations in the Philippines. Until March 1945 the First Army generally confined its role to passively guarding perimeters around the remaining enemy units in the theater's rear areas. But at a meeting with MacArthur in Manila that month, Blamey learned of the plans for the Eighth Army in the Philippines south of Luzon, which the Australian commander concluded were based on "political rather than military grounds." Forthwith Blamey began to press for, and obtained, authorization for his First Army to go on the offensive. He shrewdly argued his case, citing the Eighth Army's action as precedent: "Just as it is necessary to destroy the Japanese in the Philippines, so it is necessary that we should destroy the enemy in Australian territories where the conditions are favourable for such action and so liberate the natives from Japanese domination."[9]

Australian casualties from combat and diseases were alarmingly heavy as Blamey's troops attacked the trapped enemy forces in the dense jungles of New Guinea, Bougainville, and New Britain during the ensuing months. Why MacArthur, who had taken such pride in the lives saved earlier by bypassing these Japanese units, reversed himself and allowed Blamey to nullify the strategic value of the previous envelopments is not fully known, but probably was related to pressure on him from the Australian Government and public to either use the First Army in combat or send it home. The Australian Army's official chronicle is blunt in judging MacArthur's "complex of decisions, some contradictory and some illogical," in 1945 which resulted in the Australian I Corps, "well equipped and with powerful air and naval support, . . . fighting battles of doubtful value in Borneo," while units of the First Army in the regions to the east "were fighting long and bitter campaigns (whose value was doubted) in which they were short of air and naval support, and suffered . . . a poverty of ships and landing craft."[10]

The generous assistance that MacArthur provided the Australians in Borneo was directly related to his scheme to develop bases there for an invasion of Java—a plan that he had never dismissed despite its rejection in the first Oboe Plan he had presented to the Joint Chiefs. General Eichelberger, Eighth Army commander, said that MacArthur confided to him in late spring that "if the Navy idea of piddling around for a long time before doing anything against the Japanese homeland carries through, he still wants me to go into Java rather than have my troops sit around and stagnate."[11] Based on the evidence of similar comments in interviews with other officers close to MacArthur, together with the still tentative and confused preparations for Operation Olympic (Kyushu invasion) by early August as well as MacArthur's previous record of success in persuading or ignoring the Joint Chiefs, it is highly probable that he would have sent the Eighth Army into Java about September. In an understatement the Australian official history says, "In retrospect the wisdom of embarking upon this third thrust—westward against Japanese forces isolated in the Indies—seems doubtful."[12] It was fortunate for the lives of the Allied troops and for MacArthur's reputation that the war ended before he got his way on the Java plan, for that attack could have produced not only a tragic bloodbath in Java but also a logistical paralysis for the impending invasion of Kyushu.

If before the zenith of the Luzon-versus-Formosa debate in 1944 the Joint Chiefs had been able to foresee the tangential moves south of Luzon that MacArthur would launch, they surely would have terminated his offensive after the conquest of Netherlands New Guinea. It is regrettable that MacArthur's strategy in 1945 has gotten little scholarly notice, but it is tragic that the decisionmakers in the White House and Pentagon contemplating the North Korean invasion of the South, in June 1950, did not recall his behavior pattern of five years before. Perhaps some of them had begun to notice by April 1951 that there were similarities between MacArthur's strategic concepts and his attitude toward his superiors during the last stages of the Pacific war and during the first nine months of the Korean conflict.

Notes

1. This essay is based mainly upon a synthesis of data in D. Clayton James, *The Years of MacArthur*, Vol. II, *1941–1945* (Boston: Houghton Mifflin, 1975), especially chaps. 9, 12, 13, 16, and 17. The footnotes for the relevant passages in these chapters, in turn, cite the primary and secondary materials used in the research. Hereafter in the notes of this essay sources will be cited only when actually quoted.
2. Henry L. Stimson, Diary, 22 June 1944, Yale University Library, New Haven CT.
3. Douglas MacArthur to George C. Marshall, 18 June 1944. Records of War Department Operations Division Executive File, Record Group 165, National Archives, Washington DC.
4. Samuel E. Morison, *History of United States Naval Operations in World War II*, Vol XIII, *The Liberation of the Philippines: Luzon, Mindanao, and Visaya, 1944–1945* (Boston: Little, Brown, 1959), p. 214.
5. On Palawan, a Philippine island southwest of Luzon, Japanese guards at a prisoner of war camp panicked on 14 December 1944 when news came that MacArthur's forces were approaching (Mindoro was invaded 15 December). The guards poured gasoline on 149 American prisoners, set them afire, and machine-gunned the survivors (miraculously, nine managed to escape).
6. Robert R. Smith, *Triumph in the Philippines*, one of several works constituting *United States Army in World War II: The War in the Pacific*, volume 2 of the official history published by the Office of the Chief of Military History (Washington: Department of the Army, 1963), pp. 584–85.
7. MacArthur to Marshall, 5 February 1945, Operations Division, Executive File.
8. MacArthur to Thomas Blamey, 12 July 1944, Records of General Headquarters, Southwest Pacific Area, Record Group 3, MacArthur Memorial Bureau of Archives, Norfolk VA.
9. Blamey, Appreciation [Report] on Operations of the AMF [Australian Military Forces] in New Guinea, New Britain, and the Solomon Islands, 18 May 1945, quoted in Gavin Long, *The Final Campaigns. Australia in the War of 1939–1945*, Series I (Canberra: Australian War Memorial, 1963), p. 609.
10. Long, p. 547.
11. Robert L. Eichelberger to "Miss Em" [his wife], 28 April 1945, Robert L. Eichelberger Papers, Duke University Library, Durham NC.
12. Long, p. 547.

Military Intelligence and MacArthur, 1941–1951

A Reappraisal

Edward J. Drea

In an essay prepared for this volume the leading authority on ULTRA *intelligence in the campaigns of the Southwest Pacific, Edward Drea, assesses MacArthur's use of military intelligence in both World War II and Korea.*

Maj. Gen. Charles A. Willoughby's account of General Douglas Mac-Arthur's campaigns, *MacArthur 1941–1951*, was both more and less revealing than the author intended. An internal U.S. Army review cited Willoughby's book for a minimum of ten major security breaches, most of them having to do with his accounts of intelligence operations during MacArthur's command.[1] As MacArthur's G-2 (intelligence) officer throughout the war against Japan (1941–1945) as well as during the Korean War (1950–1951), as editor in chief of the multivolume *Intelligence Series*, and as the staff officer in charge of compiling MacArthur's four-volume historical report (1946–1950), Willoughby was certainly in a position to link intelligence to operations.

As history, however, Willoughby's published assessment of MacArthur was self-serving and uncritical to the point of embarrassment. Described by one fellow officer as having "the best hindsight of any intelligence officer in the army," Willoughby's character flaws marred the reliability of his version of Douglas MacArthur and diminished the value of the G-2's revelations.[2] Yet, for all his bombast Charles Willoughby was the pivotal staff officer from whose desk flowed much of the intelligence that reached MacArthur. Without access to Willoughby's supporting documentation it was impossible to evaluate the G-2's assertions and therefore to assess MacArthur's generalship. To a degree that condition persists to this day, although previously classified documents from the World War II and Korean War eras offer a better yardstick by which to measure G-2's record and uncover a more accurate, if less flattering, understanding of Douglas MacArthur's use of military intelligence from 1941 to 1951.

When Douglas MacArthur returned to active duty to command the newly established United States Army Forces in the Far East (USAFFE), military intelligence was not among his top priorities. The general had an army to organize, train, and equip more or less from scratch. Brimming with his usual self-confidence, he projected unjustified optimism about his forces (especially his Filipino troops who comprised the great bulk of his army) and dismissed his potential Japanese opponents as third-rate, exhausted by a debilitating four-year struggle in China.[3] His well-practiced strategic eye correctly estimated that any Japanese invasion would come along the shores of Lingayen Gulf in northwestern Luzon and push down the natural invasion corridor leading to Manila. Willoughby forecast the enemy assault along those beaches would come December 28; the Japanese army landed six days earlier.[4] Even had the G-2 predicted the exact hour of the Japanese invasion there was little that MacArthur could have done to counter it.

Before the outbreak of war with the Japanese empire MacArthur had already exhibited the traits that stamped his imprint on command intelligence over the next decade. A decorated war hero and past army chief of staff, MacArthur's public persona exuded a patrician aloofness and surety while in private he believed that cliques in Washington plotted his downfall.[5] Based on a bedrock of a half-century of military experience, his personality conditioned him to trust his own sweeping strategic assessments and commander's instinct more than any intelligence report placed before him. The general, for instance, doubted that Japan would declare war on the western powers before the spring of 1942, and at a late-November 1941 council over Washington's "war warnings" he seemed "extremely optimistic" about the course of events.[6] Still, MacArthur was a professional soldier and did take expected precautions, ordering field commanders on December 3 to hold the landing beaches at all costs and three days later putting a full alert into effect throughout the islands.[7] In the days counting down to Pearl Harbor American pilot sightings and U.S. Army radar trackings of large flights of Nipponese aircraft fifty to seventy-five miles off northern Luzon and a Japanese overflight of the U.S. air base at Clark Field on Luzon disturbed him enough to issue orders on December 5 to shoot down the next intruder sighted.[8]

Unlike the American commanders at Pearl Harbor in the Hawaiian

Islands, MacArthur received MAGIC—decrypted Japanese foreign ministry cables via the U.S. Navy intercept and decryption center located on Corregidor.[9] Only MacArthur and his chief of staff, then Brig. Gen. Richard K. Sutherland, were privy to MAGIC, whose content, it must be remembered, was diplomatic, not military, in nature. MAGIC intelligence never arrived on his desk in a timely fashion because inflexible administrative security and delivery procedures created a three-day delay between the moment intercept operators plucked a foreign ministry message from the airwaves and the time its decrypted translation arrived at MacArthur's desk. In most cases the lag hardly mattered, but occasions sometimes arose when perishable intelligence of potential value was held prisoner by regulations. Indeed, a decrypted Japanese message breaking off negotiations with the United States reached Sutherland five hours after Manila radio broadcast news of the Japanese attack on Pearl Harbor. Even assuming MacArthur received that intercept, or that he paid great attention to MAGIC intelligence sources in general, there is no reason to believe he could divine any better than the civilian and military leaders in Washington and Hawaii exactly when Japan might choose to strike against the Philippines.[10]

More damning was MacArthur's tactical failure to react to the news of Pearl Harbor by at least dispersing his warplanes or ordering them to attack the enemy. Earlier that morning (December 8 in the Philippines) American fighter aircraft were scrambled to challenge a formation of intruders tracked on radar. B-17 heavy bombers without their bomb loads were also ordered aloft to escape possible destruction on the ground. Failing to find the enemy the planes returned to base where by late morning the B-17s were being loaded with bombs and refueled in anticipation of an attack against Formosa. Radar operators and lookout posts along the northwest coast then reported approaching enemy bombers and transmitted an air raid warning to Clark Field. For reasons unclear to this day the message never got through.[11] Nine hours after the attack on the U.S. Pacific fleet at anchor in Hawaii these same planes were still lining Clark Field, refueling and awaiting orders when Japanese naval land-based bombers escorted by zero fighters roared in from the northwest. The disaster that overtook Clark Field was duplicated shortly afterward at Iba Field, forty miles to the west, as Japanese bombers and fighters destroyed the base and its P-40 aircraft that had just landed after a combat patrol. Japanese airmen destroyed eighteen of MacArthur's thirty-five precious B-17s and fifty of his seventy-two P-40 fighters, wiping out his air cover in a single afternoon. It was a lesson about air power that MacArthur took to heart. Much blame but no satisfactory answer has emerged about this disaster, but as the commander MacArthur must shoulder the responsibility for leaving his air force grounded and vulnerable to attack.

Although the navy's codebreaking unit continued to attack Japan's porous diplomatic code, after December 8 MacArthur needed tactical or combat intelligence. Much of it arrived in a time-honored manner: stripped from dead Japanese soldiers or from interrogations of live prisoners of war. But more modern technology was appearing. The U.S. Army intercept station at Fort Mills, Philippines, had monitored Japanese army radio traffic, but since early 1941 Washington had ordered the station staff to work almost exclusively against Japanese diplomatic cipher systems. On Christmas Eve the unit was disbanded. Its men and equipment moved to Corregidor where they intercepted and analyzed Japanese army radio traffic, monitored Imperial navy and army air force circuits for early warning purposes, and conducted basic cryptanalysis. Most of the detachment (eleven men) were later evacuated to Australia where the unit became the nucleus for a new cryptanalytic center.[12] A major intelligence find—the Japanese army's air-ground codebook—was recovered from the wreckage of a Japanese bomber. Loose Japanese radio discipline—pilots often broadcast in plain language—together with possession of the code book and their own radar plots enabled MacArthur's command to receive advance warning of approaching Japanese air raids. It was only a beginning, but the rudimentary early warning system showed the capabilities of tactical intelligence.

In another controversial move MacArthur opted to abandon War Plan ORANGE. Instead of withdrawing to defend the vital harbor at Manila according to the prewar plans, he decided to meet the enemy on the beaches. The order was based less on an intelligence appreciation than on MacArthur's strategic understanding of the importance of the Philippines to Pacific strategy and its value to the United States in case of war with Japan.[13] This operational decision overextended his ill-trained and ill-equipped command and exposed precious stockpiles that were prepositioned close to the beaches to support his forward-deployed forces. After the Japanese landings Willoughby vociferously supported his commander's decision not to withdraw the provisions to stock Bataan in case a withdrawal proved necessary.[14] The G-2's motivations are unknown. Although accurately characterized as a sycophant, Willoughby, as will be seen, could display independence, especially when potential setbacks loomed ahead. At this early stage of the war the less-experienced G-2's adulation of MacArthur made it natural for him to side with his commander. The result was a disaster. When the Japanese pushed back or overran Filipino and American defenders they also seized the supply dumps. MacArthur's raw forces did conduct a brilliant retreat and delaying action against a seasoned opponent, but one that culminated tragically as 80,000 troops and 26,000 Filipino refugees were herded into the harsh Bataan Peninsula where available stockages could supply but 10,000 troops for six months.

Among other reasons, Willoughby later blamed MacArthur's defeat on overwhelming enemy numbers—he claimed 191,939 Japanese versus 50,000 to 60,000 Filipinos and Americans. During the fighting, however, the USAFFE G-3 (operations) estimated the defenders were facing 120,000 enemy troops.[15] Initial Japanese forces, though, totaled 51,200, and subtracting units later transferred to the Netherlands East Indies while adding replacements and reinforcements dispatched in February and March 1942 likely totaled about half of Willoughby's exaggerated estimate.[16] This was one of the few cases throughout the Pacific War when Willoughby grossly overestimated the size of the enemy opposing Allied forces, but one of the many cases where he stubbornly clung to wartime impressions despite postwar evidence to the contrary.

Following his escape to Australia MacArthur formed General Headquarters, Southwest Pacific Area (GHQ, SWPA). Coincident with SWPA's establishment, combined Allied efforts to build an intelligence center "down under" commenced. The signals intelligence components were divided as the U.S. Navy's cryptanalysts from Corregidor formed Fleet Radio Unit, Melbourne (FRUMEL). The U.S. Army group, together with a handful of Australian and British cryptanalysts, were organized as Central Bureau. Henceforth MacArthur received naval signals intelligence from U.S. naval authorities over whom neither he nor Willoughby exercised operational control. Naval intelligence naturally focused on the radio communications of the Japanese fleet and its carrier air arm, but often detected precious information about maritime deployments of Japanese army units as well as enemy supply and reinforcement convoys.

The Central Bureau, MacArthur's personal cryptanalytic center, worked initially against the immediate threat: Japanese air power. Capitalizing on the Philippine experience and Australian cryptanalytic know-how, Central Bureau broke the Japanese land-based naval air force's air-ground code in early 1942. This feat enabled intercept sites in Papua New Guinea and northern Australia to provide early warning of Japanese air raids and important air order of battle intelligence.

The SWPA also established the Allied Intelligence Bureau (AIB) whose agents specialized in long-range reconnaissance deep behind Japanese lines. Eventually AIB supported guerrilla operations in the Philippine Islands. The anti-Japanese bands roaming the Philippines were not organized by MacArthur (who was unaware of their existence until December 1942) but rather thrived in the chaos of economic and social dislocation following the American surrender in May 1942 or appeared in reaction to harsh Japanese occupation polices. With the remarkable exception in 1944 of capturing a Japanese admiral and with him top secret plans for the Imperial navy's air campaign in the central Pacific, AIB produced tactical intelligence to support raids and guerrilla actions as well as order of battle data.

The bitter experience of Bataan exposed GHQ to the value of Japanese linguists who could exploit captured Japanese documents, interrogate prisoners of war, and monitor Japanese radio communications. The Allied Translator and Interpreter Section (ATIS) started with just two Caucasian officers, eight Japanese-American linguists, and three enlisted clerks. Indicative of its importance, by war's end it totaled approximately 3,500 billets.[17] Though appreciated at GHQ, initially field commanders had little comprehension of the intelligence potential Japanese language skills offered their headquarters. In late 1942 a Japanese-American sergeant assigned to ATIS arrived at headquarters, Thirty-second Infantry Division, in the midst of the bitter fighting at Buna, Papua New Guinea. Unsure of what to do with him, division staff officers followed a time-honored army ritual and gave him make-work: digging field latrines. On his own initiative and time permitting the sergeant translated a diary taken from a dead Japanese officer, then handed his English translation of the document (which contained a detailed description of the Buna defenses) to a surprised division staff. Once shown the tactical advantage that language skills could uncover, it was not long before Japanese-American linguists were assigned to all SWPA's U.S. armies, corps, divisions, and regimental combat teams.[18]

By the end of 1942 intelligence within the SWPA had proved its value from below—that is, developing in the combat units and percolating to general headquarters. Neither MacArthur nor Willoughby imposed a rigid administrative framework or intelligence requirements from the top. Perhaps in reaction to their experience in the Philippines, GHQ often flouted security regulations in order to act on "hot" intelligence. Other commands, especially in the U.S. Navy and War Department, often complained about SWPA's security sieve, but their criticisms did not change SWPA's modus operandi. GHQ likewise adopted a pragmatic approach to intelligence collection, showing great flexibility in allowing the tactical forces to target and exploit enemy security lapses. This was true of radio intercept work and, as assets became available, more sophisticated aerial reconnaissance programs. Success was consolidated, expanded, and generally improved upon at GHQ. The Allied Geographical Section prepared thousands upon thousands of sophisticated terrain studies, maps, charts, and booklets in support of SWPA operations. The Far Eastern Liaison Office steadily chipped away at Japanese morale through an innovative, imaginative, and persuasive propaganda campaign.[19] Issues of control of intelligence assets, especially of AIB and the Central Bureau, became sources of increasing friction between GHQ, Washington, and Allied governments, whose mutual animosity endured throughout the war and beyond. MacArthur, for example, excluded the Office of Strategic Services (OSS) from operating in his theater and similarly deflected numerous attempts from the War Department to consolidate signals intelligence functions under Washington's centralized control.[20]

When it all started in April 1942, however, the intelligence assets at Douglas MacArthur's disposal were few: a newly organized cryptanalytic center at Melbourne, a tiny translation section, haphazard aerial reconnaissance, sporadic traffic analysis of enemy radio communications, the odd prisoner of war interrogation, and, surely at that time his best internal source, the stay-behind Australian planters or reserve officers popularly known as coast watchers. Outside his headquarters FRUMEL provided the most reliable intelligence, especially after U.S. Navy cryptanalysts resumed reading various Japanese naval ciphers and codes sometime during the early spring of 1942. U.S. Navy intelligence accurately forecast the Imperial navy's seaborne attempt to invade Port Moresby, Papua New Guinea, scheduled for early May 1942. Willoughby read the same raw data and handed MacArthur an entirely different appreciation—namely, the Japanese fleet would strike directly at the northeastern Australian coastline or at New Caledonia in an effort to isolate Australia from Hawaii. Shortly afterward the G-2 reversed himself to predict a one-division amphibious assault against the Papuan port. His oscillating performance marked the beginning of the sine curve signature that characterized many of his important intelligence appreciations for the next decade. One of the greatest mysteries of Douglas MacArthur is why he tolerated, and later grew to depend on, Willoughby's tergiversation. A possible explanation may reside in the SWPA chief's concept of the role of military intelligence in operational planning.

For example, decrypted naval communications later revealed Japanese intentions to attack Port Moresby overland across the rugged Owen Stanley Range. MacArthur simply refused to believe the intelligence meant anything more than a minor raiding party.[21] Conventional military wisdom, after all, said large units could not operate in such terrain but, as they would do throughout the war, Japanese foot soldiers defied that conventional wisdom. Despite agent, radio, and aerial evidence of major enemy landings at Buna on Papua's north coast, Willoughby continued to insist from late July until October 1942 that the Japanese target was an airfield adjacent to the coastline. Either because the G-2 underestimated Japanese strength or because the enemy was not behaving in an orthodox manner, as the invaders moved inexorably inland MacArthur complained bitterly that the withdrawing Australian troops were fleeing in the face of inferior enemy numbers. In fact, the Japanese initially outnumbered the Australians two to one and by early August, after receiving fresh reinforcements, by almost four to one.[22]

Battlefield intelligence acquired by troops in contact with the Japanese- or Australian-led guerrilla bands, coupled with traffic analysis of enemy radio networks, provided basic information about the composition of the Japanese ground forces fighting their way through the Owen Stanleys. Coast watchers reported enemy convoys departing Rabaul Harbor and hugging the New Britain coast en route to Buna. The raw data was not translated into usable combat intelligence. Ambiguity, MacArthur's prejudices, and the uncertainty of warfare led GHQ to evaluate Japanese ground forces on the basis of wishful thinking not hardheaded analysis. The condition persisted throughout the Papuan campaign and accounts in part for the costly battles of attrition that finally in January 1943 reduced the Japanese stronghold at Buna. It is useful to contrast the period's lamentable performance of ground intelligence with its air intelligence complement.

Among other missions, recently established radio intercept sites in New Guinea that were manned by Australian servicemen monitored Japanese army and navy air communications. Whereas nascent radar technology provided about thirty minutes early warning of approaching hostile aircraft, intercepted radio transmissions from Japanese pilots stretched that advantage to several hours.[23] Radio intercept was a proven technology when in August 1942 then–Maj. Gen. George C. Kenney reported to GHQ to head MacArthur's Allied Air Forces and, shortly afterward, the U.S. Fifth Air Force.

Kenney was innovative, a risk taker, and a believer in technology. The intercept sites had already shown their ability to identify and track incoming Japanese air raids and were now expanding their coverage to deduce Japanese convoy movements through patterns of radio traffic. FRUMEL continued to predict accurately and regularly Japanese convoys headed for New Guinea. Kenney was a commander willing to act on the basis of intelligence revelations and one who also brought to the SWPA the determination to win—the killer instinct—so characteristic of successful wartime leaders. For all his ruthlessness he was also a student of the interplay of technology and air warfare and certainly improved the aerial reconnaissance program. He blended all the theater's intelligence sources into his plan of operations to surprise the enemy and strike when they were most vulnerable to air attack. Kenney, probably more than anyone in MacArthur's headquarters, capitalized on intelligence. He was also headstrong and, like other officers at the SWPA, hawked intelligence estimates to reinforce his own prejudice that air power alone could win wars. His convictions brought him to the edge of disaster during the preparations for the Admiralties campaign of early 1944.

During the course of the war Kenney developed a first-class tactical air force, always available to do MacArthur's bidding and, by virtue of its excellent intelligence support, seemingly able to surprise the enemy at will. MacArthur's lasting impression of air operations was less about the intelligence that undergirded Kenney's successful air strikes than of the airman's outstanding record of destruction against Japanese troop convoys, airfields, naval bases, and warplanes. Kenney sealed off MacArthur's battlefields because he preempted Japanese moves known to him in advance through signals intelligence, commonly referred to as ULTRA. MacArthur drew the lesson that air power, well led and well directed, could isolate his battlefields. He argued that case in the summer of 1945 when U.S. intelligence revealed Japanese reinforcements streaming into Kyushu and again in 1950 when pontificating on the likelihood of Chinese intervention in the Korean War.

Tactical intelligence for MacArthur's early Papuan campaigns came

from captured Japanese documents and personal diaries, prisoner interrogations, coast-watcher reports, aerial reconnaissance, guerrilla teams,
and Central Bureau–supplied signals intelligence (obtained by solving
the Japanese navy's land-based air-ground code system and analyzing the
formats but not contents of messages transmitted over Japanese military
radio networks). The U.S. Navy contributed the revelations uncovered
in deciphered Imperial navy message traffic and carrier-based air-to-
ship codes. These sources operated in concert. During the fighting at
Buna (November 1942–January 1943), for instance, captured documents
revealed the Japanese ground order of battle; prisoners disclosed tactical
dispositions; aerial reconnaissance monitored the Japanese bastion at
Rabaul for signs of naval or air reinforcements; and signals intelligence
tipped off impending Japanese resupply and reinforcement convoys as
well as impending air raids.[24] Given this awareness MacArthur finally
could seal off the Japanese garrison defending Buna by making the cost
of further enemy reinforcements prohibitive.

At the strategic level a classic use of intelligence by the SWPA to tip
the military balance in New Guinea preceded the Battle of the Bismarck
Sea fought in March 1943. Before sending the first aircraft aloft Kenney
received aerial photographs of Rabaul Harbor showing an increase in
Japanese shipping; traffic analysis data indicating a major convoy was
likely to debark at Lae on the northeast New Guinea coast; coast-watcher
reports of Japanese aircraft patrolling likely sea approaches; and naval
signals intelligence reporting the dates that a major convoy would depart
Rabaul for Lae. When a commander integrated the intelligence pieces
his staff had assembled into operational planning, the results could be
devastating for the enemy. In the Bismarck Sea, adequate intelligence
forewarning actually enabled Kenney to rehearse new low-level tactics
for the impending battle. Accurate intelligence prepared the way for
the wholesale destruction of the enemy convoy transporting an entire
Japanese division, a defeat that shifted the strategic initiative in New
Guinea to the Allies.[25]

In April 1943 Central Bureau cryptanalysts solved the Japanese army
water transport code, which handed Allied commanders advance warning of Japanese troop and resupply convoys throughout the Pacific.[26]
Allied submarines and aircraft capitalized on their secret knowledge to
intercept Japanese convoys, and in the SWPA to interdict maritime lines
of communication to isolate MacArthur's battlefields on New Guinea.
During the summer of 1943 Kenney again took advantage of intelligence,

especially data obtained by reading Japanese army air-ground codes. Allied intercept operators overheard ten of the thirteen Japanese fighter regiments deploying to the theater and identified their locations at four advance airfields in eastern New Guinea. After photo reconnaissance confirmed the airstrips were packed with Japanese warplanes, an August 1943 raid destroyed or damaged one hundred enemy aircraft, most of them on the ground. By smashing the main Japanese air bases Kenney achieved local air superiority.[27] Two weeks later, under Fifth Air Force's air umbrella, Australian infantrymen landed by sea east of the major Japanese staging base and port at Lae and U.S. paratroopers dropped west of the base the next day.

MacArthur's ground intelligence in mid-1943 remained far less precise, the major Japanese army codes still being unreadable. Nevertheless, captured documents and prisoners often revealed exact tactical details and timing of Japanese operations. Still, MacArthur's attempts mentioned above to encircle Japanese division-size formations at Lae in May 1943 and again at Saidor in January 1944 failed as the enemy escaped the envelopments to fight again. Furthermore, Willoughby's continual underestimation of Japanese ground strength, a trademark of the G-2 throughout the war, clashed with the higher totals produced by Australian staffs. Intelligence appreciation for the Finschhafen operation in September 1943 was nightmarish. Initial GHQ assessments proved woefully incorrect. Willoughby's projections immediately before the September 22 landing were off by a factor of fifteen (he estimated 350 Japanese; there were more than 5,000). Compounding this error, within three weeks Japanese reinforcements arrived at Finschhafen undetected by Allied intelligence. Willoughby insisted that the enemy was withdrawing from the area and cavalierly dismissed Australian army estimates to the contrary, ignoring the battlefield intelligence supplied by Australian infantrymen who were in the thick of the fighting.[28] Only after the Australian troops captured the Japanese army's code library at Sio, North East New Guinea, in January 1944 did ground intelligence achieve the precision and authority of its air and naval counterparts.

Central Bureau's ability to read the major Japanese army code system handed MacArthur a precious gift and he used it wisely, embracing the latest technology of warfare and altering his immediate if limited campaign plans because of the intelligence disclosures. If proof were needed of the validity of the newly available sources, operations in the Admiralties provided it. Pilots flying as low as one hundred feet above the islands reported no signs of life, leading Kenney to assert that air power had driven the enemy from the apparently deserted Admiralties. Based on ULTRA, however, Willoughby to the contrary insisted a 3,250-man garrison was defending the islands. A U.S. Sixth Army long-range reconnaissance patrol secretly put ashore in the Admiralties just before the scheduled invasion reported the islands "lousy with Japs." MacArthur still pushed ahead, perhaps reasoning that even if the Japanese were on the islands in force his air and naval advantages would cancel their numerical one. The general did hedge his bet by conducting a reconnaissance-in-force, in effect sending in enough GIS to settle the argument between his air and intelligence chiefs. In the worst case scenario he could always withdraw the ground forces (he hoped), and pound away from the air and sea at the exposed enemy. In the best case he would surprise the unprepared defenders and seize vital objectives before they could react. The landing did achieve surprise, aided by the Japanese commander who sited his defenses along the wrong beach. Still it was the type of risk-filled decision that MacArthur made confidently with little hesitation.

Willoughby's star ascended when his prebattle estimates, confirmed by a grim feature of battlefield intelligence—the body count—proved correct to within 416 of the 3,646 Japanese troops in the Admiralties.[29] The mercurial G-2 then reached his zenith by recommending the SWPA cancel a planned invasion of Hansa Bay in favor of leapfrogging more than four hundred miles up the coast to the enemy's major supply base at Hollandia, Netherlands New Guinea. The bold concept would carry MacArthur far behind the Japanese main combat units holding fast near the shoulders of Hansa Bay in eastern New Guinea and accelerate his timetable to return to the Philippines. Presenting newly available ULTRA evidence of Japanese dispositions to the joint chiefs in Washington DC, MacArthur's chief of staff was able to win their support for the dramatically revised campaign. As deciphered enemy messages revealed the operational dispositions of the Japanese Eighteenth Army, an attack on weakly defended Hollandia was a bold but carefully calculated risk. With fresh intelligence of Japanese plans pouring into GHQ, Kenney's airmen isolated the battlefield by sinking Japanese resupply convoys. Next, alerted by intelligence of another major Japanese aerial reinforcement in progress, the Fifth Air Force annihilated the Japanese air threat by destroying the main air bases near Hollandia and with them the newly arrived Japanese warplanes, again as most of the aircraft sat immobile and helpless on the ground. MacArthur's ensuing amphibious hook into weakly held enemy rear areas sliced in half the Japanese forces in New Guinea, isolated nearly 100,000 Japanese soldiers and sailors at Rabaul, cut off 60,000 troops of the Eighteenth Army, gave MacArthur excellent advance staging bases, and, best of all, was accomplished at small cost in Allied lives.[30]

Willoughby was at his apex but he was beginning an inexorable descent. His well-known tendencies to vacillate, to underestimate his foe, to offer ambiguous or even contradictory assessments, and to fit data to match his preconceptions all contributed to his slide into mediocrity. So long as the SWPA garnered one battlefield success after another Mac-Arthur could tolerate such an uneven performance. The SWPA's forces raced through western New Guinea using hastily planned amphibious outflanking maneuvers to isolate Japanese garrisons one after the other. While the SWPA commander pressed forward, convinced of his destiny and content to rely on incomplete and often minimal intelligence, Willoughby lacked such nerves of steel and often blinked. The SWPA's operations at Biak, a coral mass athwart MacArthur's line of advance to the Philippines, threw into relief both officers' personalities.

The G-2 knew little about Biak's defenders or defenses, but MacArthur needed the island's airfields to support future campaigns. He boldly pushed ahead with his invasion plans. Willoughby fretted. Biak was beyond the range of the SWPA's tactical air cover and dangerously close to Japanese naval bases in the southern Philippines. The G-2 feared that a sudden sortie by the Imperial fleet launched under cover of bad weather could reach the American landing area off Biak where MacArthur's outgunned Seventh Fleet and vulnerable transports would make inviting targets. Willoughby recommended postponing the landings to coincide with the navy and marine assault on the Marianas set for late June 1944.[31] MacArthur would have none of it. The landings went in; the land battle stalemated. Far more Japanese troops were hidden in the coral caves than Willoughby expected. To make matters worse, MacArthur's insistence on securing the island's airfields on the low ground ignored the terrain advantages of leaving the high ground in enemy hands. The stretched-out campaign pinned the fleet to the island where, due more to luck than Allied skill, three major Japanese reinforcement convoys accompanied by capital ships turned back before reaching Biak. MacArthur had ignored his G-2's warnings and pulled off another major victory. Such triumphs only reinforced the SWPA commander's sense of invincibility and he conveniently downplayed the influence of the American naval assault on Saipan in the Marianas that forced the Japanese Imperial navy to suspend efforts to retake Biak.

Willoughby meanwhile had another campaign preying on his mind. Signals intelligence, combat patrols, aerial reconnaissance, POW interrogations, and native reports all made clear that Eighteenth Army was pushing steadily westward toward an American beachhead near Aitape, about sixty miles east of Hollandia. During the painful two-month Japanese approach march Willoughby issued a series of contradictory evaluations: the enemy would attack Aitape on June 10; no, the enemy would not attack after all; yes, the enemy might attack; no, the enemy would sidestep Aitape to strike Hollandia. Throughout the G-2's seesaw performance American combat patrols fought Japanese skirmishers, watched trails well worn by hobnailed infantry boots, and reported enemy screening forces—in brief, they witnessed all the tactical-level indicators of an opponent massing for an assault. GHQ, SWPA, Sixth Army, and corps echelons all dismissed the lowly foot soldiers' reports. Willoughby declared on the morning of June 10 that the long-expected enemy attack was postponed indefinitely. That night 20,000 Japanese troops smashed through the thinly held lines of a covering force deployed about twenty miles west of Aitape.[32] It took a month of heavy fighting and 3,000 American casualties to evict the attackers and break the offensive capability of the Japanese forces in eastern New Guinea. Despite the intelligence debacle Willoughby later proclaimed his success at anticipating the attack and alerting the U.S. defenders. With neither embarrassment nor irony he displayed selective G-2 documents as "evidence" of his prescience.[33] Such duplicity became another hallmark of MacArthur's intelligence officer and surely affected his credibility within GHQ.

Why MacArthur tolerated such an inept performance one may only guess. Willoughby's misjudgments did not overly influence the conduct of the SWPA's ongoing operations nor interrupt MacArthur's timetable to return to the Philippines. Moreover, MacArthur was reluctant to relieve any senior staff officer, feeling it reflected poorly on his judgment in selecting subordinates and on his headquarters as well. Willoughby's unquestioning loyalty and uncritical admiration for his chief likely mitigated his most obvious shortcomings. MacArthur, in common with other commanders and statesmen, naturally gravitated to intelligence estimates that accorded with his interpretation of the enemy situation in regard to his latest plans. The SWPA commander relied on his intuitive strategic sense when confronted with the necessarily incomplete, contrary, and ambiguous intelligence data the G-2 provided. Unlike Willoughby he would never postpone an operation solely on the grounds of adverse intelligence reports. This analysis suggests that MacArthur frankly did not expect much from either intelligence or from Willoughby, as encapsulated in his often-quoted remark that there were "only three great intelligence officers in history and mine is not one of them."[34] Intelligence might complement but it would never dictate MacArthur's strategic campaigns.

At Leyte, despite U.S. Navy assertions to the contrary, it became known through intelligence that the Japanese were reinforcing not withdrawing from the central Philippines. Nevertheless, MacArthur's command could hardly beg off a JCS-accelerated schedule to invade the islands. Nor would MacArthur, absent from his headquarters while overseeing the landing at Morotai, have ignored such an opportunity. His goal was to liberate the Philippines to remove the stain of defeat from his escutcheon. It is not clear that he thought much beyond that goal in strategic terms. Willoughby's performance from mid-1944 onward deteriorated as his flaws magnified an already idiosyncratic and self-serving analysis of raw intelligence material that, in retrospect, forecast the shadowy outlines of later disaster. During operations in the Philippines the G-2 consistently underestimated Japanese opponents and misread their intentions.

Willoughby's initial order-of-battle information for Japanese forces on Leyte was accurate but later sullied by major blunders. Like the U.S. Navy he did not believe the Japanese main battle fleet could reach the American beachhead and landing areas, an almost fatal error. Willoughby also proved mistaken when insisting Japanese ground forces were withdrawing by sea from Leyte, when in fact the Imperial forces were throwing in thousands of reinforcements.[35] Willoughby reached this conclusion because he believed the Japanese situation on Leyte was hopeless, an interpretation that exemplified the G-2's tendency to reckon enemy intentions in a given situation as he himself might have reacted rather than trying to estimate how the Japanese might behave.

Similarly he maintained that only token resistance stood in the path of U.S. Sixth Army's drive across the island. Later during the Luzon fighting the G-2 consistently underestimated Japanese strength on the islands at 152,000 troops. Given these inferior numbers MacArthur unmercifully pushed Sixth Army to ignore its open flanks and dash straight down the

Lingayen corridor at full speed to Manila. The swpa had the air power to cover Sixth Army's exposed flanks plus the firepower and mobility of a first-class, modern, combined-arms army pitted against what amounted to a hopelessly outmatched pre–World War II infantry force. In such circumstances the G-2's assertion that only 50,000 Japanese remained alive on Luzon when there were twice that many had little effect on the campaign. On July 1 the Sixth Army commander notified MacArthur that his troops had counted 173,000 Japanese dead, or 20,000 more than Willoughby had ever acknowledged, and the Japanese were still fighting.[36]

Throughout MacArthur's Philippine campaigns intelligence was haphazard, displaying the idiosyncratic nature of its keeper and the lack of interest of its recipient. MacArthur, flush with victory and never expecting much from intelligence, overlooked G-2's errors (which were explained away or blamed on others, primarily the U.S. Navy). Willoughby, too, was becoming more impervious to criticism from subordinates. During the planning stages for the Tarakan, North Borneo, operation set for May 1945, Willoughby grew "hysterical" when a newly arrived Australian major general disagreed with him over the size of the Japanese garrison.[37] As later hard fighting discovered, the Australians were right again.

Intelligence omissions, commissions, and incompetence may have returned to haunt MacArthur had he led the invasion of Japan's home islands anticipated for November 1945. During the course of late spring and summer of 1945 decrypted enemy military communications made plain that the Japanese army had embarked on a massive reinforcement of Japan's southernmost main island of Kyushu. More to the point, Japanese units were fortifying and digging in along the very three beaches the Americans had selected for their massive invasion. As Japanese numbers on Kyushu far surpassed Willoughby's initial and largely accurate estimate, he became worried and relayed his concerns to MacArthur. Attacking at the present one to one ratio, he wrote in July, is "not the recipe for success."[38] There is no record of MacArthur's response, but circumstantial evidence from the general's later conduct strongly suggest he had no tolerance for the G-2's caution.

In Washington the War Department also grew alarmed by the Japanese buildup on Kyushu, so much so that Army Chief of Staff George C. Marshall queried MacArthur for his opinion on the intelligence revelations. MacArthur's reply typified a classic bullheaded operations officer determined to press boldly ahead regardless of intelligence reports highlighting potential hazards. First MacArthur dismissed the source of intelligence, attributing the intercepts to Japanese radio deception. Even if the Japanese were massing in southern Kyushu, he argued, Allied air and naval power would cripple them before invasion day. Although a concerned Willoughby insisted to the SWPA chief of staff that air power was not preventing the Japanese reinforcement of Kyushu (and the SWPA chief of staff reacted by ordering that the air campaign be accelerated), MacArthur insisted U.S. airmen would destroy all Japanese air defenses in southern Kyushu and immobilize enemy ground forces before the invasion. Finally he proclaimed that his G-2 had overestimated the enemy in every operation, a statement that simply turned facts on their heads.[39] Flush with victory, convinced of his destiny, and poised to culminate his military career by leading the greatest amphibious operation history ever witnessed, MacArthur reasoned away intelligence that contradicted his plans for bringing down the curtain on World War II.

Kyushu's ghost was peering over MacArthur's shoulder five years later when, despite Allied air and naval superiority, he faced another eerie November decision about advancing or withdrawing as intelligence reported enemy reinforcements moving into position to check his final offensive.

Interlude

The G-2 staff of Douglas MacArthur's Far East Command (FEC) did not escape the rapid postwar demobilization. Personnel authorizations dropped from 3,872 in January 1946 to 1,254 by January 1950, mostly in the translation and technical sections.[40] Nonetheless the War Department assigned MacArthur's command an extensive list of intelligence requirements. As might be expected, the activities of Soviet forces in Korea, Manchuria, and the so-called Far East had a high priority in the summer of 1946. In September 1947 Washington added even more targets, including "strength, state of training, morale, equipment, order of battle of the North Korean People's Army," and a similar responsibility for the emerging Chinese communist armed forces.[41] Besides these military targets the FEC also was to report on scientific and technical intelligence matters such as atomic energy or chemical warfare developments, and the Civil Intelligence Section monitored political activities in occupied Japan and detected noncompliance with Supreme Commander for the Allied Powers (SCAP) directives or opposition to Allied occupation forces. Willoughby, an open admirer of the Spanish dictator Francisco Franco, whom he described as "the second greatest general in the world,"[42] also threw himself into anticommunist activities, investigating the prewar Soviet spy Richard Sorge and hunting for communists, fellow travelers, and security risks, including high-ranking officers on MacArthur's staff like Brig. Gen. Elliott Thorpe (counterintelligence) and Maj. Gen. Courtney Whitney, who were too liberal for the G-2's tastes.[43]

It would be an error to dismiss Willoughby as a court jester. As supreme commander in Tokyo during the occupation of Japan, MacArthur's distrust of Washington resurfaced. He showed little confidence in CIA or state department intelligence sources and, instead growing ever more isolated, placed increasing trust in Willoughby's intelligence estimates.[44] G-2 did produce solid military intelligence work during the occupation period, particularly in the collection phase of the process. As was the case during the Pacific War, analysis of the raw intelligence data was colored by Willoughby's prejudices, this time his virulent anticommunism and conviction that a Moscow-directed conspiracy plotted world domination.

A measure of the FEC G-2's collection ability was its production of increasingly refined order-of-battle reports for Soviet ground, air, and naval forces in the Soviet Far East. It took time to reorient resources to new intelligence targets but by September 1948 the FEC possessed a sophisticated appreciation of Soviet forces in the region. The proportion of military intelligence that emanated from Washington versus what was generated in Tokyo cannot be determined with exactitude, but the scale seems weighed in MacArthur's favor. The Far Eastern Command drew heavily on interrogations of more than 100,000 former Japanese prisoners of war repatriated from camps in Siberia and Russian language periodicals to build its order of battle.[45] The exact sources Washington exploited remain unclear, but it is certain that an increasingly refined assessment of Soviet forces appeared in American war plans developed between 1946 and 1950.[46] In January 1947, for instance, the FEC could positively identify only one of the twenty-four Soviet divisions believed stationed in the Far East. Six months later MacArthur's G-2 laid out the Soviet command structure, named major communist commanders in the area, and reported twenty-three Soviet divisions (identifying thirteen of them).[47] The FEC's intelligence estimates appeared in "GUNPOWDER," MacArthur's general war plan that, in consonance with the JCS's war plans, envisaged evacuating South Korea to a communist onslaught in favor of defending Japan and Okinawa.[48] In the case of global war, however, JCS policy left MacArthur's Asian command a distant third behind Europe and the Middle East in the resource chain.[49] MacArthur's strategic perspective placed the priority on northeast Asia, his backyard but a faraway place of little consequence for Washington policymakers imbued with an Atlantic outlook.

Following the Soviet withdrawal from northern Korea in December 1948, U.S. intelligence agencies monitored the newly organized North Korean People's Army, crediting it with at least 125,000 personnel.[50] By 1949 rumors abounded that the northerners planned to invade the south when communist-inspired uprisings below the thirty-eighth parallel grew more widespread. American intelligence did detect communist formations deploying southward just above the thirty-eighth parallel where some three divisions were in place by February 1950.[51] In December 1949 Willoughby reported "the North Korean Government has set Mar and Apr 50 as the time to invade South Korea" but only if such an attack fit into the "over-all communist strategy" directed from Moscow.[52] A few months later, on March 10, 1950, he again warned an invasion would commence in June 1950, but two weeks later suddenly reversed himself, stating, "It is believed there will be no civil war in Korea this spring or summer."[53] The performance rivaled his bizarre intelligence estimates preceding the Aitape fighting of 1944.

Besides these flip-flops Willoughby distrusted both the Central Intelligence Agency (CIA) and state department intelligence efforts in the FEC, an attitude those agencies warmly reciprocated. Having excluded the OSS from the SWPA during the war, MacArthur and Willoughby had little to do with its successor, the CIA. The combination of leftover wartime resentments and the CIA's insistence that the Far East was not and could not be a strategic theater of operations in a future general war, poisoned relations.[54] Nor did the CIA's assessments impress MacArthur. One agency estimate, published a week before the June 1950 North Korean invasion, noted that the Pyongyang regime was deploying ground units, tanks, and artillery southward in the area of the thirty-eighth parallel but implied the regime's policy of subversion, propaganda, and infiltration by guerrilla bands into the south would continue and thereby delay an overt invasion.[55]

Around the same time the FEC's Korean Liaison Office reported six and possibly seven North Korean divisions deployed between the thirty-eighth and thirty-ninth parallels. Washington had declared Korea outside of FEC jurisdiction since June 1949, so G-2's liaison office there was regarded by some as an extralegal unit created to aggrandize MacArthur's command.[56] Although Willoughby subsequently and characteristically attempted to "prove" his G-2 branch had accurately predicted the North Korean invasion, the prosaic and sad truth is the attack surprised both American authorities in Washington and in Tokyo, who, in the words of the official army historian, "had no plans to counter an invasion, even had it been forecast to the very day."[57]

Within a month of the North Korean invasion of South Korea Mac-Arthur was preparing for a "major amphibious operation in September."[58] The role of intelligence in planning the Inchon landing or its contribution to MacArthur's enormous self-confidence about a high-risk amphibious landing deep behind enemy lines remains unknown. A month of fighting was sufficient time for captured enemy documents and prisoner of war interrogations to reveal in August 1950 that Pyongyang had committed its reserves in a desperate attempt to destroy the American and South Korean forces clinging to the so-called Pusan Perimeter. In operational terms the situation seemed similar to events preceding the Hollandia operation of April 1944—an amphibious landing in the lightly defended rear areas of an overextended enemy force that could sever the foe's line of communication and deliver what MacArthur termed "a decisive and crushing blow."[59] The brilliantly conceived and executed Inchon landing lived up to MacArthur's hyperbole. North Korean ground units, isolated deep in the south and trapped between two Allied forces, suffered heavy losses and temporarily ceased to exist as an effective conventional fighting force.[60] Amidst the congratulations few gave serious notice that in faraway Beijing Chinese communist leaders viewed their fraternal communist neighbor's reverses with alarm.

In early July 1950 the Chinese had established a Northeast Border Defense Army and ordered three armies redeployed to the new command in Manchuria.[61] A month later, as directed by Chinese Communist Party leader Mao Tse-tung, Chinese troops accelerated preparations to assist the North Koreans in defeating the Americans, if necessary. Following the Inchon landing North Korean chairman Kim Il-sung made personal appeals to China and the Soviet Union for assistance, and on October 2 Mao decided to enter the Korean War, issuing orders on October 18 for Chinese troops to cross the Yalu River into northern Korea.[62] The broad outlines of Chinese deployments were known to U.S. intelligence.

Willoughby also reported a high level meeting held in late August in Beijing at which Moscow allegedly had ordered the Chinese communists to assist North Korea. Senior members of the Central Military Commission did convene on August 26 in the Chinese capital where vice premier Zhou Enlai argued forcefully for direct intervention in Korea. Where Willoughby obtained his remarkable and partially accurate account remains unknown.[63] However, the parallels with Willoughby's blend of top-grade intelligence, speculation, and ambiguous analysis during earlier campaigns and MacArthur's advance to the Yalu are striking. The G-2, for instance, correctly reported the movement of Chinese forces into Manchuria, again on exactly what basis has yet to be revealed. Willoughby estimated that the 116,000 troops present there in July had grown to 217,000 men in early August and to as many as 463,000 by early November.[64] This intelligence was available to Washington decisionmakers as well, and they, like MacArthur and Willoughby, underestimated Chinese determination to intervene in Korea. Still, MacArthur's oft-quoted remark at the October 1950 Wake Island meeting with Pres. Harry S. Truman that he no longer feared Chinese or Soviet intervention needs qualification.

MacArthur's insistence that without air support only fifty or sixty thousand Chinese could get across the Yalu and "if the Chinese tried to get down to Pyongyang there would be the greatest slaughter," speaks more to the general's "uncritical admiration of air power" than to any intelligence estimates.[65] In early November the FEC commander reiterated his confidence to Washington that air power could isolate the Korean battlefield. He praised his airmen for accomplishing that mission on November 24, the eve of the massive Chinese second-stage offensives.[66] He also believed the war throughout Korea would be over by Thanksgiving.[67] Nor was he alone in voicing such opinions. Experts in Washington also doubted China would enter the fighting in great numbers. In October CIA analysts saw "no convincing indications of an actual Chinese Communist intention to resort to full-scale intervention in Korea" in 1950.[68]

During this critical period, from mid-October when the initial battlefield contacts were made with Chinese troops to late November and the great intervention, Willoughby's estimate of the Chinese threat fluctuated.[69] Guessing there were between 80,000 and 90,000 Chinese south of the Yalu (when in fact there were around 300,000), he concluded, as he had seven years earlier at Leyte, that the indicators pointed to the enemy preparing for a defense and withdrawal.[70] His G-2 bulletin of November 3, 1950, for instance, acknowledged that special units of 3,000 men each from Thirty-eighth, Thirty-ninth, Fortieth, and Forty-second armies had been identified in North Korea. American intelligence, however, still carried the main strength of these armies north of the Yalu River, unaware that more than 260,000 troops from these units had already secretly entered northern Korea.[71] Willoughby's and MacArthur's assessments again were in tune with those of Washington.

Following the initial clashes between UN forces and Chinese "volunteers" in late October, the CIA reported that the thirty to forty thousand Chinese troops in North Korea apparently had the mission of preventing an early United Nations victory, thereby maintaining a communist government on North Korean soil.[72] Willoughby was more reluctant to admit the intrusion by the Chinese Communist Forces (CCF) and his attitude may have influenced MacArthur who was slow to realize the CCF was now his principal adversary.[73] Soon after the first encounters the Chinese "volunteers" disappeared into the bleak, snow-covered countryside where their excellent march and camouflage discipline rendered MacArthur's aerial reconnaissance useless.

The Chinese withdrawal convinced analysts that China had the capability for a large-scale offensive, but there were no definitive indications that the communists had decided to embark on one.[74] Likewise, Willoughby believed that between seventy and one hundred thousand Chinese troops were in northern Korea, but thought the UN forces would prevail.[75] The G-2 frequently pointed out the potential for CCF intervention and expressed anxiety over the growing Chinese strength aligned against U.S. X Corps in northeast Korea, but, reminiscent of the Aitape campaign, all evidence suggests he did not think it would take place.[76] The CIA was not doing much better, concluding in its November 24 reevaluation of communist intentions that Chinese activity in Korea to date was insufficient to demonstrate a plan for major offensive operations.[77] Willoughby's estimates, though, allowed one to read *anything* into them since he seemed to be trying to have it both ways in his predictions. In such circumstances MacArthur boldly plunged ahead, accommodating the Chinese who lured the UN forces deeper and deeper into the frozen northern Korea wilderness, waiting for the best opportunity to strike.[78]

The Chinese offensive on the night of November 25 caught Washington, MacArthur, and his ill-deployed UN forces off guard, drove the Allied forces from North Korea, and ultimately recaptured the South Korea capital of Seoul. Thereafter, however, the now-overextended Chinese forces, much as MacArthur had foreseen, suffered such heavy losses during their renewed spring 1951 offensive that the initiative passed to the UN forces who took the offensive and again drove north past Seoul. Then the war settled into a bitterly fought stalemate along the thirty-eighth parallel.

In early March 1951 a MacArthur cable to the JCS identified large concentrations of Soviet and Chinese troops north of the Yalu and requested Washington activate contingency plans to employ atomic bombs if the communist forces entered the fighting. Apparently in response, B-29 heavy bombers ferried at least nine unassembled atomic weapons to Guam just before MacArthur's removal from command.[79] Although the context of MacArthur's proposal remains in a shadowy background, it appears plausible that the G-2 provided the intelligence MacArthur used to buttress his atomic proposals. In March 1944 MacArthur had used intelligence revelations of enemy dispositions to sway the joint chiefs in favor of his Hollandia concept. Seven years later he may have again employed intelligence to validate his solution to the Korean problem. It was, of course, not to be. The war in Korea would remain a limited one fought thereafter without MacArthur in command.

Lacking the full range of sources available to MacArthur during the Korean War renders any comparison of the general's use of intelligence in World War II and Korea extremely tenuous. Still, there are noticeable threads MacArthur wove into his fabric of command. Foremost among these is the role of personality and intelligence. MacArthur was a preeminent strategist who cared little for tactical detail, rightly leaving it to his subordinates. Intelligence carried cachet when it was strategic in scope, that is, capable of exerting a decisive influence on a campaign or battle. In such cases—Hollandia or Inchon—MacArthur's boldness—some might say recklessness—complemented the sweep of intelligence and produced classic victories. Yet MacArthur was capable of ignoring equally high quality intelligence when it did not comport with his estimate of the situation (Biak, Kyushu, and the advance to the Yalu come to mind). This indicates that intelligence was not central to MacArthur's operations. He valued personal experience more, yet in the end MacArthur's own experience with twentieth century warfare betrayed him.

Douglas MacArthur brought the lessons of the American war against Japan to the American war against North Korea and China. His wartime experience fighting the Japanese had convinced him of the efficacy of air power—from the helplessness of campaigning without it as he had in the Philippines in 1941-42 to exaggerating its possibilities as he had done in planning Kyushu operations in mid-summer 1945. Experience fighting the emperor's forces also displayed the shortcoming of intelligence—its ambiguity, its incompleteness, and, most of all, its inert quality unless acted upon by a decisive commander. He took brilliant advantage of the superb intelligence available to his headquarters during World War II but he also recklessly disregarded intelligence that might have retarded his operations. MacArthur's fame rightly resides in his boldness, but if he had overly depended on intelligence, waiting for the full story before acting, his audacity would turn to timidity. Victory against Japan convinced MacArthur his idiosyncratic use of intelligence was the most effective means of employing this supporting weapon of war.

The war against Japan was a theater in a global total war. The war in Korea was a limited conflict. Yet MacArthur applied his experience in the former to his conduct during the latter with disastrous results not only militarily but also politically. He never accepted Washington's postwar premise that East Asia—the Far East in the parlance of the day—was a tertiary theater of operations, just as he had never accepted such a role for the swpa during World War II. If the outbreak of war in Korea was the first stage of a general war pitting the United States against the Soviet Union (as many intelligence analysts in Washington believed was the case), then limiting the war in Korea made as much strategic sense to MacArthur as the U.S. Navy's Central Pacific drive during World War II had, that is, none at all.

Total war, not limited conflict, required the boldness of purpose at which MacArthur excelled. During World War II his intelligence sources were on the cutting edge of available American technology as national mobilization put the highly technical skills of civilian mathematicians, linguists, scholars, executives, and professionals at the military's disposal. The partial mobilization for Korea offered MacArthur nowhere near comparable in-depth talent. Was his intelligence in 1950 the same caliber of 1945's? Or had intelligence sources, like the rest of the national military establishment, decayed during the immediate postwar period?

Driven from the Philippines in 1942 he resurrected his command and ultimately sat in judgment on those generals who had humiliated him. Driven from northern Korea in 1950 he left the resurrection of the U.S. Eighth Army to subordinates, but surely burned to avenge his defeat. Posterity has rarely treated the vanquished with sympathy. In a limited war MacArthur had few options to repair his military reputation. He could again drive north to the Yalu, but what if more Chinese troops intervened? He could accept a stalemate, but what honor shone forth from a draw? If intelligence told him Chinese and Soviet forces were massing north of the Yalu he could attack them with atomic weapons, win an expanded war by carrying the fight to the enemy's homeland, and regain his diminished stature. MacArthur was a lifelong student of military history but he never appreciated the tug of history on his own actions. The experiences he accumulated during an unparalleled military career, more than any amount of military intelligence, shaped his decisions and ultimately his tragedy.

Notes

1. Maj. Gen. Charles A. Willoughby, 201-File, U.S. Army Center of Military History, Washington DC (hereafter CMH).
2. Elliot R. Thorpe, *East Wind, Rain* (Boston: Gambit, 1969), 95.
3. D. Clayton James, *The Years of MacArthur*, vol. 1, *1880–1941* (Boston: Houghton Mifflin, 1970), 583, 609.
4. James, *Years of MacArthur*, 1:604; Louis Morton, *The United States Army in World War II, The War in the Pacific: The Fall of the Philippines* (Washington DC: Government Printing Office, 1953), 122.
5. Robert Eichelberger to Samuel Milner, Mar. 8, 1954, CMH.
6. James, *Years of MacArthur*, 1:615.
7. James, *Years of MacArthur*, 1:603; Geoffrey Perrett, *Old Soldiers Never Die: The Life of Douglas MacArthur* (New York: Random House, 1996), 246–47.
8. Perrett, *Old Soldiers Never Die*, 247; Charles A. Willoughby and John Chamberlain, *MacArthur, 1941–1951* (New York: McGraw-Hill, 1954), 22–23.
9. Willoughby and Chamberlain, *MacArthur 1941–1951*, 22–23.
10. For a different interpretation of MacArthur's conduct see John Costello, *Days of Infamy: MacArthur, Roosevelt, Churchill—The Shocking Truth Revealed* (New York: Pocket Books, 1994), ch. 12.
11. Morton, *Fall of the Philippines*, 82–85.
12. Robert Louis Benson, *United States Cryptologic History*, Series 4, *World War II*, vol. 8, "A History of U.S. Communications Intelligence during World War II: Policy and Administration" (Ft. Meade MD: National Security Agency, Center for Cryptologic History, 1997), 31.
13. MacArthur's strategic views are well presented in Stanley L. Falk's, "Douglas MacArthur and the War Against Japan," in *We Shall Return! MacArthur's Commanders and the Defeat of Japan*, ed. William M. Leary (Lexington: University Press of Kentucky, 1988), 3–4.

14. D. Clayton James, *The Years of MacArthur*, vol. 2, *1941–1945* (Boston: Houghton Mifflin, 1975), 28.

15. Morton, *Fall of the Philippines*, 216.

16. Willoughby and Chamberlain, *MacArthur 1941–1951*, 17; Rikusenshi ken-kyu fukyukai, ed., *Rikusen shishu 12 (dai niji sekai daisenshi) Ruson shima shinko sakusen* (Collected works on the history of ground warfare, 12: The second world war, Offensive operations on Luzon Island) (Tokyo: Hara shobo, 1969), 22; Morton, *Fall of the Philippines*, 413–14.

17. John Prados, *Combined Fleet Decoded: The Secret History of American Intelligence and the Japanese Navy in World War II* (New York: Random House, 1995), 416–19.

18. The story was related to me by the veteran, U.S. Army Col. Sunao Phil Ishio.

19. A recently published and excellent study of FELO is Allison B. Gilmore's *You Can't Fight Tanks with Bayonets: Psychological Warfare against the Japanese Army in the Southwest Pacific* (Lincoln: University of Nebraska Press, 1998).

20. The history of AIB is comprehensively covered in Alan Powell's *War by Stealth: Australians and the Allied Intelligence Bureau 1942–1945* (Melbourne, Australia: Melbourne University Press, 1996).

21. Msg, 8th Base Force Rabaul to Naval Intelligence Division, Tokyo, May 23, 1942 (available May 27, 1942), and Msg, Naval Intelligence Division, Tokyo, May 18 (available May 19), file 5, "Kokoda Trail First Information," RG-B5555, Australian Archives, Victoria. I am indebted to Dr. David Horner for providing a copy of these documents to me.

22. Samuel Milner, *The United States Army in World War II: The War in the Pacific: Victory in Papua* (Washington DC: Government Printing Office, 1957), 65; Boeicho, Boei kenshujo, ed., *Senshi sosho, 14, Minami Taiheiyo rikugun sakusen: Pooruto Moresubi—Ga shima shoki sakusen* (Official military history, 14, Army operations in the south Pacific: First stage operations against Port Moresby and Guadalcanal Island) (Tokyo: Asagumo shimbunsha, 1968), 341; and Lida Mayo, *Bloody Buna* (New York: Playboy Press, 1974), 60.

23. Edward J. Drea, *In the Service of the Emperor: Essays on the Imperial Japanese Army* (Lincoln: University of Nebraska Press, 1998), ch. 8, "A Signals Inter-cept Site at War," 110–26, describes this early intercept work.

24. See Edward J. Drea, *MacArthur's Ultra: Codebreaking and the War against Japan, 1942–1945,* (Lawrence: The University Press of Kansas, 1992), 51–57, for a detailed description of the events.

25. Drea, *MacArthur's Ultra*, 64–65.

26. Drea, *MacArthur's Ultra*, 75–76.

27. Drea, *MacArthur's Ultra*, 80–85.

28. LTG John Coates, Australian Army (Ret.), *Bravery Above Blunder: The 9th Australian Division at Finschhafen, Sattelberg, and Sio* (Melbourne, Australia: Oxford University Press, forthcoming) will be the definitive account of these

operations. I am indebted to General Coates for sharing this information with me.

29. GHQ, FEC, MIS, GS, "Operations of the Military Intelligence Section, GHQ, SWPA/FEC/SCAP," vol. 3, Intelligence Series (part 1), 1950, documentary appendices, appendix 1, tab 2, CMH.

30. For a detailed account see Edward J. Drea, "ULTRA Intelligence and General Douglas MacArthur's Leap to Hollandia, January–April 1944," in *Intelligence and National Security* 5:2 (April 1990), 323–49.

31. Memo, LtCmdr T. E. L. McCabe to General Willoughby, May 13, 1944, and attachment, Sutherland Papers, Miscellaneous Records, 1943–1945, MacArthur Memorial Archives, Norfolk VA (hereafter MMA), RG-30, box 10, folder 5.

32. The Aitape campaign is covered in Drea, *MacArthur's Ultra*, 144–51.

33. GHQ, FEC, MIS, GS, "Operations of the Military Intelligence Section, GHQ, SWPA/FEC/SCAP," vol. 3, Intelligence Series (part 1), 1950, inserts 5 & 17, CMH.

34. Oral History, Gen. Clyde D. Eddleman, Oral History Collection, (Carlisle Barracks PA: U.S. Army Military History Institute) (hereafter USAMHI).

35. Drea, *MacArthur's Ultra*, 167–68.

36. Cited in Drea, *MacArthur's Ultra*, 200.

37. Peter Stanley, *Tarakan: An Australian Tragedy* (St. Leonards, Australia: Allen & Unwin, 1997), 14.

38. GHQ, USAFPAC, MIS, GS, "Amendment No. 1 to G-2 Estimate of the Enemy Situation with Respect to Kyushu (dated April 25, 1945)," July 29, 1945, Chamberlin Papers, box 6, USAMHI.

39. John Ray Skates, *The Invasion of Japan: Alternative to the Bomb* (Columbia: University of South Carolina Press, 1994), 142–43.

40. Memo, CofS DCS, FEC to DCS, SCAP, "G-2 Personnel Reductions in the Period Dec 45/Dec 49," March 20, 1950, in GHQ, FEC, MIS, GS, "Operations of the Military Intelligence Section, GHQ SWPA/FEC/SCAP, III, The Intelligence Series (CMH, 1950), insert 31, enclosure 2.

41. Compare GHQ, "Far Eastern Intelligence Requirements," June 11, 1946, RG-4, USAFPAC, box 23, with G-2 "Estimates June '45–Far Eastern Intelligence," MMA, and GHQ, "Far Eastern Intelligence Requirements," September 20, 1947, F-M Intelligence, MMA, RG-6, FEC, box 15.

42. Thorpe, *East Wind, Rain*, 96.

43. D. Clayton James, *The Years of MacArthur*, vol. 3, *Triumph and Disaster 1945–1964* (Boston: Houghton Mifflin, 1985), 54.

44. D. Clayton James, *Refighting the Last War* (New York: Free Press, 1993), 43.

45. GHQ, FEC, MIS, GS, ATIS, "Soviet Ground Forces and Soviet General Officers," Interrogation Report No. 75, August 5, 1949, CMH.

46. Compare the order of battle, Eastern USSR in Dept. of Army, *Military Sum-*

mary, Foreign Ground Forces No. 1, 31 May 1949 and Dept. of Army, *Military Summary of Foreign Ground Forces* No. 6, March 1950, both in USAMHI.

47. GHQ, FEC, MIS, GS, Plans & Estimates Group, "Periodic Intelligence Summary: Situation Korea-China-Manchuria," January 20, 1947, and GHQ, FEC, MIS, GS, Plans & Estimates Branch, Supplement No. 3, "Periodic Intelligence Summary: Situation Korea, China, Manchuria: Strength and Disposition of Soviet Forces, July 31, 1947, both in RG-6 FEC, box 25, MMA.

48. GHQ, SCAP & FEC, Staff Study, Operation "GUNPOWDER" 2d ed., September 8, 1948, RG-6, FEC, Series III, Ops & Plans, box 100 [97], MMA; and GHQ, FEC, Annex B (intelligence) to Staff Study Operation "GUNPOWDER," 2d ed., September 8, 1948, RG-6, FEC, Series III, Ops & Plans, box 97, MMA.

49. Joint Staff Planning Committee, "Directives for Implementation of 'HALF-MOON' Emergency War Plan," JSPC 877/3, May 3, 1948, Records of the Joint Chiefs, part 2, The Soviet Union 1946–1953 (microfilm) reel 5, f 0037 ff, USAMHI.

50. War Department Military Intelligence Division, *Intelligence Review* No. 73, July 10, 1947, USAMHI.

51. *Intelligence Review* No. 152, January 27, 1949; No. 154, February 10, 1949; and No. 165, February 1950, USAMHI.

52. HQ SCAP and FEC, "Daily Intelligence Summary," No. 2669, December 30, 1949.

53. Cited in James, *Years of MacArthur*, 3:416.

54. CIA, "The Strategic Importance of the Far East to the United States and the USSR," ORE 17–49, May 4, 1949, PSF, Truman Library, Independence MO; and "Relative U.S. Security Interest in the European-Mediterranean Area and the Far East," ORE 69–49, September 12, 1949, PSF, Truman Library.

55. Memo from the CIA, "Current Capabilities of the Northern Korean Regime," June 19, 1950, *Foreign Relations of the United States 1950* (hereafter FRUS), vol. 7, *Korea* (Washington DC: U.S. Government Printing Office, 1976), 118, 120–21.

56. Korean Liaison Office, Rpt 518, May 25, 1950; James, *Years of MacArthur*, 3:416.

57. James F. Schnabel, *The United States Army in the Korean War,* vol. 3 *Policy and Direction: The First Year* (Washington DC: Office of the Chief of Military History, 1972), 64–65; Charles A. Willoughby, "The North Korean Pre-Invasion Build-up," GHQ, FEC, MIS, GS, "Operations of the Military Intelligence Section, GHQ SWPA/FEC/SCAP, vol. 3, The Intelligence Series, 1950, CMH; Willoughby and Chamberlain, *MacArthur 1941–1951*, 350–54.

58. Memo, ACS, G-3 for Cmdt, Army War College, "Request for Communications Concerning the Inchon Landing," and inclosure "Summary of Messages Exchanged between CINCFE and the JCS concerning the Inchon Landing conducted in Korea in September 1950," May 23, 1957, USAMHI.

59. "Request for Communications Concerning Inchon Landing," May 23, 1957.
60. James, *Years of MacArthur* 3:481–82; James, *Refighting the Last War*, 175.
61. Chen Jian, *China's Road to the Korean War: The Making of the Sino-American Confrontation* (New York: Columbia University Press, 1994), 135–36.
62. Chen Jian, *China's Road to Korean War*, 171–75, 209–10.
63. Compare the facsimile titled "Intelligence Highlights" in Willoughby and Chamberlain, *MacArthur 1941–1951*, 381, and the account of the meeting in Chen Jian, *China's Road to Korean War*, 149–50.
64. Eliot A. Cohen, "'Only Half the Battle': American Intelligence and the Chinese Intervention in Korea, 1950," paper presented at 3d Annual U.S. Army War College International Conference on Intelligence and Military Operations, May 17–19, 1988, Carlisle Barracks PA.
65. Gen. Omar N. Bradley, comp., "Substance of Statements Made at Wake Island Conference on October 15, 1950," FRUS 7:953; James, *Refighting the Last War*, 4.
66. Roy E. Appleman, *The United States Army in the Korean War*, vol. 1, *South to the Naktong, North to the Yalu: June–November 1950* (Washington DC: Office of the Chief of Military History, 1961), 765.
67. "Substance of Statements Made at Wake Island Conference on 15 Oct 1950," 949.
68. Memo from the CIA, "Threat of Full Chinese Communist Intervention in Korea," October 12, 1950, FRUS, 7:933.
69. Roger Beaumont, "Flawed Soothsayer: Charles A. Willoughby, MacArthur's G-2," 15. I am grateful to Professor Beaumont for providing me with a footnoted version of his essay, which appeared in *Espionage* without notes.
70. Schnabel, *Policy and Direction: The First Year*, 276.
71. Shu Guang Zhang, *Mao's Military Romanticism: China and the Korean War, 1950–1953* (Lawrence: University Press of Kansas, 1995), 94; Willoughby and Chamberlain, *MacArthur 1941–1951*, reproduction, 394–95.
72. Memo from the CIA, "National Intelligence Estimate: Chinese Communist Intervention in Korea," November 8, 1950, FRUS, 7:1104, 1106.
73. James, *Refighting the Last War*, 194.
74. CIA, "National Intelligence Estimate," November 24, 1950, FRUS, 7:1220–22.
75. Cohen, "'Only Half the Battle,'" 25.
76. Appleman, *South to the Naktong, North to the Yalu*, 763–64; William Stueck, *The Korean War: An International History* (Princeton NJ: Princeton University Press, 1995), 117.
77. CIA, "Chinese Communist Intervention in Korea," November 24, 1950, FRUS, 7:1221.
78. Chen Jian, *China's Road to Korean War*, 211; Shu Guang Zhang, *Mao's Military Romanticism*, 99, 107.

79. "100 nin no 20 seki-Makkasa," (100 persons of the twentieth century—
    Douglas MacArthur), *Asahi shimbun*, July 5, 1998, section 2, p 3; see also
    Bruce Cumings, *The Origins of the Korean War*, 2, *The Roaring of the Cataract*
    (Princeton NJ: Princeton University Press, 1990), 750–51, for a brief discus-
    sion of MacArthur's attitudes about the use of atomic weapons in Korea.

MacArthur as Maritime Strategist

Clark G. Reynolds

Widely acknowledged as one of the leading historians of the U.S. Navy in the Pacific War, Clark Reynolds of the University of Charleston gives MacArthur high marks as a maritime strategist, during both World War II and the Korean War.

I Have Returned
When Doug MacArthur at last went back,
"I have returned,"
He followed the fox-hunting, pig-boat's track,
"I have returned."
Oh, the carrier planes were overhead
And the battleship turrets spouted lead
So the general could go ashore, it's said, singing
"I have returned."

Cincpoa [commander in chief, POA] divisions were at his side,
"I have returned."
And Phibspacfor [Amphibious Forces Pacific Fleet] provided the ride
"I have returned."
Oh, the subs went up to the sea of Japan,
And the carriers ranged from Saipan to Bataan,
So the general could land, according to plan, singing
"I have returned."

MacArthur petitioned God by prayer,
"I have returned."
But God decided He couldn't be there,
"I have returned."
But to help . . . God went to the utmost limits,
For God sent Kinkaid, Halsey, and Nimitz
And MacArthur went along to kibitz . . . singing
"I HAVE RETURNED."

Anonymous. Sung to the tune "When Johnny Comes Marching Home" by
members of Air Group Three in Yorktown (v-10), December 1944.

Such is the image, portrayed by an unknown wartime wag, that the
U.S. Navy had of "Dugout Doug" during the Pacific war—a publicity
hound and strutting blowhard who reckoned himself second only to
the Almighty, a landlubbing soldier with no real appreciation of the
Navy and its Marine Corps; guilty, more or less, on all counts. But these
superficial trappings must be peeled away from the aura surrounding
Douglas MacArthur if we are to discover the essence of his strategic
thinking, his *maritime* strategic thinking.

Maritime strategy is not naval strategy. Naval strategy may be defined as
the employment of Navy forces to a specific end. Maritime strategy has a
much broader scope: the combined use of all arms—Army, Navy and Air
Forces—in seaborne operations. Historically it has meant the "indirect
approach" of maritime nations against their continental enemies by
first winning command of the sea, destroying the enemy's seaborne
commerce, conducting a naval blockade, and making amphibious assaults
on outlying enemy territory and colonies—all designed to completely
isolate the enemy's homeland, the classic formula propounded by Sir
Julian Corbett in 1911.[1]

As employed by Britain in the Seven Years' War, in the Napoleonic
wars and, unsuccessfully, in World War I, this indirect approach had
meant a strategy of concentration: defeating or neutralizing France's
or Germany's naval and maritime power and supporting a major allied
army with money, arms, equipment and encouragement to decide the
final issue on the continent—Prussia in the 1750s and Russia in 1812
and 1914. It meant that the maritime power could not afford to make
massive commitments of her own ground forces on the continent, as
Britain had done on the Western front during World War I, at least
not until the enemy's army was in irreversible strategic retreat. Then an
expeditionary force, like Wellington's, would land to help the ally's army
administer the final blow.

Strategically, Britain has been an island nation simply incapable of
shouldering the sheer immensity of both a large-scale ground war on
the continental landmasses and a naval war. So too has been a strategic
limitation of the United States, whose maritime strategists from Alfred
Thayer Mahan at the turn of the century to Adm. Ernest J. King in

World War II worked diligently to hammer out a maritime strategy for this country.

To their names, one must add Gen. Douglas MacArthur. Though a typical U.S. Army officer of the first four decades of the century in his total concern with "occupation and pacification operations" (except for World War I), he matured into a major maritime strategist during World War II and the Korean War, alone among senior American generals to that time to do so.[2]

MacArthur's maritime field throughout his career was the Pacific. Not only did he grow up during the era of Mahan, but at the time that he entered West Point, 1899, his father, Gen. Arthur MacArthur, was fighting insurrectionists in the Philippines as was his brother, an ensign of the same name in the Navy. Upon graduation in 1903 MacArthur went directly to those islands for his first duty and thence to visit Japan, an experience, he later reminisced, "without doubt the most important factor of preparation in my entire life. . . . The true historic significance and the sense of destiny that these lands of the western Pacific and Indian Ocean now assumed became part of me. They were to color and influence all the days of my life. . . . It was crystal clear to me that the future and, indeed, the very existence of America, were irrevocably entwined with Asia and its island outposts. . . ."[3]

Thus American and MacArthur's destiny in the Pacific closely involved the general during the interwar period, with two tours of duty in the Philippines (1922–25, 1928–30) before his term as Army Chief of Staff, 1931–35, during which time Japan invested Manchuria to begin its aggression in the Pacific. MacArthur then returned to the Philippines as Military Adviser and field marshal in 1935, being recalled to active duty in 1941 as commander of U.S. military forces in the Far East. Throughout these 20 years, during which no Army generals were really contemplating strategy, and for the initial unhappy days of World War II in the Pacific, MacArthur was preoccupied with the defense of the Philippines and merely had to accept War Plan Orange which called for a Central Pacific naval relief of the islands in wartime. His involvement there, however, made the Philippine Islands into the keystone of MacArthur's future maritime strategy for the eventual defeat of Japan.

Upon the fall of the Philippines and all Southeast Asia to the Japanese during the winter of 1942, General MacArthur turned his attention to the strategy whereby the United States might defeat Japan—and liberate the Philippines in the process. From his first thoughts on the subject, he embraced a maritime strategy. That is, the United States must defeat Japan not by a direct invasion of Japan proper or even by landings on the continent of Asia, in China, but by the indirect approach of whittling down Japanese power in battles for the seizure of the Pacific islands.

Once Japan had spent her naval and air forces in futile attempts to defend the Solomons, New Guinea, Halmaheras, Philippines and Ryukyus against American landings, the home islands of the Japanese Empire could be blockaded and surrounded by superior U.S. naval and air forces. MacArthur himself would command the ground forces of these assaults. The armies of Nippon in China would be bypassed, tied down in the prolonged war against the Chinese. But under no circumstances must the United States attempt to pit its ground forces against the huge Japanese armies in China or Japan.

The frustrations of achieving this end were not in theory, but in the details of execution. Indeed, MacArthur's maritime strategy closely duplicated that of Admiral King and Gen. George C. Marshall of the Joint Chiefs of Staff. The principal opposing detail was the divided command into two main theaters—MacArthur's Southwest Pacific and Adm. Chester W. Nimitz' Central Pacific. From this division emerged two preferred routes to Japan: MacArthur wanting the single line of New Guinea–Philippines, King the dual approach of the Marshalls-Marianas-Formosa with New Guinea secondary and the Philippines to be bypassed.[4]

MacArthur's futile attempt to have the JCS subordinate Nimitz' Central Pacific Force to his own drive up the New Guinea coast during 1943 brought on the not unreasonable fear of the Navy that its new aircraft carriers would be expended guarding MacArthur's northern flank. MacArthur's ubiquitous communiques, which almost failed to recognize the Navy's contribution to the war, only confirmed Admiral King's worst fears—and cemented King's opposition to MacArthur.[5]

None of this rivalry, however, should detract from the fact that General MacArthur steadfastly maintained his commitment to a maritime strategy aimed at choking off Japan's interior sealanes at the "Luzon bottleneck." Furthermore, in January 1944, just as the dual counteroffensive was in its initial stages, MacArthur found adherents to his program in two very influential admirals, John H. Towers, Nimitz' Deputy and air commander, and Forrest Sherman, Nimitz' brilliant planner and another naval aviator. Both men argued for the Pacific drives to meet at the Philippines and convinced Nimitz to agree with them.[6]

Two months later, in March 1944, the JCS agreed on going into the southern Philippines (but with MacArthur still splitting command responsibilities with Nimitz); he to aim for Luzon in the northern Philippines and Nimitz for Formosa, both in early 1945. Admirals King and Nimitz pressed for Formosa and the adjacent Chinese coast at Amoy over Luzon for the next 6 months. Both arguments were thus discussed at length in Hawaii in July 1944 when President Franklin Roosevelt met with MacArthur and Nimitz to review the alternatives. For political as well as military reasons, MacArthur strongly opposed the Formosa plan in favor of Luzon.[7]

A flaw in the Navy's strategic preference for Formosa-Amoy lay in the second part, Amoy. To land on the mainland of Asia as well as in heavily defended Formosa, merely to have naval base facilities and airfields for closing the blockade of Japan proper, flew in the face of sound maritime strategy. Amoy would have to be defended—not as a beachhead or bridgehead but as an enclave, a blockading station, against massive concentrations of still unbeaten Japanese regular Army forces. Amoy would then have to be defended by strong continental forces to prevent a possible Dunkirk and that meant compromising the maritime strategy and fighting continental battles away from Japan's strategic center—Japan itself. Everything for Formosa-Amoy depended upon the ability of the Nationalist Chinese armies to keep open U.S. airfields in China to support this enclave.

In September 1944 General Marshall turned the Army's position against Formosa-Amoy and for the easier target of Luzon. JCS Chairman Adm. William D. Leahy agreed, and so did Admiral Nimitz as the Japanese Army began to overrun the U.S. B-29 bases in China. Admiral King finally had to go along, so that by the time MacArthur's forces landed at Leyte in the Central Philippines in late October MacArthur's maritime strategy had prevailed.[8]

The next decision involved the final campaign to defeat Japan, and here MacArthur's clear maritime strategic thinking reached its zenith. General Marshall and the Army insisted on the invasion of Japan in the traditional continental style as at Normandy in June. Although the Allied Combined Chiefs of Staff in December had suggested invasion might be unnecessary, the JCS nevertheless decided in July 1944 to plan for such an invasion one or two years hence.

Admiral King and the Navy would have none of this. Japan must be sealed off and strangled into submission by air-sea blockade—a philosophy with which the Army Air Forces thoroughly agreed. But King and the Navy still wanted an Amoy-type landing now further up the Chinese coast near Shanghai at the Chusan Archipelago, along with Okinawa Island in the Ryukyus.[9]

As this debate developed, Adm. Forrest Sherman flew to MacArthur's advanced headquarters at Leyte early in November 1944 to iron out some operational details, but during an evening of conversation Mac-Arthur spoke frankly with this man whose mind he obviously respected. (Quoting Sherman's notes in full,) MacArthur

> Expounded [his] theory of our naval and air superiority in the Pacific, and came out flatfootedly against fighting [the] Japanese Army. Particularly emphatic against invading Japan. Said his troops were keyed up to take the Philippines, but basically wanted to go home after that. Said the Fleet should be freed from amphibious war to exert its power to isolate Japan same for air. I emphasized [the] extent to which POA had done only such fighting on shore as was necessary to get bases. He emphasized [the] extent to which he had been able to advance and "cut off half a million men" "under the wing of the Fleet."

After that half million left behind on the bypassed islands, MacArthur preferred not to face the more than two million Japanese troops on the home islands or another two million–plus on the continent, in China, Manchuria, Korea and Indochina.[10]

At the very same meeting, however, the general "stressed several times the ultimate operation on the 'Plains of Tokyo.'" This seeming contradiction may be explained by MacArthur's urgent desire to eliminate as many more Navy-run amphibious operations as possible and to tighten the noose around Japan proper. So while he could not thwart Iwo Jima and Okinawa, neither of which subsequent operations during the first half of 1945 impressed him, he had no use for the Chusan operation being sought by the Navy during the early months of 1945.[11]

"The plain of Tokyo" had become the Army's avowed goal, with a preliminary assault on Kyushu during the autumn of 1945, Operation OLYMPIC, and though General MacArthur preferred not to fight the huge Nipponese Army he could see very well that OLYMPIC was in the works and that he was the logical choice to command it. And if the invasion must occur he had the answer to minimizing his losses: to implement fully a maritime strategy of concentration.

Secretary of the Navy James Forrestal at Manila in February 1945 recorded MacArthur's strategy: He

> expressed the view that the help of the Chinese would be negligible. He felt that we should secure the commitment of the Russians to active and vigorous prosecution of a campaign against the Japanese in Manchukuo [i.e., Manchuria] of such proportions as to pin down a very large part of the Japanese army; that once this campaign was engaged we should then launch an attack on the home islands, giving, as he expressed it, the *coup de main* from the rear while substantial portions of the military power of Japan were engaged on the mainland of Asia. . . . He said he felt that our strength should be reserved for use in the Japanese mainland, on the plain of Tokyo, and that this could not be done without the assurance that the Japanese would be heavily engaged by the Russians in Manchuria.[12]

He told a fellow officer that same week, " . . . we should make every effort to get Russia into the Japanese war before we go into Japan. . . ."[13]

The classic maritime strategy: blockade by the maritime power at sea and from the air while a major allied army—Soviet Russia's—fights on the continent, with the maritime power's expeditionary force—led by MacArthur—landing in the enemy's homeland to administer the *coup de grace* from the rear. Such had been the strategy of Eisenhower at Normandy while the Russians drove the Germans back on the main Eastern Front. Such had been Wellington's strategy against the French in Spain as Napoleon retreated from Russia after 1812. And such was Admiral King's identical thinking on this war in the Pacific.[14]

Given command in May 1945 of the ground forces that would land in Japan, MacArthur pressed the JCS for promoting the Russian attack on Japan, unaware that the Russians had already promised it at the Yalta Conference early in the year. He wanted more than 60 Russian divisions to be used in China as against maybe 13 American divisions to be employed in OLYMPIC and 22 for CORONET, the attack on Tokyo and Honshu in early 1946. Rejecting the idea of bogging down American forces on the mainland of Asia, in April he told the JCS that the American invasion of Japan "would continue the offensive methods which have proven so successful in Pacific campaigns. . . ."[15]

In other words, now that the air-sea blockade had isolated Japan, and assuming that the Russians would pin down the Japanese armies on the mainland, MacArthur put his trust in the maritime-amphibious forces that had so impressed him ever since the landings at Hollandia, New Guinea and at Leyte.

His biographer D. Clayton James has observed that MacArthur "never fully comprehended the principles of modern naval warfare, especially the complexities and dangers inherent in operating fast carrier groups, the Navy's most potent striking force."[16] This had changed, however, by the summer of 1945. MacArthur's considerable powers of observation, somewhat at Hollandia but most profoundly at Leyte, had schooled him in naval operations and taught him to distinguish between effective and ineffective leadership of these naval forces he was learning to respect so much.

For example, within days of Adm. William F. Halsey's near debacle at Leyte Gulf in which Halsey had perilously uncovered MacArthur's beachhead to a Japanese surface fleet attack by taking Adm. Marc A. Mitscher's fast carriers to hit the Japanese decoy carriers, the general changed his theretofore high opinion of "Bull" Halsey. In talking to 7th Fleet Commander Adm. Thomas C. Kinkaid, according to Admiral Sherman, MacArthur "apparently . . . criticized Halsey bitterly for [his] tendency to leave his covering assignment, and questioned [the] accuracy of his claims of damage inflicted." Kinkaid however calmed down MacArthur enough for him to send a congratulatory note to Halsey for his victory at Leyte.[17]

When Admiral Sherman had visited MacArthur at Tacloban on Leyte in November, MacArthur heaped praise on the escort carriers and ships' gunfire but "felt that Halsey by rushing off to watch Mitscher strike [the enemy] cvs had created a critical situation which had been retrieved by [the] magnificent work of [the] cves and their escorts, but [he] seemed to speak entirely without rancor."[18]

Contrasting the easy handling of Admiral Mitscher's 5th Fleet carriers at Hollandia in April 1944 with Halsey's 3rd at Leyte in October and November, MacArthur "spoke highly of the Fifth Fleet and [of] Mitscher's work at Hollandia [and] said: "Off the record—give me the Fifth Fleet or any other than the Third." [He] referred disparingly [sic] to Halsey's "wise cracks" which were not helpful when he wanted information. . . . Said he never knew where Halsey was—neither did Kinkaid. Referred to him as "not a team player." All this when annoyed at lack of knowledge of Halsey's plans. . . ." Two days later MacArthur "commented on Halsey's failure to reply to his messages and his complete ignorance of Halsey's position. It is noteworthy that without [radio] intercepts he has no picture of the strategic position at sea."[19]

Significantly, for the anticipated invasion of Japan, 5th Fleet under Adm. Raymond A. Spruance would provide the assault ships and close support, expanding on its successes in the Marianas and at Iwo Jima and Okinawa. And whereas before these operations MacArthur had been a notorious Marine-hater as well as ignorant of Marine and Navy close air support techniques, after them he fully accepted the superior techniques over Army Air of Navy and Marine Corps close support techniques, after them he fully accepted the superior techniques over Army Air of Navy and Marine Corps close support as well as the complete trustworthiness of the Navy-Marine assault team. For OLYMPIC, therefore, he enthusiastically included Marine Corps divisions and tactical air units and insisted upon Navy control of all close air support which would include 16 escort carriers, four with Marine groups.[20]

As his plans matured, MacArthur warmed to the prospect of the final drive into the home islands but he could not be assured that his maritime strategy would succeed completely until Russia attacked the huge Japanese army in China. When that attack came in early August, MacArthur was thrilled as he learned the details of their advance. His strategy had been rounded out.[21]

The end came within days of the Russian invasion of Manchuria and of the two atomic bombings, that final act of the air-sea blockade. A maritime strategy had defeated Japan, with the added bonus that MacArthur had never had to lead that last assault he had wanted to avoid all along. Later he described the American strategy for victory.

> By the time we had seized the Philippines, we were enabled to lay down a sea and Navy blockade so that the supplies for the maintenance of the Japanese armed forces ceased to reach Japan. . . . At least 3,000,000 of as fine ground troops as I have ever known . . . laid down their arms because they didn't have the materials to fight with . . . and the potential to gather them . . . where we would attack. . . . The [Allied] ground forces that were available in the Pacific were probably at no time more than one-third of the [Japanese] ground forces; but . . . when we disrupted their entire economic system, . . . they surrendered.[22]

Though preoccupied with reconstructing Japan in the 5 years after V-J Day, General MacArthur never deviated from his commitment to the maritime strategy which had worked for him in the Pacific war. He held fast while the cold war situation deteriorated in the Far East with the overthrow of Nationalist China by the Communist Chinese late in 1949 and several concurrent fears; the possibility that Soviet Russia might assist the Red Chinese against the Nationalists on Formosa; the threat of the Vietminh against the French in Indochina; the fighting of the Huks in the Philippines; and the North Korean menace to South Korea.

In February 1950 the JCS—led by its Chairman, Gen. Omar Bradley, but intellectually dominated by Adm. Forrest Sherman—journeyed to Japan to discuss American strategy in the Western Pacific with the Supreme Allied Commander there, MacArthur. To deter all Asian communists, the Chiefs now gave MacArthur control over all fleet units whenever they were in Japanese waters rather than just during emergencies, and reaffirmed the focus of U.S. naval forces to be Yokosuka in Japan and Subic Bay in the Philippines. MacArthur asked that amphibious units training with the Marines be diverted to the Army, but the JCS turned him down.[23] Ominous intelligence projections followed the JCS visit, but MacArthur had no firm strategic plans for any conflict in the Far East.

The bedrock of MacArthur's Far East strategy, however, lay in preserving the integrity of America's bases in the "littoral island chain" that ringed the Asian mainland. He told visiting retired Adm. Charles M. Cooke in April 1950 that the Philippines and Formosa were the keys, but Formosa occupied his attention. Whereas we had morally liberated the Philippines and remained pledged to their defense, Formosa had become a purely military asset whose importance had to be impressed upon the U.S. Government. MacArthur told the JCS this in February, and on 14 June 1950 he sent a four-and-a-half page typed single-spaced "Memorandum on Formosa" to them, adding that Formosa could be a springboard for attack to the south, as it had been for the Japanese in 1941–42.[24]

The North Korean attack across the 38th parallel within days of this memo plunged MacArthur back into the role of active strategist—a Pacific *maritime* strategist. As if the 5 years since he had been planning Operation OLYMPIC had been but a minute in time, he harkened back to his hopes for an allied Russian attack into Japanese China by advising the JCS in July to unleash Nationalist Chinese naval and air forces from Formosa for attacks on mainland amphibious targets and airfields, where Soviet advisers and airplanes were in evidence.

Meanwhile, he employed U.S. naval and air forces to isolate the fighting in South Korea while his ground forces stabilized their retreat at the Pusan perimeter. The prospect of Americans fighting the ground war in Asia that he had managed to avoid in World War II, especially now with only limited forces, did not appeal to him at all and in August he confided to the Chief of Naval Operations, Sherman, "that we must turn Korea over to Koreans as soon as [the] fighting is over and not occupy it."[25]

The association of the two kindred minds of Douglas MacArthur and Forrest Sherman was an intellectual one, stemming from their few meetings during the conduct of the Pacific war but which now reached full flower in the strategy over the Korean conflict. They were both maritime strategists who had agreed on the strategy that had defeated Japan and who now concurred in a dual goal in the new struggle: (1) to retrieve Allied reverses in Korea, and (2) to keep the war from expanding into Chinese territory.

For the first problem, winning the battle in Korea, MacArthur conceived the ingenious scheme in July of landing an expeditionary force in the communist rear at Inchon, retaking Seoul and routing the North Korean army. The sheer audacity of the plan brought Sherman and Army Chief of Staff Gen. J. Lawton Collins out to Japan late in August to study it more closely. When they arrived MacArthur had nothing but praise for the Marines, Air Force and carrier airplanes holding the line at Pusan. And now he wanted more troops for the Inchon assault, he said, namely the Army's X Corps and the First Marine Division, for a miniature OLYMPIC. To the doubts of the JCS over the wisdom of the enterprise, said MacArthur: "My confidence in the Navy is complete, and in fact I seem to have more confidence in the Navy than the Navy has in itself. The Navy's rich experience in staging the numerous amphibious landings under my command in the Pacific . . . leaves me with little doubt on that score."[26]

Sherman, marveling at the general's supreme faith in the Navy's ability to achieve victory at Inchon, took him aside for a private conversation which the CNO later recorded in his diary.

> Had a long talk with MacArthur alone. He praised the Navy and spoke in glowing terms of its future. Said the entire Pacific should eventually be commanded by a naval officer. He agreed to my proposal that in the event of general hostilities, [Pacific Fleet Commander Admiral Arthur] Radford should move forward to wherever MacArthur is and take operational command of the entire Pacific Fleet. Criticized Air Force and blamed them for

poor support of troops. Told me Marines were superb, but had a tendency to gripe. I told him again that Inchon was a dangerous enterprise if any resistance developed. He agreed it could be done only if there were none.[27]

Won over by MacArthur's genius, Sherman took his leave of the general who remarked to him in passing that the Navy was the "only service which hadn't let out a peep" of complaint.[28] As soon as he reached his office in Washington, Sherman immediately wrote to MacArthur that "I feel much better equipped to cope with problems connected with the Far East because of my visit and the opportunity to talk with you."[29] And, of course, MacArthur was correct; the assault in mid-September took Inchon by surprise, broke the back of the North Korean Army, and sent it reeling in retreat back across the 38th parallel.

For the second and larger problem, keeping the war from expanding to the Chinese mainland and thereby risking full-blown retaliation by the Red Chinese and Soviet Russia, MacArthur proclaimed his maritime strategy in which the United States (or United Nations) would maintain its ring of bases that girdled the periphery of East Asia. In a letter to a Veterans of Foreign Wars convention in late August he called this ring the "island chain . . . from the Aleutians to the Marianas . . . from [which] we can dominate with air power every Asiatic port from Vladivostok to Singapore and prevent any hostile movement into the Pacific. . . . If we hold this line we may have peace—lose it and war is inevitable."

At the heart of the chain lay Formosa, "an unsinkable aircraft carrier and submarine tender" that possessed "a concentration of operational air and naval bases potentially greater than any similar concentration on the Asiatic mainland between the Yellow Sea and Strait of Malacca." He also looked upon the Nationalist Chinese as a potential manpower reservoir for fighting on the continent. The Truman administration did not agree with the importance of Formosa, nor the possibility of using its Nationalist Chinese troops, and the President had MacArthur withdraw his already published statement, while the JCS placed restrictions on MacArthur's movements into North Korea so he would not antagonize the Communist Chinese or Russians, restrictions that MacArthur modified to his own liking. The President therefore flew to Wake Island in October to meet MacArthur and to assert his authority over his Far East commander.[30]

At Wake MacArthur conveyed to Truman erroneous intelligence estimates that Red China would not enter the war in Korea and thus was faced with embarrassing reassessments when indeed the Communist Chinese crossed the Yalu the very next month, November, and drove back the United Nations ground forces. MacArthur now began not only to fear for the ability of his limited ground forces to hold in the South in the purely defensive war that the Truman administration wanted, but he also began to doubt whether his skeleton forces in Japan could resist a Russian attack on that country. He asked that National Guard divisions be called up to reinforce his Japan garrison, and then chafed when the JCS late in December told him to evacuate Korea if he could not hold against the Communists there with his available forces.

Douglas MacArthur had been through another such evacuation in the past—the Philippines 9 years before. The nightmares of Bataan and Corregidor had led to the need for the long drive back across the Pacific, and MacArthur could never believe his situation at the end of 1950 paralleled the dark days of early 1942. Consequently he invoked his maritime strategy that had worked so well against Japan and responded to the JCS on 30 December.

He called for four measures to repel the Communist advance: (1) a naval blockade of mainland China, (2) air and naval attacks on the Chinese warmaking industry, (3) the use of Nationalist Chinese troops in Korea inasmuch as the UN could not provide the necessary manpower, and, (4) a not altogether successful strategic ploy most recently demonstrated at Dieppe in 1942, namely the creation of a "diversion" by allowing the Nationalists to make amphibious raids on the mainland at least to promote guerrilla action there and even "possibly leading to counter-invasion."

These actions he believed would save the UN military position in Korea until a political decision was forthcoming "as to whether to maintain the fight in that area or to effect a strategic displacement of our forces with the view to strengthening our defense of the Littoral Island Chain while continuing our naval and air pressure upon China's military potential." To evacuate the Korean peninsula "without taking military measures against China proper," he believed, would hurt American prestige, encourage a Communist assault on Japan, and thus require heavy reinforcements for the defense of that country, particularly against Russia.[31]

The Joint Chiefs rejected MacArthur's recommendations as at least premature and at most alarmist. The Truman administration reflected the attitude of the majority of the American people in not wanting to risk expanding the war, which the JCS felt MacArthur would be doing with his desire and strategy to destroy Red China's warmaking capacity. Furthermore, they noted that the sudden reestablishment in December of a strong UN defensive position in the South was evidence that the military situation was being stabilized.[32]

Nevertheless, MacArthur the military commander clung to his maritime strategy. At no time did he advocate projecting the U.S. Army or Marines into Chinese territory; as he often said, "Anyone in favor of sending American ground forces to fight on Chinese soil should have his head examined." Rather, he would isolate the Korean peninsula from outside supply in classic maritime strategic fashion. Then, as he said in March 1951, he would go after Chinese supply lines: "Control of the sea and the air, which in turn means control over supplies, communications and transportation, are no less essential and decisive now than in the past."[33]

After regaining the Seoul line just south of the 38th parallel, as he recalled in his memoirs,

> I would then clear the enemy rear all across the top of North Korea by massive air attacks. If I were still not permitted to attack the massed enemy reinforcements across the Yalu, or to destroy its bridges, I would sever Korea from Manchuria by laying a field of radioactive wastes—the by-products of atomic manufacture—across all the major lines of enemy supply. . . . Then, reinforced by Nationalist Chinese troops, if I were permitted to use them, and with American reinforcement on the way, I would make simultaneous amphibious and airborne landings at the upper end of both coasts of North Korea, and close a gigantic trap. . . . It would be something like Inchon, but on a much larger scale.[34]

Unfortunately for MacArthur, his completely sound military strategy involved so many political aspects—not least the new idea of using anything nuclear—that the Truman administration could simply not entertain the possibility of adopting his plan. Equally tragic, the JCS had lost confidence in MacArthur's ability to restrain himself should the Communists launch a massive air attack from Manchuria; the Chiefs concluded he would probably retaliate with airstrikes on China's Shandong (Shantung) peninsula. With none of his civilian or military superiors trusting his leadership, MacArthur faced removal from command— done finally in April when he made critical political remarks about the

Administration's prosecution of the war in a letter to Congressman Joe Martin.[35]

Politics aside, Douglas MacArthur ended his career as America's foremost amphibious general. From his initial strategic ideas of 1942 through the Pacific victory and into Korea, he had matured into a maritime strategic thinker of the first rank. And so, in his final statement before a joint session of Congress in April 1951, he repeated his strategic views of the previous August, that the Pacific is

> a protective shield for all of the Americas. . . . We control it to the shores of Asia by a chain of islands extending in an arc from the Aleutians to the Marianas. . . . From this island chain we can dominate with sea and air power every Asiatic port from Vladivostok to Singapore and prevent any hostile movement into the Pacific. Any predatory attack from Asia must be an amphibious effort. No amphibious force can be successful without control of the sea lanes and the air over those lanes. . . . With naval and air supremacy and modest Ground elements to defend bases, any major attack from continental Asia . . . would be doomed to failure. . . . Our line of defense is a natural one and can be maintained . . . [as] an invincible defense against aggression.[36]

General MacArthur's consistent advocacy of a maritime strategy for the United States in the Pacific places him along the nation's leading admirals who have similarly advocated such a strategy. Indeed, if one can excuse this bit of hyperbole (which may well cause him to turn over in his grave!), history would not be far wrong in remembering him also as *Admiral* Douglas MacArthur.

Notes

1. Sir Julian Corbett, *Some Principles of Maritime Strategy* (New York: AMS Press reprint, 1972). The term "indirect approach" is usually attributed to Sir Basil Liddell Hart during the inter–world war period.
2. Clark G. Reynolds, "American Strategic History and Doctrines: A Reconsideration," *Military Affairs*, December 1975, p. 185. For King, see my "Admiral Ernest J. King and the Strategy for Victory in the Pacific," *Naval War College Review*, Winter 1976, pp. 57–64.
3. Quoted in D. Clayton James, *The Years of MacArthur* (Boston: Houghton Mifflin, 1970, 1975), v. I, 94; Douglas MacArthur, *Reminiscences* (New York: McGraw-Hill, 1964), p. 32.
4. Maurice Matloff, *Strategic Planning for Coalition Warfare, 1943–1944* (Washington: Chief of Military History, 1959), pp. 186–191, 207–208.

5. His repeated attempts to gain control of Navy vessels are best described in Daniel E. Barbey, *MacArthur's Amphibious Navy* (Annapolis: U.S. Naval Institute, 1969), while in his forthcoming study of the War Shipping Administration Jeffrey J. Safford has discovered similar efforts with respect to the merchant marine. MacArthur "wreaked havoc with the wsa's turnaround and loading efficiency programs. At certain points he was confiscating the vast majority of the vessels the wsa sent to the South Pacific—for his own 'cross-trades' and for storage purposes." Safford to the writer, 7 May 1979.

6. Clark G. Reynolds. *The Fast Carriers: The Forging of an Air Navy*, rev. ed. (Huntington ny: Krieger, 1978), pp. 116–118; George C. Kenney, *General Kenney Reports* (New York: Duell, Sloan and Pearce, 1949), pp. 346–348; and Matloff, p. 455.

7. James, v. II, pp. 522–524; Reynolds, *Fast Carriers*, pp. 142–143, 243–245; Matloff, pp. 480–482; and Robert Ross Smith, "Luzon versus Formosa," in Kent Roberts Greenfield, ed., *Command Decisions* (Washington: U.S. Dept. of the Army, Office of Military History, 1960), pp. 465–469.

8. James, v. II, 539–541; Reynolds, *Fast Carriers*, pp. 245–246, 248–249; Matloff, pp. 486–487; and Smith, pp. 467–469.

9. Louis Morton, *Strategy and Command* (Washington: Office, Chief of Military History, 1962), pp. 668–669; Matloff, p. 487; and Reynolds, *Fast Carriers*, pp. 248–249, 322–323.

10. Forrest Sherman, "Notes on Conferences with c in cswpa," 3–10 November 1944, p. 11, Sherman papers. Operational Archives, Naval Historical Center. On Japanese strength, see David James, *The Rise and Fall of the Japanese Empire* (New York: Macmillan, 1951), p. 246.

11. Sherman, p. 8. As for Chusan, "He seemed interested, but noncommittal." For the details, see Reynolds, *Fast Carriers*, pp. 323–324.

12. Walter Millis and E. S. Duffield, eds., The Forrestal Diaries (New York: Viking Press, 1951), p. 31. Entry of 28 February 1945.

13. George A. Lincoln, quoted in James, *MacArthur*, v. II, p. 764.

14. See my King essay.

15. Quoted in James, *MacArthur*, v. II, pp. 764–768, 770.

16. James, *MacArthur*, v. II, p. 359.

17. Sherman, p. 4.

18. *Ibid.*, pp. 6–7.

19. *Ibid.*, pp. 9, 12.

20. Reynolds, *Fast Carriers*, pp. 288–289, 298, 342–343, 368; Frank Futrell and James Taylor, "Reorganization for Victory," in W. F. Craven and J. L. Cate, eds., *Army Air Forces in World War II* (Chicago: University of Chicago Press, 1953), v. V, p. 690; and Sherman, p. 8. For MacArthur's education about tactical air and naval gunfire in the Pacific, see James, *MacArthur*, v. II, pp. 281–282 and 283. For the details of olympic, see K. Jack Bauer and Alvin

C. Coox, "OLYMPIC VS. KETTSU-GO," *Marine Corps Gazette*, August 1965, pp. 32–44.

21. James, *MacArthur*, v. II, pp. 773–774, noting MacArthur's press conference 3 days before the anticipated Russian attack. In his *Reminiscences*, p. 261. MacArthur simply chose to forget his advocacy of the Russian invasion because of his displeasure over the Yalta "sell-out." "From my viewpoint, any intervention by Russia during 1945 was not required." He allowed only that he had advocated it in 1941! "See also William Manchester, *American Caesar: Douglas MacArthur, 1880–1964* (Boston: Little, Brown, 1978), pp. 438–439.

22. *Hearings on . . . The Relief of General . . . MacArthur* (Washington: U.S. Govt. Print. Off., 1951), Part I, pp. 57–58, quoted in Theodore Ropp, *War in the Modern World* (New York: Collier Brooks, 1962), pp. 381–382.

23. "JCS Visit to the Pacific, February 1950," prepared by the staff of the Commander in Chief Pacific Fleet/Admiral Arthur W. Radford/, citing JCS 1380/75 of 19 December 1949, JCS 1483/50, NCS 13/3 and NSC 49. Sherman papers. Also, *The New York Times*, 14 February 1950.

24. Omar N. Bradley, "Notes on the Visit of the JCS to the Far East," February 1950, and MacArthur to JCS "Memorandum on Formosa," 14 June 1950, Bradley papers, National Archives, Box I.091. Charles M. Cooke to Forrest P. Sherman, 14 April 1950, Sherman papers. For the detailed sequence of JCS actions over Korea, see James F. Schnabel and Robert J. Watson, *The History of the Joint Chiefs of Staff: The JCS and National Policy: Vol. III, The Korean War* (Washington: JCS Historical Division, March 1979; also Wilmington DE, 1979).

25. Sherman, "Memorandum for the Record" (actually an abbreviated diary) recording all JCS actions between 25 June 1950 and 11 April 1951, entries of 1, 8, 10, 15 and 21 August 1950, Sherman papers; and MacArthur, p. 341.

26. MacArthur, p. 349; Sherman, "Memorandum," entries of 21 and 22 August 1950; and M. W. Cagle and F. A. Manson, *The Sea War in Korea* (Annapolis, U.S. Naval Institute 1957), pp. 75–76.

27. Sherman, "Memorandum," entry of 23 August 1950; MacArthur, pp. 347–348, 350; Manson and Cagle, p.76; David Rees, *Korea: The Limited War* (New York: St. Martin's Press, 1964), pp. 82–83.

28. Quoted in Sherman, "Memorandum," entry of 24 August 1950. See also Robert Debs Heinl, Jr., *Victory at High Tide: The Inchon-Seoul Campaign* (Philadelphia: Lippincott, 1968), pp. 38–41.

29. Sherman to MacArthur, 25 August 1950, Sherman papers.

30. Quoted in *The New York Times*, 29 August 1950: MacArthur, p. 341; Rees, pp. 115ff; Lawrence J. Korb, *The Joint Chiefs of Staff* (Bloomington: Indiana University Press, 1976), pp. 143–145. In the afterglow of Inchon, Bradley wrote to MacArthur on 29 September 1950 that "we want you to feel

unhampered tactically and strategically to proceed north of the 38th parallel," which assurance he liberally interpreted. Bradley papers, Box I.091.

31. MacArthur to the JCS, 30 December 1950, Sherman papers; Sherman, "Memorandum," entries of 2, 9 and 10 January 1951; Rees, pp. 179–181; MacArthur, pp. 378–380. An interesting sidelight to his strategy, in view of the subsequent events in Vietnam, was MacArthur's view of the French crisis in Indochina. At the Wake meeting he told the President, "The French have 150,000 of the best troops there with an officer of the highest reputation in command. . . . I cannot understand why they do not clean it up—we have seen a debacle. . . . I cannot understand it." To which the Pacific Fleet commander Radford observed that the French had no popular backing in Indochina and proposed that they raise native troops. Bradley noted that Truman and MacArthur agreed on the importance of Formosa. Bradley, "Verbatim Notes of Wake Island Meeting," p. 8, Bradley papers, Box II.

32. JCS to MacArthur, 55234 of 9 January 1951; Sherman, "Memorandum," entry of 19 January 1951, Sherman papers. For the dilemma MacArthur faced, see J. Lawton Collins. *War in Peacetime: The History and Lessons of Korea* (Boston: Houghton Mifflin, 1969), pp. 248–254

33. MacArthur, pp. 387, 389.

34. *Ibid.*, p. 384. Collins, pp. 215–216, believed MacArthur placed too much faith in airpower.

35. Sherman, "Memorandum," entry of 8 April 1951; Omar Bradley statement to JCS of 23 April 1951. Copies in Bradley and Sherman papers. On the JCS reasons for MacArthur's relief, see Collins, pp. 284–285, and Manchester, p. 641.

36. Quoted in MacArthur, p. 401.

A Commentary on Dr. Clark Reynolds's Paper "MacArthur as Maritime Strategist"

Gerald E. Wheeler

Gerald Wheeler, the biographer of Admiral Thomas Kinkaid, takes strong issue with Reynolds's interpretation of MacArthur's skills as a strategic thinker.

I found this paper by Dr. Reynolds interesting and thought-provoking. It does highlight an aspect of General MacArthur's military biography that is normally handled a bit amateurishly by writers. In fact, MacArthur, in his own autobiography, spends little time with any discussion of the strategy he used to accomplish ends. Greatly simplified, what Reynolds has done is to describe how the general, in World War II and the Korean war, used the strategy of "the indirect approach." He wasn't the fist to use this strategy, nor the last, but he was the best known during World War II. By Reynolds' own admission, Admiral King and Gen. George C. Marshall led the Joint Chiefs of Staff into developing a strategy for victory in the Pacific, against the Japanese, that incorporated the use of the strategy of the "indirect approach." But King and Marshall were in Washington, and MacArthur was in the Southwest Pacific fighting the Japanese.

Throughout this paper I had to keep fighting off one of those nagging issues—*definitions*. Normally it is the lack of a definition that is bothersome; but with Dr. Reynolds it is the opposite, there is almost a surfeit of definitions. In the beginning I read that *naval strategy* concerned itself with navies, fleets, seaborne operations, amphibious operations when marines are used, all directed toward some important goal. Then I read that *maritime strategy* concerned the use of all armed forces, in an oceanic environment, to achieve some desirable end. A bit further I then read that England had used the *indirect approach* as a part of its *maritime strategy*, and so did the United States. But soon the "indirect approach" and "maritime strategy" became interchangeable. And so they were, if we constrain our study to MacArthur, or to British planning during the time of Churchill; but as an historically usable term, I object to the idea that "maritime strategy" and the "indirect approach" are the same terms and thus interchangeable.

Let me give an example of an exception to demonstrate what I mean. Japan, as an island nation like England, in three wars used a "maritime strategy" to achieve its ends; but I do not find that Japan's strategy was based on the "indirect approach." The Japanese attacked continental powers three times: China in 1894–95, Russia in 1904–05, and the Chinese again in 1937. In these three wars troops were used on the mainland of Asia and navies, transports, and later air fleets (army and navy) were involved. In the earlier wars, of course, major Japanese naval victories in the Battle of the Yalu (September 1894) and at Tsushima Strait (May 1905) made their "maritime strategy" a success. While the Japanese had no military ally nipping at the flanks or rear of the Chinese or the Russians, one might say that they had plenty of rooters on the sidelines, but these countries would hardly be equated with a second front, or something like that. Though it might be straining somewhat to use the example, Italy also employed a "maritime strategy" in Ethiopia, and there was nothing "indirect" about its approach.

When we get to MacArthur's strategic thinking, I think it might be useful to remember that his ideas were definitely evolved out of circumstances that he could not control. Like Carlyle's lady friend who declared that she "accepted the world," as if she had a choice, MacArthur's position in Australia in April 1942 left him (and the Combined Chiefs in Washington) few alternatives except a "maritime strategy"—unless he and his troops really could walk on water. His use of the "indirect approach" stemmed from accommodating to existing facts in 1942 a major land power, though a weak one, was engaged actively in combat with several million Japanese troops; I'm speaking of China, of course. For 5 years the State Department's "strategist in residence," Dr. Stanley K. Hornbeck (Chief of the Division of Far East Affairs and Special Advisor to the Secretary of State), had been pressing the Army, Navy, State, and Treasury Departments, and President Roosevelt, to continue supplying China as the Chinese were the only people resisting the Japanese with force. Some of these people thought of Russia, of course, but that nation was still a question, in terms of potential use against Japan, until the issue at Stalingrad was decided in the winter of 1942–43. Thus, to get back to the point, MacArthur's strategy for defeating Japan, when it began to be formulated, was of necessity a maritime strategy, employing the "indirect approach," but I suspect his continental ally was China and not Russia. By mid-1944, and into 1945, after having his New Guinea campaign saved from the frustrations of 1942 and 1943 by "Uncle Dan, the Amphibious Man" (RADM Daniel Barbey), and his 7th Amphibious Corps, MacArthur could begin to develop seriously a total strategy to defeat Japan.

Reynolds suggests that MacArthur gradually learned the limitations on carrier use and eventually began to appreciate the Navy's ability to shorten wars through blockade and strategic strangulation. Vice Adm. Thomas Kinkaid, the Commander of the 7th Fleet (MacArthur's Navy), wondered if the general would ever understand the way a fleet should be used. He had sacked two previous 7th Fleet Commanders (Vice Adms. Fairfax Leary and Arthur Carpender) because they worried too much (from his viewpoint) about losing their vessels in operations on New Guinea's north coast during most of 1943. Admiral Kinkaid was less worried, possibly because he had more ships during 1944 than had been available to his predecessors. Yet after the great Battle for Leyte Gulf, in October 1944, where the Japanese Navy had been decimated, he was almost fired because he asked MacArthur to delay for a month the Luzon campaign, which included capturing the island of Mindoro in December and then assaulting Luzon in Lingayen Gulf in January 1945. Kinkaid did not want to risk his fleet, including a dozen or so small escort carriers, in trying to sail among the islands between Leyte and Mindoro. He definitely was very concerned that Japanese aircraft, based ashore, might finish off his fleet before it ever got to Luzon. MacArthur had already set a timetable and to change it would result in some sort of loss of stature, or at least so he reasoned. Fortunately for the U.S. Navy, Kinkaid was persuasive, particularly since he was backed by Admirals Halsey and Nimitz. Once the Lingayen Gulf assault was launched in January 1945, and all could see that the "Divine Wind" (kamikaze attacks) would not blow them away, then it became clear to MacArthur, and the Navy, that the maritime strategy he now envisioned would work. But this "maritime strategy" would be more effective if either China or Russia (preferably both) were heavily engaging the Japanese when allied troops went ashore in Kyushu or the Tokyo Plain.

The point I'm making, from studying MacArthur close up in my own research on Admiral Kinkaid, is that MacArthur came late to the role of a genuine "maritime strategist." But once he had given the matter full thought, and with the 3 years of battle experience behind him, including a new willingness to trust the seagoing types, he did evolve a full strategy of the "indirect approach" to end the war with Japan.

When we turn to the Korean war, the interpretation laid down by Reynolds is acceptable except where he seems to agree with General MacArthur's proposals concerning the use of the Nationalist Chinese Army on Formosa (Taiwan). As I read it, it appears that MacArthur did not seem to understand that his very valid arguments used against Admiral King's proposed Formosa-Amoy strategy (trying to defend an enclave, etc.) in 1944 were equally valid when applied to his proposal to use Nationalist Chinese on the mainland, in diversionary raids or a lodgment, in 1951. MacArthur's other proposal, to use the forces of Chiang Kai-shek in Korea, might have been quite sound, except for two considerations: (1) The Joint Chiefs of Staff and the State Department wondered if such a course of action would be politically wise; and (2) the JCS questioned whether the Chinese army would be any more effective in 1951 than it had been when it fled to Formosa 2 years earlier. The first question is probably unanswerable now, and is merely speculative. The second question was answered quite fully at the hearings concerning MacArthur's recall by President Truman, but the key information was censored from the published hearings and only released in 1973. Here the Joint Chiefs and other Army generals testified about their serious reservations concerning whether the Chinese forces of Chiang could defend Formosa, let alone raid the mainland of China or render significant assistance in Korea. The Army Chief of Staff, and several others, believed that Chiang's troops would break and run about as readily as the Republic of Korea armies had already done. A strategy built around the use of possibly unreliable troops would have been a strategy of greater risk than even a General MacArthur should have been allowed to manage—at least so argued the JCS.

I conclude this critique of what I consider a first-class paper with my own bit of hyperbole. Were anyone seriously to think of an "Admiral" MacArthur, the disturbances at the gravesites of Admirals King, Nimitz, and Kinkaid might well be mistaken for earthquakes.

3. JAPAN

The Administration of Japan

Douglas MacArthur

In an address to the Allied Council for Japan on April 5, 1946, MacArthur outlined his policies for the reconstruction of the defeated nation. At the same time he made clear that the Council, which included Soviet members, had only an advisory role in the process.

Members of the Allied Council for Japan:
I welcome you with utmost cordiality in the earnest anticipation that, in keeping with the friendship which has long existed among the several peoples represented here, your deliberations throughout shall be governed by goodwill, mutual understanding and broad tolerance. As the functions of the Council will be advisory and consultative, it will not divide the heavy administrative responsibility of the Supreme Commander as the sole executive authority for the Allied Powers in Japan, but it will make available to him the several viewpoints of its members on questions of policy and action. I hope it will prove to be a valuable factor in the future solution of many problems.

To assist the Council in the fulfillment of its objectives, instructions have been given that copies of all directives issued to the Japanese Government shall promptly be furnished it, together with such background information as may be appropriate to permit a full understanding thereof, or as the Council may specifically desire. Matters of substance will normally be laid before it prior to action. Any advice the Council as a whole or any of its individual members may believe would be helpful to the Supreme Commander will at all times be most welcome, and given the most thorough consideration. As my manifold other duties will not normally permit me to sit with the Council, I have designated a deputy to act as Chairman thereof. To promote full public confidence in its aims and purposes, it is advisable that all formal sessions be open to such of the public and press as existing facilities will accommodate. There is nothing in its deliberations to conceal even from the eyes and ears of our fallen adversary. Through such a practice of pure democracy in the discharge of its responsibilities, the world will know that the Council's deliberations lead to no secret devices, undertakings or commitments. The suspicion, the distrust, and the hatred so often engendered by the veil of secrecy will thus be avoided—and in the undimmed light of public scrutiny we will therefore invite full confidence in the sincerity of our purposes and the rectitude of our aims. As Supreme Commander I can assure you that I entertain no fear that such an opportunity for public discussion will have the slightest adverse effect upon the discharge of my executive responsibilities.

The purposes of the occupation are now well advanced. Japanese forces on the home islands have been disarmed, demobilized, and returned to their homes, and in other respects the Japanese war machine has been neutralized. Dispositions have been taken to eliminate for all time the authority and influence of those who misled the people of Japan into embarking on world conquest, and to establish in Japan a new order of peace, security, and justice; to secure for the Japanese people freedom of speech, religion and thought, and respect for the fundamental human rights; to remove all obstacles to the strengthening of democratic tendencies among the Japanese people; and to readjust the Japanese industrial economy to produce for the Japanese people after reparations an equitable standard of life. All of these dispositions in implementation of principles outlined in the Potsdam Declaration have already been taken.

My policy in the administration of Japan for the Allied Powers has been to act as far as possible through existing instrumentalities of the Japanese Government. The soundness of this policy has been unmistakably reflected in the progress of the occupation. I have sought, while destroying Japan's war potential and exacting just penalties for past wrongs, to build a future for the people of Japan based upon considerations of realism and justice. Without yielding firmness, it has been my purpose to avoid oppressive or arbitrary action, and to infuse into the hearts and minds of the Japanese people principles of liberty and right heretofore unknown to them. As success of the Allied occupational purposes is dependent upon leadership as well as upon direction—as only through the firm application of those very principles which we ourselves defended on the battlefield may we, as victors, become architects of a new Japan, a Japan reoriented to peace, security and justice—this policy shall continue to be the aim of my administration and should serve to guide the Council throughout its deliberations.

Were it otherwise—were we but to insure the thoroughness of Japan's defeat, then leave her prostrate in the ashes of total collapse, history would point to a task poorly done and but partially complete. It is equally for us now to guide her people to rededicate themselves to higher principles, ideals and purposes, to help them rise to the full measure of new and loftier standards of social and political morality—that they firmly may meet the challenge of future utility in the service of mankind. In the consummation of this high purpose, we, as victors in the administration of the vanquished, stand charged to proceed in that full unity of purpose which characterized our common effort in the war just won.

It is no small hindrance that in reaching this goal there are those throughout the Allied world who lift their voices in sharp and ill-conceived criticism of our occupational policies; some, honestly inspired but with no knowledge of conditions existing in this far-distant land, who would see applied here wholly unadaptable principles and methods; some who, lacking both vision and patience, see but the end desired, being blind to the means without which that end is impossible of achievement; some who opposed the guiding principles adopted at Potsdam and who, unwilling now to join in full unity of purpose, seek to foment dissatisfaction in others to the end that such principles be reshaped to their will, or their implementation be impeded; some who, from selfish motives, would exploit as slaves a thoroughly defeated nation and people, thus serving the identical philosophy of evil which Allied soldiers opposed unto death on the battlefields of the world; and some who, for various reasons, are out of sympathy with Allied policies and aims, and seek to sabotage success of the occupation.

To the peoples of the Allied world I would say, in answer to such criticism, that history has given us no precedent of success in a similar military occupation of a defeated nation—anywhere, at any time, to serve as a guide to assist in reshaping Japan to meet the aims to which we are here solemnly committed. It thus has become necessary for us, in meeting that challenge of the past, to devise new guiding principles and new methods by which to solve the problems of the future. To serve this purpose, a wise and far-seeing policy was formulated at Potsdam, fully attuned to the noble ideals, principles and standards in defense of which the Allied nations firmly and in complete unity took their stand. Through implementation of that policy lies best hope that the errors responsible for the failures of past occupations may be avoided in the task to which we are here no less inseparably dedicated. The road ahead is not an easy one, but it is my firm purpose that, within the underlying precepts governing occupational policy, the objective be reached. I fervently hope that each member of the Council will exert his best effort in support of that purpose, eliminating insofar as possible misconceptions which but sow the seeds of disunity and serve the cause of failure.

A new constitution has been evolved, patterned along liberal and democratic lines, which the Japanese Government intends to submit for consideration to the next incoming National Diet. This proposed new constitution is being widely and freely discussed by the Japanese people, who show a healthy disposition to subject all provisions thereof to critical public examination through the media of press and radio. Regardless of changes in form and detail which may well result from this open forum of public debate and the ultimate consideration of the National Diet and the Allied Powers, if the underlying principles remain substantially the same when finally adopted, the instrument will provide the structure that will permit development in Japan of a democratic state, fully conforming to existing Allied policy. If we are firmly to implement that policy, it is incumbent upon us to encourage and assist the Japanese people in reshaping their lives and institutions thereunder—scrupulously avoiding superficial and cynical criticism of motive or purpose and destructive influence upon their will to do just that which it is our firm purpose they shall do.

While the drafting of an acceptable constitution does not of itself establish democracy, which is a thing largely of the spirit, it does provide the design for both structural and spiritual changes in the national life, without which so fundamental a reform would be utterly impossible. With it there is hope for accomplishing that reshaping of national and individual character essential to form the strong foundation of popular support upon which a democratic state must rest. It is yet too early to predict with any degree of certainty how deeply rooted the tenets embodied in such reform will become in the social and political life of Japan. It is inescapably true, however, that the course thus charted to the fulfillment of Allied policy in the democratization of Japan is the only course that points to success—that the degree of that success will depend in large measure upon the patience and encouragement with which we ourselves are willing to endow the test.

While all provisions of this proposed new constitution are of importance, and lead individually and collectively to the desired end as expressed at Potsdam, I desire especially to mention that provision dealing with the renunciation of war. Such renunciation, while in some respects a logical sequence to the destruction of Japan's war-making potential, goes yet further in its surrender of the sovereign right of resort to arms in the international sphere. Japan thereby proclaims her faith in a society of nations governed by just, tolerant and effective rules of universal social and political morality and entrusts its national integrity thereto. The cynic may view such action as demonstrating but a childlike faith in a visionary ideal, but the realist will see in it far deeper significance. He will understand that in the evolution of society it became necessary for man to surrender certain rights theretofore inherent in himself in order that states might be created vested with sovereign power over the individuals who collectively formed them—that foremost of these inherent rights thus surrendered to the body politic was man's right to resort to force in the settlement of disputes with his neighbor. With the advance of society, groups or states federated together through the identical process of surrendering inherent rights and submitting to a sovereign power representing the collective will. In such manner was formed the United States of America, through the renunciation of rights inherent in individual states in order to compose the national sovereignty; the state first recognized and stood guarantor for the integrity of the individual, and thereafter the nation recognized and stood guarantor for the integrity of the state.

The proposal of the Japanese Government—a government over people who now have reason to know the complete failure of war as an instrument of national policy—in effect but recognizes one further step in the evolution of mankind, under which nations would develop, for mutual protection against war, a yet higher law of international social and political morality.

Whether the world is yet ready for so forward a step in the relations between nations, or whether another and totally destructive war—a war involving almost mass extermination—must first be waged, is the great issue which now confronts all peoples.

There can be no doubt that both the progress and survival of civilization is dependent upon the timely recognition of the imperative need for some such forward step—is dependent upon the realization by all nations of the utter futility of force as an arbiter of international issues—is dependent upon elimination from international relations of the suspicion, distrust and hatred which inevitably result from power threats, boundary violations, secret maneuvering, and violence to public morality—is dependent upon a world leadership which does not lack the moral courage to implement the will of the masses who abhor war and upon whom falls the main weight of war's frightful carnage—and finally is dependent upon the development of a world order which will permit a nation such as Japan safely to entrust its national integrity to just such a higher law to which all peoples on earth shall have rendered themselves subservient. Therein lies the road to lasting peace.

I therefore commend Japan's proposal for the renunciation of war to the thoughtful consideration of all of the peoples of the world. It points the way—the only way. The United Nations Organization, admirable as is its purpose, great and noble as are its aims, can only survive to achieve that purpose and those aims if it accomplishes as to all nations just what Japan proposes unilaterally to accomplish through this constitution—abolish war as a sovereign right. Such a renunciation must be simultaneous and universal. It must be all or none. It must be effected by action—not with words alone—an open undisguised action which invites the confidence of all men who would serve the cause of peace. The present instrumentality to enforce its will—the pooled armed might of its component nations—can at best be but a temporary expedient so long as nations still recognize as co-existent the sovereign right of belligerency.

No thoughtful man will fail to recognize that with the development of modern science another war may blast mankind to perdition—but still we hesitate—still we cannot, despite the yawning abyss at our very feet, unshackle ourselves from the past. Therein lies the childlike faith in the future—a faith that, as in the past, the world can somehow manage to survive yet another universal conflict. In that irresponsible faith lies civilization's gravest peril.

We sit here in council, representatives of the military might and moral strength of the modern world. It is our responsibility and our purpose to consolidate and strengthen the peace won at the staggering cost of war. As we thus deal in the international sphere with some of the decisive problems I have but briefly outlined, it is incumbent upon us to proceed on so high a level of universal service that we may do our full part toward restoring the rule of reason to international thought and action. Thereby may we further universal adherence to that higher law in the preservation of peace which finds full and unqualified approval in the enlightened conscience of all of the peoples of the earth.

The Late General MacArthur, Warts and All

Faubion Bowers

Faubion Bowers, military secretary to MacArthur, provides a personal glimpse into the life of the Supreme Commander for the Allied Powers (SCAP).

We were loyal to Him. He was loyal to us, too. He never fired; for that matter, he had never hired us either. We had simply arrived, passed on by one person to another, until suddenly there we were at the top and in a job. Oh, yes, there was one exception, but of that, later. Up there we wrote each other's annual efficiency ratings. He, of course, would have given all of us "Excellent" without a second thought. That wouldn't have been right for the rest of the Army, would it?

"We" means those who were immediately around Him. We were generals, colonels, majors, and one lieutenant. I can't remember a single captain, small as the entourage was. The unique distinction we all shared, and sometimes it was unkindly said to be our only one, was direct access to The General. And that's the way we spoke of Him.

"Close to the Throne" was the expression. We ourselves occasionally used it, but, I seem to recall, we didn't smile. We were by no means humorless, though, in that rarefied empyrean air. One of the aides, for instance, was homosexual in an openly secret sort of way, and when he appeared in the company of one of the other officers, perforce, we would whisper gleefully, "There goes His aide with *his* aide-de-camp." "Camp" meant camp in those days . . . nothing literary or arty.

This was the first year of the Occupation of Japan in Tokyo—1945–1946 plus. Bedizened with stars, General Douglas MacArthur was as dazzling a figure as could be hoped for. Christ, King, MacArthur and Country! He had majesty to a degree . . . to the point of failure. But this flaw in the flawless I simply failed to see.

MacArthur wore a circle of five stars on each shirt-collar tab. As hot September gentled into cold, damp November, via October of course, he added the stars to each shoulder strap of his short jacket, and then, as the weather grew more treacherous, to his raincoat flaps as well. How dirty that raincoat was! So unused to change it wasn't waterproof anymore. Come to think of it, even the famous hallmark, that hat vizored with scrambled eggs, was tarnished, sweat-stained, almost tattered. Rather like never firing anybody, wasn't it?

One of my duties was to ride with him to and from work. We all lived in the American Embassy compound: He in the house on the hill, and we in the two buildings, one of four, the other of five apartments each, down below, where the swimming pool and garden were. Work meant the Dai Ichi Building, an undamaged insurance building, the best in town, a street, moat, and stone wall away from the Imperial Palace.

General MacArthur and I had adjacent offices on the sixth and top floor. I was, to be truthful, in an anteroom to his suite. Technically, I was a military secretary to the C-in-C, pronounced "sink" but meaning "Commander-in-Chief." He preferred the title "SCAP," or Supreme Commander for the Allied Powers, not so much, I believe, because of its exalted and extended connotations, but because it was less reminiscent . . . less competitive with the Presidential title. No man, I quickly began to feel, was more of a hater of Presidents. It seemed that no living President could be good. But I was wrong, as I often was in those days.

"Oh, Hoover," he once said to me, "wasn't so bad."

MacArthur's limousine was an old beat-up Cadillac, souvenir of some conquest from a sugar owner in the Philippines. How splendid it looked, all black and shiny! How soft was its faded grey upholstery! At least so it seemed to all of us after a diet of Jeeps and weapons' carriers— transportation's equivalent of hardtack.

The Tokyo limousine was decorated with two fender flags—one of the United States, the other with the five laurelian stars—and a license plate tersely numbered "1" and, again, glittering silver stars on a bright blue field in front and back. One cold day I counted forty-five stars.

As we drove, he rarely looked out of the window, except when soldiers saluted in the street and the motion caught his eye. He returned salutes with a succession of forefinger-to-brim tremolos. For a while I used to salute the ones he missed, and he would quickly follow suit without even looking. Japan was new to him. He had passed through it briefly once in 1936.

"I thought then . . . it was raining just like now," he soliloquized of a wet evening's ride, " . . . what a brooding race. Something menacing and nefarious about the Japs. . . ."

The oddest part of our rides was not the route, which never varied, but the pace. The ten-minute ride took twenty. "Potshot speed," or "dead-march drag" were the only descriptions. It perplexed all of us why the driver drove so slowly. It was, yes, majestic, but it was also obsequial. A tempo you could hum to, and indeed The General often hummed to himself as we moseyed along.

"He's a target," one of the colonels of our group snapped, "slower than a duck at an amusement park. . . ."

"With the current switched off," someone added.

"We're responsible for his life."

True, the street between Hibiya Park and its trees and shrubs, not to mention the moat, was ideal for a sniper.

"Your job when you're in that car is s-e-c-u-r-i-t-y," a general said, as if spelling it out for me.

"Well, sir," I said, "I can lay a carbine on the car carpet."

"He'd have a fit."

"Why?"

"The General," one of the kindlier aides explained, "doesn't like any kind of fuss. Just do what you think best, but remember, our job is to keep his mind off the little things and on the important stuff."

"What important stuff? Wouldn't you think his life, his very existence . . ."

"You don't understand yet. At the moment he's trying to work out how much money Japan used to spend on its military. He wants to turn all that money over to education."

Next day, I wore a tiny revolver in my trousers pocket. I spoke to the driver.

"Say, Corporal, what do you think of our speed?"

"Me drivin' too fas'?"

"No, not that; too slow, slow enough to get The General shot . . ." and touching wood I added, "at."

"Everything The General does gits criticized by somebody."

"He's not driving."

"All he has to do is holler if he don't like it."

"Corporal! You know The General doesn't like to make a fuss."

"Yes, sir."

There was, next day, not the slightest change in pace. I was furious, but said nothing.

I used to study him out of the corner of my eye as we drove. I welcomed those chances to turn my head and look at him directly to say, "Sir?" or "Really?" He usually sat in total repose, like a monk in a successful session of meditation. His white hands were smooth as wax, only blemished by brown spots of age. His fingers were exquisitely manicured, as if lacquered with transparent polish. He held them in his lap, peacefully. His profile, which I knew better than his full face, was granitic. He was always immaculately clean shaven, and I never saw a nick on him. The skin was tightly drawn and almost translucent. Large bones, an oversize jaw that jutted a little. From face to walk, from gesture to speech, he shown with good breeding. His eyes were a little too small for that face. They were solid brown, both iris and pupil. He was really very beautiful, like fine ore, a splendid rock, a boulder. How full of majesty. "His Majesty," those in lower echelons would sneer. They didn't understand.

He was used to sneers and even abuse.

"I've never liked the Waldorf-Astoria," he once volunteered out of the blue. "It has bad associations for me ever since World War I. I had just come back from France very much the hero. My Rainbow Division was the rage of New York and that night, after the parade, there was a big ball at the Waldorf-Astoria in my honor. I was in full uniform. And in those days full uniform meant spurs and the works. I was dancing and the maître d'hôtel came over to me. He said it was against the hotel rules to wear spurs on the dance floor. I said, 'Do you know who I am?' He said, "Yes, Colonel.' And I took my lady and we walked off the dance floor and I never set foot in that place again. . . ."

Our offices were severe—tan walls, an occasional hotel-type picture, brown leather chairs, harsh blinds. His had a huge mahogany table and across from it was a long leather sofa where visitors sat like Hudson Valley family portraits. ("This is a historic occasion," one of a visiting delegation of nine Congressmen rushed out to gasp at me. "Get a photographer! Quick!")

When he talked to visitors, he paced restlessly back and forth in front of them. He always held a pipe in his hand, and the only time I ever saw one in his mouth was at the airfield when he landed in Atsugi. It was the famous old corncob. I never saw him with it again, although it stood in the pipe rack on his desk. Nor did I ever see him light up or smoke for pleasure. Perhaps he did after dinner in the evening. But none of us ever saw that. No one was invited for the evening meal. Dignitaries were entertained at lunch only. Breakfast was the only meal he had with his son.

Meanwhile, the leather-couch visitors followed him with their eyes. They always looked spellbound, whenever I saw them as I brought in papers or responded to the buzzer. They were enraptured not only by what he said, but how he was saying it, and the fact that he was saying anything at all. A legend was talking, and the wonderment lasted until they had left our offices and were out of my hearing.

"My God," sputtered Berlin's John McCloy as he was putting on his coat in my office. "How does he do it? He's in better health than when I saw him before the war . . . more fascinating than when he was Chief of Staff. . . . What a man! What a man!"

That night I relayed McCloy's enthusiasm.

"How do you do it, sir?"

"I just give 'em a shot of truth. They're so unused to it it knocks 'em for a loop." Then, after a long pause, during which my mind had leaped on to tomorrow's details, he jerked me back to where the conversation had stopped. "A soldier's first duty is to keep fit."

Another of my duties was to sort the morning mail—the one delivery of the day. Cablegrams arrived all the time, because they took varying degrees of time to decode, and the priorities ranged widely. I put these in order of interest, keeping the insignificant ones in a drawer in my desk. Letters that I could answer—those from Japanese, GIs, or requests for simple favors—I did. A polite "No." Those that were fan mail, no matter how trivial, I gave him in a separate pile. Sometimes they came back to me with a notation: a polite yes. "The Commander-in-Chief (or SCAP) has asked me to thank you most kindly for your fine letter." A large number of Americans, GIs and Japanese were heard to say, "I got a letter from MacArthur the other day. . . . Nice guy, after all."

The daily quota of one or two autographs was quickly dispatched. Usually they were to officers who had served in the Pacific under him. I had a drawer full of pictures—always the same—full-face, stern-looking, jaw out, eyes narrowed. They were always signed to officers: "To my comrade-in-arms, Douglas MacArthur." If he was of field rank: "To my comrade-in-arms, Sincerely, Douglas MacArthur." If a fellow general: "To General so-and-so from his comrade-in-arms, Sincerely, Douglas MacArthur." He wrote in a startlingly clear, firm, legible, immaculate hand.

All the other letters he drafted in pencil, and the erasures and crossings out were remarkably few. I sent these to the typist and the holograph was carefully locked away in the "archives"—a row of filing cabinets down the hallway in the corridor.

As a rule his daily letters seldom covered more than a dozen items. One letter I remember, from Harvard's Dr. Conant, offered him an honorary doctorate. He was quite pleased and gave the matter special attention, but he misread the letter. As June approached, another letter came, to which he drafted a cablegram saying there had been a misunderstanding: he could not accept the degree "in person." "Impossible to leave my pressing duties in Japan." Apparently Harvard only gives degrees "in person," so the matter was put in abeyance.

This same reason of "pressing duties" was invoked several times. It forced Roosevelt to Hawaii in 1944, and Truman later to Wake Island. Nothing seemed to annoy outsiders more than his refusal to return to America. They found it arrogant and a gross inconvenience.

I pursued the matter of security.

"Sir, a couple of minor matters," I said as I brought in the mail. He continued reading the newspaper, as was his wont. "It's about how fast the driver drives."

"What's wrong with it?"

"It's slow."

"Leave it be."

"Sir, may I ask another question . . . about security?"

"Fire away."

"What does The General feel about carrying firearms?"

"Me?"

"No. I."

He stopped reading. He looked at me. I had the feeling he had never seen me before. "Suit yourself. Just don't make a fuss."

That evening the blush of white-helmeted MPs outside the Dai Ichi entrance did their twice-daily parade ballet of thunder and blazes: turning, stepping, snapping to, and saluting in four directions, like Tibetan lamas at prayer. MacArthur, head lowered, indifferent, tossed a massive salute to cover the guard and those civilians and Japanese who always clustered at the place, but were harshly cordoned off at a distance. The performance had never been asked for by him, nor was it ever reprimanded for being so fussy.

Homeward bound, he initiated the conversation as usual. "Conversation" to him meant a monologue. He talked out loud, and it really didn't matter, I think, who heard him or whom he was supposed to be addressing. He simply assumed that everyone within his hearing was white, gentile, and a sepulchre of silence. This was never written out *en toutes lettres*, but we all were amazingly Anglo-Saxon and Protestant. He began reminiscing, and I was again struck by the underground continuity of his mind, like a brushfire that disappears and then bursts into flame again in another place.

"Rumor," he said "is a fearsome monster. It gets out of hand and is almost indestructible." His voice deepened and was wonderfully virile. His important words reverberated. Even his mistakes had the unassailability of confidence. How often he said, "between he and I," "medeevial," "sacerligious."

"Once they start talking, everybody believes *them*, and you got to change your tack. Take that story in the Philippines. . . ."

"Which?"

"You know the one."

He wouldn't repeat the phrase "Dugout Doug," and it was only later in the context that I remembered it.

"Why, it almost cost me my life . . . I had to expose myself deliberately on Corregidor. Every time the siren went off, I had to put on my hat and walk out of headquarters' tunnel and just stand there so the men could see me. I couldn't even wear a helmet. What *would* they have said then? They wore one, though." His voice grew edgy. "I just stood there letting the bombs fall like firecrackers. You can thank the Good Lord Almighty that I wasn't hit. Finally, the story stopped. They didn't say it anymore. But at what a price! What a risk! And for what? Rumor.

"And those damn Marine rumors," he continued, as if I had prodded him with a "And then what happened?" "How could the Marines say I sent them in first to soften the battlefields? I wasted thousands and thousands of tons of bombs to counter those damn lies and to prevent anyone's being killed. I pulverized wherever we landed, marines or soldiers. I even had atomic small arms all ready before we landed on Japan. . . ."

He waved toward the weather outside. It was raining again. November was the month when the Olympic Operation—the landing on Japan—was to have begun, had the country not surrendered.

"In weather like this we could never have made it, no matter who I sent in first. The skies would have knocked out my air cover. The Navy wouldn't be able to see to bombard. They wouldn't have taken proper orders anyway."

"Why?"

"They never did . . . not throughout the war, although I said to Roosevelt that I would only get back into uniform if *all* the services were under me." He paused. "I've had hard people to get along with, but Halsey was the limit. Give him an order and he'll do the exact opposite."

Part of the train of MacArthur's thought was a headline Halsey had just made. The peace treaty had been signed on September 2; the Emperor had called on MacArthur, the real surrender. Everything was going well, and some newspaper reporter asked Halsey about once "expressing the view that you'd like to hang the Emperor. Has there been any change?" Halsey had answered, "No, no change. . . . I don't trust the vermin." While this may have read well in the States at the time, it struck at the very foundation of the MacArthur Occupation of Japan.

"Take Stassen, or whatever that commander's name is. I gave strict orders that the Advance Party would evacuate the wounded and sick prisoners-of-war. But oh no. The Navy steps in. That man waltzes into Tokyo and takes a couple of stretcher cases back to his ship and he's a hero. If he had been shot, the war would have had to be resumed. That's irresponsible. I didn't say anything. I didn't want a fuss. Now he's a hero. Let him run for President and see where he gets."

It was seven-thirty in the evening. We had reached the Embassy. We were at the doorway.

"Oh, you're back, General," cried Mrs. MacArthur in surprise. Little Arthur rushed out. He had been allowed to stay up.

"Daddy."

The General swept him up in his arms and kissed him. "Now to bed. Here Mrs. Gibbs, take Arthur. I want to talk to Mrs. MacArthur.

My main duty at the office was to filter people . . . sort them pretty much as I did the mail. Some could and some could *not* see him. My instructions were first to stall, and then, if forced, to make appointments for between six and seven in the evening only. Never at any other time. Dinner would be the excuse for breaking away. Those who had automatic appointments were the Japanese Prime Minister (the only Japanese he ever saw except for the Emperor), commanding generals under his direct command, and visiting firemen who outranked him—Chief of Staff Eisenhower, the Secretary of War, etc.

A message came to me that Danny Kaye and Leo Durocher were in Japan. They would like to call on The General for a "few moments, just to pay their respects." As I put the mail on his desk, I said, "I'm making an appointment today for Danny Kaye and Leo Durocher."

"Route them to Mrs. MacArthur. Make her give them tea."

I called Mrs. MacArthur. She was thrilled. "The General just adores them both."

"Well, not this time. He wants you to give them tea."

I made the appointment for four-thirty at he Embassy. I was to be there, because, as she said, "I don't know a thing about baseball."

We spent the half-hour ahead of time discussing whether or not to serve drinks.

"I can't have people saying they got drunk at The General's, don't you know," said Mrs. MacArthur.

"But these are show people, baseball. . . ."

We decided on sherry, but only if they refused tea.

They arrived, and the conversation consisted of eulogies of The General, how much America admired him, how great he was in war, how they admired him.

"Oh, I forgot, won't you take some tea?"

"Why, yes, thank you."

"We also have a little sherry, I believe, don't we, Major?"

"Yes, I believe so."

"A little of that, too, please."

We all drank sherry and the tea got cold. As they left, Kaye said point-blank, "Mrs. MacArthur, we would be delighted if we could just get a glimpse of The General, just to say hello and shake his hand."

"Why, of course, he'd be thrilled. We watch your movies all the time, right here in the Embassy. He hasn't time to *go* to the movies, so we have showings right here in the drawing room. The house is so big, don't you know."

"When would it be convenient for The General to see us?"

"Oh, Major, can you set a time when The General is free?"

"How about day after tomorrow? Around six? That is, if Mr. Kaye and Mr. Durocher are still here."

"Why, we'll lay over specially," Kaye said.

Mrs. MacArthur winked at me.

Next morning, I informed The General.

"Can't be helped. Can't have them hoping for a visit and then leaving saying I wouldn't see them. Don't want a fuss. Now that the war's over every Tom, Dick and his cat's coming over."

People came and went. One didn't go. There was another who also stayed. The first was a poisonous general who dropped by for a chat with me. One time he put two bottles of Suntory whiskey on my desk . . . liquid gold . . . straight from the "distilleries' officer."

"Any appointments for The General tonight?"

"None."

That general walked straight through the door, past the private bathroom, into The General himself. He stayed there happily forever after and The General never sent him away.

The second was a colonel who barged into my office one afternoon. As soon as he introduced himself, the cogs clicked in my mind. He was the man The General had fired for drinking too much. I had heard all about it during the sherry crisis from Mrs. MacArthur.

I said that The General was busy and would not see him. Would you care to write him a letter? The colonel, having been an aide himself, ordered, "Just go in the office, tell him my name and say that I am outside, on my way home, quitting the Army . . . he'll see me."

"Sure, shoot 'im in," said The General.

Ten minutes later the colonel came out. He was puffing with joy, his eyes dancing with delight.

"He just wouldn't let me go. I am staying on here in the Army. He's finding me a slot. Be seein' ya. Wow, what a man!"

Other people, of course, were visitors in the sense of transients, or persons involved with the Occupation who came on business rather than for a social look-see. One was a State Department fellow who brought a message from Joseph Grew, Ambassador to Japan at the time of Pearl Harbor. Grew had suggested to MacArthur that he not only use the Embassy as his home, but that he unpack all the crates of Grew belongings and set the house up just as it had been in his heyday. Now, the message came saying that Grew was frantically worried about an autographed photograph of Roosevelt. He had heard that some GIS guarding MacArthur at the Embassy had stolen it. They hadn't. I had packed it away myself. It read: "To Ambassador Joseph Grew, Sincerely, Franklin D. Roosevelt." Before packing it, I showed it to MacArthur. It was the first time I ever saw him angry.

Another time the callers were the Commanding General of the Soviet Occupation Forces—they fought the Japanese the last month of the war, in Manchuria—and the representative on the Allied Council which theoretically was supposed to oversee the supervision of the country.

"They're up to no good," The General said. "I've got to freeze them out. Otherwise they'll take a mile. I won't let them lay a hand on Japan."

The Soviets arrived in a cloud of officials and uniforms. Everyone crammed into The General's office. Usually, generals talked privately, while the ADCs sat with me outside. (I particularly enjoyed it when the British Commander-in-Chief of his forces came; his aide was Brigadier Profumo.)

Seven o'clock came and went. Mrs. MacArthur called.

"Dinner first burned and now it's cold."

"The Soviets are here. Shall I break in?"

"No, don't disturb The General."

At eight-thirty, MacArthur came into my office. They'd left by the other door.

"Let's wait a minute and then go in." He didn't want to run into them at the elevator.

"What took so long?" I asked, but didn't get an answer until we were in the car on our way home.

"I hate terminating an interview. They'll say I kicked them out," he began. "But the Russians sit like bumps on a log. I had to initiate the conversation. I hate opening these things, too. They come to see me. I don't lift a finger to see *them*. They didn't even bring me Stalin's greetings. Can you beat that? I took the bull by the horns and said, 'How are things in Moscow?' 'In order,' Derevyanko says. Then like a stupid parrot he says, 'How are things in Tokyo?' 'In order,' I said and I threw in, 'As you can see . . . all you have to do is look around yourself.' Finally he gets up his courage and asks if we can have our picture taken together."

"What were your impressions of him?"

"Huh?"

I had noticed that his hearing was impaired and repeated the question more loudly, as I often had to.

"Him? Just one of those peasant generals. Probably fought well in Manchuria. They learn one thing at Staff College and go on repeating it. That's why he got this post here. Tactics won't do him any good with me though. I'll nip him in the bud before he can start. Just think, I had to stop the interview or we'd still be sitting there. I told him my wife was waiting, and we had a long talk about wives. I said dinner was waiting, and we talked about Russian and American food. He invited me to Russia to taste the food there. I accepted. My, my, those Russians, all fuss, all bother, nothing but trouble-makers . . . up to no good.

"Good-night."

"Good-night, sir."

Later that night at dinner, a friend said to me, "How can you stand all that crap . . . the claptrap . . . that Honor Guard doing a jig with rifles outside the Dai Ichi when he arrives and leaves? All those references to God as if the two of them were in cahoots?"

"He is a great man, and you don't understand."

"Did you hear his speech about how Christianity was sweeping Japan since the Occupation?"

"Yes, of course, I sent down the request for the statistics."

"I supplied the figure."

"Thanks."

"Well, there were more Christians *before* the war than now. I submitted the correct figure and my boss said, 'MacArthur won't like this, it's not enough.' So I added a zero."

"Well, that's not *his* fault."

"Of course it is," he snapped, "to create such an atmosphere."

However, MacArthur's guiding axiom, as he often said, was, "If it is right at the top, it will be right at the bottom."

I know of no greater untruth than the old saw about no man being a hero to his valet. All of us were convinced of MacArthur's magnificence. We protected the image, deified the man, and as disciples became rather sanctified ourselves. One morning I read a postcard that came in the mail for him. It was from his pilot who was on leave in Manila. The exact words are etched on my memory: "Dear General, I write this card to one who talks and walks with God."

There was the time when the Son of Heaven talked with God, too, as some of the more irreverent among us put it jocularly. The Emperor in late September sent a message saying he would like to meet The General at any place, under any conditions The General set. MacArthur simply replied that, for privacy, he would receive the Emperor at the Embassy, in his home. One photograph would be taken. The Emperor could also bring his own interpreter, if he wished.

A few days later, at ten in the morning, a stream of black limousines sped out of the Imperial Palace and crowded into the Embassy driveway. I was standing at the doorway, with specific instructions to salute smartly and show every deference. Mrs. MacArthur and Arthur were allowed to hide behind the hall curtains, provided they made no sound. The Emperor bowed low. I took his top hat and motioned him inside. He was in frock coat, dressed to the hilt. MacArthur was in open shirt, no coat or tie—it was warm.

"Your Majesty," he said warmly and walked quickly to the Emperor, grasping his hand. The Emperor bowed deeper than ever. He then introduced his staff of twelve or so who had accompanied him—chamberlains, heads of protocol, keeper of the treasures, and all manner of Imperial Household Staff. MacArthur swept the Emperor and his interpreter into the large drawing room, and the assistants and we lesser aides crowded into the small library. Conversation was stiff. I spoke of the theatre. No one had seen it. One of the generals on our side said to me, "Tell them that I went duck shooting with the King of Egypt."

"Would The General like to go duck shooting in the Emperor's preserve?"

"Well, his duties are pretty pressing."

After a half hour, the Emperor and MacArthur emerged. Farewells were said with dignity and warmth. The cortège backed out, down the driveway awkwardly. Mrs. MacArthur and I stood in front of The General, waiting to hear.

"I was born a democrat, I was reared as a liberal. But I tell you I find it painful to see a man once so high and mighty brought down so low."

He marched upstairs, leaving us. We didn't go to the office that day.

Some days later, in the car, MacArthur began, "I could have humiliated him, publicly exposed him, but what for? I fought the war; he ended it. He deserves respect, the magnanimous gesture a noble defeated enemy deserves. Besides, with him as figurehead, our job is so much more easy."

Not long after, all of us aides asked the Emperor for his autograph. He sent it . . . in trembling, scrawly English script.

Another night, on our way home, The General couldn't stop talking. He went on and on, but he wasn't really angry, just annoyed.

"How dare they reprint that article? What has my paunch to do with my work? Why do they say I have special tucks in my trousers to hide it? How can they say a man of my dignity combs his hair to hide his baldness? It's downright disrespectful to a soldier who has served his country for all these years. . . . Why there I was in the Philippines, retired, my career at an end, enjoying myself for the first time in years and years and they call me up. . . . Take command. How can they mock my references to the Almighty?"

Perhaps the rockiest time of the Occupation for all of us was when General Eisenhower arrived from Washington. From the moment I put the cablegram on his desk, MacArthur was cross.

"What about General Eisenhower, sir?" I asked.

"Up to no good. He'll look for trouble and I hope he doesn't find it. Got the roar of the crowd in his ears, that boy. Can't sit still and do his job. Got to junket around. Look at that trip to Canada. What was he doing there? The Canadians didn't even recognize his visit with a parade. . . . He used to be an aide of mine in the Philippines, and he hasn't changed a whit. If I had to know something that I had forgotten, he made a good enough aide-mémoire, but if I wanted a plan of something, a scheme worked out, he would always turn up with some damn crackbrain scheme that wouldn't work in years. Hopeless."

"But in Europe?"

"He never fought in Europe. He let his generals in the field fight the war for him. They were good and covered up for him. He drank tea and coffee with kings and queens. Just up Eisenhower's alley, and that's why Rosenfeld . . . Roosevelt . . . put him there. He was told to keep the peace. His only instructions were, in case of doubt, sell the American soldier down the drain! Keep on good terms with the Allies. He did that all right. Look who our Allies were. Russians. English. Roosevelt didn't care how the war was fought, so long as the Allies were happy. Lucky he had Patton. Poor old Patton. I and him are the only generals they persecute. The press hauls us over the coals, and for what? Without us they wouldn't have a paper to write for."

"What was Roosevelt like?"

"A social butterfly. It's always the military who come in and sweep up the mess the President and those coffee-drinking diplomats make. They bungle; we extricate. There I was fighting Roosevelt's war for him and he wanted to meet *me*. For what? I didn't want to meet him. Well, I made him cross over to Hawaii. That was as far as I was going to leave my work. He's rolled down the gangway, holds out his hand, forces me to come to him, and says, 'Douglas.' How could he use my first name? I didn't know him. And now we're even worse off with that Jew in the White House."

"Which?"

"Truman. You can tell by his name. Look at his face . . ."

Eisenhower arrived, and rioting which and been going on for two weeks broke out anew. The problem at that time was that the war was over, but Washington had not provided for getting the boys out of uniform and back home.

"You see, Eisenhower can't even work out a plan to demobilize. If those men aren't home by Christmas, there won't be an Army for the next war."

That night, the generals were closeted until around ten o'clock, supperless, waiting for the cable from Washington, from Eisenhower's office, which would contain a demobilization plan. It came. I took it in.

"Thank God, at last," MacArthur said spontaneously. "Now we can issue a press release and tell our boys they're going home in these stages."

Eisenhower glowered.

Innumerable cables came across my desk during my tenure headed, "Hodge to SCAP," and marked "Top Secret." General Hodge was the commander in Korea, "if only for a day." "Your presence will stabilize the situation...." "I urgently request your active participation in my difficult position." "Calm can only be assured by your visit, no matter how short your stay." SCAP to Hodge was equally monotonous. "My pressing duties here preclude..." or words to that effect.

One day Hodge turned up in person. He waited until six, when The General received him.

"How are things in Korea?" I asked the aide waiting with me.

"Hell."

"That's too bad."

"Korea is the bottom of creation."

"I hear your general won't let Koreans ride in Army jeeps."

"If so they'd take over and we'd walk. Too damn many Koreans."

"We're better off here. We can ride the girls home anytime...."

"We don't have the girls we'd *want* to ride...."

Later, on our way home, MacArthur mused about the interview.

"I wouldn't put my foot in Korea. It belongs to the State Department. They wanted it and got it. They have jurisdiction. I don't. I wouldn't touch it with a ten-foot barge pole. The damn diplomats make the wars and we win them. Why should I save their skin? I won't help Hodge. Let them help themselves."

Suddenly we passed a GI embracing a Japanese girl, hotly.

"Look at that," The General said. "They keep trying to me to stop all this Madam Butterflying around, too. I won't do it. My father told me never to give an order unless I was certain it would be carried out. I wouldn't issue a no-fraternization order for all the tea in China."

Shortly after this, one morning The General was reading the *Stars and Stripes*, and I walked in with a handful of letters. The banner story announced that the Canadians had named a mountain after Eisenhower. The General followed my eye.

"It's a very small peak, considering the Canadian terrain."

I picked up the letters that he had hand-drafted. He handed me a letter he had earlier opened.

"Look at this."

It was from a lady in Wisconsin urging him to run for President.

"Very nice, sir."

"I just don't get it. The press spends its time tearing me down . . . and look at my fan mail. The press doesn't say what the American people are thinking. This does."

The phone in my office rang. It was one of the aides.

"Be sure to be back at three. We're having a game of musical chairs with little Arthur again."

It was his birthday. The full staff was to be there. We ranged in age from twenty-six to fifty-six, and in girth from twenty-six to a tubby forty-two. The game ended. It was long over. Arthur was fast asleep in bed. The General drove home that night . . . alone.

Success in Japan—Despite Some Human Foibles and Cultural Problems

Robert B. Textor

During 1946–48 Robert B. Textor served in Japan as Civil Information and Education Officer at First Corps headquarters and later with the Wakayama Military Government Team. In 1951 he published Failure in Japan: With Keystones for A Positive Policy, *a critical look at occupation policy. Forty years later Textor, professor emeritus of anthropology at Stanford University and courtesy professor of International Studies at the University of Oregon, had occasion to reflect on his earlier views, including MacArthur's role in the occupation.*

The last time I was in Tokyo I paid a sentimental visit to the Dai Ichi Building. I took the elevator to the fifth floor, there to find the inevitable *uketsuke* (receptionist). I asked the old man if I could see *Maakaasaa Gensui no jimusho*, and promptly—as though long accustomed to receiving nostalgic *gaijin* visitors like me—he slipped on his sandals and led me down the hallway.

There it was: a pleasant room with paneled walls. I looked everywhere for some kind of marker or plaque. There was none. Yet, out of respect for its history, the company that owned the building kept the room clean and tidy but unused, except for an occasional company reception. For this room, from 1945 to 1951, had been the office of General of the Army Douglas MacArthur.[1]

Here, I mused, was where a thousand vital decisions had been made—decisions that would impact upon the entirety of Japanese politics and economics, and indeed on the very fabric of everyday Japanese life. Here was where policies were developed that freed up liberal Japanese to initiate sociocultural change processes that might not otherwise have taken place as quickly—or at all.

I stood there alone quietly for several minutes, thinking a thousand thoughts. Then I left the building and strolled across to the plaza in front of the Imperial Palace. Thousands of school children were there on *ensoku* (school trips). They were smiling, relaxed, spontaneous. I started a conversation with some of them, and was struck by how much easier I found it to speak with these kids in 1983, than with those I had met back in 1946–48. Back then, as an Occupation official, I had made scores of school inspections, during which I had always tried to include conversations with students—but had usually found them stiff and almost ritualistic in their responses. But on this bright day 35 years later, I said to myself, "Hey, these look like the kinds of kids we *hoped* Japan would some day have, back in the Forties when we were working with Japanese educators." Here in front of me, I ruminated, stood convincing exemplars of the "New Japan" that we in Military Government had talked about with our Japanese colleagues more than a generation earlier. The future had become the present. It was a good feeling.

This article deals with one person's experience in working with Japanese educators and media communicators to help build that New Japan. It deals principally with my "grass roots" work during the first half of 1948 as a civilian official of Military Government (MG) in Wakayama Prefecture. I shall illustrate my experiences by quoting selected excerpts from my monthly reports to higher headquarters.[2]

Ironically, this article reports on events and phenomena of a nature doubtless quite foreign to Douglas MacArthur's own experience in Japan—for he defined his role from the start as that of a sort of latter-day *shoogun*, aloof from the masses of ordinary Japanese. He played that role to perfection. In my view, his aloof stance was not only one that came to him naturally, but one that he should have taken even if it had not come naturally. Given the Japanese political culture at the time, his very unreachability gave him maximal charisma, and hence tremendous influence over political, economic, and sociocultural change processes. It did, though, have the disadvantage that it permitted him no direct opportunity to observe events at the grass roots.[3]

Enter the Occupationaire

In 1943 I was a 20-year-old student at Antioch College when the Army of the United States finally decided that it wanted me, on the double, and promptly proceeded to transmogrify me into an infantry heavy weapons gunner. Then, in its wisdom, the military personnel system assigned me to the Army Japanese Language School at the University of Michigan. As the fates willed it, I spent the rest of the war either at Ann Arbor or waiting to go there.

Like millions of young Americans at that time, I believed deeply in America's war aims. When v-j Day arrived, I felt an irresistible urge to get to Japan as quickly as possible and do what I could to promote a democratic new order. I reported to my separation center three days early, hurried to Washington, and took the first War Department civilian job offered me.

On a sunny April morning in 1946, I arrived in Yokohama aboard an army troop transport ship. Our group was loaded onto busses for the trip to Tokyo. I was shocked beyond forgetting at the sight of this totally flattened city. Little else besides scattered chimneys, steel safes, and stone *kura* storehouses had survived the holocaust of American fire bombs. This shock, and others like it which followed, only strengthened my resolve to do what I could to promote democracy in Japan—on the assumption, of course, that a democratic Japan would less likely be an aggressive Japan.

I had been assigned as a civilian interpreter to the Allied Translator and Interpreter Service, Supreme Commander for the Allied Powers (ATIS/SCAP). However, it was immediately clear that if I stayed at ATIS, the odds were strong that my duties would be routine and technical—precisely what I did not want. What I did want was direct contact with those Japanese who were actively working at the intercultural synapse across which Americans and Japanese were attempting to communicate and cooperate in the process of fashioning a New Japan.

Fortunately for me there was at that time a severe shortage of trained Americans on hand to run the Occupation. Tens of thousands of military personnel chafed impatiently to return home for discharge, and only a relative handful of civilians were available to take their places and staff a rapidly expanding Occupation bureaucracy. Given this fluid situation, and the grace of the Almighty, I managed to get myself released from ATIS, and to convince the Military Government Civil Information and Education (MG CIE) Division at Eighth Army Headquarters that my qualifications as a specialist on Japanese language and culture somehow made up for my very limited experience as a teacher.

Thus, unbelievably, at the age of 23 I found myself Assistant CIE Officer, MG Section, Headquarters First Corps, Kyoto. There, my supervisor, the late Ronald S. Anderson, and I were responsible for overseeing the implementation of Occupation policy for the democratic reorientation of all schools and public media in three MG regions embracing almost one-third of the population of Japan. Similarly, we implemented Occupation policy with respect to religion and the preservation of arts and monuments. Given the priceless artistic and historic treasures of unbombed Kyoto and Nara, this last responsibility was considerable. In pursuit of all these duties, I traveled frequently throughout the three regions.

Anderson and I were also directly involved in the hiring of numerous civilian CIE officers to work in the three regions under our charge. This experience gave us a first-hand awareness of the kinds of Americans who were being posted to 20 of Japan's 46 prefectures—their widely varying competences, cultural sensitivity, values, goals, world view—and the extent of their knowledge of Japan.[4]

After a year and a half in Kyoto, I was given the opportunity to conduct my own operation, as CIE Officer in Wakayama Prefecture, near Osaka. During the following eight months, I gave guidance, assistance, and encouragement to a hard-working group of local educators who, with stunning speed and skill, succeeded in achieving a comprehensive restructuring of Wakayama's entire public school system, aimed at achieving gender and class equality of access to elementary and secondary education. This was in effect a bloodless revolution, and will serve as the center-piece for much of the analysis that follows. I also worked with a small group of college professors in designing what is today Wakayama University.[5]

During those heady days I was well aware that I enjoyed a level of responsibility far higher than I deserved, especially in terms of my "paper" qualifications. However, as one who helped hire and supervise numerous CIE officers for First Corps' 20 prefectures, I soon saw how ethnocentric and culturally naive some occupationaires were, who *did* have impressive paper qualifications—e.g., 15 years as a superintendent in an isolated monolingual rural district in the American heartland—and I felt less inadequate. "We're *all* unqualified," I told myself, "so why not just do your best, and hope it's good enough?"

Moreover, my enthusiasm for activism rose as I discovered how many key Japanese leaders, officials, and intellectuals were *ready* for change. Japan had suffered cataclysmic losses in a brutal war, had experienced the utter horror of nuclear attack, and, for the first time ever, had been occupied by foreign troops. All this trauma had certainly rendered many Japanese wide open to new ideas about how to conduct social life. And the fact that the Emperor had instructed them to lay down their arms gave a powerful legitimacy to Occupation efforts to effectuate or catalyze change.

I was also struck by what can only be termed a *cultural* characteristic of the Japanese: a tendency to search relentlessly for the *best* way to do something. This tendency had been in manifest operation throughout Japan's modern period since at least the 1870s, when the Japanese government started sending missions to the West to find out what was the best legal system, the best military system, the best education system, etc., for Japan. And now, due to the exigencies of war and surrender, I found myself besieged daily with questions about the best way to run an organization, a school system, a newspaper, or, indeed, a country. It was a unique and humbling historic opportunity.

So, in the two years that followed, I learned to consider eleven-hour days and six- or seven-day weeks to be a reasonable, and deeply satisfying, work routine. Throughout this entire period, I was in direct daily contact with Japanese educators, writers, journalists, labor leaders, intellectuals, politicians, and reform-minded citizens. I made scores of school inspections, gave countless lectures to teachers' groups, youth clubs, civic associations, PTAS, etc., and held numerous press conferences. Frequently, this contact was through the medium of the Japanese language.

Incidentally, Japan reoriented my entire life. When I returned to the States in 1948 I switched career plans and became a cultural anthropologist. In reflecting today on the grass-roots aspects of the occupation of Japan, therefore, I do so primarily as an anthropologist—though secondarily through the prisms of history and political science.[6]

Human Foibles on the American Side

The pace and profundity of daily life in MG at the grass roots readily revealed numerous human foibles on both sides, as well as the patterned ways in which each side defined the other side's foibles. I will not dwell on these human foibles very long, but a quick summary of a few of them (or more precisely, my imperfect perceptions of them) will serve to create the context for the analysis to follow.

Unprepared Personnel

In the early months of the occupation, almost all MG officers were military—I being, as I recall, the first civilian of officer rank in First Corps Headquarters' MG section.[7] Gradually, more and more civilians were hired, though the top jobs remained in military hands.

In terms of their fitness for cross-cultural work, MG's officers, military and civilian, varied from excellent to poor. At the positive end of the continuum one found, among others, a number of officers who had been trained for MG duties at various Civil Administration Training Schools (CATS schools) in the U.S. during the war.[8] Many were citizen-soldiers who could draw upon successful administrative or leadership careers in their civilian past. Some of these officers took discharges in Japan and continued their duties as civilians.

As I recall, all of the CATS alumni that I met were male. Indeed, during the first year or so, MG in the First Corps area was almost exclusively staffed by males. It was only gradually that any appreciable number of women MG officers were hired—a fact that certainly rendered prefectural and regional teams less sensitive to the needs and problems of Japanese women than would otherwise have been the case.

At the negative end of the preparedness continuum were many officers—especially career military—who often had exemplary war records, but sometimes were hopelessly unprepared by education or experience, and perhaps temperament, for anything like MG work. They lacked previous cross-cultural experience or knowledge of any foreign language, and were further handicapped by a certain narrowness that hardly fitted them to function effectively in Japan, let alone to supervise or to lead in Occupation affairs.[9] I have described this situation elsewhere (Textor 1951: 186–96), and will not belabor it here.

Looking back on all this, I sometimes find myself marveling that MG didn't do more harm. I believe that what saved the organization, in part, was that, for many domains of responsibility, MG officers were formally expected merely to "observe and report" compliance with Occupation directives. This often made it possible for an officer to satisfy higher headquarters while in fact remaining fairly passive—after all, one could always ask for some statistics from the *kenchoo* (prefectural government office), and put them into a plausible monthly report that would probably satisfy higher headquarters. Many, perhaps most, MG officers, especially military ones, (and most especially *career* military ones) were inclined to take this route—and then relax and enjoy life.[10] This is not to say that many such officers were not conscientious, but it is to say that many were scarcely inclined to go out of their way looking for problems.

By contrast, some military, and more civilian, MG officers did go farther, and became quite ardent activists. I include myself in this category. Instead of simply "observing and reporting," my philosophy—shared widely in MG CIE—was that we should assertively try to encourage positive change processes by "guiding and assisting" relevant Japanese in a consistent and persistent manner.[11]

Inefficient Structure

The MG structure was a part of the Eighth Army, with headquarters in Yokohama. Under Eighth Army were two corps: the Ninth, headquartered in Sendai, and the First, headquartered in Kyoto. Under the First Corps were three MG regions: Kinki, Tokai-Hokuriku, and Kyushu, headquartered respectively in Kyoto, Nagoya, and Fukuoka.[12] Under each region in the First Corps area were six or seven prefectures, each with its prefectural MG team. At all levels—army, corps, region, and team—the commanding and executive officers were invariably military, as were, typically, the holders of many other key posts.

Note that here was a situation of extreme shortage of qualified personnel, yet the military saw fit to maintain *five* levels of administration for military governance purposes, where three would not only have done the job faster, but saved manpower for other purposes.[13] The only justification for such redundancy was, I suppose, the unspoken one that it provided niches for military officers who might otherwise have been difficult to place![14]

Vagueness of Mission

Especially in the early days of the occupation, prefectural MG teams were plagued by the vagueness of their mission, and the difficulty of securing urgently needed policy decisions, due in part to the three layers of bureaucracy between themselves and SCAP in Tokyo. And it was SCAP *alone* which, in theory, made all policy decisions.

Perhaps this theoretical administrative model could have worked, but only in a situation in which the structure was highly efficient and the mission clearly defined and widely understood. In reality, however, such was not the situation. Only in some cases would a prefectural MG officer refer a problem to higher headquarters—and be prepared to wait weeks for an authoritative decision. In other cases the officer would simply demur, and assume that the problem at hand would somehow solve itself without MG intervention.[15]

In still other and numerous cases, however, referral or demurral were not appropriate. Such cases were those in which Japanese officials and citizens would ask MG for clarification as to whether this or that option was permitted by Occupation policy, where *not* to have given an immediate and clear response would have created more problems, or even danger, than to have referred the matter to higher headquarters. In such cases, MG officers would simply, in effect, *make* interim *ad hoc* policy. Technically, however, such officers might well have been exceeding their authority.[16]

In short, MG CIE officers often found the rigid "observe and report" approach grossly inadequate, and often felt that they had no choice but to invoke the more flexible and positive "guide and assist" approach—and to stretch it considerably.

Paranoia in the Counter Intelligence Corps

Another problem standing in the way of a fully successful Occupation was a certain negativism that pervaded both MG and the Counter Intelligence Corps (CIC), but especially the latter.[17] There was an almost paranoid concern, on the part of numerous military officers, over possible subversion among American civil servants working in Japan. Heading the entire surveillance effort was SCAP's G-2, General Charles A. Willoughby, a man who had been close to General MacArthur for many years, and who was probably the second most powerful American in Japan. It is said that General MacArthur once described Willoughby as "my lovable fascist".[18] This sobriquet is consistent with my own findings. In 1951 I wrote:

> Not long before Mussolini marched into France, Willoughby wrote a book that was generally sympathetic with Generalissimo Franco and with Japanese military activities in China, and said: "historical judgment, freed from the emotional haze of the moment, will credit Mussolini with wiping out a memory of defeat by reestablishing the traditional military supremacy of the white race, for generations to come." Had a Japanese written this sort of opinion about the Japanese "race," he would have been purged by the Occupation (Textor 1951: 191).

While the Communist threat was certainly real, and assuredly deserved to be taken seriously, General Willoughby and his sprawling national intelligence network sometimes went to absurd extremes that did serious harm to some of the basic positive goals of the Occupation itself (Textor 1951: 120–3). For example, during much of my time in Kyoto, the CIC would send representatives to "monitor" my speeches to teachers' groups, civic organizations, and the like. At one point the CIC even decided, for reasons never explained, that I could not go on a routine field trip into upcountry Kyoto Prefecture—to speak to teachers' groups, inspect schools and historic monuments, etc.—unless a CIC officer accompanied me. This decision was especially mysterious because I had been doing just such upcountry work routinely for many months. In any case, my assistant and I obligingly fitted a fourth person into our jeep—a CIC lieutenant who proceeded to attend every speech I gave, and otherwise to accompany me night and day throughout a three-day trip through back country villages so remote as to have been virtually unaware of (urban-based) Japanese Communism. Lieutenant P had actually been a class-mate of mine at Ann Arbor, and must have known that I had no reputation for being a Communist or fellow traveler. I knew him as a positive person and nice guy and it did not surprise me that he was visibly embarrassed by his assignment. At the end of the trip he apologized: "Bob, I've felt bad all during this trip, especially since it is so clear that you are contributing a lot more to the aims of the Occupation than people like me are." He later sent me a copy of his report to his superior; it not only cleared me, but was actually laudatory (Textor 1951: 154–5). Surely the Occupation could have found ways of harnessing the talents of this Japan specialist—and numerous other, similarly well-trained and -motivated officers who found themselves in the CIC—in a more positive and socially useful way.[19]

Human Foibles on the Japanese Side

Especially during the first year and a half of the occupation, Americans at the local level held great *de facto* power, and often all that was needed to get something done was to say, directly or otherwise, that "the *Shinchuugun* (Occupation forces) want this . . ."—and it would be done. Such informal edicts were gradually supplanted by more formal ones, such as the formal written "procurement demands" that were used to obtain resources to provide all sorts of facilities for occupationaires and their families—to build or refurbish office space, to hire musicians to entertain Americans in the billet dining room, or to make life more efficient, convenient, or pleasant for the Americans in a hundred other ways.

Democratically oriented change, however, cannot be obtained by procurement demand. If the Occupation was to produce positive results in its more complex, substantive goals for the Japanese future, it had to gain a more complex, more *consensual* kind of cooperation from key Japanese officials who were credible to both the Occupation and to the local Japanese power structure. In retrospect, what amazes me is not that there were so few such willing and credible Japanese, but that there were so many.

This is not to say, however, that those on the Japanese side were without their "foibles," at least as I viewed (and oversimplified) them in my American cultural terms. Many educational officials I found myself dealing with were not really educators at all, but general administrators who possessed administrative efficiency, no doubt, but who had no vision of alternative futures for Japanese education—indeed, in some cases, no apparent vision at all, other than that of a vague maintenance of the *status quo*.

What heartened me, however, was to discover many Japanese educators, often quite junior in status, who actively hungered for change, and were prepared to take risks with their own careers in order to help achieve it.[20] The challenge for the reform-minded occupationaire was to identify these liberal, change-oriented Japanese, and to work with and through them. This is exemplified by an excerpt from one of my monthly CIE reports from Wakayama to higher headquarters.

> The new chief of the Education Department, a man in his forties, appears progressive;[21] his new chief of the School Education Section, a man in his thirties, has apparently been the prime mover and planner in educational reorganization throughout the Ken. Top personnel in the Ken Social Education Section and in the education departments of Wakayama, Tanabe and Shingu cities appear hopelessly unimaginative and ill-equipped for their jobs. A new crop of "inspectors" has been appointed, including a few women. A few women have been appointed as principals, including one to a new lower secondary school. The Kencho is believed deliberately but humanely making merit promotions and gradually cleaning out dead wood. (Apr. 1948).

Liberals Versus Conservatives

As a means of bridging from human foibles to the more complex matter of cultural problems, it is first worth taking a brief look at the matter of liberalism versus conservatism among MG occupationaires—which translates, to some extent, into relative activism versus inactivism in promoting the progressive sociocultural change programs of the Occupation.

The "liberals" in MG, as in SCAP,[22] tended to be people who had matured politically during the Roosevelt period, and who endorsed the broad humanitarian and equity goals of the New Deal. They were comfortable with the general notion that government must intervene when non-governmental institutions leave important problems unresolved. In the MG context, they were not comfortable with merely "observing and reporting," and were more inclined to "guide and assist." The liberals were keenly aware of the need (as they saw it) for actively implementing in peace the very aims for which the war had been fought. Hence, they were more likely to "go the extra mile" to contain various Japanese tendencies to revert toward authoritarianism, racism, and ultranationalism—and then to follow this with positive programs aimed at democracy and peace.

The more conservative occupationaires were more inclined to regard pro-change Japanese as Communist or pro-Communist, and to try to build up conservative elements in the prefecture, so that (as they saw it) the Japanese government and society would serve as a bulwark against the spread of Communism in Asia. Building up conservative elements often meant simply doing little to actively promote many of the reforms called for by Occupation policies. And unsurprisingly, many officers and enlisted men in the Counter Intelligence Corps epitomized this extreme conservative position.

We come now to an important historical fact, namely that in the early months and years of the Occupation, its overall policy orientation was basically liberal in many respects, and frequently offered considerable latitude for Occupation officials to pursue quite liberal goals. This fact is a striking paradox, in view of the generally conservative outlook of most high-ranking military officers of the time. It is even more of a paradox in the case of General MacArthur himself, whose political views, in the U.S. domestic context, were widely known to have been staunchly conservative.[23]

At the prefectural and regional levels of MG in the First Corps area, my impression was that officers who could broadly be characterized as liberal were more likely to be civilian than military, and more likely temporary military than regular. Conversely, officers who were civilian were more likely to be liberal than those who were military. These characterizations are, though, very rough and approximate; there were many exceptional and ambiguous cases.

The MG officers I knew varied widely in how hard they worked. In general, civilian officers tended to work harder than military officers,[24] and liberals harder than conservatives. Conservatives were more likely to rely on the local Japanese prefectural officials, and to assume that reports from these officials were true and accurate, or at least satisfactory. Liberals were more likely to follow up on aspects of these reports that seemed unpersuasive or unsatisfactory. Many relatively liberal occupationaires were workaholics, and the majority of workaholics were relatively liberal. I classify myself as having been a liberal workaholic.

Though there was a good deal of genuine camaraderie in MG life at the prefectural level, it was not always easy for workaholic liberal civilian MG officers to work effectively with their non-workaholic conservative military colleagues. To the former, the latter sometimes seemed unconcerned with pursuing many of the announced positive goals of the Occupation. To the latter, the former seemed unreasonably, even suspiciously active.

Cultural Problems

It is a truism to say that when we come into contact with people from another culture, the experience makes strikingly clear to us many features of our own culture about which we had previously not been explicitly aware. The truth of this is all the more compelling when we are officially charged with promoting *change* in the other culture. In occupied Japan, even where American and Japanese foibles were not too great a problem, and even where there was good faith and some degree of consensus between the American and Japanese sides, there still remained many problems of a cultural nature. That is, there were many respects in which the two sides would consistently meet with difficulty in communicating or cooperating, because they viewed the world from different cultural stances.[25] This section will list some of these cultural problems, and illustrate them by quotations, where available, from my monthly reports.

First, however, some background. When I arrived in Wakayama in November 1947, I had an active interest in all the areas within the CIE purview. These areas ranged from fostering democratic education, and education for democracy; to promoting responsible investigative journalism; to encouraging democratic civic associations; to fostering research by faculty in tertiary institutions; to administering SCAP policy concerning religion; to preserving Wakayama's precious arts and monuments—and on and on. While I dealt actively with all these areas, it was clear to me from the beginning that I had to set priorities in order to maximize my overall effectiveness. I determined to give top priority to *structural* reform, following guidelines from Tokyo calling for a new 6–3–3–4 ladder system—six years of primary education, three years of lower secondary, three of upper secondary, and four of tertiary—to take the place of an older system. Therefore, as a matter of priority, I worked with selected Japanese officials and citizens to reform the total *system* of public elementary and secondary education at one fell swoop, which would take place at the beginning of the 1948–49 academic year in April, 1948. In short, all at once, my Japanese colleagues and I undertook to equalize access to educational opportunity across gender and class lines throughout the prefecture. Doing it all at once, I felt, would cause less net dislocation than doing it piecemeal—and, equally important, would promote irreversibility.

In the case of gender, I undertook to promote coeducation at every level—a goal that official Occupation policy broadly and loosely favored, but did not insist upon.

In the case of class, also, my efforts were broadly consistent with, but not mandated by, SCAP policy. Specifically, I undertook to promote:

1. districting of public schools, with every child in a particular district attending the school in her or his district.

2. "comprehensive" secondary schools, each to contain both a general (academic) and a vocational curriculum—as a means of democratizing the total learning atmosphere within a school, and moving away from elite bias.

The above two structural innovations were intended to replace an older system of privilege in which the education of girls was less valued and hence less emphasized, and in which certain secondary schools were widely assumed to be more or less reserved for elite children. For example, the prefecture's most prestigious secondary school, the Dai Ichi Chuu Gakkoo (First Middle School), located in Wakayama City, was *the* school to which senior bureaucrats and wealthy people would "of course" send their sons—to receive academic rather than vocational education. Some of these boys commuted daily on overcrowded trains from as far away as Tanabe, some seventy miles distant, to attend this elite school.

I realized of course, that the democratic re-drawing of school district boundaries would not bring about changes in educational *practice* immediately—but, I reasoned, it *would* help to do so in the longer run by:

1. causing better-educated and socio-politically more influential parents to give their genuine interest and support to the *local* school—rather than to a school for the privileged, located in another community; and

2. necessitating that school administrators and teachers actually *confront* the need to teach all students together: male and female, academically and vocationally oriented.

Entire ken has been districted for senior high school purposes. All senior high schools will be coeducational. Out of a total of twenty senior high schools, two will be vocational, all former old system secondary vocational schools will offer general and vocational courses, and former general education old system secondary schools will have a general course with a vocational course or two planned for the near future. . . . Particular attention has been given to securing best possible teachers for junior high schools. Principals of old system secondary schools which became new senior high schools will be transferred. (Mar. 1948)

According to the Kencho, structural change in Wakayama's school system is as thorough-going as any in Japan. Advising the Kencho, the city hall and civic groups re these structural changes was CE's biggest job this month. Governor and those whom he appears to represent are patently cool toward re-organization; young teachers, college-graduated citizens and others generally to be categorized as "progressive" are warmly supporting reorganization. (Apr 1948)

This description of the situation Wakayama MG CIE faced will serve to set the context within which we may now examine a number of key cultural problems in which American and Japanese cultural stances were often in opposition.[26]

Open Criticism versus Harmonious Silence

While most adult Japanese were doubtless shocked by their nation's defeat into feeling that some basic changes in their sociocultural system were needed, many nonetheless manifested a *general* proclivity NOT to offer overt, public criticism of the *status quo*. By contrast, the American proclivity was much more supportive of active public criticism of the *status quo*.

Perhaps the most thoroughly democratic and profitable discussion series ever held in Wakayama Ken occurred this month in the Social Education Study Conference. WMG and the Kencho wrote a provocative list of questions for each program item. Almost all program items were handled by panels. The list of questions provoked the audience into very wide participation. Some of the attitudes and remarks were caustic and in bad taste, the kind usually associated with enthusiasm mixed with immaturity. For example, one youth group member told a local judge who was serving as panel leader that he thought somebody else should immediately be selected to replace the judge who, he felt, was doing an incompetent job as panel leader. Few youth leaders in the past have ever so addressed a member of the bench. The audience developed the habit of indicating aloud that they could not hear a given speaker, or that a given speaker was long-winded or dilatory in his tactics. One enthusiastic conference participant even attempted to take control of the meeting away from the chairman. This member, who, as far as is known, does not have radical political tendencies,[27] wanted the audience to join him in his enthusiasm to form a new movement aimed at the abolition of the present marriage system and the creation of a free marriage system. WMG at this point suggested that, whatever the merits of the participant's ideas, he should not try to gain acceptance for those ideas through usurpation of the authority of the conference leader. (May 1948)

Action versus Inaction

Japanese officials in the *kenchoo* were less likely to come up with plans for sweeping action, than were their opposite numbers in MG. In part, the American position reflected a culturally typical value in favor of change-oriented activity *in general*. And in part, too, it reflected the fact that the American knew that his or her presence in Japan was temporary, and that the malleable situation in Japan, favorable to change, would exist for only a few more short years or even months. Therefore, if action was going to be taken, it had to be taken soon.[28]

Initiatory versus Maintenance Action

Although MG was officially expected, at most, to offer "guidance and assistance," in some cases MG's inclination to initiate action, and to support Japanese initiators, went further, as the following excerpt indicates. "Continued firm but gentle pressure was exerted on Japanese authorities to get consolidated junior high schools [established] wherever geographical conditions permit. Great resistance has been met from local bosses, who pander to local superstition and prejudices" (Mar. 1949).

Individual versus Group Expressiveness

Americans are a nation of individuals, or at least our mythology tells us we are. In expressing themselves and their views, occupationaires tended, relative to the Japanese, to do so as autonomous individuals.[29] Our opposite numbers among the Japanese were, in sharp contrast, not likely to express autonomous opinions that diverged from those of their colleagues, and highly likely to consult their *group* first, and to work out a group position with which all members of the group could be comfortable.

Rightness versus Appropriateness

Americans, imbued with the notion of "inalienable rights," were culturally inclined to stress the need for this or that change because it was seen
as the *right* thing to do. Japanese, to the extent that they were inclined to
stress the need for change, were somewhat more likely, in my perception,
to justify change as *tekitoo*, or proper. This, as I see it, is consistent with a
deep tendency in the Confucian tradition to equate politics with ethics,
and to preserve harmony at almost any cost.

One problem with the American cultural emphasis is that rightness can merge into righteousness, which in turn can merge into self-
righteousness. I am well aware that I was hardly immune to this problem.
In my case, the problem was deftly epitomized in the delightful inscrip-
tion to a copy of *Fuzambo's Japanese-English Dictionary*, that Wakayama's
newspaper reporters gave me as a farewell gift when I completed my
service there:

> Present to Mr. Textor
> From the M.G. Beat Men
> Hope you much idealism,
> with a little realism.

I still prize this gift, and take to heart its implied constructive advice
concerning rigid idealism and self-righteousness. *Mea culpa.*

Participatory versus Hierarchical Action

In advocating action to produce change, Americans tended to favor
a grass roots approach in which many individuals, of varying wealth
and status, would participate. To the extent that Japanese officials and
politicians favored action designed to produce sociocultural change of
any kind, they tended to prefer the kind that let the government and the
established power structure manage the action. This way, they doubtless
felt, that very structure would more likely persist through time.

> Principal [Civil Information] activities [for this month] centered on the case
> of Mr. [KW], a well known local businessman who failed to file an income
> tax return despite an obviously large income. cı backed up the team's Legal
> and Government Section with publicity on the progress of the [K] Case. [K's]
> agents attempted to lure some of the newspapers off the case with bribes.
> Military Government backed these newspapers up in their refusal to "do
> business" with [K]. It is felt that the giving of publicity to the [K] Case will

help restore the confidence of small tax payers in their government. (June 1948)[30]

Civic versus Governmental Action

Since at least the time of Jefferson, Americans have been suspicious of too much government. During his celebrated visit to the U.S. in the Nineteenth Century, DeToqueville was astounded to note the rich variety of American voluntary civic associations. This cultural tradition was readily evident in MG work; Americans, liberal and conservative alike, were far more inclined to look to civic associations to initiate or carry out change, while Japanese were more inclined to leave the initiation, and much of the execution, to governmental officials. "The principal barrier to desired development of organizations in this Ken is believed to be the officials concerned with women's activities. WMG continued to emphasize the need for separation of government and civil organizations; some of the greatest opposition to this came from the women's organizations themselves, which generally are unaccustomed to shifting for themselves" (Feb. 1948).[31]

Equality versus Special Privilege

Fundamental to the American political culture is the notion that all people have been created equal in their basic rights. On the Japanese side, the degree to which people subscribed to this value varied widely. In general, however, the then-extant polity and economy were far from emphasizing equality. "WMG encouraged the Teachers' Union to contact the Governor in an effort to receive an extra appropriation of approximately six million yen as soon as possible for the realization of the 'Equal pay for equal work regardless of sex' principle. The principle already has been achieved, the Union says, in about ten of Japan's prefectures. Since the Governor is generally in opposition to equal treatment for women, some delay and trouble are expected" (Feb. 1948).

Gender Equality versus Inequality

Many activist occupationaires—female and male—initiated action to promote gender equality. For example, in Wakayama, I stressed that women should have an equal opportunity to enter higher levels of training in the normal schools. In our attempts to incorporate this principle into serious policy, my Wakayaman colleagues and I found ourselves producing action of the type that, twenty years later, came to be called "affirmative" action in the U.S. Our efforts were, though, hardly free of problems.

> The Governor of Wakayama is opposed to co-education, and has publicly said so. The Governor and "old line" interests throughout the prefecture are these days opposing, by all sorts of spurious arguments: co-education, new senior high schools, and equality of educational opportunity. Progressive citizens throughout the Ken have been encouraged by CIE to oppose these interests. (Feb. 1948)

> The entrance examination for the current school year at the Wakayama Economics College will give maximum permitted weight to intelligence testing and minimum permitted weight to scholastic achievement testing, in an effort to admit as many female candidates as possible. (Feb. 1948)

Critical versus Rote Approach to Learning

Japanese educators were wedded to pedagogical approaches that emphasized rote learning.[32] By the time of the occupation, American educators had long since been emphasizing independent critical thinking and reasoning. "WMG has encouraged the teachers of one county to enter into an essay contest on the subject: "Workable Methods for Encouraging Spontaneous Participation, and Eliminating Memorized Answers in the Class-room." The winning essay or essays will be submitted to various education magazines for publication" (Feb. 1948).

Individual Happiness versus Social Duty

In my perception, the "ultimate" cultural difference that separated Americans from Japanese was this one. The Americans in the Occupation were culturally committed to the fundamental importance of the "pursuit of happiness," principally on an individual basis, and to the Jeffersonian notion that the duty of government is to permit and foster such pursuit. To the American, duty was also important—but not, I would argue, *more* important.

My Japanese colleagues, by contrast, seemed to me to emphasize duty, and the precise, persistent, and consistent fulfillment of obligation, vastly more than individual happiness. Individual *fulfillment*, to them, was a goal to be realized through pursuing one's duty in the context of one's group— and of the higher groups to which one's group owed fealty. The task of government was to require and facilitate the carrying out of social duty.

Looking Backward: Giving to Japan

Today, as I re-read the musty pages of my MG CIE reports of 43 years ago, I am reminded that in 1948 I was constantly asking myself whether this or that specific MG intervention was truly justified—especially changes of the type that, I suspected, the voters of Wakayama, if given the opportunity of a referendum, would not have supported. (I was quite sure at the time, for example, that Wakayamans would *not* have voted consistently to support the radical, "one fell swoop" re-structuring of their schools that in fact did occur in that year—and without incident.) Under what conditions, I would ask myself, should an occupationaire go ahead anyway, on the assumption simply that he or she was *right*—and that, in the future, the Japanese would come to agree, even if they did not agree now? Asking this question immediately places one on tricky moral ground, for rationalizations of this sort have, after all, been used by dictators and brutal rulers since time immemorial.

I countered my suspicions of excessive ego- or ethnocentrism by reminding myself that soon the Japanese would once again be in control of their own country—and then free, if they chose, to revert to older forms and practices.

I have no systematic data on the extent to which the reforms I helped to catalyze have endured or not. Thirty-five years after I left, however, I was assured by two Japanese educators with whom I had worked closely, that the structural reforms described above have indeed endured and sunk deep roots. I like to believe that this is because, at least to some extent, people have come to value the new institutions and practices, and are now prepared to defend them.[33]

Looking Forward: Learning from Japan

In approaching my closing, I cannot resist a brief commentary on the fact that in recent years thoughtful Americans have become at least as convinced that America must learn from Japan, as they were 45 years ago that Japan must learn from America. I emphatically include myself among them.

Forty-odd years ago Japan *did* indeed learn a lot from America, and much of what it learned was, I believe, useful. Today, surprising though it may seem to some, those very elementary and secondary schools that American occupationaires helped make democratic and modern, are turning out graduates whose mean achievement scores, especially in math and science, are seriously higher than the American. Today, those same schools are turning out workers who, in many instances, are appreciably more adaptable and efficient at manufacturing than American workers. And today, many Japanese industrial workers labor under conditions that are *fairer* than those of their American counterparts—a reversal of the situation 45 years ago when we in the Occupation fostered democratic unionism—and indeed a partial explanation for the Japanese industrial miracle.

And a miracle it is. I, for one, am frank to admit that if someone in Wakayama in 1948 had prophesied that within 40 years I would be driving a Japanese-manufactured automobile by choice, I would have doubted his mental stability. Yet today I do drive a Japanese car.

Japanese productive success in the automobile and many other industries has complex implications, and will force Americans to adjust to many new economic and political realities. Making this total adjustment, and making it quickly and adroitly, will certainly not be easy. But adjust we must.

Adjustment can be facilitated by understanding. In seeking understanding, I would argue that the principal reasons why the Japanese are scoring high in scholastic achievement, and in manufacturing, are rooted in Japanese *culture*. I would further argue that the *freeing up* of various proclivities that in 1945 were already deeply rooted in that culture, for which the American Occupation was in a primary sense responsible, contributed significantly to various processes of change which in turn help to explain Japan's excellence in many fields today.

Be that as it may, I regard the present widespread tendency among thoughtful Americans to try to learn from Japanese culture, as wise indeed. Any such efforts bring one quickly, of course, to the obvious conclusion that many elements of Japanese culture cannot be borrowed into American culture straightaway, because such borrowing would do damage to too many *other* aspects of our sociocultural system. Thus, to take but one of many possible examples, there is no way that several million American married women, even if they wanted to, could suddenly become stay-at-home "*Kyooiju mama*-s" (education mothers)—because most of them have jobs that they cannot afford to give up. And so forth.

Nonetheless, even though *direct* cultural borrowing is not possible in a given instance, a thorough *awareness* of how the Japanese have been successful in some particular respect can often inspire creative thinking and innovation: if the American mother cannot perform the monitoring, stimulating, and nurturing role, then perhaps American society can find someone else who can. And so forth.

Today, then, it is literally true that America cannot afford *not* to learn from Japan. At the same time, it is also arguable that Japan still has much to learn from America. Above all, I consider it a matter of the highest priority that we search vigorously, affirmatively, and creatively for new avenues toward positive Japanese-American cooperation in an increasingly interdependent and borderless world.

The Bottom Line: Success in Japan

I conclude as follows. The allied occupation of Japan, which was really an American occupation, was, in my view, the most ambitious occupation the world has seen since the emergence of the nation-state. It was an occupation that demonstrated that American leaders had learned several vital lessons from the post-World War I experience. Far from being an occupation of revenge or reciprocated plunder, it was positive in intent and relatively benign and helpful in effect.

A word is here in order concerning my 1951 book about the occupation, which was widely reviewed, often favorably. The *New York Times*, for example, selected the book for its list of "Outstanding Books of 1951." A Japanese language version was published by Bungei Shunju and immediately became a best-seller.

Forty years later, as I re-read my book, I see many things that I would change—which is hardly surprising, considering that the book was the first scholarly publication of any kind that I had ever written.

First off, I would change the ill-chosen title: *Failure in Japan*, which is only somewhat redeemed by the sub-title, *With Keystones for a Positive Policy*.[34]

However, I am still glad I wrote that book. It said some things about the occupation that I still believe needed to be said at that point in history. And Yes, it did criticize General MacArthur, who, I believed and still believe, needed to be criticized on some scores. And it did criticize U.S. foreign policy, which had reversed our policy of deconcentrating the *zaibatsu*'s (moneyed clique's) economic holdings,[35] and vitiated other policies in ways that I still think were not appropriate.[36]

But now that a post-occupation history has accumulated, now that a more tempered judgment can be rendered, let me speak as an anthropologist and say that, in an overall sense, I think the Occupation was—as occupations go—*anthropologically* well conducted. Let me speak as a philosophical democrat and say that the occupation was an epochal contribution to world democracy. And let me speak as a member of the human species and say that the occupation was, on the whole, humane. Yes, the occupation *was* a success!

Finally: however much I may have disagreed with him at the time, let me add my conviction that the record of General of the Army Douglas MacArthur as Supreme Commander of the Occupied Forces serves well to remind us of the social truth that situations do from time to time arise in which a single individual can significantly influence history. General MacArthur showed far greater wisdom and effectiveness than most other American leaders, civilian or military, of the sort that might have been given his assignment, probably would or could have shown. He achieved clear and definite success in an unprecedented undertaking. He holds a high place in Japanese history—indeed, a unique one. He deserves that place.

And he deserves honor in our memory.

Notes

This paper is dedicated to the memory of a scholar and man of action who devoted his entire professional career to building creative bridges between Japanese and American education. Prior to World War II, and shortly after graduating from Stanford University, Anderson spent six years in Japan, teaching at Aoyama Gakuin and at the higher schools in Kanazawa and Fukuoka. He then returned to Stanford for a master's degree, and taught in California secondary schools. From 1946 to 1950 Anderson served as the first and only regular Chief of the Civil Information and Education Division, Military Government Section, Headquarters, First Corps and Kinki Region, in Kyoto. In this key role, his humanity, his energy, and his deep understanding of Japanese and American education became important factors in the promotion of education for democracy in Western Japan. Ronald Anderson was one of the true unsung heroes of the Occupation.

Thereafter Ron earned his doctorate in history at the University of California, Berkeley, and taught at the Universities of Michigan and Hawaii, where he continued his lifelong involvement with education in Japan and America.

Ron's friends among the Japanese and the Americans were legion. It is an honor to have been one of them.

I wish to thank Dr. Anderson's widow, Mrs. Lucille Anderson, and the late Dr. David Kornhauser and Ms. Michiko Kornhauser for reviewing this article in manuscript form. Responsibility for all errors is, of course, mine.

1. Since my visit in 1983, I am told, a Japanese group has begun efforts to restore the office to the way it looked when General MacArthur occupied it, and to preserve it as a memorial.

2. Each month the Wakayama MG Team submitted a report of activities to higher headquarters. I was responsible for the Civil Information (CI) and Civil Education (CE) sections of each such report. I have obtained xerox copies of my reports from the U.S. National Archives for January through June, 1948. These reports were originally classified as "Restricted," but were declassified on April 12, 1974.

3. I have no direct information as to how accurate General MacArthur's knowledge of local grass roots conditions was. If I had to guess, I would speculate that his grasp of such conditions was probably greater than I thought at the time, but still considerably less than I (or he) would have preferred.

4. Perhaps equally important, for the first year or more Anderson and I, and for a while the late Warner I. ("Bud") Weil, were also in *de facto* in charge of MG CIE activities for Kyoto Prefecture. This gave us a direct window on the rapidly changing scene at the local level, ranging from that at the major universities in Kyoto city to that in isolated village schools in Oku-Tango.

5. The establishment of Wakayama University out of an economics college and two normal colleges was a fascinating experience, but space does not permit its adequate treatment here.

6. I should add that my primary anthropological specialty is Thailand, *not* Japan. I do not consider myself a Japan expert.

7. My civil service rank was that of Clerical-Administrative-Fiscal (CAF) 9, with the simulated rank of first lieutenant or captain.

8. These officers, many of whom spoke at least some Japanese and understood at least something about Japanese society and culture, included some highly qualified men. However, they constituted only a minority of the total officer personnel in MG, and most of them left Japan within a year or so.

9. For example, one regular army colonel, with authority over many MG teams, made it clear in staff meetings that he would do all in his bureaucratic power to resist the granting of permission for any Caucasian MG man to marry any Japanese woman, because such a man would thereby be "lowering" himself. However, in the case of a *Nisei* (Japanese-American) MG man, he would not resist, because such a man would be marrying "above" himself. Racist biases of this general sort were by no means rare, though the harshness of this particular stance was not typical.

10. And life could indeed be enjoyable. Virtually all occupationaires enjoyed a level of physical comfort and convenience far beyond their previous experience. There were Japanese servants to take care of all menial tasks. There were plenty of Japanese women available on one basis or another. There were ample black market opportunities for those who were interested—

and many were. In some areas, there was extremely comfortable housing. For virtually all occupationaires, there were ample sports and recreational facilities, luxurious rest hotels, and the like. Usually, occupationaires had fairly ready access to post exchanges or PX trains, where they could buy all sorts of necessities and luxuries, from liquor to wrist watches to Japanese silks or cloisonne. These amenities and luxuries, as well as room and board, were usually available at low prices, and many occupationaires could manage to bank most of their monthly salary.

11. At some point in the occupation—just when I do not remember—MG CIE officers were officially authorized to go beyond "observing and reporting," to "guiding and assisting." In fact, many of us had already been doing just that, in response to situations that arose which required some kind of immediate constructive response.

12. At that time the Shikoku and Chugoku MG regions were staffed by Americans for MG purposes, but the tactical occupying troops were those of the British Commonwealth Occupation Force.

13. As soon as it became obvious that there would be no military or physical resistance to the Occupation by the Japanese, there was really no justification for such a complex table of organization for MG activities. A suitable number of tactical troops could have been maintained to insure domestic tranquility and serve whatever other tactical or strategic purposes were considered necessary, but there was no need for MG to be under the command of tactical units.

   Of the five levels, the Eighth Army had corps levels that were obviously redundant, and often served simply to slow the process of communication between the team level and the SCAP policy level. MG affairs would have run much more efficiently and professionally if team had reported to region, and region directly to SCAP.

14. On January 1, 1950, a change did occur. Military government, re-named "Civil Affairs," was restructured. The total number of personnel was reduced drastically, especially on the military side. Only two levels were retained: the regional teams and the MG Section at Eighth Army Headquarters. The prefectural teams were abolished, thereby depriving MG of true influence at the grass roots. But by this time it hardly mattered, since the Occupation had long since run out of reforming steam (Textor 1951: 192–3).

15. With respect to the First Corps area, it was my impression that in general junior officers would demur more than senior, military more than civilian, and career military more than non-career military.

16. During the middle and later months of 1946 Ronald Anderson and I frequently made interim policy in this manner, with respect to Kyoto Prefecture, and, more provisionally, with respect to the entire First Corps area.

17. The CIC had its own structure, separate from MG, with branches down to

prefectural level and below. At least at its lower levels, the CIC was, as far as I know, composed entirely of military personnel.

18. It is difficult for me to understand why General MacArthur, a leader dedicated to fundamental human rights, kept an individual like Willoughby as a key staff officer for many years. Schaller (1989: 121) describes Willoughby thus: "A German-born immigrant with pretensions of noble birth, Willoughby brought a Prussian demeanor and extremely right-wing views to his intelligence post. MacArthur hit the mark when he once called his aide "my lovable fascist." Willoughby saw Communist and Jewish conspiracies at home, abroad, and especially in SCAP's ranks. His Counter Intelligence Corps (CIC) spied on Americans and cultivated former members of Japan's secret police and armed forces."

19. Lieutenant P as a well educated man. Many of the personnel assigned to isolated CIC posts, however, were not. Often they were the only American personnel in the city to which they were assigned. They operated in secrecy, a fact that gave them considerable *de facto* power, and ample opportunity to assume prerogatives well beyond those officially assigned to them.

20. After the occupation, some Japanese officials who had cooperated actively with Occupation officials suffered setbacks in their careers. In other cases, however, such cooperation actually resulted in career advancement to a degree greater than probably would have occurred otherwise—though they may not have been particularly concerned about, or aware of, this possibility at the time that they offered their cooperation.

21. The official I found in charge of education when I arrived in Wakayama in November 1947 had previously been associated with ultranationalistic activities, even including the administration of "thought control." It was soon clear that there was utterly no way in which he could have been expected to promote democratic education policies. I made it clear to the appropriate officials that he and I could not work together, and before long he was transferred to other duties. I was, in this sense, responsible for his transfer. I was not, however, responsible for the selection of his successor. It was simply my good luck that his successor was so excellent.

22. For a description of a quintessential liberal occupationaire in action, see Chapter 3 of Williams (1979), on Charles L. Kades, of Government Section, SCAP, who played a key role in drafting the present constitution of Japan.

23. For a thorough examination of just how conservative General MacArthur had earlier been, see Schaller (1989).

It remains to explain just why a person so conservative on American domestic issues would turn out to be so liberal when placed in the role of Supreme Commander in Japan. Two reasons seem plausible.

First, MacArthur quickly discovered, if he had not earlier known, that leading conservatives in Japan tended, unlike most of their American counterparts, to be fundamentally anti-democratic. They were what I called, for lack of a better term, the "Old Guard" (Textor 1951: 15–20). MacArthur characterized them thus: "Control was exercised by a feudalistic overlordship of a mere fraction of the population, while the remaining millions, with a few enlightened exceptions, were abject slaves to tradition, legend, mythology, and regimentation" (MacArthur 1964: 310).

Second, MacArthur's liberal policies reflected the influence of liberals in the Roosevelt and Truman Administrations, during which considerable planning for the U.S.'s post-surrender Japan policy took place. This planning was embodied in two documents: "Initial Post-Surrender Policy for Japan," SWNCC (State-War-Navy Coordinating Committee) 150/4/A, signed by President Truman on September 6, 1945; and "Basic Directive for Post-Surrender Military Government in Japan Proper," JCS (Joint Chiefs of Staff) 1380/5, dated November 3, 1945.

Schaller contends that MacArthur knew the substance of both documents *before* he landed in Japan on August 30, 1945, and argues that credit for conceptualizing the Occupation's reforms should go primarily to such officials in Washington.

Interestingly, however, in his *Reminiscences*, MacArthur gives the credit to himself. He makes no mention of either Washington document. Instead, he contends: "From the moment of my appointment as supreme commander, I had formulated the policies I intended to follow, implementing them through the Emperor and the machinery of the imperial government. I was thoroughly familiar with Japanese administration, its weaknesses and its strengths, and felt the reforms I contemplated were those which would bring Japan abreast of modern progressive thought and action. First destroy the military power. Punish war criminals. Build the structure of representative government. Modernize the constitution. Hold free elections. Enfranchise the women. Release the political prisoners. Liberate the farmers. Establish a free labor movement. Encourage a free economy. Abolish police oppression. Develop a free and responsible press. Liberalize education. Decentralize political power. Separate church from state" (1964: 282–3).

Schaller disputes this. He contends that the two directives from Washington "outlined virtually the entire reform agenda . . ." Schaller contends, therefore, that MacArthur took personal credit for conceptualizing reforms that in fact were conceptualized by planners in Washington (Schaller 1989: 123).

I find Schaller's argument convincing. In judging General MacArthur on this apparently excessive claim, however, I think one should bear in mind two points:

1. He was a very old man when he wrote his book, and died shortly after finishing his manuscript.

2. Regardless of who conceptualized these reforms (and allowing for the

possibility of a considerable amount of independent conceptualization) it was MacArthur whose leadership succeeded in *implementing* them. This, alone, was an achievement of major historical significance.

24. Informally, the standard developed that the civilian officers should be expected to do the really hard work of MG, since civilian salaries were higher. There was some resentment over these salary differentials.

25. My analysis will be somewhat confounded by the fact that it was not just two cultures that confronted each other, but also two *situations*, that of prosperous victorious nation and that of prostrate defeated nation. Consequently, there is, in this section, always the danger that I will attribute to cultural factors phenomena that can better be explained by invoking situational phenomena. On the other hand, it is sometimes true that in situations of extreme stress, the fundamental values of a culture become more evident than would otherwise be the case. Suffice to say here that I am aware of these problems and have tried to deal with them in the presentation.

26. The word "often" is important. The differences in cultural stance here outlined represent what I consider to be *statistical* tendencies only. The listing of these issues in this rough form is intended to indicate general types of situation in which American occupationaires tended to take one broad stance, and Japanese officials and leaders tended to take a different, and more or less opposing, stance. Usually there would be exceptions to these tendencies, and these exceptions sometimes provided useful common ground for negotiation. One of the key tasks of the change-oriented CIE officer was to find and utilize these areas of common ground.

27. In the MG subculture, it was always prudent, especially for a civilian liberal activist officer such as myself, to bend over backwards to make clear to one's superiors that the Japanese with whom one was dealing were not "radical" (in the sense of being Communist or pro-Communist). Otherwise, one risked incurring the suspicion of one's military superiors, and losing their support.

28. Furthermore, the American knew that his or her future career would not be disadvantaged by changes in the Japanese situation, while the Japanese official was keenly aware that he, his group, and his family would have to live with such changes for the indefinite future—perhaps at a significant disadvantage. This factor was, then, more a situational than a cultural one.

29. Riesman (1950), writing of American characterological types, classified many Americans prior to about World War II as "inner-directed." The implication here was that the American searches his or her soul, and then decides quite autonomously what to do. Clearly, Americans working in Japan in 1946–48 varied as to the extent to their inner-directedness, but I would judge that most civilian liberals were inclined to be inner-directed, and would so categorize

myself. I and other civilian liberal activist MG officers sometimes resented the military officers who were our bosses, because they tended more to be, again in Riesman's terms, "other-directed"—the "others" being, of course, other (and higher ranking) *Americans*—and certainly not Japanese. Riesman broadly classified the Japanese as "tradition-directed" (p. 10).

30. "K," by the way, owned a commodious home in Wakayama City which the local CIC had procured to serve as their residence and office. The chief CIC officer for Wakayama Prefecture once casually informed me that he relied heavily on K for intelligence information—so much so that he was considering inviting K to move in with the CIC contingent in K's old home, so as to facilitate closer "cooperation."

31. Of course it was true in 1946–48 that due to the dislocation of infrastructure, and the widespread economic hardship, it was often *only* the government that had the economic or physical resources to carry out a change. My point is, though, that even where such constraints did not exist, this Japanese cultural proclivity was still in evidence. A women's organization, for example, might see nothing particularly strange about receiving advice from a government official or non-governmental "advisor"—typically an elderly, culturally conservative male.

32. In part, this tradition clearly stems from the simple facts that the Japanese writing system is a character system, and that fully one-third of an elementary school student's time is devoted to memorizing, using, and appreciating characters.

33. Wray (1991: 473) looking at the history of Japanese education over the forty years since the occupation, concludes as follows with respect to the nation as a whole: "The introduction of the 6–3–3–4 educational ladder system achieved . . . equal educational opportunity and the vested interests of teachers and administrators who bettered their social position has prevented any retreat from the 6–3–3–4 system. [Note that Wray is here explaining permanence by referring to vested interests, rather than to ideological commitment.] Coeducation was strongly resisted by the *Monbushoo* [Ministry of Education], but it is complete at the elementary level and generally characteristic of urban public junior and senior high schools."

With respect to the comprehensive school, Wray notes: "Before the reforms had a chance to work, the occupation ended. The Americans really never achieved the essence of the 6–3–3–4 system, the comprehensive curriculum, or many other changes because there were not enough teachers, appropriate educational materials and funds, or enough time to ensure adequate follow-through."

34. Other problems with the book, viewed in retrospect, include the following:

1. The book demanded too much, and was too rigid in its standards.

2. Although the Japanese "Old Guard" were hardly a savory group by the standards most Americans would use, the book treated them as considerably more diabolical than they subsequently proved to be.

3. The decision to de-emphasize reform and increasingly emphasize the building up of Japan as a Cold War strategic resource came primarily from Washington. The book did not give MacArthur credit for *resisting* some of these decisions, simply because at that time I did not have access to adequate information that would have enabled me to do so.

4. Perhaps most important, the book was delayed in publication, due in part to the fact that I was at the time a full-time graduate student. By the time it came out, many of its policy recommendations were out of date.

35. I have not researched this point, but I suspect that it could be argued with some cogency that the current difficulties some American firms are experiencing in competing with Japanese industry are traceable to the failure of the Occupation to carry through most of its originally announced *zaibatsu* deconcentration policy.

Incidentally, in General MacArthur's *Reminiscences*, he does not mention the fact that the Occupation's original program for *zaibatsu* deconcentration was drastically reduced, in fact almost totally scuttled (Textor 1951: 50–60 and Appendix Two). He simply states that "these great trusts were partially dissolved and a truly competitive free enterprise system inaugurated. . . . The main thing was that their influence was broken."

36. I think it can be argued that some aspects of U.S. political policy toward occupied Japan contributed to a situation in which, ever since the end of the Occupation, the nation has essentially been ruled by just one political party. I do not consider this to be a healthy political condition. In my view, Japan will be more convincing as a democracy when it experiences a peaceful, responsible turnover of its ruling party at the national level.

Bibliography

MacArthur, Douglas. 1964. *Reminiscences*. New York: McGraw-Hill. Riesman, David. 1950. *The Lonely Crowd: A Study of Changing American Character*. New Haven: Yale University Press. Schaller, Michael. 1989. *Douglas MacArthur: The Far Eastern General*. New York: Oxford University Press.

Textor, Robert B. 1951. *Failure in Japan: With Keystones for a Positive Policy*. New York: John Day. Japanese version published as *Nippon ni Okeru Shippai*, in four editions, by Bungei Shunju, Tokyo, 1952, and included on *Yomiuri* Best Seller List. English version reprinted by Greenwood Press, Westport CN, 1972.

U.S. Education Mission to Japan. 1946. *Report of the United States Education*

Mission to Japan. Tokyo. Submitted to Supreme Commander for the Allied Powers.

Williams, Justin, Sr. 1979. *Japan's Political Revolution under MacArthur: A Participant's Account*. Athens: University of Georgia Press.

Wray, Harry. 1991. "Change and Continuity in Modern Japanese Educational History: Allied Occupational Reforms Forty Years Later," *Comparative Educational Review*, Vol. 35, No. 3, pp. 447–476. Note: I here use this informative article as an authoritative general summary of the fate, positive or negative, of various Occupation efforts at educational reform. Wray bases his assessments on a wide range of professional literature in both Japanese and English. I find his long "Conclusions" section convincing and valuable, in particular because he relates the relative persistence of various Occupation-sponsored reforms to Japanese culture, institutions, and history.

MacArthur's Japan

The View from Washington

Michael Schaller

In the Stuart L. Bernath Memorial Lecture, delivered in April 1985, Michael Schaller of the University of Arizona takes a critical view of MacArthur's conduct as the Supreme Commander for the Allied Powers.

Within the past decade, scholarly accounts of the American occupation of Japan have almost entirely reversed course. Most earlier studies praised the enterprise and focused on the personal role of General Douglas MacArthur, the Supreme Commander for the Allied Powers (SCAP). This "heroic" genre treated occupied Japan as if it were wholly separate from contemporary world developments. By the 1970s historians on both sides of the Pacific had begun to explore the nuances and contradictions of the occupation, the long-ignored role of planning bureaucracies, economic interest groups, and, above all, the Cold War. Collectively, all had profound impact upon postwar Japan and linked the occupation to developments in Europe and the rest of Asia. At the same time, the new accounts diminished MacArthur's importance from that of superman to bit player in a vast political drama.[1]

MacArthur's near disappearance from recent American and Japanese revisionist treatments of the occupation is remarkable given the earlier consensus. Previously the general's detractors seemed willing to concede Japan as a unique success. Even the normally outspoken Harry S. Truman and Dean G. Acheson dealt benignly with the pre-Korean War MacArthur in their memoirs, while George F. Kennan waited twenty years before publishing his attacks.[2]

Recent critiques of the occupation have tended to damn MacArthur with faint praise rather than attack him directly. While perceptive accounts by historians John Dower and Howard Schonberger reveal the importance of the so-called "Reverse Course" in occupation policy, they have tended to weigh the impact of bureaucrats, business elites, and

Japanese and American politicians more heavily than that of MacArthur. In substance, I agree fully with their analysis. It is important, however, to recall MacArthur's significant role as a "negative catalyst" in policy-making. Despite the profound institutional influences upon Japan, both friend and foe saw MacArthur as a personification of the occupation.

MacArthur's appointment as SCAP came reluctantly. Few leaders in the Roosevelt and Truman administrations voiced confidence about MacArthur's prospects in Japan. Like FDR, who posted MacArthur to Manila a decade earlier, Truman may have considered Tokyo a distant sinecure for a potential rival. Since Washington planners already had developed an elaborate reform agenda for Japan, perhaps they believed MacArthur could be entrusted to puff up his own importance while implementing orders. In any case, the most comforting aspect of Occupied Japan from Washington's perspective was its isolation from more intense trouble spots while appearing to be an important job.

Democrats and New Dealers had distrusted MacArthur since his infamous handling of the Bonus Army in 1932. Professional military officers in Washington questioned his abilities soon after the Japanese attack on the Philippines. Dwight D. Eisenhower, a former aide to the general, recorded the War Department's frustration and disillusionment with the general's blundering defense of the islands, where, with ill-prepared forces, MacArthur persisted in pursuing an impossible plan to defeat Japanese landings on the coast. His bravado left the bastions of Bataan and Corregidor unprepared for the resulting siege. The general's selection of "bootlicker" assistants, his loss of nerve, and refusal to "face facts" resulted in a military campaign that might be "suitable for plebes" at West Point but not for a real war.

MacArthur's heroic veneer tarnished further in February when he endorsed Philippine President Manuel Quezon's proposal to declare the Commonwealth "neutral" and arrange for the departure of both American and Japanese armies. The idea disgusted Roosevelt, and Secretary of War Henry L. Stimson described the logic behind Quezon and MacArthur's decision as "wholly unreal." A few months after the episode, Stimson condemned the general for supporting a "virtual settlement with the Japanese" in his desperation.

MacArthur's "hysterical" behavior, which alternated between grandiose schemes to defeat the enemy and desperate threats to surrender or die, caused Eisenhower to question Roosevelt's wisdom in evacuating the general from Corregidor. A doomed siege provided MacArthur with the "essentials of drama" he required. In a really major theater, the "love of the limelight might ruin him." Eisenhower believed that, if the general's backers had an opportunity to hear the same rantings from their idol as he had listened to in Manila, it would sound as "silly to the public [now] as they then did to us. But he's a hero! Yah."[3] Eisenhower and Stimson both feared MacArthur would recklessly parlay the public's need for a "hero" into pressure for a "Pacific first" strategy.

During the next three years, MacArthur acted precisely as Eisenhower had predicted. He parlayed public acclaim, skillful public relations, and political blackmail to make the Pacific a major theater of military operations, while nearly all Army and Navy war planners favored a "Europe first" strategy. FDR found himself in a cruel dilemma. He worried that his refusal to placate MacArthur would be seen as proof of his jealousy and political spite. Even a casual reading of the diaries of such advisers as Stimson and Interior Secretary Harold L. Ickes reveals how intensely political all decisions relating to the allocation of manpower and scarce resources for the Pacific campaigns became. The general's abortive quest for the GOP presidential nomination in 1943–44 only deepened the constant suspicion of MacArthur's motives during the war.

Even a relative outsider like Truman looked upon the general with a jaundiced eye. Late in April 1945 the new president had to choose a civilian high commissioner to take over duties from MacArthur in the Philippines. He told Ickes, who deeply disliked MacArthur, that his "only question" to a possible candidate was whether or not he was "strong enough to keep General MacArthur in line." Ickes happily decided that Truman had "definite reservations about MacArthur," a trait that convinced the testy Interior secretary to "overlook a good many things" he disliked about the new president. Even his beloved FDR, from awe or political calculation, had been "too much disposed to play along and give in to the brass hats" like MacArthur.[4]

In June, after several jousts with MacArthur over the restoration of civilian authority in the Philippines, Truman confided his diminished opinion of MacArthur in some "pretty vigorous Missouri expletives." In a note he jotted to himself, the president fretted over the many imponderables associated with the final assault on Japan, including the pressure to name MacArthur as overall commander. FDR might have given in to the public's pressure that left him few alternatives, but Truman retained his contempt for: "Mr. Prima Donna, Brass Hat, Five Star MacArthur. He's worse than the Cabots and the Lodges—they at least talked with one another before they told God what to do. Mac tells God right off. It's a very great pity we have stuffed shirts like that in key positions. I don't see why in hell Roosevelt didn't order Wainwright home and let MacArthur be a martyr. Guess he was afraid of the Sabotage Press–McCormick–Patterson Axis. We'd have had a real General and a fighting man if we had Wainwright and not a play actor and a bunco man such as we have now." Truman went on to contrast favorably such generals as Eisenhower, Robert E. Lee, and Omar Bradley to the "Custers, Pattons and MacArthurs."[5]

On 10 August, as the president weighed Japan's tentative acceptance of the Potsdam surrender terms, Senator Tom Connally (D–TX) warned Truman that he would be making a "big mistake in appointing Dugout Doug as Allied Commander in Chief to accept the Jap surrender" Connally predicted that the general would use the position to run against Truman in 1948.

Shortly after the Japanese surrender, Truman and Ickes again discussed the Philippine appointment and Tokyo's future. The Interior secretary had persuaded the president to appoint a civilian, Paul McNutt, to be high commissioner in Manila. Now that the general had bigger fish to fry in Tokyo, Ickes hoped he would leave Philippine affairs alone. In any case, the secretary recorded how Truman interrupted him, "in entire good nature," to say: "that I couldn't blame on him the appointment of MacArthur as the chief commander in the Far East area. I replied that I agreed with him thoroughly. Politically, he couldn't do anything else. That blame is due to Roosevelt. I remarked that Roosevelt had made a mistake in taking MacArthur away from the Philippines; that he should have left MacArthur to clean up his own mess and taken Wainwright out. Truman agreed, saying that Wainwright was a better soldier. He knows, as do others, that the Philippine campaign under MacArthur was a fiasco."

Nevertheless, in Ickes's opinion, the consequences of not appointing MacArthur "Chief in the Far Pacific" were probably as dismal as the results of appointing him. The general's Republican champions were eagerly anticipating an opportunity to "make a martyr out of him and a candidate for president." Ickes agreed with Truman that "MacArthur would probably be a candidate anyhow," and there was little chance of stopping him.[6]

Two months after selecting MacArthur as SCAP, the president allegedly told General Lief J. Sverdrup, one of MacArthur's subordinates, that

"FDR was always afraid of MacArthur and seemed to think he might have tremendous political power." A similar concern probably impelled the Truman administration to send the contentious political commander to Tokyo. Whatever grave doubts existed about MacArthur's abilities and intentions, Truman's advisers hoped he would adhere to the carefully scripted occupation agenda in return for their cooperation in the fiction that he "personified" the occupation.[7]

MacArthur flourished in the kind of environment he found in Tokyo. He was free from routine supervision by the War Department and assumed the fancy trappings (if hollow core) of an "international status." MacArthur relished his distance from North America and Europe; it seemed to justify his complaints that all problems in his command arose because priority went to Europe. A remarkable opportunism, rather than any consistent political ideology, dictated MacArthur's dazzling policy reversals. At various times between 1945 and the outbreak of the Korean War, he advocated both preserving and dissolving industrial combines, protecting and suppressing organized labor, forbidding and encouraging U.S. military bases, cooperating with and shunning the Soviets in a peace settlement, and ignoring and hiding behind the Allied consulting organs created in 1945. The speed with which he could strike new poses outraged and confused his many critics.

Within one month of his arrival in Tokyo, MacArthur created a controversy that foreshadowed many subsequent conflicts with Washington. On 17 September 1945 he proclaimed he had personally won one of the most significant military and political victories "in history." The general praised his decision to permit the Japanese to supervise demobilization and lavished effusive compliments on their talents, goodwill, and honor. Moreover, he predicted that his success would make it possible to implement a "drastic cut" in the size of American forces down to about 200,000 men. MacArthur insisted that, as "rapidly as ships can be made available," the boys would go home, while a subordinate suggested the entire occupation might be over in one year.[8]

America's wartime allies were outraged by their inability to influence events in Tokyo, especially now that the Supreme Commander was speaking of winding down the occupation before basic reforms had been imposed, much less achieved. Besides international complications, MacArthur's suggestion to accelerate demobilization threatened to wreck attempts to stabilize American force levels. War Department planners were certain the occupation required 400,000 men, double the troops

MacArthur claimed. They also believed that he was trying to curry favor with his soldiers by playing on their hopes of an early discharge. Worse still, MacArthur had sabotaged the president's efforts to persuade a reluctant Congress to extend the draft. The general's willingness to play politics on the issue seemed confirmed when he privately reported to Army Chief of Staff Eisenhower that he needed 400,000 men and supported the draft but then publicly denied it.[9]

MacArthur insisted that he based his troop estimate solely on objective criteria and could not endorse the resumption of the draft because he knew nothing of administration plans. In fact, he and his political allies were concerned almost exclusively with the political implications of these issues. On 4 September 1945 one of MacArthur's closest political supporters, Sears Roebuck Chairman Robert E. Wood, cautioned SCAP about a heinous plot in Washington to smear the general. The Truman administration, Wood alleged, hoped to make MacArthur the patsy in a scheme to maintain a large postwar conscript army. Talk of an extended occupation was part of a "very clever ruse on the part of the politicians in Washington" who intended to put "the burden of blame" on MacArthur. To escape being "pilloried . . . in the eyes of the public," Wood urged SCAP immediately to release a statement declaring his minimum aims and requirements. According to General Bonner Fellers, secretary to SCAP, MacArthur shared Wood's suspicions and issued the 17 September statement as a preemptive strike against the "State, Navy and War departments."[10]

MacArthur compounded this snub to the administration by rejecting a presidential request to return home. On 17 September, while making his unauthorized comment on troop levels, and again the next month, SCAP received invitations from Truman, through Chief of Staff George C. Marshall, to come to Washington for a ceremony honoring the nation's ranking commanders. Although he had just boasted about his success in pacifying the enemy, MacArthur declined, citing the "extraordinarily dangerous situation in Japan."

MacArthur's unauthorized statements and refusal to accept Truman's invitations outraged the president. He ordered the State and War departments to instruct MacArthur to avoid public speculations about policy and to adhere strictly to existing directives. Privately, Truman characterized that episode as a "political statement" or gambit by the general, designed to boost his own standing while humbling the president. In a rage, Truman insisted he was "tired of fooling around" and would "do something with that fellow [MacArthur] who had balled things up."[11]

Spurred on by Marshall and Acheson, whom Truman would nominate as undersecretary of state on 19 September, the president sent Assistant Secretary of War John J. McCloy to visit MacArthur. McCloy told Ickes that the administration wanted him to visit both Germany and Japan "to muzzle the talkative Generals." To appear evenhanded, he would go first to Frankfurt to confer with Eisenhower about the removal of General George S. Patton for his pro-Nazi remarks. "However," McCloy added, "the real objective was MacArthur in Tokyo." By sending McCloy to Europe first, the War and State leaders hoped they would soften the public blow to MacArthur, but they were still determined to discipline him. Ickes applauded the move and later told Acheson "how much I thought of him for setting Gen. MacArthur back on his heels."[12]

Despite this flurry of activity, the president took no decisive action against the general. Truman continually fumed and sputtered but ultimately tolerated MacArthur's scoring political points from his sinecure in Tokyo. A troublesome MacArthur on the far side of the globe seemed preferable to having him closer to home.

Not surprisingly, most observers of the occupation have commented on the apparent contradiction of the "conservative" MacArthur supporting a "liberal" reform program while the liberal administration eventually pushed through a more conservative agenda. This dichotomy oversimplifies and obscures the real dynamics between the general and the administration. As on almost every issue, political calculation, not principle, defined the general's policy. For example, it is common to emphasize MacArthur's crusade against Japan's giant industrial combines, the Zaibatsu, in defiance of Washington. In 1947 and 1948 the general spoke eloquently about the dangers of monopoly capital and the likelihood of a revolutionary upsurge unless the occupation restructured the economy. During 1945 and 1946, however, the Truman administration through study commissions had pushed structural economic reform, while SCAP opposed it. Not until Washington changed course in mid-1947 did MacArthur fully commit himself to an anti-Zaibatsu program. The Truman administration, to be sure, altered its basic economic policies, but it did to because of perceived changes in the Japanese and international situation. MacArthur, in contrast, acted almost entirely for opportunistic reasons.

MacArthur's discussions with presidential envoy Edwin A. Locke, during an October 1945 meeting in Tokyo, reveal his political opportunism. MacArthur, typically, tried to overwhelm his visitor with hyprbole about "oriental psychology." He proceeded to debunk many of the democratic political reforms recently imposed by SCAP staff. MacArthur emphasized his own concern with keeping a tight lid on Japanese politics and preventing "so-called liberals," who were really Soviet agents, from targeting the nation for a "successful communist revolution."

Locke asked why SCAP had not pressed forward more vigorously with antimonopoly, purge, and reparations programs mandated by the Potsdam Declaration and postsurrender directives. The general and his current economic adviser, Colonel Raymond C. Kramer, believed that SCAP should enact only cosmetic reforms which gave the appearance of change but left most economic power in "identical hands." Kramer condemned all other Asians as inferior and incapable of managing modern industry. The title to Japanese property abroad should not be transferred to Asians, he insisted, but leased to American corporations that would manage them in ways which complemented Japanese requirements. MacArthur and Kramer both urged that the United States give Japan what they called a "green light" to resume economic expansion in Asia and predicted that, under an American umbrella, the nation would soon become the "natural leader in Asia."

In his report to the president, Locke expressed amazement with MacArthur's apparent defiance of the basic reform agenda. He suggested that perhaps the general merely misspoke his plans or was carried away by "poetic license." MacArthur, however, revealed his intentions in November 1945, when SCAP announced tentative approval of a plan, originating among the Zaibatsu, to enact a limited antimonopoly program. While superficially reshuffling some elements of the giant combines it left the basic operating structure and ownership intact. Similarly, SCAP colluded with Japanese industry to reclassify many military facilities as peaceful and not subject to reparations.[13]

Few in the Truman administration accepted the validity of MacArthur's poetic license. With the president's implicit support, the State, Treasury, and War departments dispatched two special missions to Tokyo in November and December 1945 to ensure formulation of a major economic reform program. Edwin Pauley led a reparations commission, first organized to investigate German cartels, to identify major industrial facilities for transfer to victims of Japanese aggression. Economist Corwin

Edwards led the second mission, which was charged with developing a comprehensive antimonopoly program to supersede SCAP's paltry efforts.

The parallel recommendations issued by the two missions early in 1946 radically attacked the economic status quo. Central to both reports was a desire to end Japan's regional economic predominance by assisting the industrial development of colonial and neocolonial areas in Asia. Initially, Truman, the State Department, and the military establishment all heartily endorsed this concept, but MacArthur's top staff condemned it as "idealistic," "too sweeping," "too liberal," and "unwise."[14]

Neither the administration nor SCAP energetically implemented the proposed structural reforms of the economy during 1946. SCAP focused primarily on imposing a democratic political structure on Japan, an agenda acceptable to Washington. MacArthur still attributed the pronounced downward economic spiral of the economy to wartime dislocation and immediate postwar disruptions. American relief aid from the Army Department's Government and Relief in Occupied Areas program (GARIOA), and expectations for the revival of world trade, were anticipated to tide Japan over the transition from war to peace.

During 1945–46 high-level administration visitors to Tokyo, including McCloy, Eisenhower, W. Averell Harriman, and James V. Forrestal, typically received MacArthur's lecture on "oriental psychology," the dangers of Chinese communism and its appeasement by Marshall, the possibility of Eisenhower's presidential candidacy, and Japan's utility as a spearhead of Christian proselytizing in Asia. Neither he nor his guests seemed overly concerned about Japan's dire economic straits, and few made recommendations about altering policy.[15]

For sheer nastiness, almost nothing rivaled the talk between the general and former President Herbert Hoover, who visited Tokyo on a food aid mission. The two men continued a long-standing vituperative attack on FDR, whom they blamed for most of the world's outstanding problems. Roosevelt had willfully provoked war with Japan, pursued a military strategy for political purposes, and ensured a Soviet advance. Hoover offered to lead a political movement for MacArthur, while the general promised to consider returning home for a speaking tour sometime in late 1947 "when the time was right."[16]

The crisis of the Greek civil war drastically affected Washington's view of Occupied Japan, and the insularity of the general's response to global developments outraged the Truman administration. A virulent anti-Communist, MacArthur nonetheless seemed certain that the Soviet

Union posed little physical threat to Japan. Broad notions of security, the world economy, connections between centers of supply and production, or links among the European, Japanese, and American economies did not trouble him. MacArthur's idea of resisting communism projected greater involvement in China's vast civil war, even though most of the administration considered China's fate irrelevant to the world power balance.

As the president's leading foreign policy advisers debated a new course early in 1947, MacArthur continued to call attention to his religious and spiritual transformation efforts in Japan. He ignored its faltering economy (sustained by nearly $500 million per year in relief aid) and paid scant attention to the question of restoring trade and production. SCAP headquarters never asked how Japan would ever recover economically in an Asian environment beset by revolutionary nationalism.

Despite growing misgivings, the administration seemed unable to challenge MacArthur directly in early 1947. The State Department drifted under the leadership of James F. Byrnes, while a divided military establishment recoiled from making any demands of SCAP. Within six months, however, the reorganization of the State and Defense departments brought forth a group of confident officials willing and able to challenge MacArthur's authority. In the State Department, Marshall, Acheson, and Kennan harbored few illusions about MacArthur's abilities. Defense Secretary Forrestal, Army Secretary Kenneth Royall, and Army Undersecretary William Draper were determined to assert civilian authority over SCAP, whatever MacArthur's objections. The administration's new team pushed to bring occupation policy into line with the evolving containment doctrine in Europe. Essentially, they sought to link an industrially revived Japan to Southeast Asia and Western Europe.

Fearful that this new agenda would leave him on the sidelines, MacArthur devised a strategy to dominate the immediate future of Japan and prevent the administration from implementing its policies. During the spring of 1947, in an abrupt reversal, he called upon the Japanese government to enact quickly a comprehensive antimonopoly program centered on the dissolution of the Zaibatsu. Such massive structural economic reform would block efforts by Washington to promote, or take credit for, economic recovery. In addition, the assault on the industrial combines promised to provide MacArthur with a new image of reformer and trustbuster which would be important if the general decided to challenge Truman for the presidency. Since the administration had steadily moved away from support of the Zaibatsu dissolution, the contrast between the general and the president could be sharpened. Along with this major economic innovation, MacArthur intended to pronounce "his" Japan so great a success that it deserved a quick peace settlement. Not only would such an assertion be dramatic, it also would highlight the contrast between MacArthur, the "peacemaker," and Truman, the exponent of expensive new aid programs for occupied Germany and Western Europe.

Never a subtle man, the general hammered home this theme in conversations "leaked" to the outside. In Tokyo he frequently revealed his plans to British Representative Sir Alvary Gascoigne, and, on 3 March 1947, MacArthur lectured him on the "three phases of the Occupation." MacArthur boasted of his "miraculous" success in demilitarizing and democratizing Japan. The failure to revive the economy was not his, however. Instead, he blamed all the Allied governments whose trade restrictions would "completely and irretrievably kill the Japanese economy." Since only a change in the restrictions would help Japan, he claimed it was ridiculous to provide new foreign assistance or to delay further a peace settlement. Unfortunately, MacArthur believed, Marshall and his aides "paid heed" only to "Wall Street whose main holdings were in Europe." Consequently, the administration focused on Germany and ignored Japan.

The general condemned this Europe first strategy and argued that occupation forces could be withdrawn easily from Japan. Such outstanding issues as reparations, levels of production, and trustbusting were merely "technical problems." Japanese security could be assured by a "simple article . . . providing UN responsibility for future protection." MacArthur insisted that nearly all of Japan's alleged problems were the fault of Truman and his staff, whose petty jealousies led them to inflate their own successes in Europe while denigrating his achievements in Asia. Unless Marshall made progress toward a treaty during the upcoming Moscow meeting of the Council of Foreign Ministers, he told Gascoigne, he would shatter the "Pacific air" with his "cries" to "conclude an early peace treaty with Japan."[17]

Not only did the Moscow conference fail to make the progress MacArthur desired, but the president's announcement of the Truman Doctrine on 12 March also ended any likelihood of Soviet-American cooperation. MacArthur quickly made a rare visit to the foreign press club in Tokyo, where, without informing Washington first, he told reporters that recovery was impossible until a peace treaty ended the "economic warfare" against Japan which had inflicted even more damage than the atomic bomb. With a flourish, the general claimed that he was powerless to revive the economy and dismissed any initiatives from Washington.

MacArthur praised the Japanese government, the fruit of his "spiritual revolution," and blithely explained away fifty years of aggression. Japan was merely a poor country that took a wrong turn in "reach[ing] out to get resources." Defeat in war the loss of overseas investments were sufficient punishments for past transgressions. Tokyo owed nothing to its victims and already had earned an honored place in the world community through its "advanced spirituality." MacArthur concluded this remarkable statement by paraphrasing Winston Churchill's remark that the West's major European problem was "not to keep Germany down, but to keep it up." America's greatest problem in Asia, he insisted, was to "keep Japan up."[18]

As so often before, both MacArthur's blanket absolution of Japan and his demand for a peace treaty collided with opposite initiatives from Washington. Even as the general spoke, the president sought to rally Congress, the public, and the European allies behind a new major foreign aid program. The administration, the general implied, already had botched affairs in Europe, while he had built a new Japan at bargain rates. Now Washington seemed determined to export its mistakes across the Pacific by needlessly extending the occupation and throwing away money.

Shocked by MacArthur's latest grandstanding, Marshall, Forrestal, Acheson, Kennan, the Joint Chiefs of Staff (JCS), and technical specialists in the cabinet departments feared that the general had set the stage for Japan's collapse. Unless basic policy were changed quickly, the collapse might come while America remained in control. Some officials guessed that MacArthur realized this and therefore hoped to reach a peace that would get him out of Tokyo before a politically disastrous crisis.

Forrestal, soon to be named Defense secretary, mobilized the administration against MacArthur. While initially one of the general's foremost admirers, Forrestal had grown disillusioned with, and then cynical toward, him. Like others in the administration, Forrestal believed the greatest threat of Soviet expansion might follow the economic collapse of Western Europe and Japan. He also believed that the strength of American capitalism and a solution to the chronic postwar trade imbalance appeared to be linked to the health of the world economy. Occupation policies and fears, which suppressed German and Japanese recovery, threatened to spread economic chaos and facilitate a possible Soviet breakthrough, Forrestal argued. If "we are to have a run for our side in the competition with the Soviets," he asserted, the United States had to "harness all the talents and brains in the country just as we had to do during the war." Containing the Soviets required a business-led recovery abroad. "Specifically," this meant putting "Japan, Germany and other affiliates of the Axis . . . back to work."[19]

During March and April 1947, Forrestal coordinated discussions among the cabinet secretaries in order to build a consensus favoring a reversal in occupation policies for both Germany and Japan. Former President Hoover, invited to join the ad hoc group, argued that European recovery absolutely depended upon lifting the "ceiling on German heavy industry." Secretary of Commerce Harriman advocated making Germany the economic center of Europe and the core of an integrated regional economy. Forrestal noted that everything the group said about "Germany and the need for making some restoration of its industry possible applied with equal force to Japan." Existing occupation policies drained American resources, undermined industrial strength, and promoted the uncertainty and chaos most likely to invite Soviet meddling.

To Forrestal the solution required silencing MacArthur's "defeatist rhetoric" and restoring "hope of recovery to the Japanese" before a "complete economic collapse." This would necessitate stopping the anti-Zaibatsu campaign, followed by a quick move to implement a new economic agenda. While Secretary of War Robert P. Patterson agreed in theory, he believed he lacked the power to order MacArthur to accept new advisers or new ideas. Forrestal fumed that the Army and War departments seemed to exert no control whatsoever over MacArthur, lacking both the will and ability to "issue a single order."[20]

Forrestal's complaint was more than rhetorical, as Army Secretary Royall discovered late in 1947. When Royall ordered MacArthur to delay Diet consideration of the controversial Zaibatsu dissolution bill, a Pentagon official quickly informed him that it was the "policy of the Department of the Army not to issue an order to General MacArthur." Royall quickly conferred with Chief of Staff Eisenhower, who said that others might be wary of doing so but that he would back up Royall's direct order. Moreover, Eisenhower urged the secretary to speak directly with the president about this problem. Truman, more courageous in private than in public, angrily declared to Royall that, if the "so-and-so hesitated one minute" in following an order, he personally would "bust him to a corporal." Although Royall issued the directive, MacArthur ignored it without any change being made in his rank.[21]

Because of incidents of this sort, a broad consensus developed among planners during 1947 to lessen MacArthur's power and to effect a major shift in occupation policy. State Department officials hammered home to Truman's assistants a clear warning that SCAP's opportunistic push for a treaty and his radical economic agenda would play havoc with the emerging "containment program." Truman was told he must dispatch a "super diplomat" to break the grip of "MacArthur, his chief of staff, and that 'Bataan Group'" in Tokyo. The U.S. government had a choice between "saving the face of SCAP or wrecking its whole economic policy in the Far East."[22]

A new program for Japan, coupled with a move to reduce MacArthur's authority, gathered momentum by piggybacking atop the Truman Doctrine and the Marshall Plan. The concept of an integrated union of industrial capitalist nations could not exclude Japan. The preparation of several comprehensive aid recovery proposals drafted in Washington during 1947 by the State Department, the JCS, and the State-War-Navy Coordinating Committee (SWNCC) each shared parallel proposals calling for this fundamental "shift in emphasis" in occupation policy.

In the State Department the Japan-Korea Economic Division chief, Edwin F. Martin, argued that only an industrially revived Japan could solve the many "related problems" of East Asia. Without a crash program to restore Japanese industry and trade by loaning capital and providing raw materials, a descending economic spiral would shatter democratic reforms and undermine the chance of stability in non-Communist Asia. The State Department program urged canceling reparations, abandoning the anti-Zaibatsu campaign, and promoting Japanese industrial production for export to the rest of Asia. In this scheme, Japan would emerge as the industrial-commercial hub for less developed regional states, especially those in Southeast Asia which could provide vital raw materials. Conceptually, this model consciously evoked the recreation of a new "co-prosperity sphere." Citing a powerful Japan as the key point in a "circle" of Asian recovery, the State Department plan favored a $500 million recovery package extended over several years.[23]

During the spring and summer of 1947 both the JCS and SWNCC expanded on their new ideas for occupation policy. The Joint Staff planners compared Japan's role in Asia to that of Germany in central

Europe and viewed a program of industrial recovery as essential to military security in the region. SWNCC, in an extensive analysis, argued that the United States must assist the Japanese to develop a regionally integrated trade network in non-Communist Asia. State Department, JCS, and SWNCC planners all focused on the need to extend temporary recovery aid while developing a permanent Asian market for Japan.[24]

The drift in administration policy, and its refutation of MacArthur's call for a quick peace treaty, became clear on 8 May 1947. While delivering a major public address, Undersecretary of State Acheson described the "grim facts of life" which could not be ignored. The "greatest workshops of Europe and Asia—Germany and Japan—remained idle." In direct contrast to MacArthur's demands, the administration had determined to abandon the search for an early peace settlement. It would not longer press for economic reforms until the "two great workshops" had been restored. In effect, Acheson opened the administration's assault upon MacArthur's domain.[25]

Much to the general's astonishment, his gambit failed. His sudden push for the peace treaty and Zaibatsu dissolution did not overwhelm the divided administration or boost his presidential candidacy. The challenge from Tokyo, in fact, had united squabbling civilian and military planners. As a result, over the next eighteen months, the president and the State and Defense departments regained control of policymaking for Japan and reduced MacArthur to something of a figurehead.

SCAP's attempt to manipulate public opinion in favor of a peace settlement had backfired. MacArthur's crusade found no large American constituency, and his actions propelled State and Defense planners to unite against him. Although some area specialists, led by Hugh Borton in the State Department, already had drafted a treaty, the general did not like it. The "Borton draft" reflected the liberal reform agenda of 1945 and called for prolonged international supervision of the Japanese economy and political system. Army planners, who resented the idea of any international controls, denigrated Borton's approach but took even greater exception to MacArthur's call for cooperation with the Soviets to secure a "neutral" Japan. The Army's Plans and Operations Division insisted that Japan be considered a permanent American "potential" military base. Colonel S. F. Giffen, spokesman for P&O, told Kennan that MacArthur had failed to consult the Army Department and was completely unprepared to deal in international relations. His behavior forced Washington to spend "vast sums" to undo the damage he already had caused. Since the American military expected to use Japan as a major base in case of war with the Soviet Union, the possibility that Moscow might accept a neutral Japan was especially upsetting.[26]

The actions of the coalition against MacArthur were directed by Kennan, head of the State Department's Policy Planning Staff (PPS), and Army Undersecretary Draper. Royall, Forrestal, Acheson, and Marshall also supported their efforts. Kennan's staff began questioning SCAP policy in August 1947, after first assessing European problems. Kennan and his chief assistant for Asia, John P. Davies, expressed horror with both the Borton draft treaty and MacArthur's proposals. Current SCAP reforms, if followed by an American withdrawal, practically encouraged "Sovietized totalitarianism," Davies wrote. Instead of rushing out of Japan, Davies and Kennan urged a program to "crank-up" Japanese industry, promote its integration into a "Pacific economy," assure "internal stability," and make it a "ready and dependable ally" amenable to "American leadership." Since Japan must "inevitably gravitate into the orbit of one or the other of the superpowers," America must delay a treaty until the direction of the drift was confirmed.[27]

Throughout the autumn of 1947, Kennan and his staff worked tirelessly to piece together an anti-MacArthur coalition within the State Department, with Army and Defense department cooperation. They pushed for sending a high official to Tokyo to survey the damage already done by MacArthur in encouraging "communist penetration" of Japan. In meetings with Forrestal, Royall, and other military administrators, Kennan denounced SCAP policy and its antimonopoly program as "socialization." MacArthur's plan to turn over power to the Japanese now, he warned, would mean "economic disaster, inflation . . . near anarchy, which would be precisely what the communists want."[28]

In September 1947, Draper returned from a brief trip to Japan and told his associates that MacArthur had turned the country into an economic "morgue." The general seemed determined to push through the deconcentration program, which Royall and Forrestal described as "socialism, pure and simple, if not near communism." SCAP had simply ignored the army secretary's orders that he delay Diet consideration of the plan; Forrestal complained that MacArthur was unaware of "what is involved in running a country." The general "scrambled" everything he touched, and Japan faced ruin unless the administration got "some business people over there to administer the law."[29]

MacArthur's defiance not only embarrassed the administration but also threatened to undermine congressional support for the Economic Recovery in Occupied Areas (EROA) bill introduced early in 1948. If economy-minded members of Congress believed that reparations and deconcentration were to continue in Japan, they were not likely to appropriate hundreds of millions of dollars for industrial recovery.

While MacArthur might have believed in the justice of an early treaty and the anti-Zaibatsu program, his enemies in Washington were convinced that political calculus underlay all SCAP's actions. Late in 1947 and early 1948, Truman spoke at length with Royall about MacArthur's anticipated presidential candidacy. The president feared that he could not beat the general and that publicly rebuking the commander might only augment MacArthur's popularity. Instead, he asked Royall to request Eisenhower to consider the possibility of running for president in order to stop MacArthur. Royall later claimed that only after MacArthur's quest for the nomination collapsed in the spring of 1948 did Truman feel confident enough to rein in the general.[30]

Although MacArthur did not declare his candidacy formally until March 1948, he had begun working for the nomination much earlier. When his treaty gambit failed in the fall of 1947, he had then focused on the anti-Zaibatsu deconcentration campaign. At the same time, he began leaking derogatory statements about both Truman and his Republican rivals. In a December 1947 conversation with British diplomat Gascoigne, he condemned Truman for "losing" China and boasted that he could have defeated the Communists had he, rather than Marshall, been sent in 1946. He deprecated Thomas Dewey as "shopworn" and called Robert Taft a "provincial" politician. His cruelest jabs, however, were reserved for Eisenhower. MacArthur accused his former aide of secretly having "Jewish blood in his veins," disqualifying him as either a "real" Republican or true American. Much to the astonishment of an aide, MacArthur also referred to Truman as "that Jew in the White House."[31]

Such remarks filtered back to Washington late in 1947, further convincing Truman administration officials that almost all the general's gambits had been motivated purely by politics. This conclusion seemed confirmed when an anonymous source in Tokyo, a "Mr. Wm. W," sent Draper a confidential report on MacArthur's tactics to force passage of the deconcentration bill. The report alleged that the law originated among a "radical" antibusiness clique in SCAP and that, although MacArthur had selfish reasons for promoting it, he cared little about its substance. In July his aides threatened the reluctant Socialist prime minister, Katayama Tetsu, by informing him that MacArthur interpreted any deviation from SCAP policy as an insult. Unless the legislation were introduced promptly, SCAP "would not be so kind in the future."

Just before the final vote, SCAP officials issued another warning to the prime minister. The law must be "passed so as not to embarrass" MacArthur "who expected to be nominated for president." The general did not care much about enforcing the law, only that there be no "sign to the world of dissension" in Japan. Dissent would tarnish his image and "prejudice the future of Japan when the Supreme Commander became President."

To complicate matters further, MacArthur told influential American conservatives a different story. According to the report given Draper, in November or December 1947 MacArthur had met with two prominent executives from an American corporation, one of whom sat on the Republican National Committee. MacArthur claimed he had "nothing to do with the reforms." All the radical, antibusiness initiatives came from Washington and the Far Eastern Commission. He was a "proponent of capitalism, but the men under him [in SCAP] . . . well, he could not do anything about it, because Washington Democratic Reds sent them." Outraged by this duplicity, Draper circulated the report widely within the administration.[32]

In December 1947, Draper also initiated a publicity campaign against the general's popular image. Turning first to *Newsweek*, he urged the magazine to print portions of a scathing attack on SCAP, extracted from a report compiled in September by lawyer James Lee Kauffman. The *Newsweek* account trumpeted its conclusions with leads that accused MacArthur of pushing Japan "far to the left" by promoting the "lethal weapon of socialism."

The Army undersecretary encouraged such Republican stalwarts as Senator William F. Knowland (R-CA) to denounce SCAP for implementing the most "socialistic" ideas "ever attempted outside Russia." The senator threatened to open a wider investigation into the whole occupation unless radical reforms were stifled. Soon, such conservative newspapers as the *Chicago Tribune*, *Washington Times Herald*, and *San Francisco Chronicle* began charging that their erstwhile hero had permitted "New Deal Socialists" to take over his headquarters.[33]

In January 1948, Royall publicly questioned MacArthur's actions and highlighted the "differences of opinion" between the administration and the general. Washington opposed extreme deconcentrations, favored the revival of mass industrial production, and believed that the leaders of Japan's pre-1945 economy were best qualified to lead the postwar recovery. MacArthur, in turn, responded by denouncing his critics as defenders of the "traditional economic pyramid" who would bring about a "revolutionary bloodbath" in Japan by blocking reform.[34]

Increasingly frustrated by MacArthur, the secretaries of State and Defense resolved to send their own special missions to Tokyo in March 1948. Marshall sent Kennan, while Forrestal selected Draper to lead a business delegation. Both cabinet secretaries hoped that their aides would strongly recommend changes in occupation policies, frighten MacArthur, and create an opportunity for Truman to become involved more directly in Japanese affairs. While the planners in both agencies already viewed SCAP critically, a visit to Japan was expected to legitimize their recommendations further.

Before he left Washington, Marshall urged Kennan to avoid damaging MacArthur's fragile ego, even if, as he predicted, the general tried to humiliate the diplomat. Marshall suggested that Kennan humor MacArthur and make him feel that new proposals were his own. Unfortunately for Kennan, Draper's office leaked provocative news reports about the upcoming visits. Under such headlines as "Drastic Change in Policy of U.S. envisaged—Kennan Visit Seen as Move to Build up Japan as Anti-Red Bulwark," the stories claimed that Kennan and Draper were being sent to order MacArthur to reverse his economic policies and to support Japanese rearmament, long favored by Forrestal, Draper, and the JCS.[35]

MacArthur dreaded the arrival of both missions, knowing they signaled the beginning of the administration's assault on his freedom of action. He spoke bitterly to Gascoigne about the "plot" by "American Tycoons," such as Forrestal, Royall, Draper, and Harriman, to reverse his economic initiatives "because they thought they would conflict with their own business interests." MacArthur insisted that his authority as an "international official" should protect him from errand boys like Kennan and Draper who treated him as if he were a "purely American official."[36]

Kennan's *Memoirs* give a partial account of the cavalier, even demeaning, reception MacArthur first accorded him. Later, by submitting patiently for hours to the general's oratory, he managed to elicit some cooperation. The two men shared a few ideas about the importance of holding a defensible island perimeter, and, for somewhat different reasons, they agreed that Japanese rearmament was not warranted. MacArthur labored to convince Kennan that his economic program, in practice, would be far less radical than his critics charged. He blamed misperceptions and any "extreme" aspects on a few "academic theorizers of a left-wing variety at home and in Tokyo" whom he would like to purge. Charging that a similar subversive clique operated in the State Department, the general implied that, if Washington only left him alone, he would not push deconcentration much further.[37]

MacArthur's belated effort at civility did not impress Kennan. In private letters to Marshall, W. W. Butterworth, and others, he remarked how SCAP headquarters had the same "fragile psychic quality" as the Kremlin under Stalin. He lambasted the "stuffiness" and "degree of internal intrigue" around MacArthur which resembled "nothing more than the latter days of the court of the Empress Catherine II, or possibly the final stages of the regime of Belisarius in Italy." SCAP foisted on Japan a crude "American brand of Philistinism," a "monumental imperviousness to the suffering and difficulties" of the Japanese. the occupation possessed a selfishness which "monopolized everything that smacks of comfort or elegance or luxury." The idleness and boredom of nearly all Americans in Tokyo filled Kennan with despair. MacArthur and his staff seemed determined to exhibit the very worst of their culture, the "monotony of contemporary American social life, its unbending drinking rituals," the "obvious paucity of its purposes," and "absence of inner content" which appeared "pathetic" to the Japanese and visitors alike.

The social habits of American dependents particularly offended Kennan. They behaved, he complained, as if the war had been fought so that officers' wives might have "six Japanese butlers with the division insignias on their jackets," or enjoy skiing lessons at Hokkaido at the taxpayers' expense. It seemed that the ultimate "fate of the Japs" in defeat was to "have the tastes and habits of American suburbia imposed upon them." SCAP had contaminated Japan, Kennan lamented; it had wrecked the old conservative hegemony, disrupted Japanese lifestyles, and substituted no intelligible alternative. Despite MacArthur's rhetoric about a treaty, Kennan suspected that most SCAP officers trembled at the prospect of leaving the posh life they enjoyed. When the occupation ended, Kennan feared, MacArthur's program would virtually ensure a radical leftward swing after the U.S. departure.[38]

While in Tokyo awaiting the arrival of Draper's business mission (named after its nominal leader, Percy Johnston), Kennan composed a terse forty-two-page commentary on SCAP's failures and what Washington must do to correct them. The draft became PPS 28 and, later, NSC 13. The diplomat described SCAP as a parasite, rotting the vitals of Japan and leaving it susceptible to revolution. A multiyear economic recovery program, along the lines already discussed by State and Army planners, was essential. For recovery to take place, however, SCAP's entire agenda must change. Plans for reparations and deconcentration had to be shelved, labor had to be disciplined, and social and political liberalization must be tightly controlled. The "prime objective" of all American activity must be economic growth and political stability.[39]

The findings of Draper's business delegation supplemented Kennan's recommendations. The corporate executives and the Army administrator closeted themselves with Japanese political and business leaders who had been purged or threatened with it. The delegates told journalists that their visit signaled the adoption of a "businessman's solution to Japan's economic ills." The group discussed the need to curb labor unions, protect industrial combines, cancel reparations, and target recovery aid for export-oriented industry. They intended to rebuild Japan as the "workshop of the Far East." Promising that the occupation would never again "go to extremes," Draper incorporated all these views into the delegations' official report, released in April 1948.[40]

During the summer and fall of 1948, Kennan and Draper pushed their recommendations into formal policy. Congress funded the EROA program in June, allocating at least $125 million for an initial recovery program, with additional credits available from related programs. That same month the State Department forwarded Kennan's report on Japan to the National Security Council, which approved it in October.

MacArthur continued to rage about plots by Wall Street tycoons and claimed immunity from Washington's orders, but he backed down in the face of a united administration. The Army and State departments appointed a Deconcentration Review Board in the spring of 1948, promptly cancelling most of the cases brought against the Zaibatsu. SCAP itself turned more conservative during the summer by purging alleged radicals from its ranks and pressing the Japanese government to impose new strict limits on labor union agitation.

MacArthur's de facto capitulation to the administration's program probably stemmed from the collapse of his presidential bubble. Almost as soon as he declared himself a candidate, a string of losses in Wisconsin and the Midwest shattered the general's image as a public hero. His support did not extend widely or deeply in domestic politics. Without a political base, he could neither sustain his resistance to the State and Army offensives nor deter further attack. In effect, the general proclaimed victory and retreated. As the Deconcentration Review Board terminated all cases against the Zaibatsu, MacArthur characterized the event as marking the successful completion of the antimonopoly campaign.

SCAP veterans returning to Washington in search of other government jobs in the summer of 1948 discovered that their association with MacArthur doomed them. They had hoped that service with the occupation would facilitate finding employment with the Economic Recovery Program, then hiring its staff. As Guy Swope reported to his colleagues, SCAP veterans were marked as part of the "small group of long haired boys . . . who have helped General MacArthur put over his socialistic schemes." Both Democrats and Republicans shunned him, Swope complained. Whether Truman or Dewey took office in November, Washington planned to take revenge on the "Big Chief" and those around him for his program in Japan.[41]

Following Truman's election, Army and State department officials quickly hobbled MacArthur's freedom of action. Draper and Acting Secretary of State Robert Lovett signed a "memorandum of understanding," pledging their departments to monitor MacArthur's compliance with new directives. Draper still worried that SCAP would twist or try to wriggle out of guidelines set by NSC 13/2. Accordingly, he prepared a formal directive for Truman's signature which ordered MacArthur and the Japanese government to take "whatever measures may be required . . . to achieve fiscal, monetary, price and wage stability in Japan and to maximize production for export." It mandated a balanced internal budget, tax reform, limits on government credit, wage and price controls, and the allocation of raw materials for export industries even if this required a sacrifice in living standards. Truman then appointed a special emissary, banker Joseph Dodge, to oversee implementation of the guidelines.[42]

MacArthur continued his threats to defy civilian authority. In a testy exchange with Draper, he promised to ignore both the NSC guidelines and the presidential directive, protesting that they had been transmitted to him through improper channels. The new plans so undermined the "fundamental rights and liberties" of the Japanese, the general believed, that they would create "explosive consequences." Even more remarkable the general again insisted that he was under no compulsion to obey orders from the American government. On matters of policy, SCAP, as an "international authority," was subject solely to the Far Eastern Commission and the Allied Council for Japan. Since both NSC 13 and the stabilization decree which altered basic policy came from Washington, he felt justified in ignoring them.

Stunned Army and State department officials declined to challenge the general directly. They guessed, correctly, that he needed to vent his spleen and save face by threatening to defy orders. Administration officials ignored the puffery and simply reiterated the new policy directives. Although he periodically bickered with Washington, and at times stretched the limits of the administration's patience, MacArthur largely accepted its policies after 1948.[43]

The administration's victory over SCAP's independence did not resolve all problems with occupation policy. Throughout 1949 and 1950 State Department planners clashed with their military counterparts over the thorny problems of a peace treaty, bases, and rearmament. MacArthur, however, played a surprisingly small role in these debates. Indeed, he tended to support the proposals put forward by Acheson over those of Defense Secretary Louis A. Johnson and the military establishment.

Increasingly, MacArthur seemed uninterested in the details of occupation policy and turned his attention toward new issues in East Asia. As the Chinese civil war reached its climax, the general advocated the development of Taiwan as an anti-Communist bastion. Even before the Korean War he suggested that his command might be extended to include the island; Taiwan might become the seat of a new unencumbered SCAP headquarters. The fighting which erupted in June 1950 both rescued MacArthur from near oblivion and set in motion a new round of conflict with the Truman administration which, in its style, closely resembled the confrontations of the previous five years.

Notes

1. Carol Gluck, "Entangling Illusions—Japanese and American Views of the Occupation," in Warren Cohen, ed., *New Frontiers in American–East Asian Relations* (New York, 1983), pp. 169–236. Gluck's illuminating survey of the field is filled with insights regarding the evolution of occupation studies by both Western and Japanese historians. She demonstrates how both the style and substance of the literature have moved through distinct stages during the last three decades.

2. D. Clayton James, the most important biographer of MacArthur, recently has

completed a three-volume study of the general's life, *The Years of MacArthur, 1880–1964*, 3 vols. (Boston, 1970–85). The latest volume, which appeared after this essay was written, is far more positive about MacArthur's role in Japan than most recent accounts. Overall, James is more critical of other aspects of the general's career than of the occupation period. Carol M. Petillo's "psycho-history," *Douglas MacArthur—The Philippine Years* (Bloomington IN, 1981), raises fascinating questions about MacArthur's character but implies that the occupation years were an unusually successful aspect of his career. See also Harry S. Truman, *Memoirs*, 2 vols. (Garden City NY, 1955–56); Dean Acheson, *Present at the Creations: My Years in the State Department* (New York, 1969); George F. Kennan, *Memoirs*, 2 vols. (Boston, 1967–72); William Manchester, *American Caesar* (Boston, 1978); John W. Dower, *Empire and Aftermath* (Cambridge MA, 1979); and Howard Schonberger, "The Japan Lobby in American Diplomacy, 1947–52," *Pacific Historical Review* 46 (August 1977): 327–60, as well as his "The General and the Presidency: Douglas MacArthur and the Election of 1948," *Wisconsin Magazine of History* 57, no. 3 (1974): 201–19.

3. Robert H. Ferrell, ed., *The Eisenhower Diaries* (New York, 1981), pp. 43–44, 46–47, 49, 54; Henry L. Stimson diary, 9 and 12 February and 8 April 1942, Stimson Papers, Yale University Library, New Haven CT.

4. Stimson diary, passim; Harold L. Ickes diary, multiple entries, 1941–45 Ickes Papers, Library of Congress, Washington DC. Ickes relished collecting and circulating scathing criticism of MacArthur. In 1942 he discovered evidence of MacArthur's suspicious acceptance of large cash gifts from Philippine President Manuel Quezon. Probably, he passed this information on to FDR and others. Ickes diary, 5 April 1942; James, *Years of MacArthur*, vol. 2: passim.

5. Robert Ferrell, ed., *Off the Record: The Private Papers of Harry S. Truman* (New York, 1980), p. 47; Ickes diary, 9 June 1945.

6. Ferrell, *Off the Record*, p. 61; Ickes diary, 26 August 1945.

7. Clark M. Eichelberger diary, 20 October 1945, quoted in James, *Years of MacArthur*, 3:23–24.

8. Statement by SCAP, 17 September 1945, *Foreign Relations of the United States, 1945* (Washington DC, 1966), 6:715 (hereafter cited as *FRUS*, followed by the appropriate year and volume).

9. Eisenhower quoted in Stephen E. Ambrose, *Eisenhower, 1890–1952* (New York, 1983), pp. 440–41.

10. Robert E. Wood to MacArthur, 4 September 1945, MacArthur file, Wood Papers, Herbert Hoover Presidential Library, West Branch IA; General Bonner Fellers to Wood, 1 October 1945, ibid. See also James, *Years of MacArthur*, 3:21–24.

11. The flap over MacArthur's troop level statement is covered in *FRUS, 1945*,

6:716–21; Truman, *Memoirs*, 1:520–21; diary entry, 18 September 1945, Harold Smith Papers, Harry S. Truman Presidential Library, Independence MO; diary entry of 18 September 1945, Eben Ayers Papers, Truman Library.

12. Ickes diary, 7 October and 14 November 1945. McCloy prepared only a sketchy account of his meeting with MacArthur. See note 15 below.

13. Edwin A. Locke to Truman, 19 October 1945, President's Secretary's file, Harry S. Truman Papers, Truman Library, SCAPIN 244, Supreme Commander for the Allied Powers, *The Political Reorientation of Japan*, 2 vols. (Tokyo, 1948), 2:565, app. B; *Report of the Mission on Japanese Combines* (Washington DC, 1946).

14. The recommendations of the Pauley and Edwards missions are discussed in Michael Schaller, *The American Occupation of Japan: The Origins of the Cold War in Asia* (New York, 1985), pp. 20–51.

15. W. Averell Harriman and Elie Abel, *Special Envoy to Churchill and Stalin* (New York, 1975), pp. 541–45; John McCloy, memorandum for General George A. Lincoln, "Visit to Japan," 17 February 1946, box 222, Records of the Far Eastern Commission, RG 43, National Archives, Washington DC; Ambrose, *Eisenhower*, pp. 440–41; Walter Millis, ed., *The Forrestal Diaries* (New York, 1951), pp. 177–79.

16. Memoranda of conversations with MacArthur by Herbert Hoover, 4, 5, and 6 May 1946, "Famine Emergency Comm—World Mission, Gen., H. H. diary 1946 Journey," Hoover postpresidential subject file, Hoover Papers, Hoover Presidential Library.

17. Record of conversation with MacArthur, Sir Alvary Gascoigne to Foreign Office, 4 March 1947, FO 371/63766, Public Record Office, London, England (hereafter cited as PRO).

18. MacArthur interview with press correspondents, 17 March 1947, in SCAP, *Political Reorientation of Japan*, 2:765–67, app. F.

19. Forrestal diary, 3 March 1947, James Forrestal Papers, Seeley Mudd Library, Princeton University, Princeton NJ.

20. Diary entry, 16 April 1947, ibid.; minutes of the Meeting of the Secretaries of State, War, and Navy, 16 April 1947, ibid.

21. Kenneth Royall Oral History, Oral History Collection, Columbia University, New York City NY.

22. Minutes of the Meeting of the Secretaries of State, War, and Navy, 16 April 1947, Forrestal diary; Dean Acheson to Robert Patterson, 14 April 1947, filed with 740.0019 Control (Japan) 9–1347, Department of State Records, RG 59, National Archives; Patterson to Acheson, 21 April 1947, ibid; note to Locke, ibid.

23. See reports on Japan in SWNCC 360, 21 April 1947; SWNCC 360/1, 12 May 1947; SWNCC 360/2, 3 June 1947; SWNCC 360/3, 11 October 1947, all in SWNCC 360 file, State-War-Navy Coordinating Committee Records, RG 353,

National Archives; E. F. Martin to John Hilldring, 26 February 1947, box 22, FEC Records, RG 43.

24. Ibid.; Joint Chiefs of Staff 1769/1, 20 April 1947, *FRUS, 1947* (Washington DC, 1972), 1:738–50.

25. Dean Acheson, "The Requirements of Reconstruction," speech of 8 May 1947, Department of State *Bulletin* 16 (18 May 1947): 991–94.

26. Colonel S. F. Giffen to Policy Planning Staff, 14 August 1947, Policy Planning Staff Records, Freedom of Information Act request.

27. John P. Davies to George Kennan, 11 August 1947, *FRUS, 1947,* 6:485–86; Kennan to Robert Lovett and Lovett to Kennan, 12 August 1947, ibid., pp. 486–87; W. W. Butterworth to George C. Marshall, 22 September 1947, ibid., pp. 523–25; minutes of discussion of treaty draft, meeting 48, 25 August 1947, box 32, Policy Planning Staff Records, RG 59, National Archives; meeting 54, 4 September 1947, ibid.; meeting 65, 22 September 1947, ibid.

28. Kennan to Lovett and Marshall, 14 October 1947, *FRUS, 1947,* 6:536–43; memorandum by Carlisle Hummelsine to Willard Thorp et al., 29 October 1947, PPS Records, Freedom of Information Act request; Hummelsine to General Marshall Carter, 16 October 1947, ibid.; Forrestal diary, 31 October and 7 November 1947, Forrestal Papers.

29. Memorandum by O. J. McDiarmid to Roswell H. Whitman, 7 January 1948, PU 894.50/1-848, Department of State Records, RG 59; Department of the Army to MacArthur, 20 and 21 October 1947; SCAP to Department of the Army, 25 October 1947, all in memorandum of 9 December 1947 by Robert Blum, CD 3–1-9, Records of the Office of the Secretary of Defense, RG 330, National Archives. Blum, an aide to Forrestal, compiled an extensive file on the disputes between SCAP and Washington. Defense officials passed on MacArthur's cable to former Secretary of War Stimson, hoping he would press the general to curtail the anti-Zaibatsu campaign. While sympathetic to the administration, Stimson declined to enter the fray. Kenneth Royall to MacArthur, 6 December 1947, CD 3–1-9, ibid.; telephone transcript of Forrestal-John Biggers conversation, 5 December 1947, ibid.; William H. Draper History, Truman Library.

30. Kenneth Royall Oral History, Columbia University.

31. Gascoigne to British Prime Minister Clement Attlee, 26 December 1947, FO 371/63830, PRO; Faubion Bowers Oral Histories, MacArthur Memorial Bureau of Archives, Norfolk VA, and Columbia University. These two oral histories overlap but each contains novel details.

32. Memorandum, 12 December 1947, in Draper to Gordon Gray, 14 December 1947, Undersecretary of the Army, General Correspondence—Security Classified, August 1947-January 1949, SAOUS 004, Japan, Records of the Office of the Secretary of the Army, RG 335, National Archives.

33. *Congressional Record,* 80th cong., 1st sess., 19 December 1947, II:686–88;

William Knowland to Royall, 29 December 1947 and Royall to Knowland, 31 December 1947 and 10 January 1948, in Office of the Secretary of the Army, Unclassified General Correspondence, July 1947-December 1950, "Japan" Foreign Country File, Records of the Office of the Secretary of the Army, RG 335. During this period the State Department's Office of Public Opinion Studies surveyed the large amount of published criticism of SCAP. See "U.S. Opinion on Japan and Korea," December 1947-January 1948, in Records of the Office of Public Opinion Studies, RG 59.

34. Speech by Royall, 5 January 1948, printed in Jon Livingston et al., eds., *Postwar Japan: 1945 to the Present* (New York, 1973), pp. 116–19; Royall to speaker of the House of Representatives, 17 January 1948, U.S., House of Representatives, Committee on International Relations, Selected Executive Session Hearings of the Committee, 1943–50, *U.S. Policy in the Far East* (Washington DC, 1976), pt. 1, 6:277–78; MacArthur to Senator Brien McMahon, 1 February 1948, in SCAP, *Political Reorientation of Japan*, 2:783; MacArthur to J. H. Gipson, 1 February 1948, ibid., pp. 780–81.

35. Hummelsine to Kennan, 9 February 1948, box 19, PPS Records, Freedom of Information Act request; Kennan memorandum of conversation with Marshall, 19 February 1948, ibid.; Stewart Hensicy, 27 February 1948, United Press release; Theodore Koslow, 26 February 1948, International News Service release. SCAP censored these stories in Tokyo, claiming they represented Draper's efforts to undermine MacArthur. See William Sebald to Niles Bond, 3 March 1948, filed with 740.0019 Control (Japan) 3–348, Department of State Records, RG 59, National Archives; Royall to Forrestal, 18 May 1948, 091 Japan TS, sec. 1A, P&O, Army Department Records, RG 319.

36. Gascoigne to Foreign Office, 6 April 1948, FO 371/69886, PRO.

37. Kennan report, in FRUS, *1948* (Washington DC, 1974), 6:697–99; Kennan, *Memoirs*, 1:384; Kennan to MacArthur, 5 March 1948, box 19, PPS Records, Freedom of Information Act request; Kennan memorandum of conversation with MacArthur, 5 March 1948, FRUS, *1948*, 6:699–706.

38. Kennan to Butterworth, 9, 14, and 16 March 1948, box 19, PPS Records, Freedom of Information Act request.

39. PPS 28, 25 March 1948, PPS Records, RG 59. For an edited version see FRUS, *1948*, 6:691–98.

40. *Pacific Stars and Stripes*, 12 April 1948; *New York Times*, 20 April 1948; memorandum by Draper aide, Colonel T. N. Depuy, to director, CAD, with enclosures of 15 April 1948, CAD 1948 decimal file, CAD 014 Japan, sec. 2, 1 March 1948–31 May 1948, Records of the War Department General and Special Staffs, RG 165; memorandum for General William Marquat, in memorandum given to Paul G. Hoffman, 13 April 1948, box 6396, SCAP Records, RG 331, National Archives and Federal Records Center, Suitland

MD; memorandum on final reparations program for Japan, 1 April 1948, box 5977, ibid.; report by General C. V. R. Schuyler on Economic Study of Japan by Civilian Advisory Group, April 1948, 091 Japan TS, sec. 1, case 4, P&O, Army Department Records, RG 319; British Embassy Counselor H. A. Graves to D. F. MacDermot (Foreign Office), with enclosures, 1 May 1948, FO 371/69887, PRO; Percy Johnston et al., "Report on the Economic Position and Prospects of Japan and Korea, and the Measures Required to Improve Them," copy in Joseph Dodge Papers, Detroit Public Library, Detroit MI; Jerome Cohen, "Japan: Reform vs. Recovery," *Far Eastern Survey* 17 (23 June 1948): 137–42.

41. Guy Swope to Justin Williams, 17 March, 21 May, and 13 September 1948, file 106, Justin Williams Papers, University of Maryland Library, College Park MD.

42. "Informal Memorandum of Understanding" between State and Army departments concerning implementation of NSC 13, 7 December 1948, Undersecretary of the Army, Draper-Voorhees Project decimal file, 1947–50, 091 Japan, Records of the Department of the Army, RG 335; Draper-Lovett exchange, 13 December 1948, *FRUS, 1948*, 6:1060; statement on economic stabilization of Japan, ibid.; William H. Draper Oral History, Truman Library.

43. Sebald to John Allison, 29 November 1948, 820.02, Records of the Foreign Service Posts of the Department of State, 59 A 543, pt. 9, RG 84; MacArthur to Army Department, 4 December 1948, Draper-Voorhees Project File, RG 335; Draper to SCAP, 10 December 1948 and SCAP to Draper, 12 December 1948, both in "Japan-1947–48: MacArthur Communications," File 42, Admiral William Leahy Files, Joint Chiefs of Staff Records, RG 218; MacArthur to Draper, 18 December 1948, P&O, 091 Japan TS, sec. 1B, pt. 2, Records of the Department of the Army, RG 319; Max Bishop to Butterworth, 28 December 1948, PPS Records, Freedom of Information Act Request; Lovett to National Security Council, 29 December 1948, ibid.; MacArthur to Prime Minister Yoshida Shigeru, 19 December 1948, *FRUS, 1948*, 6:1066–67.

The Occupation of Japan, 1945–1952

Ikuhiko Hata

Ikuhiko Hata, professor of history at Takushoku University and author of a history of the U.S. Occupation of Japan, traces the course of American policy under MacArthur. "In a profound and basic way," he concludes, "it set the course of Japanese history in the second half of the twentieth century."

In the last year, two books have appeared in Japan which are particularly relevant to a study of the American occupation of Japan. One of these is by Etō Jun, the other by Shimizu Ikutaro.[1] Etō, angered that the Japanese have completely forgotten the humiliation of the occupation, maintains that the Americans completely ignored the Hague Convention on Land Warfare and forced a spiritual revolution—under the name of reform—upon the people of an occupied nation. Shimizu, who was once a leader of anti-American progressive intellectuals, has now turned into a right-wing hawk. He argues that the Japanese, who have a foreign-made constitution, including the restrictions on armaments outlined in Article Nine of that constitution, have no right to be called a nation, and that Japan is merely a community. He appeals for the Japanese to recover their existence as a nation by nuclear armament.

For many Japanese intellectuals, an article of faith since World War II has been the belief that "postwar democracy is our fundamental and supreme principle which should be protected," as the greatest intellectual theorist of the postwar era, Maruyama Masao, stated. In this case, "postwar democracy" means the best part of American democracy with the qualification that it does not include the "dirty America" after the "era of reverse courses" [see sec. 3].

Both Etō and Shimizu were most distraught because it was no doubt true that the occupation of Japan by the United States, which lasted six and one-half years from 1945 to 1952, satisfied the majority of Japanese.

It was a "generous occupation" from the Japanese point of view and a "successful occupation" from the American.

When Japan surrendered in 1945, some radical young Army and Navy officers tried to stage a *coup d'etat* and to demand forcefully an "imperial decision" from the Emperor to continue the war. After the coup failed, they organized several underground organizations which watched the behavior of the occupying forces. Their plan was to resist through a guerrilla war, with a young royal prince at their head, once the emperor system was abolished or harsh occupation policies were implemented. They abandoned this project within a year; the underground organization was dissolved. It was the American method of occupation under General MacArthur and his subordinates in the Far Eastern American Army which led to the melting away of feelings of revenge in the most tough and narrow-minded militarists. Friction sometimes occurred in later years, but fraternity, as the basic tone of U.S.-Japanese relations, has never been shaken. However, the return of nationalism due to Japan's attainment of the status of an economic super-power has awakened some suspicions concerning the "legacy of occupation," as represented in the arguments of Etō and Shimizu.

It is difficult to predict what influence this tendency will have in relations between Japan and the United States in the future. Before venturing into prediction, however, this paper looks back on the development of the occupation era, which has become an important historical context for the present age.[2]

Initial Phase of the Occupation

There is no evidence that Japanese officials gave any thought during World War II to contingency planning for the postwar period, particularly with regard to Japan's position vis-à-vis the Allied powers. In striking contrast, the planning carried out by the Allies, particularly the United States, was meticulous. Japan specialists in the U.S. State Department began research on postwar policies toward Japan and East Asia as early as August 1942, scarcely nine months after the attack on Pearl Harbor.[3] This beginning coincided roughly with a U.S. counterattack on the Solomon Islands, about one year earlier than the Japanese had anticipated. In 1942, U.S. Army and Navy Japanese-language schools were also established, designed to train intelligence and military government officers.

The basic Allied policy line for the postwar period was first made public in the Cairo Declaration of 1 December 1943, according to which Japan had to renounce all colonies, grant independence to Korea, and surrender unconditionally. Once defeat of the Axis powers seemed certain, in 1944, concrete measures were drafted in preparation for the occupation of Japan and Germany. The State-War-Navy Coordinating Committee (swncc) was set up as a central policy planning agency in December of that year, with its initial efforts concentrated on policy for Germany. In April and May 1945, however, a group of Japan specialists drafted a comprehensive occupation policy for Japan, which formed the basis of the final plan approved by President Harry Truman at the end of the war.

A central figure in the formulation of occupation policy toward Germany at this time was Secretary of the Treasury Henry Morgenthau.[4] He advocated a severe policy of direct Allied rule under which German industrial capacity would be dismantled. Morgenthau insisted upon a similarly stern policy toward Japan, and was supported both by a group of State Department officials known as the "China crowd" and a number of liberals associated with the Institute of Pacific Relations. The views of President Franklin Roosevelt were influenced by this kind of thinking. However, the sudden death of Roosevelt in April 1945 came as a setback for advocates of a strict occupation policy, and it temporarily enhanced the voice of the "Japan crowd," led by Undersecretary of State Joseph C. Grew, former ambassador to Japan, and Councillor Eugene H. Dooman. These men felt that "the democratization of Japan should be promoted, but the purge and dissolution of moderate, responsible forces must be minimized in order that Japan become a staunch ally of America."[5]

An early draft of the Potsdam Declaration, which was based on recommendations from Grew and Stimson, specifically referred to retention of the emperor system in postwar Japan. This reference was eliminated from the final version announced on 26 July 1945, however, as a result of an "in-house" compromise with the hard-liners. In Japan, as well, this deletion became a subject of heated contention in the Imperial Conference, where the terms of surrender were discussed. Acceptance of the Potsdam Declaration was finally possible only after an "imperial decision" overrode efforts of the military to secure inclusion of specific guarantees that the emperor system not be abolished. Once that obstacle had been cleared, Japan accepted the terms of the declaration unconditionally.

A final decision on the Emperor's status was withheld at the time the

"Basic Initial Post-Surrender Directive to SCAP [Supreme Commander for the Allied Powers] for the Occupation and Control of Japan" (JCS 1380/15) was issued in November 1945. This directive instructed the supreme commander "not to remove the Emperor or take any steps toward his removal without prior consultation with and advice issued you through the JCS." The question was finally resolved during the first phase of the occupation when the United States, recognizing the depth of national feeling surrounding the imperial institution, incorporated it in the new Japanese constitution.

The fundamental principles of occupation policy for the demilitarization and democratization of Japan were dispatched by President Truman on 6 September 1945 in the "U.S. Initial Post-Surrender Policy Toward Japan" (SWNCC 150/44). The wording of this document, however, was vague and open to interpretation. Therefore MacArthur and the civil administrators of SCAP retained considerable freedom in the formulation and execution of precise policy measures. Two additional bodies were established to coordinate Allied policies: the Far Eastern Commission (FEC), set up in Washington in late 1945, consisting of representatives of eleven United Nations countries and theoretically the highest policy-making organ for the Allied Occupation; and the Allied Council for Japan, set up in Tokyo in the spring of 1946 to perform an advisory function, including representatives of the U.S., the Soviet Union, China, and the British Commonwealth. Since neither of these bodies was active until early 1946 their influence was limited. As a SCAP announcement confirmed, by the time these bodies began operations, the basic orders for the democratization of Japan had been outlined.

In fact, the FEC was never in a position to play more than an indirect role, at best. In the first place, intervention in occupation policy could take place only through the executive channels of the American government and SCAP. The U.S. government, furthermore, was in a position to make *ad hoc* policy by issuing "interim directives" and therefore did not need to depend upon the authority of the FEC. The Allied Council for Japan had only an advisory role from the beginning, and its authority was further diminished by MacArthur's tendency to ignore it. Power therefore remained largely in the hands of MacArthur himself, proud senior general of the American military establishment. John Gunther likened him to Caeser, with good reason.

The SCAP staff was composed of persons from a wide diversity of backgrounds. One group, referred to as the "Bataan Boys," consisted of close associates of MacArthur who had served on his staff since the start of the war. Others were career officers who had fought in the Pacific theater. SCAP also included technical experts, academicians, government officials, "old [prewar] Japan hands," and a number of second-generation Japanese-Americans.

Prominent "Bataan Boys" were Courtney Whitney, a lawyer from Manila who served as chief of the Government Section; William F. Marquat, once a journalist, who headed the Economic and Scientific Section; and Charles A. Willoughby, chief of the Intelligence Section. Career officers included Lieutenant General Robert L. Eichelberger, commander of the Eighth Army, and Chief of Staff Richard Sutherland, both of whom had served in the field during the Pacific campaign. Civilians in SCAP included Hubert G. Schenck, chief of the National Resources Section, who came to SCAP from a position as professor of geology at Stanford University; Crawford F. Sams, chief of the Public Health and Welfare Section, who had been a noted neurologist in St. Louis; and Ken R. Dyke, chief of the Civil Information and Education Section, who came from the advertising industry. Governmental officials included such persons as William J. Sebald, chief of the Diplomatic Section. A foreign service officer married to a woman of mixed Japanese and British parentage, Sebald had practiced law in Japan before the war.

Those personnel of the middle echelon who were called liberal or radical "New Dealers," headed by Charles Kades, included Edward C. Welsh, chief of the Antitrust and Cartels Divisions; James S. Killen and Theodore Cohen, each of whom served for a time as head of the Labor Division; Sherwood M. Fine, advisor to the Economic and Scientific Section; and Harry F. Alber, chief of the Price and Rationing Division. All of these men had experience in executing reforms in the U.S. under the Roosevelt administration and had proved themselves able administrators.

It was perhaps inevitable in a bureaucracy large enough to include SCAP and all local military authorities, that some officials would be less than well qualified. Others took advantage of Japanese pliancy and receptivity to wield the powers of their office oppressively. Nevertheless, the vast majority of the Japanese people believed that the occupational reforms were beneficial. The leaders of the occupation administration must be given the credit for this success. The SCAP bureaucracy has occasionally been dismissed as a group of second-rate malcontents who could not succeed in their own country; that view is not correct. Occupation officials on the whole, including members of the special missions which frequently visited Japan, displayed a level of ability and confidence superior to that of the people they governed.

Years of Reform and Starvation

The occupation cannot be understood apart from the personality of the supreme commander, General Douglas MacArthur. John Gunther portrays MacArthur as a colorful personality who, on the one hand, was a "man of providence," an "idealist," and a "reformer." He was "hard working," a man who "exercised formidable power with moderation," yet on the other hand, was "narcissistic," "theatrical," "histrionic," "a man of nineteenth-century virtues," and "one who dictatorially imposed democracy on Japan."[6] Gunther was obviously at a loss to sum up the various facets of this complex personality. From the standpoint of the Japanese, who were the governed, MacArthur's rule was a form of "benevolent despotism." It follows that everything American, and the entire corpus of postwar democracy passed down to the Japanese through the hands of MacArthur, may have been only an illusion.

The general outline of early occupation policy was established by directives from Washington, while concrete implementation was largely entrusted to the judgement of MacArthur and SCAP. During his flight into Japan, MacArthur discussed with Major General Whitney the main objectives of the early stages of the occupation. He listed them under eleven headings: (1) destruction of military power; (2) establishment of representative government; (3) granting women suffrage: (4) release of political prisoners; (5) liberation of farmers; (6) freedom for the labor movement; (7) encouragement of a free economy; (8) abolition of police oppression; (9) development of a free press; (10) liberalization of education; and (11) decentralization of political power. These objectives were all elaborated in SCAP's policy directives issued shortly after MacArthur's arrival in Japan. On 11 October 1945 MacArthur instructed newly appointed Prime Minister Shidehara to proceed with five major reforms: granting women suffrage; encouragement of labor unions; liberalization of education; abolition of oppressive institutions; and democratization of the economy.[7]

During the half-year between MacArthur's landing at Atsugi Air Base and February 1946, SCAP ordered numerous democratic reforms, including the arrest of war criminals (September 1945), granting freedom of speech (September), release of political prisoners (October), dissolution of the *zaibatsu* (November), land reform (December), revision of the election law to grant suffrage to women (December), guarantees of freedom in religion and education (December), and the purge of public officials (January 1946). The reforms came to a climax with the issuance of MacArthur's draft of the new constitution in February 1946.

The Japanese government, not anticipating that SCAP's policy of "demilitarization and democratization" would be instituted so thoroughly and quickly, tried to ride through the period with only lukewarm reforms. This behavior can be attributed to two factors. On the Japanese side, old-line government leaders misjudged the climate within SCAP and in Washington by overestimating the influence on decision-making of Grew and the "Japan crowd." SCAP officials, for their part, wished to rule only indirectly and therefore sought some signs of reformist zeal on the part of Japanese leaders. It soon became evident to those in SCAP, however, that the scale and extent of the reforms it considered necessary were beyond the range of vision of the Japanese government and the old, established class. Attempts to enact land reform, to dissolve the *zaibatsu*, and to draft a new constitution brought these limitations clearly to light. While the Japanese side did not deliberately seek to resist or sabotage SCAP directives, their slowness and cursory responses were sufficient to raise doubts within SCAP about their enthusiasm for reform.

The reforms came to a climax in February 1946 with the issuance of the new Japanese constitution. On 3 February, General MacArthur summoned Courtney Whitney, Chief of the Government Section, and ordered him to develop a draft constitution which would include the following: retention of the emperor system, renunciation of war, and abolition of the peerage.[8] Charles Kades and twenty-five members of the staff of the Government Section completed a draft to these specifications after a week's nonstop labor. It was proclaimed to the Japanese Government on 13 February. The drafting of a constitution in such a short interval is a record which remains unequaled.

Whitney explained that the document was based on American political concepts, utilizing elements of the Meiji Constitution and the Weimar and other European constitutions as well. In fact, however, it has been pointed out that several articles were borrowed almost literally from the United States Constitution, the American Declaration of Independence, the Gettysburg Address, and the Atlantic Charter.[9] Nevertheless, the constitution was liberal and progressive, and a first-class performance for that era. For that reason the majority of the present

Japanese population is satisfied with this constitution, although even the drafters of the constitution anticipated it would be replaced by the Japanese as soon as the occupation ended.

MacArthur stated that the two main features of the new constitution were "the system of the Emperor as symbol and Article Nine which regulated the abandonment of war." Even today, Article Nine remains a feature peculiar to the Japanese Constitution, not to be found in any other country, with the perhaps notable exception of Costa Rica. It is interesting to note, however, that it was not perceived to be a curiosity in the atmosphere of that time. There were rosy expectations concerning the role of the United Nations as the world police force, while the security of Japan was guaranteed, for a time, by the U.S. occupation forces. Furthermore, the drafters at SCAP expected that Article Nine would be abolished by the Japanese as a matter of course, once the occupation had come to an end.

When the United States later came to regret the inclusion of Article Nine in the Japanese Constitution, MacArthur wrote in his *Reminiscences* that the idea had been proposed by Prime Minister Shidehara. Historical opinion remains divided as to whether Shidehara or MacArthur himself was the originator. It is most likely that both the retention of the emperor system and the inclusion of Article Nine were the result of an exchange or a bargain made in meetings between the General and Shidehara. In any event, when Article Nine became a *fait accompli*, MacArthur became its ardent supporter.

It was MacArthur who, for two years, kept rejecting a limited rearmament for Japan as requested by Washington after 1948 during the intensificaiton of the Cold War. It might be said that the original proponent of "unarmed neutrality," which remains popular and influential even today, was General MacArthur.

The fact that the general public in Japan, which had long endured a militaristic rule, looked upon the occupation force as a "liberation army," prevented nationalistic reaction to the barrage of SCAP directives. Hence, democratic reforms were enthusiastically instituted and enthusiastically received. The Japanese economy, however, because of the war, reached a nadir. Inflation was rampant and food shortages were so common that prophesies circulated of ten million people dying of starvation in the winter of 1945–1946. Meanwhile, labor union struggles over the right to livelihood intensified. A people "liberated" spiritually was tottering on the edge of starvation. The economy was further weakened by the heavy burden of wartime reparations. Japan's external assets had been promptly confiscated and the initial policy toward domestic economic recovery, as set forth in November 1946 in the final Pauley Report, limited Japan's productive capacity to 1930 levels. The harsh recommendations of this report, furthermore, provided for the transfer of most of the factories surviving the wartime devastation to countries such as China and the Philippines. The second Strike mission, under Clifford S. Strike, which visited Japan in the summer of 1947, eased Japan's reparations burdens. It recommended that production standards be raised to the 1935 level, allowing Japan's economy to recover and become self-reliant.

Reparations provisions were subsequently modified again in accordance with changes in American policy toward Japan; indeed, except for interim deliveries to the Philippines and elsewhere, reparations were finally discontinued altogether. There was little indication that the assets already transferred were being put to use by the recipient countries. One illustration of this fact is given by George F. Kennan, who, upon visiting Shanghai in the spring of 1948, noted that various kinds of machines, still unpacked, were piled up on the wharves and were corroding with rust. For Japanese industry, on the other hand, the fact that worn and dated machinery was removed from their factories meant, ironically, that economic recovery required its replacement by the most modern equipment, paving the way for later rapid growth.

Given the needs of the Japanese economy in the immediate postwar years, one finds fanciful the ideas of Pauley and Strike. Hampered by mounting inflation, industrial recovery was slow. As late as 1948 industrial production was still limping along at about 30 percent of the prewar level. Both the first Yoshida cabinet and the Katayama cabinet attempted to break this vicious circle of inflation and low production by promoting a "Priority Production Program" whereby important industries such as coal production (with a target of thirty million tons) and iron production were fostered. Under this policy food was specially rationed to mine workers and large sums of capital were invested in both industries by the Reconstruction Finance Bank (RFB). Unfortunately, however, this also stimulated the "RFB inflation."

A widespread debate broke out over whether priority should be given to rapid industrial recovery or to economic stabilization through control of inflation. Views also differed as to whether stabilization could be achieved in one sweep through the implementation of drastic measures or whether a more moderate policy, aimed at gradual stabilization, would be necessary. For all the debate, the Japanese government was in no position to take any decisive action. The control of inflation and the recovery of the economy depended on external factors and could come only with a change in American policy toward Japan.

The Cold War and the "Reverse Course"

Change in American occupation policy in 1948 came as a by-product of the Soviet-American Cold War confrontation which had begun to unfold the previous year. Conflict between the United States and the Soviet Union over the form and control of the occupation began with Japan's surrender, but strong American opposition blocked a Soviet attempt to partition Hokkaido. In sum, at least as far as the occupation of Japan was concerned, Soviet intervention was successfully prevented. In Europe, on the other hand, the circumstances were quite different. Germany had been divided into four zones, with the United States, the Soviet Union, Britain, and France each occupying one of the zones. The struggle over occupation policy that ensued between the United States and the Soviet Union matured into the Cold War by way of the Greek civil war of 1946–1947 and the Berlin blockade of April 1948.

The United States, with its monopoly of the atomic bomb, had expected to enjoy supremacy in a postwar Pax Americana which would encompass even the Soviet Union. Forced to revise this optimistic outlook, the Truman administration adopted a new strategy, the containment policy, as set forth in the Truman Doctrine of March 1947. The United States, in the face of the Communist threat, began by the end of that year to extend military aid to Greece and to Turkey and inaugurated the Marshall Plan to provide large scale aid to the war-ravaged economies of western Europe. According to this plan, Europe's economic recovery was to be based on the resuscitation of Germany's industrial capacity. Toward this end the Joint Chiefs of Staff, in July 1947, issued to General Lucius Clay, commander of the American occupation force in Germany, a new directive (JCS 1779) that fundamentally revised existing occupation policy toward Germany.

The de-Nazification policy of the U.S. occupation force during the early stages of the German occupation was implemented through direct military rule, which was much stricter and more thorough-going than was the occupation of Japan. As the influence of the New Deal officials began to wane in early 1946, however, decartelization policies were relaxed and emphasis was placed on promoting a self-reliant German economy. It is apparent, therefore, that American occupation policies toward Germany and Japan evolved in similar directions, with the change in Germany preceding that in Japan by more than a year.

In light of the global confrontation between the United States and the Soviet Union, it was natural that the U.S. should eventually reevaluate Japan's significance and consider Japan as a pro-Western bulwark against Communism in Asia. In late February 1948, George Kennan consulted with MacArthur in Japan. In the wake of these talks Kennan presented a report to the National Security Council (NSC) which provided the guiding principles for subsequent policy toward Japan. The main points of this report included relaxation of SCAP control, development of a self-supporting economy and a halt to reforms, discontinuation of the purge, an end to reparations payments, strengthening and reorganizing the Japanese police, and postponement of an early peace treaty.[10]

The question of signing an early peace treaty had already become a focal point of discussion in the United States. MacArthur was a keen advocate of an early treaty, fearing that prolongation of the occupation would invite the resistance of the Japanese people. In February 1947 he had dispatched Diplomatic Section Chief George Atcheson to Washington with a proposal that a peace treaty be concluded by July of that year. Opinion was divided among the various groups in Washington. The Army and Navy were unenthusiastic about an early peace, owing to their desire to maintain bases in Japan. In the State Department, however, Hugh Borton's group produced the first outline of a peace treaty in March 1947, and revised drafts were prepared in July and again in January 1948. These drafts included such essential points as: prohibiting the maintenance of a regular military force, with the exception of police and coast guard; prohibiting any aircraft industry; prohibiting military research; continuing the purge; rigorously collecting reparations; and establishing a supervisory committee under the FEC which would oversee the execution of the above measures for twenty-five years.[11] The underlying tone of these objectives was, in the words of Frederick Dunn, "that of World War II and not of the cold war."[12]

The State Department's Cold War strategists, led by Kennan, believed that the SCAP "Pinkers" (as they called the New Deal group) had drastically weakened Japan under the banner of reform. To conclude a peace with Japan under such circumstances, they argued, would be tantamount to delivering Japan into the hands of the Communists. Kennan supported a continuation of the occupation until Japan achieved economic self-sufficiency and became, as in the case of Germany, the "workshop of Asia" and a bulwark against Communism. Another year passed, however, before the changes in occupation policy proposed by Kennan were made final.

Several missions were dispatched to Japan in 1948, which, in addition to having to analyze the situation, had to overcome internal SCAP resistance in order to bring about a gradual change in policy. Along with Kennan, a central figure in this policy shift was Undersecretary of the Army William Draper, a former Wall Street investment banker who had served in the German occupation. At almost the same time as Kennan's visit, Draper brought to Japan a delegation of businessmen headed by Percy H. Johnston. The recommendations submitted by this delegation, which included drastic reduction of reparations, increased aid to Japan, and measures for the expansion of trade, set the goal of self-sufficiency for the Japanese economy.

Further recommendations for revisions in economic policy came in May 1948 from the Young Mission, headed by Ralph A. Young of the Federal Reserve Board, which urged the adoption of a single exchange rate to pave the way for Japan's reentry into the international economy. Then, in October 1948 came the epoch-making reorientation of policy toward Japan by the National Security Council paper NSC-13/2.[13] The three essential elements of this NSC decision called for: reducing SCAP controls and transferring a large measure of authority and responsibility to the Japanese government; entrusting reforms to voluntary efforts by Japanese; and strengthening and reorganizing the national police.

From the standpoint of MacArthur and SCAP, the NSC decision came as an "unwelcome interference" implying a cutback in their operation. Kades, leader of the "Pinkers," was dispatched to Washington by MacArthur in an attempt to reverse the new policy. Failing in this effort, the disappointed Kades resigned without returning to Tokyo.

SCAP's resistance to the change in occupation policy was manifested in several ways. MacArthur disapproved in particular of strengthening and reorganizing the national police, and he disapproved of an additional request for a limited Japanese armed force. A strong supporter of Article Nine of the Constitution, he adopted a "wait-and-see" attitude, despite constant urging from Washington. Finally, with the outbreak of the Korean War, a police reserve of seventy-five thousand men was created.

The clearest example of SCAP's recalcitrance in the face of change was the struggle that ensued over the deconcentration law (the Law for

Elimination of Concentrations of Excessive Economic Power). Following the appearance of an article in *Newsweek* magazine in December 1947, criticisms were raised in the United States against the "Pinkers" in SCAP, who, it was felt, were so completely dismantling Japanese enterprises that recovery would be impossible. This protest that SCAP reforms were "going too far" was based on a document (FEC 230) which had been submitted by the State Department in May to the FEC, but on which action had been deferred.[14]

Taking advantage of the American protests, the Japanese government maneuvered to block passage of the deconcentration law by aligning with SCAP conservatives. Despite this effort, the Japanese Diet was forced to adopt the bill when, on the night of 9 December 1947, under the vigilance of SCAP Antitrust and Cartels Division Chief E. C. Welsh and Legislative Division Chief Justin Williams, the clock was set back to forestall the closing of the Diet session.[15]

In May 1948, Army Undersecretary Draper dispatched a five-man review board of businessmen to Japan to review conditions for implementing the deconcentration law, by virtue of which 314 of the 325 designated firms were exempted. In essence, as Robert Textor points out, this action meant the end of the deconcentration program.

Washington next ordered SCAP to implement the nine-point Economic Stabilization Plan. Joseph M. Dodge, president of the Detroit Bank and the man who had planned currency reform in Germany in 1946, was sent to Japan as financial advisor in charge of the nine-point plan. Concurrent with this appointment was the announcement that since the objectives of anti-monopoly and deconcentration policies had been achieved, these policies would be terminated. The occupation entered a new stage.

The Last Phase of the Occupation

As the occupation continued, a fraternity developed between the administrative bureaucracies of Japan and SCAP. From the Japanese standpoint, there was, during this period, no business more important than that of "liaison" with SCAP. Whenever Japanese officials alluded to "SCAP sources," Diet members could no longer question their views. Never has the Japanese bureaucracy exercised greater authority than it did during the occupation.

On the American side, MacArthur secluded himself from the Japanese people, meeting prime ministers and few others. By shrouding himself in the mystery of an imperial aura, MacArthur sought to preserve his prestige. Scrupulously cautious, he warned SCAP officials against "collusion" with the governed. Among lower SCAP officials, however, close personal relations with their Japanese counterparts grew as a natural consequence of the daily "liaison." Beyond this, there was, of course, "fraternization" between American soldiers and Japanese women. The Japanese "liaison bureaucrats" felt that their toilsome contact with SCAP officials offered the latter an opportunity to become more familiar with conditions in Japan.

This closeness at the working level explains, in part, why it took so long for changes adopted in Washington to be reflected in the occupation administration. For example, the unified exchange-rate plan (one dollar to three hundred yen, plus or minus thirty yen) as recommended by the Young Mission, and measures to combat the inflation, both met with strong resistance from the SCAP bureaucracy. The ten principles of economic stabilization passed in a directive to the Ashida cabinet in July 1948 received no more than a lukewarm response from the Economic Stabilization Board. In light of such deliberate resistance to the guidelines offered by Washington, the nine economic principles policy was issued in December. This policy, later known as the "Dodge Line," was enforced by Dodge upon his arrival in Japan in February 1949. Dodge was supported by Washington officials, who now realized that effective action on economic problems was impossible as long as it was left in the hands of SCAP.

The two main pillars of the Dodge Line were a balanced budget for fiscal year 1949 designed to curb "RFB inflation," and the establishment of a single exchange rate of 360 yen to the dollar. Saddled with these policies, the Yoshida cabinet was unable to fulfill most of its election promises. Finance Minister Ikeda-Hayato made a plea for relaxation of these policies, but made no headway against Dodge's stubborn insistence on strict enforcement. A sudden deflation was therefore anticipated, and it was feared that corporations and export industries might go bankrupt. Layoffs also intensified labor problems. The start of the Korean War in June 1950, however, produced a sudden boom that enabled the stagnant economy to recover its vitality and to sustain high growth rates in the last half of the 1950s. Rescued by happenstance, the Dodge Line brought inflation to a halt. Stopping inflation provided a basis for industrial recovery during the war boom; the "stabilization policy" should perhaps be regarded as successful.

The Korean War also prompted the revival of military power in Japan. Article Nine of the constitution may be considered to be the product of the collaboration between MacArthur and Prime Minister Shidehara. MacArthur, to be sure, was breezily optimistic about the security prospects of a demilitarized Japan. The Japanese government, however, began to examine Japan's security requirements early after independence was regained. Even within SCAP, General Willoughby, Chief of the Intelligence Section, sought to maintain the nucleus of a rehabilitated Japanese Army by carefully cultivating the group led by Colonel Hattori Takushiro and elite members of the former Japanese Army General Staff.

Until about 1947 the Shidehara and Yoshida cabinets favored making Japan a neutral state like Switzerland. The United States, the Soviet Union, China, and Great Britain would guarantee that neutrality; therefore this plan was premised on the conclusion of a peace treaty with all the former Allied powers, including those in the Socialist bloc. This was MacArthur's personal view as well. In the spring of 1947, when the Japanese government learned of the possibility of an early peace, Prime Minister Yoshida ordered the Central Liaison Office to study Japan's security. That June, Foreign Minister Ashida, representing the Socialist Katayama cabinet, put forward a plan whereby Japan's security would be entrusted to America in exchange for military bases on Japanese soil. Atcheson and Whitney, however, quickly disapproved this proposal as being inappropriate.

Ashida prepared a second memorandum in September 1947 according to which Japan, by virtue of a special agreement with the U.S., would be dependent on American military strength to prevent external aggression until the United Nations was functioning effectively. A Japanese national police force would be created to deal with the danger of civil insurrection. Ashida requested that Lieutenant General Robert Eichelberger, who was returning temporarily to the United States, hand-carry the proposal to Washington.[16] Under the circumstances, however, this plan was also ignored.

Despite these early failures, Ashida's proposals concerning a peace only with the Western powers and dependence on the United States for defense were almost identical to the provisions later included in the San Francisco peace treaty and the U.S.-Japan Administrative Agreement.[17] The idea of a national police force was likewise incorporated into the NSC decision and realized in July 1950 in the form of the Police Reserve.

The change in U.S. policy took place within the framework of further intensification of the Cold War in 1949, exacerbated in Asia by the victory of the Chinese Communist Army, leading to the establishment of the People's Republic of China, and by Soviet development of the atomic bomb. There were repeated statements, by Secretary of State Acheson and others, to the effect that the U.S. defense perimeter in Asia should run from Japan through Okinawa, Taiwan, and the Philippines.

The lack of clear reference to the Korean peninsula left the status of this area open to question, and it is frequently suggested that it was a fatal omission, helping to induce the North Korean Army to invade South Korea. MacArthur himself once remarked to William Sebald that he "considered a United States pullout sensible because Korea was militarily indefensible."[18] When the Korean War actually broke out, however, the United States, under the banner of the United Nations, was quick to send reinforcements to fight against North Korean and Chinese armies. The tide of the war ebbed and flowed, but by the second half of 1951 the two sides had settled into positional warfare in the vicinity of the 38th parallel. It was during this stage of the conflict that Japan's role as a rear supply area became indispensable to the United Nations' troops. Consequently, for better or for worse, Japan's position in the Western camp was a foregone conclusion.

In July 1950, General MacArthur ordered that the Japanese create a National Police Reserve to number seventy-five thousand men. This force was to maintain domestic security in Japan to take the place of the four divisions of American ground forces which were to leave Japan for Korea. Through SCAP and Dulles, the U.S. Government requested that the Japanese expand this force to 300,000–350,000 but this was rejected by Prime Minister Yoshida on the grounds that the Japanese economy, still weak from the war, could not support such numbers.

The National Police Reserve was expanded to 110,000 in 1951, and to 130,000 the year after that in response to constant pressure from the U.S. The Maritime Security Force—in reality a small navy—was founded in 1952. In 1954, these ground and maritime forces were united with a newly created air force and the current Self-Defense Forces were born.

The discordance between United States demands for large-scale rearmament and the Japanese Government's reluctance to carry it out resulted in a compromise in the Ikeda-Robertson Talks of October 1953. The strength of the Ground Self-Defense Force was fixed at 180,000, where it remains today. The setting of this limit in size of ground forces made possible the creation of three well-balanced modern conventional services, albeit compact ones, and was a result of the rejection of large-scale rearmament.[19]

Once the prospects had dimmed for a peace treaty that would embrace all the former combatants in World War II, the process of regaining independence for Japan accelerated. In September 1950 President Harry Truman directed the State Department to prepare a peace treaty; the following January, John Foster Dulles, an advisor to the State Department, arrived in Japan to begin framing the document. Following a joint British-American proposal drafted in July, the San Francisco Conference convened in September 1951. Forty-eight nations, excluding the Soviet Union and China, signed the peace treaty which took effect in April 1952. The American occupation of Japan, which lasted more than six years, had come to an end, and Japan was again independent.

The termination of the occupation in 1952 was hardly a dramatic moment in Japanese history. Beginning in 1950, SCAP bureaucrats had progressively reduced their own organization and had encouraged the gradual transfer of power to the Japanese government. The Japan-U.S. security treaty, which had been signed simultaneously with the peace treaty, further heightened the sense of continuity. It provided for the stationing of American troops in Japan for an unspecified period of time.

The restoration of Japan's independence in this fashion left a residue of dissatisfaction and uneasiness, not only in the Soviet Union and China, but also among members of the British Commonwealth and other Asian countries, who feared a revival of Japanese militarism. To ease these misgivings the United States entered into mutual defense treaties with the Philippines, and with Australia and New Zealand (ANZUS).

The forceful demands of Dulles, who was the embodiment of Cold War ideology, led Japan to favor the Taiwan regime, thereby precluding a restoration of diplomatic relations with the Chinese mainland. Problems such as relations with China, which were caused or at least left unsolved during that period, would return to haunt Japan in later years. Under the international circumstances of the time, however, Yoshida felt it wisest to go along with Dulles and in so doing to secure at an early date independence and a self-supporting economy.

It is unfortunate that the personal role of the Emperor, which has been overlooked to the present time, has not been touched upon in arguments concerning the occupation by such scholars as Etō and Shimizu. This writer believes that the keynote of occupation policy was formed by the eleven meetings between the Emperor and MacArthur. Other than these two persons, only a diplomatic interpreter who accompanied the Emperor participated in the talks. It is certain that memoranda of these talks were prepared by the interpreter, and the Ministry of Foreign Affairs and the Imperial Household Agency admit the existence of the memoranda. Unfortunately, these documents have yet to be released. The reason given is that it would give rise to political arguments if it were proven that a personal diplomacy had developed between MacArthur and the Emperor at a time when the Emperor had supposedly lost all political power and become merely a political symbol.

From fragmentary information it is possible to reconstruct the contents of the talks, however, and the Emperor seems to have given his positive support to occupation policies concerning demilitarization and democratization and the anti-Communist policy, while on the other hand he requested the relaxation of the purge and expressed concern over how the security of Japan would be protected under Article Nine of the Constitution. The Emperor, through his aides, offered some advice concerning the Asian policies of the United States.

There are indications that MacArthur paid serious attention to the Emperor's requests and advice, as MacArthur recognized that the Japanese people's support of the Emperor was overwhelming. It seems, however, that when the conflict between the General and Washington intensified, the Emperor and his aides opened a new channel of communication, through the Japan lobby, which led to Dulles. The court circle quietly abandoned the General more than a year prior to the dismissal of MacArthur by President Truman in April of 1951.[20] This led to the anticlimactic atmosphere surrounding the twelfth and final meeting between MacArthur and the Emperor. MacArthur refused the request from the Japanese side that he pay a visit to the Emperor immediately before returning to the United States after his recall. Instead, MacArthur demanded that the Emperor come to greet him. This last meeting was purely ceremonial.

The American occupation of Japan, however, was anything but ceremonial. In a profound and basic way, it set the course of Japanese history in the second half of the twentieth century.

Notes

1. Etō Jun, *Wasureta koto to wasuresaserareta koto* [Things We Have Forgotten and Things We Were Made to Forget], (Tokyo, 1979), and Shimizu Ikutaro, *Sengo o Utagau* [Doubts on the Postwar Japan], (Tokyo, 1980).

2. See *Amerika no Tainichi Senryo Seisaku* [History of the U.S. Occupation of Japan], (Tokyo, 1976). Book review by Roger Dingman, *The American Historical Review*, (April 1978).

3. Hugh Borton, *American Presurrender Planning for Postwar Japan* (New York, 1967).

4. *Morgenthau, Diary*, 2 vols. (Washington, 1967).

5. Waldo H. Heinrichs, *American Ambassador* (Boston, 1966), pp. 363–370.

6. John Gunther, *The Riddle of MacArthur* (New York, 1951), pp. 10–12, 15.

7. GS, SCAP, *Political Reorientation of Japan*, I, pp. 102–103.

8. Courtney Whitney, *MacArthur: His Rendezvous with History* (New York, 1956), p. 213.

9. Ikuhiko Hata, *Shiroku Nippon Saigunbi* [History of Japan's Postwar Rearmament], (Tokyo, 1976).

10. George F. Kennan, *Memoirs, 1925–1950* (Boston, 1967), pp. 391–392.

11. U.S. Dept. of State, *Foreign Relations of the United States, 1948*, VI, pp. 656–660.

12. Frederick S. Dunn, *Peace-making and the Settlement with Japan* (Princeton, 1963), p. 59.

13. NSC-13/2, 13/3, National Archives of the U.S.

14. Elenor M. Hadley, *Antitrust in Japan* (Princeton, 1970), p. 130.

15. Interview with Justin Williams.

16. *Eichelberger Diary*, 7 Sept. 1947, Duke University.

17. Martin E. Weinstein, *Japan's Postwar Defense Policy, 1947–1968* (New York, 1971).

18. W. J. Sebald, *With MacArthur in Japan* (New York, 1965), p. 179.

19. Hata, pp. 198–200.

20. See Howard Shonberger, "The Japan Lobby in American Diplomacy 1947–1952." *Pacific Historical Review* (Aug. 1977).

4. Korea

Old Soldiers Never Die

Douglas MacArthur

In a nationally televised address before a joint session of Congress on April 19, 1951, the recently dismissed MacArthur defended his conduct in Korea and set forth his views on the strategic importance of Asia to the United States.

Mr. President, Mr. Speaker, and distinguished Members of the Congress: I stand on this rostrum with a sense of deep humility and great pride— humility in the wake of those great American architects of our history who have stood here before me, pride in the reflection that this forum of legislative debate represents human liberty in the purest form yet devised. Here are centered the hopes and aspirations and faith of the entire human race.

I do not stand here as advocate for any partisan cause, for the issues are fundamental and reach quite beyond the realm of partisan consideration. They must be resolved on the highest plane of national interest if our course is to prove sound and our future protected. I trust, therefore, that you will do me the justice of receiving that which I have to say as solely expressing the considered viewpoint of a fellow American. I address you with neither rancor nor bitterness in the fading twilight of life with but one purpose in mind—to serve my country.

The issues are global and so interlocked that to consider the problems of one sector, oblivious to those of another, is but to court disaster for the whole.

While Asia is commonly referred to as the gateway to Europe, it is no less true that Europe is the gateway to Asia, and the broad influence of the one cannot fail to have its impact upon the other.

There are those who claim our strength is inadequate to protect on both fronts—that we cannot divide our effort. I can think of no greater expression of defeatism. If a potential enemy can divide his strength on two fronts, it is for us to counter his effort.

The Communist threat is a global one. Its successful advance in one sector threatens the destruction of every other sector. You cannot appease or otherwise surrender to Communism in Asia without simultaneously undermining our efforts to halt its advance in Europe.

Beyond pointing out these simple truisms, I shall confine my discussion to the general areas of Asia. Before one may objectively assess the situation now existing there, he must comprehend something of Asia's past and the revolutionary changes which have marked her course up to the present. Long exploited by the so-called colonial powers, with little opportunity to achieve any degree of social justice, individual dignity, or a higher standard of life such as guided our own noble administration of the Philippines, the peoples of Asia found their opportunity in the war just past to throw off the shackles of colonialism and now see the dawn of new opportunity, a heretofore unfelt dignity and the self-respect of political freedom.

Mustering half of the earth's population and 60 percent of its natural resources, these peoples are rapidly consolidating a new force, both moral and material, with which to raise the living standard and erect adaptations of the design of modern progress to their own distinct cultural environments. Whether one adheres to the concept of colonization or not, this is the direction of Asian progress and it may not be stopped. It is a corollary to the shift of the world economic frontiers, as the whole epicenter of world affairs rotates back toward the area whence it started. In this situation it becomes vital that our own country orient its policies in consonance with this basic evolutionary condition rather than pursue a course blind to the reality that the colonial era is now past and the Asian peoples covet the right to shape their own free destiny. What they seek now is friendly guidance, understanding, and support, not imperious direction; the dignity of equality, not the shame of subjugation. Their prewar standard of life, pitifully low, is infinitely lower now in the devastation left in war's wake. World ideologies play little part in Asian thinking and are little understood. What the peoples strive for is the opportunity for a little more food in their stomachs, a little better clothing on their backs, a little firmer roof over their heads, and the realization of the normal nationalist urge for political freedom. These political-social conditions have but an indirect bearing upon our own national security, but form a backdrop to contemporary planning which must be thoughtfully considered if we are to avoid the pitfalls of unrealism.

Of more direct and immediate bearing upon our national security are the changes wrought in the strategic potential of the Pacific Ocean in the course of the past war. Prior thereto, the western strategic frontier of the United States lay on the littoral line of the Americas with an exposed island salient extending out through Hawaii, Midway, and Guam to the Philippines. That salient proved not an outpost of strength but an avenue of weakness along which the enemy could and did attack. The Pacific was a potential area of advance for any predatory force intent upon striking at the bordering land areas.

All this was changed by our Pacific victory. Our strategic frontier then shifted to embrace the entire Pacific Ocean, which became a vast moat to protect us as long as we hold it. Indeed, it acts as a protective shield for all of the Americas and all free lands of the Pacific Ocean area. We control it to the shores of Asia by a chain of islands extending in an arc from the Aleutians to the Marianas held by us and our free allies. From this island chain we can dominate with sea and air power every Asiatic port from Vladivostok to Singapore and prevent any hostile movement into the Pacific. Any predatory attack from Asia must be an amphibious effort. No amphibious force an be successful without control of the sea lanes and the air over those lanes in its avenue of advance. With naval and air supremacy and modest ground elements to defend bases, any major attack from continental Asia toward us or our friends of the Pacific would be doomed to failure. Under such conditions the Pacific no longer represents menacing avenues of approach for a prospective invader—it assumes instead the friendly aspect of a peaceful lake. Our line of defense is a natural one and can be maintained with a minimum of military effort and expense. It envisions no attack against anyone nor does it provide the bastions essential for offensive operations, but properly maintained would be an invincible defense against aggression.

The holding of this littoral defense line in the Western Pacific is entirely dependent upon holding all segments thereof, for any major breach of that line by an unfriendly power would render vulnerable to determined attack every other major segment. This is a military estimate as to which I have yet to find a military leader who will take exception. For that reason I have strongly recommended in the past as a matter of military urgency that under no circumstances must Formosa fail under Communist control. Such an eventuality would at once threaten the freedom of the Philippines and the loss of Japan, and might well force our western frontier back to the coasts of California, Oregon, and Washington.

To understand the changes which now appear upon the Chinese mainland, one must understand the changes in Chinese character and culture over the past 50 years. China up to 50 years ago was completely nonhomogeneous, being compartmented into groups divided against each other. The war-making tendency was almost nonexistent, as they still followed the tenets of the Confucian ideal of pacifist culture. At the turn of the century, under the regime of Chan So Lin, efforts toward greater homogeneity produced the start of a nationalist urge. This was further and more successfully developed under the leadership of Chiang Kai-shek, but has been brought to its greatest fruition under the present regime, to the point that it has now taken on the character of a united nationalism of increasingly dominant aggressive tendencies. Through these past 50 years, the Chinese people have thus become militarized in their concepts and in their ideals. They now constitute excellent soldiers with competent staffs and commanders. This has produced a new and dominant power in Asia which for its own purposes is allied with Soviet Russia, but which in its own concepts and methods has become aggressively imperialistic with a lust for expansion and increased power normal to this type of imperialism. There is little of the ideological concept either one way or another in the Chinese make-up. The standard of living is so low and the capital accumulation has been so thoroughly dissipated by war that the masses are desperate and avid to follow any leadership which seems to promise the alleviation of local stringencies. I have from the beginning believed that the Chinese Communists' support of the North Koreans was the dominant one. Their interests are at present parallel to those of the Soviet, but I believe that the aggressiveness recently displayed not only in Korea, but also in Indochina and Tibet, and pointing potentially toward the south, reflects predominantly the same lust for the expansion of power which has animated every would-be conqueror since the beginning of time.

The Japanese people since the war have undergone the greatest reformation recorded in modern history. With a commendable will, eagerness to learn, and marked capacity to understand, they have, from the ashes left in war's wake, erected in Japan an edifice dedicated to the primacy of individual liberty and personal dignity, and in the ensuing process there has been created a truly representative government committed to the advance of political morality, freedom of economic enterprise, and social justice. Politically, economically and socially Japan is now abreast of many free nations of the earth and will not again fail the universal trust.

That it may be counted upon to wield a profoundly beneficial influence over the course of events in Asia is attested by the magnificent manner in which the Japanese people have met the recent challenge of war, unrest and confusion surrounding them from the outside, and checked Communism within their own frontiers without the slightest slackening in their forward progress. I sent all four of our occupation divisions to the Korean battlefront without the slightest qualms as to the effect of the resulting power vacuum upon Japan. The results fully justified my faith. I know of no nation more serene, orderly and industrious—nor in which higher hopes can be entertained for future constructive service in the advance of the human race.

Of our former ward, the Philippines, we can look forward in confidence that the existing unrest will be corrected and a strong and healthy nation will grow in the longer aftermath of war's terrible destructiveness. We must be patient and understanding and never fail them, as in our hour of need they did not fail us. A Christian nation, the Philippines stand as a mighty bulwark of Christianity in the Far East, and its capacity for high moral leadership in Asia is unlimited.

On Formosa, the Government of the Republic of China has had the opportunity to refute by action much of the malicious gossip which so undermined the strength of its leadership on the Chinese mainland. The Formosan people are receiving a just and enlightened administration with majority representation on the organs of government, and politically, economically and socially they appear to be advancing along sound and constructive lines.

With this brief insight into the surrounding areas I now turn to the Korean conflict. While I was not consulted prior to the President's decision to intervene in support of the Republic of Korea, that decision, from a military standpoint, proved a sound one, as we hurled back the invader and decimated his forces. Our victory was complete and our objectives within reach when Red China intervened with numerically superior ground forces. This created a new war and an entirely new situation— a situation not contemplated when our forces were committed against the North Korean invaders—a situation which called for new decisions in the diplomatic sphere to permit the realistic adjustment of military strategy. Such decisions have not been forthcoming.

While no man in his right mind would advocate sending our ground forces into continental China and such was never given a thought, the new situation did urgently demand a drastic revision of strategic planning if our political aim was to defeat this new enemy as we had defeated the old.

Apart from the military need as I saw it to neutralize the sanctuary protection given the enemy north of the Yalu, I felt that military necessity in the conduct of the war made mandatory:

1. The intensification of our economic blockade against China;
2. The imposition of a naval blockade against the China coast;
3. Removal of restrictions on air reconnaissance of China's coastal areas and of Manchuria;
4. Removal of restrictions on the forces of the Republic of China on Formosa with logistical support to contribute to their effective operations against the common enemy.

For entertaining these views, all professionally designed to support our forces committed to Korea and bring hostilities to an end with the least possible delay and at a saving of countless American and Allied lives, I have been severely criticized in lay circles, principally abroad, despite my understanding that from a military standpoint the above views have been fully shared in the past by practically every military leader concerned with the Korean campaign, including out own Joint Chiefs of Staff.

I called for reinforcements, but was informed that reinforcements were not available. I made clear that if not permitted to destroy the enemy build-up bases north of the Yalu; if not permitted to utilize the friendly Chinese force of some 600,000 men on Formosa; if not permitted to blockade the China coast to prevent the Chinese Reds from getting succor from without; and if there were to be no hope of major reinforcements, the position of the command from the military standpoint forbade victory. We could hold in Korea by constant maneuver and at an approximate area where our supply line advantages were in balance with the supply line disadvantages of the enemy, but we could hope at best for only an indecisive campaign, with its terrible and constant attrition upon our forces if the enemy utilized his full military potential. I have constantly called for the new political decisions essential to a solution. Efforts have been made to distort my position. It has been said that I was in effect a warmonger. Nothing could be further from the truth. I know war as few other men now living know it, and nothing to me is more revolting. I have long advocated its complete abolition as its very destructiveness on both friend and foe has rendered it useless as a means of settling international disputes. Indeed, on the 2d of September, 1945, just following the surrender of the Japanese nation on the battleship *Missouri*, I formally cautioned as follows:

> Men since the beginning of time have sought peace. Various methods through the ages have been attempted to devise an international process to prevent or settle disputes between nations. From the very start, workable methods were found insofar as individual citizens were concerned, but the mechanics of an instrumentality of larger international scope have never been successful. Military alliances, balances of power, leagues of nations, all in turn failed, leaving the only path to be by way of the crucible of war. The utter destructiveness of war now blots out this alternative. We have had our last chance. If we will not devise some greater and more equitable system, Armageddon will be at our door. The problem basically is theological and involves a spiritual recrudescence and improvement of human character that will synchronize with our almost matchless advances in science, art, literature, and all material and cultural developments of the past 2,000 years. It must be of the spirit if we are to save the flesh.

But once war is forced upon us, there is no other alternative than to apply every available means to bring it to a swift end. War's very object is victory—not prolonged indecision. In war, indeed, there can be no substitute for victory.

There are some who for varying reasons would appease Red China. They are blind to history's clear lesson. For history teaches with unmistakable emphasis that appeasement but begets new and bloodier war. It points to no single instance where the end has justified that means—where appeasement has led to more than a sham peace. Like blackmail, it lays the basis for new and successively greater demands, until, as in blackmail, violence becomes the only other alternative. Why, my soldiers asked of me, surrender military advantages to an enemy in the field? I could not answer. Some may say to avoid spread of the conflict into an all-out war with China; others, to avoid Soviet intervention. Neither explanation seems valid. For China is already engaging with the maximum power it can commit and the Soviet will not necessarily mesh its actions with our moves. Like a cobra, any new enemy will more likely strike whenever it feels that the relativity in military or other potential is in its favor on a world-wide basis.

The tragedy of Korea is further heightened by the fact that as military action is confined to its territorial limits, it condemns that nation, which it is our purpose to save, to suffer the devastating impact of full naval and air bombardment, while the enemy's sanctuaries are fully protected from such attack and devastation. Of the nations of the world, Korea alone, up to now, is the sole one which has risked its all against Communism. The magnificence of the courage and fortitude of the Korean people defies description. They have chosen to risk death rather than slavery. Their last words to me were "don't scuttle the Pacific."

I have just left your fighting sons in Korea. They have met all tests there and I can report to you without reservations, they are splendid in every way. It was my constant effort to preserve them and end this savage conflict honorably and with the least loss of time and a minimum sacrifice of life. Its growing bloodshed has caused me the deepest anguish and anxiety. Those gallant men will remain often in my thoughts and in my prayers always.

I am closing my 52 years of military service. When I joined the Army, even before the turn of the century, it was the fulfillment of all my boyish hopes and dreams. The world has turned over many times since I took the oath on the Plain at West Point, and the hopes and dreams have long since vanished. But I still remember the refrain of one of the most popular barrack ballads of that day, which proclaimed, most proudly, that "Old soldiers never die. They just fade away."

And like the old soldier of that ballad, I now close my military career and just fade away—an old soldier who tried to do his duty as God gave him the light to see that duty.

Goodbye.

Inchon

The General's Decision

H. Pat Tomlinson

MacArthur's dramatic landing at Inchon on September 15, 1950, was hailed at the time—and later—as a brilliant strategic move. Military analyst H. Pat Tomlinson stresses the opposition that MacArthur overcame in launching Operation Chromite.

On 15 September 1950, as the gray shoreline adjacent to the South Korean port city of Inchon became visible in the morning haze, the stillness was shattered by earsplitting sounds and sheets of flame that belched forth from the cruisers and destroyers. A major amphibious assault against the invading North Korean People's Army (NKPA) was beginning. So deep behind the lines was the attack that only a few had confidence in the feasibility of the daring scheme. This operation was the brainchild solely of one of the most controversial military leaders of modern times, General of the Army Douglas MacArthur, Commander in Chief, Far East (CINCFE).

General MacArthur's plan was based largely on terrain. An evaluation of terrain would be necessary because Korea is essentially a peninsula of mountains. The east coast consists of ranges running its length with spur ranges deviating westward across the peninsula. These ranges are characterized by their ruggedness and steep ridges; however, they are not notably high. They definitely curtail mobility for mechanized forces. Therefore, motor movement was restricted to a few primitive roads, mainly in the lowlands along the west side of the peninsula. The same restrictions applied to railroads. Thus, Korea's primary communications were centered in the west with the main roads and rails converging on Seoul from the south and following the western lowlands to the north.

Amphibious Landing

The general planned an amphibious landing at Inchon, a seacoast town

25 miles west of Seoul, to be followed by a lightning advance on the capital city to cut the NKPA's main communication routes. Simultaneously, the 8th U.S. Army in the south would mount a counterattack northward, presenting the NKPA with a two-front war. Inchon, the second largest port in Korea, would be in United Nations hands.

Finally, the recapture of Seoul would be a psychological and political blow of great significance. General MacArthur envisioned winning the war with this one bold stroke. Any doubts that might have crept into his mind were quickly subdued by his overwhelming self-confidence.

Considering the tides that limited an Inchon landing to one of four dates—15 September, 11 October, or 2 or 3 November—he chose 15 September because it would more quickly relieve the pressure on his outnumbered troops on the Pusan perimeter and spare them a bitter winter campaign. A longer wait would permit the enemy additional time to improve his defenses. An early liberation would give the South Koreans an opportunity to harvest their October rice. A frontal assault from the perimeter was dismissed because, even if successful, the heavy casualties would outweigh any advantage in simplicity.

In July the CINCFE transmitted his plan to the Pentagon, calling for a two-division amphibious landing at Inchon.

Optimism versus Pessimism

There was evidence of skepticism among his own staff in Tokyo. They thought that two divisions were insufficient and were worried over what might happen in Japan with the occupation forces removed. They agreed with the Navy that the poor landing conditions at Inchon made the plan too risky. Further, reinforcements could not be provided from Pusan.

So enthusiastic was General MacArthur, however, that, early in July, planning for Operation *Bluehearts* to put the 1st Cavalry Division ashore at Inchon as early as 20 July was initiated. This endeavor was scuttled when the cavalry had to be committed to Korea at an earlier date.

At a meeting in Tokyo on 10 July, Lieutenant General Lemuel C. Shepherd, Jr., Commander, Fleet Marine Force, Pacific, told General MacArthur that the 1st Marine Division with necessary air support could be ready for a landing by 15 September. This was a big order. The only possible method of bringing the division to full strength was to call in the Reserves. Soon many civilians, who just five years before had said "never again," were receiving clothing issue at Camp Pendleton, California.

Opposition to General MacArthur's plan was not confined to his own staff. The Navy Department presented a sound case. Hydrographically, Inchon was one of the least desirable ports. Tide varied from 25 to 33 feet. The approach to the objective was restricted by a narrow channel with a five-knot current studded with natural obstacles and easily mined.

The port only offered limited facilities for handling cargo. Further, the Marines would land in the middle of a city with an added obstacle of 12-foot seawalls to scale. The small islands of Wolmi and Sowolmi were located in commanding positions and were linked to Inchon by causeways. As the bad conditions in the channel precluded night assembly of the fleet, the main landing force would have to hit the beaches in the afternoon daylight, allowing only about two hours in which to secure the city.

Operation "Chromite"

By early August, General MacArthur had his units—the 1st Marine Division commanded by Major General Oliver P. Smith and the 7th Infantry Division under Major General David G. Barr. the 5th Marine Regiment would be withdrawn from the Pusan perimeter, bringing the Marines to division strength. The two divisions and support would form the 10th Corps, to be commanded by Major General Edward M. Almond. Rear Admiral James H. Doyle was Navy amphibious commander, and Vice Admiral Arthur D. Struble was over-all commander of the invasion armada. Admiral Struble answered to Vice Admiral C. Turner Joy, Commander Naval Forces, Far East. The Operation was assigned the code name *Chromite*.

The final debate on Operation *Chromite* was held 23 August. The meeting was attended by General J. Lawton Collins, Chief of Staff, U.S. Army; Admiral Forrest P. Sherman, Chief of Naval Operations; General Shepherd; and Lieutenant General Idwal H. Edwards, U.S. Air Force; as well as other Pentagon representatives and General MacArthur's own staff. General Collins later said: "We went out to discuss it with General MacArthur. We suggested certain alternate possibilities and places. . . ."

The Navy had a group of eight amphibious experts representing every specialty. Each was allowed eight minutes to present his case. They spoke of navigational, hydrographic, geographic, and other obstacles that made the doubtful plan seem impossible.

Then General Collins voiced his doubts. He did not like removing the Marine regiment from Pusan, and wondered if the 10th Corps might be pinned down ashore. He suggested Kunsan as the place to land, and Admiral Sherman agreed.

General MacArthur conceded that Kunsan would be safer, but, at best, it was a flanking attack, at worst, a bloody affair that could fail. Rather than that, he would commit his troops to Lieutenant General Walton H. Walker for a frontal assault, but he would not assume responsibility for such action. He was confident the Navy could overcome the difficulties of tide and terrain. Noting the objections from the Joint Chiefs of Staff (JCS), he told them the: " . . . *very arguments you have made as to the impracticabilities involved will tend to insure for me the element of surprise. For the enemy commander will reason that no one would be so brash as to make such an attempt.*"

He recalled Wolfe's impossible victory at Quebec and assured the Joint Chiefs that Inchon would be another. He argued that the combined effort would put 90 percent of the NKPA between a hammer and an anvil. He ended his defense with an argument that reflected his view of the global struggle in which the United States was engaged.

If the war in Korea were lost, Europe would be jeopardized. The anti-Communist front did not lie in Europe or Washington, but along the Naktong River in Korea. In Europe, it was a war of words—in Asia, it was a war with bullets. He warned that millions of Asians were watching the outcome of battle. "I can almost hear the ticking of the second hand of destiny . . . we must act or we will die." As his voice sank to a whisper, he ended with, "We shall land at Inchon and I shall crush them."

The historic conference concluded. He did not ask nor did he receive the approval of the Joint Chiefs present.

The Navy still doubted the soundness of General MacArthur's plans. On 24 August, Admirals Sherman, Arthur H. Radford, Joy, and Doyle met with General Shepherd and decided to propose the more favorable P'osung-Myon area, south of Inchon, for the landing point. General Shepherd approached General MacArthur in a last minute plea for reconsideration, but the general would not alter his plan.

A reluctant JCS approval was transmitted from Washington, but their reluctance was confirmed when they again queried the general on 7 September. Their concern was based on the fact that nearly all reserves would be committed. On 8 September they reapproved, but only after obtaining an endorsement over the President's signature. This gesture might well be interpreted as written insurance in case the mission were disastrous. General MacArthur labeled it "pessimism at its worst." However, he was well aware of the tremendous gamble.

Initial Phase

With clocklike precision, the hammer fell, and the initial phase of Operation *Chromite* was executed on 15 September 1950. The Marines landed, and the 7th Division followed in their wake. On 29 September, General MacArthur, in a dramatic ceremony, turned Seoul back to South Korean President Syngman Rhee.

General Walker launched the 8th Army's offensive on 16 September. Soon the hammer and anvil met. On 26 September the UN forces made contact. The North Koreans were beaten, disorganized, and suffered heavy losses. The formidable NKPA, which had all but overrun the entire peninsula, ceased to exist as an organized force below the 38th Parallel by the end of September. The old soldier had scored another spectacular success.

Viewing the Inchon operation in retrospect, military students and scholars generally agree that *Chromite* was a brilliant maneuver—that it was a spectacular success cannot be doubted. Even those who tried the hardest to convince the general that other landing points would be the wiser choices readily praised its outcome. General Shepherd praised the operation when he said, "The Inchon landing was a major amphibious operation, planned in record time and executed with skill and precision."

Only a man possessed of self-confidence to a degree beyond that of most men could have refused to alter or compromise under such pressure. The Navy's skepticism was based on sound research by specialists in amphibious operations. The hydrographic obstacles were real. The Marines were right—the geographical features lent advantage to the defenders. The enemy had excellent topographical command of the landing area, and the seawall was a difficult obstacle. Even his own staff had sound reasons for their hesitancy.

The Joint Chiefs were unable to shake General MacArthur with their doubts. He listened as some of the most reputable and high-ranking professional soldiers literally tore his plan apart for more than six weeks. He listened with interest. He considered—even doubted at times—but, from the conception, he did not waver from his prediction of complete success. Luckily for General MacArthur, the two men who had confidence in him were the two men who could have overruled his decision—President Harry S. Truman and Secretary of Defense Louis Johnson.

Considering that the arguments against the general's plan were sound, one might easily conclude that the entire affair was just plain luck. Battles have been decided by unforeseen circumstances that have been referred to as "luck." However, a brief look at the nine principles of war and an analysis of their application to the Inchon operation leads to a different conclusion.

Objective. The ultimate military objective of the war was General MacArthur's—to destroy the enemy and his will to fight. His plan would accomplish the ultimate objective by cutting the main north-south line of communication, immediately securing Inchon, presenting the enemy with a two-front war, and psychologically damaging the Communists by retaking the South Korean capital.

Offensive. Originally, the defense was forced by the overwhelming advance of the NKPA forces. UN-held territory had shrunk to a 140-mile perimeter around Pusan. General MacArthur's conception of a two-front war and double-offensive thrusts would give his forces the initiative.

Simplicity. The over-all planning and execution were accomplished without violating this principle. This was most difficult due to the limited availability of resources for the operation.

Unity of Command. This principle was achieved and maintained. The command structure from the general down to the smallest elements was sound enough to minimize confusion.

Mass. To attain the maximum available combat power, he asked for the 1st Marine Division. To attain a full division, the 5th Marines were taken from Pusan. Careful planning, firepower, tactics, and morale contributed to the effectiveness of the principle of mass.

Economy of Force. There is no evidence that excessive numbers of men or materiel were devoted to unnecessary secondary efforts during the operation.

Maneuver. Operation *Chromite* was a classic example of maneuver being used to alter the relative combat power of the enemy. Envelopment, severance of communication lines, and confronting the enemy with a two-front war were planned and executed in such a manner as to place the NKPA forces at a costly disadvantage.

Surprise. General MacArthur based much of his planning on the element of surprise. This was evident at the conference on 23 August when he informed the skeptical representatives of the various services that their arguments as to the impracticability of his plan tended to insure its success since the enemy would reason in the same way.

Security, the last principle, is essential to the application of the other principles. So much depended on the element of surprise that a major effort at securing positive intelligence for planning was initiated. Agents worked in the landing area, aerial photographs were taken by the hundreds, and tides and hydrographic conditions of the narrow approach through the channel were studied. Lieutenant Eugene F. Clark, U.S. Navy, established rapport with the natives, rowed a dinghy to Inchon Harbor to confirm the height of the seawall and bottom conditions of the harbor, and repaired the harbor lighthouse, turning the beacon on to guide the invasion fleet through the narrow channel. Deception measures, such as bombardments and decoy invasions, were planned to enhance security of the invasion fleet.

Strategically, the most dangerous situation involved in the operation was the commitment of nearly all of the available reserves, even those in the continental United States. The general was confident that nothing would go wrong. Nothing did go wrong.

The success of the operation was based on his self-confidence, ability, and qualities of leadership, and on the abilities and leadership of the hundreds of individuals who were involved in the over-all planning and execution of the maneuver.

Inchon has to be recorded as one of the great battles of military history, and General MacArthur's brave decision earned him a place among the great captains of the past.

The Inchon Invasion

Karl G. Larew

MacArthur's Inchon landing, as with just about everything else he undertook, is not without its critics. Karl Larew, of Towson State University, contends that Operation Chromite was both risky and unnecessary. It reflects ill on MacArthur's inflated reputation.

The August issue contains two separate references to Gen. of the Army Douglas MacArthur's landing at Inchon on 15 September, 1950—Operation Chromite. Gen. William E. DePuy's article, "Concept of Operation: The Heart of Command, The Tool of Doctrine," speaks of the Eighth Army's having been "penned into the Pusan Perimeter" until that "incandescent moment" when Gen. MacArthur carried out his stroke of genius at Inchon, thereby meeting the "demands of the crisis." Bevin Alexander, in his review of James L. Stokesbury's *Short History of the Korean War*, "Korea: Bravery and Blunder, Right and Wrong," says that it was a "bizarre fact that Gen. MacArthur had to fight a fierce battle with the Joint Chiefs of Staff (JCS) to get approval for the Inchon landing," the obvious target. I question the tone and implications of both these passages.

My quarrel is not only with Gen. DePuy and Mr. Alexander, but also with the general tendency among military historians and others to exaggerate the brilliance of the Chromite plan—as distinct from its execution—and to exaggerate the benefits that flowed from the operation. Only by ignoring the plan's faults can one make the case that the reluctance of the JCS to agree with it was bizarre, and only by exaggerating the benefits derived from Chromite can one make the case that it met the demands of the crisis in an incandescent way. Gen. MacArthur was great enough not to need such exaggerations—although he himself, of course, gave impetus to the mythmaking about Inchon that has been and continues to be so common even to this day.

In the first place, it is not true that the Inchon landing saved Eighth Army from destruction. (I do not contend that Gen. DePuy or Mr. Alexander say this, but it is a widespread misapprehension, one that Gen. MacArthur himself helped to create by implication in his memoirs.) The truth is that Eighth Army was no longer in danger as of 15 September—even Gen. MacArthur admitted that—and in fact was able to counterattack on the following day, a counterattack whose purpose was in part to assure the success of Chromite—*not* the other way around! Moreover, far from saving Eighth Army, Chromite placed the Pusan Perimeter in its greatest peril, because the buildup for Inchon could only be accomplished by withholding troops from Gen. Walton Harris Walker at the very moment when his Eighth Army really *was* in serious danger—that is, in late August and very early September. In addition, of course, Chromite posed a very grave risk to X Corps, which made the landing, because of the extraordinary physical and hydrological problems involved in assaulting Inchon.

In the second place, Chromite was not a necessary operation. A landing could have been made at Inchon at a later date, thereby avoiding the dangerous withholding of troops from Gen. Walker during his most difficult time. Or a landing could have been made at a less hazardous place on the Korean coast, thereby avoiding the problems inherent in assaulting Inchon. Either course would have enabled Eighth Army to break out of its perimeter.

Alternatively, X Corps could have been given to Gen. Walker for a breakout offensive. In any case, victory was certain—given the growing weight of American manpower and materiel in late September and early October. Gen. MacArthur, however, insisted on underestimating the effect of such strategies and pressed for his Chromite plan.

It is true, of course, that Chromite did lead to a swifter and more complete victory than any of the alternative scenarios could have produced. But—and this is crucial—a swift and smashing victory, while certainly gratifying, was not necessary to achieve the original and rationally limited goal of the United States, that is, the salvation of South Korea.

Indeed, the nearly total victory that followed Chromite proved in the long run to be counterproductive and in vain—counterproductive because it gave Gen. MacArthur and President Harry S. Truman such swelled heads that they invaded North Korea, ignored China's warnings and ended up with a disaster on their hands; vain because the war ended with North Korea still under communist rule. A slower advance to the 38th Parallel just may have brought about truce talks before the intervention of the Chinese—or at least might have tempered our enthusiasm for a headlong dash toward the Yalu.

If Chromite, then, was extremely risky on the one hand and yet not really necessary on the other, we must ask ourselves why it was ever launched. The answer lies in the psychological and ideological makeup of Gen. MacArthur and of those who supported him. To an extreme conservative like Gen. MacArthur, the Korean War was a monumental turning point in what he believed was a religious, indeed apocalyptic, crusade against communism. From this viewpoint, an enormous victory was vital enough to justify an enormous risk. The Truman Administration, on the other hand, saw the Korean War as a highly regrettable distraction from the really important areas of the world, Europe and the Middle East. Agreeing with President Truman, the members of the jcs were understandably reluctant to risk most of America's combat-ready forces (Eighth Army and X Corps) merely to achieve a smashing victory in a second-rate war.

Whether President Truman or Gen. MacArthur was correct—or whether they were both being overly paranoid and therefore incorrect— is still a matter for debate. In the context of my present argument, however, it does not really matter which philosophy was correct, if either. In any case, it was Washington's right to determine the place of the Korean War in America's global strategy, not Gen. MacArthur's. It was rather Gen. MacArthur's duty to make his plans in accordance with the spirit as well as the letter of America's overall policy, not in accordance with his own ideology. Nor can MacArthur-apologists offer the excuse that Chromite was a purely military matter not related to politics or ideology. The truth is that Chromite presented such a risk to so many of America's few combat-ready forces (both X Corps *and* Eighth Army, remember) as to make it a matter of global policy far beyond the prerogative and competence of a theater commander or even of the Pentagon.

Chromite was, or should have been, a matter for the President and his cabinet to decide. If Gen. MacArthur had been willing to accept that obvious fact in spirit as well as in law, he might not have been so ready to utilize all of his powers of persuasion and coercion so as to get his way. (I say coercion not just in the sense that he bombarded the jcs with his eloquence—men much junior to him in age, fame and grade—but that *anything* he did or wanted to do had political overtones in those frenzied days when the American right wing was behind him all the way and just itching for opportunities to crucify President Truman.)

It seems to me that there are two circumstances in which enormous risks can be justified. One is the kind of situation where the resources one risks are not vital and can be replaced. It is not madness for a rich man to bet $100 on a horse with 30 to one odds against it, but that was not the situation of the United States in the summer of 1950. Gen. MacArthur was gambling with the majority of America's combat strength at a time when the Administration had determined that much more important areas in the world might suddenly be endangered, and he made that gamble at what he himself called 5,000 to one odds! (Doubtless this was merely hyperbole—only a madman would have invaded Inchon if the odds had really been that horrifying—yet the real dangers of Chromite were serious enough, even when viewed from hindsight.)

The other circumstance in which an enormous risk is justified is when one might just as well gamble because one faces inevitable disaster unless the gamble is made. It is not irrational for a man facing his would-be murderer to make a break for freedom even at 5,000 to one odds because, without such a gamble, he would be killed anyway. Again, this was not the situation of the United States in August and September of 1950. We were not headed for inevitable defeat at Pusan, and therefore, a desperate gamble was not necessary or rational. Moreover, as noted above, the risk of defeat at Pusan was *increased*, not decreased, by the Chromite buildup.

The worst that can be said of the JCS, apart from a certain weakness of will in dealing with Gen. MacArthur, is that they were overly pessimistic about the "purely" military aspects of the Inchon operation—but such pessimism was hardly "bizarre," nor was Inchon the "obvious" spot to attack, especially when the entire problem is seen in the context of global considerations.

On the other hand, what is the worst that might be said of Gen. MacArthur? That the difference between a daring genius and a foolhardy grandstander is that a daring genius is a foolhardy grandstander who just happened to get lucky? Gen. MacArthur may not have been foolhardy—since his 5,000 to one odds calculation was mere bombast and soon recanted—but he did leave too much to luck considering that Chromite was not a vital operation. Also, he was too much guided by his own political and ideological ideas rather than those of the U.S. government.

All of this was brought out later in the context of his fall from power, but the same faults that led to his dismissal when he quarreled with

President Truman over what to do about China can be found at the root of his Chromite plan. The Inchon operation therefore cannot be said to have met the "demands of the crisis," however "incandescent" it may have been, because the "crisis" (over by 15 September in any case) called for a different kind of politico-military response.

Gen. MacArthur was a great general, but not so great as he thought he was—nor so great as his starry-eyed worshipers still believe. His reputation has been elevated by adolescents of all ages, thrilling to the lone wolves and Rambos of this world who defy their superiors for the sake of heroics. His reputation has also been puffed up beyond reason by ultra-conservatives determined to turn their darling into a demigod.

More to the point—and here I address Gen. DePuy and Mr. Alexander, not the adolescents or the right wingers—we should understand that the gutsy willingness to take great risks on the battlefield, while often a good attribute in a combat leader, is not necessarily what we should demand of those responsible for global policy nor is hero worship an appropriate component of historical analysis.

Truman and MacArthur

The Wake Island Meeting

John Edward Wiltz

As John Wiltz of Indiana University makes clear, MacArthur's meeting with President Truman in October 1950 has been the subject of much controversy. In this essay he attempts to clear away the many myths that have arisen about the Wake Island conference, while offering his own interpretation of events.

The Korean War was in its fourth month in mid-October 1950 when President Harry S. Truman flew to Wake Island in the Western Pacific to confer with the Commander-in-Chief of United Nations forces in Korea, General of the Army Douglas MacArthur. Scarcely the momentous event that contemporary observers made it out to be, the so-called Wake Island Conference nonetheless has occupied an enduring niche in the literature of the Korean War and the celebrated controversy involving the two men.

In a book published less than a year after the conference, Arthur M. Schlesinger, Jr. and Richard H. Rovere asserted that a disagreement between Truman and MacArthur on policy toward Formosa (as Taiwan was generally called in those days) had prompted the Wake meeting, and took due note of MacArthur's assurance during the conversations with the President that an intervention in the war by the Communist Chinese was unlikely. A few years later Major General Courtney Whitney, a close friend and former subordinate of MacArthur, dismissed the Wake affair as a political ploy to link Truman and the Democratic party with MacArthur's recent victory at Inchon. As for MacArthur's assessment that the Chinese were not apt to intervene in Korea, Whitney contended that it rested on the assumption that the UN Command would respond to a Chinese thrust into Korea by blockading the coast of China and launching attacks against Chinese bases and supply routes in Manchuria. Had MacArthur suspected that retaliation would not follow a Chinese intervention, he was certain that the general would have offered no assurance at Wake that an intervention was improbable. In a book published at the end of the 1950s, John Spanier disputed Whitney's contention that domestic politics prompted the Wake meeting. According to Spanier, the evidence indicated that Truman "flew out to Wake Island to establish a more cordial and harmonious relationship with his field commander, and thereby deny Peking any reason for intervention." Spanier also surmised that a mistaken attack on a Soviet air base in Siberia by American planes on 9 October 1950 may have triggered Truman's announcement on 10 October that he would confer with MacArthur.[1]

Other commentaries followed. Carefully noting MacArthur's assurances about the Chinese, Trumbull Higgins wrote in 1960 that Truman went to wake "to still any doubts regarding the settlement of the Korean problem by means of a personal interview with General MacArthur." Cabell Phillips conceded in 1966 that Truman "had a lesser and concealed motive—namely, that he wanted, for personal political reasons, to warm up his own image within the radiant MacArthurian nimbus."[2] He intimated, however, that the President's main purpose in traveling to Wake was to make certain that "his headstrong field commander" understood American policy in the Far East, the more so in view of reports that Chinese troops were massing on the Manchurian border.

In the 1970s, with publication of Merle Miller's best-selling book *Plain Speaking*, the Wake Island meeting achieved new prominence. Based on interviews with Truman in the early 1960s, the account in Miller explained that the President traveled to Wake to make certain that MacArthur understood the limited objectives of the war in Korea. The Miller book also included a colorful description of the meeting of the two men. According to the account in Miller, the Truman and MacArthur airplanes arrived at Wake simultaneously, and MacArthur landed first only when so ordered by the President. MacArthur was nowhere in sight, Truman told Miller, when the presidential plane rolled to a stop on the Wake air strip, and appeared 45 minutes late for a private meeting with his Commander-in-Chief. When the "son of a bitch" finally showed up for the latter meeting, the presidential temper erupted, and thenceforth—while declaring that under no circumstances would the Communist Chinese enter the Korean War—MacArthur behaved like "a little puppy." In addition to providing a dramatic high point in Miller's book, Truman's recollection of the events on Wake during his meeting with MacArthur was similarly expressed in Samuel Gallu's hit stage play *Give 'em Hell, Harry!*, which opened in 1975, and in a television dramatization entitled *Collision Course: Truman vs. MacArthur*, beamed to a national audience by the American Broadcasting Company on 4 January 1976.[3]

Save for that by Whitney—and Whitney is easily dismissed as an inveterate sycophant of MacArthur—all of the aforementioned accounts of the Wake Island meeting present the view that serious considerations of high policy prompted Truman to fly out to the Pacific to confer with his Far Eastern commander. Their prevailing theme is that the President, concerned about the possibility of an intervention in Korea by the Communist Chinese and fearful that MacArthur might do something rash, journeyed to the Pacific to make certain that the general understood America's Far Eastern policy, and that he also understood that the President indeed was America's Commander-in-Chief. But an examination of the record discloses that Truman's motive for flying to Wake in autumn of 1950 may have been considerably less exalted.

Apart from the World Series, the principal preoccupations of Americans in the first days of October 1950 seemed to relate in one way or another to the war in Korea: soaring prices, the draft, civil defense (in event the East Asian conflict escalated into a global holocaust). Of course, 1950 was an election year, and a central issue in the political campaign by early October was the Korean War—not whether the United States should have entered the conflict, for a recent Gallup poll had indicated that a majority of the citizenry approved the decision to intervene in Korea,[4] but whether mindless or even treasonous policies by the Democratic leadership in Washington had prompted the war in the first place.

Whatever their anxiety about inflation and the draft and their conflicting ideas about the origin of the Korean War, Americans seemed triumphant during the first days of October 1950. After enduring a succession of defeats in the first weeks of their intervention in Korea, American troops had dramatically turned the tide of combat on the Korean peninsula by the brilliant amphibious operation orchestrated by General MacArthur at Inchon in mid-September. Within two weeks the onrushing division of the UN Command had nearly cleared the North Korean invaders from South Korea. Sanctioned by an overwhelming vote in the General Assembly of the world organization, UN troops thereupon pressed their attack across the 38th parallel into North Korea, and by 10 October South Korean soldiers had entered the port of Wonsan on the Sea of Japan.

The man credited with making early October 1950 a time of triumph for America, of course, was the 70-year-old MacArthur, the defender of the Philippines in the dark days after Pearl Harbor, the architect of the Allied sweep through the Southwest Pacific in 1942–1945, the bearer of democracy to Japan in the years after World War II. Now MacArthur had turned defeat into victory in Korea, and was about to climax a half-century of military service by completing the expulsion of communism from the Korean peninsula. He was indeed the hero of the hour. Truman wrote the general on the last day of September: "I know that I speak for the entire American people when I send you my warmest congratulations on the victory which has been achieved under your leadership in Korea. Few operations in military history can match either the delay action where you traded space for time in which to build up your forces, or the brilliant maneuver [at Inchon] which has now resulted in the liberation of Seoul."[5]

A nettlesome question nonetheless remained as UN troops pressed across the 38th parallel in the first days of October 1950: might the Red Chinese enter the war? That question had taken on a special urgency on 30 September when Premier Chou En-lai of the People's Republic of China announced that his government would not stand aside if UN forces entered North Korea. Alas, most noncommunist observers dismissed Chou's broadside as a bluff, or—noting his comments about "persistent long-term resistance"—concluded that at most the Chinese might support protracted guerrilla activities by Korea's communists. Such views rested largely on the assumption that the UN Command would meet any intervention with bombing attacks against the territory of China, and as observers in Hong Kong explained, such reprisals would strike hard at an already dislocated Chinese economy that was just beginning to show signs of revival.[6]

If inclined to share the view that the Chinese would not enter the war, and hence a UN victory in Korea was assured, America's leaders had not dismissed the possibility of Chinese intervention. In the first week in October, MacArthur asked a naval intelligence unit in Taipei to collect additional information concerning a press report from Formosa that General Lin Piao's Fourth Field Army had crossed the Yalu and encamped in northernmost Korea. A day or so later he received an intelligence summary from Washington disclosing that the recent deployment of experienced Chinese forces in Manchuria had increased China's ability to intervene. Next, on 10 October the Joint Chiefs of

Staff reminded MacArthur of the possibility of a Chinese intervention, then amplified his operational directive to cover that possibility: should the Chinese enter the war he was to continue present operations so long as action with existing UN forces offered a reasonable chance of success, but he was to obtain authorization from Washington before attacking objectives in Chinese territory. Meanwhile, on 6 October American and British representatives at UN headquarters pledged that UN forces would not threaten the Soviet Union or China and that non-Korean troops would leave Korea as soon as order was restored throughout the peninsula.[7]

Where was Harry Truman in those early days of October 1950? He assuredly was not on the front page—not conspicuously, at any rate. Monopolizing the headlines of America's newspapers at that point was the General Assembly's vote authorizing UN ground forces to cross the 38th parallel in Korea, the surge of South Korean troops up the east coast of North Korea, and a surrender ultimatum issued by MacArthur to the communist enemy. In the first days of October, in truth, the President was cruising Chesapeake Bay aboard the yacht *Williamsburg*.

By 7 October Truman was back in the capital, which was quiet inasmuch as Congress had recessed for the political campaign. Then, just before noon on 10 October his press secretary Charles G. Ross handed reporters a statement announcing that during the next weekend the President would meet with MacArthur somewhere in the Pacific. The following men would accompany the chief executive: W. Averell Harriman, Special Assistant to the President on Foreign Affairs; Philip C. Jessup, Ambassador-at-Large; Dean Rusk, Assistant Secretary of State for the Far East; Frank Pace, Secretary of the Army; General of the Army Omar N. Bradley, Chairman of the Joint Chiefs of Staff; Charles S. Murphy, special counsel; Charles Ross and Matthew J. Connelly, secretaries; Major General Harry Vaughan, military aide; and Brigadier General Wallace H. Graham, personal physician. On returning from the Pacific, Ross announced, the President would deliver a foreign policy address in San Francisco's War Memorial Opera House.[8] Within hours the occupant of the White House was back on page one—in boldface headlines.

Why did Truman wish to meet with MacArthur? The next days brought widespread speculation. Since the White House had taken care to emphasize that no "sudden emergency" required a consultation with the general, a prevailing assumption was that Truman wanted to exchange views on such topics as the concluding phase of the Korean War, the rehabilitation of Korea in the aftermath of the UN victory, and a peace treaty with Japan. Then there was Formosa. Recalling that less than two months before, in a message to the Veterans of Foreign Wars, MacArthur had taken issue with Truman's policy of "neutralizing" Formosa pending a decision by the UN about its disposition—only to be ordered by an angry President to withdraw the message—nearly everyone guessed that Truman intended to take up the future of that island with his Far Eastern commander.

White House spokesmen naturally refused to concede that the presidential meeting with MacArthur had the slightest partisan political purpose. The view nonetheless was universal that the conference would yield political dividends to the President and his party, and perhaps increase the Democratic vote in the election three weeks hence. The columnist Joseph C. Harsch wrote that for Democratic politicians the presidential trip "is the perfect answer to prayer and fasting." Democratic operatives, according to Harsch, had been trying to figure out a way to put Truman back in the headlines and regain the publicity initiative in the electoral campaign without arranging for him to make an unabashed campaign tour, inasmuch as such a tour might be viewed as bad form so long as the fighting continued in Korea and thus might hurt rather than help the Democrats on election day.[9]

While speculation about the purpose of his trip continued, Truman on the afternoon of 11 October boarded the DC-6 *Independence* and flew to St. Louis. Following in a chartered Pan American World Airways Stratocruiser were 18 press people (all males). That evening the President witnessed the installation of his 61-year-old sister, Mary Jane Truman, as worthy matron of the Missouri Grand Chapter, Order of the Eastern Star. The next morning he led reporters on a 27-block walk, during which he waved to honking motorists and returned a snappy salute to a Negro soldier. That afternoon he reboarded the *Independence* and within a few hours as at Fairfield-Suisun (now Travis) Air Force Base in California where he was joined by Harriman, Rusk, Pace, Bradley, and Murphy who had arrived from Washington aboard an Air Force Constellation. After visiting with wounded evacuees from Korea in the base hospital, Truman returned to his aircraft, and shortly after midnight on 13 October was airborne, destination, Honolulu. Three high-speed destroyers and three coast guard cutters with special weather and search and rescue equipment patrolled the 2,470-mile route, while B-17 and B-29 aircraft circled the flight and escorted it part of the way.[10]

Landing at Hickam Air Force Base at 8:00 AM, Truman was met by an array of dignitaries, caused a stir when he refused to allow the governor of Hawaii to put a lei of white carnations around his neck (insisting that it be put around his arm), and received the usual military honors. In mid-morning, while newsmen and photographers scrambled aboard another boat, the presidential party embarked in a launch for a tour of Pearl Harbor. Next came a lunch at the Pearl Harbor Officers' Club, during which Press Secretary Ross announced that Truman and MacArthur would confer on Wake Island. After that came a 55-mile tour of military and naval installations on Oahu. After dinner the President conferred for two hours with his staff and diplomatic and military advisers on the impending discussion with MacArthur. By midnight he was in bed aboard his aircraft, and at 12:12 AM on 14 October, the *Independence* took to the air. (The press plane and the Constellation already had departed.) Five hours later the presidential conveyance crossed the 180th meridian (the international date line). It now was Sunday, October 15.[11]

As for MacArthur, he already was on Wake, having arrived at 6:10 PM on 14 October. Accompanying him were America's Ambassador to the Republic of Korea, John J. Muccio (brought along at the request of leaders in Washington), Brigadier General Whitney, MacArthur's aide-de-camp Colonel Laurence Bunker, his personal physician Colonel Charles C. Canada, and his pilot Lieutenant Colonel Anthony Story. On leaving the four-engine *scap*, MacArthur and his party made their way to the quonset living quarters of the maintenance manager of the Civil Aeronautics Administration on the desolate little island.[12]

One can only speculate about MacArthur's mood as he awaited the President. Viewing the conference as nothing more than a political junket, he had felt annoyance on receiving the summons to meet Truman. On takeoff from Haneda Airport outside Tokyo he had sat down on the arm of Muccio's seat, and the ambassador later recalled, "He appeared irked, disgusted, and at the same time somewhat uneasy. In the course of his exposition, he used such terms as 'summoned for political reasons' and 'not aware that I am still fighting a war.'" Whitney would remember that the general "paced restlessly up and down the aisle of the plane."[13]

When the presidential aircraft arrived at 6:30 AM, virtually the entire population of the island, and also servicemen awaiting planes to and from the Far East, pressed against a strand of wire near the runway.

The morning was humid, and great cumulus clouds towered above the Pacific.[14] Waiting motionless and solemn-faced as the President, dressed in a business suit and wearing his familiar gray fedora, made his way down a mobile stairway, were MacArthur, his aides, and the officials who had arrived in the Constellation. In a memorandum dictated a few months later Truman recalled that the general was wearing "a greasy ham and eggs cap that evidently had been in use for twenty years." More notable perhaps, the general did not salute and instead offered a handshake, smile, and the greeting: "Mr. President." Grinning, Truman responded: "How are you, General? I'm glad you are here. I have been a long time in meeting you, General." Replied MacArthur: "I hope it won't be so long next time, Mr. President."[15]

A few moments later the two men, arm in arm, walked to a well-worn two-door automobile. After motioning MacArthur into the rear seat, Truman entered the car and sat down beside the five-star general, and while aides attached American and presidential flags to the front fenders the two men engaged in what appeared to be amiable conversation. Then, after a ride of a few hundred yards, they arrived at the quonset hut where MacArthur had spent the night.[16]

Inside the tiny structure the two men conferred for perhaps 40 minutes. Nobody else was present, and neither made any notes. A few years later, in his memoirs, Truman recalled that MacArthur had told him victory was assured in Korea, the Communist Chinese would not enter the war, and Japan was ready for a treaty of peace. According to Truman, MacArthur brought up his vfw message on Formosa and apologized for any embarrassment, to which Truman replied that the incident was closed. As the President remembered, MacArthur said he was in no way involved in domestic politics, unlike in 1948 when he allowed supporters to campaign in his behalf for the Republican presidential nomination. He said he would not permit politicians to make a "chump" of him again. Truman then outlined the administration's plans for strengthening Europe, and MacArthur responded that he believed he would be able to send a division to Europe in early 1951. Recalled the President: "The general seemed genuinely pleased at this opportunity to talk with me, and I found him a most stimulating and interesting person. Our conversation was very friendly—I might say much more so than I had expected." In a paragraph on the private meeting, presumably resting on conversation with MacArthur, Whitney confirmed Truman's recollection of the colloquy on the VFW incident. Otherwise, he wrote, the private talk was a "relatively unimportant conversation," much of it taken with, "of all things at this time, the fiscal and economic problems of the Philippines." In his *Reminiscences*, published more than a decade after the Wake encounter, MacArthur did not dwell on the private meeting, but of the entire discussion at Wake wrote, "I had been warned about Mr. Truman's quick and violent temper and prejudices, but he radiated nothing but courtesy and good humor during our meeting. He was an engaging personality, and quick and witty tongue, and I liked him from the start."[17]

Members of the respective entourages of Truman and MacArthur meanwhile had moved by bus to a one-story concrete and frame building at the southeast tip of the island. A wind sock floated over the little structure, and on a coral reef beyond the adjacent beach the foaming water of the Pacific splashed over the hulks of two Japanese landing boats knocked out by marines in the combat at Wake in December 1941. At length Truman and MacArthur arrived from their private meeting, and by 7:45 AM, the general discussion was underway. Seated about the rectangular table were the President, MacArthur, Harriman, Jessup, Rusk, Muccio, Pace, Bradley, Admiral Arthur W. Radford (Commander-in-Chief of American forces in the Pacific, who had joined the presidential party in Hawaii), and Colonel A. L. Hamblen (Deputy Special Assistant to the Secretary of the Army for occupied areas). Others present in the room included Vaughan, Murphy, Ross, Whitney, and Story.[18]

Informality prevailed. In deference to Wake's humidity Truman removed his jacket, while MacArthur pulled a briar pipe from his pocket and inquired, "Do you mind if I smoke, Mr. President?" As the other participants laughed, Truman replied, "No, I suppose I've had more smoke blown in my face than any other man alive." The President then asked MacArthur for a resumé of the situation regarding the rehabilitation of Korea. After explaining that rehabilitation could not take place until the termination of hostilities, the general remarked that "formal resistance will end throughout North and South Korea by Thanksgiving." The North Koreans were continuing to fight only to save face, he said, for "Orientals prefer to die rather than to lose face." The general hoped to return the Eighth Army to Japan by Christmas and remove all remaining American and non-Korean UN detachments from Korea in early 1951. To secure Korea and deter a southward thrust by the Chinese—a threat which he thought "cannot be laughed off"—he would leave behind a well-equipped ROK (Republic of Korea) army of perhaps ten divisions and also a KMAG (Korean Military Advisory Group) of some 500 American officers and enlisted men. As for rehabilitation, he portrayed Korea as a land of poverty which could not absorb more than $150 million annually in economic assistance, an estimate confirmed by Muccio.[19]

Consideration of Korea's rehabilitation continued, and that topic indeed consumed half of the general discussion. When Harriman asked about psychological rehabilitation, Muccio urged that noncommunist messages be communicated in rural districts and village centers by sound trucks, a proposal that prompted Truman (in only his second interjection to that point) to evoke a round of laughter by commenting: "I believe in sound trucks. I won two elections with them."[20]

What of a two-day-old UN resolution on the postwar government of Korea? The conferees were adamant that the resolution must not be used to undermine the regime of President Syngman Rhee of the Republic of Korea. Said Muccio, "The last election [in South Korea, in the Spring of 1950] was an honest election, about as honest as any ever held in the Far East. How are you going to ignore that?" MacArthur agreed: "It would be bad to turn out of office a government which had stood up so well and taken such a beating, and to treat them just like the North Koreans." Unfortunately, according to Rusk, "there has been an effective propaganda campaign against the Rhee Government which has infected some of the UN delegations." Snapped Truman, "We must make it plain that we are supporting the Rhee Government and propaganda can 'go to hell.' "[21]

The President asked about the chance of Chinese or Soviet intervention in the war. Responded MacArthur, "Very little. Had they interfered in the first or second months it would have been decisive. We are no longer fearful of their intervention. We no longer stand hat in hand." He explained that the Chinese had 300,000 troops in Manchuria, not more than 125,000 of them deployed along the Yalu, not more than 60,000 of whom could be moved across that river. Observing that the Chinese had no air force, he surmised that "if the Chinese tried to get down to Pyongyang there would be the greatest slaughter." As for the Soviets, they had few ground forces immediately available for combat in Korea—and could not assemble substantial forces before the onset of winter. Thus MacArthur thought the most likely form of a Soviet intervention would be aerial support of Chinese ground troops. Would Soviet air support of Chinese soldiers be effective? MacArthur thought not.[22]

With the Chinese and Soviets disposed of in barely five minutes, the conferees turned to war criminals, relations with Japan, and the possibility of a pact binding the noncommunist governments of the Western Pacific. War criminals consumed not more than a minute when MacArthur said, "Don't touch war criminals. It doesn't work. the Nurnberg trials and Tokyo trials were no deterrent." Regarding Japan, MacArthur urged that the United States get on with the task of negotiating a Japanese peace treaty, with or without cooperation by the Soviets and Chinese. From relations with Japan (which consumed perhaps 15 minutes), the conferees turned briefly to the idea of a defense pact in the Pacific similar to the North Atlantic Treaty. Both MacArthur and Radford thought poorly of the idea.[23]

The discussion then drifted to Indochina, where the French were faltering in their campaign against the Vietminh. MacArthur thought the situation puzzling: "The French have 150,000 of their best troops there with an officer of the highest reputation in command. Their forces are twice what we had in the [Pusan] perimeter and they are opposed by half of what the North Koreans had. I cannot understand why they do not clean it up." Said Truman, "This [the situation in Indochina] is the most discouraging thing we face. Mr. Jessup and others have worked on the French tooth and nail to try to persuade them to do what the Dutch had done in Indonesia but the French have not been willing to listen. If the French Prime Minister comes to see me, he is going to hear some very plain talk. I am going to talk cold turkey to him. If you don't want him to hear that kind of talk, you had better keep him away from me."[24]

The Indochina discussion consumed perhaps seven minutes. The conferees next devoted about five minutes to the offers of other members of the UN to send troops to Korea. Then, a few minutes after 9:00—after barely 80 minutes—Truman terminated the discussion. Observed the President, "No one who was not here would believe we have covered so much ground as we have been actually able to cover." He proposed that while staff people were preparing a communique, members of the groups from Washington and the Far East hold informal discussions. At noon everyone would gather for lunch, and after that, following the awarding of some medals, the Truman and MacArthur parties would fly off in their separate directions. Interjected MacArthur, "If it's all right, I am anxious to get back as soon as possible and would like to leave before luncheon if that is convenient." Truman replied that the general could leave as soon as the communique had been submitted, then concluded. "This has been a most satisfactory conference."[25]

Truman now motored to the quonset quarters of Pan American's manager on Wake, where he rested while staff personnel drafted a communique. At 10:45 MacArthur and his aides joined Truman, whereupon the President and general quickly approved the communique. In 780 words the document lauded the conference, claimed that "the very complete unanimity of view which prevailed enabled us to finish our discussions rapidly," and reported that MacArthur had given Truman "a clear picture of the heroism and high capacity of the United Nations forces under his command." The communique approved, Truman and MacArthur returned to the air terminal where the President awarded the general a fourth oak leaf cluster for his Distinguished Service Medal, pinned a Medal of Merit on Muccio, and promised to do something about making Whitney a two-star general as soon as he returned to Washington.[26]

Having abandoned plans for a luncheon on Wake, Truman now boarded the *Independence*, and at 11:35 A.M., while MacArthur waved, the presidential aircraft took off for Hawaii. The President spent the next day touring Oahu, and on the following day flew to San Francisco where he was greeted by a group of dignitaries, including Vice President Alben W. Barkley. The next evening he delivered a foreign policy speech which was carried by the four major American broadcasting networks and beamed across the world in 26 languages by the Voice of America. Praising MacArthur as "a very great soldier," he explained that he had gone to Wake to "give emphasis to the historic action taken by the United Nations in Korea" and make clear that "there is complete unity in the aims and conduct of our foreign policy." After the speech Truman motored to the airport, and within minutes was winging toward Washington. During the flight he received a telegram from MacArthur declaring that "public reaction throughout the Far East to your San Francisco speech will be electric." At 9:00 A.M. on 18 October, Truman landed at Andrews Air Force Base where he was greeted by Mrs. Truman, Secretary of State Dean G. Acheson, Secretary of Defense George C. Marshall, and other officials.[27]

Clearly much that has been written about the Wake Island meeting abounds with inaccuracy and mistaken assumption. Unfortunately, inasmuch as it has reached an audience of tens of millions, no commentary or account is so distorted and error-ridden as that set out in Miller's best-selling book and its theatrical spinoffs. As demonstrated in the present essay, the Truman and MacArthur planes did not arrive at Wake at the same time, and MacArthur did not keep Truman waiting, either in the *Independence* or in the quonset building before their private meeting. One cannot disprove passages in Miller *et al.*, describing a presidential "dressing down" of MacArthur at the start of the private conversation. But individuals who were on Wake on 15 October 1950—Harriman, Rusk, Muccio, Pace, and Bunker—have dismissed the proposition that Truman tongue-lashed the general.[28] Wrote Muccio: "On the return flight [from Wake to Tokyo] . . . he [MacArthur] was his sparkling best, and, for MacArthur effervescent. . . . MacArthur, always the consummate actor . . . could not have been so flawless at the conference and for seven hours so good humored on the return flight had he been 'slapped down' by the President at their only private session."[29]

Alas, serious students also have been wide of the mark in their musings about the Wake meeting. They have erred in asserting that Truman summoned MacArthur to Wake for an earnest discussion of American policy. In his memoirs, written more than a decade and a half after the Wake encounter, Dean Acheson, the official most responsible after the President for foreign policy, wrote that he did not learn of Truman's "intended pilgrimage" to Wake until after the President had decided to make the trip. Invited to go along, Acheson declined. Nor did the secretary of state offer any suggestions regarding what the President and general ought to discuss. He recalled, "The whole idea was distasteful to me. I wanted no part of it, and saw no good coming from it." Foreign policy adviser Harriman reportedly had no part in the decision that the President would meet with MacArthur, nor apparently did Secretary of Defense Marshall and the Joint Chiefs of Staff.[30]

That serious policy concerns did not prompt the Wake meeting is borne out by other observations. There was no conference agenda, and no extensive preliminary discussions between the President and his advisers, only the brief talk in Hawaii the evening before the flight to Wake. Then the meeting on Wake was ridiculously short, inspiring the entertainer Al Jolson (who died ten days after the Wake affair) to quip that he recently had enjoyed a lengthier audience with MacArthur than had the President, and during the rambling and superficial conversations the conferees moved rapidly from topic to topic, making no effort to probe complicated questions. As MacArthur later observed, "No new policies, no new strategy of war or international politics, were proposed or discussed." Although near the end of the general discussion the President announced that in their private meeting he and the general had talked "fully" about Formosa and were in "complete agreement,"[31] the evidence, including Truman's memoirs, indicates that the delicate question of what to do about Chiang Kai-shek's island—a question that nearly everybody had assumed would command serious attention during the meeting—was not taken up at all except in the context of the recent flap over MacArthur's message to the VFW.

At the center of Truman's decision to travel to Wake, it seems fair to say (as the sycophantic Whitney believed), was public relations—or, more to the point, domestic politics. As one who thoroughly enjoyed travel, and also one who had an abiding interest in military affairs, the President doubtless found the prospect of flying out to the Pacific to meet the illustrious MacArthur most appealing. And it is not improbable that he persuaded himself that a get-acquainted encounter with the general would serve the national interest.[32] The weight of evidence nonetheless indicates that the cardinal purpose of the meeting was "P-R." Plans for the trip to Wake and a foreign policy speech in San Francisco were concocted in the first days of October 1950 while Truman was cruising Chesapeake Bay. Who dreamed up the trip? As Charles Murphy subsequently conceded, the idea originated with the President's administrative assistant George Elsey and was promoted by the White House staff.[33] Speculation on their reasoning comes easily. MacArthur presently was enjoying the national (indeed international) spotlight, the President was not. An important election was at hand. Could one imagine a better ploy to put Truman back at the center of the public vision and strengthen the electoral chances of Democrats than to have the President, in the guise of the Chief of State weighing high policy with his Far Eastern commander, move into the spotlight which was beaming on the general who recently had turned frustrating defeat into a glorious victory?

If mistaken about its purpose, have commentators on the Wake meeting also erred in intimating that MacArthur misled his superiors concerning the likelihood of China's entry in the war? That question does not lend itself to an easy answer. As demonstrated in the present essay, nearly every observer of the Korean War reckoned in early October 1950 that the end of the conflict was in sight. Despite a continuing uneasiness, manifested in messages between Washington and Tokyo in the first days of October (and by the fact that the question was taken up at Wake), leaders of the American government and military establishment shared that conviction. What MacArthur probably brought about by his assertion that a Chinese intervention was unlikely was reinforcement of a view which his superiors already held. Lending credence to that assertion, in addition to the sheer power of his Olympian personality, was MacArthur's renewed reputation for wisdom and insight in the aftermath of Inchon, an operation about which his superiors in Washington had felt misgiving.

But what of Whitney's contention, recently reaffirmed by Dean Rusk,[34] that MacArthur's confidence that China would not intervene rested on the assumption that the UN Command would meet an intervention by retaliating against the territory of China? As noted, Whitney was sure that MacArthur would have expressed a different view had he foreseen the policy which subsequently took shape when China threw itself into the war, namely, that of rigidly confining the actions of the UN Command to the Korean peninsula. Here is another question that does not lend itself to an easy answer. In his Wake Island commentary on the chance of a Chinese intervention, MacArthur gave no hint that his estimate that China would not enter the war was predicated on the assumption that such entry would provoke instant retaliation. Rather, it seemed to rest on his gross underestimate of the strength of Chinese forces deployed along the Yalu frontier and his certainty—a certainty which he apparently thought the Chinese shared—that the UN Command, mainly by air power, would bring the Chinese to disaster if they did intervene. If the Chinese were planning a thrust into Korea, he seemed to say, it probably would come after American and other non-Korean troops had departed the peninsula and the army of the Republic of Korea was left alone to guard the south bank of the Yalu—a danger that the conferees might well have considered at length if the purpose of the Wake encounter had been to weigh serious questions of policy.

Whatever the explanation of MacArthur's comments about China, the Wake Island meeting as an exercise in public relations—or, more politely, presidential theater—seemed highly successful. Although that segment of the news media that tended to be hostile to the Truman administration depreciated the meeting (the *Indianapolis Star* of 15 October 1950 bannered the defeat of Purdue University's football team rather than the Truman-MacArthur rendezvous), the presidential stopovers in St. Louis, Hawaii, and San Francisco, as well as the meeting on

Wake, produced reams of front-page coverage, pictures, background stories, editorials, editorial cartoons, and commentaries by syndicated columnists. Whether such publicity was of much help to the Democrats on election day in early November is another question, for the balloting resulted in serious reverses for the President's party.

In conclusion, what was the historical importance of the Wake Island meeting?

Inasmuch as the meeting produced no discussion or decisions that had any discernible bearing on America's approach to problems in the Far East or in the world at large, the student of military affairs or foreign policy need spend little time with the affair on Wake. Contrary to a widespread belief, the meeting resulted in no serious discussion of the likelihood of a Chinese intervention in the Korean War and had no important bearing on the decision to press the UN attack in Korea to the Yalu. Leaders in Washington already had made the decision to expel communism from Korea—a decision they did not alter less than a fortnight after the Wake meeting, in the last days of October 1950, when UN troops first encountered Chinese soldiers in Korea, *i.e.*, UN forces continued to push forward for another month, until the Chinese unleashed their massive counterattack at the end of November 1950. (Thus it is manifestly unfair to intimate, as President Truman and writers friendly to him later intimated, that MacArthur's assurances at Wake that the Chinese would not enter the war prompted the decision to press on to the Yalu; hence MacArthur was principally to blame for the disaster that befell the UN command when the Chinese threw themselves into the conflict.)

As a piece of presidential theater, however—one that succeeded in fooling later-day scholars no less than contemporaries into believing that the meeting of the President and the general represented a serious attempt to deal with serious questions of policy—the Wake Island meeting ought to command the interest of students of the post-1945 presidency. Similarly, it ought to provide an object lesson to historians that they should be careful not to assume that historical personages generally exalted by history—in this instance, President Truman—always acted on the basis of exalted motives.

Otherwise, the Wake meeting marked a moment of high national euphoria that preceded the terrible letdown brought by the intervention of the Chinese in the Korean War—a moment when it appeared that

America had registered a magnificent victory over its adversaries and dramatically seized the initiative in the Cold War.

Notes

1. Schlesinger and Rovere, *The General and the President, and the Future of American Foreign Policy* (New York, 1951), 131–134; Whitney, *MacArthur: His Rendezvous with History* (New York, 1956), 384–395; and Spanier, *The Truman-MacArthur Controversy and the Korean War* (Cambridge MA, 1959), 105–112.

2. Higgins, *Korea and the Fall of MacArthur: A Précis in Limited War* (New York, 1960), 56–58; and Phillips, *The Truman Presidency: The History of a Triumphant Succession* (New York, 1966), 318–321.

3. Miller, *Plain Speaking: An Oral Biography of Harry S. Truman* (New York, 1973), 293–296; Gallu, *"Give 'em Hell Harry," Reminiscences* (New York, 1975), 56–60; and Ernest Kinoy, *Collision Course: Truman vs. MacArthur, A Drama Based on Historical Fact* (Los Angeles, 1975), manuscript prepared by Wolper Productions, 58–77.

4. George H. Gallup, *The Gallup Poll: Public Opinion, 1935–1971*, Vol. 2 (New York, 1972), 942.

5. Truman to MacArthur (30 Sept. 1950), in compilation of messages exchanged between the President, the Joint Chiefs of Staff, and General MacArthur, RG-6, Official Correspondence, Box 1A, MacArthur Memorial, Norfolk, Virginia.

6. *New York Times*, 2 and 5 Oct. 1950.

7. CINCFE TOKYO JAPAN to ALUSNA TAIPEI, C-65574 (5 Oct. 1950), RG-9, Navy, MacArthur Memorial; DA (ARMY-NAVY-AIR) to CINCFE, W93505 (6 Oct. 1950) RG-9, DA WX, MacArthur Memorial; and *New York Times*, 7 Oct. 1950.

8. *New York Times*, 11 Oct. 1950.

9. *Christian Science Monitor*, 12 Oct. 1950.

10. *Washington Post*, 12 Oct. 1950; *Log of President Truman's Trip to Wake Island, October 11–18, 1950*, compiled by Lieutenant Commander William M. Ridgon, United States Navy, Truman papers, Harry S. Truman Library, Independence, Missouri (also in Papers of General of the Army Omar N. Bradley, Special Collections Division, United States Military Academy, West Point), 13–23; *St. Louis Post-Dispatch*, 12 Oct. 1950.

11. *Log of President Truman's Trip*, 24–25; *New York Times*, 14 Oct. 1950.

12. *Log of President Truman's Trip*, 47.

13. Muccio to author (18 Feb. 1976); see also William J. Sebald, *With MacArthur in Japan: A Personal History of the Occupation in Japan* (New York, 1965), 217. Whitney, 385.

14. *Log of President Truman's Trip*, 45; *New York Times*, 15 Oct. 1950; *Indianapolis Star*, 15 Oct. 1950; *Washington Post*, 15 Oct. 1950.

15. *Log of President Truman's Trip*, 45–47; memorandum by Truman entitled "Wake Island" (6 April 1951), Truman papers, President's Secretary's File—General File, Harry S. Truman Library; *New York Times*, 15 Oct. 1950; *Washington Post*, 15 Oct. 1950.

16. *Log of President Truman's Trip*, 47; *New York Times*, 15 Oct. 1950; *Washington Post*, 15 Oct. 1950.

17. *Log of President Truman's Trip*, 47; *Memoirs by Harry S. Truman*, II. *Years of Trial and Hope* (Garden City, 1965), 365; Whitney, 387; MacArthur, *Reminiscences* (New York, 1964), 361.

18. *Log of President Truman's Trip*, 47; *Washington Post*, 15 Oct. 1950; *Substance of Statements Made at Wake Island Conference on 15 October 1950, Compiled by General of the Army Omar N. Bradley, Chairman of the Joint Chiefs of Staff, From Notes Kept by the Conferees from Washington*, RG-5, CL-1, 1, MacArthur Memorial; Whitney, 387–388. Another individual was within earshot of the conference table: Vernice Anderson, Jessup's secretary. According to subsequent recollections by Bradley and Rusk, Miss Anderson had accompanied the presidential party to the conference building to help draft the post-conference communique. When the President and general appeared she retired to an adjacent room. Since the door between the two rooms remained ajar she could easily hear the general discussion, and knowing that a memorandum of the discussion would be drafted took it upon herself to jot down detailed notes of what was being said. On the flight back to the United States, as the conferees under the direction of Bradley were putting together their notes for the memorandum which she had anticipated, Miss Anderson came forward with her own notes. Delighted, her superiors used the Anderson notes to augment their own in the preparation of a 23 page memorandum (almost a verbatim transcript of the general discussion), a copy of which went to MacArthur's headquarters in Tokyo. MacArthur later testified that the memorandum probably offered an accurate recounting of the general discussion on Wake Island. (*Military Situation in the Far East. Hearings before the Committee on Armed Services and the Committee on Foreign Relations, United States Senate, 82nd Cong., 1st Sess. to Conduct an Inquiry into the Military Situation in the Far East and the Facts Surrounding the Relief of General of the Army Douglas MacArthur from His Assignments in that Area* [Washington, 1951], Part I, 27, 28–29, Part II, 926–928, 959–960, 979–980; Rusk to author [12 Jan. 1976]. The so-called Bradley memorandum is cited above as *Substances of Statements Made at Wake Island Conference on 15 October 1950*.)

19. *MacArthur*, 361; and *Substance of Statements Made at Wake Island Conference*, 1–4.

20. *Substance of Statements Made at Wake Island Conference,* 5–9.

21. *Ibid.,* 9–10, 22.

22. *Ibid.,* 10–12.

23. *Ibid.,* 12, 12–17.

24. *Ibid.,* 17–18, 19.

25. *Ibid.,* 23.

26. *Log of President Truman's Trip,* 49–55; Whitney, 390.

27. *Log of President Truman's Trip,* 55–75; *Public Papers of the Presidents of the United States, Harry S. Truman, Containing the Public Messages, Speeches, and Statements of the President, January 1 to December 31, 1950* (Washington, 1965), 673–79; *New York Times,* 18 Oct. 1950; MacArthur to Truman (8 Oct. 1950), Truman papers. President's Secretary's File, General File, Harry S. Truman Library.

28. Harriman to author (19 dec. 1975); Rusk to author; Muccio to author; Pace to author (23 Jan. 1976); interview of Bunker by United Press International, *Athens* (Georgia) *Daily News,* 6 Jan. 1976.

29. Muccio to author.

30. Acheson, *Present at the Creation: My Years in the State Department* (New York, 1969), 456; and column by Joseph C. Harsch, *Christian Science Monitor,* 19 Oct. 1950.

31. *Washington Post,* 25 Oct. 1950; MacArthur, 362; and *Substance of Statements Made at Wake Island Conference,* 20.

32. More than a decade and a half after the Wake meeting Charles Murphy recalled that Truman had "a distaste for public relations stunts," and when members of the White House staff proposed a trip to the Pacific to talk with MacArthur, he felt "some distaste" for the idea. Charles T. Morrissey and Jerry N. Hess, *Oral History Interview with Charles S. Murphy, May 21, 1969,* Harry S. Truman Library.

33. *Ibid.* At the time of the announcement that Truman and MacArthur would meet in the Pacific, Charles Ross explained that the idea of such a meeting had "jelled" the previous week while the President was aboard the *Williamsburg. St. Louis Post-Dispatch,* 11 Oct. 1950.

34. Rusk to author.

The MacArthur Plan

Edgar O'Ballance

From a purely tactical point of view, observes the British military analyst Edgar O'Ballance, MacArthur's plan to win the war in Korea deserves high marks. Whether it made sense in terms of Cold War global strategy, he adds, remains questionable.

The abrupt dismissal of General MacArthur by President Truman on 11th April, 1951, at the height of the Korean war was generally regarded with satisfaction in Western democracies because it demonstrated the principle of supremacy of the civilian administration over the military. The official reason given for the removal of the General was that "he was unable to give his wholehearted support to the Administration and the UN."

It is well known that General MacArthur had a plan which he was convinced would bring a speedy and victorious end to the war in Korea, but it involved risks that were politically unacceptable at the time. Today, the art of generalship includes not only defeating an enemy on the field of battle but also of doing so within the political brief laid down by his government.

After a suitable lapse it may now be an appropriate time to examine some aspects of the MacArthur Plan, to discuss the likelihood of its success, and to consider implications that might have arisen had it been adopted.

Situation in Korea—February, 1951

The MacArthur Plan was formulated in mid-February, 1951, when the UN line in Korea had stabilized south of Seoul, the capital of the country, which had just been occupied by Chinese Communist troops. There were nearly one million Chinese Communist troops in the Korean Peninsula, and in the background, in China, were another four million. Ranged against this formidable array were about half-a-million UN troops. The estimate that there were one million Chinese Communist soldiers in Korea was General MacArthur's; perhaps 850,000 might have been a more accurate figure.

It will be remembered that on 25th June, 1950, the Soviet-trained North Korean Army struck south over the 38th Parallel, the boundary between North and South Korea, seizing Seoul four days later, and then pushing the smaller South Korean Army, which was little more than an armed gendarmerie, into the Pusan perimeter, on the southern tip of the peninsula. The UN decided to intervene, and on 1st July, U.S. troops landed in Korea, to be followed later by detachments from other UN countries.

In September, U.S. troops made a big amphibious landing at Inchon, on the west coast, and after some fierce fighting, took Seoul. A land column of UN soldiers pushed northwards from the Pusan perimeter, and the invaders were bundled backwards over the 38th Parallel. UN forces harried them further, halting only a few miles to the south of the River Yalu, which forms the boundary between North Korea and China for a greater part of its length. Here the remnants of the North Korean regiments huddled.

In early October, Chinese Communist troops massed to the north of the River Yalu, and during the following four or five weeks, over 300,000 of them crossed into North Korea. On 27th November, General Lin Piao, who was in command of what became the Chinese People's Volunteer Army (CPVA), launched his men into battle against the UN forces, sheer weight of numbers pushing them back southwards. With only a brief halt and check, the Chinese Communists were able to continue doing this until they entered Seoul on 4th January, 1951. UN forces managed to stabilize a line across the peninsula just to the south of Seoul.

That was the background against which General MacArthur formed his controversial plan for a quick victory in the "shooting war" in Korea.

The Plan
General MacArthur's plan was only partially revealed by himself in his *Reminiscences*, but sufficient additional evidence is available from interviews, articles, and speeches, and also from his reports to Congress, to enable its outline to be determined. Briefly it included:—

a) Using 20 to 30 atomic bombs to destroy Chinese air installations and supply bases in Manchuria. (*b*) Laying a belt of radio-active nuclear material across the upper "neck" of North Korea. (*c*) Using 500,000 Chinese Nationalist troops from Formosa (with two U.S. Marine divisions) to make amphibious and air landings simultaneously on both the west and the east coasts near the northern part of the "neck," to join up, cut off, and so contain the one million Chinese Communist soldiers then in the Korean Peninsula. (*d*) Moving reinforced UN troops northwards to crush the trapped CPVA in a gigantic nutcracker.

General MacArthur estimated that this plan would have forced the surrender of the CPVA within ten days.

The outstanding, and to some extent unusual, features of the Mac-Arthur Plan were the use of Chinese Nationalist troops, the use of nuclear weapons, and carrying the war outside the confines of the Korean Peninsula. In turn these would bring risks of reopening the Chinese Civil War between the Communists and the Nationalists, drawing Red China into open conflict with America (and incidentally the UN as well), and the fact that the use of nuclear weapons might project the Soviet Union into counter-action, which might precipitate World War III.

As is well known, American and UN political leaders decided against the Plan because they calculated that the risks it involved were too great.

Re-Opening the Chinese Civil War

By the end of 1949, Chiang Kai-shek had taken refuge on Formosa, where he had an army of over 500,000 men, equipped with American material and arms. Red China planned to attack Formosa, probably in July, 1950, as in the preceding June the strength of the Communist troops on the mainland just across from the island suddenly rose from about 40,000 to over 156,000. The outbreak of the Korean War stopped this.

Even so, this was perhaps the only moment that Chiang Kai-shek could have invaded the mainland, either across the Straits of Formosa or through Korea, with any chance of success. The Red Chinese régime was still unsteady, bewildered, and more than slightly surprised at its victory over the Nationalists. Although there were some five million troops still mobilized, the Chinese Red Army had been diluted by huge infusions of "turn-coat" Nationalist soldiers, who at that stage, before Communist indoctrination had taken full effect and the essential weeding out had been done, could just as easily have been persuaded to turn their coats again and rejoin Chiang Kai-shek had they though the had a chance of winning. The Chinese Red Army had many men, but few guns, few armoured vehicles, and few aircraft; and Soviet military material had hardly started to flow in any volume towards the CPVA.

Up to one million, perhaps far more, Chinese Communist soldiers were engaged in "bandit suppression," which meant fighting the many groups of Nationalist guerillas that remained at large and active in many parts of the country. Also, many non-Han peoples were not reconciled to a Communist government; the unruly Moslem groups in the north-west were discontented; and the welter of traditional secret societies was a serious menace. Chinese Communist troops suffered a bad set-back when they failed in their assault on Quemoy in October, 1949; Hainan Island was not seized until April, 1950; and the invasion of Tibet had not yet taken place. If one million of the best Chinese Communist soldiers, the cream of Mao Tse-tung's army, were eliminated in Korea, as the MacArthur Plan envisaged, an inspiring lead and impetus could be given to the tens of thousands of Nationalist resistance fighters on the mainland. The possibilities of instigating and stirring up guerilla warfare on a large scale inside China, and so taking a leaf from Mao Tse-tung's manuals, were staggering and opportune.

It was widely alleged that the Nationalist troops were ageing, demor-alized, ill-organized, poorly led, and so untrustworthy that it would be folly to allow them to come into contact with Communists in battle. But General MacArthur, who had inspected them and who was prepared to use them, was not of this opinion, and his military assessment must be seriously considered.

Had the Civil War in China been resumed, America would not have been any more involved than in the past, her aid being limited to supplying Chiang Kai-shek with money, arms, and material. Chiang Kai-shek's chances of success, or at least of securing Manchuria, or a large section of the eastern seaboard, would have been good. If Nationalist Chinese troops had been let loose there might have been "two Chinas" today, which might have counter-balanced each other in the world power struggles. Then, like the Soviet Union, America could have fought its main enemy by proxy.

Drawing Red China Openly into the War

There was considerable anxiety that the MacArthur Plan would project Red China into openly declaring war on America (and perhaps the UN too), which in retrospect seems to have been a most unlikely course.

Initially, Red China crept into the Korean War secretly, silently, and cautiously, apprehensively expecting swift retribution. Air raid shelters were constructed in the main cities of Manchuria, and air raid drills were carried out by the people. She only became bolder when no action was taken by UN forces north of the River Yalu. When she could no longer hide her true numbers fighting in Korea, Red China continued to fight by "proxy," claiming that the members of the CPVA were merely "volunteers," a pretence that was maintained until the end. There may have been some justification for taking the view that Red China was only reluctantly persuaded to attack South Korea and the UN forces by Stalin, who wanted to draw the West to test its reaction, and that Red China only agreed on the condition that the Soviet Union supplied modern war material and helped in other ways, economical and financial.

Had Red China declared war, or entered it openly, she would not have been able to do any more than she did, as most of her remaining four million soldiers were required for pacification and labour duties, or were far too unreliable to be trusted in battle. Had she done so, she would have forfeited the sanctuary of the River Yalu and exposed her territory to American retaliatory air action. Entering the war openly would almost certainly have caused America to allow Chiang Kai-shek to reopen the Civil War, which he was itching to do, and to bomb bases and cities in Manchuria and perhaps other parts of China.

In support of this opinion of Red China's cautious and unwilling attitude, General MacArthur, who was convinced that there was a security leak from Washington, through Moscow, to Peking, tells in his *Reminiscences* of an official leaflet by General Lin Piao, the commander of the CPVA, published in Red China, which indicated that the Chinese General would not have risked his "reputation and his men" (it is interesting to note the order in which they are mentioned) if he had not been assured that the Americans would not take retaliatory measures against his supply lines. In other words, the CPVA would not have been committed to battle in Korea had it not been almost certain that the Americans would not attack, nor allow Chiang Kai-shek to attack, Red Chinese territory.

Starting World War III

Throughout, America was meticulously careful not to do anything at all to provoke the Soviet Union, or even Red China, into open war with her. General MacArthur, for example, was not allowed to destroy the bridges over the River Yalu, over which poured men, supplies, and arms to the CPVA, and Chiang Kai-shek was penned up on Formosa. the great fear was that the Soviet Union might be persuaded, or feel morally obliged, to support her Communist partner, and in doing so resort to nuclear weapons, thus instigating World War III.

America exploded her first test atomic bomb in June, 1945, and since had been experimenting and stockpiling. The size of her nuclear stockpile in 1951 has naturally not been publicly revealed, but General MacArthur, whom it might be presumed would be most likely to have a good idea exactly how many atomic bombs his country possessed, was prepared to expend between 20 and 30 of them on his Plan. It could not be expected that by so doing he would have deliberately denuded the American nuclear capability, so these numbers must have been only a proportion of the American nuclear stockpile, and perhaps only a small one at that. Also, America had a huge functioning fleet of strategic bombers, able to deliver atomic bombs to any part of the world.

In contrast, the Soviet Union had not been able to explode her first atomic bomb until August, 1949, a time-lag of over four years. The Soviet Union was still at an experimental stage and technically unsure in many ways. Her nuclear stockpile must have been quite small in comparison with that of America. It is of interest to note that the Commandant of the U.S. Air War College was suspended about this period for saying, "I can break up the five Russian A-bomb nests in a week."

The Soviet Union had far fewer strategic bombers, as she had not carried out much strategic bombing during World War II. She was only in the earlier stages of building a large fleet of strategic bombers, and the Soviet Air Force could not match the American Air Force in techniques or experience in this respect. H-bombs had yet to appear on the scene. In brief, the Soviet Union was a long way behind America in nuclear capability.

All the indications were that the Soviet Union wanted to avoid open conflict with America, and one's guess is that the selfish Stalin had not the slightest intention of precipitating World War III on behalf of Red China, or any other Communist ally. In fact, he would probably have liked to see American—and UN—strength sapped by protracted war with Red China, which would have been to his advantage. It was thought that Stalin had urged Red China to march into Korea for this very purpose.

It was an era of timid counsels and politics, and the plain fact is that most Western statesmen misjudged Stalin and his intentions. At one point General MacArthur was instructed to withdraw his forces from Korea if he thought that to stay there was to endanger the safety of Japan.

Fears were probably exaggerated, and it was not known how far advanced America was with the H-bomb. (She exploded her first in November, 1952.) But fear of Soviet aggression was real and understandable. There was acute tension in Europe, where only the NATO doctrine of total nuclear retaliation kept the powerful Soviet Army at bay. We now know that the "deterrent" was a success, but there were many uncertainties in those days when no one could be really sure of the strength of the Sino-Soviet alliance, and how far it was prepared to go.

Military Feasibility

Political and national objections and interests apart, would the Mac-Arthur Plan have worked? There is no disputing the fact that General MacArthur was a shrewd, calculating, clear-thinking commander and planner, and it should be accepted that the means for putting the Plan into operation were, or could quickly have been made, available to him. On the weapons and logistical side this would have meant that there were at least 30 atomic bombs available (and many more left over for NATO purposes), the aircraft to drop them, and sufficient shipping and transport aircraft to lift half-a-million men swiftly to the "neck" of Korea.

The planned nuclear radiation belt may have been the only part of the Plan that may not have come up to expectation. It was to consist of cobalt and was to be about five miles in width. General MacArthur thought cobalt had a "half-life" of 60 years and that it could be spread equally well by aircraft, trucks, and carts, but in fact its actual life was nearer five years, and it could only have been dropped in "flakes" from aircraft. It could not have been spread by trucks and carts. However, although it may have taken longer to lay than envisaged, once formed, the nuclear belt would have served its purpose, which was both to stop Chinese supplies and reinforcements arriving from the north and to prevent massed break-outs by trapped detachments of the CPVA.

The CPVA relied completely on its supply lines through Manchuria, there being absolutely nothing available in devastated Korea, and it had only ten days' supplies of food and ammunition in hand. If the supply lines were cut and kept blocked, after that period of time it would have starved and become impotent owing to lack of ammunition. In addition the CPVA had a huge disease problem, especially of typhoid, with which its primitive medical service was having difficulty in coping. It was extremely short of medicines and drugs.

Could the one million strong CPVA have been contained and crushed by General MacArthur's forces, which were numerically much smaller? The answer must surely be that the fire and air power of the UN forces were so much greater that in battle the CPVA would have certainly come off second best. There might have been desperate massed break-outs through the nuclear radiation belt, but the spectacle of thousands of Chinese Communist soldiers returning to Chinese territory only to die shortly afterwards would have had an immensely adverse effect on morale.

From a purely military point of view the MacArthur Plan was a bold one that would have probably produced victorious results in Korea.

The Verdict

The MacArthur Plan was quashed, and a UN land push began in mid-March, 1951. Seoul was re-taken and the UN line stabilised about the 38th Parallel, where both sides dug in and a stalemate settled on the war.

General Bradley, the Chairman of the Joint Chiefs of Staff at Washington, voiced the opinion of the majority of Western strategists when he said that the Korean War "was the wrong war, at the wrong place, at the wrong time, with the wrong enemy." Strategically he was correct—the real enemy was the Soviet Union, and the key potential battleground was in Europe.

The MacArthur Plan was a tempting one that was attractive in many ways, especially as it could have netted some million of the best of Mao Tse-tung's soldiers, and done much to enhance Western military prestige in Asian eyes. It was perhaps the only occasion when nuclear weapons might have been used without precipitating World War III.

The obituary of the MacArthur Plan must be that it was a good tactical one, but one that did not take into consideration many extremely relevant and vital factors, or fit in with the wider political and strategical situation in the major struggle of the cold war between the West and the Communists.

Command Crisis

MacArthur and the Korean War

D. Clayton James

In his Harmon Memorial Lecture at the U.S. Air Force Academy on November 12, 1981, D. Clayton James argues that the Truman-MacArthur controversy was rooted in a failure to communicate. Too much has been made of the episode, he contends, and many questions remain to be answered.

When General of the Army Douglas MacArthur delivered his moving address before the joint session of Congress on April 19, 1951, I was watching and listening with bated breath before a television set in a room packed with excited college students at Southwestern-at-Memphis. Most of us were convinced at the time that President Harry S. Truman was a foolish politician who had dared to rush in where the Joint Chiefs of Staff had feared to tread. It seemed to us that the most momentous issues since World War II were at stake in the President's relief of the general. The torrent of abusive mail that Truman received, the charge by otherwise responsible public leaders that the President was guilty of offenses just short of treason but deserving impeachment, the tumultuous welcome accorded MacArthur upon his return, the lengthy and sometimes dramatic Senate hearings on his relief from command, the gradual shift in public support from MacArthur to Truman as the testimony continued into June 1951, and the countless arguments in newspapers and magazines, as well as over television and radio, on whether the President or the general had been right—all this surely demonstrated the crucial nature of the Truman-MacArthur controversy to those of us who lived through this great excitement of 1951.

In the hearings before the Senate's Armed Services and Foreign Relations committees in the late spring and early summer of 1951, two issues of the dispute emerged as dominant and have remained so in most later writings about the episode: MacArthur's alleged challenges to the strategy of limited warfare in Korea and to the hallowed principle of civilian supremacy over the military. American history textbooks for high school and college students may abbreviate or ignore many aspects of the Korean War, but it would be difficult to find one that does not emphasize the Truman-MacArthur confrontation as a major crisis of that period. Disappointingly few scholarly works on the subject range beyond the supposed threats to limited-war strategy and civil-military relations. In their efforts to show that the Korean War was instigated by South Korean aggressors or American imperialists, the New Left historians so far have not paid much heed to the affair.

The notion that the Truman-MacArthur controversy was rooted in disagreement over whether the Korean conflict should be kept a limited war is a myth that needs to be laid to rest. Many contemporary and later critics of MacArthur cleverly employed the false-dilemma argument, presenting the case as if only two alternatives existed—World War III or the war with the limitations that actually evolved. But other alternatives may have existed, including controlled escalation that might have prevented a frustrating stalemate and yet might not have provoked the Soviet Union into entering the fray. MacArthur surely desired escalation but only against the nations already at war against South Korea and the United Nations Command. At various times he requested permission to allow his aircraft to enter Manchurian air space to pursue enemy planes and bomb their bases, to attack bridges and hydro-electric plants along the Yalu River, to blockade Communist China's coast and conduct naval and air bombardments against its industrial centers, and to use Nationalist Chinese troops in Korea or in limited assaults against the Chinese mainland. But all such requests were peremptorily rejected, and MacArthur retreated from each demand. He simply had no other recourse; disobedience would have meant his instant removal, as he well understood. It is interesting that in their deliberations on these proposals by MacArthur, the Joint Chiefs either turned them down because they were tactically unsound and logically unfeasible or postponed a decision until further consideration. In truth, most of MacArthur's requests for escalation could not have been effectively executed. Not until their testimony before the Senate committees after MacArthur's relief did the Joint Chiefs assert that their main reason for rejecting MacArthur's proposals was that their implementation might have started a new global war.

Contrary to persisting popular belief, MacArthur never advocated an expansion of the land war into Manchuria or North China. He abhorred the possibility of a war with the Soviet Union as much as did his superiors in Washington. While the latter viewed the North Korean invasion as Moscow-directed and anticipated a massive Soviet response if MacArthur's proposed actions were tried, MacArthur did not believe the Soviet Union would become involved on a large scale in order to defend North Korea or Communist China. In view of the Sino-Soviet conflict that erupted not long after the Korean War, who is to say, especially with the sparse Western sources on strategic planning in Moscow and Peking, that MacArthur was altogether wrong?

No matter what MacArthur might have advocated in the way of escalation, the President and his military and foreign policy advisers were firmly committed to keeping the war limited because they were more concerned with a potential Soviet armed incursion into Western Europe. Washington focused on implementing the overall military build-up called for in the NSC-68 document of early 1950 and on quickly organizing deterrent forces under the NATO aegis. Knowing this and realizing it was unlikely that he would receive further reinforcements in Korea, MacArthur would had to have been stupid, which he was not, to nourish dreams of ground offensives above the Yalu, as some of his detractors have claimed.

MacArthur was not involved in the decision-making responsible for unleashing the United Nations forces' invasion of North Korea, which, in turn, brought Communist China into the conflict—the only two significant escalations of the Korean War. MacArthur's troops crossed the 38th parallel into North Korea on October 1, 1950, only after he had received a Joint Chiefs' directive four days earlier authorizing such a move. And on October 7, the United Nations General Assembly passed a resolution that, in essence, called for the reunification of Korea by force. In many works, even textbooks that our youth must study, MacArthur is still portrayed as unilaterally deciding to conquer North Korea. In truth, MacArthur merely executed the policy made in Washington to seize North Korea, which turned out to be perhaps the most important decision of the war and produced the only escalation that brought a new belligerent into the conflict. For the decision-makers behind this startling change in policy, one must look to Washington, not Tokyo. In summing up this point, the Truman-MacArthur controversy, as far as strategic difference were concerned, was not a real disagreement on *whether* the war should be limited, only on *how* it should be done.

The other persisting notion is that MacArthur's actions produced a crisis in American civil-military relations. But he actually was not an "American Caesar" and was not interested in spearheading a move to overturn the long-established principle of civilian supremacy over the military, which, with his masterful knowledge of American military history, he knew was strongly rooted and widely endorsed by the people. There is no question that he issued public statements sharply critical of the Truman administration's military and foreign policies and expressly violated the Joint Chiefs' directive of December 6, 1950, requiring theater commanders to obtain clearance from the Department of Defense on statements related to military affairs and from the Department of State on releases bearing on foreign policy. His defiance was also manifest when on March 24, 1951, he issued unilaterally a surrender ultimatum to the Communist Chinese commander after having just been informed by Washington that the State Department was beginning diplomatic overtures that could lead to truce negotiations. But MacArthur's disobedience and arrogant gestures were a far cry from constituting a threat to the American system of civil-military order.

To call a spade a spade, MacArthur was guilty of insubordination toward his Commander-in-Chief, and therefore he was relieved, though perhaps belatedly and certainly rudely. General of the Army George C. Marshall, then Secretary of Defense, explained it in straight-forward terms at the Senate hearings:

> It is completely understandable and, in fact, at times commendable that a theater commander should become so wholly wrapped up in his own aims and responsibilities that some of the directives received by him from higher authority are not those that he would have written himself. There is nothing new about this sort of thing in our military history. What is new, and what has brought about the necessity for General MacArthur's removal, is the wholly unprecedented situation of a local theater commander publicly expressing his displeasure at and his disagreement with the foreign and military policy of the United States.[1]

The President himself said in his memoirs that "MacArthur left me no choice—I could no longer tolerate his insubordination."[2] Probably the major reason MacArthur was not court-martialed stemmed from Truman's weak political base at the time. In short, an officer disobeyed and defied his superior and was relieved of command. The principle of civilian control over the military was not seriously threatened by MacArthur's statements and actions; the President's exercise of his power as Commander-in-Chief should have made it clear that the principle was still safe and healthy.

If not limited-war strategy or a civil-military crisis, then what was the fundamental issue at stake in the Truman-MacArthur controversy? In essence, it was a crisis in command that stemmed from failures in communication and coordination within the chain of command and was exacerbated by an unprecedented political-social phenomenon called McCarthyism.

The failure in communication between Truman and MacArthur was due, in part, to the absence of any personal contact with each other prior to their brief and only meeting at Wake Island on October 15, 1950, and to the stereotypes each had accepted of the other based primarily on the views of their respective confidants. In his reminiscences and elsewhere Truman admits that he was miffed by the general's rejection of his invitation at the end of World War II to return home and receive the customary hero's welcome and visit at the White House. Truman had also expected to confer with MacArthur on issues in Japan when various congressional committees in 1946 48 requested his personal testimony, but each time the general remained in Tokyo, claiming that the pressures of occupation matters prevented him from returning to the States.

In his rise in politics, Truman had carefully cultivated a public image of himself as a representative of the common man. Unassuming and possessing a down-to-earth friendliness, he was completely without pose and affectation. As President, he continued without inhibition his poker and piano playing, bourbon drinking, and, when aroused, profuse cursing. Many people were deceived into thinking that this "little man" who spoke with a Missouri twang and dressed like a Main Street shopkeeper was not up to the demands of the nation's highest office and surely was not able to walk in the footsteps of Woodrow Wilson or Franklin D. Roosevelt in providing dynamic leadership. MacArthur and his GHQ confidants in Tokyo since 1945 had accepted this impression and had never had the personal connections with Truman necessary to disabuse them or to discover that the real Truman was a shrewd, intelligent, and skilled political master who, as chief executive, could be as aggressive and tough as necessary. And they did not learn that Truman's public image and the actual person meshed when it came to at least one important trait: his deep-seated contempt for pretension and arrogance.

While MacArthur and his Tokyo entourage underestimated Truman as a decisive leader, the President, at least until the autumn of 1950, held considerable respect for the general. After all, it was Truman who appointed him as supreme commander in Japan in 1945 and as head of the United Nations Command in the Korean conflict. Truman's earliest impressions of MacArthur derived from World War I where MacArthur, already a general officer, had won fame as a bold, courageous combat leader. When Truman came to Washington as senator in 1934, MacArthur was serving as military head of the Army and often was called upon to testify before congressional committees and not infrequently to confer with President Roosevelt. While MacArthur's name was in the headlines many times during World War II, Truman did not really achieve national prominence until his vice-presidential nomination in mid-1944. As President, however, Truman's respectful attitude toward the "Big General," as he sometimes called him, was tempered by his innate dislike of egotistical, aloof, and pretentious persons, among whom MacArthur began to stand out in his mind as the Japanese occupation continued to appear like a one-man act and particularly after the general's thinly disguised bid for the Republican presidential nomination in 1948.

The first rounds of the Truman-MacArthur clash began in July August 1950 with the general's allegedly unauthorized trip to Taiwan and his message to the Veterans of Foreign Wars attacking American policy in the Far East. The final rounds came in late March and early April 1951 with MacArthur's brazen announcement of his terms for a cease-fire and Minority Leader Joseph W. Martin's reading before the House of Representatives a letter from MacArthur critical of the Truman administration's conduct of the war. On April 11, six days after the House heard MacArthur's letter, Truman, upon consulting with the Joint Chiefs and members of the National Security Council, announced the general's removal from his commands. By then Truman had discounted MacArthur's long and sometimes brilliant career, as well as his many positive leadership traits, and was ready to accept the negative side of his public image: the "Beau Brummell" of the AEF, the "political general" that FDR in 1932 had paired with Huey Long as "the two most dangerous men in the country," the producer of self-seeking communiques from the Southwest Pacific theater, the "Yankee Shogun" in Japan, and now the haughty, insubordinate theater chief in the frustrating war in Korea. Unlike MacArthur's previous differences with Roosevelt, his confrontation with Truman would not be ameliorated by a long and deep, if enigmatic, friendship. This time there were no personal ties between the two, and each fell back on misperceptions based on stereotypes of the other. Each man incorrectly judged the other's motivation, and each erroneously estimated the impact of his actions (or lack of actions) upon the other's image of his intentions. The outcome marked the sudden end of MacArthur's career, and the clash played no small part in killing Truman's chance for another term as President.

The Truman-MacArthur relationship vis-à-vis the Korean War started and ended with decisions that might have had happier alternatives. The President's appointment of MacArthur to head the United Nations Command on July 7, 1950, was based largely on the grounds that, as chief of the American Far East Command, he had been handling the piecemeal commitment of American forces to Korea since shortly after the war began two weeks earlier and, as commander over the Japanese occupation, he was in position to prepare Japan as the principal staging base for later operations. But MacArthur was a half year beyond his seventieth birthday and, though not senile or in ill health, was beginning to show natural signs of aging. It was not as if the nation had gone many years without a war and lacked a supply of proven high-level commanders. Truman could have chosen the United Nations commander from a generous reservoir of able officers who had distinguished themselves in World War II, while perhaps leaving MacArthur to continue his direction of the occupation of Japan. Unlike some of the top commanders of the wartime European theater who had been in on the evolution of the containment strategy since 1945, MacArthur had not been in Washington since 1935 and was not acquainted with the twists and turns of Pentagon thinking nor with the officials who had been developing Cold War strategy. From his days as a West Point cadet at the turn of the century onward, MacArthur had been disciplined to think in terms of winning on the battlefield. As he remarked at the Senate hearings, "The only way I know, when a nation wars on you, is to beat her by force."[3] In retrospect, then, the first mistake was in selecting MacArthur rather than a younger but fully capable officer who was known to be in accord with current Pentagon strategic thinking, such as General Matthew B. Ridgway.

The Truman-MacArthur affair ended in a manner that surely did not surprise the general for its lack of consideration and tactfulness. However people may differ on the various facets of the controversy, most would agree that the relief of the distinguished old warrior could have been handled in a different manner. Although Truman had intended for Secretary of the Army Frank Pace to interrupt his tour in Korea and bring the orders of relief to MacArthur in Tokyo personally, there were mixups and the general learned of it through a public radio broadcast. Truman's orders stated that MacArthur was relieved immediately of his duties, with Ridgway, head of the Eighth Army in Korea, to succeed him in charge of the United Nations Command, the Far East Command, and the occupation of Japan. Always viewing himself as a soldier-aristocrat and a professional par excellence, MacArthur later opined, "No office boy, no charwoman, no servant of any sort would have been dismissed with such callous disregard for the ordinary decencies."[4] To him it seemed that a commoner without "breeding" or professional credentials had dismissed an aristocrat and premiere professional. Truman would have missed such nuances, for to him it was simply a matter of the boss firing an unruly, disobedient subordinate. If, as he claimed, Truman lost no sleep over his decision to use atomic bombs in the summer of 1945, it is doubtful that he suffered insomnia after ousting MacArthur.

If lack of effective communication marred the relationship between the President and his theater chief in the Far East, failures in both communication and coordination flawed relations between the Joint Chiefs and MacArthur, as well as between the Chiefs and the President. In 1950 51 the Joint Chiefs of Staff consisted of General of the Army Omar N. Bradley, Chairman; General J. Lawton Collins, Army Chief of Staff; General Hoyt S. Vandenberg, Air Force Chief of Staff; and Admiral Forrest P. Sherman, Chief of Naval Operations. All of them had distinguished records from World War II and postwar commands, but none had ever served with or under MacArthur and, like Truman, had only secondary impressions of him—and vice versa. During the planning stage of Operation CHROMITE, the Inchon assault, the Joint Chiefs had been annoyingly conservative in their approach to MacArthur's risky proposal. But with the operation's startling success in mid-September 1950, the Joint Chiefs, along with the new Secretary of Defense, General Marshall, seemed to throw caution to the wind and authorized MacArthur's crossing the 38th parallel into North Korea without assessing the much higher risk factors with the care they had exercised in analyzing the Inchon plan. Indeed, MacArthur was given a virtual free hand in October and November as his forces fanned out across North Korea and pushed toward the Yalu River boundary with Manchuria. In the dazzling light of the Inchon success, few could see that the poorly planned amphibious operation at Wonsan a few weeks later, which logistically crippled the Eighth Army's offensive, may have been more indicative of MacArthur's strategic thinking at this stage than the Inchon assault. But the lessons of Wonsan never seemed to penetrate Washington minds until too late. Besides, the Joint Chiefs and Marshall were probably more absorbed in planning overall rearmament and NATO's new military structure than in what transpired immediately after MacArthur's seemingly decisive triumph over the North Korean Army.

During the advance above the 38th parallel the Joint Chiefs tried to limit MacArthur only to the extent of requiring him to use South Korean units solely in the approach to the Yalu. Armed with an ambiguous message from Marshall that he interpreted as giving him freedom to decide whether American forces should spearhead the advance, Mac-Arthur boldly rejected even this slight attempt at control by the Joint Chiefs. Astonishingly, the Joint Chiefs offered no rejoinder and quietly yielded to the discretion of the theater commander—a practice that had usually been proper in World War II but which would prove disastrous in the Korean War. In an unprecedented conflict like that in 1950, where limited fighting could and did escalate dangerously, the Joint Chiefs should have kept a much shorter leash on their theater commander.

After the initial Chinese attacks of late October and early November there was an ominous lull while MacArthur began preparations for an offensive to consummate the conquest of North Korea and flush out any Chinese volunteer forces. By mid-November the Joint Chiefs and their planners were deeply worried by MacArthur's failure to concentrate his forces: the Eighth Army was heading up the west side of North Korea toward Sinuiju, while the X Corps was pushing to the Chosen Reservoir and northeastward to Chongjin, with a huge gap in the middle between the tow forces. Not only the Joint Chiefs but also Marshall, Secretary of State Dean G. Acheson, and National Security Council advisers were becoming alarmed, but none proposed to change MacArthur's directive and none went to Truman to share his anxiety with the Commander-in-Chief. Since there was no overwhelming evidence on the Peking regime's intentions or the whereabouts of its armies, these key advisers to the President chose not to precipitate a confrontation with MacArthur. Just before MacArthur launched his fateful "end-the-war" offensive on November 24, even Truman commented, "You pick your man, you've got to back him up. That's the only way a military organization can work."[5] Actually a revision of MacArthur's directive was urgently needed, but his Washington superiors hesitated because of the intimidating impact of the Inchon "miracle" and because of their outmoded trust in the principle of not reversing a theater or field commander without solid grounds. They were still searching for substantial evidence to do so when the Chinese forces struck in mass shortly after MacArthur's troops had started forward.

There were also problems of coordination between American intelligence outfits, although in most writings on the war MacArthur is held liable for the intelligence blunders that failed to provide the signals of the impending North Korean invasion in late June 1950 and the Chinese intervention that autumn. It is nothing short of astonishing that at the Wake Island conference the President should ask MacArthur whether the Communist Chinese were going to enter the conflict. The general's sadly flawed ego prompted him to respond with some ill-informed remarks reminiscent of his regrettable and uncalled-for comments in 1932 charging that the Bonus Army was a Communist-led menace. Actually MacArthur's intelligence staff was responsible only for intelligence concerning the enemy at war, and the opposing belligerent in mid-October was North Korea, not Communist China. Intelligence on the intentions and activities of a nonbelligerent in time of war was the responsibility of the non-military agencies in that field. Yet, inexplicably, no known writings on the war seriously fault either the State Department's intelligence arm or the Central Intelligence Agency. If and when the documents of those agencies for 1950 become available to outside researchers, it is predicted that those two bodies will be judged the chief culprits in the failure to provide advance warning of the North Korean and Red Chinese attacks. All that is now known is that there was little cooperation and coordination between them and MacArthur's intelligence staff, which was headed by Major General Charles A. Willoughby, who, in turn, rarely welcomed "outside" opinions. The smoke created by MacArthur's overly confident pronouncements led later writers to anoint him as the scapegoat and hid the lamentable failure to coordinate intelligence data.

The only long-term friend MacArthur had in the Washington "inner circle" in 1950 was Secretary of Defense Louis Johnson, but on September 12, 1950, Truman removed him and appointed Marshall in his stead. Despite the fact that Marshall had been MacArthur's immediate superior in World War II and the two had exchanged hundreds of messages on Southwest Pacific plans and operations, they had conferred personally at length only once, when Marshall visited him on Goodenough Island in December 1943. For the most part, Marshall can be excused from blame for the command crisis of 1950 51 because not only was he new to the job but also the role of the Secretary of Defense was not then as clearly defined or powerful as it would later become. Marshall's relations with the Joint Chiefs were close and cordial, no doubt assisted by his close friendship with Bradley and Collins. The Secretary of Defense's chief failure, as mentioned earlier, was shared by his colleagues, namely, failing to insist on closer control over MacArthur after Inchon and not having his directive revised or countermanded once the Chinese made their preliminary move against the United Nations forces in late October. Marshall's most controversial mistake was his message of September 29 to MacArthur stating, "We want you to feel unhampered tactically and strategically to proceed north of the 38th parallel."[6] Thereupon MacArthur used this against the Joint Chiefs when they tried to inhibit his employments of units other than South Korean in advancing to the Yalu. It is hoped that Marshall's distinguished biographer, Forrest C. Pogue, will provide in his forthcoming volume a satisfactory explanation of this action by Marshall that was so uncharacteristic of his dealings with the Joint Chiefs. Whatever Marshall's intentions were, however, his message contributed to the dissonance in the chain of command.

Secretary of State Acheson had a well-known and hearty distaste for MacArthur, though the two were not personally acquainted. The feeling was mutual and began with an exchange of barbs in press statements about the troop strength required in Japan in the fall of 1945. It was hardly coincidental that shortly after Acheson became Secretary of State in 1949 a move was underway in the State Department to try to remove MacArthur as supreme commander in Japan. In September 1950, Truman appointed John Foster Dulles as the chief negotiator of a draft peace treaty for Japan (the final document to be eventually signed a year later); Acheson was not pleased thereafter when Dulles often solicited input from MacArthur. Acheson's role in the Truman-MacArthur controversy appears to have been that of a significant contributor to the President's shift to an almost totally negative image of MacArthur. As arrogant in his own way as MacArthur, Acheson later commented in his book on the Korean War: "As one looks back in calmness, it seems impossible to overestimate the damage that General MacArthur's willful insubordination and incredibly bad judgment did to the United States in the world and to the Truman Administration in the United States."[7] This is sheer hyperbole as far as MacArthur's lasting impact on world opinion is concerned, though his feud with the President probably did some damage to Truman's political future. What was said in informal talks between Truman and Acheson, who undoubtedly was "on the inside" with the President, cannot be documented precisely, but, in understated language, the secretary's input did not likely contribute to better understanding between Truman and MacArthur. Moreover, Acheson was instrumental in the decision that led to one of the worst blunders of the war in the wake of MacArthur's removal: the indication to North Korea and Red China that the United States was ready to begin negotiations on a truce with a cease-fire line in the proximity of the 38th parallel, while at the time, early June 1951, Ridgway's unit commanders were reporting that Chinese troops were surrendering in unprecedented numbers and that the Communist forces appeared to be on the verge of collapse.

The command crisis at the level of Washington and Tokyo had its counterpart in microcosmic form on the Korean peninsula. There, thanks to an unwise decision by MacArthur, his GHQ chief of staff and crony, Major General Edward M. Almond, was given command of X Corps, whose operations were independent of General Walton Walker's Eighth Army. Almond and Walker developed a deep-seated animosity toward each other, as did Almond and his main division commander, Major General O. P. Smith of the First Marine Division. Apparently MacArthur never became fully aware of the friction and lack of cooperation and coordination between these key field commanders. The results were that MacArthur either was not accurately informed on the situation at the front or received contradictory reports. Even when Ridgway took over the Eighth Army after Walker's death in late December 1950, the channel between MacArthur and his new army commander was not satisfactory, though primarily the fault of the former. MacArthur was still rendering gloomy, alarmist reports to the Joint Chiefs long after Ridgway had turned the Eighth Army around. It is little wonder that Chief of Staff Collins was pleasantly surprised when he visited the Eighth Army's front in mid-January 1951 and found the troops preparing for a major counteroffensive.

Besides the failures in communication and coordination within the chain of command, there were also political factors that impinged upon command relations and decision-making. In the November 1950 congressional elections, the Truman administration and the Democratic Party suffered serious reverses that indicated, among other things, considerable voter dissatisfaction with the conduct of the war. The Democratic majority in the Senate dropped from twelve to two, while in the

House the Democratic margin was reduced by two-thirds. It has been alleged, and not without some justification, that an important reason for Truman's trip to Wake Island in mid-October had been his desire to identify his administration more amiably with MacArthur, who still enjoyed a large following in the States as a hero and continuing support from a sizable number of conservative Republicans who still hoped to get him into the Oval Office. No scholarly study has been published yet on how much the impending presidential election of 1952 affected the Truman-MacArthur controversy.

Unlike the Second World War, when an earnest, if not altogether successful, effort was made at bipartisanship, the politics of the Korean War was highly partisan. Many Republican leaders felt free to assail savagely the Truman administration's management of the war and, of course, the President's handling of MacArthur. Senator Robert A. Taft, often called "Mr. Republican" by his conservative colleagues, commented after MacArthur's relief that he could no longer trust Bradley's judgment because he allegedly sided with Democrats. The distinguished journalist Walter Lippmann took an unfair slap at the Joint Chiefs when he deplored what he called "the beginning of an altogether intolerable thing in a republic: namely a schism within the armed forces between the generals of the Democratic Party and the generals of the Republican Party."[8] There is little evidence for such alarm, but political considerations undoubtedly intruded upon the thinking of the main actors in both the Truman and MacArthur camps.

An area that still awaits in-depth research is the impact of McCarthyism on the Truman-MacArthur affair. It seems more than coincidental that Senator Joseph R. McCarthy's ship had already developed a full head of steam when the Truman-MacArthur controversy began and that both phenomena were making headlines in 1951. Unfortunately, my research for the third volume of my biography of MacArthur is not yet complete for this period. The evidence gathered thus far does not indicate any connections between the general and the volatile senator from Wisconsin, except for occasional laudatory remarks by the latter about MacArthur. Both men appeared to draw support from those citizens who were concerned about the loyalty issue, the menace of communism, and the allegedly faltering position of the United States globally that had led to the "loss" of China. Both men were strong on Americanism, though neither lucidly defined it, and both were critical of Truman's Fair Deal as an effort to continue and expand the liberal reforms of

Roosevelt's New Deal, though MacArthur's criticism of domestic policies was reserved until after the Senate hearings. Truman surely took the mounting excitement of McCarthyism with more seriousness than he indicated publicly.

Several recent scholarly writings have maintained that the principal reason for Truman's decision to hurl American forces into the gauntlet in Korea in June 1950 was that the President felt compelled politically to demonstrate that his administration, especially in the wake of the ouster of the Nationalists from mainland China, was prepared to act decisively and aggressively against world communism. But if the hypothesis is valid regarding Truman's motivation in this case, it is difficult to explain on similar grounds his relief of MacArthur. While the former action may have stolen some thunder from Senator McCarthy and his devotees, the latter action provoked their displeasure as well as the wrath of many citizens who had not endorsed McCarthyism. The dismissal of MacArthur still appears as an act of personal courage on Truman's part, taken at considerable political risk to himself. All such observations must be qualified, however, by a reminder that my research on the possible links between McCarthyism and the Truman-MacArthur episode is still underway.

As each year passes, the controversy between the President and the general seems less momentous. It is not likely that it can ever be called a tempest in a teapot, but the question of whether Truman or MacArthur was right no longer appears as important. This is especially true in light of a number of fundamental questions that were not pursued carefully at the time, such as the following: To what extent was the Korean conflict a civil war? Were there signs available during the Korean War that portended the coming Sino-Soviet clash? Was American policy on French Indo-China and Formosa significantly altered by Truman's actions in late June 1950 dispatching more military aid to the French and units of the Seventh Fleet to the Formosa Strait? How important is bipartisanship in time of war? Should investigations like the Senate hearings on MacArthur's relief be conducted in the midst of war? Can the will and endurance of a democratic government and society stand the strain of a protracted limited war? Were there flaws in the American command structure that affected the prosecution of the war in Korea and perhaps were carried over into the Vietnam War also?

These and other important questions needed asking in view of the way history unfolded during the ensuing decade, but the publicity and excitement of the Truman-MacArthur controversy drew attention to its relatively less vital questions and shrouded the crisis in command of that era. In closing, I propose that, besides the previous questions, one may ponder anew Bradley's famous statement at the 1951 Senate hearings as applicable not only to MacArthur's strategic ideas but also to the sad confrontation between the President and his theater commander. In their lamentable feud that inadvertently served to screen more crucial issues, Truman and MacArthur had been engaged against each other in "fighting in the wrong war, at the wrong place, at the wrong time, and with the wrong enemy."[9]

Notes

1. Testimony of Secretary of Defense George C. Marshall, May 7, 1951, in U.S. Senate, Committees on Armed Services and Foreign Relations, *Military Situation in the Far East: Hearings Before the Committee on Armed Services and the Committee on Foreign Relations, United States Senate, Eighty-second Congress, First Session, to Conduct an Inquiry into the Military Situation in the Far East and the Facts Surrounding the Relief of General of the Army Douglas MacArthur from His Assignments in That Area* (5 pts. in 2 vols., Washington: U.S. Government Printing Office, 1951), pt. I, p. 325.

2. Harry S. Truman, *Memoirs*, Vol. II: *Years of Trial and Hope* (Signet ed., New York: New American Library, 1956), p. 501.

3. Testimony of General of the Army Douglas MacArthur, May 3, 1951, in U.S. Senate, *Military Situation in the Far East: Hearings*, pt. I, p. 67.

4. Douglas MacArthur, *Reminiscences* (New York: McGraw-Hill Book Co., 1964), p. 395.

5. Richard E. Neustadt, *Presidential Power: The Politics of Leadership* (New York: John Wiley and Sons, 1960), p. 128.

6. Secretary of Defense George C. Marshall to General of the Army Douglas MacArthur, September 29, 1950, JCS 92895, RG 218, Records of the U.S. Joint Chiefs of Staff, National Archives, Washington DC.

7. Dean G. Acheson, *The Korean War* (New York: W. W. Norton and Co., 1971), p. 111.

8. *New York Herald Tribune*, April 30, 1951.

9. Testimony of General of the Army Omar N. Bradley, May 15, 1951, in U.S. Senate, *Military Situation in the Far East: Hearings*, pt. II, p. 732.

New Light on the Korean War

Barton J. Bernstein

Barton Bernstein of Stanford University, a leading practitioner of New Left history, reexamines American policy during the Korean War in light of new documentary evidence and finds that the relationship between MacArthur and the Truman administration was much more complex than generally viewed.

Thirty years ago, on 25 June 1950, war erupted on the Korean peninsula. The President, Harry S. Truman, and his key advisors promptly concluded that it was a Soviet-inspired attack, probably a test of American will. In the next five days, he committed American forces and prestige to the conflict in an effort to repel the North Korean troops. Savouring success during the summer and fall, the administration, the Joint Chiefs of Staff and General Douglas MacArthur, American commander in the Pacific, endorsed plans, first to cross the thirty-eighth parallel and, then, to march towards the Yalu River to reunited Korea and vanquish communism.

American hopes briefly dimmed but revived in mid-November after the small Chinese entry into the war. In late November, however, American hopes speedily collapsed when massive Chinese forces entered the war and routed America and its allies. It was, MacArthur stated, "an entirely new war" against a new enemy. At first, American leaders feared that the United States might have to evacuate the peninsula. By mid-winter, the tied of war turned. As the United States began to regain territory in 1951, having surrendered all hopes of unifying the peninsula militarily, American leaders planned to offer the communists negotiations for a truce. On 24 March, MacArthur torpedoed that strategy and publicly criticized the administration for giving up its earlier quest for victory. He still sought victory, not compromise, and even wanted to extend the war across the Yalu to Manchuria and China, a strategy that the administration publicly condemned as reckless.

In July 1951, the warring nations finally opened truce negotiations, which dragged on for two years. A public debate in America continued to rage about whether Truman had invited communist aggression and whether the nation should pull out of Korea or escalate the war by attacking Manchuria and China. Embittered partly by the prolonged war, voters repudiated the Democrats in November 1952 and elected Dwight D. Eisenhower. Within seven months of entering the White House, after using nuclear threats and escalating conventional bombing, Eisenhower ended the war and forced the obstreperous Syngman Rhee, President of the Republic of Korea, to accept the armistice.

Recently declassified materials throw new light and raise questions about some of these subjects—attitudes about war with the Soviets, reports of Chinese intervention, the drive to the Yalu, the military conduct of the war, the Truman administration's position on bombing across the Yalu, the Truman-MacArthur controversy, the attitude of both the Truman and the Eisenhower Administrations to atomic war in the Pacific, the Eisenhower Administration's uneasiness about the armistice, and a top American general's dealings with Rhee. Though most of these subjects might support at least a substantial essay, the purpose of this analysis is more modest: to examine important parts of these issues in the light of new evidence and to suggest new ways of viewing critical aspects of the war.

Truman and his principal advisers committed American forces to the war to stop what they interpreted as Soviet-instigated aggression. The developing American commitment came to seem safer on 29 June 1950, when the Soviets responded in moderate words to the American message of the 27th. American advisers, including George Kennan, the noted Soviet expert, found this Kremlin reply generally reassuring, since, in the words of the minutes paraphrasing Kennan, the USSR was "indicating that [it] was not directly involving itself."[1]

The recently declassified minutes of the meeting at which Kennan spoke, a session of the National Security Council Consultants on 29 June, reveal some unsettling information. Advisors were talking about bombing Manchuria if China entered the war, the possible use of the A-Bomb in future situations and that it might not be a bad time for war with Russia. "[If] we caught Chinese Communists in South Korea we could . . . even bomb in Manchuria" Kennan concluded in the words of the minutes. Major General Richard Lindsay, Deputy Director for

Strategic Plans, "warned that if we bombed in Manchuria with conventional bombs we would lose some of our capability of using atomic weapons if they later became necessary." He implied that the best targets would have been destroyed and thus the A-bomb would not have the same dramatic impact.[2]

When the group discussed Soviet plans, Kennan emphasized that the Soviets would probably exploit "Asiatic satellites against us . . . because there was no risk involved for the USSR." A global war, he contended, was very unlikely since Russia did not have "the capability to attack North America successfully." On the other hand, Kennan "thought if the Russians got into a world war now they would have stumbled in, and in the long run this might be the best situation for us." Apparently he meant that the Soviet Union was weaker in 1950 than it would be later, and therefore it could do less damage to the United States and be defeated more easily. So far as the minutes and other documents indicate, no one at the meeting probed Kennan's analysis.[3]

According to most interpreters and archival sources, Chinese forces did not intervene until about mid-October 1950, and American Headquarters did not discover their presence for about another week. Then, after some bitter battles, the Chinese withdrew from combat in early November. When the United Nations forces continued their march towards the Yalu, however, the Chinese reentered the fray in late November and threw back the UN armies.

But some recently declassified documents from July 1950 raise some questions about part of this accepted view that MacArthur did not discover PRC [People's Republic of China] troops in the war until October. On 9 July 1950, in a message requesting four more divisions, he informed the Joint Chiefs of Staff [JCS] that the enemy force included Chinese Communists. As he put it in outlining the new threat, "this force more and more assumes the aspect of a combination of Soviet leadership with Communist ground elements."[4]

His message raised some doubts for at least one State Department official, Fisher Howe, a Deputy Special Assistant in Intelligence. Howe pointed out that there was no confirming evidence for MacArthur's message of the 9th and that it was ambiguous. "The actual presence of Chinese Communists . . . has not been confirmed in any other reports. MacArthur says that operations *assume* the aspect of having Chinese Communist personnel."[5] But army intelligence that day saw no ambiguity, concluding that MacArthur "reports the presence of Chinese Communist forces among the North Koreans."[6]

MacArthur's message was passed on to Dean Acheson, the Secretary of State, and used in the next few days in some key JCS papers discussing the need for expanded American forces in the war.[7] On 14 July, for example, a JCS planning committee stressed that "MacArthur has now reported that elements of Chinese Communist forces have already appeared in the battle areas . . . Chinese Communist troops are in fact being employed in strength in Korea." This committee report expressed uneasiness, concluding that "the appearance of these elements may well presage the entry of significant numbers of Chinese Communist forces into and a widening of the present conflict, a capability which cannot be disregarded." In view of "the situation which in fact now exists, i.e., Chinese Communist troops employed in Korea," the committee recommended that MacArthur, who had already received a commitment of four divisions and was requesting four more, would need "1 Field Army of 9–12 divisions."[8]

Despite these military documents of July, high-ranking State Department officials and the Joint Chiefs, as well as MacArthur, stated from late July to October, that China would not enter the war.[9] How then do we explain their later optimism? Perhaps key officials decided that MacArthur's report of the 9th was wrong and that his officers had confused North Korean forces, who had returned from Manchuria, with Chinese ones. Maybe MacArthur himself sent a later dispatch cancelling the one of 9 July. Curiously, though, neither the official military histories nor the declassified cables include such a message.[10]

Most likely, Washington viewed MacArthur's report as a useful gambit in the effort to expand the American troop commitment to the war. That theory would explain why there is no trace among the declassified State Department papers of the alarm that should have been felt if MacArthur's message had been treated as an announcement of China's entry. Even the declassified military files reveal no sense of immediate danger, of the need to reappraise strategy. When General J. Lawton Collins, Army Chief of Staff, and General Hoyt Vandenberg, Air Force Chief of Staff, conferred in Tokyo with MacArthur on 13 and 14 July, they apparently did not even discuss his report of Chinese intervention.[11] At the same time, MacArthur's plea of the 9th for more troops helped push the Administration to increase American forces in Korea.[12]

On 13 July, just four days after reporting the presence of Chinese troops, MacArthur assured Washington that he could block a massive Chinese entry into the war by bombing key routes. "The only passages leading from Manchuria and Vladivostok have many tunnels and bridges," he explained to General Vandenberg, while implying that he might bomb across the Yalu. "I see here a unique use for the atomic bomb—to strike a blocking blow—which would require a six months repair job," said MacArthur. "Sweeten up by B-29 force." Vandenberg promised to provide more B-29s but apparently sidestepped the issue of the A-bomb.[13]

With American forces still pinned in the South, MacArthur was already planning on the 13th to destroy North Korean forces and hoping to unify Korea. As his successes grew, many Republicans, the Joint Chiefs and Administration leaders looked forward to the reunification of Korea. While they worried about Soviet entry into the war, they were usually sanguine that the Chinese would not intervene.

Among the more cautious proponents of unification was John Foster Dulles, the Republican adviser to the State Department. In mid-July, he suggested that it might be too dangerous to try to reunify the northern-most Korean provinces, for that effort might threaten the Soviet Union. "[The] portions of North Korea which are close to Vladivostok and Port Arthur are particularly sensitive areas from the standpoint of the Soviet Union," he privately explained.[14]

Like most other Washington officials, he did not anticipate China's entry into the war when America crossed the thirty-eighth parallel in early October and moved northwards. By early November, after China's small-scale entry, however, he claimed that he had foreseen the PRC's intervention and he warned privately against further expansion toward the Yalu. Disagreeing with MacArthur and the administration, Dulles was willing to settle for stopping short of the northern areas. "My guess is," he privately stated on 9 November, "that if we try by military means to get control of *all* of Korea we shall become bogged down in an interminable and costly operation like Japan's 'China Incident.' "[15]

Apparently he never tried to restrain MacArthur, Acheson, and the Joint Chiefs in their optimistic venture—even after the first PRC intervention—to unify the entire peninsula. Probably because Dulles did not want to risk dividing the Republican party or estranging himself from those who supported the continued march to the Yalu, he never publicly disclosed that he had wanted to halt the effort at reunification. He knew that his counsel of prudence would not win friends, either before or after the PRC's massive intervention of late November.

Even since Truman's early armed intervention in the Korean War, planners have thought about the conditions under which the United States might use the atomic bomb. In mid-July, when American forces were still struggling in the south, members of the State Department's Policy Planning Staff at the request of Paul Nitze, its Director, analyzed the conditions for using the bomb. On 15 July, a staff member contended that American citizens would support the use of nuclear weapons if civilian and military leaders deemed them "essential for reestablishing peace and for saving the lives of American boys, and if the atomic bombs were used against military objectives without resultant wholesale destruction of civilians." He concluded that these weapons should be used if Chinese and Soviet forces were *overtly* committed in Korea; if the weapons would restore "the situation in Korea," assure a decisive military success, and not appreciably deplete the nuclear arsenal; if "the bombs could be used without excessive destruction of noncombatants"; and if the UN approved or the government decided that the disadvantages of seeking approval outweighed the advantages.[16]

Paul Nitze discussed these conditions on 16 July with General Kenneth D. Nichols, chief of the Pentagon's special weapons project and deemed by Nitze as "probably the principal Pentagon military authority on the bomb." Nichols thought that the bomb should be used, in Nitze's words, "to prevent our being pushed off the peninsula even though there was *no overt* Soviet or Chinese [intervention in the war]."[17] Nitze reported these conclusions to Acheson, but there is no evidence that the Secretary then chose to pursue the matter any further. Probably he regarded Nitze's inquiries as simply an essential part of wise contingency planning, the consideration of unlikely and unpleasant possibilities.

On 4 November, about a week after China's small-scale intervention, Nitze invited General Herbert B. Loper, an army specialist on atomic energy, to discuss the possible use of nuclear weapons against the Chinese. Nitze learned that the primary use of the bomb in Korea would be against troop concentrations and artillery, but "such targets would probably not come about normally." The bomb would probably not be militarily decisive in Korea. While it might deter further Chinese intervention, "its use might bring the Soviet Union into the war [and] arouse the peoples of Asia against us," Nitze reported. If the bomb was used against Manchurian cities, "it would almost certainly bring the Soviet Union into the war."[18]

Prompted partly by the first Chinese intervention, General J. Lawton Collins, Army Chief of Staff, warned the Joint Chiefs on 20 November that they might be required on short notice to make recommendations on the use of the A-bomb in Korea. "it is . . . conceivable," he told the other Chiefs, that "in the event of an all-out effort by the Chinese Communists, the use of atomic bombs against troop and material concentrations might be the decisive factor in enabling the UN forces" to hold their position or resume their drive to the Yalu. Since there was no formal policy, he called for a study of the conditions for using the bomb and the selection of suitable targets.[19]

On 30 November, five days after China's entry but before the Joint Chiefs had defined their own policy on the bomb, President Truman implied at his press conference that he might use the A-bomb in the Korean War.[20] His statement alarmed Allies, captured headlines, unleashed a flood of hostile mail to the White House[21] and won support among Americans.[22] Fearing nuclear war, Clement Attlee, the British Prime Minister, rushed to Washington to urge a more cautious American policy. The result was, in part, a joint British-American communiqué. It was an uneasy document designed to ease Allied anxieties. It expressed the President's "hope that world conditions would never call for the use of the atomic bomb."[23] That statement kept secret America's policy on the use of the bomb and provoked continued speculation.

Truman's dislike of MacArthur preceded the Korean War, for the President resented the General's unwillingness to bend to the White House's inclinations. Twice in the years before the war, Truman had invited MacArthur to visit Washington, and each time the General had refused explaining that his work in Japan was too important to allow any interruption.[24]

During the early days of the war, Truman expressed his resentment at the General's arrogance. On 29 June 1950, Truman directed the Joint Chiefs to send MacArthur "an order from the President . . . telling him that the President wanted full reports every day." Truman told the members of the National Security Council [NSC] that during the Second World War "he practically had to telephone General MacArthur to get information from him."[25]

In the words of a presidential aide, Truman felt "that MacArthur is a supreme egotist, who regards himself as something of a god." Truman pointed to the fact that MacArthur had escaped from the Philippines to Australia while leaving General Joseph Wainwright behind to be captured. "Wainwright has never recovered from the experience while MacArthur has become a hero and dictator of Japan," Truman complained.[26]

According to Truman, John Foster Dulles, who had been visiting the General when the war erupted on the 25th, was appalled that, when the first word reached Tokyo of the outbreak in Korea, nobody on the General's staff would call MacArthur. "All of them were afraid to," Dulles had reported. According to Truman, Dulles wanted "MacArthur hauled back to the United States." The President rejected Dulles's advice, explaining that the General was so involved politically, as a possible Republican presidential candidate, "that he could not recall MacArthur without causing a tremendous reaction in this country."[27]

Truman and his advisers, including the Joint Chiefs, knew that they were dealing with a politically powerful general. In August 1950, when MacArthur sent the Veterans of Foreign Wars [VFW] a statement for their annual convention criticizing Truman's Formosa policy, Administration leaders faced the problem of how to handle the General. The President later claimed that he considered removing MacArthur from command in the Korean War but decided against it because "I had no desire to hurt [him] personally."[28] More likely, the President was deterred chiefly by his fears of provoking a political battle at home that would further aid the GOP in attacking the administration's unclear China policy.

On 26 August, dealing with the General's VFW statement, Truman hit upon moderate tactics. He directed Louis Johnson, his Secretary of Defence, to order MacArthur to withdraw his statement, though it had already been published in a magazine. Fearful of combat with MacArthur, Johnson asked Acheson whether "we dare send [MacArthur] a message that the President directs him to withdraw the statement." Even after Truman dictated the exact words for Johnson, he still tried to squirm away from the task. Maybe, Johnson suggested, the administration could simply say that MacArthur's "statement is the statement of one individual only and is not the policy of the United States Government." Acheson would not support Johnson in this venture, but Ambassador W. Averell Harriman, who had earlier negotiated with the General on behalf of Truman, was inclined to ask Truman to reconsider his tactics. When Harriman talked to Truman, according to a recently declassified memorandum, "the President had said . . . that he had dictated what he wanted to go and he still wanted it to go."[29] When MacArthur received this rebuke, he feigned innocence, claiming that he had supported (not criticized) Truman's China policy.[30]

Not until MacArthur had injured his own reputation through a dramatic failure could the President risk dismissing or demoting him. And that occurred with the debacle of the "home by Christmas" offensive, when the Chinese routed American forces in Korea. The administration skilfully blamed MacArthur for the debacle and sought to avoid joint responsibility.[31]

Most analysts of the Korean War have treated MacArthur as a reckless, arrogant, self-righteous leader, eager to expand the war, unduly optimistic that the Soviets would not retaliate, and indifferent to constitutional and legal restraints upon the military. Therefore, few analysts would be surprised to learn that, when American forces were nearly pushed off the peninsula in January 1951, MacArthur wanted to use gas warfare. (After all, General George C. Marshall, a more cautious man, had wanted to use it against Japan in 1945.)[32] The surprising fact is, however, that MacArthur actually resisted pleas for the use of gas, and that the plan came instead from General Matthew Ridgway, the American commander in Korea.

On 6 January 1951, Ridgway admitted that he had first considered using gas, as he explained, to regain the initiative in the war. Because of the danger of retaliation, he had rejected gas except "as a last resort to cover [American] withdrawal and evacuation from a final beachhead where pressure might be so great as to justify resorting to such extreme measures." Under such circumstances, he argued, it could be safely used because the enemy would not have time to retaliate. Would MacArthur approve? Ridgway asked.[33]

Rather than sending Ridgway's request to Washington, MacArthur bluntly turned him down. American "inhibitions on such use are complete and drastic," MacArthur stressed. "[Even if our government should change this attitude], it is most improbable that the membership of the United Nations would be in accord."[34]

Wily and vainglorious, MacArthur had long acted as America's proconsul in the Pacific. He had patronized the President, pressured the Joint Chiefs, and surrounded himself with sycophants. On 24 March 1951, he sabotaged the Administration's plan for seeking a truce when he demanded that the Communists surrender and pledged otherwise to defeat them. At almost the same time, he sent to Speaker Joe Martin, a Republican leader, a letter (likely to be made public) assailing the administration's stated policy of limited war in Korea. MacArthur pleaded for using Nationalist Chinese troops and for attacking the PRC. "[If we lose this war to communism in Asia] the fall of Europe is inevitable," he warned. "[Win it and] Europe most probably would avoid war and yet preserve freedom . . . we must win. There is no substitute for victory."[35]

The administration's public case against an expanded war, in the famous phrase of General Omar Bradley, Chairman of the Joint Chiefs, was that it would "involve us in the wrong war, at the wrong place, at the wrong time, and with the wrong enemy."[36] MacArthur's strategy, Dean Acheson publicly argued, might also lead to war with Russia. How could the Soviets stay on the sidelines if America attacked the PRC? Acheson asked.[37]

Traditionally, analysts of the Truman-MacArthur controversy have treated the dispute, on the policy level, as a conflict between a cautious administration and a reckless general.[38] Such a framework fails to accommodate some recently declassified material: MacArthur's proposals of March, when American forces had regained the initiative, were similar to the advice of the Joint Chiefs and of W. Stuart Symington, Chairman of the National Security Resources Board, in mid-January, when America had been *near defeat*.

In mid-January 1951, the Joint Chiefs recommended imposing a naval blockade in China, unleashing and aiding Chiang Kai-shek's forces against the PRC, assisting guerrilla forces against the PRC, and maintaining air reconnaissance of Manchura and coastal areas of China. Like MacArthur, the Joint Chiefs wanted to expand the war to China, but they did stop short of proposing the bombing of Manchuria and China *unless* it was necessary to save American troops in Korea or to retaliate against Communist attacks on American forces outside Korea.[39]

In mid-January, Symington moved beyond the vigorous JCS proposals. He offered a bold global plan that included attacks on China and a nuclear ultimatum to the Soviet Union. Like MacArthur, he wanted to blockade and bomb China and unleash Nationalist forces against the PRC. He also urged the "extension of fullest possible support to all anti-Communist elements in the Far East, including Southeast Asia." For Symington, America and its allies were "fighting a war for survival against the aggression of Soviet Russia [and] are losing the war, on both the political and military fronts."⁴⁰

Like MacArthur, Symington chafed under the restraints imposed by America's allies. If the UN or the Allies opposed his strategy for expanding the war, Symington argued, the United States should proceed unilaterally. He wanted the administration to issue an ultimatum: "Any further aggression, in areas to be spelled out, would result in the atomic bombardment of Soviet Russia itself." Such a warning, he wrote, would deter Soviet aggression, assert American leadership in the "free world," and "establish moral justification for the use of . . . atomic bombs in retaliation against Soviet aggression."

With his own channels to Washington, MacArthur had probably learned of the Joint Chiefs' proposals and Symington's even more bellicose recommendations.⁴¹ If so, even though the gloom of January had lifted by March, MacArthur had reason to believe that his strategy would find support within sections of the government, as well as in parts of the Republican party.

In his self-righteousness, MacArthur may have believed that he could force Truman to change his policy. MacArthur certainly had no respect for the President and saw him as weak and even mentally ill. He thought the President was losing his mind. On 12 April, the day after his dismissal, MacArthur told General Matthew Ridgway that he had learned from a physician who had gotten if from the President's own doctor that Truman "was suffering from malignant hypertension: that this affliction was characterized by bewilderment and confusion of thought; and that . . . he wouldn't live six months."⁴² Put bluntly, as MacArthur saw it, a sick, erratic Chief Executive was making the wrong policy and cashiering his top general. MacArthur may well have believed that his own dismissal would backfire on Truman and finally force the President to endorse both the General and his policy. . . .

Notes

1. "Memorandum of National Security Council Consultants' Meeting," 29 June 1950, Policy Planning Staff [PPS] Files, D[epartment of] S[tate Records, Department of State]; also printed in Department of State, *Foreign Relations of the United States* (Washington DC, 1950), 1, 327–30.
2. Ibid.

3. Ibid. Also see NSC 73, 1 July 1950, NSC box, M[odern] M[ilitary] R[ecords,] N[ational] A[rchives].

4. General Douglas MacArthur to Joint Chiefs of Staff, 9 July 1950, CX 57481, File 795.00/ 7–905, DS.

5. Fisher Howe to Dean Rusk, 9 July 1950, File 795. 00/ 7–950, DS (emphasis added). See also the calm response in AMG, no title, 9 July 1950, CCS 383.21 Korea (3–9-45), R[ecords of the] J[oint] C[hiefs of] S[taff] RG 218, [NA].

6. "G-2 Estimate of Enemy Capabilities in Korea (090800 July 1950)," attached to Howe to Rusk, 9 July 1950.

7. Joint Intelligence Committee to Joint Chiefs of Staff, "Estimate of North Korean Capabilities," 11 July 1950, JCS 1924/16; and ibid.; 12 July 1950, JCS 1924/19, CCS 383.21 Korea (3–19-45), RJCS.

8. Report by the Joint Strategic Plans Committee (in collaboration with the Joint Intelligence Committee) to the Joint Chiefs of Staff, JCS 1924/20, 14 July 1950, TS G-3 091 Korea, R[ecords of the] A[rmy] S[taff,] RG 319, [NA].

9. Barton J. Bernstein, "The Policy of Risk: Crossing the Thirty-Eighth Parallel and Marching to the Yalu," *Foreign Service Journal*, LIV (1977), 16–21.

10. James Schnabel, *Policy and Direction: The First Year* (Washington DC, 1972), pp. 84–5 et seq.; James Schnabel and Robert J. Watson, "The History of the Joint Chiefs of Staff: The Joint Chiefs of Staff and National Policy," vol. III, pt. 1, 'The Korean War,' 184–98, MMA, NA.

11. D. D. Dickson to Bolte on "Report of Trip to the Far East Command (10–15 July 1950)," 17 July 1950, G-3 333 Pacific TS, Sec. 1, Case 3 (1950–51), RAS; Arthur W. Radford memoir, 919–23, Hoover Institute, Stanford.

12. Schnabel and Watson, "The Korean War," pp. 182–8.

13. "Questions and Answers, First Conference (0900 13 July 1950)," attached to D. D. Dickson to Bolte on "Report of Trip to the Far East Command (10–15 July 1950)."

14. John Foster Dulles to William Mathews, 24 July 1950, Dulles MSS, Princeton University Library; cf., Dulles to Paul Nitze, 14 July 1950, File 795.00/ 7–1450, DS.

15. Dulles to Ferdinand Lathrop Mayer, 9 Nov. 1950, Dulles MSS (emphasis added).

16. "The Question of U.S. Use of Atomic Bomb in Korea," 15 July 1950, attached to Paul Nitze to Secretary [Acheson], 17 July 1950, PPS Files, DS (emphasis added).

17. Ibid. (emphasis added).

18. Nitze, memorandum to files, 4 Nov. 1950, PPS Files, DS.

19. Chief of Staff, Army, to Joint Chiefs, on "Possible Employment of Atomic Bombs in Korea," 20 Nov. 1950, CCS 383.21 Korea (3–19-45), RJCS. The same day, General J. Lawton Collins received a report from General Reuben Jenkins, "Department of the Army Policy Concerning the Employment of

Atomic Weapons in the Korean Operations," 20 Nov. 1950, G-3 335.2 TS, RAS. For a discussion of the staff studies, see Schnabel and Watson, "The Korean War," pp. 372–3.

20. Truman's press conference, 30 Nov. 1950, in *Public Papers of the Presidents: Harry S. Truman, 1950* (Washington DC, 1965), pp. 727, 738–40.

21. Miss Ruckh to George Elsey, 12 Dec. 1950, "Analysis of Public Comment Contained in Communications to the President, received December 4 to 8, 1950"; and Ruckh to Elsey, 4 Dec. 1950, "Analysis of Public Comment Contained in Communications to the President, received November 28 to December 1, 1950," Elsey MSS, Truman Library.

22. Gallup polls of 11/12–11/17/50 and 11/11–11/16/51, in *The Gallup Poll*, ed G. Gallup (New York, 1972), II. 950, 1027.

23. Attlee-Truman Communiqué in *Public Papers: Truman*, p. 740.

24. Harry S. Truman, *Memoirs: Years of Trial and Hope* (Garden City NY, 1956), p. 447.

25. Philip Jessup "Meeting of the NSC in the Cabinet Room at the White House," 29 June 1950, file 795.00/ 6–2950, DS.

26. Eben Ayers, diary, 1 July 1950, Ayers MSS, Truman Library.

27. Ibid.

28. Truman, *Memoirs*, II, 355–6.

29. L. D. Battle, "Memorandum for the Record of the Events of Saturday, August 26, 1950," Dean Acheson MSS, Truman Library.

30. Courtney Whitney, *MacArthur: His Rendezvous with Destiny* (New York, 1968), p. 380; Douglas MacArthur, *Reminiscences* (New York, 1964), pp. 341–2.

31. Barton Bernstein, "The Policy of Risk," pp. 16–22, 29.

32. John J. McCloy, "Memorandum of Conversation with General Marshall," 29 May 1945, Records of the Secretary of War, RG 107, NA; David Lilienthal, *The Journals of David Lilienthal: The Atomic Energy Years* (New York, 1964), p. 199.

33. M. B. Ridgway to MacArthur, 6 Jan. 1951, box 20, Ridgway MSS A[merican] M[ilitary] H[istory] I[nstitute], Carlisle PA.

34. Douglas MacArthur to Matt [Ridgway], 7 Jan. 1951, box 20, Ridgway MSS.

35. MacArthur to Joseph Martin, 20 Mar. 1951, in Joint Senate Committee on Armed Services and Foreign Relations, *Military Situation in the Far East*, 82nd Cong., 1st Sess., 3182 (hereafter *Military Situation*).

36. Bradley, in *Military Situation*, p. 732.

37. Acheson, in *Military Situation*, pp. 741, 751.

38. Trumbull Higgins, *Korea and The Fall of MacArthur* (New York, 1960) and John Spanier, *The Truman-MacArthur Controversy and the Korean War* (New York, 1959).

39. NSC 101, 12 Jan. 1951, JCS memorandum for the Secretary of Defence,

"Courses of Action Relative to Communist China and Korea," P[resident's] S[ecretary's] F[ile], Truman Library. For background, see JCS 2118/10, 12 Jan. 1951, "Note by the Secretary to the Joint Chiefs of Staff," G-3 (1950–51) 381 China Sect. 1-A, Case 4/3, RAS; cf., Bradley, in *Military Situation*, pp. 735–8.

40. NSC 100, 11 Jan. 1951, Chairman, NSRB, "Recommended Policies and Actions in Light of the Grave World Situation," PSF, Truman Library.

41. For a summary of some administration positions, see NSC 100/1, 15 Jan. 1951, "US Action to Counter Chinese Communist Aggression," PSF, Truman Library.

42. Ridgway, memorandum for diary, 12 April 1951 (paraphrase of MacArthur), box 20, Ridgway MSS. Also see Ridgway oral history, 81, AMHI.

5. Assessments

Duty, Honor, Country

Douglas MacArthur

MacArthur received the Thayer Award, presented by the Association of Graduates of the U.S. Military Academy, on May 12, 1962. In his remarks to a luncheon audience at West Point that included the entire Corps of Cadets, the general spoke extemporaneously about the values that were closest to his heart.

No human being could fail to be deeply moved by such a tribute as this. Coming from a profession I have served so long and a people I have loved so well, it fills me with an emotion I cannot express. But this award is not intended primarily to honor a personality, but to symbolize a great moral code—a code of conduct and chivalry of those who guard this beloved land of culture and ancient descent. For all hours and for all time, it is an expression of the ethics of the American soldier. That I should be integrated in this way with so noble an ideal arouses a sense of pride, and yet of humility, which will be with me always.

Duty, honor, country: Those three hallowed words reverently dictate what you ought to be, what you can be, what you will be. They are your rallying point to build courage when courage seems to fail, to regain faith when there seems to be little cause for faith, to create hope when hope becomes forlorn.

Unhappily, I possess neither that eloquence of diction, that poetry of imagination, nor that brilliance of metaphor to tell you all that they mean.

The unbelievers will say they are but words, but a slogan, but a flamboyant phrase. Every pedant, every demagogue, every cynic, every hypocrite, every troublemaker, and, I am sorry to say, some others of an entirely different character, will try to downgrade them even to the extent of mockery and ridicule.

But these are some of the things they do. They build your basic character. They mold you for your future roles as the custodians of the nation's defense. They make you strong enough to know when you are weak, and brave enough to face yourself when you are afraid.

They teach you to be proud and unbending in honest failure, but humble and gentle in success; not to substitute words for actions, not to seek the path of comfort, but to face the stress and spur of difficulty and challenge; to learn to stand up in the storm, but to have compassion on those who fall; to master yourself before you seek to master others; to have a heart that is clean, a goal that is high; to learn to laugh, yet never forget how to weep; to reach into the future, yet never neglect the past; to be serious, yet never to take yourself too seriously; to be modest so that you will remember the simplicity of true greatness, the open mind of true wisdom, the meekness of true strength.

They give you a temperate will, a quality of the imagination, a vigor of the emotions, a freshness of the deep springs of life, a temperamental predominance of courage over timidity, of an appetite for adventure over love of ease.

They create in your heart the sense of wonder, the unfailing hope of what next, and the joy and inspiration of life. They teach you in this way to be an officer and a gentleman.

And what sort of soldiers are those you are to lead? Are they reliable? Are they brave? Are they capable of victory?

Their story is known to all of you. It is the story of the American man-at-arms. My estimate of him was formed on the battlefield many, many years ago, and has never changed. I regarded him then, as I regard him now, as one of the world's noblest figures; not only as one of the finest military characters, but also as one of the most stainless.

His name and fame are the birthright of every American citizen. In his youth and strength, his love and loyalty, he gave all that mortality can give. He needs no eulogy from me, or from any other man. He has written his own history and written it in red on his enemy's breast.

But when I think of his patience in adversity, of his courage under fire, and of his modesty in victory, I am filled with an emotion of admiration I cannot put into words. He belongs to history as furnishing one of the greatest examples of successful patriotism. He belongs to posterity as the instructor of future generations in the principles of liberty and freedom. he belongs to the present, to us, by his virtues and by his achievements.

In twenty campaigns, on a hundred battlefields, around a thousand campfires, I have witnessed that enduring fortitude, that patriotic self-abnegation, and that invincible determination which have carved his statue in the hearts of his people.

From one end of the world to the other, he has drained deep the chalice of courage. As I listened to those songs [of the Cadet Glee Club], in memory's eye I could see those staggering columns of the First World War, bending under soggy packs on many a weary march, from dripping dusk to drizzling dawn, slogging ankle-deep through the mire of shell-pocked roads; to form grimly for the attack, blue-lipped, covered with sludge and mud, chilled by the wind and rain, driving home to their objective, and, for many, to the judgment seat of God.

I do not know the dignity of their birth, but I do know the glory of their death. They died, unquestioning, uncomplaining, with faith in their hearts, and on their lips the hope that we would go on to victory.

Always for them: Duty, honor, country. Always their blood, and sweat, and tears, as we sought the way and the light and the truth. And 20 years after, on the other side of the globe, again the filth of murky foxholes, the stench of ghostly trenches, the slime of dripping dugouts, those boiling suns of relentless heat, those torrential rains of devastating storms, the loneliness and utter desolation of jungle trails, the bitterness of long separation from those they loved and cherished, the deadly pestilence of tropical disease, the horror of stricken areas of war.

Their resolute and determined defense, their swift and sure attack, their indomitable purpose, their complete and decisive victory—always victory, always through the bloody haze of their last reverberating shot, the vision of gaunt, ghastly men, reverently following your passwords of "Duty, honor, country."

The code which those words perpetuate embraces the highest moral law and will stand the test of any ethics or philosophies ever promulgated for the uplift of mankind. Its requirements are for the things that are right and its restraints are from the things that are wrong. The soldier, above all other men, is required to practice the greatest act of religious training—sacrifice. In battle, and in the face of danger and death, he discloses those divine attributes which his Maker gave when He created man in His own image. No physical courage and no greater strength can take the place of the divine help which alone can sustain him. However hard the incidents of war may be, the soldier who is called upon to offer and to give his life for his country is the noblest development of mankind.

You now face a new world, a world of change. The thrust into outer space of the satellite spheres and missiles marks a beginning of another epoch in the long story of mankind. In the 5 or more billions of years the scientists tell us it has taken to form the earth, in the 3 or more billion years of development of the human race, there has never been a more abrupt or staggering evolution.

We deal now, not with things of this world alone, but with the illimitable distances and as yet unfathomed mysteries of the universe. We are reaching out for a new and boundless frontier. We speak in strange terms of harnessing the cosmic energy; of making winds and tides work for us; of creating unheard-of synthetic materials to supplement or even replace our old standard basics, to purify sea water for our drink; of mining ocean floors for new fields of wealth and food; of disease preventives to expand life into the hundreds of years; of controlling the weather for a more equitable distribution of heat and cold, of rain and shine; of spaceships to the moon; of the primary target in war no longer limited to the armed forces of an enemy, but instead to include his civil populations; of ultimate conflict between a united human race and the sinister forces of some other planetary galaxy; of such dreams and fantasies as to make life the most exciting of all times.

And through all this welter of change and development your mission remains fixed, determined, inviolable. It is to win our wars. Everything else in your professional career is but corollary to this vital dedication. All other public purposes, all other public projects, all other public needs, great or small, will find others for their accomplishment; but you are the ones who are trained to fight.

Yours is the profession of arms, the will to win, the sure knowledge that in war there is no substitute for victory, that if you lose, the nation will be destroyed, that the very obsession of your public service must be duty, honor, country.

Others will debate the controversial issues, national and international, which divide men's minds. But serene, calm, aloof, you stand as the nation's war guardian, as its lifeguard from the raging tides of international conflict, as its gladiator in the arena of battle. For a century and a half you have defended, guarded, and protected its hallowed traditions of liberty and freedom, of right and justice.

Let civilian voices argue the merits or demerits of our processes of government: Whether our strength is being sapped by deficit financing indulged in too long, by Federal paternalism grown too mighty, by power groups grown too arrogant, by politics grown too corrupt, by crime grown too rampant, by morals grown too low, by taxes grown too high, by extremists grown too violent; whether our personal liberties are as thorough and complete as they should be.

These great national problems are not for your professional participation or military solution. Your guidepost stands out like a tenfold beacon in the night: Duty, honor, country.

You are the leaven which binds together the entire fabric of our national system of defense. From your ranks come the great captains who hold the nation's destiny in their hands the moment the war tocsin sounds.

The long grey line has never failed us. Were you to do so, a million ghosts in olive drab, in brown khaki, in blue and grey, would rise from their white crosses, thundering those magic words: Duty, honor, country.

This does not mean that you are warmongers. On the contrary, the soldier above all other people prays for peace, for he must suffer and bear the deepest wounds and scars of war. But always in our ears ring the ominous words of Plato, that wisest of all philosophers: "Only the dead have seen the end of war."

The shadows are lengthening for me. The twilight is here. My days of old have vanished—tone and tint. They have gone glimmering through the dreams of things that were. Their memory is one of wondrous beauty, watered by tears and coaxed and caressed by the smiles of yesterday. I listen vainly, but with thirsty ear, for the witching melody of faint bugles blowing reveille, of far drums beating the long roll.

In my dreams I hear again the crash of guns, the rattle of musketry, the strange, mournful mutter of the battlefield. But in the evening of my memory always I come back to West Point. Always there re-echoes and re-echoes: Duty, honor, country.

Today marks my final roll call with you. But I want you to know that, when I cross the river, my last conscious thoughts will be of the corps, and the corps, and the corps.

I bid you farewell.

The MacArthur I Know

George C. Kenney

In the midst of the Truman-MacArthur controversy General Kenney, Mac-Arthur's innovative air commander in the Southwest Pacific, published a glowing tribute to his former boss. Needless to say, not everyone associated with MacArthur agreed with Kenney's appraisal.

Like most great men who have left their mark on the pages of History and who have had to reach their goals against heavy odds, MacArthur is a controversial figure. There are those who worship him and those who dislike him intensely. He has received extravagant praise and has been just as extravagantly censured. He has been awarded every decoration of his country for bravery—and christened "Dougout Doug."

A brilliant character, with a superb command of English and a gift for expressing himself, he is an interesting man to listen to for five minutes or five hours, and MacArthur can keep you interested that long. If he is planning something or speculating about some future move, he thinks best on his feet, pacing back and forth across the room. When he talks about something that has already taken place, he relaxes in a chair while he talks, pausing only to light his pipe, which is almost as much a part of him as his uniform. He has an astounding knowledge of ancient, modern, and current history, but it never obscures the present. While he can discuss the campaigns of Genghis Khan, Napoleon, or Mao Tse-tung with equal facility, his knowledge of the current situation in every part of the globe shows that, while he knows the past, he is thinking and living in the present. His analysis of what the future holds may not always prove to be correct in all its details, but the percentage of his predictions that have come true is surprisingly high. If we don't use them as guides for future action, we should at least weigh them carefully before discarding them.

MacArthur has always had definite ideas of what he should or should not do under any circumstances. He will fight as a matter of principle whenever he feels that his rights are being infringed. When he believes that he is right he will argue long and eloquently in defense of his action or decision. At such times he may become quite impatient with anyone who opposes him. This trait, of course, intensifies the constant controversy about the man. When he wins the argument his friends give him credit for persevering on a matter of principle. When he loses his critics accuse him of being stubborn or obstinate. His reputation for insisting on his rights, and incidentally for winning most of his arguments, started almost at the beginning of his Army career. During his second year at West Point, Cadet Douglas MacArthur had some trouble with his eyes and spent considerable time in the hospital. As a consequence he missed a few of the weekly mathematics tests. One afternoon, as he came back to his room from the hospital, he saw on the bulletin board a notice that several of the class "goats," or students whose records in mathematics were below par, were to take a special examination the next morning at nine o'clock. MacArthur's name was on the list.

He announced to his roommate that he was going to see the mathematics professor and have his name taken off the list.

"But you can't do that," said his fellow cadet. "You haven't permission to see the professor and besides it's an order. You can't argue about an order."

"I'm going to get my name off that list," replied MacArthur.

He put on his best uniform and called on the mathematics professor to protest against being required to take the test. He claimed that his marks had been so high on the exams that he had already taken that he had a passing average for the course and therefore should not be included with the goats. He considered it an insult to have his name on that list. It had nothing to do with any desire on his part to shirk work or any fear that he might not get a passing mark. It was the principle of the thing and he wanted to be excused from taking the examination.

The professor reminded him that he had not given him permission to see him, that he was not on very firm ground challenging a direct order, and that furthermore there was a rule that required a student to take a certain number of these tests. MacArthur replied that he had never heard of any such rule. If he had known of its existence he could have turned in a piece of paper with nothing on it except his name, accepted a zero for that particular test, and still have passed the course. He concluded,

"Sir, I will not take the test," saluted, and walked out of the professor's office.

He returned and told his roommate what had happened. The latter remonstrated with him most of that evening, but Douglas MacArthur was adamant. "I will not take that test," he reiterated. "I know it is an order, but it is an unreasonable one. I have not failed my mathematics course and I will not have my name listed with those who have failed. Orders can be rescinded and if my name is not removed from that list by nine o'clock tomorrow morning, I will resign."

"But what will your father say?" protested his roommate.

"He will be terribly disappointed," said Douglas, "but I believe he will see my attitude in the matter and approve my action."

He turned in and slept for eight solid hours. His roommate worried about the situation all night and hardly closed his eyes. About ten minutes of nine the next morning, an orderly came into the room with a notice that the name of Cadet Douglas MacArthur had been removed from the list.

One of his great characteristics, however, is his willingness to admit his mistakes. He has made some, as anyone will who does things. He can see both sides of an argument and when events show that things have not worked out as he expected they would, he surprises you with his ready frankness in saying, "Yes, I was wrong."

He has no regular schedule of staff meetings. When he wants to discuss a matter with his staff he sends for them. On such occasions he outlines the problem and listens carefully to the arguments and presentations of each member of his staff who has anything to say. He asks many questions to draw out opinions and wants to know a lot of details. Contrary to what most people think, he does not like to have people "yes" him. He does not like people who say what they think he would like to hear. When he has once rendered the decision, he promptly dismisses the subject from his mind and lets his subordinates carry it out.

His forecasts on coming events have been generally excellent, but he has been wrong too.

He foresaw the rise of Germany and that her aggressions were to bring another World War. From the very beginning of Hitler's invasion of Russia, he was almost the only military man I know of who thought that the Russians would be able to hold out. He was quite critical of the North African campaign of 1942, as he believed that Spain would be persuaded by Germany to enter the war and our forces would suffer a colossal disaster. Spain did not join Hitler, but there is little question that, if she had, MacArthur's forebodings would have been justified.

He underestimated Japan in 1941—according to John Hersey who interviewed him in May of that year. In his *Men on Bataan*, Hersey says MacArthur told him that, if Japan started a war in the Pacific, the American, British, and Dutch forces already there could handle her. He predicted that the Jap navy would be destroyed or bottled up. He believed that the long war in China had cut down the Japanese effectiveness and burned out Japan's resources. He estimated that about one half of the Japanese army had become reduced from first-class to third-class troops.

None of our responsible leaders in either the Army or the Navy, including MacArthur, foresaw the disaster at Pearl Harbor which, in a few minutes on December 7, 1941, eliminated the United States Pacific Fleet sufficiently to make possible the quick conquest by Japan of Hong Kong, Singapore, the Dutch East Indies, and the Philippines.

When it came to fighting, however, MacArthur's defense of the Philippines was the one creditable episode of the whole first five months of the war in the Pacific. The battle of Luzon stands out like a beacon of hope in comparison with the incredible debacle at Singapore, the easy fall of the Dutch East Indies, and the confusion in Washington. No wonder MacArthur proudly named his airplane Bataan. The pages of our military history contain few stories more dramatic, more stirring, more heroic than the epic of Bataan. It is a story that America and the Philippines can be proud of for all time.

One day in Hollandia in September 1944, just a month before he returned to the Philippines, MacArthur said that those islands were the key to victory in the Pacific War. He believed that the Japs realized that their loss would cut them off from the essential raw materials in the Netherlands East Indies and that when we retook the Philippines the Nips would sue for peace. The General qualified his forecast with one reservation. Japan would not quit before Germany—their pride would not let their allies have a chance of accusing the Japs of letting them down. MacArthur also said that the break would come from Tokio, not from the Japanese army.

When I asked how long it would take to reconquer the Philippines, he replied, "Six weeks after I land in Luzon I'll have Manila and in eight months the Philippines will be cleared."

We landed in Luzon on January 9, 1945. On February 5 we entered Manila and had cleared the Japs out of the city by the 25th. When the Emperor threw in the sponge on August 14, 1945, it was just in time to save the last remnants of Yamashita's forces from surrender or annihilation.

When I was in Washington in March 1945, I repeated MacArthur's ideas, but everyone I talked to in the War Department and even among the Air crowd disagreed. The consensus was that Japan would hold out for possibly another two years. They seemed sure that we would have to invade China to get rid of the Japanese army there and that the war would finally end only when we destroyed them in Japan itself, where the Nips would go down in a wild orgy of killing and mass suicide. It was that belief more than anything else that was responsible for the insistence upon the entry of Russia into the war to take care of the Japs in Manchuria. The belief that Japan would resist to the end also had a lot to do with the decision to drop atomic bombs on Japanese cities to try to bring them to terms. In the meantime, however, the Japanese had been putting out peace feelers for several months before Hiroshima. They were trying to get the Russians to act as intermediaries to discuss the terms under which hostilities would cease. The Russians, however, would have nothing to do with them. They were already committed to a declaration of war against Japan as soon as Stalin could transfer his troops and supplies from Europe to the Manchurian border. It was quite evident from a study of the context of the messages from Tokio to their ambassador in Moscow that the Japanese realized further resistance was futile and were willing to grant almost any concessions to halt the war, providing the Emperor remained as the spiritual head of the country.

While the dropping of the two atomic bombs may have hurried the Japanese decision to quit, there is little doubt that MacArthur was right in July when he told me that the projected Operation Olympic—to invade Japan on November 1, 1945—would never take place. At that time he was confident that the capitulation would come by September 1 at the latest and perhaps even sooner. He made that prediction two weeks before we learned that the atomic bomb would be used against the Japanese cities.

Some day, when the complete history of his campaigns from New Guinea to Luzon is written and analyzed, the world will realize the magnitude of the tasks confronting him, the paucity of men and resources that he had to work with, and the true genius of the man who gained that unbroken string of victories with an astoundingly low casualty list. In three years of vicious fighting against a desperate and determined enemy, and combatting the heat and diseases of the tropical jungles, the war in the South West Pacific Area cost us only 20,000 of the 325,000 American lives expended in World War II. MacArthur drives hard but he precedes those drives by careful planning that saves lives.

Confronted with the situation facing him when he arrived in Australia from Corregidor in March 1942, MacArthur without fear of criticism might have decided to remain on the defensive until sufficient forces could be made available to start his movement back to the Philippines. With insufficient naval forces to insure his supply line to New Guinea, with a vastly outnumbered Air Force, and with the apprehension of the people of Australia in regard to invasion of that continent by the enemy, a lesser general might even have considered the abandonment of Port Moresby, his only base in New Guinea.

His first announcement was characteristic of the man. He would defend Australia in New Guinea. He would drive the enemy back. He ordered the Port Moresby harbor facilities extended, more airdromes built in that area, roads constructed, and campsites laid out. It would be his main base of operations. Troops were sent to Milne Bay to hold the eastern flank of his New Guinea position and there, too, engineers were ordered to build more airdromes, more docks, more base facilities. As Australian troops were returned from the Middle East he moved them to New Guinea with instructions to hurl back the enemy then driving on Port Moresby over the Kokoda Trail from Buna and Gona on the north coast.

His next move was characterized by a boldness and audacity coupled with adaptability and flexibility of purpose that was evidenced throughout all his Pacific campaigns and which stamp him as one of the great military captains of all time. Here was no narrow concept of rule-book warfare rigidly based on the past. Here was the vision of a clear thinking, open-minded leader who correctly estimated his capabilities and those of the enemy, made his decision, and had the courage to carry it through to victory.

Lacking naval forces and amphibious equipment to dislodge the Japanese from the Buna-Gona area, he made the first air envelopment in history. There was no precedent for his seizure by air of landing areas within a few mils of the enemy positions. There was nothing in the books that advocated or even suggested the flying of two divisions of infantry with their light artillery across the Owen Stanleys and landing them on the flank and in rear of the enemy position. To depend upon air supply for food, ammunition, evacuation, replacements, and even for the installation of a field hospital during the major portion of the campaign would have been and actually was considered foolhardy by many officers who considered themselves military experts. His own staff did not approve of the operation and at one time became so worried about the ability of the Air Force to supply the troops in combat that they actually recommended withdrawal.

It has been called a MacArthur gamble. It was not a gamble at all. MacArthur had the winning hand. If he played it properly, he would win. It would take a skilled player, of course, but MacArthur was that player. He didn't have all the cards, by any means, but under his leadership and impelled by his inspiration, soldier, sailor, and airman performed prodigies of valor and gained the victory over a brave and tenacious enemy, while enduring hardships as great as ever have confronted any military force in the history of warfare. That spirit and leadership carried his forces along the long road back to the Philippines and placed him finally in Tokio as Supreme Commander of the Allied Powers.

In the case of Korea, when they are written, the histories will, I believe, add still more to the luster of MacArthur's reputation as a military leader. There are few withdrawals by green troops under attack by a well-disciplined, well-equipped, hard-driving enemy that have been executed more skillfully, with as low losses to themselves and as heavy losses by the enemy, as MacArthur's withdrawal to the Pusan beachhead. There his forces took a terrible toll of the North Koreans for over a month. When he sensed that his opponent had been sufficiently weakened, his landing at Inchon was made and the end of the Korean war was in sight, unless Mao Tse-tung or the Russians intervened. That intervention cost MacArthur a quick victory, but it did not dim his reputation as a general to any fair-minded student of military operations. What course the future will take in Korea, no one can forecast; but, in any event, we were fortunate to have had a commander of the ability of Douglas MacArthur on the spot when the Reds crossed the 38th parallel on June 25, 1950.

As a general thing MacArthur's publicity has not been good. This has not been his fault, unless he should be blamed for the mistakes of his public-relations officers and censors. He has had several of them, none of whom were experts at their trade, but they did him a lot of harm.

His public-relations officers invariably adored MacArthur almost to the point of idolatry. To them unless a news release painted the General with a halo and seated him on the highest pedestal in the universe, it should be killed. No news except favorable news, reflecting complete credit on an infallible MacArthur, had much chance of getting by the censors. They seemed to believe that they had a sacred mission, which was to "sell" the General to the world, and they didn't trust the newspapermen to interpret MacArthur properly. They never seemed to realize that they didn't have to sell Douglas MacArthur. The General was a brilliant, colorful, likable personality, who would sell himself much better without any help. He was not a demigod, he was human.

A military censor has a difficult task. He must see that military secrecy is not violated. One word may inadvertently give the enemy a clue to some future operation. An interview from a single disgruntled soldier may lead the people back home to believe that the morale of the whole army has gone when actually it is excellent. There are hundreds of difficult decisions that have to be made that call for tact, diplomacy, and the wisdom of Solomon. None of his public-relations officers had all of these characteristics. Sometimes they tended to be arrogant and almost insulting to the representatives of the press, of whom they did not have a high opinion.

The General got the blame, especially back home, and the newspaper reaction too often was far from favorable. At one time he was criticized "for applying dictatorial powers to the world's press." Every one of his public-relations officers worked hard for his commander and believed that what he was doing was for MacArthur's best interests; but practically every one of the newspapermen who were accredited to the South West Pacific had no use for MacArthur's public-relations department during the war and have not changed their minds since.

MacArthur's loyalty to those who are loyal to him and work for him is a wonderful trait. It marks the leader whose men trust him and follow him. In MacArthur's case it will even tolerate a degree of inefficiency. He cannot hurt a loyal friend. I believe that is why he kept some people around, in spite of the fact that they were largely responsible for the bad press that he had during World War II.

At seventy-one, MacArthur is still tall, erect, graceful, and a handsome figure of a man. His step is firm. His eyes are clear and alert. His face and hands are without wrinkles. His dress is meticulous. He has the vigor and stamina of a man at least ten years younger than the records show him to be. His hair is thin on the top of his head, but there is no gray in it. I have often heard people say that he dyes it. I don't know where they got their information and it wouldn't disturb me in the least if it were true. To me it would be in the same class with wearing a wig or toupee.

However, the story does not agree with the facts as I know them from over three years' association with MacArthur during the war and several visits to the Far East since.

One day in New Guinea I was talking to the General while he was taking a shower. He had just had a haircut and was washing his head. The dark hair looked blacker than ever. As a joke, I said:

"General, I wish you would tell me what brand of hair dye you use. My hair is beginning to show quite a bit of gray."

He laughed and, reaching for the soap, vigorously lathered his head and massaged the soap into his hair for a couple of minutes. He then rinsed it off, stepped out of the shower, and dried his head with more vigorous rubbing with the towel which he then held out for my inspection.

"It is good at that," he said. "See, it doesn't even stain the towel, but I'll not tell you what it is."

The last time I saw him was in October 1950. I looked at his still black hair and repeated the old remark. He laughed as usual at my pretended curiosity. It is a standing joke between us.

He has tremendous personal charm that captivates anyone he likes or wishes to impress. His conversation is vivid and colorful as well as interesting, and the way that he puts emphasis and feeling into what he says makes you remember the man, but you also retain the message that he is trying to put across to you. He is sentimental, emotional, and deeply religious. He is innately shy and retiring. While at ease with close friends, he does not enjoy the mob scenes which so many of our modern cocktail and dinner parties seem to have turned into. He is not a thick-skinned individual who laughs off criticism, regardless of whether it is just or not. If he feels that he does not deserve it, he is extremely sensitive to criticism, although he can take it and ignore it when he has a job to do.

MacArthur is a positive individual. There is nothing vacillating about him. He believes in himself, his destiny, and in his place in history. While he will freely admit his mistakes after they have happened, he is sure that his decisions are correct at the time he makes them.

He is inordinately proud of his distinguished father and the wonderful record that General Arthur MacArthur had as a soldier and as an administrator in the Philippines, where his name is revered along with that of General Douglas MacArthur. I believe that he is also proud of the fact that his record as a soldier and an administrator has caught up with that of his father. General Arthur MacArthur was the first military governor of the Philippines and first introduced *habeas corpus* in that country. General Douglas MacArthur held a similar position in Japan for five and a half years and to him is due the introduction of *habeas corpus* to the Japanese people. However, if you suggested to him that his career has surpassed that of General Arthur MacArthur, he would quite sincerely argue the point with you.

His devotion to his mother is one of MacArthur's remarkable traits. When he was Army Chief of Staff in Washington from 1931 to 1935, after lunch before returning to his office, he invariably spent an hour or so with her discussing his problems and talking over with her what he intended to do about them. Putting his thoughts into words seemed to fix them in his mind in their proper orderly sequence so that later on at a staff conference they would appear as a smooth and finished presentation that was the envy of his listeners. These daily discussions with his mother as confidant were of tremendous help to MacArthur. They had no secrets from each other. Both had strong convictions, they never compromised on matters of principle, and both had the courage to fight for what they believed in. Each had strong likes and dislikes, but in spite of the fact that they were both exceedingly positive characters, MacArthur and his mother were seldom on opposite sides of an argument.

When in 1919 he was sent to West Point as Superintendent, his mother accompanied him and presided as hostess at the Commandant's quarters. There she took care of her son, but she looked after the interests of the cadets too. It wasn't long before she was a real favorite with all of them. There is a story of two "plebes," or first-year men, who were sent out for ice cream by some upperclassmen. On the way back they passed by the Commandant's House, MacArthur, who happened to be walking across the lawn as they approached, engaged them in conversation. After several minutes had elapsed, the General still showed no sign of terminating the discussion. Suddenly Mrs. MacArthur called from a window upstairs, "Douglas, you must stop talking to those boys and let them go. Don't you see that their ice cream is beginning to melt?"

MacArthur smiled and said, "I guess you'd better hurry along." For the first time he had noticed that, from the looks of the bottoms of the paper bags the lads were carrying, his mother was undoubtedly right. They exchanged salutes and the two cadets hurried off with their oversoft ice cream, but with another story to tell about their Commandant and his vivacious mother.

When he was offered the job of military adviser to the Philippine Government in 1935, MacArthur asked his mother, whose health had not been good for some time, to go with him to the Far East and said that otherwise he would not take the position. She said of course she would go and MacArthur accepted President Quezon's offer.

The General didn't know it and his mother never mentioned it to him, but she had already been told by her doctor that she would be signing her own death sentence if she went to the Philippines to live. Her devotion to her son was only matched by his adoration of his mother. Mrs. Arthur MacArthur accompanied Douglas to Manila that summer and remained with him until her death at the age of eighty-two in December 1935.

Every once in a while, someone used to ask me when MacArthur was coming back to the United States. I asked him that question in July 1946, when I saw him in Manila at the inauguration of Roxas as the first president of the Republic of the Philippines. MacArthur had been given a tremendous ovation that day by the Filipinos and I was speculating on the number of tons of ticker tape that New York would have to clean up if MacArthur should return and receive the keys to that city.

He smiled and said, "When I have finished here, or they fire me. This is my last job for my country." His pride would never let him ask to be relieved from an unfinished job. He had finished everything he ever started and would not step out of character now.

I asked him what he was going to do when he did come home.

"I expect to settle down in Milwaukee," he replied, "and on the way to the house I'm going to stop in at a furniture store and buy the biggest red rocker in the shop. I'll set it up on the porch and alongside it put a good-sized pile of stones. Then I'll rock."

"What are the stones for?" I asked expectantly. His eyes twinkled.

"They are to throw at anyone who comes around talking politics," he replied.

I don't believe that MacArthur was ever really interested in running for any public office, even for the presidency.

I remember one evening in early 1944 with Jean MacArthur and the General in their hotel apartment in Brisbane. At one stage in the conversation we got on the subject of the political situation in the United States. I had heard a lot of conversation among members of his staff to the effect that MacArthur would not only be a candidate but would sweep the country. This was the first time that the General and I had even mentioned politics. I didn't think anyone could defeat Roosevelt while the war was going on and I hoped that MacArthur wouldn't listen to the politicians in or out of the service who might try to persuade him to throw his hat in the ring. In the first place I suspected that most of them wanted to ride his coattails for their own interests more than his.

I remarked that back home people seemed to be doing a lot of speculating about him as a candidate for the presidency in the coming election. I added that I hoped he would keep out of the race. Some day, when we entered Tokio, I wanted to ride down the main street with him instead of wondering what had happened to the man who had lost to Roosevelt in 1944.

He smiled and said, "Don't worry, I have no desire to get mixed up in politics. The first mission that I want to carry out is to liberate the Philippines and fulfill America's pledge to that people. Then I want to defeat Japan."

I probably registered relief. I believe Jean did too. Regardless of all the statements that have appeared to the effect that MacArthur wanted to run for the presidency in 1944, I am convinced that his statement to me that evening was sincere. He was a soldier with a soldier's mission and he wanted to carry it out.

In 1948 there was much more talk about MacArthur as a candidate on the Republican ticket. For a while, a number of his followers tried to start the ball rolling with the hope that a landslide would develop by the time the convention was held that summer in Philadelphia. Some newspapers came out strongly for him and "MacArthur for President" clubs sprang up all over the country. The campaign collapsed, however, as he refused to come home to put himself back of the effort and—beyond a message which said that he would accept the nomination if the country wanted him—refused to issue anything else even remotely resembling a campaign statement. When the boom did not develop he asked his supporters to withdraw his name from consideration. if there had been a real national demand for him to take the job, I believe he would have accepted it, just as he has accepted other duties as a matter of service to his country. MacArthur, above all, is an American, passionately fond of America, its heritage of freedom, its ideals, and its principles. He believes sincerely in democracy as defined by Abraham Lincoln, "government of the people, by the people, for the people," but he would never stump the country and campaign for votes as any presidential candidate must do if he expects to get elected.

MacArthur's headquarters in Japan was in the Dai Ichi Building, a modern office building overlooking the moat around the Emperor's palace. His office on the sixth floor was small and simply decorated. A picture of Lincoln was there. It was the same picture that had been on the wall of every one of MacArthur's offices from Australia to Japan. With it was this quotation attributed to Lincoln while he was President: *"If I were to try to read, much less answer, all the attacks made on me, this shop might as well be closed for any other business. I do the very best I know how, the very best I can, and I mean to keep doing so until the end. If the end brings me out all right, what is said against me won't amount to anything. If the end brings me out wrong, ten angels swearing I was right would make no difference."*

The office had no telephone. MacArthur did not use one. His aide in an outer office took all calls and made appointments after consultation with his commander. The General had no secretary. He read all his own mail. He seldom dictated replies to the mass of correspondence he received. Some of the letters he took care of himself, preparing the answers in longhand for the typist. Others he turned over to his aide who prepared the letters for his signature.

He lived in the American Embassy in Tokio. It is a handsome, well-built, attractive house with beautiful gardens and shrubbery. He lived quite simply, although his hours were almost as irregular as they were during the war. He read a lot at home, sometimes until quite late at night, but he got enough sleep, ate moderately, and in general took good care of himself. Jean, quite skillfully and unobtrusively, helped out along that line. The General went to no parties, paid no calls, and saw no outsiders socially. Once in a great while, he would have some visitors in for dinner at home in the evening but most of the time luncheon was reserved for such occasions. That meal began about one-thirty, and with eating and conversation, lasted about two hours. At that point the General, who never worries about what time it is, got a signal from Jean that it was time for his afternoon nap, which he takes religiously, war or no war. That signal terminated the luncheon and MacArthur said goodbye to his guests and retired. He has the gift of being able to relax and fall asleep almost instantly when his head touches the pillow. Around five o'clock he is back in the office, refreshed and ready for another half day's work.

He and his wife are both Episcopalians, but while MacArthur is profoundly religious, in Japan Jean and his son Arthur did the churchgoing for the family. MacArthur's schedule operated seven days a week. Sunday was just another day as far as his office hours were concerned.

In the evening he liked to relax at a movie in the Embassy. He and his son Arthur both like Westerns.

Jean MacArthur, dark-haired, animated, neat, and pretty, a charming hostess, was extremely popular with the Japanese women and the American wives alike. The word petite describes her better than any other description I can give. She is just over five feet and weighs about a hundred pounds.

She neither asked for nor received any privileges over the other American women in Tokio. She stood in line and awaited her turn at the Army stores and shopping centers like everyone else. When talking about MacArthur she refers to him as "the General" and she calls him "General" when they are together. An exceedingly nice person is Jean MacArthur.

The boy Arthur, a handsome, alert, attractive lad of thirteen, looks a lot like Jean but from all present indications will have the tall, graceful figure of his father when he grows up. He has lived in Manila, where he was born in February 1938, on Corregidor for a short time during the siege of that fortress in early 1942, in Melbourne and Brisbane, Australia, and in Tokio, but until this year he had never seen the United States. About four and one half years of his life have been spent in the Philippines, three in Australia, and five and one half years in Japan. He has been educated so far by tutors and is well abreast the level of youngsters of his age, but both his father and mother for some time have wanted to come home so that Arthur's education and his environment would be more like that of the average American boy. This, however, could only be when MacArthur himself came back. The three members of the family are agreed on this one subject above all others—they will not be separated.

To say that he is "the apple of his father's eye" is an understatement. the only break in MacArthur's work schedule since Arthur was born came a few years ago when the boy broke his arm while skating. It was a simple fracture with no complications, but during the whole time his son was in the hospital the General paid a daily visit to see how Arthur was getting along. The hospital staff liked the youngster and liked his famous father, but they were glad when the boy could be sent home. Doctors, nurses, and patients all found it difficult to maintain routine procedures when at any time during the day they were liable to have as a visitor five-star General of the Army Douglas MacArthur, Supreme Commander of the Allied Powers in Japan.

Arthur likes to read and does quite a lot of it. He is especially interested in history. Music attracts him enough so that the piano competes with his three dogs for his attention, although so far the dogs are well ahead. While in Japan he had a few playmates from the American officers' families stationed in Tokio who used to join him playing the usual boys' games around the spacious Embassy grounds. As an only child, under the circumstances in which he has lived, one might expect him to be a bit spoiled, but his parents have taken care of that angle remarkably well. Arthur MacArthur is just another normal, healthy, attractive American boy.

MacArthur takes an occasional glass of wine, but except for that his alcoholic intake is practically zero. He likes good cigars after dinner but during the rest of the day he smokes a pipe. The way he lives agrees with him so well that it is easy to believe that Douglas MacArthur will be available to serve his country for many more years to come.

Douglas MacArthur has worn the uniform of his country continuously, on active duty, for fifty-two years—longer than most of his critics have been alive. Thirty-three of those years he has been a general officer. Since December 1, 1941, until he left Japan in April 1951, he had worked seven days a week without a single day's vacation.

He was made a temporary brigadier general in 1918 because General Pershing considered him to be a superior leader. After World War I, MacArthur did not go back to his permanent rank as did many others. His record was too brilliant to be ignored. He was made a permanent brigadier general and assigned as Superintendent at West Point in 1919. In 1925 he was made a major general and, by 1930, at fifty, he donned the four stars of a full general and became Chief of Staff of the United States Army.

There was only one reason for his rapid promotion and his assignment to the most important jobs in the Army. He was good.

He was a smart, able, and brilliant leader then, but World War II saw him emerge as one of the great generals of all time. He is a smart, able, and brilliant general today.

But whatever MacArthur is to us, we should remember that we are the ones who have created the man the world knows. When we say that he is a hero and a military genius, in our impulsive way we hoist him to the highest pedestal we can find. When something goes wrong and the search for a scapegoat points the finger at MacArthur, we just as impulsively try to tear him down. He hasn't changed. He is the same MacArthur all the time. We are the ones who have changed.

We seldom think about his own personal reactions to this weathervane treatment. As a normal, rather sensitive human being, he cannot lightly brush aside adulation and condemnation alike. A lesser character would have become a cynic long ago, but some of the shafts of criticism—especially the unjust ones—have found their mark and they have hurt. MacArthur tries and succeeds remarkably well in not showing the hurt, but more and more he tends to rely upon and trust only those people who have proven their loyalty to him. He does not like to remember the occasions when self-seeking fair-weather friends have gained his confidence and later tried to knife him.

Perhaps once in a while we should pause and reflect upon our methods of utilization and our treatment of our preeminent leaders. In normal times we may not feel that we need them, but when emergencies arise, we find to our consternation that the supply of them is limited.

No Substitute for Virility

Douglas MacArthur, Gender, and the Culture of Militarism

Laura A. Belmonte

In an essay prepared for this volume Laura Belmonte, a diplomatic historian at Oklahoma State University, uses gender analysis to examine MacArthur's public and private life.

In the 1956 Evander Childs High School yearbook, my mother listed Douglas MacArthur as her hero. She was far from alone. MacArthur's masterful construction and manipulation of his public image convinced millions of Americans that he exemplified courage, patriotism, and honor. Sympathetic biographers refer to him as "American Caesar," "Man of Destiny," "MacArthur the Magnificent." While other writers have offered less laudatory portraits of MacArthur, all studies share a common thread. They describe a man thoroughly immersed in the culture of the most "masculine" of American institutions, the military. Yet no one has applied gender analysis in examining the private life and public persona of MacArthur.[1]

This essay explores how MacArthur's conception of manhood affected his relationships, career, and policies.[2] It speculates that MacArthur's notions of his masculinity were inextricably linked to his military service. MacArthur presented himself as an aristocratic warrior possessed of stunning bravery, intelligence, and foresight. Unable to realize his ambitions outside of the military, MacArthur was determined to forge a military career that sustained his self-image. He interpreted restrictions on his military ambitions as attacks on his masculinity. Both personally and professionally he surrounded himself with people who accepted his grandiose vision of himself. The military, consequently, became MacArthur's forum for defining his masculinity and his refuge from changing conceptions of gender roles.

Any exploration of MacArthur's private life is challenging. Most of his personal papers were destroyed during the Second World War.

Although scores of biographers have documented MacArthur's life, most focus on his military prowess, administrative capabilities, and leadership skills.[3] MacArthur and his close associates offer error-laden treatises that perpetuate the myth of MacArthur as a flawless hero.[4] By carefully drawing on these sources, however, one can construct a narrative of the general's private relationships, conception of self, and policies on gender-related issues.

No portrait of MacArthur is complete without an analysis of his family relationships. The MacArthur family prided itself on its moral ideals and reputation. Douglas's father, Arthur MacArthur Jr., served courageously in the Civil War. After recovering from his war injuries and making a brief foray into law, Arthur enlisted in the regular army as a second lieutenant. He quickly reached the rank of captain, but twenty-three years passed before he received another promotion. In rapidly industrializing America, professional soldiers received little remuneration or respect for their services. Arthur remained mired in marginal military assignments ranging from supervising Reconstruction in Louisiana to patrolling Native Americans along the western frontier.

In 1875 he married Mary "Pinkie" Pinkney Hardy. From a wealthy Virginia family, Mary shared her husband's aristocratic ethical code. The MacArthurs had three sons: Arthur II, Malcolm, and Douglas, born in 1876, 1878, and 1880, respectively. For over a decade the family lived on isolated military posts. The boys adored the rugged life of the West. They ran, hunted, and fished. They loved the soldiers' tales of martial adventures. Pinkie, however, chafed at the austere, lonely conditions. After Malcolm's death from measles at the age of five she focused her attentions on tutoring Arthur II and Douglas in basic rudiments and moral principles. "We were taught to do what was right," Douglas later recalled, "no matter what the personal sacrifice might be. Our country was always to come first. Two things we must never do. Never lie, never tattle."[5]

Despite Pinkie's dedication Douglas was an unmotivated student. When the family moved to Fort Leavenworth in 1886 he performed poorly at the post school and found formal education stifling. After the family moved to Washington DC in 1889 Douglas grew even more depressed. Detached from a military environment for the first time Douglas found the glitz of Washington politics and society a poor substitute for the excitement of the frontier. When his father was reassigned to Fort Sam Houston in 1893 Douglas was thrilled.

In Texas Douglas began to mature. At age 13 he entered the Texas Military Academy and dramatically improved his grades. He played baseball, football, and tennis. His sense of spirituality burgeoned. Although he dated a variety of young girls, the relationships were brief and casual. For years afterward romance remained a low priority for Douglas. West Point, not marriage, was his ultimate aspiration.[6]

After he graduated in June 1897 the MacArthurs devoted themselves to getting Douglas into the U.S. Military Academy. His influential grandfather and father convinced several prominent politicians, generals, and clergymen to recommend him for a presidential appointment. But most of the referees knew little about Douglas and instead extolled his father. Sen. Redfield Proctor (R-VT), for example, argued: "I know of no officer who better deserves the privilege of having his son educated at West Point than MacArthur." Neither Grover Cleveland nor his successor, William McKinley, responded positively.

In October 1897 Douglas and his mother prepared an alternate plan. When Colonel MacArthur was assigned to St. Paul, Minnesota, Pinkie and Douglas moved to the stylish Pinkerton Hotel in Minneapolis. From there Douglas hoped to attain a congressional appointment from Rep. Theabold Otjen, a close friend of his recently deceased grandfather. With the assistance of two tutors Douglas spent the next eighteen months preparing for the grueling West Point entrance exam. When not studying he received medical treatment for the slight scoliosis which had caused him to fail his first physical examination for admission.

The months spent in Minneapolis shed light on Douglas's relationship with Pinkie. With Colonel MacArthur absent, Douglas's mother focused all of her attentions on her son. When Douglas suffered from insomnia and nausea, she urged him to persevere. "Doug," she said, "you'll win if you don't lose your nerve. You must believe in yourself, my son, or no one else will believe in you. Be self-confident, self-reliant, and even if you don't make it, you will know you have done your best. Now, go to it." In June 1898 their joint efforts paid off in Douglas's receipt of a congressional appointment. Throughout her life Pinkie served as Douglas's primary source of encouragement to the detriment of his forging intimate bonds with women his own age. He, however, appears to have needed Pinkie as much as she needed him. Even if he worried about being called a "mama's boy," Douglas remained devoted to his mother.[7]

While Pinkie and Douglas toiled in Minneapolis, Colonel MacArthur's life dramatically changed. When the United States began war with Spain in April 1898, Arthur was promoted to brigadier general of volunteers. He gained national renown for his victories over Spanish forces in the Philippines. General MacArthur oversaw the occupation of Manila and was named military governor of the Philippines in May 1900. After a bloody guerilla war erupted between American troops and Filipino rebels, General MacArthur began to clash bitterly with William Howard Taft, the civilian appointed by Pres. William McKinley to oversee the pacification program.

In July 1901 the War Department recalled MacArthur to the United States. Taft's efforts to build coalitions with local elites successfully defused the rebels. As the guerilla war subsided, disturbing allegations about the treatment of Filipinos by American soldiers prompted a congressional inquiry. Although the hearings did not implicate him, Arthur MacArthur viewed his transfer as an unjust punishment for his outspokenness. For the remainder of his life he told Douglas that truly brave soldiers sometimes questioned the decisions of their superiors.[8]

General MacArthur's reputation complicated Douglas's years at West Point. While the MacArthur name attracted the attention of Academy administrators it also drew the enmity of upperclassmen. Throughout their plebe year Douglas MacArthur and Ulysses S. Grant III endured brutal hazing. Viewed as an essential part of the transition from boyhood to manhood, hazing represented boys' rejection of the maternal value of restraint in favor of manly independence. When the cadre learned that the mothers of Ulysses and Douglas resided in Craney's Hotel near the West Point campus, they singled them out for even more abuse. No one with such a doting mother, they reasoned, could be a real man.

Douglas had additional strikes against him. While leading troops in the Philippines General MacArthur received a great deal of media coverage. Upperclassmen forced Douglas to recite his father's military record and endure calisthenics until the onset of convulsions. Douglas's tremendous good looks were another disadvantage. Cadets assumed that he was a dandy as well as a mama's boy. Nonetheless, Douglas survived these travails and earned the respect of many cadets.

The following year the hazing-induced death of a plebe prompted a congressional inquiry that placed Douglas in a moral quandary. Deeply imbued with an ethos of duty and honor, he was forced to choose between naming his tormentors or facing possible expulsion from West Point. Plagued by the nausea he experienced at stressful times, Douglas welcomed a poem from Pinkie. Although the origin of the poem is unknown, it does provide insight into their relationship:

> Do you know that your soul is of my soul such a part
> That you seem to be fiber and core of my heart?
> None other can pain me as you, son, can do;
> None other can please me or praise me as you.
> Remember the world will be quick with its blame
> If shadow or shame ever darken your name.
> Like mother, like son, is saying so true
> The world will judge largely of mother by you.
> Be this then your task, if task it shall be
> To force this proud world to do homage to me
> Be sure it will say, when its verdict you've won
> She reaps as she sowed: "This man is her son!"

Its dubious literary merits notwithstanding, the poem inspired Douglas to cooperate with the investigators. When Douglas recalled this incident in his 1964 memoirs he claimed to have concealed the names of the hazers. He may have conveniently forgotten his exposure of his persecutors, but he always remembered his mother's code of honor.[9]

Comforted by daily visits with Pinkie, Douglas performed brilliantly at West Point. For three of his four years Douglas ranked first in his class. He reached the top of the cadet military ranks and played sports. Classmates noted his admiration for his father and determination not to disappoint General MacArthur. They also stopped teasing him about his mother. Offered few social outlets at the Academy, cadets relished her hospitality at Craney's Hotel. They especially appreciated her services as a lookout during their clandestine romantic encounters in the hotel's parlor. Douglas continued his pattern of short, casual romances, but rumors about his love life abounded. When later asked if he had been engaged to eight different women he retorted, "I do not remember being so heavily engaged by the enemy."[10]

After Douglas graduated in 1903 he was assigned to the Philippines. His engineering duties enabled him to immerse himself in the culture and beauty of the islands. He got a taste of adventure after killing two bandits who attacked his survey team. While in Manila Douglas befriended two promising Filipino politicians, Manuel Quezon and Sergio Osmeña. Later in his career the pair became vital allies to MacArthur's efforts in Asia. Douglas even formed an intimate relationship with a woman named Florence Adams. But his first opportunity to experience life away from his parents was brief. In October 1904 a persistent case of malaria forced his return to the Untied States.

While Douglas worked in the Philippines General MacArthur escaped the frustrations of his battle with Secretary of War Taft by attaining a post as a military attaché in Tokyo. Although he arrived too late to observe most of the Russo-Japanese War, General MacArthur received approval for an extensive military survey of China, the Far East, and India. Despite his clashes with Taft, General MacArthur persuaded him to assign Douglas as an aide on the Asian tour. In October 1905 Douglas joined his parents in Tokyo.

For nine months the MacArthurs traipsed from country to country. Savoring the diversity and hospitality of Asia, Douglas considered the trip "the most important factor of preparation in my entire life." He concluded that "the future and, indeed, the very existence of America, were irrevocably entwined with Asia and its island outposts." Although sixteen years passed before he again visited the region, the Far East became an integral element in Douglas's definition of himself as a military authority and a man.[11]

The tour marked the twilight of General MacArthur's career. After returning to the United States he realized that he would never be promoted to army chief of staff. Following Taft's election to the presidency in 1908 Arthur retired. For the remaining three years of his life he railed against the Army's failure to reward him adequately. He died so embittered that his will prohibited a military funeral or interment at Arlington National Cemetery.

Upon returning from Asia in August 1906 Douglas enrolled in the prestigious Engineers School at Washington Barracks DC. But he focused his energies on his extra duties as a White House ceremonial aide. He relished his discussions with Pres. Theodore Roosevelt and other influential people. Not surprisingly, the commandant of the Engineers School reported that Douglas appeared distracted.

His problems in the Engineering Corps continued. In August 1907 Douglas was transferred to Milwaukee, where his parents lived. His supervisor, Maj. William V. Judson, included Douglas in important engineering projects along Lake Michigan and helped him complete the requirements for his Engineering School diploma. But Douglas remained unsatisfied. Expecting the special privileges that the MacArthur name always elicited, he demanded frequent visits to his parents' home and refused assignments outside of Milwaukee. He neglected his duties for months. Nonetheless, the army chief of staff, an old friend of Arthur's, rewarded Douglas with a troop command at Fort Leavenworth, Kansas. Judson was incensed and submitted a harsh evaluation of Douglas's performance. All of Douglas's former superiors received copies of Judson's remarks for comment, but all of them (except the commandant of the Engineering School) praised MacArthur.

Sharing his father's propensity for challenging army superiors, Mac-Arthur vociferously denied Judson's claims. He offered to take a written or oral test of his engineering skills and displayed hyperbolic sensitivity to criticism. "I feel keenly the ineradicable blemish Major Judson has seen fit to place up my military record," he asserted. Ignoring proper channels MacArthur sent his response directly the chief of engineers. MacArthur's arrogance backfired. The chief of engineers upbraided him for disregarding army procedures and warned him about the perils of shirking assigned duties.[12] The army chief of staff, however, did not rescind MacArthur's first troop command.

A failed romantic endeavor may explain some of MacArthur's behavior during this time. His pursuit of Fanniebelle Stuart illustrates MacArthur's difficulties in balancing his intense attachment to his parents, his military ambitions, and his attempts to form intimate relationships with women. After meeting Fannie in Milwaukee Douglas sent her several love poems. The first was a twenty-six-page epic filled with his characteristic flowery prose. Reflecting his attitudes about marriage and the military, the poem described the life of an army wife. When her husband is called to war she begs him not to leave. He explains that he is fighting

For home, and for children, for freedom, for bread
For the house of our God—for the graves of our dead
For leave to exist on the soil of our birth—
For everything manhood holds dearest on earth.

Bowled over by her beloved's honor and patriotism, the wife urges him to "die rather than yield."

Drawing on his childhood memories of Indian wars and his father's war stories, MacArthur describes his poetic soldier's combat against "brown beggars." After recovering from severe injuries, the warrior returns to the front to lead a spectacular charge:

His hoarse voice rang aloft through the roar

Of the musketry poured from the opposite shore;
—"Remember Wisconsin!—remember your wives!
And hold on to your duty, boys!—on—with your lives;'
He turned, and he paused, as he uttered the call
Then reeled in his seat, and fell—pierced by a ball.

The hero dies in his army hospital bed while gazing upon his wife. Not impressed with Douglas's melodrama, Fannie traveled to New York and on to Paris. But MacArthur persisted. He sent other poems describing his pain at her departure and demanded to know why she did not love him. Ignoring his letters Fannie threw herself into a world of fun and parties alien to Douglas MacArthur.

By April 1908 MacArthur's anguish turned to cynicism. He sent a final poem rejecting romantic entanglements. His accompanying letter announced that he was going to Fort Leavenworth only because he and the army could not agree on a more prestigious assignment to Panama or West Point. The story was patently false. He seems to have convinced himself that his military ambitions, not Fannie's rejection, doomed the relationship. It would not be the first time MacArthur used the military to shield his masculinity from romantic rejection.[13]

The incidents with Judson and Fannie behind him, MacArthur flourished at Fort Leavenworth. But Pinkie was unsatisfied. Embittered by the army's treatment of her husband, Pinkie decided that Douglas was wasting his talents in the military. She wrote to railroad magnate Edward H. Harriman whom she had met in Tokyo three years earlier. Stressing Douglas's mathematical, technical, and administrative capabilities, Pinkie asked Harriman to consider hiring him. "Frankly, I would like to see my son filling a place promising more of a future than the Army does," she admitted. She did not know if Douglas would surrender his military career but "maternal solicitude" compelled her to intercede on his behalf.

After investigating Douglas's background Harriman's assistants went to Fort Leavenworth and offered him a position. To their surprise and annoyance MacArthur said he was uninterested. Harriman's aide wrote: "It is evidently a case where the mother wants to get her son out of the army, and not where the son is figuring on getting out himself." Pinkie's response to Douglas's refusal is unknown but it is clear that MacArthur valued the independence the military accorded him enough to disobey his mother's wishes. While Pinkie's love and support encouraged him to succeed, Douglas must have recognized that her incessant demands frequently conflicted with his military obligations. The decision not to abandon the army paid off and MacArthur was promoted to captain in 1911.[14]

He did not, however, maintain his independence from Pinkie for long. In September 1912 the sudden death of his father brought Douglas and his brother to her side. Worried about Pinkie's frail health Douglas asked for a transfer to an urban center with good medical facilities. Impressed by Douglas's maternal loyalty, army chief of staff Leonard Wood asked him to work in his office in Washington DC. MacArthur's request for special consideration did not backfire this time. Instead it catapulted him into the army's most influential circles.[15]

MacArthur's time in Washington was tranquil and productive. He enjoyed frequent visits with his brother's family. Pinkie's health improved. She and Douglas shared a home in a stylish neighborhood. The dashing young captain dated many women, but remained focused on his military career.

International affairs soon gave MacArthur more opportunities to ascend the army ranks. After American troops occupied Vera Cruz, Wood sent MacArthur on a reconnaissance mission behind enemy lines. Determined to solve the troops' transportation problems, MacArthur led a reckless raid in search of railroad engines. They found the locomotives but encountered armed resistance from Mexican rebels and army troops. Although the hostile action could have sparked a war between the United States and Mexico, Wood recommended MacArthur for the Congressional Medal of Honor. But the War Department rejected the nomination and criticized MacArthur's "error of judgment" in ignoring his local commander. Furious, MacArthur fired off a rash and arrogant response. Not only did MacArthur fail to change the committee's decision, he also convinced many officers that he was self-righteous and thin-skinned.

The outbreak of the First World War soon overshadowed the Vera Cruz incident. During the three years of American "neutrality" Douglas received a promotion to major and worked on the national preparedness campaign. His duties as press officer in the new Bureau of Information yielded media contacts that proved valuable for the rest of his life. But he, like all ambitious soldiers, knew that combat was the surest way to reach the military's highest levels. Ironically, MacArthur's willingness to challenge his superiors resulted in his attaining a combat position. He persuaded his skeptical supervisors to deploy a "Rainbow Division" of National Guard units from all fifty states rather than wait for regular army units to finish training. Promoted to full colonel for his ingenuity, MacArthur was given a choice between remaining in the Engineering Corps or transferring to the infantry. With his dreams of battlefield glory MacArthur chose the infantry without hesitation.[16]

The Great War permitted MacArthur to prove his courage and cultivate a heroic image. From October 1917 to April 1919 he enjoyed splendid success. Fighting in eight major engagements, MacArthur won two Distinguished Service Crosses, seven Silver Stars, two Purple Hearts, and several French military honors. In June 1918 he was promoted to brigadier general. Unlike most high officers MacArthur chose to fight at the front lines rather than remain in the safety of command headquarters.

But bravery alone did not bring MacArthur notice. His clashes with John J. Pershing, the commander of the American Expeditionary Forces (AEF), reached U.S. newspapers. MacArthur adopted a distinctive style of dress. He removed the metal band from his cap to give it a rakish appearance. He wore bright mufflers and shiny puttees. Though he was nowhere near a calvary unit, MacArthur carried a riding crop at all times. Other soldiers christened him "the Dude," "the Stick," and "Beau Brummell of the AEF." MacArthur's courage was even more conspicuous than his attire. He refused to wear a gas mask or helmet and went into battle unarmed.[17]

Following the armistice on November 11, 1918, MacArthur spent six months commanding a small occupation force stationed in the Rhineland. He placed his headquarters in an elegant chateau. Although ill much of the time, he gave reporters frequent interviews. The journalist William Allen White recalled that MacArthur had "the grace and charm of a stage hero. . . . I had never before met so vivid, so captivating, so magnetic a man. He was all that John Barrymore and John Drew hoped to be."[18] At long last MacArthur was a hero in the mind of America, not just in his own fantasies.

Yet he faced an uncertain future when he returned to the United States in April 1919. Once again his family connections helped him. Chief of Staff Peyton March, an old comrade of his father's, selected Douglas to be superintendent of West Point. The post not only enabled MacArthur to retain his wartime rank but provided an exciting opportunity to modernize the antiquated curriculum of his beloved alma mater.

MacArthur's reform agenda illustrated his broad notion of the proper role of military officers. MacArthur wanted West Point graduates to be more than narrowly trained combat experts. He envisioned soldiers as military leaders who understood the world and the people around them. He called for more creativity and independent thinking in the classroom. Although his pedagogic reforms drew the ire of the conservative faculty, MacArthur persisted.

MacArthur instituted changes that reflected his aristocratic warrior ideal. Convinced that sports fostered the qualities vital to successful soldiers, MacArthur created an intramural sports program. His formalized the honor code and made it a proud element of the West Point tradition. He curtailed hazing and offered cadets a grossly expanded variety of extracurricular activities. These reforms, MacArthur hoped, would create the type of soldier who embodied his ideals of courage, intelligence, independence, and honor.

Facing peacetime cutbacks and outraged West Point alumni, the army general staff gave superintendent MacArthur little encouragement or financial assistance. Although he lived with Pinkie Douglas grew distant and lonely. Pershing's promotion to chief of staff did little to raise his spirits. In January 1922 Pershing announced that Brig. Gen. Fred Sladen would succeed MacArthur. Irritated by MacArthur's reforms, Pershing ordered him to the Philippines.

Contrary to popular myth, Pershing did not transfer MacArthur because of the latter's engagement to Mrs. Louise Cromwell Brooks, a wealthy divorcee with whom Pershing had been romantically linked.[19]

Louise was an unlikely match for MacArthur. The socialite and mother of two possessed far more romantic experience than her forty-two-year-old fiancé. Louise's powerful personality may have reminded Douglas of a younger version of his mother. However similar, the two women disliked one another instantly. When Louise and Douglas married on February 14, 1922, Pinkie did not attend the ceremony nor did she accompany the newlyweds to Manila. The MacArthurs immersed themselves in Filipino society. After she tired of decorating, flamboyant Louise organized an orphanage and championed animal rights. Relations with her mother-in-law, however, remained strained especially after Pinkie's health declined in 1923. Although he tried to bury himself in his work, MacArthur could not escape familial tensions. In December the unexpected death of his brother from appendicitis increased Douglas's unhappiness. Now the weight of all of his parents' dreams for MacArthur glory rested solely on him. Pinkie wasted little time before lobbying for her remaining child. Despite MacArthur's conviction that Pershing detested him, Pinkie prevailed upon the chief of staff to promote Douglas to major general. Ten days following Pershing's retirement Douglas received his second star. It is unclear whether Pinkie's intervention prompted the promotion.[20]

After returning to America MacArthur commanded the III Corps from 1925 to 1927. He and Louise enjoyed living in the Baltimore area. MacArthur's fame grew when he served on the controversial court marshal of Billy Mitchell. In 1927 Douglas's role as president of the American Olympic Committee provided a perfect forum for his proselytizing on patriotism, sport, and character.

Amidst these successes MacArthur's private life was a disaster. Louise may have had unresolved feelings for an old boyfriend, Col. John G. "Harry" Quekemeyer, whom she dated prior to marrying to MacArthur. She complained about MacArthur's sexual performance, telling her brother that the general was "a buck private in the bedroom." Although MacArthur doted on her children, Louise found him inattentive as a husband. Appalled at his suggestion that they live only on his military salary, Louise begged MacArthur to leave the army and become an investment banker. Upset by her failure to understand his love for the military, Douglas rejected Louise's suggestions. In 1927 the couple separated, and they were divorced two years later.

Although Douglas remained silent about their marital problems, Louise provided plenty of gossip to MacArthur's political enemies. Columnist Drew Pearson detested MacArthur and adored repeating Louise's stories. "Doug didn't think that his penis was for anything except to pee with," Louise claimed, imitating Douglas's potency with a limp forefinger. Whether or not these rumors were true, they embarrassed and hurt MacArthur. He returned to the Philippines and threw himself into building an effective division.[21]

MacArthur restored his sense of masculinity by beginning an affair with a vaudeville star named Isabella Cooper, a nonthreatening Filipina woman. Her biracial background and the thirty-year age difference between them compelled MacArthur to hide their romance. Yet MacArthur clearly cared for her deeply. In November 1930, when President Herbert Hoover offered him the coveted post of army chief of staff that had eluded his father, MacArthur hesitated to return to the United States. Pinkie, who knew nothing about Isabel, told Douglas that Arthur would be ashamed of his temporizing. Chastened by Pinkie's remarks, MacArthur accepted the position.

But MacArthur was determined to keep Isabel. He made intricate arrangements for her to accompany him to Washington DC. He lived with his mother but rented Isabel a lovely apartment. He waited several months before sending for her. During the separation the two exchanged letters which reflect MacArthur's pressing need to have his masculinity validated. Addressing Isabel as "my own darling baby girl," MacArthur signed his notes "Daddy." Perhaps adopting a paternal tone enabled MacArthur to triumph over the insecurities he experienced with more domineering women like Louise and his mother. He also seems to have overcome the Victorian sexual reticence Louise found so off-putting. Douglas wrote Isabel of the powerful lust that sent him "groping, blindly in the dark" for "my own true little fellah."[22]

MacArthur's tenure as chief of staff was infinitely less satisfying. The Great Depression not only prompted more cuts in an already low military budget but also fostered a social climate that rankled MacArthur's traditional conservatism. However, MacArthur did forge friendships with Hoover and Secretary of War Patrick J. Hurley, who echoed his belief in individualism and opposition to federal antipoverty programs.

MacArthur's views on gender contributed to his distrust of social radicalism and pacifism. In 1931 the Japanese invasion of Manchuria created an upsurge of pacifist activism. After the religious journal *The World Tomorrow* published a survey demonstrating widespread opposition among Judeo-Christian clergy to military preparedness and war, MacArthur seized the journal's invitation to respond. Addressing "all those who would refuse to take up arms in defense of their country," MacArthur asserted:

> I can think of no principles more high and holy than those for which our national sacrifices have been made in the past. History teaches us that religion and patriotism have always gone hand in hand, while atheism has invariably been accompanied by radicalism, communism, bolshevism, and other enemies of the government . . .
>
> I confidently believe that a red-blooded and virile humanity which loves peace devotedly, but is willing to die in the defense of the right, is Christian from center to circumstance, and will continue to be dominant in the future as in the past.

The implication was clear: in MacArthur's view opposition to war placed one's spirituality and and masculinity in doubt. No "red-blooded, virile" American man would support the effeminate values espoused by communists and pacifists. Similar motives fueled MacArthur's overzealous response to the Bonus Army in 1932.[23]

Although MacArthur's hypermasculine militarism drew widespread condemnation, others recognized his tremendous magnetism. In a meeting with his advisors, Democratic presidential nominee Franklin D. Roosevelt described MacArthur and Huey Long as "the two most dangerous men in the country." Roosevelt explained that "people wanted strong leadership, they were sick of uncertainty, anxious for security, and willing to trade liberty for it." The American people needed "the familiar symbolic figure—the man on horseback," and there "was none so well endowed with charm, tradition, and majestic appearance as MacArthur." Cognizant that a "man" of MacArthur's symbolic power could capture the American imagination, Roosevelt urged his advisors to "tame these fellows and make them useful to us."[24]

Once elected Roosevelt "tamed" MacArthur by retaining him as army chief of staff. Roosevelt and MacArthur shared aristocratic backgrounds, determined mothers, and boundless ambition. Whatever their political differences they respected one another and developed a friendship. Despite his disdain for the New Deal, MacArthur cooperated with the army's recruitment and training of young men in the Civilian Conservation Corps. His compliance, however, did not convince Roosevelt to stop slashing the military budget.[25]

MacArthur also experienced personal difficulties during this time. His military duties permitted few free hours to spend with Isabel. He traveled often and when he returned Pinkie demanded his attentions. Isabel grew bored and convinced Douglas to grant her more freedom. She traveled to Cuba, took art classes, and enrolled in law school. MacArthur eventually decided that she was more trouble than she was worth. In early 1934 MacArthur sent Isabel a return ticket to Manila in an envelope marked "From the Humane Society." She, however, refused to leave America. Frustrated by Isabel's obstinacy and worried about his ailing mother, MacArthur lashed out at his critics. After Drew Pearson and Robert S. Allen derided the general's "dictatorial leanings" in their newspaper column, MacArthur filed a $1.75 million libel suit. Marshaling their defense, Pearson and Allen asked their sources for damaging information about MacArthur.

Shortly thereafter Pearson tracked down Isabel. Pretending to be sympathetic to her plight he persuaded her to surrender MacArthur's letters. As the pretrial hearing opened Pearson's lawyer, Morris Ernst, announced his intention to call Isabel as a defense witness and submitted excerpts from her planned testimony. When MacArthur heard this news he immediately dropped the suit. He also paid sixteen thousand dollars in defense legal fees and gave Isabel fifteen thousand dollars in order to retrieve his letters. Although Pearson kept several copies he promised not to print them while MacArthur was alive. Isabel married a fellow law student and became a Hollywood actress. After a futile attempt to sell her story she died of a barbiturate overdose in 1960.[26]

The incident deeply shook MacArthur. Humiliated by another woman MacArthur took rather extreme measures to reconstruct his tattered sense of manhood. T. J. Davis, one of MacArthur's aides, claimed MacArthur entertained prostitutes. But MacArthur wanted flattery not sex. Sitting across the room MacArthur would order the prostitutes to "admire what a great man he was." Occasionally MacArthur would praise a prostitute then call her "a little whore" and depart. MacArthur obviously harbored misogynist feelings and profound insecurities. He often complained about Pinkie's expectation that he be "glorious Apollo, Roland, and George Washington, all in one." His frequent suicide threats indicated deep depression.[27]

In 1935 with few friends and an uncertain future, MacArthur welcomed appointment as the top military advisor to the new commonwealth government in the Philippines. The assignment saved MacArthur from retirement at age fifty-five. It also played to his romantic conception of himself as guardian of Asian security. But MacArthur wanted more. Never one to cloak his ambitions with modesty, MacArthur pushed Roosevelt to name him high commissioner of the Philippines. After Roosevelt refused MacArthur claimed that the job was only a ceremonial position not worth his talents.

When he and Pinkie sailed for Manila in October, MacArthur's personal life took unexpected turns. During the voyage Pinkie's health declined precipitously. MacArthur rarely left her bedside. But his concern for his mother did not quash his interest in Jean Faircloth, a thirty-seven-year-old Tennessee native. MacArthur was drawn to Jean's bubbly personality. Jean held MacArthur in awe. The two quickly developed a strong bond and began a courtship.

After Pinkie died in December 1935, MacArthur was devastated. All of his immediate family members were now gone. Without his "devoted comrade" MacArthur found himself "groping desperately but futilely." For months he refused almost all social invitations. His only solace came from Jean. Following their marriage in April 1937, Jean and Douglas enjoyed a happy union. Like Pinkie, Jean provided MacArthur constant encouragement and support. Unlike Louise, Jean loved the regimen of army life and called her husband "General" instead of "Douglas." Jean made MacArthur's career the center of her life and let him dictate their social activities. She shared his code of honor, patriotism, and duty. After the birth of their only child, Arthur III, in February 1938, the MacArthurs became devoted parents. Disregarding all his talk about manly toughness, Douglas doted on his son.[28]

But a happy personal life did not diminish MacArthur's need for military glory. He formulated grand defense schemes for the Philippines and bragged incessantly about the strength of his forces. He repeatedly ignored staff members who warned that his defensive plans were unworkable. Instead he retreated into delusional displays of masculinity and militarism. He even persuaded Philippine president Manuel Quezon to appoint him field marshal of the Philippines. The position possessed only symbolic importance but MacArthur designed an elaborate sharkskin uniform and demanded a lavish awards ceremony for the appointment.

Philippine newspapers and the Roosevelt administration roundly condemned MacArthur's vanity, outspokenness, and obstinacy. Disillusioned he retired from the U.S. military in December 1937. With no job prospects in America he remained in Manila as a military advisor to the Philippine Army. Impervious to criticism, MacArthur continued to proffer improbable defense plans. His best staffers, including Davis and Dwight D. Eisenhower, abandoned him. Onlookers ridiculed him as the "Napoleon of Luzon" who "cut no more ice in this U.S. Army than a corporal." MacArthur had become a public joke.[29]

But international events saved MacArthur from irrelevancy. Throughout the 1930s U.S.-Japanese relations deteriorated as the Japanese invaded China and Indochina. Preoccupied with the war in Europe, U.S. officials failed to develop clear defense plans for the Pacific. But by mid-1941 the threat of a Japanese assault on southeast Asia forced the Roosevelt administration to reevaluate its strategy for the region. Military leaders lacked the troops and equipment to build a substantial

American force in the Pacific. As an alternative to significant military assistance they embraced the symbolic gesture of appointing a famous general to lead a new Far Eastern command.

MacArthur was the only logical choice. Although controversial, Mac-Arthur had a worldwide reputation as a heroic leader. He knew Asia far better than most of the U.S. military establishment. Accordingly, the War Department yanked MacArthur out of retirement, elevated him to the temporary rank of lieutenant general, and appointed him commander of U.S. Army Forces in the Far East (USAFFE). With the stroke of a pen MacArthur reentered the army's most elite circles. The symbiotic relationship between his masculinity and his military career was flourishing once again.

MacArthur surrounded himself with staff members who believed in his heroic image. He appointed Col. Richard Sutherland and Lt. Col. Richard Marshall as chief of staff and deputy chief of staff, respectively. Other appointees included Brig. Gen. Courtney Whitney, Lt. Sidney Huff, and Col. Charles Willoughby. Several of these men formed the core of what became the "Bataan Gang," the close-knit group of advisors who became MacArthur's closest confidants for the rest of his life. Despite enormous logistical problems in the Philippine military MacArthur bragged about his impregnable defenses.[30]

On December 7, 1941, the Japanese shattered MacArthur's dreams of easy victory. Shortly after their devastating attack on Pearl Harbor the Japanese prepared to strike the Philippines. Amidst the ensuing confusion among his commanders MacArthur retreated into his office. By the time he launched a belated response to the Japanese assaults over half of his vaunted air forces lay in ruins on the ground. Within two days the Philippine Army collapsed. By December 24 MacArthur ordered a military evacuation of Manila and withdrew American and Filipino forces and supplies to the Bataan Peninsula and Corregidor Island. For the next five months American troops valiantly resisted the Japanese advance.

Amazingly the siege transformed MacArthur into the first major hero of World War II. MacArthur's staff issued a deluge of press statements, many written by MacArthur personally. The error-laden missives rarely mentioned either fellow officers or the front-line troops. Instead they made it appear that MacArthur alone was fighting Japan. Privately Mac-Arthur complained that the Roosevelt administration had abandoned him and his troops.

The exact opposite was true. U.S. military and civilian authorities heaped praise upon MacArthur. Instead of publicly criticizing Mac-Arthur's inept defense of the Philippines they extolled his leadership. The War Department ordered MacArthur to leave the Philippines only after the magnitude of the Japanese offensive and the imperatives of the European theater left no alternative. Even then Army Chief of Staff George Marshall awarded MacArthur a Congressional Medal of Honor in order to discredit Japanese propaganda deriding MacArthur's bravery.

In the interim the situation on Bataan grew desperate. While MacArthur and his staff were ensconced in the relative safety of Corregidor's tunnels, the men on Bataan fought disease, starvation, and exposure. Many soldiers bitterly resented the tone of MacArthur's press statements. Although veterans of Corregidor attest to MacArthur's bravery, his decision to visit Bataan only once demoralized the peninsula's defenders. In February 1942 an anonymous soldier composed a satiric verse set to the tune of "The Battle Hymn of the Republic." The song circulated widely and spoke volumes about how the men on Bataan viewed MacArthur. Its first verse read:

> Dugout Doug MacArthur lies ashaking on the Rock
> Safe from all the bombers and from any sudden shock
> Dugout Doug is eating all the best food on Bataan
> And his troops go starving on

Desperate to prove he was not a coward MacArthur blasted the Roosevelt administration for failing to bolster his forces. On February 22, although loath to make MacArthur a martyr, Roosevelt ordered him to retreat to Australia.[31]

Roosevelt's decision fueled the "MacArthur craze" sweeping the United States. Beginning in January 1942 and led by anti-Roosevelt publications, Americans fawned over MacArthur in countless ways. Parents named their babies after him. People danced the "MacArthur glide." Cities across the country christened MacArthur streets, buildings, and schools. Scores of honorary awards and memberships were bestowed upon him. Journalists wore out their thesauri searching for superlatives to describe MacArthur.

MacArthur and his staff contributed to the flood of hero worship. While traveling to Melbourne on March 21 he told a group of reporters that he would be planning "the American offensive against Japan; a primary object of which is the relief of the Philippines. I came through and I shall return." Although censors at the Office of War Information tried to change the "I" to "we," the phrase gave MacArthur worldwide notoriety. In the Philippines, however, soldiers lampooned MacArthur's arrogance by declaring "I am going to the latrine, but I shall return." In America not even the surrenders of Bataan and Corregidor quelled the public's hunger for tales of MacArthur's heroism.[32]

Reluctantly the Roosevelt administration catered to the popular fascination with MacArthur. Working with their British counterparts the Joint Chiefs of Staff divided the Pacific region into two theaters of operation. They placed Adm. Chester Nimitz in charge of the Pacific Ocean Areas and assigned MacArthur command of the Southwest Pacific Area. The decision to reward MacArthur in the wake of the Philippine disaster irritated several military and civilian officials who found his actions deplorable, not heroic. They considered MacArthur's attempts to blame the defeat on others particularly contemptible. Yet they recognized his symbolic value even if they detested the problems he created.

For the remainder of the war MacArthur and his staff exploited his heroic image to the hilt. Backed by his allies in the media and business community, MacArthur derided Roosevelt's "Europe First" strategy. His complaints proved so effective that by December 1943 the Joint Chiefs of Staff had committed as many supplies and troops to the Pacific as to Europe. Nonetheless, MacArthur indulged in paranoid speculation that naval strategists and New Dealers were opposing him at every turn.

MacArthur shielded himself with a phalanx of public relations officers. Led by Brig. Gen. LeGrande A. Diller, MacArthur's press aides published scores of reports detailing the general's battlefield exploits. In the typical "MacArthur communiqué" all of the field commanders, the navy, and the marines virtually disappeared. The grossly inaccurate releases fostered the impression that MacArthur "was the field commander himself, in tactical command of every jungle and on every beachhead." Premature declarations of victory obscured the fact that thousands of troops died in brutal "mopping up operations" in New Guinea.

Soldiers and sailors in the Pacific often parodied the self-righteous missives. The poem "Doug's Communiqué" mocked:

"My battleships bombard the Nips from
  Maine to Singapore
My subs have sunk a million tons;
  They'll sink a billion more.

My aircraft bombed Berlin last night."
   In Italy they say
"Our turn's tonight, because it's right in
   Doug's Communiqué . . ."
And while possibly a rumor now,
   someday it will be fact
That the Lord will hear a deep voice say
   "Move over, God—it's Mac."
So bet your shoes that all the news
   that last great Judgement Day
Will go to press in nothing less than
                     DOUG'S COMMUNIQUÉ!

But cutting verses like this did not undo the fact that MacArthur received credit for the hard-won battles in the Southwest Pacific.[33]

MacArthur's supporters hoped that his reputation would propel him into the White House. Conservative and isolationist Republicans led by Sen. Arthur Vandenberg (R-MI) and Sears, Roebuck Company chairman Robert Wood championed MacArthur as the candidate to unseat Roosevelt in 1944. Although MacArthur publicly denied having political aspirations his aides communicated on his behalf with Republicans hoping to draft him. Ever mindful of his public image, MacArthur cooperated with many of the authors producing reverential books and articles about him. MacArthur enjoyed posing with a cane. But after an aide worried that it might make him look "feeble" MacArthur abandoned the cane in favor of a corn cob pipe.

Not everyone responded positively to these ploys. Determined not to "martyr" MacArthur, Roosevelt and his aides avoided public actions that could alienate the general. Instead they awarded him a medal and supported his continued service beyond the mandatory retirement age of sixty-four. Privately, however, administration officials gathered damaging information that could be used to discredit a MacArthur candidacy.

In early 1944 the War Department found itself enmeshed in a difficult situation with MacArthur. In the January edition of *American Mercury* journalist John McCarten published the first critical assessment of MacArthur's leadership. Without revealing his sources McCarten debunked many of the heroic myths surrounding the general. He exaggerated the role of right-wing extremists like Gerald L. K. Smith and Father

Charles Coughlin in the MacArthur-for-president movement. He corrected many of the inaccuracies found in MacArthur communiqués. The magazine, however, did not have a wide readership.

But after the Army War College library service included the McCarten piece on its list of recommended readings it reached servicepeople throughout the world. MacArthur and Vandenberg blasted the War Department for circulating "libelous" material to the troops. The administration quickly withdrew the article from circulation and suppressed a second anti-MacArthur story scheduled to appear in *Harper's Magazine*.

At the same time MacArthur tried to deflect McCarten's accusation that he rarely visited the front lines with a visit to an Australian training camp. Exiting his Packard limousine MacArthur asked I Corps commander Robert Eichelberger to drive him in a jeep to a jungle warfare exercise. Days later MacArthur's headquarters released a picture portraying "General MacArthur and General Eichelberger at the New Guinea Front." After Eichelberger noticed "the unmistakable nose of a Packard automobile in one corner of the picture" he observed wryly, "There weren't any Packards in the New Guinea jungle in early 1944."

Fake photographs and censorship did little for MacArthur's presidential aspirations. Polls demonstrated widespread enthusiasm for MacArthur's military abilities but little excitement about his civilian leadership. By April New York Governor Thomas Dewey had emerged as the overwhelming front runner for the Republican nomination. After embarrassing letters detailing his political ambitions emerged, MacArthur made the situation worse by issuing unconvincing proclamations about his disinterest in politics. At the Republican convention in June MacArthur endured the final indignity of receiving only one vote.[34]

But the assault on the Philippines soon restored MacArthur's image to its heroic glory. In the years following the defeat of Bataan and Corregidor MacArthur insisted that the Philippines were an ideal base for launching attacks on Japan. In the fall of 1944 the pressing need for Allied military bases in China convinced the joint chiefs that he was right. On September 8 they directed the general to prepare an assault on Leyte. On October 20 MacArthur waded ashore and proclaimed "People of the Philippines, I have returned! By the Grace of Almighty God, our forces stand again on Philippine soil . . . Rally to me!" Despite persistent rumors to the contrary the dramatic landing was unplanned. But after MacArthur realized the impact it had on the American people he repeated it when other islands were secured.[35]

By v-j Day MacArthur was a legend. To many Americans victory over Japan was inextricably linked to the five-star general's administrative and leadership skills. Unaware of MacArthur's military blunders, most Americans viewed him as the only choice to lead the occupation of Japan. But in the final months of the war neither Roosevelt nor his successor Harry S. Truman kept MacArthur informed about plans for postwar Japan. They did not include him in crucial deliberations on the Potsdam Declaration and the use of the atomic bomb. Yet Truman, like Roosevelt, hoped to exploit MacArthur's authoritative presence. On August 15, 1945, Truman named MacArthur the Supreme Commander for Allied Powers (SCAP) and charged him with accepting the Japanese surrender and supervising the Allied occupation of Japan. No longer just a hero, now MacArthur had a kingdom.[36]

MacArthur immediately projected the demeanor befitting such a role. On September 2 he accepted the Japanese surrender and promised an era of peace and hope. He established headquarters in the Dai Ichi building, a grand edifice near the Imperial Palace in central Tokyo. MacArthur's spacious office featured two portraits—one of Abraham Lincoln and one of George Washington—whom the general sometimes called "my major advisors." He and his family lived in an elegant house in the U.S. embassy compound. Each morning during MacArthur's five-minute ride to the Dai Ichi building masses of Japanese lined the streets and cheered the SCAP. He treasured a postcard addressed to "His most gracious majesty, the old friend, the Most Honorable General MacArthur, Sahib, Bahadur, Military Governor and Crowned King of Japan" encapsulating this adulation.[37]

But did MacArthur's role in Japan warrant all this celebration? Did his policies on gender-related issues reflect the liberal reformer ideals he expounded? For decades MacArthur and his admirers fueled the myth that he had almost singlehandedly reconstructed Japanese politics and society.[38] Historians have countered these assessments by sketching a more complex portrait of the occupation in which the role of MacArthur is greatly diminished. They argue that MacArthur supported the "controlled revolution" in order to position himself as a candidate for the 1948 presidential election. But the Truman administration's response to the cold war frustrated MacArthur's political ambitions and pushed him into a more conservative, less influential role in Japan.[39]

These differing interpretations all reflect MacArthur's need to define himself beyond the confines of the military. He yearned to be remembered as a visionary, not simply a warrior. His sycophantic staff certainly catered to this desire. MacArthur's closest advisors offered him unquestioned loyalty and shielded him from outsiders. They continued to censor all but the most positive accounts of MacArthur and his achievements. But these arrangements complicated MacArthur's attempts to leave his imprimatur on the occupation. Since he never left Tokyo and did not speak Japanese his knowledge of the inner workings of the Japanese Diet was limited. Although MacArthur presented himself a reformer, most reforms were implemented by bureaucrats, not the scap commander.[40]

Nonetheless, one can assess MacArthur's views on gender by evaluating his statements on militarism and women's issues. In late 1945 MacArthur issued several prohibitions on displays of ultranationalism and militarism in Japan. Like many of his contemporaries he viewed the Japanese as a brutal people. MacArthur's efforts to propagate Christianity and support for provisions in the Japanese constitution outlawing war and the armed forces reflected his desire to tame this "warrior race." By 1951 MacArthur compared the Japanese not to savages but to "a boy of twelve" who required the tutelage of mature Anglo-Saxons. MacArthur's gendered metaphor echoed the paternalism evident in his correspondence with Isabel Cooper. By stripping the Japanese of their masculine posture of "warrior" MacArthur negated the threat they posed.[41]

Similar factors motivated MacArthur's support of Japanese women's rights. Occupation officials viewed equal rights for women as part of "a larger effort to reform an antidemocratic family system considered by the Americans to be a root cause of the militarism and fascism that had led to the war."[42] Prior to the occupation the Japanese patriarch exercised virtually absolute authority over his immediate family and the families of his children. He arranged marriages and controlled all family assets. Mid-level scap bureaucrats working with a core of Japanese women's activists hoped to replace this patriarchal system with a more equitable nuclear family structure. Overcoming formidable resistance from the all-male hierarchies in scap and the Diet they gained passage of reforms that ranked among the most progressive in the world.

Articles Fourteen and Twenty-four of the Japanese Constitution were their boldest initiatives. The provisions state:

> All people are equal under the law and there shall be no discrimination in political, economic or social relations because of race, creed, sex, social status or family origin.

Marriage shall be based on the mutual consent of both sexes and it shall be maintained through mutual co-operation with the equal rights of husband and wife as a basis. With regard to choice of spouse, property rights, inheritance, choice of domicile, divorce and other matters pertaining to marriage and the family, laws shall be enacted from the standpoint of individual dignity and the essential equality of the sexes.

In his memoirs MacArthur describes these reforms as the most "heart-warming" of all the changes enacted during the occupation of Japan.

But MacArthur was hardly the liberator of Japanese women. Few of his SCAP directives were directed at women or addressed sex discrimination. He hated to see women in his Dai Ichi office and rarely did so. Although MacArthur advocated universal suffrage and coeducational schools, neither of these actions indicated progressive views on women's rights. Instead, MacArthur's views on gender-related issues reflect his political ambitions and conservatism.

Advocating women's equality offered MacArthur a means to appeal to a wide spectrum of American voters. The constitutional reforms encompassed a broad conception of democracy supported by most Americans. Furthermore, they offered MacArthur a *malleable* social issue. Promoting women's rights promised to gain MacArthur support from moderate Republicans and Democrats. If, however, the conservative Republicans who formed the core of his constituency protested such "radical" views, MacArthur was also secure. Until the 1960s the Equal Rights Amendment drew the bulk of its support from Republicans and conservative Southern Democrats. Depending on the audience, MacArthur could position himself as a New Deal–style reformer or as a defender of classically liberal notions of individual rights. In 1948 the collapse of MacArthur's presidential hopes made these political calculations moot.

On policies less likely to garner public notice, MacArthur's views remained strikingly conservative. Wary of collective actions for social change he "strongly cautioned" female Diet members "against the temptation to form a women's bloc to influence legislation." MacArthur did little to prevent U.S. servicemen from frequenting Japanese brothels. Instead, his public health officers quietly treated the cases of VD that were rampant among American troops. MacArthur adopted a similar laissez-faire stance on birth control. But in mid-1949, when American religious groups protested the use of contraceptives MacArthur announced that "the problem of Japanese population control . . . does not fall within the prescribed scope of the Occupation, and decisions thereon rest entirely with the Japanese themselves." He then barred famed contraception advocate Margaret Sanger from entering Japan in order to give a series of lectures. Whatever the status of Japanese gender relations, neither MacArthur nor any other American working for the occupation was directly affected by the restructuring of Japanese laws on marriage and gender-related issues.[43]

During MacArthur's tenure at SCAP, Jean and his staff ensured that his personal life remained orderly and pleasant. His daily schedule rarely varied and he worked seven days a week. When an observer noted that his long workweeks were "killing" the SCAP staff, MacArthur responded, "What better fate for a man than to die in the performance of his duty?" The comment attested to the profound sense of honor and patriotism that animated MacArthur throughout his life.[44]

On June 25, 1950, the outbreak of war in Korea shattered MacArthur's tranquil routine. At seventy MacArthur assumed command of the United Nations forces resisting the North Koreans in addition to his duties as SCAP and commander of the U.S. troops in the Far East. The Truman administration once again cast aside its doubts about MacArthur in favor of exploiting his heroic reputation.

But the Korean War marked a new era in warfare. In the delicate world of cold war rivalries, nuclear weapons, and fragile congressional relations MacArthur's bold individualism proved too volatile. Although the Inchon landing in September 1950 gave MacArthur a final taste of military glory, the entry of the communist Chinese into the war signified his greatest defeat. While his aggressive support of Jiang Jieshi and calls for raids on communist China resonated with right-wing Republicans, MacArthur's statements frightened other Americans. On April 11, 1951, MacArthur's overconfidence, overt partisanship, and rash public comments prompted Harry S. Truman to dismiss the iconoclastic general.[45] MacArthur learned of his recall from a radio broadcast. The snafu offended his sense of aristocratic privilege greatly. "No office boy, no charwoman, no servant of any sort would have been dismissed with such callous disregard for the ordinary decencies," he recalled.

News of his dismissal prompted a tremendous uproar in the United States. Reactions ranged from ecstasy to rage. In San Gabriel, California, the president was burned in effigy. At the University of Washington students lynched a dummy wearing an army uniform and clenching a corn cob pipe in its teeth. Right-wing Republicans quickly exploited the clamor and began to press for the impeachment of the president and the secretary of state. Initially popular opinion overwhelmingly favored MacArthur.

When MacArthur returned to the United States following a fourteen-year absence, America's controversial hero received an incredible welcome. Millions attended parades honoring him and bought MacArthur souvenirs. When he addressed a special joint session of Congress on April 19, millions more listened to or watched the thirty-seven-minute speech. The rhetoric was classic MacArthur. In a calm, powerful voice he denied being "an advocate of any partisan cause" and stressed his patriotism. He then launched into an extended discussion of his strategic aims in the Far East, reminding his audience that "[t]here can be no substitute for victory." He concluded with a bathetic reference to an old army ballad that proclaimed, "Old soldiers never die, they just fade away."

MacArthur had no intention of fading away before trying to redeem his heroic image, however. After moving his family into a lavish suite at the Waldorf-Astoria Hotel in New York City he appeared before a senate inquiry exploring "the military situation in the Far East." The Truman administration, however, zealously defended its decision to dismiss Mac-Arthur. Throughout May and June administration spokesmen criticized MacArthur's plan for extending hostilities beyond Korea. Claiming that such actions would involve the United States in a general war with the Soviet Union and would consequently destroy the NATO alliance, these witnesses discredited MacArthur's strategy and supported limited combat in Korea. As the hearings continued Americans rapidly lost interest in the MacArthur-Truman affair.

Determined to keep himself in the public eye, MacArthur began a national speaking tour that lasted until June 1952. While wearing his uniform MacArthur blasted the foreign and domestic policies of the Truman administration. The speeches offended many Americans. Little popular support for a MacArthur presidency appeared. After MacArthur's keynote address at the 1952 Republican National Convention flopped, he stopped his public appearances for several months. MacArthur finally realized that while Americans might praise him as a hero and military leader they did not accept him as an authority on domestic issues.[46]

MacArthur spent the remainder of his life in privileged circumstances. In addition to his military retirement package he received substantial benefits from his position as chairman of the board for the electronics firm Remington Rand. His residence at the Waldorf provided a controlled environment mirroring his years in the Philippines and Japan. Jean continued to fawn over the general and cater to his every wish. Although Arthur III embraced music and not the military as his primary interest, MacArthur remained close to his son. Their visitors consisted of people who still viewed MacArthur as an American icon. In May 1962, two years prior to his death, MacArthur made a final trip to his beloved West Point. After an elaborate ceremony he received the Sylvanus Thayer award honoring his personification of "duty, honor, country." It was a fitting tribute for a man so imbued with military ideals.[47]

MacArthur's conception of manhood affected virtually every aspect of his professional and personal lives. At a young age he latched onto the aristocratic warrior ideal to define himself. Under the sway of his mother for most of his adult life, MacArthur used the military as a means of meeting—and occasionally escaping—Pinkie's overwhelming expectations. Deeply insecure outside a martial milieu, MacArthur rejected anyone who failed to accept privately his public persona as brave hero. As he ascended the military hierarchy MacArthur grew more isolated from the profound changes American men and women experienced during his lifetime.[48]

The disjuncture between the public and private MacArthur testifies to our profound need for heroes. MacArthur's contemporaries recognized that Americans wanted to believe in the persistence of courage and honor in a troubling, unstable world. Accordingly, military and civilian authorities often overlooked MacArthur's failings in order to exploit his heroic image.

Notes

1. For examinations of the connections between masculinity and the military, see Allen Berubé, *Coming Out under Fire: The History of Gay Men and Lesbians in World War Two* (New York: The Free Press, 1990); Susan Jeffords, *The Remasculinization of America: Gender and the Vietnam War* (Bloomington: Indiana University Press, 1989); James William Gibson, *Warrior Dreams: Paramilitary Culture in Post-Vietnam America* (New York: Hill and Wang, 1994); Carol Cohn, "Wars, Wimps, and Women: Talking Gender and Thinking War," in *Gendering War Talk*, ed. Miriam Cooke and Angela Woollacott (Princeton: Princeton University Press, 1993): 227–48; and Marc Fasteau, "Vietnam and the Cult of Toughness in Foreign Policy," in *The American Man*, ed. Elizabeth H. Pleck and Joseph H. Pleck (Englewood Cliffs NJ: Prentice-Hall, 1980): 377–416.

2. See, for example, Michael Kimmel, *Manhood in America: A Cultural History* (New York: Free Press, 1996); Anthony Rotundo, *American Manhood: Transformations in Masculinity from the Revolution to the Modern Era* (New York: Basic Books, 1993); and Joan W. Scott, *Gender and the Politics of History* (New York: Columbia University Press, 1988).

3. For some of the finest examinations of MacArthur, see D. Clayton James, *The Years of MacArthur*, 3 vols. (Boston: Houghton Mifflin Company, 1970–1985); Michael Schaller, *Douglas MacArthur: The Far Eastern General* (New York: Oxford University Press, 1989); and Carol M. Petillo, *Douglas MacArthur: The Philippine Years* (Bloomington: Indiana University Press, 1981).

4. See Douglas MacArthur, *Reminiscences* (New York: McGraw-Hill, 1964); George C. Kenney, *The MacArthur I Know* (New York: Duell, Sloan, and Pearce, 1951); Courtney Whitney, *MacArthur: His Rendevous in History* (New York: Knopf, 1955); and Charles Willoughby and John Chamberlain, *MacArthur, 1941–1951* (New York: McGraw-Hill, 1954).

5. Schaller, *Douglas MacArthur*, 3; James, *Years of MacArthur*, 1:14–53; MacArthur, *Reminiscences*, 15. In the Victorian era mothers commonly bore responsibility for the moral education of their sons. See Rotundo, *American Manhood*, 29.

6. James, *Years of MacArthur*, 1:54–65.

7. James, *Years of MacArthur*, 1:63–66; Petillo, *MacArthur: Philippine Years*, 30–33. On contemporary fears of being denigrated as a "mama's boy" see Rotundo, *American Manhood*, 51.

8. Petillo, *MacArthur: Philippine Years*, 4; James, *Years of MacArthur*, 1:44; Schaller, *Douglas MacArthur*, 5–7.

9. Petillo, *MacArthur: Philippine Years*, 33–35; James, *Years of MacArthur*, 1:67–71. On the role of hazing as a transition to manhood see Rotundo, *American Manhood*, 28–61.

10. James, *Years of MacArthur*, 1:78–82; Petillo, *MacArthur: Philippine Years*, 35–37.

11. Schaller, *Douglas MacArthur*, 7–8; MacArthur, *Reminiscences*, 31–32; Petillo, *MacArthur: Philippine Years*, 65–66, 76–77.

12. James, *Years of MacArthur*, 1:95–101.

13. Petillo, *MacArthur: Philippine Years*, 100–106.

14. Petillo, *MacArthur: Philippine Years*, 107–11; James, *Years of MacArthur*, 1:103–5.

15. James, *Years of MacArthur*, 1:107–9; Schaller, *Douglas MacArthur*, 8–9.

16. James, *Years of MacArthur*, 1:115–35; Petillo, *MacArthur: Philippine Years*, 112–15.

17. James, *Years of MacArthur*, 1:139–246; Petillo, *MacArthur: Philippine Years*, 117–23.

18. James, *Years of MacArthur*, 1:244–55.

19. Although Sladen reversed most of MacArthur's innovations, his reforms were eventually restored. See James, *Years of MacArthur*, 1:287–94.

20. James, *Years of MacArthur*, 1:304–5; Petillo, *MacArthur: Philippine Years*, 123–37.

21. Schaller, *Douglas MacArthur*, 11–12; James, *Years of MacArthur*, 1:319–24.

22. Schaller, *Douglas MacArthur*, 13–14; Petillo, *MacArthur: Philippine Years*, 150–54.

23. James, *Years of MacArthur*, 1:375–77, 384–403; Schaller, *Douglas MacArthur*, 14–15. For gendered analyses of pacifism and communism see Susan Zeiger, "She Didn't Raise Her Boy To Be a Slacker: Motherhood, Conscription, and the Culture of the First World War," *Feminist Studies* 22 (spring 1996): 7–39; Frank Costigliola, "'Unceasing Pressure for Penetration': Gender, Pathology, and Emotion in George Kennan's Formation of the Cold War," *Journal of American History* 83 (March 1997): 1309–39; Robert Dean, "Masculinity as Ideology: John F. Kennedy and the Domestic Politics of Foreign Policy," *Diplomatic History* 22 (winter 1998): 29–61; and Jeffords, *The Remasculinization of America*.

24. James, *Years of MacArthur*, 1:405–14; Schaller, *Douglas MacArthur*, 15–16.

25. James, *Years of MacArthur*, 1:415–35; Schaller, *Douglas MacArthur*, 17–18.

26. Schaller, *Douglas MacArthur*, 18–20.

27. Joseph C. Goulden, *Korea: The Untold Story of the War* (New York: Times Books, 1982), xxii–xxiii.

28. Petillo, *MacArthur: Philippine Years*, 175–77, 186–88; James, *Years of MacArthur*, 1:494–95, 553–60.

29. Schaller, *Douglas MacArthur*, 21–42.

30. Schaller, *Douglas MacArthur*, 42–54; James, *Years of MacArthur*, 2:76–81.

31. Schaller, *Douglas MacArthur*, 55–61; James, *Years of MacArthur*, 2:3–99, 125–33; Richard H. Rovere and Arthur Schlesinger Jr., *General MacArthur and President Truman: The Struggle for Control of American Foreign Policy* (1951; reprint, New York: Transaction Publishers, 1992), 50–63.

32. James, *Years of MacArthur*, 2:141–54; Schaller, *Douglas MacArthur*, 61–62.

33. Schaller, *Douglas MacArthur*, 62–78; Rovere and Schlesinger, *General MacArthur and President Truman*, 70–81; James, *Years of MacArthur*, 2:100–402; William M. Leary, ed., *We Shall Return: MacArthur's Commanders and the Defeat of Japan* (Lexington KY: University of Kentucky Press, 1988).

34. Schaller, *Douglas MacArthur*, 78–84; James, *Years of MacArthur*, 2:403–40; John McCarten, "General MacArthur: Fact and Legend," *American Mercury* 58 (January 1944): 7–18.

35. James, *Years of MacArthur*, 2:537–59.

36. James, *Years of MacArthur*, 2:775–92; Schaller, *Douglas MacArthur*, 108–19.

37. James, *Years of MacArthur*, 3:58–60; John Gunther, *The Riddle of MacArthur:*

Japan, Korea, and the Far East (New York: Harper and Brothers, 1950), 22–24.

38. MacArthur, *Reminiscences*, 282–83; Whitney, *MacArthur: His Rendezvous with History*, 213; Justin Williams, *Japan's Political Revolution under MacArthur: A Participant's Account* (Athens: University of Georgia Press, 1979), 263–82.

39. Carol Gluck, "Entangling Illusions: Japanese and American Views of the Occupation," in *New Frontiers in American–East Asian Relations*, ed. Warren I. Cohen (New York: Columbia University Press, 1983), 179–80, 196–98; Michael Schaller, *The American Occupation of Japan: The Origins of the Cold War in Asia* (New York: Oxford University Press, 1985); Howard B. Schonberger, *Aftermath of War: Americans and the Remaking of Japan, 1945–1952* (Kent OH: Kent State University Press, 1989); Schaller, *Douglas MacArthur*, 120–57.

40. James, *Years of MacArthur*, 3:9–66; William J. Sebald and Russell Brines, *With MacArthur in Japan* (New York: W. W. Norton, 1965), 111; Schlesinger and Rovere, *General MacArthur and President Truman*, 89–95.

41. John Dower, *War without Mercy: Race and Power in the Pacific War* (New York: Pantheon Books, 1986); James, *Years of MacArthur*, 3:114–19, 129–30; Schaller, *Douglas MacArthur*, 125–29; Schaller, *American Occupation of Japan*, 124.

42. Susan J. Pharr, "The Politics of Women's Rights," in *Democratizing Japan: The Allied Occupation*, ed. Robert Ward and Sakamoto Yoshikazu (Honolulu: University of Hawaii Press, 1987), 222.

43. James, *Years of MacArthur*, 3:134–35, 193–217, 275–87; Pharr, "Politics of Women's Rights"; Hugh Davis Graham, *Civil Rights and the Presidency: Race and Gender in American Politics, 1960–1972* (New York: Oxford University Press, 1992), 47–50; Gunther, *Riddle of MacArthur*, 53, 130–37; MacArthur, *Reminiscences*, 305.

44. James, *Years of MacArthur*, 3:355–75.

45. On the Truman-MacArthur affair see Laura A. Belmonte, "Anglo-American Relations and the Dismissal of MacArthur," *Diplomatic History* 19 (fall 1995): 641–68; John W. Spanier, *The Truman-MacArthur Controversy and the Korean War* (Cambridge MA: Harvard University Press, 1959); Robert Smith, *MacArthur in Korea: The Naked Emperor* (New York: Simon and Schuster, 1982); and Schlesinger and Rovere, *General MacArthur and President Truman*.

46. MacArthur, *Reminiscences*, 394–95; James, *Years of MacArthur*, 3:600–652.

47. James, *Years of MacArthur*, 3:652–90.

48. On changing gender roles see Sara Evans, *Born for Liberty: A History of American Women* (New York: Free Press, 1991); Elaine Tyler May, *Homeward Bound: American Families in the Cold War* (New York: Basic Books, 1988); and Kimmel, *American Manhood*, 223–67.

Douglas MacArthur

Norman Cousins

In an editorial written following MacArthur's death in 1964, Norman Cousins, editor of the Saturday Review, *complained both about the extravagant praise of MacArthur by his "extremist supporters" and the harsh criticism of the general by his vociferous detractors. While he recognized the magnitude of the task, Cousins expressed his hope that a balanced biography of MacArthur might some day be written.*

They demanded for him the highest honors but they saw to it that he was deprived of a decent burial. They intoned the articles of his integrity but no sooner was he unable to speak than they put foul words in his stilled mouth, causing him to say things he had never been known to say in life. They said he was a man to be respected and venerated, but even before he was laid to rest they jumped up and down on his casket with microphones and amplifiers, involving him in the kind of sordid controversy he rigorously avoided in retirement. They pointed to his towering nobility but they pulled him down to their own level where the smells of the political gutter were rankest. They acclaimed him as a hero but they did their best to make him sound like a knave.

Who are "they"? Only superficially are "they" the scoop-hungry newsmen. More basically, "they" are the extremist supporters who never really understood him. They never understood him in life or death. They had a craving for someone who could be proud and powerful, a military hero who would symbolize both the national honor and glory. He symbolized all these things but he was not a militarist. He was not a lover of big bombs or a brandisher of hot swords. He was not fitted to a white horse or to any of the extremist platforms from which a strong man would pronounce and denounce, propose and dispose. Yes, there was grandeur to the man. He could be hard, haughty, impatient. He could drive forward when he had an objective to reach, and he was disdainful of obstructions. And no one surpassed his genius for invoking patriotism. But he was not a tub-thumping jingoist who contrived to juxtapose the national cause against the human cause. He may have been autocratic in manner but he was democratic in purpose. His main job in life was done in soldier's uniform but this was not the way he wanted ultimately to be remembered.

"Could I have but a line a century hence crediting a contribution to the advance of peace," he once said "I would gladly yield every honor which has been accorded me in war."

And again, he had expressed the hope that if a future historian should judge him worthy "of some slight reference," it would be not as a military commander but as a man determined to create a genuine basis for justice and peace.

But in the headlines and in the flaming newspaper stories after his death, what he had prayed would not happen did happen. They extolled him as a great military figure, which he was, but they gave very little notice to the things of which he was proudest and which may help to change history for the better. He was proud to be called the liberator of the Philippines but he was at least equally proud of his insistence that the civilian government of the Philippines come ahead of the military. He was proud to have received the articles of military surrender from the Japanese but he was even prouder that the central purpose of his occupation was to create civilian rule within the shortest possible time. And he was especially proud that Japan was the first nation in human history to renounce war and the means of war.

This renunciation was written into the new Japanese Constitution that took shape under the Occupation. Two other features of that Constitution he believed were also of historic significance. One was the clause decreeing the end of feudalism and the social injustices inherent in it. The second was a bill of rights and the establishment of an independent judiciary.

He regarded the Japanese Constitution not merely as an expression of ultimate aspiration but as a statement of working principles. He didn't come to Japan for the purpose of helping to lay down a superficial veneer but to participate in the making of a profound revolution in the democratization of a nation—and he never hesitated to use the word "democracy" even though the extremists at home who professed to worship him had the strongest contempt for the term. He sponsored a program of land reform under which millions of acres were turned over to the peasants who had worked the land for absentee owners. He fought against the usury that impoverished countless numbers of farmers and tradesmen. He helped to set free the largest politically and socially disfranchised group in Japan—women. He made it possible for Japanese laborers to be represented through organized collective bargaining.

All these were substantial achievements, and they were all interrelated but it is possible that the clause in the Japanese Constitution renouncing war was the achievement that meant the most to him personally.

He liked to recall the time that Prime Minister Shidehara came to him and agreed that the best way of serving and saving Japan was by abolishing war as an international instrument. "The world will laugh at us as impractical visionaries," the Prime Minister said, "but a hundred years from now we will be called prophets."

He spoke at a joint session of the Congress of the Republic of the Philippines three years ago in what was perhaps his last important public appearance. He said the great question of our time is whether war could be outlawed from the world. "If so, it would make the greatest advance in civilization since the Sermon on the Mount. It would lift at one stroke the darkest shadow which has engulfed mankind from the beginning."

He was never called a visionary, yet he felt most at home with visions of a better world.

"Many will say, with mockery and ridicule," he declared, "that the abolition of war can be only a dream—that it is but the vague imagining of a visionary. But we must go on or we will go under. And the great criticism that can be made is that the world lacks a plan that will enable us to go on."

His main rebuke of leaders in government was not so much that they interfered with the military but that they weren't sufficiently imaginative in creating the design for a world under law.

"Leaders must not be laggards," he said. "They have not even approached the basic problem, much less evolved a working formula to implement this public demand. They debate and turmoil over a hundred issues; they bring us to the verge of despair or raise our hopes to utopian heights over the corollary misunderstandings that stem from the threat of war. . . . Never do they dare to state the bald truth, that the next great advance in the evolution of civilization cannot take place until war is abolished."

The term "common man" may sit awkwardly on the lips of many extremists, but he had no hesitation in using the expression or in investing it with uncommon significance. The common man, he said, understands that there is no greater issue before the world than the need to outlaw war. But his leaders are at least fifty years behind him.

"We are told we must go on indefinitely as at present," he said. "With what at the end? None say; there is no definite objective. They but pass along to those that follow the search for a final solution. And, at the end, the problem will be exactly the same as that which we face now.

"Must we live for generations under the killing punishment of accelerating preparedness without an announced final purpose or, as an alternative, suicidal war . . . ? Sooner or later the world, if it is to survive, must reach a decision. The only question is, when? When will some great figure in power have sufficient imagination and moral courage to translate this universal wish, which is rapidly becoming a universal necessity, into actuality?

"We are in a new era. The old methods and solutions no longer suffice. We must have new thoughts, new ideas, new concepts, just as did our venerated forefathers when they faced a new world. There must always be one to lead, and we should be that one. We should now proclaim our readiness to abolish war in concert with the great powers of the world. The result would be magical."

He carried these ideas into assemblies where they needed most to be heard. In January 1955, at a banquet meeting of the Los Angeles County Council of the American Legion, he talked about the implications of atomic warfare. He began by saying that many of those present had been his comrades-in-arms. Then he asked: "How is it that the institution of war has become so integrated with man's life and civilization? How has it grown to be the most vital factor in our existence?"

He asked his listeners to recognize that as soldiers they could no longer regard war as a relevant way of safeguarding values or defending a nation. The reality of scientific annihilation, he said, had destroyed the possibility of war being used "as a medium of practical settlement of international differences. Science has clearly outmoded war as a feasible arbiter. War has become a Frankenstein to destroy both sides. No longer is it the weapon of adventure whereby a short cut to international power and wealth—a place in the sun—can be gained. If you lose, you are annihilated. If you win, you stand only to lose. No longer does it possess the chance of the winner of a duel. It contains rather the germs of double suicide."

This was what he believed, yet they are now trying to make it appear that he was prevented by politicians from using atomic bombs against China in the Korean War.

He had deplored the use of the atomic bomb against Japan and had no intention of using it in the Korean War. He believed that victory was possible in both cases without nuclear bombs, and he said so. Yet he has now been made to say the opposite in death.

A President of the United States is Commander-in-Chief of the Armed Forces. It is his right and responsibility to make ultimate decisions concerning America's politics and actions in the world. In 1951, the President could no longer countenance opposition in the field to his decisions about Korea. No man could be more opposed than was Douglas MacArthur to the President's basic decisions about Korea, but no man who understood as clearly as he did the need for the primacy of the civilian over the military in a free society would argue against the obligations of a President, once having made a difficult decision, to implement it as fully as possible.

It is possible to disagree severely with MacArthur over Korea, but it is unfair to allow even so substantial an event to blot out a view of the whole man. For if it is true that his extremist supporters have an incomplete view of Douglas MacArthur, the same is equally true of his critics. Both groups have reacted to the military posture, to the rakish tilt of the cap, to the mystique of the man. And both groups have failed to see beyond the clusters of medals. They have never taken the trouble to find out who he was philosophically; they have never gone into his library and observed the esteem he had for men like Thomas Jefferson, John Stuart Mill, Abraham Lincoln.

Some day, a biographer will succeed in writing a full-length portrait of Douglas MacArthur. It will not be an easy undertaking. It will require an almost superhuman capacity for balance and perspective. But it is clearly in the national interest that it be written. And it is in the human interest that it be read.

A Unique General

MacArthur of the Pacific

Brian Loring Villa

While many scholars believe that D. Clayton James met Cousins's challenge, Brian Loring Villa of the University of Ottawa, in his review of the second volume of James's biography, praises the author's efforts to be objective and dispassionate in his treatment of the general but concludes that James fell short of his goal.

A statue of General Douglas MacArthur, with jaw set in grim determination, now stares out across the plain at West Point. Characteristically, there were those who quietly refused invitations to attend the unveiling. MacArthur has long been and will continue to be a symbol of division for the cadets who parade by his statue, for the army, and for the citizenry at large.

MacArthur's provocative character derived in part from the fact that he was born in 1880 and was one of the few theater commanders in World War II to have been educated in the nineteenth century.[1] He had a second (and even a third) career after most of his contemporaries had gracefully retired. Like de Gaulle, MacArthur derived his concept of leadership from the nineteenth century. It was an aloof and dominating, if not domineering, form of leadership. Total loyalty was the least he would accept. And, most gratingly in an American officer, it was aristocratic. D. Clayton James, in the second volume of this very well-researched biography, quotes an illuminating account of one of MacArthur's visits to the Balikpapan beachhead on Borneo. In the midst of blazing heat, MacArthur stepped forward, "immaculately dressed with well pressed khaki trousers and carrying light tan gloves." To the "prespiry troops" at the front he asked, "How goes it gentlemen?" The ensuing silence can easily be imagined (pp. 761 62).

But MacArthur also had the great strengths of a man of the nineteenth century. He was uncommonly literate and had a truly marvelous command of his mother tongue. His martial orations, fearlessly touching on the great themes of life, are among the most stirring of our era. (It is one of the fine features of James's biography that at the right times he lets the general himself speak.) Then too, like most great men produced in the century dominated by the image of Napoleon, MacArthur believed in his star with remarkable constancy. This faith in himself paid off handsomely until the inevitable denouement. In the classic model, MacArthur was destined to be rejected at the end of an illustrious career. Retirement would have a certain bitterness.

But the imprint of the nineteenth century was not alone responsible for the hostility MacArthur aroused. There was something distinctly un-American about MacArthur. It was not just that he would spend decades outside of his native country. He seems not to have understood that new experience is the American idea and that the character and quality of lives on this continent were supposed to change drastically from one generation to another. MacArthur, however, followed in his father's steps so closely that it is difficult to distinguish between the early careers of Arthur and Douglas MacArthur. True, America has known other dynasties, but the least liked are military. They are few and far between. The more appreciated pattern is that demonstrated by General Pershing's son, Warren, whom MacArthur wanted to have as an aide. The young Pershing chose to enter the war as a private.

MacArthur was also one of the most political generals in the American army, something that was always meant to be a contradiction in terms in the American scheme of things. Roosevelt, at least, thought MacArthur was one of the two most dangerous men in America, someone who might lend his name to a right-wing dictatorship.[2] This appraisal was probably unfair. MacArthur did choose to fade away like a soldier while Eisenhower became president. Even if MacArthur had sought the presidency, at his worst he would have been a de Gaulle. But as James shows, MacArthur was, in the midst of a difficult war, uncommonly interested in domestic politics. James is inconclusive about MacArthur's motivation, but the evidence seems unambiguous; MacArthur trotted out his political interests to blackmail Washington into following his plans and alloting more to his theater than otherwise would have been the case. Roosevelt evidently felt the price was well worth paying and almost without exception backed MacArthur. It all seems to have paid off handsomely, as MacArthur, in charge of an essentially secondary theater, frequently succeeded in obliging the Joint Chiefs to back down.

Though James is too cautious to suggest it, it may well have been a mark of Roosevelt's fear of MacArthur that General Marshall was denied command of the European invasion to prevent the most obvious successor, MacArthur, from returning to Washington. In all this maneuvering there is something plainly contrary to American civil-military traditions. Divisions of opinion about MacArthur are not likely to disappear.

James has tried to avoid polemics and produce a balanced account of the general. And, at first glance, this well-researched study seems to be supremely judicious. MacArthur is shown in moments of glory but the rest of the record is there also. James concedes the kernel of truth in the "Dugout Doug" stories, which proclaimed that MacArthur lacked the courage or wisdom to visit the front at Bataan as often as he should have. Why MacArthur should always choose to call his planes "Bataan," as though it were a badge of honor, is to James "a phenomenon that will be left to the psychologists to explain" (p. 55). The myth about MacArthur being outnumbered in the defense of the Philippines is clearly exposed and so also is MacArthur's brazen lying in his communiqués and reports to Washington.

But on closer examination it is evident that James has conceded only what he has been obliged to concede. The myth about MacArthur's forces being outnumbered in the Philippines was exposed more than twenty years ago in the official histories; so also was much of MacArthur's prevarication in his communiqués and reports. While conceding the undeniable, James has managed to build a structure of excuses for MacArthur that, on the whole, is very hard to accept. In the first volume of his biography James suggested that MacArthur's lying might have been the result of his seeing what price Hoover paid for candor during the bonus march.[3] In the second volume James tends to excuse MacArthur in much more questionable fashion, suggesting that MacArthur was no better or worse than Franklin Roosevelt: "Just as the Hudson Valley aristocrat in the White House could skillfully play other parts as the occasion required, so the swpa [South West Pacific Area] leader could project a different image to suit each scheme or maneuver in which he was engaged. He seemed no more able to refrain from role playing than Roosevelt, and either man, it was said, would have rivaled John Barrymore as an actor" (p. 666).

While accepting the possibility of other interpretations, James implicitly asks us to believe that the mendacious communiqués were simply the "personal performances" of a "supreme actor" (pp. 666–67). Accepting this FDR-MacArthur analogy at face value, one still has to note the differences between deceit in politics and war. It must be kept in mind that the lying nature of MacArthur's communiqués was clear to every major commander during World War II, as was the glory that MacArthur seemed to reap from them. Recognizing the damaging nature of the precedent, Washington sought at one point to take the general to task. An investigation was launched which succeeded in proving the falsity of MacArthur's reports. The general brazenly denied all and successfully dodged a final accounting. James, with uncalled-for even-handedness, refers to the "mischief-making on both sides in this prolonged and eventually ridiculous controversy" (p. 303). This most decorated general was thus left to school a whole generation of commanders in questionable techniques of reporting. One has but to read Sam Adams's brilliant piece on Vietnam in the May 1975 issue of *Harper's*, "Cover-Up, Playing War with Numbers," to understand how far from ridiculous the controversy was, how tragic the effect of lying about the facts of battle could be.

James also reveals his pro-MacArthur bias in his treatment of the George Marshall Douglas MacArthur relationship (which has always been the touchstone of objectivity for anyone writing on the Pacific commander). For most of the volume James is scrupulously fair. But on the subject of Marshall's (and Roosevelt's) cables encouraging MacArthur to resist in the Philippines, James refers to "false encouragement" perhaps intended to make MacArthur and his men fight longer than if "told the truth." James adds: "If so these words were an insult to the garrison's bravery and determination" (pp. 51–52). That such a charge should be made in so detailed a volume without any reference to Stimson's and Marshall's valiant effort to block British proposals for the abandonment of the Philippines during the Washington Conference (at the time the cables were sent) is incomprehensible.[4] The record is sufficiently clear that Stimson and Marshall hoped to save the Philippines and honor their promises to MacArthur. So one-sided is James that, after having questioned Marshall's sincerity in promising aid, he can casually criticize Marshall some ninety pages later for his desperate and vain efforts to get that aid to MacArthur (p. 144). This sort of "heads I win, tails you lose" treatment puts James squarely in the MacArthur camp.

Though very reasonable for the most part, this is a decidedly pro-MacArthur biography. James admits as much. Closing the chapter on the Papuan campaign, he writes: "He had acquired a large number of critics, but, with the exception of King and some of his staff, no one in high level positions with whom he had differed—from Roosevelt, Stimson and Marshall to Halsey, Blamey and Eichelberger—would have suggested in early 1943 that a better theatre commander could be found for the South West Pacific than MacArthur. "Warts and all," he still had their trust, as well as that of the vast majority of people in America and Australia. As a commander, he would more than repay their faith in him, for the Old Man's finest hours still lay ahead" (p. 286). It is hard to argue with that statement, but for some, particularly Marshall, the warts would always be troubling. Equally troubling must be any interpretation that seeks, even in a small way, to rationalize those flaws.

But James's work is undoubtedly one of the most important biographies of recent years and will, almost certainly, be the definitive biography of MacArthur. It deserves a very wide reading despite some stylistic warts of its own. Unlike the first volume, the second moves along a bit slowly at times. One has to question James's decision to stretch the biography from two to three (and one suspects probably four) volumes for the sake of so much detailed military history, particularly when he universally agrees with major conclusions of the official army histories. The general reader surely does not read a biography for military history in this detail. And if James were going to go into such detail he might well have tried to plow into some new ground. One of the most interesting questions that should have been explored was the relationship between MacArthur and the planners in Washington, who virtually held MacArthur's destiny in their hands. Some were MacArthur backers, some were not. James lumps them all together as "the planners" (see, for example pp 307, 330, 507.) The principal army planner for the final defeat of Japan and chief of the strategy and policy section of the General Staff (Operations Division [OPD]) is referred to only once and then simply as Brigadier General George A. Lincoln of "Marshall's staff" (p. 764). This is a little bit better than describing him as "one of the Marshall crowd," as MacArthur was wont to do with almost anyone out of OPD, but not much. In fact there seems to be an interesting story here worth exploring, for the two men developed some mutual antipathy by war's end, despite Lincoln's early admiration for MacArthur's battlefield competence. When Lincoln returned to West Point after the war and while he sat on the Academic Board, MacArthur returned only once officially to the academy he had once headed. For both men that seemed to be more than enough. MacArthur's other visits were made as a private citizen. MacArthur's relationship with some of the other planners was more felicitous but there is none of this either in James's biography. Not surprisingly, James's remarkably full bibliography does not mention the official Joint Chiefs of Staff histories, among the best sources on the planning disputes.[5]

One also has to register some disappointment with James's reluctance to rise above the detail and draw out the implications of his narrative. With so controversial a man as MacArthur some distance is wise, and no doubt many readers will prefer it this way. Still, there should have been room for a broad, interpretive overview of MacArthur's relations with the Philippine people and government from Pearl Harbor to VJ Day. The pattern, if James had chosen to bring it out explicitly, was one of generous paternalism which foreshadowed MacArthur's Japanese reign. Such a delineation is all the more called for since James's principal interest is in MacArthur the civil administrator and statesman. It is in these roles in Tokyo that James sees MacArthur's greatest success (p. x). The account of that Tokyo reign, once promised for volume 2 and now to be volume 3, should set the lines of James's portrait more clearly still. But the outlines of a too-favorable image are already visible.

Notes

1. General "Vinegar Joe" Stilwell, Commander of U.S. Forces, China-Burma-India, is the other. I am indebted to Lieutenant Colonel John Bradley of the Department of History, West Point, for an interesting and useful exchange of views on MacArthur. We disagree to a considerable extent but his knowledge of MacArthur's career is very extensive and his reflections on that career were helpful.

2. Rexford G. Tugwell, *The Democratic Roosevelt* (New York: Doubleday, 1957), pp. 349–50.

3. D. Clayton James, *The Years of MacArthur*, vol. 1 (Boston: Houghton Mifflin, 1970), p. 413.

4. Henry L. Stimson, "Diary," December 25, 1942, in Yale University Archives, New Haven CT.

5. Most noticeably absent is Grace P. Hayes, *History of the Joint Chiefs of Staff in WW II, The War against Japan*, 2 vols. (Washington DC: Historical Division, Joint Secretariat, Joint Chiefs of Staff, 1953).

A Successful Postrevisionist Synthesis?

Charles M. Dobbs

Although not without some criticism of James's third volume of The Years of MacArthur, *Charles Dobbs of Metropolitan State College, Denver, concludes that the author has succeeded in writing an even-handed treatment of the controversial general.*

In recent years historians of American foreign policy have sought a postrevisionist synthesis for 1940s U.S. diplomacy much as medieval Europeans hunted for the Holy Grail—with great effort and little success. The desire to bring together views of scholars divided by values, approach, and interest areas has been strong. While the confrontations of the 1970s apparently have muted, differences between various groups of scholars remain great.

The divisions are significant. The generation that came to maturity in the 1950s buoyed by victory in World War II and disillusioned by the onset of cold war blamed the Soviet Union for the glacial chill. Perhaps reflecting their ethno-European origins, they examined diplomacy over the German question, Eastern Europe, Greece and Turkey, and the like. In the 1960s and 1970s younger scholars, influenced by the Vietnam conflict and a sense that American actions might not appear abroad as they seem at home, wrote with doubt of American policies and looked to economic and trade relations to explain the onset of cold war. While the Soviet Union undoubtedly installed favorable regimes in areas overrun by Red Armies, perhaps it had a right to a security sphere, and perhaps America wrongfully or mistakenly challenged that need. So-called New Left scholars changed the debate, making consideration of economics a *sine qua non* for future studies, but they too concentrated on Europe. Lately a group of young scholars influenced not only by the flawed and failed effort in Vietnam but the decline of political consensus, Watergate, and the economy, have come of age. Many of these historians have labored to bring their dissertations into print, but one can see that this group has shifted its focus somewhat to East Asia, Southeast Asia, South Asia, the Middle East, and Latin America.

Differences have spawned attempts to span them. In 1971 John Lewis Gaddis published his highly-regarded *The Origins of the Cold War*, one of the first monographs based upon recently declassified documents, and somewhat of a revisionist effort. Gaddis sought to bring together so-called court and New Left historians by concluding that America and Russia each deserved a measure of blame for the origins of the cold war. But Gaddis too had a European orientation. Later as document collections, primarily at the National Archives and Harry S. Truman Library, were opened to scholarly research, historians published many monographs and even broader studies without common approach or conclusion. In 1984 at the Organization of American Historians Convention, Gaddis suggested a new postrevisionist synthesis, perhaps a common approach if not common conclusions. But, as comments of respondents indicated, few accepted the attempted synthesis. Lawrence Kaplan, for example, wondered whether historians who did not live through the 1940s could understand the fears, worries, and perceptions of the period. Other commentators suggested that the inclusion by scholars of international economics and trade relations did not form the basis for a successful synthesis—if anything, it meant a triumph for the New Left.[1]

Perhaps without intending to, D. Clayton James has finally written the long-awaited postrevisionist synthesis with Volume 3 of the *The Years of MacArthur*. This magnificent tome is at least two books: MacArthur and the occupation of Japan (384 pages plus notes) and MacArthur and the first year of war in Korea (265 pages plus notes). It certainly is evidence of a historian in control of his material, for James has mastered a vast amount of secondary literature and a goodly amount of primary materials (especially at the MacArthur Archives in Norfolk, Virginia). The notes are stunning in their detail; James seems as familiar with the origins of the Korean War, or Japanese War Crimes Tribunals, or American domestic politics, as specialists in those fields. At least as important as mastery of material is James's careful balancing: each set of opinions—favorable to MacArthur or not—receives due attention. He presents a considered and detailed opinion of MacArthur, while treating others—especially President Truman and the Joint Chiefs of Staff—with respect; and he manages to focus on MacArthur and his area of command without giving it undue weight or overlooking events elsewhere in the world. James not only understands the complex situation in Eastern Asia, but he can set events in Asia and Europe into perspective. In balancing events, in judiciously evaluating opinions of various scholars, and in keeping the focus on MacArthur without exaggerating the man, James points the way to a successful postrevisionist synthesis.

In chronicling MacArthur's greatest triumph and worst defeat, James gives MacArthur deserved credit for his magnificent job as head of the American occupation of Japan, but he also notes problems. As he had done throughout his career, MacArthur imposed his army command structure and long-serving army officers on SCAP, while giving others— Americans, foreign observers—short shrift. MacArthur also probably erred in the trials and executions of some senior Japanese officials soon after the war ended. James agrees with legal studies that found that MacArthur encouraged trial officers to violate rules of evidence, and despite pleas by many Japanese he not only consented to executions but, in the case of General Tomoyuki Yamashita who commanded Japanese troops in the Philippines in 1944 45, he ordered death by hanging, highly insulting in that culture, rather than death by firing squad or ritual *hara-kiri* as requested in a petition signed by 86,000 Japanese. James also concluded that "the blame must be shared not only by MacArthur . . . but also by the American and Philippine supreme courts and President Truman" (p. 98). James faults MacArthur for the attempt to secure the Republican party presidential nomination, and his amazingly limited contact with the Japanese people (or their American occupiers) during the occupation. "In sixty-eight months in one of the most fascinating countries on earth the only sights of Japan he [MacArthur] saw were from his automobile as he was driven between the Dai Ichi Building [SCAP Headquarters] and the embassy and on the Haneda Airport route" (p. 357). James also criticizes MacArthur's misplaced attempt to force evangelical Christianity on the Japanese, who as it turned out did not want it.

Still, MacArthur generally deserves credit for his command of the occupation. Not so with his command of UN armies in Korea. Again, James is careful to fault MacArthur, to present views of his contemporaries, and to make judgments, including pointing out errors of omission and/or commission by others. As UN commander in Korea, MacArthur regularly exceeded, ignored, or violated directives from the Joint Chiefs, his superiors in Washington. But James blamed the JCS for permitting such unparalleled independence. When Army Deputy Chief of Staff Matthew Ridgway demanded that orders be sent to MacArthur telling him what he could do, the response was "What good would that do? He wouldn't obey the orders. What *can* we do" (p. 537)? Yet for all of MacArthur's errors in Korea, including generally doing what he pleased, inadequately informing his Washington superiors, discounting early reports of Chinese intervention, seeking to transfer blame for the intelligence failure to others, and his dire warnings of disaster (unfounded) after the People's Republic intervened in force, MacArthur receives a sympathetic treatment from his biographer.

James notes that it was unfortunate that Truman and his military chiefs "felt compelled to add another enormous command to a general who was only a half-year away from his seventy-first birthday.... The first step leading to the Truman-MacArthur confrontation of 1950 1951 may well have been the selection of the difficult, aging, and overburdened MacArthur, who should not have been ordered to prove his leadership ability in another military crisis" (p. 438). As the Truman-MacArthur controversy became more heated, and as MacArthur's actions became less defendable, James becomes more critical. He notes that, at first, Truman and MacArthur sought to lessen the differences between them and that the Wake Island Conference should have provided an opportunity for MacArthur to give the president a detailed military accounting, and for the president to make clear the constraints on MacArthur. Instead their private meeting was brief, the meeting of the two parties was superficial and undirected, and aside from political gain to the president's party for the 1950 midterm elections, the benefits were difficult to gauge. After his dismissal, MacArthur lost any remaining sense of perspective. James rightly has demonstrated that while the Senate's MacArthur hearings sought mostly to refight the China policy of 1947 1950, administration witnesses proved the spurious nature of MacArthur's charges. It was a sad ending to a long and glorious career.

It seems that James, in noting that "the reader will find no concluding chapter . . . on the measure of MacArthur" (p. vii), indicates his view of a possible postrevisionist synthesis: carefully set forth the facts, the discoveries of various scholars representing differing schools of thought, and let the reader "form his or her judgments, using the many facts and the small guideposts I have provided" (p. vii).

Perhaps that is the only possible, workable synthesis: to represent fairly the opinions of all those who have come before, do so without apparent prejudice, and let the reader decide.

Ultimately, it seems an unsatisfying result. While presenting various arguments, James frequently refers to a scholar as a "distinguished" or "knowledgeable" historian; however, one must search the notes to learn the identity. In considering arguments of various groups of scholars, whether he accepts views of rejects them, James blends them into an account largely devoid of historiographical argument. He is more willing to note contemporary criticisms of MacArthur than he is to admit to debate among present historians, some of whom might not care to see their opinion on one point neatly folded into another scholar's view on a different but related matter. It very likely is a matter of choice, between a puree of opinions and a stew where the opinions are distinct and some may be more palatable than others. for consensus historians of the 1950s and early 1960s, this approach may be welcome. But, if this approach is a sign of the future postrevisionist synthesis, I would rather have a common understanding of the grounds for disagreement than a loss of a sense of the issues and the debate.

Regardless, this third volume about MacArthur sets a standard that scholars may find difficult to attain; it is a commanding work on a commanding individual by a scholar at the height of his powers.

Notes

1. Gaddis's paper and comments by panelists—the entire session—were published in the Winter 1986 issue (Vol. 10, 1) of *Diplomatic History*.

Military Biography without Military History

Russell F. Weigley

William Manchester has written the most widely read biography of MacArthur. In this review essay the distinguished military historian Russell Weigley takes Manchester to task for his inadequate and uncritical treatment of MacArthur's military leadership.

A soldier's biography should assess him as a soldier: if it concerns a general it should focus upon his generalship. Strangely enough, American military biography has tended to lack such focus, often failing to assess generalship critically. William Manchester's biography of General Douglas MacArthur is a case in point.

To carry paradox further, it is the most quintessentially military figures whose biographies especially have not grasped firmly the distinctively military aspects of their subjects' lives. The soldiers in our country's history who are most thoroughly and completely soldiers, the ones who are too much so to be elected president—the Pershings, the Pattons, the MacArthurs—are the very figures with whom American military biography has found it most difficult to cope.

A Dwight D. Eisenhower, a general whose principal distinction even while in uniform may not have been essentially military but rather diplomatic, and who not being a man-on-horseback type could be trusted enough by his fellow citizens to win the presidency, has enjoyed in addition to several comprehensive biographies a good distinctively military biography, Stephen E. Ambrose's *The Supreme Commander: The War Years of General Dwight D. Eisenhower* (1970). The genuine men on horseback, in contrast, tend to lack distinctively military biographies and, particularly, critical studies of their generalship. John J. Pershing, for instance, was recently the subject of a two-volume, highly acclaimed biography that won a National Book Award. But this work, Frank E. Vandiver's *Black Jack: The Life and Times of John J. Pershing* (1977), is uncritical in its assessment of all things through Pershing's eyes. Its dedication to Pershing's perspective prevents it from relating Pershing's career adequately to the history of the United States Army in Pershing's time, and this Pershing-centeredness also stands in the way of a satisfactory evaluation of Pershing as commander of the American Expeditionary Forces, either in his administrative role or to the admittedly limited extent to which he could display tactical or strategic capacities. General George S. Patton, Jr., a similarly soldierly figure, similarly does not have a critical biography studying and assessing Patton the general. The principal biography published so far, Martin Blumenson's two-volume *The Patton Papers* (1972–74), is an admirable work; but by design it is a different kind of biography, an exploration of Patton's character rather than his generalship, as revealed mainly through his own writings. And now with MacArthur, though a comprehensive biography is in progress—D. Clayton James's *The Years of MacArthur* (2 volumes to date, 1970)—the work that attracts major publicity and reaches the best-seller lists falls short in its portrayal of MacArthur as a general.

William Manchester might have been expected to deal well with the most particularly military aspects of his military subject. Manchester saw combat in the Pacific and was badly wounded as a marine during World War II. As a marine, he might also have been expected to judge MacArthur critically, because the Marine Corps habitually believed that MacArthur misunderstood and misused the special capacities of marine divisions for amphibious assault. Manchester has overcome any biases that might have lingered from his Marine Corps years in his portrait of MacArthur, but the escape from a negative bias is less impressive when it leads toward the opposite deficiency, adulation.

In fact, Manchester offers virtually uncritical acceptance of MacArthur's own lofty estimation of his generalship. Manchester finds MacArthur "unquestionably . . . the most gifted man-at-arms this nation has produced" (p. 3). "The General's gifts were those of a strategist, an architect of warfare. There, quite simply, he had no peer in any World War II theater, in any army" (p. 332). MacArthur's Hollandia campaign "would have been beyond the talents of all but a few history's great captains. In retrospect it looms as a military classic, comparable to Hannibal's maneuvering at Cannae and Napoleon's at Austerlitz" (p. 344). It is with Hannibal and Napoleon, and above all other American generals, that Manchester consistently ranks MacArthur. Such sweeping comparative judgments obviously are dubious under any circumstances. They have to raise eyebrows when they rest on such drastic simplification of the evidence as they do in Manchester's book.

For despite the large size of the book, Manchester compresses MacArthur's campaigns into exceedingly brief segments of the narrative. The Hollandia operation, for example, so highly praised, occupies only pages 344–48. The compression of strategic and tactical materials assists Manchester in depicting MacArthur's leapfrogging advance up the north coast of New Guinea, bypassing Japanese strongpoints, and particularly the leap past Wewak to Hollandia, as products of an almost unique strategic genius. In this depiction Manchester ignores much of the substantial evidence presented by D. Clayton James's fuller analysis of MacArthur's generalship, by the Australian writer Gavin Long's *MacArthur as Military Commander* (1969), and by the United States Army official histories that MacArthur accepted the strategy of leapfrogging and bypassing strong enemy bases only late and hesitantly. The first bypassing in the Pacific Ocean was by the Japanese against MacArthur's forces in the Philippines, whom they enveloped and virtually isolated by means of their offensive into the Dutch East Indies. The first leapfrogging by the Allies occurred in May 1943 in the Aleutians, when Kiska was hopped over to get at Attu. The process was repeated in the Solomons in August 1943 when the navy leapfrogged Kolombangara to assault Vella Lavella. MacArthur did not begin leapfrogging until the Hollandia campaign, the plans for which he outlined to General George C. Marshall, the army chief of staff, on March 5, 1944. Once having adopted the leapfrogging strategy utilizing amphibious turning movements, MacArthur became addicted to it, and in time he came to employ it repetitively and mechanically, without much question of its appropriateness.

If a case is to be made for MacArthur as a general of brilliant originality, the case has to rest largely on his famous leapfrogging maneuver of the Korean War, the landing at Inchon on September 15, 1950. Not only was this amphibious envelopment spectacularly successful, it was also accomplished at MacArthur's lonely insistence, over the objections of the Joint Chiefs of Staff, the navy, and almost every other responsible officer concerned. It was MacArthur's design, almost alone. The objections argued that Inchon was too far from the United Nations forces in the Pusan perimeter, so that a landing there was likely to become another fiasco like Anzio, because the Inchon and Pusan troops would be beyond mutual supporting distance. More immediately pertinent, the tides, a narrow channel, and a seawall at Inchon all made amphibious assault there highly precarious. To wrest from Inchon the success that he did, MacArthur had to be lucky; but this is not necessarily a count against him, because good fortune seems to be an essential element of superior generalship. The more serious charge against Inchon as a foundation of MacArthur's military greatness is that the success was merely short-run and that it paved the way to disaster.

With Inchon behind him, and now infatuated with leapfrogging maneuvers, MacArthur insisted on performing the feat yet again, this time at Wonsan, above the thirty-eighth parallel on the east coast of Korea. To prepare for Wonsan, the divisions that had landed at Inchon had to be withdrawn through Inchon and through Pusan. The withdrawals so overtaxed the limited port facilities of Inchon and the transport facilities of South Korea more generally that the logistical support of MacArthur's offensive into North Korea never caught up with the resulting deficit in tonnage. Before the 1st Marine Division sailed from Inchon for Wonsan, South Korean troops advancing overland had already captured Wonsan anyway. Of this episode Manchester says practically nothing. Of the disaster to which it was a prelude, he says remarkably little.

Manchester is too honest to pass quietly over all of MacArthur's military deficiencies. He concedes that in Papua the general returned perilously close to head-on assaults in the style of World War I. He concedes that it was not MacArthur but the Joint Chiefs, over MacArthur's dissent, who applied the leapfrogging strategy to Rabaul. But more often Manchester remains the apologist and the advocate. Without noting the differences in numbers of troops engaged, he offers such a comparison as: "In the Battle of Normandy, Eisenhower lost 28,366. Between MacArthur's arrival in Australia and his return to Philippine waters over two years later, his troops suffered just 27,684 casualties . . ." (p. 339). This reckoning conveniently omits the dubious campaigns in the Philippines after Luzon and on Borneo, in which MacArthur backslid from the bypassing strategy and methodically reconquered one island after another, with heavy casualties in the process. Embarrassed by the backsliding, Manchester claims of the fights for a dreary succession of islands that "each of the operations was a strategic masterwork, magnificently executed" (p. 429). It is more accurate to emphasize, as James does, that "it is hard to understand why MacArthur . . . committed [as large a force as] five divisions . . . to the Eighth Army's operations south of Luzon," that the operations assumed a repetitive pattern in which MacArthur's troops would try in vain to force the enemy to decisive battles, the Japanese would withdraw into interior mountains, and then there would have to be a slow "mopping-up, which was sometimes still costly" (*Years of MacArthur*, 2: 741, 746).

Except in this negative instance of the obstinacy with which MacArthur insisted on the direct reconquest of all of the Philippine Islands, there persists through the available two volumes of James's biography of MacArthur, unlike Manchester's, a nagging implication that the great man's presence in the Southwest Pacific Area in World War II did not make much difference. Despite MacArthur's self-advertised brilliance, James seems to suggest that tactics, strategy, and the course of the war would have been much the same without him. He was not the hero in history, the man who personally wrenches events from the direction they would otherwise have followed. It is difficult to emerge from a reading of James's biography without thus concluding that MacArthur made little difference. Manchester never so much as hints at any such conclusion.

To miss capturing MacArthur the general is to leave a conspicuous empty center in a MacArthur biography. Nevertheless, Manchester's concerns are largely with the character of the man and with his activities apart from generalship, and especially with the proconsular years in the Philippines and Japan. The title of the book reflects this preoccupation with MacArthur as proconsul. It was the breadth of his career, not generalship alone, that made MacArthur the American Caesar. And in approaching the nonmilitary aspects of MacArthur, Manchester is much more willing to be critical than he is in the presence of the strategist.

In dealing with personal shortcomings Manchester indeed is more critical and candid than James, the reverse of James's greater frankness in military criticism. Manchester probes more deeply than James, for example, into MacArthur's uncommonly close relationship with and dependence on his mother, to her death almost on the eve of World War II. Manchester tries to look further than James into the troubles of the general's failed first marriage. Manchester recounts with relish how MacArthur may have kept a Eurasian mistress while he was chief of staff of the army, while dropping a suit against Drew Pearson and perhaps paying $15,000 to an agent of Pearson's for fear the columnist would reveal the liaison—not so much out of fear of the public's learning about it as fear of Mother's learning. James, in contrast, refers to this episode with only the most discreet obliqueness. Manchester similarly offers no concealment of the fact that MacArthur was an incorrigible liar, sometimes perversely injuring his military reputation itself when the dissimulations in his press releases raised unrealistic hopes about what his troops were accomplishing. MacArthur's mendacious version of Manuel Roxas's wartime collaboration with the Japanese in the Philippines had far more serious consequences, helping to undermine liberal democracy among the Filipinos at the beginning of their independence.

With the personal MacArthur, Manchester's candor sometimes extends into persuasive insight. Manchester's literary skills permit him to do more than merely state, but to invest with poignant feeling, the plight of the old army man who as proconsul in Japan and United Nations commander in Korea had to make decisions in a world so completely different from that of the frontier garrisons in which he had grown up during the last days of the Indian wars. The mere span of MacArthur's life and the contrasting circumstances of its beginning and end go far to explain the latter-day Douglas MacArthur.

Yet there remains the problem of MacArthur's accomplishments. Manchester praises the general's achievements in reforming Japan almost as lavishly as he does the alleged strategic abilities. In doing so, Manchester takes particular note of the paradoxical contrasts between the social conservatism of MacArthur's views in American politics and the liberal reforms in Japan that tore away at the old industrial oligarchy on the one hand while elevating the status of women, modernizing public health, reorganizing schools, and conducting dozens of additional positive programs of social change on the other. But Manchester never gets to the bottom of the paradox. If the Japanese programs diverged so much from MacArthur's usual political and social opinions, how much were they genuinely his? There were far too many of the programs for the Supreme Commander, Allied Powers, to give most of them more than passing attention anyway. How much were the changes credited to MacArthur the work of the numerous staffs that labored under him? Again, as with his military leadership, beyond prestige and ceremony how much difference would it have made had MacArthur not been there? These questions take on more pertinence because of indications, ignored by Manchester, that MacArthur's health was already in considerable decline between 1945 and 1950 and that MacArthur was an aged man whose grip on affairs was no longer that of the World War II years even before the Korean War began.

Noting Edwin O. Reischauer's observation that some of MacArthur's qualities "are less admired by Americans than by Japanese," Manchester comments: "That was perceptive. The Nipponese still believed in heroes;

MacArthur's countrymen had grown distrustful of them" (p. 496). But while he has written a sensitive, engrossing, sometimes moving biography, Manchester fails to convince us that Douglas MacArthur finally was a hero. The question implied by D. Clayton James's biography—what difference did MacArthur make, what did his accomplish?—haunt Manchester's efforts to avoid them.

Egotist in Uniform

Louis Morton

MacArthur wrote his Reminiscences *shortly before his death in 1964. As Louis Morton of Dartmouth College and official U.S. Army historian points out in this review, the appearance of MacArthur's autobiography only contributed to the controversies surrounding his career.*

When, on August 21, 1963, it was revealed that General MacArthur had at last written his autobiography, the news was greeted in some quarters as the promise of a publication event of the first magnitude. For years the General had resisted offers to write a book or to take advantage of an open invitation by the Army to publish his report of operations in World War II and the Occupation of Japan. As a matter of fact, this report, in the form of an oversized and elaborately illustrated three-volume history, had already been completed (and printed in five copies) before he left Tokyo in 1951. But by arrangement with MacArthur, it had not been published and access to it had been restricted to official users.

Announcement of the autobiography had somewhat the nature of a revelation. All 220,000 words of it, we were told, had been written over a period of six months in the General's own hand on fourteen-inch yellow pads. General Courtney Whitney had "caught him" at it and passed the word to Henry Luce, who immediately made arrangements for serial publication in *Life*. Ranking the *Reminiscences* with the greatest historical writings of any age, Mr. Luce declared, "The General is as clearly a master of narrative and language as he is of strategy and statesmanship."

If MacArthur's reputation as a strategist and statesman rested on the *Reminiscences*, the task of the historian would be relatively simple, for MacArthur is certainly not a "master of narrative and language." But the problem is more complex. The fact is that here, as in everything else involving MacArthur, we are faced with a contradiction. The General's talents were considerable and his contribution in peace and war undeniably large. But he had serious weaknesses, and many of his actions were not above criticism. He had the capacity to inspire both love and hate, admiration and fear. He had a strong personality, a flamboyant style, great moral and physical courage, a high sense of patriotism and duty, and a profound belief in his own destiny. But he was also a supreme egotist who could brook no criticism. He seemed unable to take advice, always quarreled with his superiors, demanded complete obedience and loyalty from his staff, but rationalized his own opposition to authority as responsive to a higher need.

Unfortunately, it is mostly the negative side of MacArthur's character that emerges in the *Reminiscences*. One is surprised that a man who was generally conceded even by his critics to have been brilliant, a genius, "packed with brains," could have written so poor a book. There is in it little sign of high intellect, of noble purpose, and of a grand vision of the future of mankind. The writing is undistinguished, pompous, and self-righteous in tone. There are long testimonials, some in the text, some in footnotes, from numberless public figures extending over half a century bearing witness to the greatness of his deeds—as though he needed such testimonials. Virtually every decoration and honor he received—and he was the most decorated soldier in American history—is noted.

The ego, the sensitivity to criticism, the conviction in his own rightness, the tendency to place himself in the center of affairs, to take credit for himself and place blame on others—all the traits that mar MacArthur's greatness are evident in the *Reminiscences*. He speaks of "my forces," "my plan," "my Alabama cotton-growers," "my Iowa farmers." He writes about his decisions and actions as though he were a sovereign unto himself. He pictures himself constantly beset by difficulties, the hostility of unnamed enemies, the stupidity of smaller men, and opposition from a government that has fallen under the influence of Communists. Alone and unaided he goes to Pearl Harbor, where the Navy has assembled a vast paraphernalia of plans, maps, and talent, to persuade the President that his strategy for returning to the Philippines is correct, the Navy's wrong. Similarly at Wake Island in October 1950 he faced alone the array of talent that the President brought with him, and conquered.

The almost paranoiac quality that marked MacArthur emerges clearly in this volume. It can be noted as early as 1932, when he personally led the troops against the Bonus Marchers, whom he regarded as tools of a communist conspiracy. His role then, he believed, made him a major target of the Communists, as did his advocacy of military preparations in the 'twenties and early 'thirties. This conviction was strengthened in the years that followed and emerges finally as a full-blown plot led by unnamed persons high in government in Washington, aided by the British. He is shocked by the order to take transports from him at Luzon to send supplies to Russia and sees in this evidence of communist influence in Washington. "The Communists," he writes, "had never ceased their violent attacks against me and with the liberal extremists joining them, the crescendo was rising." His candidacy for the Presidency in 1948, he believed, made retaliation against him only "a question of time," and his opposition to Soviet efforts to secure a voice in the Occupation led finally to his relief. "It took several years," he writes, "but their day finally came."

MacArthur's propensity for individual action, for challenging his superiors is evident here also. A lesser man would have been broken quickly, but MacArthur used the technique as a means for his own spectacular advancement. A major on the general staff in 1917, he wrote the single dissenting opinion on a troop study for World War I. When Secretary of War Newton D. Baker called him in, he boldly recommended the use of a National Guard division and before long was named chief of staff to the division and promoted to colonel. Undoubtedly, there was more to it than this, as there was to his version of how, single-handed, he frustrated the attempt to break up the Rainbow Division in France and use its elements as replacements for other units. As chief of staff, he opposed President Roosevelt on budget cuts, and, by his own account, used very hard words indeed to get the President to withdraw his program. More than once in World War II he used his special position with the Australian Prime Minister to secure more men and material for his theatre than the Joint Chiefs of Staff was willing to grant on the basis of military priorities. When he became Allied commander of the Occupation, he proved more difficult to control and in the Korean War virtually set his policies against those of his government. Yet he claims at the end that he does not understand why he was relieved by Truman.

The promise of additional light on some of the more controversial aspects of MacArthur's career is, unfortunately, not fulfilled in the *Reminiscences*. For those who have followed his career, the book holds few surprises. No new chapters of his life, personal or public, are revealed, few new incidents or encounters with the great and near-great. Even the anecdotes have been told time and again. Perhaps that is part of the MacArthur legend.

But if it adds little that is new, the *Reminiscences* omits much that is an essential part of the MacArthur story. Curiously, it contains only a single brief reference to his first marriage, even though it lasted nine years. The lady's name is not even mentioned! Protesting his own admiration for the Navy, MacArthur quotes a conversation in which General Marshall criticized the Navy and Admiral King. His own much stronger criticism of the Navy he withholds. One would scarcely be aware from this book that Admiral Nimitz played a major role in the defeat of Japan. For MacArthur, the Joint Chiefs of Staff as the directing agency of the war against Japan does not seem to exist. In the *Reminiscences*, it is MacArthur who makes all the plans, except those that go badly, and who, from time to time, advises Marshall, rather than the other way round. Though he quotes extensively letters of congratulations, citations, and similar material, he often fails to include—or quotes only small portions of— more important dispatches and communications.

Nor is he always entirely open with his reader. On several occasions he refers to the lack of a unified command in the Pacific and says that he sought vainly to persuade the Joint Chiefs to establish such a command. What he had in mind was his own elevation to this command, and he quotes with approval a letter from Senator Lister Hill to this effect. No one was more concerned about unity of command than General Marshall, but he knew, as did everyone else, that it would be impossible to establish a unified command without giving it to MacArthur, and the Navy would never accede to this. At various times General Marshall and General Arnold were proposed for the command, and one officer searching for a solution to the problem even suggested that MacArthur be made Ambassador to Russia to get him out of the Pacific.

General MacArthur had a strong sense of history, and frequently calls on history in support of his policies, using such phrases as "history clearly shows" and "history teaches." Yet he ignores and distorts much of the history of the events in which he was involved. His version of the events surrounding the Japanese surprise attack on Clark Field in the Philippines on December 8, 1941, does little justice to the labors of historians and settles none of the outstanding problems. He blames the United States for failing to provide him, when he was Military Adviser to the Philippine Commonwealth, with materials for defense of the Islands, but never mentions that there existed in the Philippines a large U.S. Army command (which he himself once commanded) that had the mission of defending the Islands from attack. He implies he had no knowledge of the Germany-first strategy adopted in 1941, although it is a matter of record that he received a copy of the plan embodying this concept. He charges Washington with "managed news," although his theatre was regarded by most correspondents as having stricter censorship rules than any other. He declares that Australian defense plans in 1942 were defeatist, that he was responsible for placing the defenses forward to Port Moresby, and that his relations with the Australian political and military authorities were excellent. The Australian official history denies all these assertions and claims that MacArthur deliberately avoided giving the Australians their proper place in the conduct of the war and the command of their troops.

There may be a particular value in having a MacArthur view of events, but it is a view that most historians would accept only with major reservations and qualifications. "Among President Truman's many weaknesses," writes MacArthur, quoting an unnamed source, "was his utter inability to discriminate between history and histrionics." This characterization would seem to fit the General better than the President.

MacArthur is fond of quoting himself, and does so frequently. He also paraphrases himself, as quoted by others, and often repeats what he apparently told other biographers. Sometimes, even the words are similar. Thus he writes: "We numbered four in our little family when orders shortly came for K Company to march overland 300 miles from Fort Wingate to tiny Fort Selden," (p. 14). In Frazier Hunt's *The Untold Story of Douglas MacArthur* (1954) appears the following: "The MacArthur family numbered only four when orders came for K Company to march overland from Fort Wingate the 300 miles to tiny Fort Selden" (p. 10). There is more of the same in the next few pages, and on page 61 Hunt describes Newton D. Baker as having "a clear, brilliant mind, with the fine ability to make instant and positive decisions," but needing a young man near him "who could match his own swift and uninhibited mind and answer the innumerable questions of a purely military nature that were constantly cropping up." Obviously MacArthur was the man, and in his *Reminiscences* writes: "I found him . . . with a clear, brilliant mind and a fine ability to make instant and positive decisions . . . . I spent much time . . . trying to match his swift and uninhibited mind and answer the innumerable questions of a purely military nature that were constantly cropping up" (pp. 43–44).

The similarity between the *Reminiscences* and General Whitney's *Mac-Arthur: His Rendezvous with History* (1956) is even more striking. Each quotes the other extensively and many pages of the two books, especially those dealing with the Occupation and the Korean War, are very much alike. In many cases, the only differences are in the substitution of "I" for "he." MacArthur's description of his arrival by air in Japan in August 1945 is taken, with acknowledgment, from Whitney. But MacArthur makes one revealing addition to Whitney's text. Whitney wrote, as the plane came down to Atsugi airfield, "I held my breath" (p. 214). MacArthur's version, identical in all other respects, adds "I think the whole world was holding its breath" (p. 270). Both men also use the same long quotation from a third published source to describe the surrender aboard the *Missouri*.

The similarities in language and organization become more pronounced in the Korean sections of the two books. "It was early morning Sunday, June 25, 1950," writes Whitney, "when the telephone rang in his bedroom in the American Embassy in Tokyo . . . it rang with the note of urgency that can sound only in the hush of a darkened room" (p. 315). The same words appear in the *Reminiscences* (p. 327) except that "his" is changed to "my." MacArthur's description of the conference in which he won the Joint Chiefs over to the Inchon landing (pp. 348–351) is almost identical with Whitney's version of the meeting (pp. 345–50). The differences are slight, sometimes amusing. Whitney writes, in reference to the approach to Inchon: "Then I noticed a flash. . . . Evidently we *were* taking the enemy by surprise. The lights were not even turned off. I felt much relieved as I went to my cabin and turned in" (p. 359). MacArthur uses virtually the same words, except it is *he* who notices the flash, *he* who concludes that they were taking the enemy by surprise, *he* who goes to his cabin and turns in (p. 353). One wonders whether MacArthur and Whitney are not one and the same person.

In Whitney, April 11, 1951, the day MacArthur was relieved, is described in the following terms: "And as the sun rose, as it had since time immemorial upon this land of the chrysanthemum with its deep shadows and brilliant hues, with its majestic peaks and low-lying valleys . . ." (p. 470). (According to the *New York Times* story on MacArthur's relief, it rained heavily on April 11, 1951.) And when MacArthur leaves Japan at daybreak of the sixteenth, he writes: "We took off as the sun rose. . . . Beneath us lay this land of the chrysanthemum with its deep shadows and brilliant hues . . ." and so on in the same words (p. 399).

The similarities of the two books, not only in wording but in organization and point of view, are too frequent to be accidental. Only a few have been noted here; many more could have been cited. The most probable explanation is that there exists a single source that both men used, probably MacArthur's personal files or a diary, and that neither bothered to check back to see what had been used before. This explanation would account also for the occasional similarities with other authors. It is possible also that both men worked together on both books and did not notice the similarities.

A further question raised by the *Reminiscences* is the addition of ten pages (408–418) sometime between the printing of the galleys, which this reviewer received at the end of July, and the completed book. Four of these pages (410–413) deal with MacArthur's plan for ending the Korean War, and appeared without explanation as a postscript to the final installment of the book in *Life* (July 24, 1964). But the rest, including a statement by MacArthur of his political and economic beliefs that would put him in the extreme right wing of the Republican party, are entirely new. Since the General died last April 5, one cannot help but wonder how these pages, added sometime between July and September, got into his autobiography, and who wrote them.

All his life MacArthur was the center of controversy. Even before his burial, while his body lay in state, the controversy was renewed by the publication of two interviews he had given some years before, charging Washington and the British with obstructing his plans in Korea. (These charges, incidentally, are quite consistent with the point of view expressed in his and Whitney's books.) The *Reminiscences*, far from stilling the controversies, will only add fresh fuel to the fire. Those who admired and revered him during his lifetime will find in it evidence to support the charges he made and the policies he advocated. Others will find in it confirmation of their worst fears. He was always his worst enemy, and his autobiography will add nothing to his reputation. He should be remembered by his deeds, not his words.

Bibliographical Essay

This essay is not intended to be comprehensive. For a more complete, annotated listing of material on MacArthur see Eugene L. Rasor, *General Douglas MacArthur, 1880–1964: Historiography and Annotated Bibliography* (Westport CT: Greenwood Press, 1994). The reader is also referred to the Bibliographical Notes in D. Clayton James, *The Years of MacArthur*, 3 vols. (Boston: Houghton Mifflin Company, 1970–1985).

Biographies and Memoirs

MacArthur published his *Reminiscences* (New York: McGraw Hill, 1964), shortly before his death. Generally considered reliable for the years prior to 1942, the memoirs become defensive and polemical for the later period of his life. Support for the general's conduct also can be found in the biography-memoirs of two of his senior associates: Charles A. Willoughby and John Chamberlain, *MacArthur, 1941–1945* (New York: Knopf, 1954), and Courtney Whitney, *MacArthur: His Rendezvous with Destiny* (New York: Knopf, 1955). MacArthur's doctor and aide-de-camp provide personal insights: Roger Olaf Egeberg, *The General: MacArthur and the Man Called "Doc"* (New York: Hippocrene, 1983), and Sid Huff and Joe Alex Morris, *My Fifteen Years with General MacArthur* (New York: Paperback Library, 1964).

There were a number of biographies of MacArthur written during World War II but the only one worth mentioning is John Richard Hersey, *Men on Bataan* (New York: Knopf, 1942). A talented reporter and novelist, Hersey interspersed his account of the fighting on Bataan with chapters on MacArthur's early life. The quality of biographies published during MacArthur's lifetime remained poor. The best of a mediocre lot is Frazier Hunt, *The Untold Story of Douglas MacArthur* (New York: Devin-Adair, 1954). A friendly reporter who was close to the general, Hunt had

498 BIBLIOGRAPHICAL ESSAY

access to some of MacArthur's private records. Nonetheless, the highly laudatory biography is rife with errors.

One of the first scholarly treatments of MacArthur was done by Gavin Long, official historian of Australia's role in World War II. His *MacArthur as Military Commander* (London: B. T. Batsford, 1969), took a balanced view of the general's martial talents. While praising Mac-Arthur's courage, patriotism, persistence, and ability to inspire subordinates and comfort anxious Australians in 1942, Long sees the general as extraordinarily lucky. MacArthur, he concludes, "will be written into history as an advocate of politico-military doctrines and as one-time ruler of Japan rather than a great captain" (p. 226).

A watershed in the study of MacArthur came in 1970 with the appearance of the first volume of D. Clayton James's biography. *The Years of MacArthur, 1880–1941* (Boston: Houghton Mifflin, 1970) was followed by *The Years of MacArthur, 1941–1945* (Boston: Houghton Mifflin, 1975), and *The Years of MacArthur: Triumph and Disaster, 1945–1964* (Boston: Houghton Mifflin, 1985). The product of exhaustive research, James's temperate and insightful approach to his controversial subject ranks as one of the finest products of historical biography in the American century. All students of MacArthur owe him an enormous debt.

One of the first authors to exploit James's research was William Manchester. *American Caesar: Douglas MacArthur, 1880–1964* (Boston: Little, Brown, 1978) found a responsive audience, and the book remained in print (in paperback) more than two decades after first publication. Readers responded to Manchester's vivid prose. Prone to taking strong positions, Manchester viewed MacArthur as the greatest soldier in American history. Reviewers, however, pointed out that the volume contained numerous factual errors; also, Manchester's coverage was weak for the period after 1945 (James's third volume had not yet appeared).

Less positive in its treatment of MacArthur but equally dependent upon James's work is Michael Schaller, *Douglas MacArthur: The Far Eastern General* (New York: Oxford University Press, 1989). A diplomatic historian usually associated with the New Left, Schaller finds little to admire in MacArthur's career. His negative views represent the dominant scholarly judgment on MacArthur during the last quarter of the twentieth century.

While academic authors in general have been critical of MacArthur, writers who reach a larger audience have been less so. Geoffrey Perret, *Old Soldiers Never Die* (New York: Random House, 1996) is a more balanced treatment of MacArthur than Manchester, but nonetheless positive. "At his best," Perret concludes, "he was probably the second-greatest soldier in American history, second only, that is, to Ulysses S. Grant" (p. 589).

Growth to Maturity

The starting point for insights into MacArthur's formative early years is Kenneth Ray Young, *The General's General: The Life and Times of Arthur MacArthur* (Boulder co. Westview Press, 1994). Unfortunately there is no individual monograph on MacArthur during World War I. The official history of the Forty-second Infantry ("Rainbow") Division is by Henry J. Reilly, *Americans All: The Rainbow at War* (Columbus OH: Heer, 1936). For MacArthur's tour of duty as superintendent of West Point see Stephen F. Ambrose, *Duty, Honor, Country: A History of West Point* (Baltimore: Johns Hopkins University Press, 1966), and the memoirs of William Ganoe, adjutant of cadets in the 1920s, *MacArthur Close-Up* (New York: Vantage Press, 1962).

The treatment of the Bonus Expeditionary Force has received a good deal of scholarly—and non-scholarly—attention. The best account of the incident and one that is critical of MacArthur's conduct is Roger Daniels, *The Bonus March: An Episode of the Great Depression* (Westport CT: Greenwood Press, 1971). Carol Morris Petillo, *MacArthur: The Philippine Years* (Bloomington: Indiana University Press, 1981), is the standard work on the topic. Petillo's documentation is impressive; her psychoanalytic musings are less so. For the context of MacArthur's association with the Philippines see H. W. Brands, *Bound to Empire: The U.S. and the Philippines* (New York: Oxford University Press, 1992), and Brian McAllister Linn, *Guardians of Empire: The U.S. Army and the Pacific, 1902–1940* (Chapel Hill: University of North Carolina Press, 1997).

World War II

There is a tremendous amount of literature on the war in the Southwest Pacific. For a comprehensive listing see Eugene L. Rasor, *The Southwest Pacific Campaign: Historiography and Annotated Bibliography* (Westport CT: Greenwood Press, 1996).

MacArthur's headquarters produced its own version of the general's campaigns: Charles A. Willoughby, ed., *Reports of General MacArthur*, 2 vols. in 4 parts (Washington: Government Printing Office, 1966). The volumes contain valuable material, especially on the Japanese side of the war, but omit items critical of MacArthur.

The official U.S. Army histories of World War II, known as the Green Books, are essential for studying the war in the Southwest Pacific. The pertinent volumes, all published by the Government Printing Office, are Louis Morton, *The War in the Pacific: Strategy and Command: The First Two Years* (1962) and *The Fall of the Philippines* (1953); Samuel Milner, *Victory in Papua* (1957); John Miller Jr., CARTWHEEL: *The Reduction of Rabaul* (1959); Robert Ross Smith, *The Approach to the Philippines* (1953); Hamlin Cannon, *Leyte: The Return to the Philippines* (1954); and Robert Ross Smith, *Triumph in the Philippines* (1963).

For the early phases of the New Guinea campaign the Australian Army's official histories should be consulted: Dudley McCarthy, *Southwest Pacific Area: First Year: Kokoda to Wau* (Canberra: Australian War Memorial, 1959), and David Dexter, *The New Guinea Offensives* (Canberra: Australian War Memorial, 1961).

The best one-volume history of the war in the Pacific is Ronald H. Spector, *Eagle against the Sun: The American War against Japan* (New York: Free Press, 1985). Gunter Bischof and Robert L. Dupont, eds., *The Pacific War Revisited* (Baton Rouge: Louisiana State University Press, 1997), is a worthwhile collection of essays, including one by Michael Schaller on MacArthur. Schaller concludes that MacArthur had superb public relations talents but only limited military ability.

David Horner has written three excellent studies that cover the Australian dimension of the war in the Pacific and contain much valuable information about MacArthur's relationship with his Allied partner: *Crisis of Command: Australian Generalship and the Japanese Threat* (Canberra: Australian National University Press, 1978); *High Command: Australia and Allied Strategy, 1939–1945* (Canberra: Australian War Memorial, 1982); and *Blamey: The Commander-in-Chief* (St. Leonards: Allen & Unwin, 1998).

For two excellent volumes on aspects of MacArthur's war see Stanley L. Falk, *Bataan: The March of Death* (New York: Norton, 1962), and *Decision at Leyte* (New York: Norton, 1966). Both studies are sharply critical of MacArthur's conduct, as is Lida Mayo, *Bloody Buna* (Garden City NY: Doubleday & Company, 1974). By contrast, Stephen R. Taaffe, *MacArthur's Jungle War: The 1944 New Guinea Campaign* (Lawrence: University Press of Kansas, 1998) presents a balanced but generally favorable picture of MacArthur's leadership. Not to be missed is Edward

J. Drea, *MacArthur's Ultra: Codebreaking and the War against Japan, 1942–1945* (Lawrence: University Press of Kansas, 1982), by far the best book on this important topic.

William M. Leary, ed., *We Shall Return! MacArthur's Commanders and the Defeat of Japan, 1942–1945* (Lexington: University Press of Kentucky, 1988), is a collection of essays on MacArthur's senior commanders. Robert Eichelberger, commander of Eighth Army, has attracted a good deal of attention. For his own version of events see Robert L. Eichelberger and Milton McKaye, *Our Jungle Road to Tokyo* (New York: Viking Press, 1950). Jay Luvaas, ed., *Dear Miss Em: General R. L. Eichelberger's War in the Pacific, 1942–1945* (Westport CT: Greenwood Press, 1972), is a valuable collection. Two biographies can be recommended: John F. Shortal, *Forged in Fire: General Robert L. Eichelberger and the Pacific War* (Columbia: University of South Carolina Press, 1987), and Paul Chwialkowski, *In Caesar's Shadow: The Life of General Robert Eichelberger* (Westport CT: Greenwood Press, 1993). For Walter Krueger, commander of Sixth Army, there is only his *From Down Under to Japan: The Story of Sixth Army in World War II* (Washington: Combat Forces Press, 1953), which focuses more on the actions of Sixth Army than on Krueger's role. A biography of Krueger would be a welcome addition to the literature.

George Kenney, MacArthur's innovative air commander, has his say in *General Kenney Reports* (New York: Duell, Sloan and Pearce, 1949). There is also a fine scholarly biography: Thomas E. Griffith, *MacArthur's Airman: General George C. Kenney and the War in the Pacific* (Lawrence: University Press of Kansas, 1998).

For the naval side of the war in the Southwest Pacfic see Daniel E. Barbey's memoir, *MacArthur's Amphibious Navy: Seventh Amphibious Force Operations* (Annapolis: Naval Institute Press, 1969), and Gerald E. Wheeler's excellent biographical study, *Kinkaid of the Seventh Fleet* (Washington DC: Naval Historical Center, 1995).

In addition to the volumes by Willoughby, Whitney, Ogeberg, and Huff cited earlier, two other members of MacArthur's official family have written their memoirs: Weldon E. Rhodes, *Flying MacArthur to Victory* (College Station: Texas A & M University Press, 1987), and Paul P. Rogers, *The Good Years: MacArthur and Sutherland* (New York: Praeger, 1990), and *The Bitter Years: MacArthur and Sutherland* (New York: Praeger, 1990).

Japan

Robert E. Ward and Frank J. Shulman, eds., *The Allied Occupation of Japan, 1945–1952: An Annotated Bibliography of Western Language Materials* (Chicago: American Library, 1974), reviews the literature on the topic but covers publications only until 1971. For recent historiographical essays see Carol Gluck, "Entangling Illusions: Japanese and American Views of the Occupation," in *New Frontiers in American–East Asian Relations*, ed. Warren Cohen (New York: Columbia University Press, 1983), and William M. Tsutsui, "The Domestic Impact of War and Occupation on Japan," in *World War II in Asia and the Pacific and the War's Aftermath, with General Themes*, ed. Loyd E. Lee (Westport CT: Greenwood Press, 1998). For general accounts of the occupation from two different perspectives see Walter Shelton, *The Honorable Conquerors: The Occupation of Japan* (New York: MacMillan, 1965), and Kazuo Kawai, *Japan's American Interlude* (Chicago: Chicago University Press, 1960). Not to be missed is John W. Dower, *Embracing Defeat: Japan in the Wake of World War II* (New York: Norton, 1999), a critical look at MacArthur and the occupation by a perceptive historian.

A number of participants in the occupation have published their views of events. Among the more significant accounts are William Sebald and Russell Brines, *With MacArthur in Japan* (New York: Norton, 1965); Theodore Cohen, *Remaking Japan: The American Occupation as New Deal* (New York: Free Press, 1983); Richard B. Finn, *Winners in Peace: MacArthur, Yoshida, and Postwar Japan* (Berkeley: University of California Press, 1992); and Justin Williams, *Japan's Political Revolution under MacArthur: A Participant's Account* (Athens: University of Georgia Press, 1979).

Two early evaluations of the occupation, sponsored by the Institute for Pacific Relations, are Edwin M. Martin, *The Allied Occupation of Japan* (Stanford: Stanford University Press, 1948), and Robert A. Fearey, *The Occupation of Japan: Second Phase, 1948–1950* (New York: Macmillan, 1950). The works of two leading revisionist scholars, both emphasizing the conservative nature of occupation policy, are John W. Dower, *Empire and Aftermath: Yoshida Shigeru and the Japanese Experience, 1878–1954* (Cambridge: Harvard University Press, 1954), and Michael Schaller, *The American Occupation of Japan: The Origins of the Cold War in Asia* (New York: Oxford University Press, 1985). Howard B. Schonberger, *Aftermath of War: Americans and the Remaking of Japan, 1945–1952* (Kent OH: Kent State University Press, 1989), reviews the scholarly debate over the occupation from a revisionist perspective. For a more balanced view see Robert Ward and Yoshikazu Sakamoto, eds., *Democratizing Japan* (Honolulu: University of Hawaii Press, 1987).

Korea

Although sometimes labeled "the forgotten war," the Korean conflict has not lacked for both scholarly and popular studies. For a survey of literature see Keith D. McFarland, *The Korean War: An Annotated Bibliography* (New York: Garland, 1986).

Two volumes in the army's official history of the war cover the MacArthur period: Roy E. Appleman, *South to the Naktong, North to the Yalu, June–November 1950* (Washington: Government Printing Office 1961), and Billy Mossman, *Ebb and Flow, November 1950–July 1951* (Washington: Government Printing Office, 1990). Appleman has gone on to write a detailed military history of the war. Four volumes, all published by Texas A & M University Press, have appeared: *East of Chosin: Entrapment and Breakout in Korea, 1950* (1987); *Escaping the Trap: The U.S. Army X Corps in Northeast Korea, 1950* (1988); *Disaster in Korea: The Chinese Confront MacArthur* (1989); and *Ridgway Duels for Korea* (1990). D. Clayton James and Ann Sharp Wells, *Refighting the Last War: Command and Crisis in Korea, 1950–1953* (New York: Free Press, 1993), contains additional thoughts on the topic by MacArthur's premier biographer.

The best scholarly study of the Korean War that places the conflict in the broader context of the cold war is William Stueck, *The Korean War: An International History* (Princeton: Princeton University Press, 1995). For a fine narrative account of military events, see Stanley Weintraub, *MacArthur's War: Korea and the Undoing of an American Hero* (New York: Simon & Schuster, 2000). Two popular histories that emphasize its military dimension can also be noted. Joseph C. Goulden, *Korea: The Untold Story* (New York: Times Books, 1982), and Clay Blair, *The Forgotten War: America in Korea* (New York: Times Books, 1987), are both critical of MacArthur. Francis H. Heller, ed., *The Korean War: A 25-Year Perspective* (Lawrence: Kansas University Press, 1977), contains the recollections of major participants in the war.

The Inchon invasion has its own bibliographical volume: Paul M. Edwards, *The Inchon Landing, Korea, 1950: An Annotated Bibliography* (Westport CT: Greenwood Press, 1994). Most studies of the operation are favorable to MacArthur. See, for example, Robert D. Heinl Jr. *Victory at High Tide: The Inchon-Seoul Campaign* (Philadelphia: Lippicott, 1968), and Michael Langley, *Inchon: MacArthur's Last Triumph* (New York: Times Books, 1979).

The Truman-MacArthur controversy also is a popular topic, with most authors taking Truman's side. Richard H. Rovere and Arthur M. Schlesinger Jr., *The General and the President, and the Future of American Foreign Policy* (New York: Farrar, Straus and Young, 1951), set the tone for the early anti-MacArthur literature, while John W. Spanier, *The Truman-MacArthur Controversy and the Korean War* (New York: Norton, 1959), and Trumbull Higgins, *Korea and the Fall of MacArthur: A Precis in Limited War* (New York: Oxford University Press, 1960), became the standard accounts of the episode. For a collection of documents and public statements see Richard Lowitt, ed., *The Truman-MacArthur Controversy* (Chicago: Rand McNally, 1967).

As Geoffrey Perrett notes in his biography of MacArthur, the drama of the general's life "makes him a gift to biographers and a subject of enduring interest to Americans" (p. 589). Even novelists continue to find MacArthur's career a rich source for their creative imaginations, as witnessed by the appearance of James Webb's delightful *The Emperor's General* (New York: Broadway Books, 1999). The literature on Douglas MacArthur, both fictional and nonfictional, is certain to grow in the twenty-first century, and a consensus on his actions is unlikely to be achieved.

Source Acknowledgments

Part 1

Douglas MacArthur, "Let Us Remember," address to the Veterans of the Forty-second Infantry Division, Washington DC, July 14, 1935, MacArthur Memorial Archives and Museum, Norfolk VA.

Stephen A. Ambrose, "MacArthur as West Point Superintendent," in *Duty, Honor, Country: A History of West Point* (Baltimore: Johns Hopkins University Press, 1966), 261–83. © 1966, The Johns Hopkins University Press.

Dwight D. Eisenhower, "Douglas MacArthur," Dwight D. Eisenhower Presidential Library, Abilene KS.

John W. Killigrew, "The Army and the Bonus Incident," *Military Affairs* 26 (summer 1962): 59–65.

Douglas MacArthur, "The Defense of the Philippines," address to the Command and General Staff School, Baguio, Philippines, August 3, 1936, MacArthur Memorial Archives and Museum, Norfolk VA.

Carol M. Petillo, "Douglas MacArthur and Manuel Quezon: A Note on an Imperial Bond," *Pacific Historical Review* 48, no. 1 (February 1979): 107–17. © 1979, American Historical Association, Pacific Coast Branch. Reprinted by permission.

Paul P. Rogers and Carol M. Petillo, "An Exchange of Opinion," *Pacific Historical Review* 52, no. 1 (February 1983): 93–102. © 1983, American Historical Association, Pacific Coast Branch. Reprinted by permission.

Part 2

Douglas MacArthur, "The Lessons of History," Columbia University address, April 19, 1963, MacArthur Memorial Archives and Museum, Norfolk VA.

Duncan Anderson, "Douglas MacArthur and the Fall of the Philippines, 1941–1942," in *Fallen Stars: Eleven Studies of Twentieth Century Military Disasters*, ed. Brian Bond (London: Brassey, 1991), 164–87.

Stanley L. Falk, "The Army in the Southwest Pacific," *Army* 42 (June 1992): 54–61. © 1992 by the Association of the U.S. Army and reproduced by permission.

D. Clayton James, "MacArthur's Lapses from Envelopment Strategy in 1945," *Parameters* 10 (June 1980): 26–32.

Clark G. Reynolds, "MacArthur as Maritime Strategist," *Naval War College Review* 33 (March 1980): 79–91.

Gerald E. Wheeler, "A Commentary on Dr. Clark Reynolds's Paper 'MacArthur as Maritime Strategist,'" *Naval War College Review* 33 (March 1980): 99–102.

Part 3

Douglas MacArthur, "The Administration of Japan," address to the Allied Council for Japan, April 5, 1946, MacArthur Memorial Archives and Museum, Norfolk VA.

Faubion Bowers, "The Late General MacArthur, Warts and All," *Esquire* 67 (January 1967): 90–95, 164–68. By permission of *Esquire* magazine. © Hearst Communications, Inc. *Esquire* is a trademark of Hearst Magazines Property, Inc. All rights reserved.

Robert T. Textor, "Success in Japan—Despite Some Human Foibles and Cultural Problems," in *The Occupation of Japan: The Grass Roots*, ed. William F. Nimmo (Norfolk VA: General Douglas MacArthur Foundation, 1991). Reprinted by permission of the author.

Michael Schaller, "MacArthur's Japan: The View from Washington," *Diplomatic History* 10 (winter 1986): 1–23.

Ikuhiko Hata, "The Occupation of Japan, 1945–1952," in *The American Military and the Far East*, ed. Joe C. Dixon (Colorado Springs: United States Air Force Academy, 1980), 92–108.

Part 4

Douglas MacArthur, "Old Soldiers Never Die," address before a joint session of Congress, April 19, 1951, MacArthur Memorial Archives and Museum, Norfolk VA.

H. Pat Tomlinson, "Inchon: The General's Decision," *Military Review* 47 (April 1967): 28–34.

Karl G. Larew, "The Inchon Invasion," *Army* 38 (December 1988):

15–16. © 1988 by the Association of the U.S. Army and reproduced by permission.

John Edward Wiltz, "Truman and MacArthur: The Wake Island Meeting," *Military Affairs* 42 (December 1978): 169–75.

Edgar O'Ballance, "The MacArthur Plan," *Journal of the Royal United Service Institution* 110 (August 1965): 248–53.

D. Clayton James, "Command Crisis: MacArthur and the Korean War," *The Harmon Memorial Lectures in Military History: Number Twenty-Four* (Colorado Springs: United States Air Force Academy, 1982).

Barton J. Bernstein, "New Light on the Korean War," *The International History Review* 3 (April 1981): 256–77.

Part 5

Douglas MacArthur, "Duty, Honor, Country," acceptance of the Thayer Award speech, West Point, May 12, 1962, MacArthur Memorial Archives and Museum, Norfolk VA.

George C. Kenney, "The MacArthur I Know," in *The MacArthur I Know* (New York: Duell, Sloan and Pearce, 1951), 226–59.

Norman Cousins, "Douglas MacArthur," *Saturday Review* 47 (May 2, 1964): 18–19.

Brian Loring Villa, "A Unique General: MacArthur of the Pacific," *Reviews in American History* 3 (December 1975): 494–98. © 1975, The Johns Hopkins University Press.

Charles M. Dobbs, "A Successful Postrevisionist Synthesis?" *Reviews in American History* 14 (June 1986): 284–88. © 1986, The Johns Hopkins University Press.

Russell F. Weigley, "Military Biography without Military History," *Reviews in American History* 7 (December 1979): 571–76. © 1979, The Johns Hopkins University Press.

Louis Morton, "Egotist in Uniform," *Harper's* 229 (November 1964): 138, 142, 144–45. © 1964 by *Harper's* magazine. All rights reserved. Reproduced from the November issue by special permission.

Index